DEVELOPING
CROSS-CULTURAL
COMPETENCE

DEVELOPING CROSS-CULTURAL COMPETENCE

A Guide for Working with Children and Their Families

Third Edition

edited by

Eleanor W. Lynch, Ph.D.
Department of Special Education
San Diego State University

and

Marci J. Hanson, Ph.D.
Department of Special Education
San Francisco State University

PAUL·H·
BROOKES
PUBLISHING Co.®

Baltimore • London • Sydney

Paul H. Brookes Publishing Co.
Post Office Box 10624
Baltimore, Maryland 21285-0624

www.brookespublishing.com

Typeset by Integrated Publishing Solutions, Inc., Grand Rapids, Michigan.
Manufactured in the United States of America
by Edwards Brothers, Ann Arbor, Michigan.

The individuals described in this book are composites or fictional accounts based on the authors' actual experiences. Individuals' names have been changed and identifying details have been altered to protect confidentiality.

Readers may access free of charge from the Brookes Publishing Course Companion Web Site for *Developing Cross-Cultural Competence, Third Edition,* various resources that support instructors and students using the book in college courses. These materials are available at the following address: http://textbooks.brookespublishing.com/lynch. Use of these materials is granted for educational purposes only; the duplication and distribution of these materials for a fee is prohibited.

Permission to reprint the following is gratefully acknowledged:

From *The Unquiet Grave* by Cyril Connolly. Copyright © 1981 by Dierdre Levi.
Reprinted by permission of Persea Books, Inc. (New York).

Second printing, June 2006.

Library of Congress Cataloging-in-Publication Data

Developing cross-cultural competence : a guide for working with children and their families / edited by Eleanor W. Lynch and Marci J. Hanson—3rd ed.
    p.   cm.
  Includes bibliographical references and indexes.
  ISBN-13: 978-1-55766-744-1
  ISBN-10: 1-55766-744-6 (perfect bound : alk. paper)
  1. Social work with children with disabilities—United States—Cross-cultural studies.
2. Family services—United States—Cross-cultural studies. 3. Minorities—United
States. I. Lynch, Eleanor W. II. Hanson, Marci J.
HV888.5.D48 2004
362.7'086'930973—dc22   2004009543

British Library Cataloguing in Publication data are available from the British Library.

CONTENTS

ABOUT THE EDITORS

Eleanor W. Lynch, Ph.D., Department of Special Education, San Diego State University, San Diego, California 92182

For nearly 35 years, Eleanor W. Lynch has been involved in teaching, research, and community and family services that focus on improving the lives of young children who have, or are at risk for, disabilities. Prior to joining the faculty at San Diego State University (SDSU), Dr. Lynch received her doctorate in teaching exceptional children in 1972 from The Ohio State University and then joined the faculties of Miami University and the University of Michigan. She is currently Professor Emerita at SDSU, after chairing the Department of Special Education, directing the Early Childhood Special Education graduate program, and serving on the faculty of the SDSU–Claremont Graduate University joint doctoral program.

Over the course of her career, Dr. Lynch has directed a model demonstration project and personnel preparation grants in early intervention and early childhood special education as well as a series of research grants on topics such as parental perspectives on special education, the status of educational services for children with ongoing medical conditions, individualized family service plan (IFSP) development, and the use of behavioral data and reflective practice to improve novice teachers' skills. She has served on numerous local and statewide committees and was one of the national collaborators on the Culturally and Linguistically Appropriate Services (CLAS) Early Childhood Research Institute. Most recently, she served as one of the Regional Coordinators of the federally funded Early Intervention Distance Learning Program, a collaborative project involving five California state universities and state partners. In 2003, she was honored by SDSU as one of the Top 25 on the campus and as the Outstanding Faculty Member from the College of Education.

Dr. Lynch has lived in and taught special education to college instructors in Indonesia, taught in American Samoa, given invited presentations in Australia and Taiwan, and lived in India while her husband served on a U.S. Agency for International Development project. She is the author or co-author of numerous books, articles, and chapters and is a frequent presenter and workshop leader in the area of cultural competence.

Marci J. Hanson, Ph.D., Department of Special Education, San Francisco State University, 1600 Holloway Avenue, San Francisco, California 94132

In addition to her duties as Professor at San Francisco State University (SFSU), Marci J. Hanson directs the SFSU Joint Doctoral Program in Special Education with University of California, Berkeley, and is a member of the Child and Adolescent Development faculty of the Marian Wright Edelman Institute for the Study of Children, Youth, and Families at SFSU. Dr. Hanson received her doctorate in special education with a minor in developmental psychology in 1974 from the University of Oregon. Prior to joining the faculty at SFSU, she worked as a research scientist in charge of the Early Intervention Unit of the Institute for the Study of Exceptional Children, Educational Testing Service, in Princeton, New Jersey.

For many years, Dr. Hanson has been actively involved in teaching, research, and community service related to young children who are at risk for or have disabilities and their families. She was one of the principal investigators of a national research institute, the Early Childhood Research Institute on Inclusion. She also has directed a number of federally funded personnel preparation and research grants in early childhood and has directed two model demonstration early intervention programs. The graduate training programs and the early intervention programs reflect the cultural diversity of the San Francisco Bay Area.

Dr. Hanson has lived in Austria and has presented and consulted widely in the United States and in India, Italy, Egypt, Spain, Australia, and New Zealand. Dr. Hanson has contributed actively to the peer-reviewed professional literature, and she has authored, co-authored, or edited several books including *Teaching the Young Child with Motor Delays: A Guide for Parents and Professionals* (PRO-ED, 1986), with Dr. Susan Harris; *Teaching the Infant with Down Syndrome: A Guide for Parents and Professionals, Second Edition* (PRO-ED, 1987); *Homecoming for Babies After the Intensive Care Nursery: A Guide for Parents and Professionals in Supporting Families and Their Infants' Early Development* (PRO-ED, 1993), with Kathleen VandenBerg; *Atypical Infant Development, Second Edition* (PRO-ED, 1996); the *Me, Too! Series,* with Dr. Paula J. Beckman (Paul H. Brookes Publishing Co., 2001); and *Early Intervention Practices Around the World* (Paul H. Brookes Publishing Co., 2003), with Dr. Samuel L. Odom, Dr. James A. Blackman, and Dr. Sudha Kaul.

Drs. Lynch and Hanson have also collaborated on *Early Intervention: Implementing Child and Family Services for Infants and Toddlers Who Are At-Risk or Disabled, Second Edition* (PRO-ED, 1995); and *Understanding Families: Approaches to Diversity, Disability, and Risk* (Paul H. Brookes Publishing Co., 2004).

ABOUT THE CONTRIBUTORS

Sam Chan, Ph.D., Los Angeles County Department of Mental Health (Children, Youth, and Family Services), 550 South Vermont Avenue, 4th Floor, Los Angeles, California 90020

Sam Chan is a clinical psychologist and division chief with the Los Angeles County Department of Mental Health (LACDMH). During the past 25 years, he has held senior administrative and faculty positions at the California School of Professional Psychology; the University Affiliated Program at Children's Hospital, Los Angeles; the University of Southern California School of Medicine; and the University of California, Los Angeles, Department of Psychiatry. Dr. Chan has focused much of his career on early intervention with children with special needs and parent education, advocacy, and leadership programs predominantly for Asian and Latino immigrant families.

Namita Jacob, Ph.D., Tamil Nadu, India

Namita Jacob, born and raised in India, is a consultant in a variety of areas including education, rehabilitation, program development and evaluation, and research. She works with a variety of national and international agencies such as Hilton Perkins, which promotes and supports the development of services across the world for individuals with visual and multiple impairments; and SENSE, a United Kingdom–based organization founded by parents of children with deafblindness.

Jennie R. Joe, Ph.D., M.P.H., Native American Research and Training Center, University of Arizona, 1642 East Helen Street, Tucson, Arizona 85719

Jennie R. Joe is a professor in the Department of Family and Community Medicine (DFCM) at the University of Arizona and is also a director of the Native American Research and Training Center (NARTC), an organization involved in a variety of research and educational programs that focus on the impact of chronic diseases and disabilities for American Indian communities.

Evelyn Lee, Ed.D., L.C.S.W.

Dr. Lee, who passed away in 2003 shortly after completing the chapter she co-authored with Sam Chan, served as Executive Director of RAMS, Inc. She also was Clinical Professor of Psychiatry at the University of California, San Francisco. Her career spanned more than 30 years of clinical, management, administrative, teaching, and supervisory experience in the mental health and human services fields. A prolific writer, Dr. Lee was internationally recognized for her expertise in cultural competence and immigrant and refugee trauma. She was appointed to more than 50 government and community boards, and she helped found and develop innovative programs in the United States, China, Hong Kong, Taiwan, and Vietnam.

Randi Suzanne Malach, M.Cl.Sc., CCC-SLP, Abrazos Family Support Services, 412 Camino don Tomas, Bernalillo, New Mexico 87004

Randi Suzanne Malach serves as a director and speech-language therapist with a home-based, birth-to-3 early intervention program in a rural, multicultural county in New Mexico. In previous years she has served as the director of several Maternal and Child Health Bureau (MCHB) special projects addressing cross-cultural communication issues between families and providers and addressing the coordination of services between birth-to-3 early intervention programs and medical homes at a community level.

Noreen Mokuau, D.S.W., School of Social Work, Henke Hall, 1800 East-West Road, University of Hawai'i at Manoa, Honolulu, Hawai'i 96822

Noreen Mokuau is Professor and Chair of the doctoral program in the School of Social Work at the University of Hawai'i at Manoa. Her primary interests lie in Native Hawaiian health and well-being, particularly as they relate to cancer, substance abuse, and mental health. Author of numerous journal articles and book chapters, she has also edited three books focusing on Asian and Pacific Islanders. She has recently been awarded a grant from the National Cancer Institute to do pilot work on family interventions for Native Hawaiian women with cancer.

Rosa Milagros Santos, Ph.D., Department of Special Education, University of Illinois at Urbana-Champaign (UIUC), 288 Education Building, 1310 South 6th Street, Champaign, Illinois 61820

Rosa Milagros (Amy) Santos was born and raised in the Philippines. Prior to moving to the United States in 1990, she was an early childhood special education teacher and program administrator. After completing her doctoral studies at Utah State University in 1997, she coordinated the Early Childhood Research Institute on Culturally and Linguistically Appropriate Services (CLAS). Dr. Santos is Assistant Professor at UIUC and is Coordinator of the Early Childhood Special Education master's program there. She also is involved in several grant projects, including the Cross-Cultural Study of Parent–Child Interactions.

Virginia-Shirin Sharifzadeh, Ph.D., 4130 Bandini Street, San Diego, California 92103

Virginia-Shirin Sharifzadeh holds a bachelor's degree in psychology from the American University of Beirut, Lebanon, and a doctoral degree with a focus on special and multicultural education from the Joint Doctoral Program in education at San Diego State University (SDSU) and Claremont Graduate University. Born in the United States of Iranian parents, she grew up in Iran and worked at the John F. Kennedy Center for Mentally Handicapped Children in Tehran, an organization founded by her mother. Her years spent in the Middle East, Europe, and the United States and her command of several languages, have helped Dr. Sharifzadeh gain knowledge and insight into many different cultures.

Pemerika Tauili'ili, M.A., American Samoa Community College, Pago Pago, Samoa 96799

Pemerika Tauili'ili is Chairman of the American Samoa Community College Board of Higher Education. He was the former Dean and Director of the American Samoa Community College Land Grant Programs and the Agriculture Department. He holds two *Matai* (i.e., high chief) titles: *Tauili'ili* and *Leiataua*. As head of two extended families and a lay preacher, he is actively involved in Samoan village cultural activities including serving as Chairman of the Goodwill Industries Board of Directors.

Winnie O. Willis, Sc.D., Graduate School of Public Health/Institute for Public Health, San Diego State University, 6505 Alvarado Road, Suite 112, San Diego, California 92102

Winnie O. Willis, Professor of Public Health at San Diego State University (SDSU), has been in the broad field of public health for more than 30 years. With particular expertise in maternal and child health, Ms. Willis has been an educator, researcher, and advocate for better health and social services for low-income families. Her work with multiethnic communities, families, and infants at high risk has encompassed clinical services, program planning and administration, policy development, research, and education.

Maria E. Zuniga, Ph.D., M.S.W., School of Social Work, Retired, San Diego State University, 2557 C Street, San Diego, California 92102

Maria E. Zuniga has trained social workers for more than 25 years, 16 of them at San Diego State University. She has consulted at the national, state, and local levels on how to provide culturally competent services for professionals in the health care, education, and social services systems and how to increase service delivery for individuals in hard-to-reach groups. Her recent publications have focused on the needs of Latino immigrants.

PREFACE

When the first edition of this book was published in 1992, we believed that programs and services for young children with disabilities and their families were at an important crossroads. The diversity of the families being served was dramatically increasing while the field was undergoing its own metamorphosis from child-centered to family-centered approaches. We were struck with how much more we, and the students whom we taught, needed to learn in order to effectively implement these new approaches, especially to implement them in family contexts that were unfamiliar to many service providers. With encouragement from our students, we began to look for published material that would contribute to our understanding of the many issues involved in cross-cultural service delivery; however, we found that little was available that combined a strong conceptual framework with the kinds of specific information that we felt our students needed to know.

When the second edition was published in 1998, we found that family-centered approaches had been adopted throughout service delivery systems, and nearly every program in the United States had experienced an increase in diversity. Still, we knew the work was not finished; we had simply reached another crossroads. At that juncture, it was no longer enough to understand one's own worldview and the worldviews of others. We argued that it was time to consider the larger context of our similarities and differences and to understand the impact that each of us has on the children and families with whom we work as well as the world in which we all live. We encouraged readers to speak with stronger voices, to take thoughtful action on behalf of children and families, and to commit to creating programs and services that would open the circle and welcome others.

RATIONALE FOR THIS EDITION

The world has changed in dramatic ways since the last edition of this book was published. The Human Genome Project has confirmed our universal similarities, but our differences have led to terrorism and war. The population of the United States has grown at an unprecedented rate, and the composition of that growth predicts a very different mix of culture, ethnicity, and race in the future. Perhaps at no other time has diversity played such an important role in our daily lives, collectively and individually, nor has there ever been such a need for people to gain knowledge, convey respect, and take positive action. So it is with a sense of both timeliness and urgency that this book has evolved.

We are fortunate to live in cities and teach at universities where the mixing of customs, colors, and languages makes daily life a kaleidoscopic experience. We are equally fortunate to be surrounded by friends, families, and colleagues who share our passion for high-quality programs and services for *all* children and their families. High quality can only be achieved when service delivery systems are designed to meet the needs of an increasingly diverse group of individuals, when service providers work effectively with families across cultures and languages, and when the sociopolitical climate supports *all* children and their families.

Our work with our own students and colleagues, special projects related to diversity, and travel around the United States and other nations discussing cultural issues have convinced us that our collective journey is just beginning. We have met people who do not believe that they have a culture as well as people who identify strongly with their own heritage but know little about different lifeways. We have seldom, however, met anyone who did not want to learn more and be more effective with the children and families they serve. We offer this edition as one way to learn more.

Like its predecessors, this edition is based on literature that describes recommended practices in human services, literature on intercultural effectiveness, and insights and information from the contributing authors who are bicultural, often bilingual, and always strong advocates for improving programs and services. Its primary purpose is to be of use to the full range of professionals who provide educational, health care, and social services (e.g., educators, nurses, speech-language pathologists, audiologists, occupational and physical therapists, physicians, social workers, psychologists) to families of children who have, or are at risk for, disabilities. Its secondary purpose is to speak to those who influence service delivery—to reach the administrators, politicians, and policy makers whose attitudes and beliefs affect service providers and families alike. Regardless of the program, the service, or one's professional discipline or role, facilitating cross-cultural competence is an obligation because it is prerequisite to quality services.

Although children with disabilities and their families are highlighted in this edition, much of the information and many of the examples are equally applicable to all children, families, and service providers across many other programs and settings. Teachers, child care providers, clinic staff, spiritual leaders, and volunteers who work with children without disabilities and their families will find new ways of considering their roles and their actions when working cross-culturally. We also hope that this edition, like previous editions, will be used and enjoyed by individuals in other fields—from world cultures to world music to sociology.

PHILOSOPHY

In the development of this and previous editions, we have articulated a philosophy that grounds our thinking and our work. This philosophy is based on five perspectives or principles. It is our intent that these principles are clear throughout the book:

1. A prerequisite to any successful intervention is an understanding of our own cultural, ethnic, and language background and the values and beliefs that we hold about individuals who are different from ourselves.

2. All families, children, and individuals are unique. Although their ethnic, cultural, racial, and language backgrounds influence them, they are not fully de-

fined by them. Many sociocultural factors powerfully affect each family and family member. Therefore, cultural and sociocultural differences should be used to enhance our interactions rather than to stereotype or to serve as the sole determiner of our approach to intervention.

3. Culture is not static. Cultural beliefs and behaviors are always being influenced by new information and new experiences. Therefore, culture is fluid and dynamic, not something about which one can reach understanding in a single experience. Rather, learning about one's own and others' cultures is a lifelong process—a journey with many destinations.

4. Our role as service providers is twofold. It is our obligation to work with families to develop interventions that are culturally competent. It is also our obligation to interpret the new or mainstream culture to families and help them find ways to negotiate it effectively.

5. All interactions and interventions take place in a larger sociopolitical context. This context varies from family to family and is powerfully influenced by one's culture, race, language, and economic status. Many of our assumed differences do not spring from the individual but from the sociopolitical boundaries within which people are forced to live. The ultimate goal of cultural competence is to recognize and rectify political and societal barriers that artificially separate us.

SUMMARY

We hope that our readers will share our goals for helping to foster more culturally competent service systems and service providers. We also hope that readers will take active roles in their own communities to create and maintain a sociopolitical climate that supports *all* children and their families and that this book will contribute to each of these goals.

ACKNOWLEDGMENTS

We continue our grateful acknowledgment of Paul H. Brookes Publishing Company. We thank Melissa Behm for her ongoing personal and professional support, Heather Shrestha for her guidance as this edition has evolved, and Leslie Eckard for her editorial expertise. We also thank Erin Geoghegan and the design team for creating a design that supports our message and all of the other Brookes staff members whose time, talent, and teamwork make publishing a positive process.

We sincerely thank the many families who shared photographs that bring life to the pages that follow. Special appreciation is given to Catharine Ayala, professional photographer, whose work appears on page 190; Terry Joseph Sam, whose work appears on page 252; and Ken Kobre, professional photographer, whose work appears on page 260.

We also acknowledge the "family" of contributing authors for the significant role that each has played in the creation of this edition. They continue to be our cultural guides; to teach us to speak with stronger voices; and to help us see the world through different lenses. They have brought wisdom, insight, and sensitivity to the task. Their clear, passionate voices have taught thousands of people about the strengths that diversity brings to our world, and their perspectives have enriched all of us. On our personal journeys toward increased cross-cultural competence, we thank you for being our companions on the road.

Finally, we express our sadness at the loss of Dr. Evelyn Lee in March 2003. Dr. Lee spent her life creating culturally competent systems of care and working as an activist for families. In this edition, she joined Dr. Sam Chan as co-author of Chapter 8, Families with Asian Roots. Her wisdom, experience, passion, and collaborative nature were evident in every interaction, and these characteristics reverberate throughout the chapter.

FOR THE READER

Developing Cross-Cultural Competence: A Guide for Working with Children and Their Families, Third Edition, is organized into three parts. Part I introduces the issues that surround working with families from diverse cultural, ethnic, and language groups. Recommended practices for working with families of young children in intercultural training and understanding are the basis for Chapters 1–3. Examples and suggestions are provided to help service providers work more effectively with families whose cultural, sociocultural, ethnic, racial, or language background differs from their own.

Part II is the core of the book. It introduces cultural information about a number of groups that make up the population of the United States. Each group is described in terms of its history, values, and beliefs; particular emphasis is placed on issues related to family, child rearing, health and healing, and disability. In addition to being expanded and updated from the second edition, Part II includes a new chapter, Families with South Asian Roots (Chapter 12), which discusses the range of cultural beliefs and practices among individuals and families with roots in countries such as India and Pakistan who are living in the United States.

The cultural groups that were selected for inclusion in this volume are not exhaustive nor do they represent the range of cultural and ethnic groups in the United States. Instead, groups were selected because they represent a large portion of the population and/or reflect more recent immigration patterns that affect programs and services in more than one area of the United States. The contributing authors who describe these groups were carefully selected for their dual expertise and knowledge of the culture and their experiences in working with families of children who have, or are at risk for, disabilities. They come from many different professional disciplines including education, public health, nursing, psychology, speech-language pathology, administration, social work, and medical anthropology.

The Postlude in Part II, Children of Many Songs, addresses the growing number of bicultural, biracial, and multiethnic children and families. It discusses the increasing number of multicultural families and issues for service providers to consider in providing culturally competent services for these families.

Part III, the final section of the book, synthesizes the information presented in Parts I and II and provides recommendations for service providers and the service delivery systems in which they work. The intent of these recommendations is to enhance service providers' cultural awareness and responsivity to the variability across all families in matters of child rearing, communication, health care, and attitudes toward intervention. These recommendations emphasize interactions with families whose culture, ethnicity, race, and/or language differ from that of the service provider. The goals of the recommendations are to increase service providers' skills and comfort as they interact with families from diverse groups and to help programs, agencies, and organizations serving families to make their services more responsive to the children and families that they serve.

The Suggested Readings and Resources section has been expanded in this edition. Books, films, theater, and other media that provide insight, information, and entertainment to enhance cultural understanding are included. This section's contents can help readers at all levels of cultural competence increase their awareness of themselves and of the many others with whom they share the world. Forming book groups or viewing videos may provide opportunities for colleagues to read and think together about similarities and differences among themselves and the families they serve in an organized but less formal way.

TERMINOLOGY

The terminology used in this edition differs in some ways from the terminology used in the second edition. The decision to change the language is an example of the evolving nature of culture, professional standards, and the interaction of language and the sociopolitical context. The chapter authors, in keeping with accepted terminology, selected the terms that were chosen to describe each of the cultural groups represented in the book. For example, *Native American* has been changed to *American Indian* to reflect current preferences across the diverse groups being addressed. In Chapter 6, two terms—*African American* and *black*—continue to be used to acknowledge the variation of preference within the group. In Chapter 10, the spelling of Hawaii sometimes appears as Hawai'i to reflect the Hawaiian language cadences, in keeping with the recent Hawaiian sovereignty movement. The spelling and capitalization of terms were also determined by contributing authors. Whenever possible, native spellings and pronunciation are provided; however, in cases in which understanding was compromised, this practice was not followed. Throughout this edition, non-English words are set in italics. Because many of the terms were selected to reflect what is accepted within the United States, readers in various regions of the country may use, prefer, or be more familiar with another term (e.g., *Hispanic* or *Chicano* rather than *Latino*). The terms used to refer to Anglo-Europeans who make up the dominant culture in the United States vary throughout Part II. This inconsistency of terms was preserved because it exemplifies the differing cultural perspectives and points of view. Language is a powerful tool in any interaction and the way that it is used is full of lessons. As in the previous edition, the primary lessons related to terminology in this edition are that terms change and the ones chosen should describe groups of individuals based on their preferences.

Once again with love,
to Leo J. Whiteside (1907-2000) and Mary Virginia Whiteside (1912-2003),
and
Max and Maxine Hanson,
who gave us roots and wings

and to Patrick Harrison,
who understands and appreciates both
—EWL

and to
Laura and Jillian,
that I might do the same for them
—MJH

DEVELOPING
CROSS-CULTURAL
COMPETENCE

INTRODUCTION

Part I of this text introduces the reader to issues that surround culturally competent practice with families from diverse cultural, ethnic, racial, and language groups. Readers are challenged to examine their own values, beliefs, biases, and behaviors and the ways in which their professional practice is influenced by their own perspectives. Following this personal reflection, readers are invited to consider a range of worldviews and the ways in which these views may affect families' perceptions of and receptivity to programs and services. Particular emphasis is placed on communicating effectively and understanding different interpretations of the same behavior, approach, or event. Suggestions are provided throughout the chapters to help service providers increase their effectiveness as they work with families whose culture, ethnicity, race, or language may differ from their own.

CHAPTER 1

ETHNIC, CULTURAL, AND LANGUAGE DIVERSITY IN SERVICE SETTINGS

Marci J. Hanson

Culture is the sum of all the forms of art,
of love and of thought, which, in the course of centuries,
have enabled man to be less enslaved.
—ANDRÉ MALRAUX (AS QUOTED IN SELDES, 1960)

A walk through a garden reveals the panoply of lovely plants—all varied in form, blossoms, and size. All share such basic needs as soil, water, and sunlight; yet each plant may have different needs as to the type of soil, the amount of water, and the degree of sunlight required for life and growth. Each type of plant is of interest to the observer and offers its own beauty and special characteristics. Seen together, as a whole, the plants form a wondrous garden to behold. Like the garden, communities are made up of individuals, all of whom contribute their own unique characteristics to the sense of place in which they live. Just as plants share certain common needs for survival, so, too, do the individuals within communities. Each member of the community, similar to the garden plants, has different needs and avenues for growth that are essential if these individuals are to reach their full potential.

Communities, however, are highly interactive, dynamic enterprises in which individuals are constantly interacting and responding to one another and in which the characteristics of those individuals are being modified through those interactions. Although communities are neither static nor planned, societies do have cultural mores and practices that guide human behavior and provide a socialization framework that shapes interactions.

Culture is this framework that guides and bounds life practices. According to Anderson and Fenichel, "Cultural framework must be viewed as a set of tendencies of possibilities from which to choose" (1989, p. 8). Thus, culture is not a rigidly prescribed set of behaviors or characteristics, but rather, a framework through which actions are filtered or checked as individuals go about daily life. These cultural frameworks are constantly evolving and being reworked (Anderson & Fenichel, 1989). Although people of the same cultural background may share tendencies, not all members of a group who share a common cultural background and/or history will behave in the same manner. Rather, behavior is governed by many factors, such as socioeconomic status, gender, age, length of residence in a locale, and education. Finally, individuals may differ in the degree to which they choose to adhere to a set of cultural patterns. Some individuals identify strongly with a particular group; others combine practices from several cultural groups.

Cultural practices as well as the individual characteristics of the person or family may influence the interactions between service providers and the families receiving services. Similar to the plants in the garden, the individuals within a community all share basic needs but differ as to their specific needs and the types of environments that support growth. The service provider, similar to the gardener, must individualize interventions for each family to address families' concerns and priorities and tailor services to families' needs and resources. Being sensitive, knowledgeable, and understanding of the families' cultural practices enhances this process and relationship.

CULTURAL CONSIDERATIONS
FOR CHILD AND FAMILY SERVICE PROVIDERS

In a single day or two, a train traveler crossing a continent would mostly likely be struck by the range of cultural practices encountered. While sitting in the same berth, this passenger may experience vast differences with each border crossing. These differences are noted in the language of the passengers, the degree of formality or informality of communication, the dress of the conductors, the style or maintenance of trains and buildings, and the scheduling, to name only a few.

Service providers work with a variety of families through the provision of a range of education, health, and social services. In the course of their work, they may "travel," much like the train passenger, through many cultures in a given day. The differences among the families they encounter are usually much more pronounced, however.

Many practitioners enter the homes of the families with whom they work, which brings them into close and potentially intrusive contact with family members. This contact often occurs at a sensitive period in the child's and the family members' lives. The child is young, and the family may still be adjusting to the inclusion of a new family member or the presence of a disability, illness, or other at-risk condition that has necessitated that the family interacts with professionals and people outside of the family. Thus, the service provider comes to the family because someone perceives a need for services related to the child's developmental and/or health status. This referral for services may be sought or welcomed by the family, or the family may hold significant reservations about the need and desirability of such services. Coming at a time that often is emotionally charged, this close contact can be difficult for families and stressful for the professionals who provide services to them. When the service provider and family are from different cultures, either party may misunderstand routines and recommendations. The potential for "cultural clashes" emerges.

This book has been designed to assist service providers who are working with families from various cultural groups. Given the diversity of the population of the United States, it is likely that practitioners will work with families from cultural, ethnic, and linguistic groups that differ from their own. The information provided helps service providers to become more sensitive to cultural differences and to develop effective skills for working with families from diverse backgrounds and identities.

Part II, the Cultural Perspectives section of this book, provides information about many of the major cultural groups that make up the population of the United States. This information is not meant to serve as a comprehensive cultural guide to or "cookbook" about different groups. Rather, it provides basic information on historical background, values, and beliefs often shared by members of these cultural communities as a way to assist service providers in working with and forming relationships with families. Service providers are cautioned against using this information to overgeneralize or characterize all members of a cultural group as alike. Instead, they are advised to use this knowledge to form a base for respectful interaction. As Anderson and Fenichel related,

> Cultural sensitivity cannot mean knowing everything there is to know about every culture that is represented in a population to be served. At its most basic level, cultural sensitivity implies, rather, knowledge that cultural differences as well as similarities exist. . . . For those involved in early intervention, cultural sensitivity further means being aware of the cultures represented in one's own state or region, learning about some of the general parameters of those cultures, and realizing that cultural diversity will affect families' participation in intervention programs. Cultural knowledge helps a professional to be aware of possibilities and to be ready to respond appropriately. (1989, pp. 8–9)

An appreciation and respect for cultural variations, as well as group and individual differences, is crucial for service providers. It is hoped that the information garnered from this section will enable practitioners to work more effectively with families.

CHANGING DEMOGRAPHICS IN THE UNITED STATES

The following poem, written in 1883, is inscribed on the base of the Statue of Liberty. It was written by an immigrant of Russian-Jewish ancestry and was submitted in a literary campaign to raise funds for completing the statue's pedestal. For years this statue and poem have served as a beacon for immigrants arriving in the United States. The poem's message offers promise to newcomers and underscores core values for which this country stands.

The New Colossus

Not like the brazen giant of Greek fame,
With conquering limbs astride from land to land,
Here at our sea-washed, sunset-gates shall stand
A mighty woman with a torch, whose flame
Is the imprisoned lightning, and her name
Mother of Exiles. From her beacon-hand
Glows world-wide welcome, her mild eyes command
The air-bridged harbor that twin-cities frame.

"Keep, ancient lands, your storied pomp!" cries she,
With silent lips. "Give me your tired, your poor,
Your huddled masses yearning to breathe free,
The wretched refuse of your teeming shore;
Send these, the homeless, tempest-tost to me,
I lift my lamp beside the golden door!"

—Emma Lazarus (November 2, 1883)

The United States, for the most part, is a nation of immigrants. Throughout its history, immigrants have contributed greatly to the country's population. Situations around the world such as famine, lack of economic opportunity, and political and/or religious persecution, as well as historical events such as the California Gold Rush, have fueled a dramatic immigration influx during particular eras. For example, the period from the 1840s to 1914 marked the greatest immigration to the United States, and the majority of immigrants were from Europe and Asia (Chiswick, 1998). More recently, immigrants tend to have non-European roots and have included individuals from Mexico, Latin America and the Caribbean, and Asia (including the Philippines, India, China, and Vietnam) (Chiswick, 1998).

Immigrants to this country have adapted to the existing cultural structures and mores and have added their own unique contributions. Many immigrants have been quickly acculturated and absorbed into the dominant culture, whereas others have elected to maintain a more primary identification with their native culture. Many immigrants have been welcomed with open arms. Others, such as the Irish and Chinese, during the mid- to late 1880s faced extreme hardship and discrimination. Africans brought to this country involuntarily as slaves were for many years regarded as property rather than citizens and were denied even the most basic of human rights. Regardless of country of origin and immigration circumstances, immigrants have exerted crucial influence on the economic, political, and social structures of this country.

The cultural composition of the United States continues to shift toward ever increasing diversity. According to the U.S. Census Bureau, whereas one in eight Americans was a member of a race other than Caucasian at the turn of the last century, at the beginning of the 21st century, the ratio of people who were nonwhite to people who were white was one in four (Hobbs & Stoops, 2002). According to the 2000 Census, nearly 89% of the population was born in the United States and 11% was foreign born. The breakdown of birth origin of the foreign born is as follows: Latin America, 51.7%; Asia, 26.4%; Europe, 15.8%; Africa, 2.8%; North America, 2.7%; and Oceania, .5%. According to the same census, in nearly 18% of U.S. homes, a language other than English was spoken.

On April 1, 2000, during Census 2000, the population of the United States was 281,421,906. Of that number, more than 30% of individuals were of nonwhite, non–Anglo-European ancestry (with the breakdown being white, not Hispanic, 69.1%; Hispanic of any race, 12.5%; black or African American, 12.3%; Asian, 3.6%; American Indian and Alaska Native, .9%; Native Hawaiian and other Pacific Islander, .1%) (U.S. Bureau of the Census, 2000b). These data contrast with 1970 census figures in which approximately 12% of the population was nonwhite (U.S. Bureau of the Census, 1973). The population of races other than white or black grew markedly between 1970 and 2000, and many individuals identified themselves as belonging to two or more races (identified for the first time in the Census 2000) (Hobbs & Stoops, 2002). In the period from 1980 to 2000, the white, non-Hispanic population increased by only 7.9%, whereas the population who identified themselves as nonwhite or Hispanic grew by 88%.

Another burgeoning population group was "children and young adults." According to the 2000 Census, 26% of the population, or 174.1 million individuals, were 18 years old or younger (Meyer, 2001). In Census 2000, the younger age groups were characterized by greater racial and ethnic diversity than were the older age groups (Hobbs & Stoops, 2002). Asian and Hispanic/Latino populations, as noted previously, experienced the greatest growth from 1970 to 2000, and this was attributed chiefly to immigration patterns and birth rates (Hobbs & Stoops, 2002). The trends in age distribution by race and ethnicity have shifted from 25% of the population younger than age 25 in 1980 to 39% of the population younger than age 25 in 2000 (Hobbs & Stoops, 2002). In the Census 2000, the "two or more races" populations had the highest percentage of people younger than age 15 years (36%), whereas white, non-Hispanics had the lowest percentage younger than 15 from 1980 to 2000 (Hobbs & Stoops, 2002). The majority of individuals who reported in Census 2000 to be a combination of two or more races had Hispanic roots (Grieco & Cassidy, 2001). An examination of each racial category by age indicates that the percentage of members younger than 18 years old within each race are the following: Native Hawaiian and Other Pacific Islander, 35.8%; black or African American, 32.5%; American Indian and Alaska Native, 33.6%; Asian, 27.1%; white, 24%; and some other race, 36% (U.S. Bureau of the Census, 2000a). The Hispanic or Latino population accounts for the greatest percentage (90%) of those listed in the "younger than 18" category (Grieco & Cassidy, 2001). As is apparent from these data, a growing proportion of the U.S. population is composed of children and families from nonwhite racial and ethnic groups.

THE IMPORTANCE OF CROSS-CULTURAL EFFECTIVENESS

As U.S. society has become more heterogeneous, cross-cultural effectiveness has emerged as an essential skill for all service providers who work with children and their families. The need to be cross-culturally competent is just as critical for neonatal intensive care nurses, social workers, or physicians in health care environments as it is for child care providers, educators, psychologists, physical therapists, occupational therapists, speech-language pathologists, and aides in educational environments. For instance, the health care provider must be aware of the meaning that families assign to the use of surgery and drugs for medical treatments, just as educators must be knowledgeable of family beliefs about child rearing and developmental expectations. All service providers must be sensitive to differences across families in communication style, decision making, and the need or willingness to seek assistance from members outside the family.

Because of the young age of the children, the issues on which families and professionals focus in providing services for infants, toddlers, and preschoolers are closely related to the family's values, beliefs, and traditions. The most basic issues—health care, sleeping, eating, regulating body states, building relationships, and exploring the environment—are central concerns for those who work with young children. They also are primary concerns for families and ones for which typically no "outside" interference takes place unless there has been some evidence of gross mistreatment. When a child has a disability, however, many outsiders may become involved with the child and family. The potential for conflict related to child-rearing practices thus emerges. Developing a respect for the values and beliefs of different cultures can help diminish these possible clashes.

Although the diversity of children and their families has increased, training programs for professionals who are most likely to work with children and their families still have relatively few students who represent cultures with non–Anglo-European

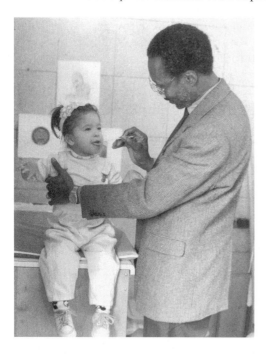

roots (Hanson & Lovett, 1992). Personnel preparation programs must address this discrepancy by establishing priorities both for recruiting students and/or trainees from groups under-represented previously and by expanding training curricula to reflect skills in cross-cultural competency. Service providers and the families with whom they work may not be matched culturally in all cases, and the cultures to which each adheres will not be changed. However, the styles and methods used by practitioners in working with families *can* be altered to enhance their respect for families and their effectiveness in working with children and families from a variety of backgrounds.

Contemporary philosophies of service delivery for children and their families typically highlight the need for family-centered or family-focused approaches (Hanson & Lynch, 2004). Children and other family members must be viewed as part of a larger family system, and the importance of working closely with parents and other family members is essential to success. This renewed focus on the family—their concerns, priorities, strengths, and resources—in the delivery of service underscores the need for respect, knowledge, and awareness of the family's cultural, ethnic, and linguistic heritage.

NATURE OF INTERVENTION IN THE EARLY YEARS

The term *early intervention* implies the provision of a set of services in the early years of a child's life. The goal of intervention is change, and the assumption is made that change is both possible and valued. Thus, even as families begin contact with service professionals in the helping sciences, they encounter mainstream American cultural values regarding the benefits of action and change. In some cultures, change may not be deemed so necessary or desirable; an acceptance of this fate or a "wait-and-see" approach to the issue of a disability or illness may predominate.

The concept of intervention may be foreign to some families. Even initial inquiries to families in terms of the availability of services and the need for their participation may prove an undesirable and upsetting intervention to family dynamics and beliefs. Understanding the cultural beliefs and practices to which families adhere may help prevent unfortunate misunderstandings.

The following discussion highlights several notions about intervention services that may produce confusion or differences between service providers' practices and family members' beliefs. These notions are organized around the following categories:

- Why intervention is done—attitudes regarding intervention

- What methods are used and where services are located

- Who provides service delivery

- How services are provided—styles of interaction and communication

Why Intervention Is Done—Attitudes Regarding Intervention

Different cultures attach very different meanings to the presence of disabilities or at-risk conditions. Views related to disability and its causation range from those that emphasize the role of fate to those that place responsibility on the person or his or her family (Hanson, Lynch, & Wayman, 1990). People who ascribe to the more fatalistic view of disability see little recourse or remedy. For example, Green (1982) noted that in the Vietnamese culture, individuals might see that they have little power to escape from their fate and, thus, seek mainly to achieve harmony in this life.

In some cultures, blame for a child's disability may be attached to the parents. Some may see the disability as a punishment for sins; others may view it a result of some action the mother or father took while the mother was pregnant. Still other groups may attribute causation to mind–body imbalances or the presence of evil spirits in the child's body (Hanson et al., 1990).

Causative factors for various disabilities have long been debated in American culture. Causation may be assigned to a variety of factors, such as disease, brain injury, genetic disorders, chemical imbalances, or environmental factors (e.g., child abuse). For some types of disabilities, multiple factors may account for difficulties, whereas for others no single factor or specific cluster of factors can be identified. Regardless of causation, however, in mainstream American culture, typically some sort of intervention is viewed as possible and desirable. The key is finding the appropriate methods.

Certainly, the views held by families about causation and disability will influence their need or willingness to seek help or intervention. These views also will affect the degree to which the family elects to participate and the type of participation. If families who ascribe to a less direct and action-oriented path to change than that found in the mainstream American culture do seek to participate in services, then their level of comfort during the process of help-seeking and intervention may be compromised. For instance, for some family members, just being asked about their concerns and areas of need may be viewed as shaming. As service providers become more effective at working cross culturally, they will be able to individually tailor information-gathering techniques and interventions to address these cultural differences.

What Methods Are Used and Where Services Are Located

Mainstream American cultural strategies regarding educational and therapeutic practices in children's early years have focused on planned and active interventions that include the involvement of their families (Lynch, 1987). Historically, early intervention practices have moved from placing little value on parental involvement, to viewing parents as teachers of their youngsters, to viewing parents more broadly as partners in the intervention process (Hanson & Lynch, 1995).

Service delivery systems for young children with disabilities typically bridge multiple professions, agencies, and places of service delivery. Interventions may be carried out in hospitals, clinics, or the child's home. Families of these children are required to make some adaptations that are not required of families who do not have a child with a disability. For example, frequent visits to hospitals or clinics in which the family's concerns and behavior are made public may be disconcerting to those whose child-rearing practices differ from those of the dominant culture. Furthermore, many service programs provide services in the family's home. The degree of

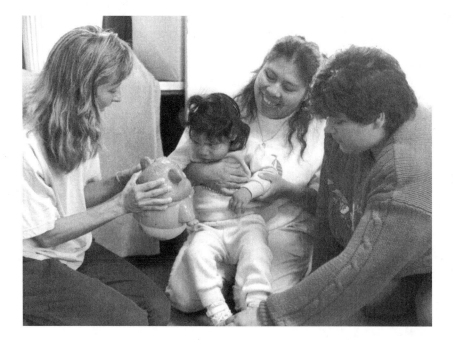

intrusion and forced intimacy this entails may cause discomfort for both the family and the service provider. The discussion that follows illustrates these points.

Children with disabilities or those who are at risk for disabilities may have serious medical problems that require intervention. Because medical practices are integrally linked to cultural traditions, service providers and family members may find that there is conflict about the recommended course of action. For example, the mainstream American culture places a high value on prevention of disease and the use of high technology in medical practice. The majority of Americans view the latest diagnostic techniques and the most aggressive approaches to managing illness as important advancements. Surgery and prescription drugs are typical treatments (Lynch, 1987).

In the United States, people generally assume that good health is a basic right and that medical science should be able to cure everything. These beliefs are far from universal. Among some American Indian tribes, for instance, the medicine man or shaman and the tribal community are considered essential to the healing process. As described in Lynch (1987, p. 85),

> The family discusses the illness with the medicine man, determines the cause of the sickness (for example, contact with a ghost), and organizes a community sing, which attempts to eliminate the cause and the disease. It is not uncommon for Navajos to use both Western medical practices and indigenous treatments to heal members of the community. (R.B. Lewis & J. Lewis, personal communication, Dec. 16, 1985)

The nurse, the physician, and the hospital social worker who are advocating for surgery, drug treatments, or other medical procedures need to be aware of these families' beliefs and practices and also the value and significance of these rituals to the families and the community.

Once a young child is medically stable, he or she often is referred to a developmentally or educationally oriented intervention program. These interventions also may produce cultural conflicts. The earliest learning experiences of young children are centered on their own senses and perceptions and are mediated by the reactions of their primary caregivers. Because early learning focuses on such basic behaviors as eating, sleeping, communicating, and establishing relationships, learning in this period is inextricably bound to cultural values, beliefs, and traditions. As a result, some of the interventions that may seem innocuous to one family may seem strange and unusual to others with different child-rearing practices. The following examples illustrate this point.

Independence and privacy are highly valued in mainstream American culture, and children typically are encouraged to become independent almost from birth. Families strive to have separate rooms for each child, and infants sleep alone, often in rooms by themselves. To many families (e.g., families from Mexico, Central and South America, and Asia), however, isolating young children in a separate room, in a crib, or in a single bed is considered inappropriate. Infants typically sleep in the same bed with the parents and are not left alone during sleep.

Feeding practices for young children also may be quite varied. For some families, mealtimes are highly structured; for others, there is much less definition. The meal may be prepared and kept out for family members, with each person taking whatever he or she wants whenever it is desired. When there is neither a formal mealtime nor specific preparations for it, suggesting that a family work on language skills for a child when the family sits down to dinner is not an intervention that can be incorporated into that family's daily routine. For interventions to be effective, they must respect and, to the extent possible, incorporate the practices of the family.

Professionals and assistants who work with families from cultures different from their own are in a unique position to bridge the two cultures. For families who have recently immigrated to the United States, service providers may assist them as they learn to function in a new environment by 1) interpreting the mainstream culture; 2) learning about the family's practices related to child rearing, health care, and socialization; and 3) helping to design interventions that match the family's preferences and concerns. Interpreting the mainstream culture may be the most difficult role because service providers may be called on to explain why some cultural practices are discouraged in the United States. For example, some healing techniques, such as *bat gio* (pinching) or *cao gio* (coining—the striking or scratching of the skin to rid the body of disorders such as headaches and colds), which are most common among the Mien, Vietnamese, and ethnic Chinese in Southeast Asia, are not considered acceptable practices in the United States because of their perceived potential to cause harm to the child (Schreiner, 1981). It may be the service provider's role to provide information about the new culture that will help the family adapt to new demands and beliefs while helping the family maintain the elements of their traditional culture. This is not an easy task, and the difficulties encountered by both the family and the service provider are made more challenging by cross-cultural differences.

In other instances, the service provider must accept the practices of families as valid and important, although these practices may be different from those practiced by the service provider or by the dominant culture in that geographical area. For example, in the United States, toilet training between the child's second and third birthday is a fairly common practice and is—in fact—highly valued by many families; however, this practice may be viewed by many other cultural groups as unnecessary and too early. Expectations for children concerning feeding, sleeping, and speaking, as well as the use of discipline, to mention only a few, vary widely across cultural groups.

Who Provides Service Delivery

Recommended practices in early intervention services in the United States typically define the providers as a team of professionals from a variety of disciplines who work collaboratively with one another and in partnerships with family members (Hanson & Lynch, 1995). The professional disciplines that most commonly provide early intervention services include education, medicine, nursing, nutrition/dietetics, occupational therapy, physical therapy, psychology, social work, and speech-language pathology and audiology. Individuals from many of these professional backgrounds may specialize in serving young children and their families.

These mainstream cultural notions of service providers may differ widely from those held by certain cultural groups. Members of particular cultural groups may turn to elders, other family members, friends, or folk healers for assistance in child health and behavioral issues. To illustrate differences across cultural groups, Randall-David (1989, p. 26) provided a list of therapeutic agents or people whose help is sought for psychosocial disorders (see Table 1.1). Thus, the people to whom a family turns for help, support, or intervention will vary with the family's cultural expectations and values.

Table 1.1.   List of therapeutic agents or people sought by various cultural groups for help with psychosocial disorders

Mainstream white American	Mexican American
Counselors	Curanderos
Psychiatrists	**Puerto Rican**
Psychologists	Espiritistas
Social workers	Santerios
Ministers	**Cuban**
African American	Santerios
Ministers	**Southeast Asian American**
Root workers	Herbalists
Voodoo priests	Family/friends
Native American	Diviners
Medicine men	**Haitian**
"Singers"	Voodoo priests

From Randall-David, E. (1989). *Strategies for working with culturally diverse communities and clients* (p. 26). Washington, DC: Association for the Care of Children's Health.

How Services Are Provided— Styles of Interaction and Communication

The styles in which individuals exchange information and converse may differ widely for various cultural groups. Particularly when dealing with sensitive issues such as the disability or illness of a family member, communication style may play a key role in establishing effective interactions with families. The dominant communication style in mainstream American culture is often characterized as direct and fairly informal. With respect to intervention services, family input and participation is typically highly valued. Family involvement throughout the intervention process is encouraged, from defining goals to participating in the treatment or teaching. For some families, direct confrontation and questioning may bring shame or discomfort. Inquiries and informal questions surrounding these personal issues may be deemed highly inappropriate. Other families, however, may seek opportunities to discuss their children's conditions with professionals.

Preferences and practices may differ dramatically from culture to culture with regard to method of greeting (formal versus informal); type of dress (professional versus informal); degree of eye contact when interacting (direct contact versus looking down or away); person to whom inquiries are directed (mother, father, elder, other family member, other); and method through which information is gathered (orally versus written, structured versus open-ended questions). The service provider's first interactions with families may determine whether an effective working relationship will be established. "Getting off on the right foot" by understanding and recognizing the communication styles practiced by various families will facilitate the process.

CONCEPT OF CULTURAL IDENTITY

Although the purpose of this book is to help the reader become more sensitive to cultural differences and more knowledgeable about variations in cultural practices, a person's cultural identification cannot be viewed as the exclusive determinant of one's actions. Many other factors also influence an individual's actions. In addition, individuals vary in the degree to which they identify with a cultural group. Such factors limit the role that culture may play in influencing behavior. Some of these factors are discussed briefly in the following sections.

Factors that Interact with the Influence of Cultural Identity

Regional labels (e.g., "southerner," "midwesterner") may connote a set of characteristics noted in an area's inhabitants. Although some people may hold strong chauvinistic regard for their geographical region, most resist being labeled and stereotyped on the basis of their place of residence. Likewise, generalizations cannot be made about the characteristics and behaviors of any given cultural or ethnic group. Although members of the groups may hold some beliefs and life practices in common, many other factors influence their behavior and how they define themselves as individuals. In fact, some of these factors may play a more significant role in determining a person's behavior at any given moment than will his or her cultural identity. For example, if a family is homeless, the absence of consistent shelter and food is likely to have a strong influence on the day-to-day practices of the family. Indeed, the "culture of poverty" likely will define an individual's and family's lifeways and possibilities to a far greater extent than cultural and linguistic identity (Hanson & Lynch, 2004).

Other influences or factors that affect an individual's cultural identity include socioeconomic status; length of residence in the United States or in a particular region of the country; the type of region (e.g., urban, suburban, rural); the person's age and gender; the amount and type of education; the number and type of resources or family support systems; and, in the case of immigrants, the reason for the immigration and/or the "wave" of immigration with which the person is associated. The language spoken by the individual or family and the level of linguistic competence will influence opportunities and access to information and services, as well. The constel-

lation of the family (e.g., mother only, no parents, two parents, parents plus extended family members, same-sex parents) will play a role in how the family members define themselves and their access to and acceptance in society. Any of these factors may exercise a powerful effect on the individual's lifeways and, in many cases, may play a more dominant role than the cultural framework in which the individual was socialized.

Within-Group Differences

Cultural group labels are used to identify groups of individuals who share many dimensions of their lifeways, values, and beliefs. Group identification helps to create bonds between individual members of the group and continues the group socialization process with children and others who join that group. However, these labels only point to tendencies of members of that group. Such labels or groupings fail to distinguish the wide variation of practices of individuals within the group. For example, in the United States the terms *Anglo* or *Anglo-European* are used to refer to individuals who typically have historical roots associated with Great Britain or Europe and who are members of what is considered the mainstream or dominant culture in the United States. To a European, these labels are sometimes amusing because the European continent comprises an array of countries, each with different languages, religions, governments, and lifestyles. To group these populations under a single label may not provide much meaning. Even in the United States, many individuals hold tight bonds to their Anglo or European roots and identify with being Italian or Irish or German rather than Anglo-European. Likewise, this tendency to label fails to recognize the differences and distinguishing characteristics within the group. For instance, several hundred tribes and villages of American Indians reside in the United States. Although tribal interests and lifeways may be similar in many respects, these people's individual tribal customs, languages, and life practices are obscured by a more general representation.

For each of the groups identified in the Cultural Perspectives section (Part II) of this volume, this variability holds true. Within each group are distinct groupings, and within those "subgroups" are individuals. Authors have been challenged to describe some central or common tendencies found within these overall cultural or ethnic identifications, but variation in terms of behaviors and beliefs is marked within each group. As service providers meet family members, this awareness of individual differences and within-group variability must be appreciated.

Continuum of Cultural Identification

Assumptions about an individual's behavior based on a cultural label or a stereotype may result in inaccurate, inappropriate, or harmful generalizations. Although individuals may identify with a given cultural, ethnic, or racial group by way of birthplace, skin color, language, or religious practices, these factors will not determine the degree to which individuals see themselves as members of a group.

America has long been characterized as a "nation of nations" (Marzio, 1976); this characterization emphasizes the immigrant history of this country. Despite the tremendous variability in the historical, linguistic, ethnic, racial, and cultural backgrounds of the immigrants who shaped American culture throughout its history, a mainstream culture has evolved and predominated. In *American Ways: A Guide for Foreigners in the*

United States, Althen stated, "The predominant ideas, values, and behaviors of 'Americans' are those of the white, middle class. People in that category have long held the large majority of the country's most influential positions" (1988, p. xiii). Althen reviewed some general notions about American "culture"—notions that are derived from how many Americans see themselves, as well as how foreigners see Americans. Predominant American values and assumptions, according to Althen, include emphases on 1) individualism and privacy; 2) equality; 3) informality; 4) the future, change, and progress; 5) goodness of humanity; 6) time; 7) achievement, action, work, and materialism; and 8) directness and assertiveness (see discussion in Chapter 4). Many long-term residents of the United States subscribe to these values; some do not. Likewise, many new immigrants will adopt all or some of these mainstream values, whereas others will choose to retain the major values of their native culture, particularly when those values differ from those of mainstream or dominant U.S. society.

Sanday (cited in Green, 1995) discussed four categories of cultural integration that reflect the degree to which the members of a cultural or an ethnic group have integrated their values with those of the dominant or mainstream culture in the place in which they live: 1) mainstreamers, 2) bicultural individuals, 3) culturally different individuals, and 4) culturally marginal individuals. *Mainstreamers* have assimilated or adopted the standard values accepted by the dominant or mainstream culture. *Bicultural individuals* may participate dually in both the dominant culture and in a nondominant culture (e.g., their culture of origin). These individuals may have a commitment to both cultures. It also should be noted that some individuals might comfortably negotiate and maintain commitments to more than two cultures. *Culturally different individuals* are those people who have been exposed to the dominant or mainstream culture but choose to remain apart in their enclave of cultural origin. These people may interact on occasion with institutions of the dominant culture (e.g., health care services), but they maintain most of their activity within their contained or isolated group. People identifying as members of enclaves such as "Chinatowns" and "Little Italys" may fall into this category. English may or may not be spoken in these cultural enclaves, and, if spoken, it may not be used in daily practice in the homes. Members of these groups may be recent immigrants or long-term residents of the United States. Finally, *culturally marginal individuals* are those individuals who essentially follow their own way and who hold no attachment to any particular cultural group.

Although this paradigm may be helpful in understanding differences in the degree of identification among individuals, a more interactional or transactional approach to cultural identification is needed from the standpoint of the service provider. Green explained that the degree to which people are acculturated is "situational rather than absolute and can be modified to suit the needs of different kinds of cross-cultural encounters" (1982, p. 13). For example, a family may adhere to most practices and proponents of the dominant culture (e.g., work, lifeways, housing standards, recreational practices) but may differ radically on one dimension (e.g., health care). For instance, several court cases involving parents' choices related to health care illustrate this notion of situational cultural identification. In one instance, parents who were Christian Scientists elected to use prayer rather than surgery to treat their child's bowel obstruction; in another case, a Chinese mother elected to use Chinese medicine rather than Western practices (i.e., drugs and surgery) to treat her child's juvenile rheumatoid arthritis ("Does Doctor Know Best?" 1990). Thus, family members may adopt some but not all aspects of the dominant culture(s) in which they reside; these beliefs may even shift over time. Families may opt at one point, for instance, to send their children to a "mainstream" school that represents the ways of the dominant culture but later decide to educate their children in a "native" school operated by and for members of their particular cultural group.

Sanchez-Hucles discussed the potential difficulties experienced by people with bicultural identification. These difficulties include the pressure felt by individuals to "select the 'right' response from their repertoire of two cultures" (1990, p. 13) and to minimize their ethnicity and act like members of the dominant culture.

Historically (as reviewed by Marsella, 1990), ethnocultural identity was viewed from the degree of "assimilation" or "acculturation" to the dominant culture. In the United States, as the population has become increasingly diverse, a more pluralistic view has been adopted. This view acknowledges the contributions of the many cultures that make up this society, but it fails to describe the dynamic and interactional perspective of cultural identity.

In summary, whereas our culture or ethnicity plays a role in defining who we are as people and how we conduct our lives, multiple dimensions form that identify and influence our lifeways. The degree to which we identify with a particular group(s), under what situations or circumstances we identify, and the dimensions or aspects we choose, along with other social and demographic factors, all play a role as well. Cultural or ethnic identification is but one facet, albeit a very instrumental facet, in shaping our behavior. The service provider who is able to value and respect these differences among families will find his or her job more understandable and infinitely more rewarding.

CHALLENGES AND PROMISES FOR SERVICE PROVIDERS

For years, the United States was characterized as a great melting pot where people from various lands and cultures met to forge a new and homogeneous society. That characterization has been replaced by a pluralistic view that recognizes the many and varied contributions made by the members of this society. However, Green (1995) cautioned that neither the melting pot nor the pluralistic categorical approaches to understanding ethnicity are particularly useful. Rather, he argued for a more transactional or interactional approach that examines the relationships between individuals and the larger society. Cultural modifications and mixing will occur as groups recognize value in each other's practices.

For service providers, a transactional and situational approach is particularly applicable. Each child with whom they will work is an individual with unique characteristics, strengths, and needs. Similar to the individual children, families also have unique concerns, priorities, and resources. As individuals and as families, these characteristics, concerns, and priorities are not static; rather, they are constantly shifting and changing.

Our cultural and ethnic identities help to shape our beliefs and practices and who we are as individuals and as family members. These identities are not the script for our behavior, but they do provide a texture and richness. They can both bind us together in groups and separate us from one another. Knowledge and understanding, sensitivity, and respect for these cultural differences can significantly enhance the effectiveness of service providers in the helping professions.

Service providers are required to adjust and adapt strategies continuously to work effectively with families that may adhere to radically different and individualized values, beliefs, and practices. These challenges can be frustrating and can necessitate further study and information gathering. They also produce unparalleled opportunities to the service provider. They provide the practitioner opportunities to be exposed to a richness of human experiences, to learn new information, and to grow as an individual. Like the gardener, the application of individualized and appropriate interventions or strategies will result in a wonderful array of outcomes—children and their family members will be nurtured and supported to reach their full potential as individuals.

REFERENCES

Althen, G. (1988). *American ways: A guide for foreigners in the United States.* Yarmouth, ME: Intercultural Press.

Anderson, P.P., & Fenichel, E.S. (1989). *Serving culturally diverse families of infants and toddlers with disabilities.* Washington, DC: National Center for Clinical Infant Programs.

Chiswick, B.R. (1998). Immigration: The latest wave. In *The 1998 World Book Year Book: The annual supplement to The World Book Encyclopedia* (pp. 238–247). Chicago: World Book, Inc.

Does doctor know best? (1990, September). *Newsweek,* p. 84.

Green, J.W. (1982). *Cultural awareness in the human services.* Upper Saddle River, NJ: Prentice Hall.

Green, J.W. (1995). *Cultural awareness in the human services: A multi-ethnic approach* (2nd ed.). Boston: Allyn & Bacon.

Grieco, E.M., & Cassidy, R.C. (2001). *Overview of race and Hispanic origin, Census 2000 brief,* C2KBR/01–1, Washington, DC: U.S. Bureau of the Census. Available online: http://www.census.gov/prod/2001pubs/c2br01.1.pdfx

Hanson, M.J., & Lovett, D. (1992). Personnel preparation for early interventionists: A cross-disciplinary survey. *Journal of Early Intervention, 16*(2), 123–135.

Hanson, M.J., & Lynch, E.W. (1995). *Early intervention: Implementing child and family services for infants and toddlers who are at-risk or disabled* (2nd ed.). Austin, TX: PRO-ED.

Hanson, M.J., & Lynch, E.W. (2004). *Understanding families: Approaches to diversity, disability, and risk.* Baltimore: Paul H. Brookes Publishing Co.

Hanson, M.J., Lynch, E.W., & Wayman, K.I. (1990). Honoring the cultural diversity of families when gathering data. *Topics in Early Childhood Special Education, 10*(1), 112–131.

Hobbs, F., & Stoops, N. (2002). *Demographic trends in the 20th century: Census 2000 special reports,* CESR-4. Washington, DC: U.S. Census Bureau. Available online: http://www.census.gov/prod/2002pubs/censr-4.pdf

Lynch, E.W. (1987). Families from different cultures. In M. Bristol & C. Kasari (Eds.), *The Family Support Network series: Monograph One* (pp. 80–88). Moscow: University of Idaho, Family Support Network Project.

Marsella, A.J. (1990). Ethnocultural identity: The "new" independent variable in cross-cultural research. *Focus, 4*(2), 14–15.

Marzio, P.C. (Ed.). (1976). *A nation of nations: The people who came to America as seen through objects and documents exhibited at the Smithsonian Institution.* New York: Harper & Row.

Meyer, J. (2001). *Age: 2000, Census 2000 brief,* C2KBR/01–12. Washington, DC: U.S. Census Bureau. Available online: http://www.census.gov/prod/2001pubs/c2br01.12.pdf

Randall-David, E. (1989). *Strategies for working with culturally diverse communities and clients.* Washington, DC: Association for the Care of Children's Health.

Sanchez-Hucles, J.V. (1990). Biculturalism in American ethnic minorities: A direction for a society that values diversity. *Focus, 4*(2), 13–14.

Schreiner, D. (1981). *Southeast Asian healing practices/child abuse?* (Available from Peck Health Center, 2415 SE 43rd Street, Portland, OR 97206.)

Seldes, G. (Compiler). (1960). *The great quotations.* New York: Pocket Books.

U.S. Bureau of the Census. (1973). *Characteristics of the population: Vol. 1.* Washington, DC: United States Department of Commerce.

U.S. Bureau of the Census (2000a). *Population by age, sex, race, and Hispanic or Latino origin for the United States: 2000; Table 4. Population by race alone or in combination and age for the United States.* Available online: http://www.census.gov/population/cen2000/phc-t9/tab04.pdf

U.S. Bureau of the Census (2000b). *Profile of general demographic characteristics: 2000,* Table DP-1. Available online: http://censtats.census.gov/data/US/01000.pdf

CHAPTER 2

CONCEPTUAL FRAMEWORK

From Culture Shock to Cultural Learning

Eleanor W. Lynch

The river of truth is always splitting up into arms which reunite.
Islanded between them the inhabitants argue for a lifetime
as to which is the mainstream.
—CYRIL CONNOLLY (AS QUOTED IN GROSS, 1987)

Many of us in this country are only a few generations removed
from the immigrant ancestors who made the long journey to this
new world. Most who made that move would call it a success. . . .
But regardless of the successes and benefits, the immigrant
experience often exacted a considerable price for that first
generation, the ones with only partially acculturated minds
and bodies, the ones who forever carried those
wispy memories of their world left behind.
—ROBERT M. SAPOLSKY (1997)

Recognizing what we have done in the past is a recognition
of ourselves. By conducting a dialogue with our past,
we are searching how to go forward.
—KIYOKO TAKEDA (AS QUOTED IN DORMANN, 1987)

Everyone has a cultural, ethnic, linguistic, and racial identity. All of us are products of one or more cultural, language, and ethnic groups. For some individuals, cultural, language, ethnic, and racial origins continue to be a major part of their overt identity. The foods served; the celebrations of major holidays and life events; and the values held regarding family, child rearing, time, independence, authority, responsibility, and spirituality reflect their cultural and ethnic heritage. These individuals' roots are very near the surface, and day-to-day life tends to be shaped by their global place of origin, its culture, its language, and sometimes by the color of its people's skin. Although shaped by a global place of origin, the ways of being in a new place differ in some ways from the original, just as the global place of origin itself differs from the memories of it that immigrants and sojourners carry in their hearts and minds.

For other people, roots are deeply buried; layers of adjustment and adaptation have blunted these people's awareness of their origins. They may think of themselves as products of the American culture with little reference or connection to an ethnic, cultural, or global heritage. Regardless of how long ago or how recently our ancestors came to the United States, however, our roots—in subtle and not-so-subtle ways—influence our attitudes and behaviors.

The influence of culture, language, ethnicity, and race is always easier to see in other people than in ourselves. Culture, similar to a second skin, is something to which we have grown so accustomed that we have ceased to notice that it exists; however, it is not surprising that culture has such a profound influence on our behavior. It is a part of our life from inception—our mother's practices during pregnancy, the way we are cared for as infants, how and what we are named, the language and sounds that surround us, and the rules that we are taught as we grow.

Guthrie's (1975) insights from several decades ago still aptly describe five reasons for the difficulties that people experience when they try to understand or function in a culture other than their own.

1. *Cultural understanding in one's first culture occurs early and is typically established by the time a child is 5 years old.* Culture, similar to language, is acquired very early in life (Brown & Lenneberg, 1965). Every interaction, sound, touch, odor, and experience has a cultural component that is absorbed even when it is not directly taught. Lessons learned at such early ages become an integral part of thinking and behavior. Table manners, the proper behavior when interacting with adults, and the rules of acceptable emotional response are anchored in culture. Many of the behaviors and beliefs learned at an early age persist into adulthood and achieve the status of "truth." Perhaps an individual, as a child, had to adhere to certain rules about how to dress in different environments—for example, a place of worship versus school. Learning to eat may have involved using a knife, fork, and spoon; chopsticks; or one's right hand. There may have been rules related to speaking to adults: As children, some people were not allowed to initiate a conversation with an adult; some may have been required to use titles of respect; some may have been taught to look at the adult while speaking, whereas others may have been taught to look down. For others, some groups and beliefs were to be revered, whereas others were to be reviled. These rules of interaction and ways of being are inculcated early and persistently. They surround the developing child and form guidelines, ways of thinking and viewing the world, and boundaries that are deeply embedded in behavior and the psyche.

2. *Children learn new cultural patterns more easily than adults.* As in language learning, children are more adept than adults at acquiring new cultural skills. Whether it is because they have the ability to be more flexible, because their patterns of behavior are less established, or because they have less information to manage, children tend to cross cultures more easily than adults. In most instances, when children of varying ethnic, racial, or language groups play together, they find constructive ways to adapt to new rules, to different languages, and to different behaviors. They may act out what is supposed to happen, negotiate a resolution verbally and nonverbally, ignore behavior that they do not understand, or confront the other child about the behavior. Although the interactions do not always go smoothly, children are typically able to make cross-cultural interactions work.

3. *Values are determined by one's first culture and may have to be revised to be effective in a second culture.* Values are responsible for many of our built-in biases. The importance that individuals ascribe to cooperation versus competition, action versus passivity, youth versus age, family versus friends, or independence versus interdependence reflects cultural values. The concept of competition is a good example. In the mainstream U.S. culture, children are encouraged from an early age to excel in whatever they do, which is often interpreted as encouragement to be better than everyone else. Contests are held for everything from spelling to selling fundraising items to hog calling. The free enterprise economy is built on entrepreneurial competition. Newspapers are filled with the latest records set in high and low temperatures, sports, and the stock market. In the United States, then, competition is highly prized; however, the reverse is true in many American Indian, Hispanic/Latino, Pacific Island, and some Asian and Southeast Asian cultures. Competition is viewed as self-serving, and the emphasis is on cooperation and teamwork. Because competition is a negative trait in these cultures, being viewed as competitive rather than cooperative brings shame rather than pride.

    Views related to gender roles provide another example. In the United States, considerable effort is placed on gender equity and equalizing opportunity for both sexes across educational, athletic, and career paths. Encouraging girls to enter professions such as math, science, and engineering is an ongoing issue and area of emphasis; and hiring male professionals in elementary education, nursing, and elder care, though not the norm, is a goal of many. Not all cultural, religious, and/or ethnic groups seek gender equality, however. Goals for girls and boys, men and women may differ considerably from culture to culture. As a result of these differences in attitudes, American schools' expectations and offerings for boys and girls (e.g., competitive sports for girls, home economics for boys, family and child care for boys and girls together) may be quite surprising and disquieting to some families and students whose views of male and female roles focus on differentiation rather than equality.

4. *Understanding one's first culture introduces errors in interpreting the second culture.* Individuals interpret situations based on their past experience, and those interpretations are never culture free. In the work of Moll and Greenberg (1990) and Velez-Ibañez and Greenberg (1992), that is applied to early childhood by Barrera and Corso (2003), the phrase "funds of knowledge" is used to describe specific knowledge that holds strategic importance to members of a particular culture or community. These funds of knowledge provide a framework for values, beliefs,

interactions, and understandings within the community or culture and for individual members (Barrera & Corso, 2003). For example, the rules for touching differ from culture to culture. In the United States, it is quite common to see members of the opposite sex holding hands, walking with their arms around one another, or kissing in public. In many other parts of the world, such public displays of affection between men and women are not tolerated; however, it would be commonplace to see members of the same sex walking hand-in-hand or with their arms around one another. In the United States, such behavior is a signal of sexual orientation; in other countries, it is more likely to be a demonstration of friendship. Likewise, most Americans interpret laughing and giggling as expressions of enjoyment—signals that people are relaxed and having a good time. Among other cultural groups, such as Southeast Asians, the same behavior may be a sign of extreme embarrassment or discomfort or what Americans might call "nervous laughter" taken to the extreme.

Confusion may also arise when interpreting spoken interactions across cultures. In the United States it is considered unusual, if not rude, to ask people their religion, their political affiliation, or how much money they make. These topics are off limits in most social conversations, and sometimes issues of money are off limits even within the family. The same is not true throughout the world. In the author's experience living and working in Indonesia, the first questions posed to her were "How many children do you have?" "What kind of birth control do you use?" and "How much money do you make?" Often, people asked about the author's religion. These questions, interpreted from a U.S. perspective, were initially startling and embarrassing. When experienced again and again, they became routine and unremarkable.

5. *Longstanding behavior patterns are typically used to express one's deepest values.* Old habits are not easily changed. People often revert to old behaviors out of habit or in times of high emotion or stress. From the caller who realizes she is saying thank you to a computer voice on the telephone to the American in England who discovers himself looking for the steering wheel on the left side of the car, individuals discover that behaviors they have practiced for years are difficult to modify. We as individuals behave as we have been culturally programmed to behave, and sometimes our cultural program conflicts with someone else's. For example, careful time management and punctuality are important and widespread values in the dominant U.S. culture. The majority of people wear a watch, and nearly every professional (and many parents) carry bulky calendars full of appointments that must be kept and responsibilities that must be fulfilled within a certain time. Everyday conversations are replete with comments about time— "I don't have time," "When I have time," "What a time waster that was," "I can't— I'll be late," and "Check your calendar." This preoccupation with time as a commodity that can be bought, sold, or apportioned is not typical in much of the rest of the world, however. In Central and South America, parts of Asia, Southeast Asia, the Middle East, Africa, the Mediterranean, the Pacific Islands, and among many ethnic groups within the United States, time is generously shared. People are more important than clocks; individuals operate on their sense of priority rather than on predetermined times. This difference is particularly problematic when people from the two cultures attempt to work together. The service pro-

vider is infuriated when families are late for or do not keep their appointments, and the family does not imagine that clock time would take precedence over everything else.

Because cultural influences are such an integral part of our lives, they are often invisible and elusive. When we are out of touch with our own culture and its influence on us, however, it is impossible to work effectively with people whose cultures differ from our own. Cultural self-awareness is the first step in intercultural effectiveness (Harry, 1992b; Locke, 1992). Only when we examine the values, beliefs, and patterns of behavior that are a part of our own cultural identity can we distinguish truth from tradition. (To examine your own cultural values and beliefs, consider and complete Appendix A, A Cultural Journey, in Chapter 3.) Such an examination is not easy. It requires a consideration of all of the things that we have learned from childhood and an acknowledgment that those beliefs and behaviors represent only one perspective—a perspective that is *not* inherently "right." To begin to understand one's self, one's culture, and the range of worldviews that others bring to every situation, it is important to keep the following five points in mind:

1. *Culture is not static; it is dynamic and ever-changing.* The cultural practices that individuals remember and practice from their country or place of origin are often different from the practices that are occurring in that same place today.

2. *Culture, language, ethnicity, and race are not the only determinants of one's values, beliefs, and behaviors.* Socioeconomic status, educational level, occupation, personal experience, personality, and the larger social and political contexts of the time combine to create sociocultural factors that exert a powerful influence over the way individuals view themselves and how families function. Although this chapter focuses on culture, it should be understood that culture is only one of many elements that family members use to define themselves; and for many, it is not the most salient.

3. *In describing any culture or cultural practice, within-group differences are as great as across-group differences—sometimes greater.* In other words, no cultural, ethnic, linguistic, or racial group is monolithic. Wide variations exist in attitudes, beliefs, and behaviors. To assume that people who share a common culture or language are alike is to make a dangerous mistake.

4. *Discussions of culture and ethnicity are typically framed in terms of differences in relation to another group.* In the United States, "diversity" all too often is used to refer to individuals who are not Anglo-European Americans. Diversity is relative (Barrera & Corso, 2003). To Anglo-European Americans, Latinos, African Americans, Cambodians, Guatemalans, and Tahitians may be considered to be diverse. To each of the groups listed, Anglo-European Americans would be diverse, however. As Barrera and Corso pointed out,

> When a person names particular children and families as being culturally diverse, that individual must simultaneously name himself or herself as being diverse from them. Calling "them" diverse without also calling oneself culturally diverse fails to recognize the relational aspect of diversity. It implicitly assumes a hierarchy of power within which only the namer has the privilege of setting the norm and naming the other(s) in reference to that norm. (2003, p. 7)

5. *Everyone is the product of one or more cultures, and everyone has a culture.* Culture is neither something exotic nor something that only others have. It is a part of each person in the world. Just because one may not be able to articulate his or her culture does not mean that it does not exist. As Samovar and Porter pointed out,

> At any given moment our behavior is a product of millions of years of evolution, our genetic makeup, the groups we have been affiliated with, our gender, age, individual histories, our perception of the other person, the situation we find ourselves in, and a long list of other factors. Although culture is the cardinal context, and also offers us a common frame of reference, none of us is ordinary. Simply put, we are our culture and much more. (1991, p. 16)

Throughout this book, we emphasize the constructs of cultural, ethnic, and linguistic diversity and identity. Racial identity, although discussed in various places, is not a focal point. Some readers will see this decision as a strength; others will view it as a shortcoming. The choice was based on the overall goal of the book—to help service providers be more effective in their day-to-day interactions with children and families whose life experiences differ from their own. However, some words about the potency of race must be said because this construct has played such a significant role in shaping interactions and opportunities. For more than 200 years, anthropologists used race as a way to describe the physical characteristics of groups of people that they studied (Gollnick & Chinn, 1997). In early history when people of the world had few interactions and little commerce, anthropological categories of Caucasoid, Mongoloid, and Negroid may have served some descriptive function. It is important, though, to remember that the categorization was developed by Caucasoids and tended to favor those with lighter skin in almost every dimension. As the world has changed and become more accessible through exploration, conquest, and commerce among nations, city-states, and tribes, the original racial groups have blended. As the Human Genome Project has clearly affirmed, there is no biological relevance to the construct of race. No significant differences exist in the genetic make-up of humanity (Olson, 2001; Smith & Sapp, 1996).

Although scientifically unsubstantiated, race continues to be the first thing that many people see when they look at others (Helms, 1994). The physical differences that have no biological relevance have historically placed some people at a disadvantage in America (Taylor, 1994) and throughout the world. Therefore, a book that emphasizes race would need to be about power differentials and sociopolitical change rather than about building relationships between families and service providers. As service providers work with families from different racial backgrounds, it is essential to consider the larger ecology and to ask themselves these questions: What are the societal barriers that each family historically and currently encounters? How have institutional racism and unequal access affected their lives and the lives of their forebears? What are the effects of educational and economic barriers? And, perhaps most important, what can we do to eliminate these inequities?

CONCEPT OF CULTURE SHOCK

Anyone who has traveled outside his or her own hometown has probably experienced some form of culture shock. Whether it is a New Yorker trying to adjust to the language and lifestyle of Mississippi, a Western rancher negotiating a city subway, or an Alaska native in Hawai'i, each is confronted with unfamiliar sounds, sights, odors, and behaviors. The unfamiliarity that each of these travelers experiences may produce interest, excitement, fear, anger, frustration, confusion, or disgust; regardless of the emotion that it evokes, it is certain to have an impact. The farther that individuals travel from their home, the greater the likelihood that they will be confronted with the unfamiliar. Thus, an American in Jakarta, a Cambodian in Fiji, an American Indian in Bombay, or an Italian in Beijing is more likely to experience confusion, frustration, or anger with the unfamiliar than the New Yorker in Mississippi, the Texan in New York, or the Alaskan in Hawai'i. It is these confrontations with the unfamiliar that create culture shock. Barrera and Corso (2003), citing the work of Archer (1986), described the feeling of discomfort when interacting with individuals from another culture as a culture bump. There is no question that these culture bumps occur when individuals are facing the unfamiliar, and they influence the ways in which service providers and families relate to one another. Culture shock is more than a bump, however, and may profoundly influence the ways in which all parties perceive, feel, and behave.

In the academic literatures of anthropology, sociology, psychology, and communications, the concept of culture shock and its stages and characteristics continue to be debated (Brislin, 1981). Although some of the early work that described the stages of culture shock (Gullahorn & Gullahorn, 1963) has not been successfully replicated in subsequent studies (Klineberg & Hull, 1979), individuals who have worked, studied, or traveled extensively in cultures different from their own are usually able to describe their experiences on this curve of cultural adjustment and learning. Those preparing others to work cross culturally use the concept of culture shock as a framework for helping individuals understand what they are experiencing emotionally and physically. Thus, the concept of culture shock has been included in this book as a conceptual framework that can assist service providers as they work with families who have recently arrived in the United States and are ex-

periencing it, as well as a framework for examining the service provider's own feelings when faced with unfamiliar values, beliefs, and practices.

Culture shock was first described by Oberg (1958, 1960). Although many investigators have elaborated on Oberg's work and used other words to describe the phenomenon and explain its cause and manifestations (e.g., Ball-Rokeach, 1973; Byrnes, 1966; Guthrie, 1975; Smalley, 1963), in this chapter, the term *culture shock* is used to describe a normal and universal response to the unfamiliar. Culture shock is most often discussed and studied when businesspeople, students, project staff members, or government officials are being prepared to live and to work or study outside of their own country; however, the concept of culture shock may also "be experienced by individuals who have face-to-face contact with

out-group members within their own country" (Brislin, 1981, p. 155). Thus, culture shock may occur when families and service providers from different backgrounds work together. Understanding the concept of culture shock and its characteristics and stages provides a framework that enables individuals to recognize their feelings, analyze the cause of the shock, alter their approach, consciously manage their own behavior, and regain emotional equilibrium.

The sections that follow examine the concept of culture shock and apply its stages and principles to the transactions between service providers and families when the service provider and family do not share the same ethnic or cultural heritage. Culture shock is conceptualized as a two-way street—one that both families and service providers travel as they work together. Service providers play a dual role on that street: They must acknowledge, respect, and build on the cultural values and beliefs that the family brings to the relationship, and they must interpret the new cultures— the culture of the United States (recognizing its many variations) as well as the culture of the service delivery system—to the families. For example, if a family engages in a cultural practice (i.e., from its first culture) such as physical punishment that may be legally governed in the United States, the service provider must explain the problems that could arise and provide the family with alternatives.

Defining Culture Shock

Culture shock is the result of a series of disorienting encounters that occur when an individual's basic values, beliefs, and patterns of behavior are challenged by a different set of values, beliefs, and behaviors. Although values are typically unacknowledged until challenged, they are the cornerstones of our being and behavior (Bohm, 1980). Once values are internalized, they become standards for guiding our personal behavior and evaluating the behavior of others (Samovar & Porter, 1991).

> Since values are the products of basic human and societal needs, the number of human values is small, and they focus on similar important concepts the world over. Values reflect a culture's view toward such central issues as politics, economics, religion, aesthetics, interpersonal relationships, morality and the environment. Cultural differences and conflicts arise from the fact that individuals and societies order these values in differing hierarchies. (Brislin, Cushner, Cherrie, & Yong, 1986, p. 299)

Culture shock occurs when the strategies that the individual uses to solve problems, make decisions, and interact positively are not effective, and when the individual feels an overwhelming sense of discomfort in the environment (Draine & Hall, 1986). The discomfort may manifest itself in emotional or physical ways, such as frustration, anger, depression, withdrawal, lethargy, aggression, or illness. In any of these states, it is difficult for the individual to take constructive action.

Families who have recently arrived in the United States typically experience culture shock as they attempt to negotiate a new culture, language, and set of behaviors. What was accepted behavior in their homeland may be misunderstood, disdained, laughed at, or even illegal in their new country. For example, in many countries outside of the United States, spitting or blowing nasal mucus onto the ground is commonplace. Capturing saliva or mucus in a tissue or handkerchief that would then be put back into a pocket or purse is considered a filthy habit. No one would carry something like that with them! In the United States, expectorating on the ground is viewed with disgust; in some cities, it is even a misdemeanor. Although both cultures have placed a value on personal hygiene, their interpretations are drastically different. Another example has to do with giving gifts in the hope of receiving preferential treatment. In the United States, gifts to government officials are legislatively regulated. Such gifts, at least ostensibly, are described as "bribes" and are illegal. In most of the rest of the world, such gifts are commonplace and even expected. Therefore, placing large-denomination bills in a book for a teacher, proffering money at a border crossing, or giving a lavish gift for someone who may have a positive or negative influence over one's career opportunities is neither considered inappropriate nor illegal. In these examples, both cultures have placed a value on interpersonal interactions within a business, governmental, or educational context; but the rules of interaction are very different.

Behaviors that were appreciated and valued in a family's country of origin may be confusing to individuals in the United States. For example, a service provider may be frustrated by a family's desire to chat over a cup of tea before "getting down to business" in the home visit; the service provider may interpret the behavior as avoidance rather than as an important cultural practice. As a result of different behaviors and interpretations of those behaviors based on culture, ethnicity, or language, tensions may emerge between families and service providers in their interactions with one another. Confusion and tension lead to discomfort and may cause both parties to withdraw. Consider this example: Typically in the United States, when an infant or a toddler attracts the attention of a stranger in a supermarket, an office, or another public place the adult usually engages with the baby in some way such as playing Peekaboo or making faces at or talking in a sing-song fashion to the baby. When the adult or the child tires of the game, the adult usually turns to the child's parents or caregivers and comments on the child's attractiveness, alertness, or delightfulness. The parents or caregivers express pleasure at the compliment and are pleased that the stranger has recognized the superiority of their child. In many other cultures, however, this would be a very disquieting interaction for the parents. In some Mexican and Central American, Islamic, American Indian, and Southeast Asian cultures, calling attention to the child's positive traits is thought to cause the evil spirits to become jealous, and the evil spirits may then cause harm.

Different values and interpretations of behaviors introduce confusion and discomfort into cross-cultural interactions. The discomfort is often heightened by limited ability to verbalize the conflict. Families who are not conversant in English and service providers who speak no other language may quickly encounter barriers that are difficult to overcome.

NAVIGATING THE STAGES OF CULTURE SHOCK

Gullahorn and Gullahorn (1963) described a predictable set of stages of adjustment that long-term, overseas sojourners experience. The ups and downs of their experience can be depicted in a W-shaped curve. At the beginning of the experience, spirits and expectations are high and individuals feel extremely satisfied. During the middle phase of the experience, individuals become dissatisfied. By this time, they have discovered that their problem-solving strategies are ineffective in the foreign environment and their expectations are not being met; as a result, they often become angry and lash out. This period of anger and frustration is followed by an improvement in outlook and a general upswing in mood and effectiveness that peaks near the end of the experience. The return to being highly satisfied with the experience is a period during which the individuals begin to function comfortably in the environment.

It is interesting to note that many long-term sojourners experience reverse culture shock when they return to their home country and go through a shorter series of readjustments or relearning that mirror those they experienced in the overseas experience. For example, the author of this chapter had a difficult readjustment period following a 5-month assignment in Indonesia. In the first few weeks back in the United States, on several occasions, trips to the grocery store were abandoned because other shoppers seemed so large, so loud, and so aggressive—opposites of the Indonesian people with whom she had interacted.

The time it takes an individual to pass through the hypothesized stages of culture shock is not predictable. Each person brings different needs and different resources to the situation and finds ways to cope that slow or hasten the passage. Similar to the grief cycle that is frequently used to describe parents' reactions to the birth of a child with a disability (Solnit & Stark, 1961), culture shock is an experience without temporal norms.

The Family's Viewpoint

Imagine the stages of culture shock as they might apply to a family with a young child with a disability who has recently arrived in the United States. The family has chosen to emigrate to the United States and has high expectations for success. Although they recognize that the streets are not paved with gold, they are imagining a land of opportunity that will welcome them and the many skills they bring. However, the feelings of enthusiasm and great expectation that they have are slowly eroded by everyday experiences. For example, only the father speaks English, and his skills in the language were learned from a textbook rather than through conversations with

native speakers. Every interaction is a struggle that leaves him very tired at the end of the day. Because he is the family's only communicator with the new environment, he is constantly in a position of trying to make himself understood, as well as trying to explain what is going on to other members of the family. Individuals experience problems not only with spoken English but also with written English. It seems that every interaction results in the need to complete a stack of forms, and comprehending and completing the forms is even more difficult than speaking. The mental energy that is required is exhausting and sometimes overwhelming.

In the family's homeland, family members arose with the sun, rested in the heat of the day, and returned to work late in the afternoon. In the United States, however, all activity seems to be governed by the clock instead of by any natural rhythm. Even though they have conquered jet lag, these family members have not yet adjusted to these new patterns. Getting things done also is very different than it was in their home country and leads to unpleasant exchanges or yields no results. For example, in their native country, everyone crowded around the windows in post offices and banks to get stamps or money, yet in the United States, several people have spoken to them very rudely for not standing in line. Similar things have happened while they were driving. On several occasions, people have yelled and gestured angrily just because they did not come to a full stop or caused a pedestrian to jump back onto the sidewalk. They were driving just as they had learned to drive in their homeland, where they had never had an accident, but the reactions to their style in the United States were very disconcerting.

It also is difficult for the family members to be expected to do things in their new home that servants did in their homeland—washing, cleaning, caring for the children, shopping. How can anyone of their background be expected to do these menial tasks for themselves? Another source of frustration is the father's discouragement regarding employment. Though educated as a physician in his homeland, his training is not acknowledged in the United States; and the work that he is offered is considerably below his knowledge, skills, and financial needs. Another area that has caused the family real frustration is related to their child with the disability. Everyone keeps suggesting programs and services for this "baby," but she is only 4 years old. Why should a 4-year-old child go to school? And why do all of these well-educated people keep asking the family's opinion, wanting them to participate, to set goals? That is a job for them, not a job for the family. How presumptuous it would be to tell those professionals what they should do to help! The professionals are the experts.

At this point, the family has probably reached the low point on the W-shaped curve of culture shock, and expectations are not being met. Patterns of behavior that have worked for family members for years in their home country do not produce the expected results in their new home; everything about the United States seems almost too demanding to endure. If the family members persevere, continue to interact, and learn about the new culture, it is likely that they will ultimately have better experiences and feel more confident and positive. They will learn what is expected in the many situations that they encounter, and each day their lives will become easier. This does not mean that they should abandon their own culture's values, beliefs, and practices, but it does mean that their success in the new culture may depend on learning new behaviors and strategies that can be used to meet the demands of the new culture.

The Service Provider's Viewpoint

Imagine this same scenario, but now try to see it from the service provider's point of view. The nurse on the intervention team was assigned to the family because of the child's medical problems. After she made many attempts to contact the family, they reluctantly allowed her to make a home visit. Everyone in the family was there, but only the father spoke. He knew almost nothing about the child's eating and sleeping patterns and the care that she had received in the family's home country. Also, he continually referred to her as "the baby," even though she was 4 years old. ("Imagine a 4-year-old child who has never received intervention; what would have happened if they had tried to enroll her in kindergarten next year without our help?" the service provider thinks to herself.) Family members seemed to turn to stone when the service provider asked what their goals were and how they would like to be involved in their daughter's education. The nurse was also very upset by a sense of hostility that seemed to be a palpable presence in the home. Everyone was polite, but they seemed angry. ("If they're going to be that hard to work with, why bother? After all, there are a lot of other families who appreciate what service providers do and want to be part of their child's program," the nurse might think.)

Now try to see the situation from a family's point of view. You may be meeting family members when they are unhappy, confused, and discouraged by their experiences in the United States, that is, when they are at the lowest point in the culture shock curve. They may appear angry, uncooperative, uncommunicative, resistant, or withdrawn; many of the verbal and nonverbal cues may be inconsistent with your expectations of involved and caring families. The whole situation may be tense and uncomfortable, and it may be very tempting to give up. This is a time when helping families understand and negotiate the new culture is most needed, however. Strategies may include acknowledging the difficulties that they are encountering and finding ways to reduce those problems through enlisting the help of translators, professionals, or paraprofessionals who share the same background; or watching, listening, and making small gestures of support. Such strategies may be the key to serving both the child and the family. It will certainly be the key to serving both effectively.

Another Family's Viewpoint

Imagine another family who has recently entered the United States from a country divided and destroyed by civil war. The family members fled their small, rural village in which they had sustained themselves through subsistence farming and small amounts of money from family members working in the city. After witnessing the guerilla attack that killed more than half of the village's residents, including all of their kin, the family members made their way across a border to an overcrowded refugee camp. After 6 months in the camp with little food, poor sanitation, and almost no medical treatment, the family was sent to the United States.

The family's youngest son was born in the refugee camp during a long and difficult labor; he remained weak and hard to feed throughout his infancy. Although his parents knew that he was not developing like other children, they did not know that he had a disability until he was examined in the United States. The U.S. doctors now say that he has cerebral palsy, but the closest translation that the family has understood is that he is "sick and crippled forever." In the family's homeland, such a diagnosis would have meant that nothing could be done and that the child would probably die at a very early age. Confronted with a language that they do not understand, a diagnosis of disability that they interpret as a death sentence, the violent loss of their family, and a world in which nothing is familiar, the family members are frightened, withdrawn, depressed, and seemingly uninterested in any of the services available for their son.

Another Service Provider's Viewpoint

The referral for this family has come from social services and a community health clinic. When the service provider met the child and his parents at their last clinic appointment, it was clear that the son needed early intervention. After spending more than 2 hours with the family and a translator, the service provider still did not get any indication that the family was interested in anything that the program had to offer. The parents hardly spoke, had almost no affect (i.e., expression of emotion), and appeared to have no attachment to their son. ("Given the family's limited abilities, the difficulty in getting a translator, and the family's apparent disinterest, what in the world could the program do?")

Unfortunately, this is not an uncommon example. Not only is this family experiencing culture shock but also they are probably suffering from posttraumatic stress disorder (PTSD). War, terrorism, violence, and displacement are occurring in countries throughout the world. Prior to the United States-Iraq war, in 2003, 53 million people throughout the world had been displaced by recent wars. Of those, women and children accounted for 42 million (Save the Children, 2004). The effects of war are long lasting. In 1993, before some of the more recent and genocidal conflicts in Africa and the Balkans, the United Nations Children's Fund (UNICEF) estimated that "10 million children worldwide suffer psychological trauma from wars" (Boyden, 1993, p. 122). According to the Armed Conflicts Report 2002 (Project Ploughshares, n.d.), 31 armed conflicts were in progress throughout the world, and at least some refugees fleeing those conflicts will enter the United States.

The apathy, lack of affect, and resignation that the service provider in this example saw are common among those who have witnessed such violence—whether they are children or adults. The family's behavior is not surprising given its new and vastly different surroundings and its discovery that its youngest boy has a disability. It also is not surprising that the service provider should feel overwhelmed. In this situation, a team of mental health professionals and cultural mediators may be the most valuable, immediate resource for the family. With the family's agreement, service providers may work with the child until his parents become emotionally available to be a part of the team.

AMELIORATING CULTURE SHOCK FOR THE FAMILY

Culture shock requires adjustment—on the part of families who are unfamiliar or inexperienced in the ways of the service systems that they encounter and on the part of the service providers who are unfamiliar and inexperienced in the ways of the families whom they meet. Culture shock is most pronounced when individuals initially discover that dramatic differences exist between their beliefs and values and those of the people around them. Thus, families who have recently arrived in the United States may be most affected by culture shock. Some families who have spent many generations in the United States may still find the predominant culture unfriendly and frustrating, however. Likewise, service providers may experience greater degrees of culture shock when they are working with families who have recently immigrated from other countries and cultures. They also may experience some degree of culture shock when they work with families who have been in the United States for many years but have beliefs, values, and practices that are foreign to those of the service provider. The following section focuses on culture shock from the perspective of families who are new immigrants and from those who have spent many generations in the United States apart from the mainstream.

New Immigrants

Families who have recently arrived in the United States are most affected by culture shock. Even those immigrants who are financially secure and skilled in English typically experience a period of adjustment that may resemble a ride on a roller coaster.

For those who have limited resources, who are unfamiliar with English, and who have experienced considerable trauma leaving their country of origin, the shock of a new culture is magnified. Although culture shock is very personalized, several issues may interfere with effective interventions during this period of time: language barriers, systems barriers, differing perceptions of professional roles, family priorities, the family's belief system, and sociopolitical barriers. Each is briefly elaborated in the sections that follow.

Language Barriers   Language is the primary means of access to understanding, relationships, and services. It also is "one of the most significant markers of ethnic diversity" (Green, 1982, p. 68). Whenever someone is conversing in a second language, he or she is putting more effort into the communication. Thus, families may be frustrated by difficulties in communication. Even if family members speak and understand English, the language of service providers is often highly technical. When family members do not speak the language of the service provider, they must rely on interpreters who may or may not provide accurate information. (That "something got lost in the translation" is an understatement in many situations.) Because few programs are able to call on interpreters who have both the language and the intervention skills, translations are often imperfect. Many times, younger or extended family members are asked to interpret, and their own concerns may shape the information being transmitted. In other instances, adequate translations do not exist for the concepts that are being shared. Just as English speakers are unable to express the fine distinctions among the kinds of snow that Alaskan Inuits or Greenlanders describe easily, so, too, is it difficult to explain the nuances of behavior management to someone who has never felt that it was necessary to change a young child's behavior or thought in terms of baselines and reinforcement schedules. (See Chapter 3 for additional discussion of working with translators and interpreters.)

Systems Barriers   Families from developing countries or regions destroyed by armed conflict may have little or no understanding and certainly no experience with prevention and intervention programs for young children. Coming from a world in which 10.5 million children, most from developing countries, die each year before their fifth birthdays (Lopez, 2000) from preventable or treatable conditions such as whooping cough, measles, diarrhea, pneumonia, influenza, tetanus, and malaria (World Resources Institute, 1992), family expectations for children's healthy growth and development are low. When 90% of all infant disability is attributable to poverty and disease rather than to genetic causes, the luxury of early intervention programs may be difficult to comprehend (Boyden, 1993). Many families, particularly those who have been in refugee camps, have come from situations in which basic sanitation, nutrition, and health care were nonexistent. In many instances, even basic safety and security was threatened on a daily basis. To arrive in a country in which specialized services exist for young children with disabilities is almost unbelievable; it may take time for families to accept the services. Focusing so much attention on a situation that tradition tells them has no solution may be part of the culture shock that some family members experience when they encounter service providers.

In addition, systems typically are not organized to be responsive to cultural differences (Walker, Saravanabhavan, Williams, Brown, & West, 1996). Translating agency brochures into Farsi, Spanish, Vietnamese, Tagalog, Swahili, or other languages and leaving them in agency reception rooms does not respond sufficiently to family needs. Strategies for reaching out to groups using the structures that are part of their culture, such as sharing information about services with older adults, religious or spiritual leaders, healers, political leaders, cultural advocacy groups, patriarchs, or matriarchs, may be the most effective way to infuse information into the entire cultural community (Lynch, 1987).

Differing Perceptions of Professional Roles Family–professional partnerships in intervention, education, and health care have become important across service delivery systems in the United States (Beckman, 1996; Capone & DiVenere, 1996; Dunst, Trivette, & Deal, 1988; Erwin, 1996; Hanson, Lynch, & Wayman, 1990; Kroth & Edge, 1997; McGonigel, Kaufmann, & Johnson, 1991; Turnbull & Turnbull, 1990). This focus on including parents and other family members as full participants on the intervention team has not been the typical perspective of many agencies; such participatory decision making is uncommon in many other countries and cultures. Among people from the majority of world cultures, professionals are held in high esteem, particularly teachers and healers. Thus, expecting families from many cultural groups to be assertive, talkative participants in developing and evaluating services for their children is unrealistic. In fact, the implied definition of an active participant typically varies from one culture to another (Lynch & Stein, 1987). Directly asking parents to state their concerns and priorities to the service provider in a formal meeting may be an upsetting and embarrassing request that adds to the family's confusion and culture shock; however, this does not mean that their concerns, priorities, and resources should be ignored. Rather, a slower approach, more informal strategies, and careful observation of what each family prefers will probably be more effective than direct approaches (Harry, 1992b; Leung, 1988). Barrera and Corso's (2003) work in the area of skilled dialogues provides some specific strategies for approaching and working effectively with families who differ in multiple ways from the service provider.

Family Priorities Family priorities should guide all interventions with young children with disabilities, especially when the family's culture differs from that of the service provider. Culture shock may emerge as families who have recently arrived in the United States encounter priorities that differ dramatically from their own. For example, many mainstream United States families regard toilet training as a crucial milestone that should occur as soon as possible, they regard independent feeding as an important step in development, and they are eager to enroll their children in toddler and preschool programs that emphasize educational activities and experiences. In other cultures, there is typically less pressure placed on toilet training. In many Asian, Southeast Asian, and Pacific Island cultures, young children are not diapered. Adults expect young children to relieve themselves freely, and both the child and the adult are simply washed as needed. Breastfeeding may continue much longer among some cultural groups and then may be followed by an extended period in which adults or older children feed the youngest child. Because *interdependence* rather than *independence* is more often the value in some cultures, caring for a younger child or a child who has a disability is not viewed as a burden. In addition, home and family are viewed as the appropriate place for young children; educational programs for children younger than age 6 or 7 are not commonplace, and families prefer not to send their children away from home at such an early age. Any intervention that is designed will have a much greater likelihood of success if family priorities form the foundation of the plan.

Family's Belief System   The family's belief system will affect the degree of culture shock that family members experience. If a family believes that everything that happens is attributable to fate or is in the hands of God, seeking to control any situation will seem contradictory, if not blasphemous. If a family believes that women should be shielded from all outside influences, then the service provider's desire to make home visits or to have both parents participate in program activities may cause conflict or confusion. If a family believes that a traditional shaman has the power to exorcise the evil spirits that cause illness, they may not see the need for sophisticated medical, diagnostic tests. The recommendations that service providers make so readily may seem extremely strange to the family and may increase culture shock.

Sociopolitical Barriers   In spite of the Statue of Liberty's call, "Give me your tired, your poor, your huddled masses yearning to breathe free," the United States does not always welcome new immigrants with open arms. "Foreign" ways of thinking, worshiping, and raising children; darker skin; and languages other than English have resulted in sociopolitical barriers that have made it difficult for many families to seek and find the supports and services that they need. These barriers are often greatest when the U.S. economy is weak. The fear of job loss to "foreign" workers who may work for lower wages and the perception that government benefits are being used to support new immigrants have created sociopolitical barriers that have, at times, resulted in very restrictive immigration policies, unfounded suspicions about people who have come to the United States legally, harsh treatment of undocumented individuals, and negative stereotypes. When attitudes become narrower, so does the legislation that provides a safety net for newcomers.

Long-Term Residents

In many areas of the United States, service providers work with families from diverse cultures who have been in the country for many years. Although the parents often

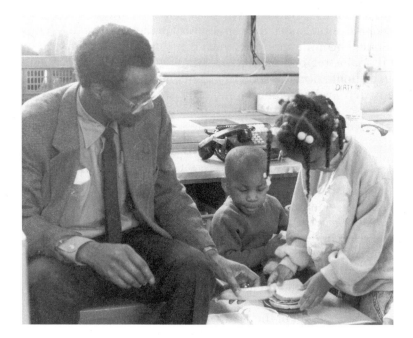

were born in the United States, these families have not adopted the beliefs, values, and language of the dominant culture. In many *barrios*, Spanish is the primary language, and customs are an amalgamation of those from the residents' original culture and the mainstream U.S. culture. Many large cities have Chinatowns that have existed for decades with few changes. Although the concept of culture shock does not make sense when describing the reactions of long-term residents who have maintained such close ties to their original culture and language, explanations do exist for their reluctance to get involved with the new culture and the system. Lack of trust of the system, different priorities, and decisions about the degree of acculturation that they desire may interfere with effective relationships with intervention programs (e.g., Harry, 1992a, 1992c; Harry & Kalyanpur, 1994).

When many of these families first came to the United States, considerably less attention and value was placed on cultural pluralism. Immigrants were expected to assimilate, and little was done to assist them. As a result of this policy, many families were extremely successful in joining the American mainstream; others were not. Across the nation, many families, particularly those of color, who have been here for many years still have not been included in "the American dream." Families who are not able to participate in the American dream may have had negative experiences with various systems that caused them to remain isolated and enculturated. As time passes, change becomes even more difficult; and individuals, whole families, and some groups remain outside the mainstream culture in both thought and opportunity. Initial lack of opportunity caused by sociopolitical barriers and prejudice catapult some families into generational cycles of poverty, poor heath, despair, and sometimes anger. With the many strides that have been made in equal opportunity in housing, education, and employment, inequities still exist that make it more difficult for some families to succeed than others. These inequities are exacerbated by the sad but true fact that in the year 2002, there were 708 active hate groups in the United States and 443 active hate web sites (Southern Poverty Law Center, 2003a, 2003b). These groups who target skin color, religion, lifestyles, and/or belief systems make it more difficult for some families to feel safe in their communities and to seek and use services.

Other families may believe that systems are not the appropriate vehicle for taking care of their needs. In many cultures, families are responsible for providing for any family member who cannot provide for him- or herself; using the services of "outsiders" would represent a loss of face in the cultural community. Finally, some families may have consciously chosen to isolate themselves from the mainstream culture. Considerable evidence points to the fact that "sizable numbers of people prefer a single set of values and behaviors" (Brislin, 1981, p. 290). Maintaining the values, beliefs, language, and practices that are understood and comfortable is more attractive to some families than risking loss of some of those aspects of their lives through exposure to another culture.

SENSITIZING THE SERVICE PROVIDER TO THE IMPACT OF CULTURE SHOCK

Throughout this chapter, the concept of culture shock has been viewed as a two-way street. Just as families from different cultures may be confused, frustrated, or upset by their encounters with the mainstream culture, service providers also may be uncomfortable with their encounters with practices that differ from their own. Service providers may discover that they disapprove of practices that they encounter, or they may find that some families engage in behaviors that generally are not accepted in the United States. In addition to the culture shock that they may experience, service providers also may have concerns about their lack of cross-cultural training and the lack of time to assist families to the extent that they would like.

In the United States, for example, the majority of service providers are women. They are accustomed to lives in which they are free to make decisions, earn money, and speak openly on any subject. In many other countries, however, women do not have the same rights. Even within the United States, groups may differ radically in their views of women's rights and roles. In some families, wives may defer to husbands or to their mothers-in-law. Although it is their responsibility to carry out whatever is decided, they may have little or no role in decision making. For service providers, these situations may be very difficult; however, advocating for the rights of the mother would be a direct affront to the cultural tradition and that may be upsetting to her and to the rest of the family.

In rare instances, a service provider may encounter cultural practices that he or she finds difficult to accept. Unfamiliar foods such as snake, squid, sweetbreads, or Rocky Mountain oysters; healing practices such as coining or exorcism; gender-based practices such as circumcision and ear piercing of infant girls; or purification rituals that keep mother and newborn separate for several weeks following delivery are often difficult for the mainstream service provider to understand. Consequently, the service provider may experience some of the same emotional turmoil in working with the family that the family is feeling toward the new culture. Anger, frustration, and a desire to pull away are typical. These sensations and feelings are not wrong or even unusual; however, they do signal a need for the service provider to assess his or her feelings, seek consultation from colleagues, and decide whether he or she can continue to work effectively with the family. In most instances, a short time-out and a discussion with a colleague who is knowledgeable about the culture are all that is needed to regain one's equilibrium. Now and then, however, another service provider may need to be assigned to the family.

Separate from the issues of culture shock, many service providers express concern about their lack of cross-cultural training and the time demands of effective intercultural interactions. Although professionals are typically well trained in their own disciplines, few have been trained to work with families from cultures different from their own. Even those families who come from the same culture or speak the same language as the service provider often represent different socioeconomic strata or educational levels, and, as a result, the service provider may find it difficult to relate to these families with complete comfort. One of the goals of this book is to assist service providers in the field as they develop and expand their cross-cultural skills; another goal is to provide a book that can be used in university classes so that students in training will enter their professions with the skills and the knowledge that will be needed in a changing world.

It takes time to learn cross-cultural skills and to work with families from diverse cultures. Many service providers are already overburdened by increases in the numbers of families that they serve and the increases in the requirements of the service systems in which they work. The range and extent of many families' needs strain the capability of the service delivery system; however, the time spent working respectfully and sensitively with families from different cultures is a sound investment, and it may be the only way to ensure that needed intervention occurs.

SUMMARY

Working effectively with families from cultures that differ from one's own requires an understanding of one's own beliefs and values as well as recognition that one's language, culture, and ethnicity do influence interactions. As the demographics of the United States change to include growing numbers of people from Mexico, Central and South America, Central and Southeast Asia, Africa, Central and Eastern Europe, Russia, and the Middle East, the need for effective cross-cultural interactions increases. This brings new opportunities as well as new demands. Families and service providers may experience confusion, alienation, and general discomfort as they struggle to understand and appreciate each other's perspectives. This discomfort, sometimes referred to as culture shock, typically occurs in predictable phases. After initial excitement and enthusiasm about the new culture, people may become overwhelmed and disenchanted. Positive feelings may turn negative; enjoyment of the new challenges may be replaced by withdrawal, anger, and frustration. Neither families nor service providers can be effective when they are experiencing the negative aspects of culture shock; however, the disillusionment can be overcome. Time, understanding, continued exposure, and a sensitive mediator can be crucial to success for everyone involved. As service providers expand their understanding of other worldviews and their ability to work cross culturally, new doors open—not only for families but also for service providers.

REFERENCES

Archer, C.M. (1986). Culture bump and beyond. In J.M. Valdes (Ed.), *Culture bound: Bridging the cultural gap in language teaching* (pp. 170–178). New York: Cambridge University Press.

Ball-Rokeach, S.J. (1973). From pervasive ambiguity to a definition of the situation. *Sociometry, 36,* 3–13.

Barrera, I., & Corso, R.M. (with MacPherson, D.) (2003). *Skilled Dialogue: Strategies for responding to cultural diversity in early childhood.* Baltimore: Paul H. Brookes Publishing Co.

Beckman, P.J. (1996). Theoretical, philosophical, and empirical bases of effective work with families. In P.J. Beckman (Ed.), *Strategies for working with families of young children with disabilities* (pp. 1–16). Baltimore: Paul H. Brookes Publishing Co.

Bohm, D. (1980). On insight and its significance for science, education, and values. In D. Sloan (Ed.), *Education and values* (pp. 7–22). New York: Teachers College Press.

Boyden, J. (1993). *Families: Celebration and hope in a world of change.* London: Gaia Books Limited.

Brislin, R.W. (1981). *Cross-cultural encounters: Face-to-face interaction.* New York: Pergamon Press.

Brislin, R.W., Cushner, K., Cherrie, C., & Yong, M. (1986). *Intercultural interactions: A practical guide.* Beverly Hills: Sage Publications.

Brown, R., & Lenneberg, E. (1965). Studies in linguistic relativity. In H. Proshansky & B. Seidenberg (Eds.), *Basic studies in social psychology* (pp. 244–252). New York: Holt, Rinehart and Winston.

Byrnes, F.C. (1966). Role shock: An occupational hazard of American technical assistants abroad. *Annals of the American Academy of Political and Social Science, 368,* 95–108.

Capone, A.M., & DiVenere, N. (1996). The evolution of a personnel preparation program: Preparation of family-centered practitioners. *Journal of Early Intervention, 20,* 222–231.

Dormann, H.O. (1987). *The speaker's book of quotations.* New York: Fawcett Columbine.

Draine, C., & Hall, B. (1986). *Culture shock! Indonesia.* Singapore: Times Books International.

Dunst, C.J., Trivette, C.M., & Deal, A.G. (1988). *Enabling and empowering families: Principles and guidelines for practice.* Cambridge, MA: Brookline Books.

Erwin, E.J. (Ed.). (1996). *Putting children first:*

Visions for a brighter future for young children and their families. Baltimore: Paul H. Brookes Publishing Co.

Gollnick, D.M., & Chinn, P.C. (1997). *Multicultural education in a pluralistic society* (4th ed.). New York: Merrill.

Green, J.W. (1982). *Cultural awareness in the human services.* Upper Saddle River, NJ: Prentice Hall.

Gross, J. (1987). *The Oxford book of aphorisms.* New York: Oxford University Press.

Gullahorn, J., & Gullahorn, J. (1963). An extension of the U-curve hypothesis. *Journal of Social Issues, 19*(3), 33–47.

Guthrie, G.M. (1975). A behavioral analysis of culture learning. In R.W. Brislin & W.J. Lonner (Eds.), *Cross-cultural perspectives on learning* (pp. 95–115). New York: John Wiley & Sons.

Hanson, M.J., Lynch, E.W., & Wayman, K.I. (1990). Honoring the cultural diversity of families when gathering data. *Topics in Early Childhood Special Education, 10*(1), 112–131.

Harry, B. (1992a). An ethnographic study of cross-cultural communication with Puerto Rican-American families in the special education system. *American Educational Research Journal, 29,* 471–494.

Harry, B. (1992b). Developing cultural self-awareness: The first step in values clarification for early interventionists. *Topics in Early Childhood Special Education, 12,* 333–350.

Harry, B. (1992c). Restructuring the participation of African-American parents in special education. *Exceptional Children, 59,* 123–131.

Harry, B., & Kalyanpur, M. (1994). Cultural underpinnings of special education: Implications for professional interactions with culturally diverse families. *Disability and Society, 9*(2), 145–165.

Helms, J. (1994). The conceptualization of racial identity and other "racial" constructs. In E.J. Trickett, R.J. Watts, & D. Birman (Eds.), *Human diversity: Perspectives on people in context* (pp. 285–311). San Francisco: Jossey-Bass.

Klineberg, O., & Hull, F. (1979). *At a foreign university.* New York: Praeger.

Kroth, R.L., & Edge, D. (1997). *Strategies for communicating with parents and families of exceptional children* (3rd ed.). Denver: Love Publishing Co.

Leung, E.K. (1988). *Cultural and acculturational commonalities and diversities among Asian Americans: Identification and programming considerations.* Paper presented at the Ethnic and Multicultural Symposia, Dallas. (ERIC Document Reproduction Service No. ED 298 708)

Locke, D.C. (1992). *Increasing multicultural understanding: A comprehensive model.* Beverly Hills: Sage Publications.

Lopez, A.D. (2000). Reducing child mortality. *Bulletin of the World Health Organization, 78,* 1173.

Lynch, E.W. (1987). Families from different cultures. In M. Bristol & C. Kasari (Eds.), *The Family Support Network series: Monograph one* (pp. 80–88). Moscow: Family Support Network Project, University of Idaho.

Lynch, E.W., & Stein, R.C. (1987). Parent participation by ethnicity: A comparison of Hispanic, Black, and Anglo families. *Exceptional Children, 54,* 105–111.

McGonigel, M.J., Kaufmann, R.K., & Johnson, B.H. (Eds.). (1991). *Guidelines and recommended practices for the individualized family service plan* (2nd ed.). Bethesda, MD: Association for the Care of Children's Health.

Moll, L.C., & Greenberg, J.B. (1990). Creating zones of possibilities: Combining social contexts for instruction. In L.C. Moss (Ed.), *Vygotsky and education: Instructional implications of sociohistorical psychology* (pp. 319–348). New York: Cambridge University Press.

Oberg, K. (1958). *Culture shock and the problem of adjustment to new cultural environments.* Washington, DC: Department of State, Foreign Service Institute.

Oberg, K. (1960). Cultural shock: Adjustment to new cultural environments. *Practical Anthropology, 7,* 177–182.

Olson, S. (2001, April). The genetic archeology of race. *The Atlantic Monthly,* 69–80.

Project Ploughshares (n.d.). *Armed conflicts report 2002.* Retrieved April 28, 2003 from http://www.ploughshares.ca/CONTENT/ACR/ACR00?/ACR00.html

Samovar, L.A., & Porter, R.E. (1991). *Communication between cultures.* Belmont, CA: Wadsworth.

Sapolsky, R.M. (1997). The dangers of fallen soufflés in the developing world. In R.M. Sapolsky, *The trouble with testosterone: And other essays on the biology of the human predicament* (pp. 197–210). New York: Simon & Schuster.

Save the Children (n.d.). *Children and war: The crisis.* Retrieved April 2, 2004 from http://www.savethechildren.org/emergencies/war.asp

Smalley, W. (1963). Culture shock, language shock, and the shock of self-discovery. *Practical Anthropology, 10,* 49–56.

Smith, E., & Sapp, W. (Eds.). (1996). *Plain talk about the Human Genome Project: A Tuskegee University conference on its promise and perils . . . and matters of race.* Tuskegee, AL: Tuskegee University Publications Office.

Solnit, A., & Stark, M. (1961). Mourning the birth of a defective child. *The Psychoanalytic Study of the Child, 16,* 523–527.

Southern Poverty Law Center. (2003a, Spring). Active hate groups in the United States in the year 2002. *Intelligence Report,* 109, 38–41.

Southern Poverty Law Center. (2003b, Spring). Active hate web sites in the United States in the year 2002. *Intelligence Report,* 109, 42–47.

Taylor, R.L. (1994). Minority families in America: An introduction. In R.L. Taylor (Ed.), *Minority families in the United States: A multicultural perspective* (pp. 1–16). Upper Saddle River, NJ: Prentice Hall.

Turnbull, A.P., & Turnbull, H.R. (1990). *Families, professionals, and exceptionality: A special partnership* (2nd ed.). Columbus, OH: Charles E. Merrill.

Velez-Ibañez, C.G., & Greenberg, J.B. (1992). Formation and transformation of funds of knowledge among U.S. Mexican households. *Anthropology & Education Quarterly, 23,* 313–335.

Walker, S., Saravanabhavan, R.C., Williams, V., Brown, O., & West, T. (1996). *An examination of the impact of federally supported community services and educational systems on underserved people with disabilities from diverse cultural populations.* Unpublished manuscript, Howard University Research and Training Center for Access to Rehabilitation and Economic Opportunity, Washington, DC.

World Resources Institute. (1992). Population and human development. In *World resources 1992–1993: A guide to the global environment—toward sustainable development.* Retrieved April 29, 2003, from http://www.ciesin.org/docs/001-233/001-233.html

CHAPTER 3

DEVELOPING CROSS-CULTURAL COMPETENCE

Eleanor W. Lynch

Most cultural exploration begins with the annoyance
of being lost. The control systems of the mind signal that
something unexpected has arisen, that we are in uncharted
waters and are going to have to switch off the automatic
pilot and man the helm ourselves.
—EDWARD T. HALL (1976)

Never try to take the manners of another as your own, for the
theft will be immediately evident and the thief will appear as
ridiculous as a robin with peacock feathers hastily stuck on.
—MAYA ANGELOU (1993)

Culture, with its processes and functions, is a subject
on which we need all the enlightenment we can achieve . . . .
—RUTH BENEDICT (1934)

Culture is akin to looking through the one-way mirror; everything we see is from our own perspective. It is only when we join the observed on the other side of the mirror that it is possible to see ourselves and others clearly; however, getting to the other side of the glass presents many challenges. Achieving cross-cultural competence requires that we lower our defenses, take risks, and practice behaviors that may feel unfamiliar and uncomfortable. It requires a flexible mind, an open heart, and a willingness to accept alternative perspectives. It may mean setting aside some beliefs that are cherished to make room for others whose value is unknown; it may mean changing what we think, what we say, and how we behave. But there are rewards—the reward of assisting families who need someone who can help them bridge two disparate cultures, as well as the reward of knowing more about ourselves and becoming more effective in all of our interactions.

This chapter focuses on the knowledge and skills that service providers can use to help build bridges between themselves and the families who come from different cultures. It is organized into the following five major areas: 1) defining cross-cultural competence; 2) self-awareness; 3) awareness and understanding of others' cultural perspectives; 4) sociocultural factors; and 5) communication issues, including working with interpreters and translators. The material presented suggests specific strategies that can be used to assist service providers in improving their ability to work sensitively and effectively with families from cultures and life circumstances different from their own and to help agencies and organizations develop more culturally competent approaches to serving children and their families. It is designed to be used by those who are just beginning to develop cross-cultural competence and to provide a refresher for those who are skilled in cross-cultural interactions. Although built on openness and a willingness to try new ways of interacting, the strategies are not just an experiential splash into unknown waters; they are, instead, the beginning steps in a long journey toward discovering new ways of knowing oneself and others. These strategies require action, practice, review, feedback, and evaluation. As Storti so aptly stated in *The Art of Crossing Cultures,* "The old proverb notwithstanding, we cannot put ourselves in someone else's shoes; or, rather, we can, but it's still our own feet we will feel" (1989, p. 51). Although it may be impossible to feel or experience what someone else is feeling, becoming more culturally competent can help service providers understand, appreciate, and support families more effectively.

DEFINING CROSS-CULTURAL COMPETENCE

Cross-cultural competence is important in professional and interpersonal interactions and an area in which every service provider should be educated initially and throughout his or her career. Defining what cross-cultural competence is, however, is considerably more difficult. Cross, Bazron, Dennis, and Isaacs (1989) described cross-cultural competence in terms of behaviors, attitudes, and policies that are congruent, converge, and result in effectiveness in cross-cultural situations. In their definition, the notion of cross-cultural competence can be applied to individuals, agencies, and systems.

Barrera and Kramer used the term broadly to refer to "the ability of service providers to respond optimally to all children, understanding both the richness and the

---

The section of this chapter titled "Working with Interpreters and Translators" was originally contributed by Sam Chan, Ph.D. It has been expanded for this edition by the chapter author.

limitations of the sociocultural contexts in which children and families as well as the service providers themselves, may be operating" (1997, p. 217). They cautioned that their definition does not refer to a specific set of skills, nor is it based on a cultural, ethnic, or racial paradigm in which one group is considered normative and all others diverse. Rather, it encompasses a wide range of possible diversities and differences and focuses on knowing oneself in a cultural context in order to relate to individuals operating in different cultural contexts. As defined by Barrera in a discussion of assessment practices,

> Diversity is deemed to be present whenever there is the probability that, in interaction with a particular child or family, the assessor might attribute different meaning or values to behaviors or events than would the family or someone from that family's environment. (1994, p. 10)

In other words, socioeconomic status, religion, education, political affiliation, and language may be as predictive of different interpretations as culture, ethnicity, or race. More recently, Barrera and Corso referred to cultural competency as "practitioners' ability to respond respectfully, reciprocally, and responsively to children and families in ways that acknowledge the richness and limitations of families' and practitioners' sociocultural contexts" (2003, p. 34).

Another definition that incorporates a broader range of diversity is that of Mestas and Petersen (personal communication), developed with the assistance of the U.S. Department of Education's Committee for Enhancing Cultural Competence in Colorado. They define cultural competency as

> Having the evolving knowledge and skills used for maintaining a process to increase one's respect, understanding and knowledge of the similarities and differences between one's self and others. This includes the values, lifestyles, abilities, beliefs and opportunities that influence every aspect of how people relate to each other. Culture includes and is extended beyond race and ethnicity by focusing on values, behaviors and attitudes.

This definition places emphasis on the process as well as a wide range of potential differences and similarities between and among individuals. It does not limit cultural competence to working effectively across racial and ethnic groups but incorporates values, behaviors, and attitudes that occur across all groups.

In discussing cultural competence in health care for women, Rorie, Paine, and Barger defined cultural competence as "a set of behaviors, attitudes, and policies that enable a system, agency, and/or individual to function effectively with culturally diverse clients and communities" (1996, p. 93). Their conceptualization of diversity is inclusive, addressing economic differences, sexual orientation, and the social context in which an individual lives. Of equal importance is their emphasis on policies that enhance cross-cultural effectiveness—the need for agencies, organizations, and systems to redefine their approaches to service to become more culturally competent. This perspective is echoed by Mederos and Woldeguiorguis (2003), who suggested systemic approaches to cultural competence in the field of child protective services that involve changes in organizational policies and practices and efforts to eliminate structures that are advantageous to some and disadvantageous to others.

For the purposes of this book, *cross-cultural competence* is defined as "the ability to think, feel, and act in ways that acknowledge, respect, and build on ethnic, [socio-] cultural, and linguistic diversity" (Lynch & Hanson, 1993, p. 50). This definition assumes that all individuals and groups are diverse and does not imply that one group is normative. It is founded in the belief that cultural competence is a process, not an endpoint. It also acknowledges that sociocultural factors are as, or more, influential in people's shared or unshared experience as their ethnicity, language, or culture. While acknowledging the many critical dimensions of cultural competence, this text focuses on ethnic, cultural, and linguistic dimensions of diversity because information about these dimensions has not been as widely available to service providers as information about sociocultural factors (e.g, economic status, the effects of parental education on children's development).

Various authors have discussed the process of developing cross-cultural competence. Harry (1992) underscored the critical nature of self-awareness when working with children and families from different cultural and experiential contexts. Cross, as cited by Chan (1990), suggested that there are three critical elements: 1) self-awareness, 2) knowledge of information specific to each culture, and 3) skills that enable the individual to engage in successful interactions. Hanson, Lynch, and Wayman (1990) identified four slightly different but related elements: 1) clarification of the service provider's own values and assumptions, 2) collection and analysis of ethnographic information related to the community in which the family resides, 3) determination of the degree to which the family operates transculturally, and 4) examination of the family's orientation to specific child-rearing issues. Authors such as McIntosh (1988), in discussing white privilege, suggested that true cultural competence can be achieved only when those who have been privileged in a society recognize that their advantages are based on systems that disadvantage others, and, once they have realized this, they actively work against those systems. Regardless of the process that one selects, it is apparent that personal awareness, knowledge of other cultures and lifeways, and application of that knowledge are common elements.

Researchers and theorists in intercultural communication continue to work toward unified theories of cross-cultural competence and communication, particularly in relation to effective functioning in overseas assignments (e.g., Abe & Wiseman, 1983; Hammer, 1989; Ruben, 1989; Spitzberg, 1989; Spitzberg & Cupach, 1984). This chapter does not presume to provide answers to questions that these theorists posed, nor does it discuss successful interactions outside of the United States. Instead, it focuses on strategies that have been demonstrated to be effective through research and clinical experience working with families in the United States whose cultural, racial, ethnic, or language background is different from that of the service provider. According to Brislin, Cushner, Cherrie, and Yong (1986), the goals of cross-cultural competence are threefold. When applied to service providers who work with families from diverse cultures and life experiences, the goals are to assist service providers to 1) feel comfortable and effective in their interactions and relationships with families whose cultures and life experiences differ from their own, 2) interact in ways that enable families from different cultures and life experiences to feel positive about the interactions and the service providers, and 3) accomplish the goals that each family and service provider establish.

SELF-AWARENESS

Everyone has a culture, but individuals often are not aware of the behaviors, habits, and customs that are culturally based (Althen, 1988). According to Hall,

> There is not one aspect of human life that is not touched and altered by culture. This means personality, how people express themselves (including shows of emotion), the way they think, how they move, how problems are solved, how their cities are planned and laid out, how transportation systems function and are organized, as well as how economic and government systems are put together and function. (1976, pp. 16–17)

Although this is true for all people, Anglo-Europeans who are part of the dominant U.S. culture may have the least awareness of the ways in which their culture influences their behavior and interactions. This is true because Anglo-Europeans have predominated in the United States since the country was colonized. Because of the positions of power and influence that Anglo-Europeans have held, their culture, customs, and habits have shaped the society more than any other single group. The "melting pot" to which America aspired during the early waves of immigration took its toll on the diversity of all groups including Anglo-Europeans. The diminishing of these early immigrants' roots has resulted in some Anglo-European Americans feeling that they do not have a culture, that they are "just American" or that they are "cultureless." During the past few years in workshops throughout the country, the editors of this book have often heard from Anglo-European participants, "I don't have a culture; I was raised American." This is not unique. Hammond and Morrison (1996) suggested that one of the most common char-

acteristics of Anglo-European Americans is their denial of any sort of collective culture.

To understand and appreciate fully the diversity that exists among the families served, service providers must first understand and appreciate their own culture. Self-awareness is the first step on the journey toward cross-cultural competence (Barrera & Corso, 2003; Chan, 1990; Harry, 1992). But how does cultural self-awareness begin and develop? And how does cultural self-awareness lead to improved understanding of other cultures? This section of the chapter addresses these questions.

Cultural self-awareness begins with an exploration of one's own heritage. Issues such as place of origin or indigenous status, time of immigration, reasons for immigration, language(s) spoken, the place of the family's first settlement in the United States, and extent of identity with both the original and new culture all help to define one's own cultural heritage. The political leanings, religion, jobs, status, beliefs, and values of the first immigrants provide a sketch of one's family and heritage. Information about the economic, social, and vocational changes that subsequent generations have undergone complete the picture. Perhaps the most enriching way to gather this information is through the recollections of the oldest family members as they tell stories of their early lives and the lives of their grandparents and great-grandparents. Although oral history often has been neglected in the rush of daily life, it can provide a wonderful bridge between generations. In some families, photographs, journals, family albums, or notes of important events in family books such as bibles may supplement oral traditions. When none of these are available, a document search in county courthouses can reveal clues to the family's past through marriage records; records of births and deaths; and titles to lands bought, sold, or occupied. In some areas of the country, church, parish, temple, mosque, or synagogue records provide a wealth of information about family history. Some public libraries also contain extensive collections specifically for those interested in genealogy. In the 1990s, computer-based search strategies have become available through electronic genealogy forums, bulletin boards, and web sites providing increased access to examining one's heritage.

For African Americans in search of their roots, information is often impossible to obtain because of the institution of slavery; however, records from the Freedmen's Bureau established in 1865 can sometimes provide information, as can military records that include the names of African Americans who fought in all of the nation's wars. Other historical documents, such as treaties and military records and accounts, contain information about American Indian people and their holdings. For example, the names of the *Dineh* (The People)—Navajo in English—can be found in military history. The 420 Navajo Code Talkers, whose language is one of the few unbroken codes in military history, were instrumental in ensuring that top-secret communications could be sent to the Pacific Front in World War II. Ironically, the Code Talkers who, in 1945, sent the message that the United States flag had been raised on Iwo Jima, had to wait another 3 years to receive the right to vote in Arizona (Watson, 1993).

Learning about one's own roots is the first step in determining how one's values, beliefs, customs, and behaviors have been shaped by culture. This new knowledge helps individuals separate the ways of thinking, believing, and behaving that have been assumed to be universal from those that are based on cultural beliefs and biases. When one has explored and developed a deeper understanding of one's own cultural heritage, the second step of discovery can begin.

The second step is to examine some of the values, behaviors, beliefs, and customs that are identified with one's own cultural heritage. Although the sociocultural variables such as education level, socioeconomic status, and degree of identification and affiliation with one's culture are potent forces in shaping one's value system and behavior, cultures are known for certain salient characteristics. (For a more in-depth description of the values and beliefs often shared by members of various cultural groups addressed in this book, see Part II, Chapters 4–12.) For example, in addition to the values described by Althen (1988) (see Chapter 1), Robertiello and Hoguet (1987) discussed 39 values that underpin the culture of white Anglo-Saxon Protestants in the United States. Among these are stoicism in adversity, honesty, courage, frugality, resourcefulness, optimism, fairness, wit and sense of humor, physical attractiveness, cheerfulness, and good taste. In developing a new framework for productivity and profitability for business and industry, Hammond and Morrison (1996, pp. 5–6) described seven cultural forces that they believe define Americans:

1. Insistence on choice

2. Pursuit of impossible dreams

3. Obsession with "big" and "more"

4. Impatience with time

5. Acceptance of mistakes

6. Urge to improve

7. Fixation with what is new

It is instructive to compare one's own perspectives to these generalizations about Americans. To what extent do these characteristics describe you? To what extent do they describe the families that you or your organization serve(s)? Service providers who are members of the Anglo-European American culture or who are strongly influenced by it may want to examine these values to determine their degree of identification with each and the extent to which each affects their practice. For example, service providers who value punctuality and careful scheduling may need to examine their frustration with families who place less emphasis on clock and calendar time. Service providers who value optimism and humor may discover that they are uncomfortable with individuals who are depressed or those whom they perceive as complainers. Service providers who value frugality may have trouble understanding why a family with very limited resources has just purchased a DVD player or sport utility vehicle. Service providers who pride themselves in sensitive but direct communications may have difficulty with families who do not look them in the eye or those who nod "yes" when the answer is "no." Service providers who value privacy may have difficulty understanding why a preschooler is still sleeping in the parents' bedroom. Service providers who create extensive "menus" of services may not understand why some families are reluctant or unable to choose. A family who does not share their enthusiasm may frustrate service providers who are ecstatic about the latest technology or technique.

Likewise, service providers who do not come from or identify with the dominant U.S. culture must examine their values and beliefs in relation to the families that they serve. Service providers from cultures that value interdependence over independence, cooperation above competition, authoritative rather than permissive child rearing, and interaction more than efficiency may need to examine how these values affect their practice. For example, families who are striving to toilet train their child at a very young age, who are encouraging self-feeding, or who are leaving the child with nonfamily babysitters starting at infancy may be puzzling to service providers who place a higher value on interdependence than independence. When a young child talks back or interrupts adult conversations, many Anglo-European American parents view the child's behavior as his or her right to personal expression, whereas many American Indian, Asian, Latino, and African American parents and service providers may see the same behavior as disrespectful and obnoxious. Parents who want to get right to the point in planning meetings and who do not engage in "small talk" may be viewed as brusque, rude, or generally insensitive by service providers who are more used to connecting interpersonally before conducting business.

The examples in the previous paragraphs illustrate the ways in which cultural beliefs may affect practice. All cultures have built-in biases, and there are no right or wrong cultural beliefs; however, there are differences that must be acknowledged. Cultural self-awareness is the bridge to learning about other cultures. It is not possible to be truly sensitive to someone else's culture until one is sensitive to one's own culture and the impact that cultural customs, values, beliefs, and behaviors have on practice. For a further examination of one's personal cultural heritage, the reader is encouraged to review the activity in Appendix A, A Cultural Journey, at the end of this chapter.

AWARENESS AND UNDERSTANDING
OF OTHERS' CULTURAL PERSPECTIVES

After service providers become familiar with their own culture and its effects on the ways in which they think and behave, the foundation for learning about other cultures has been laid. The next step is to learn about other cultures through readings, interactions, and involvement.

> The success of any interaction, in or outside our own culture, rests primarily on our ability to anticipate the behavior of others, including their reactions to our behavior. If we cannot do this . . . then even the possibility of successful interaction is largely precluded. (Storti, 1989, p. 92)

Information about cultures other than one's own helps explain the values, beliefs, and behaviors that may be encountered in cross-cultural interactions. This information provides a framework of possibilities to consider. It does not provide a fail-safe prediction of any individual's or family's beliefs, biases, or behaviors. In fact, when general information about any culture is used as a recipe for expectations and interactions, it is likely to cause rather than resolve problems. *The belief in culture-specific information is no longer viable.* Instead, service providers must look to information about cultures as a guideline rather than a template for understanding individuals and families whose life experience is different from their own. Because Part II of this book provides a wealth of general information about cultures to consider when interacting with children, families, friends, neighbors, and colleagues, this section offers only a brief introduction to the topic.

Learning About Other Cultural Perspectives

People can learn about other cultures in many ways. Perhaps the four most effective are 1) learning through books, the arts, and technology; 2) talking, socializing, and working with individuals from the culture who can act as cultural guides or mediators; 3) participating in the daily life of another culture; and 4) learning the language of the other culture. Although reading is not sufficient, it may be the best place to start when gathering information about other cultures. Readings and other media may range from history and geography to poetry, biography, and fiction. Authors and artists may be from the culture or writing about the culture, but a key to developing a new understanding is to view the culture from its members' point of view. Therefore, books, plays, films, poems, and performances by individuals from the culture provide critical insights and perspectives that are not available through other sources. It has been said that biography and fiction are often more telling than history; a list of books and other media that focus on cross-cultural interactions from many points of view is provided in the Suggested Readings and Resources section at the end of this book. Some of these resources focus on encountering mainstream culture in the United States; others focus on encounters with other cultures. In some resources, culture is the major theme; in others, it is the backdrop. Although the list is neither exhaustive nor complete, it does give the reader an opportunity to explore cultural encounters and other worldviews through literature and the arts.

Technology is playing an increasingly important role in providing information about culture, particularly issues of cross-cultural health care. Web sites such as Diversity Rx (http://www.diversityrx.org/HTML/DIVRX.htm), sponsored by the National Conference of State Legislatures, Resources for Cross Cultural Health Care, and the Henry J. Kaiser Family Foundation, provide numerous health and medical resources to support access and quality in health care for traditionally underrepresented groups. EthnoMed (http://www.ethnomed.org), sponsored by the University of Washington's Harborview Medical Center, provides health information in multiple languages, features articles on cross-cultural health issues, and provides general cultural information about groups who have recently immigrated to the United States. Organizations that focus on advocacy for social justice can also be found online. Although each varies in its specific focus, all are committed to creating a society in which diversity is valued and social justice is the norm. Examples of these organizations are the Southern Poverty Law Center (http://www.splcenter.org/splc.html) and the Children's Defense Fund (http://www.childrensdefense.org/).

A second way to learn about other cultures is through open discussion and interpersonal sharing with members of another culture. These cultural mediators or guides can highlight feelings, beliefs, and practices that may be unfamiliar. From their own experiences of living bi- or transculturally, they can describe the world in a way that allows monocultural people to reframe their perceptions. Friends, colleagues, and neighbors all can serve as cultural guides; the important prerequisites are trust and respect for each other and each other's cultures. It also is important to recognize that both parties will filter their information through a personal lens that has been affected by all of their life experiences; thus, no individual can accurately portray the range of his or her own culture's beliefs, values, and practices.

Participating in the life of the community of diverse cultures is a third way to increase cross-cultural understanding. Celebrating holidays, joining in worship, and getting involved in community projects are several ways in which individuals can increase their understanding and appreciation of different cultures. This involvement is different from entering the community as a helpful professional, an observer, or an academic voyeur (Green, 1982). Participating in the life of the community means entering as a guest of friends or colleagues from the culture with the express purpose of increasing one's own participation, awareness, understanding, and involvement. Although a cultural plunge may provide new information and new perspectives, this participation represents a sustained commitment to growing, learning, and giving back.

Finally, learning the language of another culture is one of the most powerful ways to learn about and understand that culture. Because so much of every culture is reflected in its language, language learning is a hallmark of cross-cultural competence. In addition to gaining knowledge about the culture, being bi- or multilingual opens many doors to additional opportunities. It also provides immediate access to conversations, discussions, and sharing with families and colleagues with other language backgrounds. We caution, however, that learning the language of another culture or country does not necessarily guarantee that cultural competence will be enhanced. Without concomitant changes in attitudes and beliefs about the culture and behaviors that indicate respect and reciprocity, knowing the language is insufficient.

Cultural Continua

General information about the ways in which values, beliefs, and behaviors may differ across cultures is essential to overall awareness and understanding of cultural differences and similarities. Lists of contrasting values and beliefs often have been presented as a way of illustrating cultural differences; however, these lists can be misinterpreted if the reader makes the assumption that one value or belief is normative or inherently right and the other is deviant or wrong. Instead of contrasting values and beliefs, we propose that service providers consider value sets that are common across cultures and view each as a continuum. For example, independence and interdependence represent a value set with independence at one end of a continuum and interdependence at the other end. Neither perspective is mutually exclusive, and each individual may be at any point on the continuum. Furthermore, one's position on the continuum is not fixed. Age, education, socioeconomic situation, friends, family members, one's life experiences, place in the family life cycle, and many other variables contribute to one's position at any given time. Seldom are family members at the same place, and often a group of service providers may find that they would place themselves in very different positions. Although some cultures may be closer to one end of the continuum than the other, individuals within the culture will represent the entire spectrum. How could such a model help service providers? We propose that it 1) reduces the likelihood that any culture will be viewed stereotypically, 2) reduces the likelihood that differences will be construed as "us versus them," 3) provides a set of working hypotheses that can be used to consider how families and service providers may differ in their views, and 4) increases the likelihood that service providers will develop a better understanding of the many ways of being in the world—all of which have merit.

Table 3.1 presents examples of some of the cultural continua that are most likely to emerge when working with families of young children. When communication is not going well or the family's and the service provider's goals appear to be in conflict, it is often because those involved are making different assumptions or are operating from a different position on one of the cultural continua. Examining the concerns in light of the continua can be helpful in determining each person's perspective and developing resolutions. Each of the seven value sets listed in Table 3.1 is defined and illustrated in the paragraphs that follow. (Values related to communication—high context and low context—are discussed in this chapter under the heading of General Principles of Effective Cross-Cultural Communication.)

Family Constellation Continuum Some families are large, with extended kinship networks that are actively involved in almost all aspects of daily life; others are small, with one or two adults responsible for decisions and activities. Members of large, extended families may provide support for one another through child care, shared housing, socializing, cash contributions, and helping with the many tasks of daily life. This built-in assistance can help considerably, especially when a child requires extra or special care. Large family networks, however, may exert pressure on certain family members that interferes with these family members' own develop-

Table 3.1. Cultural continua

Extended family and kinship networks	Small unit families with little reliance on the extended family
Interdependence	Individuality
Nurturance of young children	Independence of young children
Time is given	Time is measured
Respect for age, ritual, and tradition	Emphasis on youth, future, and technology
Ownership defined in broad terms	Ownership is individual and specific
Differentiated rights and responsibilities	Equal rights and responsibilities
Harmony	Control

ment. For example, the eldest daughter may be expected to care for aging parents at the expense of her own education or career, or the eldest son may be expected to begin contributing to the family income as an adolescent in order to send a younger brother or sister to college. Small families may have more independence in decision making and life choices but may also have fewer sources of support. For families with a child with a disability, especially one- or two-parent families living in relative isolation, life can be particularly challenging. Because most people grow up closer to one end of the continuum, typically they are more familiar and more comfortable with one kind of family constellation.

Service providers may want to consider where each family is on the continuum and tailor their approaches accordingly. They may consider whether the right people (i.e., the decision makers and implementers) are involved in planning the intervention. It also helps to know whether the family already has a strong network of natural supports that makes formal, agency-based support less important to them. In some instances, service providers' requests for follow-through may be too demanding because of the family's other obligations. In other instances, suggested interventions (with the parents' permission) may need to be shared with several family members, child care providers, or others who play a major role in the child's daily life.

Interdependence/Individuality Continuum Individuality, the explicit expression of self, is a value that some families prize highly. Children are encouraged to "be who they are" and stand out from the crowd. Individual characteristics that result in praise are particularly valued. Thousands of articles and books have been written about fostering self-esteem and self-worth. In other families, however, interdependence is the primary value. Contributing to the functioning of the family as a whole is far more important than expressing one's individuality. In fact, to become fully independent is viewed as selfish and as a rejection of the family. Self-esteem is based on one's contributions to the whole rather than on individual characteristics or behaviors. This continuum is particularly important in intervention programs that focus on one family member, spotlighting his or her needs to the exclusion of the needs of other family members.

In some instances the goals for independence are inconsistent with the family's desire for interdependence. For example, a service provider's goal for getting a toddler out of diapers through toilet training may be less important to family members than their goal to take the child to a cousin's wedding without worrying that he will wet or soil his clothes. For other families the attention focused on one family member may be interfering with the balance and the interdependence of the entire family. Some children who may appear to have special needs in an educational environment play an important and valued role within the family, and their disability is masked or nonexistent in the family context. As a result, families may find the label of disability difficult to understand. Programs also may want to consider whether the activities that are planned for children foster individuality or cooperation. Do games and physical activities focus on individual winners or do they encourage cooperation and teambuilding?

Nurturance/Independence Continuum Like they do in all of the continua, families and family members as well as service providers may differ on the nurturance/independence continuum. Although most people nurture young children, the behaviors attributed to nurturance vary markedly from individual to individual and from group to group. What one person views as nurturance, another may view as spoiling. For example, the majority of people throughout the world have nurtured children for centuries by having them sleep in their parents' bed; following them around in order to feed them; keeping them in close physical proximity through holding, touching, and carrying long after they can walk alone; or taking them wherever the adults go. Many families in the United States would describe themselves as nurturing, but they expect more independence. Infants may sleep alone in rooms of their own soon after birth; feedings may be scheduled and take place in a particular chair or area; children may spend more time in infant seats, car seats, and strollers than on the laps of their caregivers; and child care provided by non–family members is not unusual for infants and young children. Throughout most of the world, children are catered to throughout the preschool years. They may be fed, held, dressed, kept in almost skin-to-skin proximity, and tended to whenever there is any hint of unhappiness until they are 6 or 7 years old. At that point, expectations change dramatically. Adults expect children to behave according to societal norms. In the United States, child rearing is typically less demarcated.

If the family is closer to the end of the continuum that encourages nurturance and the service provider is closer to the end that encourages earlier independence, conflicts may arise. The service provider may see the family as too indulgent, and the family may view the service provider as unnecessarily harsh. Because developing independence is such a central feature of many early intervention and early childhood programs, some families may feel that their core values are being questioned. Service providers may want to examine their own beliefs about nurturance. Why are the family's differences in nurturance upsetting? Is the concern based on a behavior that could have negative consequences for the child, or is it because of a difference in personal preference and worldview? What could we learn from the family's approach to child rearing?

Time Continuum   The way that individuals or groups of people perceive time differs tremendously within and across cultures. The following expressions represent one end of the continuum that measures time:

- "Time is money"

- "The early bird gets the worm"

- "Let me check my calendar"

- "Wasting time"

- "Time flies"

Much of the daily life of professionals in the United States is governed by time. Watches that beep, clocks, calendars, appointment books, personal digital assistants, and a local number that can be called to get the exact time all emphasize the importance of measuring and apportioning time. Imagine the difficulties that are encountered when a family believes that time is to be given, not measured. Within this framework, the amount of time necessary for any task or interaction, not the clock, determines the time that will be given. For example, a family member may have a 2:00 p.m. planning meeting with a service provider, but if a neighbor appears on the doorstep and wants to talk or get help solving a problem, the planning meeting may

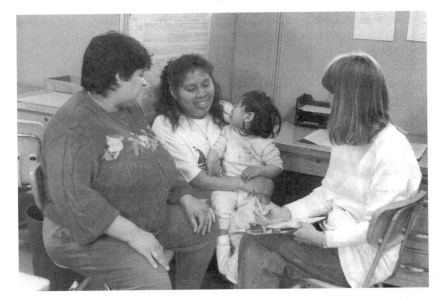

be missed. The service provider who was "stood up" only sees the behavior as disrespectful instead of understanding that the family was honoring the neighbor.

Resolving differences on the time continuum is seldom easy; within families differences often arise that make daily life even more complicated. Between service providers and families, the differences may be even more complex. When families are not available at the appointed time, service providers may want to first consider whether the family's behavior is based on a difference in the way time is viewed or whether there is another reason that they are not connecting. In some instances it is possible to make the schedule more flexible. In other situations it may be necessary to let the family know that you respect their approach to time but that other families and your organization need to operate on a schedule.

Tradition/Technology Continuum   Consider the United States: The emphasis on future, technology, and youth is everywhere—from the "new and improved" labels on nearly every grocery store product to magazine covers promoting youth, physical beauty, technology, and the world of the future. New computers and the latest diet become old in a few months. The United States has had a long-standing love of whatever is new. We have been taught to look to the future, forgetting that when we face only the future, we turn our back on the past. Not every individual or every culture is as enamored with the future, however. For many people of the world, the past is more important. The ritual, tradition, and wisdom of the ancestors form a solid base for contemporary life. As a result, the latest technology, the newest approach to teaching, or the most advanced medical intervention may be regarded with disinterest or suspicion.

Service providers who pride themselves on being on the cutting edge may discover that in these cultures, their knowledge is not regarded as highly as the folk wisdom of the elders. When this occurs, it is easy to assume that the family is ignorant, disinterested, or uncooperative; however, it is more useful to learn about the family's beliefs and the wisdom that they are using to make decisions. Understanding the family members' value system and their reliance on tradition and ritual often enables the service provider to incorporate other approaches into the family's practices and to blend current practice with the family's beliefs and values.

Ownership Continuum   One of the first words that English-speaking children learn is "mine." The same is sometimes true for adults from the United States living in a new country and learning the language. The most common approach to ownership within the predominant culture of the United States is individual and specific. Things are "mine," "yours," or "someone else's." Property is often labeled with the owner's name; and elaborate legal documents exist to define what belongs to whom. Property law occupies a significant portion of the corpus of law in the United States. Starting in the early years, children in the United States are given their own cubbies and/or their own rooms, as well as all of the other material things that their parents can afford. Not everyone, however, shares this view of ownership. Among many cultures of the world, ownership is defined in much broader terms. The family or the entire community, not individuals, owns property and material goods. When one person purchases a car or CD player, all may use it, with no priority given to the purchaser.

Although property rights may seem far from issues of intervention with children and families, they may surface in programs that have toy-lending libraries or those that leave materials in the home. When the toy is not returned and the materials are not there at next week's home visit, it does not necessarily mean that the family is careless or that they have purloined the materials. It may simply mean that the toys and materials are in another household for other children and families to enjoy. Service providers may want to ask themselves where a family is on the ownership continuum. They also may want to develop some strategies so that expensive materials are not lost to the program. In some cases, it may be a matter of explaining to families that the material is important to other children in the program. In others, it may be necessary to create expendable materials that the program can live without. In still others it may mean holding "make it, take it" workshops in which families come together and make things they can take home for their children.

Rights and Responsibilities Continuum   The United States was founded on the principle of equality. Although the goal has not been reached, it is one of the most important underpinnings of life in the United States. As a nation, the United States has placed an emphasis on equal rights and responsibilities rather than on differentiated rights and responsibilities. Equal rights apply across gender as well as across other characteristics. In many other parts of the world and in other cultures and religions, gender roles are differentiated. Women may be responsible for children and home life, whereas men may be responsible for financial support and acting as the intermediary between the family and the community. In the United States such arrangements are often considered old-fashioned. Differentiated roles have existed for centuries, however, and working cross culturally often brings service providers into families in which roles are defined by gender. Because women predominate in the service provider role in education, social services, and many areas of health care, differentiated roles may be particularly difficult for them to accept. The hierarchies that exist in many families challenge both equality and the feminist perspective.

When working with families who have a different way of organizing and assigning roles and responsibilities, it is easy for a female service provider to want to "liberate" the mother. Instead of deciding on this course of action, it is important to learn how the family prefers to function; provide opportunities and information; and support the family members in the care, intervention, and education of their children.

Harmony/Control Continuum   The last of the continua discussed here is the harmony/control continuum. Harmony is the goal of many individuals, families, and cultures; that is, these individuals want to live in synchrony with their surroundings and circumstances. For others, controlling their surroundings and circumstances is the goal. In general, the mainstream U.S. culture falls closer to the controlling end of the continuum. There is little that people in this group think they cannot control and less that they do not try to control. From heating and cooling systems in houses, malls, and cars to life-extending medical interventions, most Americans are constantly seeking to bring the cosmos under control. Early intervention in itself is an assertion that all things can be changed, managed, or controlled through human action.

Consider the difficulties that may arise when family and service provider are at different ends of this continuum. The service provider may view the family that is attempting to incorporate the child with a disability and regain harmony as denying the child's problems or as uncooperative. The family may see the service provider as disrupting the peace that is of central importance to them. As in every other interaction, it is advisable to suspend judgment of the family members' behavior and try to understand their motivation. Service providers can offer many things that support harmony, but they must be offered and incorporated on the family's terms.

These continua are provided as examples of the many values and beliefs that occur across cultures. Often it is not the values themselves that differ from group to group but the behaviors that express the value. All cultures nurture their children, but nurturing behaviors differ dramatically. All groups of people use the past and the future to make decisions, but some put more emphasis on the past, whereas others emphasize the future. Thinking about one's own position on the various continua, the program's implicit or explicit position, and the position of family members can help increase both understanding and the likelihood of culturally competent intervention.

SOCIOCULTURAL FACTORS

In addition to the cultural continua described, many sociocultural factors influence interactions among and between families, family members, and service providers. It is not uncommon for these factors to be more powerful than cultural factors or to be intertwined with dimensions of the cultural continua in ways that increase the complexity of interactions and the potential for misunderstanding. Although a wide range of sociocultural factors could be identified, three seem to be particularly salient when working with young children and their families: socioeconomic status (SES), education, and personal efficacy.

Like the cultural continua, sociocultural factors are dynamic; they may vary over time. Families and service providers may also perceive the impact of these factors differently. For example, some adults realize when reflecting on their childhood that, by objective standards, their family was poor and had very limited material resources. They may, however, have fond memories about the closeness of their family—the things they did together and the warmth that they felt from grandparents, aunts, uncles, cousins, brothers, and sisters. No socioeconomic status, educational level, or sense of personal efficacy is right or wrong; however, doors are more easily opened to those who have financial resources, are educated, and believe that they have influence over their own lives. The following paragraphs discuss these socio-cultural factors in relation to their impact on family service provider interactions.

Socioeconomic Status

In the United States and throughout the world, poverty has a profound effect on families. It is associated with threats to healthy child development because of the in-creased risk of inadequate nutrition, poor-quality child care, exposure to environ-mental toxins, impaired parent–child interactions, trauma, abuse, and parental sub-stance abuse (National Center for Children in Poverty, 2002). One cannot assume that poverty affects the love that family members have for one another, nor does being poor make a family inadequate. It does, however, make life far more difficult. Poverty limits access, opportunity, and energy. It interferes with a family's ability to make plans and to carry them out. Poverty often overshadows hope. For families liv-ing in poverty, it may be more difficult to find and participate in intervention ser-vices. Families may be uncomfortable with home visits because of their living situa-tions. They may find transportation to programs and services an unaffordable luxury and sustaining participation nearly impossible because of the overwhelming de-mands that they face to survive.

Although the old adage says that money cannot buy happiness, it can buy assis-tance and creature comforts that make life easier. Financial security helps guarantee that families will have food, shelter, clothing, medical and dental care, transporta-tion, safety, recreation, education, and opportunities for leisure. Being financially se-cure or affluent does not mean that one is a better parent, but it does provide access to many things that support good parenting. For example, money provides access to the best child care available, various services for children with disabilities, and con-nections through friends and colleagues who can help find services and supports.

The majority of families are neither impoverished nor wealthy. Most are some-where in between; and many have been affected by upward or downward financial mobility. Some may have been financially secure until they had a child with signifi-cant medical needs, until an earning parent lost his or her job, or until it became nec-essary to financially support a grandparent. Others are struggling to stay afloat and provide their families with the basics; still others are gradually gaining resources or have become financially comfortable. Even "free" services such as early intervention programs or Medicaid require clothes and shoes for children to wear, time for ap-pointments and meetings with professionals, and transportation. As service provid-ers work with families with limited resources, they will want to consider the extent to which this may affect their interactions with family members.

Education

Early intervention is based on a belief that education is important and that it facili-tates positive change. Those in early intervention and other professions have typi-cally spent many years in training to gain the knowledge and skills that they possess, and many have sacrificed to reach their educational goals. Professionals are educated and value education, but not all families have shared in educational opportunity and experience. Some may highly respect and value education but have little formal education. In the multidisciplinary and highly complex world of early intervention, lack of education may limit a family member's ability to understand the child's diagnosis, prognosis, options for interventions, and the reasons for the specific interventions being recommended. Lack of education does not translate into lack of judgment or lack of desire to do the very best for a family member's son, daughter, grandson, or niece. It may, however, reduce the amount and kinds of material that can be used to gain information about services and interventions that are being proposed. When working with families with limited education and literacy, service providers will need to be particularly sensitive and share information in ways that are respectful and accessible to families.

Personal Efficacy

Personal efficacy is a psychological construct that describes an individual's sense of personal empowerment. For example, individuals who believe that they have little control over the events of their lives and that their actions make little difference in determining outcomes are considered to have a limited sense of personal efficacy or of feeling disempowered. Those who view themselves as influencing life events and being able to take actions that change outcomes are described as having a sense of personal efficacy or of being empowered. Individuals who feel empowered and capable of influencing their lives are more likely to seek and participate in prevention and intervention services. Those who do not feel that their actions will make a difference may be less willing because they assume that the intervention will not make a difference.

Individuals and families who do not have a strong sense of personal efficacy may be viewed as passive, or uninvolved, or even disinterested. This, however, may not be an accurate characterization. Believing that one's actions influence outcomes is something that we learn. When infants squeeze a stuffed toy and it squeaks, they are learning that their action caused something to happen. Preschoolers given a choice of grape or apple juice learn that their choice makes a difference in what they get to drink. When a third grader studies hard for a spelling test and is praised for getting all of the words correct, he is learning that his effort paid off. Not all individuals, as children or adults, have consistent experiences that link their actions with outcomes. A child who studies hard but does not do well on the spelling test, an adult who completes a vocational training program but cannot get a job in that field, or a family that complains to their landlord about broken plumbing but gets no response, learn over time that their actions do not make a difference—that they do not have control or influence over their lives. Service providers must consider what lessons life has taught each family member. If family members have learned that they do not have the power to change their situation, one role of the service provider may be to assist them to become more empowered.

Each of the sociocultural factors mentioned are a part of each individual's and each family's life. They may assist families to cope, to learn, and to face the challenges that they encounter. They also may work against families, making it more difficult to survive and provide the level of support that families would like to provide for their children. Sociocultural factors do not stand alone. Each is influenced by every other, by the cultural continua, the community, and each family's approach to life. Understanding the role that these factors play in each family's life is, however, integral to working effectively with children and their families.

Gathering Family Information

In addition to general information about cultural similarities and differences, the continua of values and beliefs, and some of the sociocultural factors that affect families, it also may be helpful for service providers to have more specific information related to cultural views of children and child-rearing practices, family roles and structure, views of disability and its causes, health and healing practices, and views of change and intervention (Hanson et al., 1990). These issues are so intertwined with culture and so critical in working with families who have a child with a disability that they merit special attention. Although each is addressed in the chapters included in Part II of this book, the following paragraphs provide a conceptual framework for determining what questions to ask.

Wayman, Lynch, and Hanson (1990) suggested a set of Guidelines for the Home Visitor that can be used to learn more about the family's cultural values and preferences within the context of a family systems approach to intervention. Designed for use in early childhood environments, these guidelines could easily be modified to fit families whose children are older (see Table 3.2). Although the guidelines are not to be used as a checklist or interview protocol, they do include questions about family attitudes, beliefs, and practices that could influence the services and the approach to providing services. They can be used to help service providers determine the kinds of questions and the issues that often are mediated by culture and to assist in matching the interventions to the family's way of life.

A cardinal rule in working with all families is to make no assumptions about their concerns, priorities, and resources. This is even more critical when the family's cultural and sociocultural background and identification are different from that of the service provider. However, becoming familiar with information about other cultures and life experiences and determining their relevance to individual families and family members can reduce the potential for tension between service providers and families from different cultural backgrounds.

Cautions

Throughout this book, several caveats especially relevant to gathering and using information about various cultures are emphasized. Culture is only one of the characteristics that determine individuals' and families' attitudes, values, beliefs, and ways of behaving. Socioeconomic status, educational level, degree of affiliation and identification with their roots, the language(s) spoken, the length of time that they have been in the United States, and their reasons for emigrating all are important variables that shape who individuals are and what they believe and desire. Assuming that cultural information gathered from books, cultural mediators, or language learning applies to all individuals from the cultural group is not only inaccurate but also dangerous; it can lead to stereotyping that diminishes rather than enhances cross-cultural competence. The goal of cultural learning is insight, not stereotype. When applying cultural information to an individual or a family, it is wise to proceed with caution. It also is critical to realize that families and family members all are part of the larger sociocultural and sociopolitical context. Part of this context in the United States is institutionalized racism. As Sowell pointed out, "Future improvements depend on how much of present efforts go into developing the internal resources of a group and how

Table 3.2. Guidelines for the home visitor

Part I—Family structure and child-rearing practices

Family structure

Family composition
- Who are the members of the family system?
- Who are the key decision makers?
- Is decision making related to specific situations?
- Is decision making individual or group oriented?
- Do family members all live in the same household?
- What is the relationship of friends to the family system?
- What is the hierarchy within the family? Is status related to gender or age?

Primary caregiver(s)
- Who is the primary caregiver?
- Who else participates in the caregiving?
- What is the amount of care given by mother versus others?
- How much time does the infant spend away from the primary caregiver?
- Is there conflict between caregivers regarding appropriate practices?
- What ecological/environmental issues impinge on general caregiving (i.e., housing, jobs, etc.)?

Child-rearing practices

Family feeding practices
- What are the family feeding practices?
- What are the mealtime rules?
- What types of foods are eaten?
- What are the beliefs regarding breastfeeding and weaning?
- What are the beliefs regarding bottle feeding?
- What are the family practices regarding making the transition to solid food?
- Which family members prepare food?
- Is food purchased or homemade?
- Are there any taboos related to food preparation or handling?
- Which family members feed the child?
- What is the configuration of the family mealtime?
- What are the family's views on independent feeding?
- Is there a discrepancy among family members regarding the beliefs and practices related to feeding an infant/toddler?

Family sleeping patterns
- Does the infant sleep in the same room/bed as the parents?
- At what age is the infant moved away from close proximity to the mother?
- Is there an established bedtime?
- What is the family response to an infant when he or she awakens at night?
- What practices surround daytime napping?

Family's response to disobedience and aggression
- What are the parameters of acceptable child behavior?
- What form does the discipline take?
- Who metes out the disciplinary action?

Family's response to a crying infant
- Temporal qualities—How long before the caregiver picks up a crying infant?
- How does the caregiver calm an upset infant?

(continued)

Table 3.2.   *(continued)*

Part II—Family perceptions and attitudes

Family perception of child's disability

Are there cultural or religious factors that would shape family perceptions?

- To what/where/whom does the family assign responsibility for their child's disability?
- How does the family view the role of fate in their lives?
- How does the family view their role in intervening with their child? Do they feel they can make a difference or do they consider it hopeless?

Family's perception of health and healing

- What is the family's approach to medical needs?
- Do they rely solely on Western medical services?
- Do they rely solely on holistic approaches?
- Do they utilize a combination of these approaches?
- Who is the primary medical provider or conveyer of medical information? Family members? Elders? Friends? Folk healers? Family doctor? Medical specialists?
- Do all members of the family agree on approaches to medical needs?

Family's perception of help-seeking and intervention

- From whom does the family seek help—family members or outside agencies/individuals?
- Does the family seek help directly or indirectly?
- What are the general feelings of the family when seeking assistance—ashamed, angry, demand as a right, view as unnecessary?
- With which community systems do the family interact (educational/medical/social)?
- How are these interactions completed (face-to-face, telephone, letter)?
- Which family member interacts with other systems?
- Does that family member feel comfortable when interacting with other systems?

Part III—Language and communication styles

Language

To what degree

- Is the home visitor proficient in the family's native language?
- Is the family proficient in English?

If an interpreter is used,

- With which culture is the interpreter primarily affiliated?
- Is the interpreter familiar with the colloquialisms of the family members' country or region of origin?
- Is the family member comfortable with the interpreter? Would the family member feel more comfortable with an interpreter of the same or opposite sex?

If written materials are used, are they in the family's native language?

Interaction styles

- Do family members communicate with each other in a direct or indirect style?
- Does the family tend to interact in a quiet manner or a loud manner?
- Do family members share feelings when discussing emotional issues?
- Does the family ask you direct questions?
- Does the family value a lengthy social time at each home visit unrelated to the early childhood services program goals?
- Is it important for the family to know about the home visitor's extended family? Is the home visitor comfortable sharing that information?

From Wayman, K.I., Lynch, E.W., & Hanson, M.J. (1990). Home-based early childhood services: Cultural sensitivity in a family systems approach. *Topics in Early Childhood Special Education, 10*, 65–66; adapted by permission.

much into seeking political changes in the surrounding society" (1996, p. 383). Cross-cultural competence also includes both elements—working to increase one's own skills and working to create a society that is culturally competent.

CROSS-CULTURAL COMMUNICATION

Communication, both verbal and nonverbal, is critical to cross-cultural competence. Both sending messages and understanding messages that are being received are prerequisites to effective interpersonal interactions. Because language and culture are so inextricably bound, communicating with families from different cultural and/or sociocultural backgrounds is very complex. When the language of the family and that of the service provider are different, it is clear that communication will be severely compromised; however, speaking the same language does not guarantee communication. In fact, linguists have suggested that more than 14,000 meanings can be gleaned from the 500 most commonly used English words (Samovar & Porter, 1991). Therefore, this section of the chapter focuses on general principles of effective cross-cultural communication, nonverbal communication, and working with interpreters and translators.

High-Context and Low-Context Cultures

Cultures differ in the amount of information that is explicitly transmitted through words versus the amount of information that is transmitted through the context of the situation, the relationship, and the physical cues (Hall, 1976, 1984). High-context cultures rely less on verbal communication than on understanding through shared experience, history, and implicit messages (Hecht, Andersen, & Ribeau, 1989). Fewer words are spoken and less emphasis is placed on verbal interactions. As might be expected, high-context cultures are more attuned to nonverbal cues and messages. Asian, American Indian, Arab, Latino, and African American cultures are examples of this in that meaning does not have to be communicated through words. Hecht and colleagues described high-context communication by stating, "thus facial expressions, tensions, movements, speed of interaction, location of the interaction, and other subtle 'vibes' are likely to be perceived by and have more meaning for people from high-context cultures" (1989, p. 177).

High-context culture is best understood by considering examples in one's own life in which high-context communication is used. For instance, couples who have lived together for many years, families, twins, and long-term colleagues often use abbreviated forms of communication that are very meaningful to them but nearly uninterpretable by outsiders. A look, a word, or a gesture may convey the equivalent of paragraphs of spoken words.

Individuals from low-context cultures, such as Anglo-European Americans, Swiss, Germans, and Scandinavians, typically focus on precise, direct, logical, verbal communication and are often impatient with communicators and communications that do not get to the point quickly (Hecht et al., 1989). Members of low-context cultures may not process gestures, environmental clues, and unarticulated moods that are central to effective communication in high-context cultures. Thus, communication between high-and low-context cultures often leads to misunderstanding and dissatisfaction for both parties.

High-context cultures tend to be more formal, more reliant on hierarchies, and more deeply rooted in the past (Hall, 1976). In contrast, low-context cultures are more informal, allow more equality in interaction, and have less knowledge about and reverence for the past. As a result, high-context cultures may change more slowly but provide a healthy stability for group members. Low-context cultures may be more responsive to and more comfortable with change but may lack a sense of continuity and connection with the past.

When families and service providers differ in the level of context that they use in communication, misunderstandings may arise. On the one hand, lots of talking, clearly specified verbal directions, and detailed demonstrations may seem insensitive and mechanistic to individuals from high-context cultures. They may feel that the talking is proof that the other individual does not truly understand them and cannot, therefore, be of help. On the other hand, members of low-context cultures may be uncomfortable with long pauses and silences, cryptic sentences, and indirect modes of communication such as storytelling. They may feel that these are time wasters or are signs of resistance. These interactions are further complicated by the fact that under pressure or when confronted with a communication style that they do not understand, people rely on patterns of behavior that reflect their own zone of comfort. Thus, low-context communicators talk more, speak more rapidly, and often raise their voices; whereas high-context communicators say less, make less eye contact, and withdraw from interaction.

To help bridge this gap, it is the service provider's responsibility to become aware of the level of context that families use in their communication with outsiders and to adapt to the style that is comfortable for the family. Service providers may need to slow down, listen more than they talk, observe family communication patterns, and consult with cultural guides or mediators to begin to pace their interactions to the family's communication style.

Nonverbal Communication   Nonverbal behavior often speaks louder than words, and the same nonverbal behaviors often have very different meanings from one culture to another. A gesture or a facial expression that is accepted as positive or complimentary in one culture may be viewed as negative or even obscene in another. Although no one can be knowledgeable about the cultural and regional interpretations of all nonverbal behavior, some of the basic issues warrant discussion. The following paragraphs highlight differences that service providers may encounter, but the discussion is in no way exhaustive. Because nonverbal behavior, like verbal behavior, changes meaning over time and place, one cannot assume that it is everlasting. To learn more about the meaning and the use of nonverbal behavior across cultures, service providers may consult members of the culture, read the chapters in Part II of this book, and consult guidebooks describing cultural do's and don'ts, such as _Multicultural Manners_ (Dresser, 1996).

Eye Contact and Facial Expressions   In Anglo-European American culture, eye contact is valued in interpersonal interactions. When one is speaking or being spoken to, one is expected to make eye contact with brief glances in another direction throughout the exchange. Among Anglo-European Americans, trustworthiness, sincerity, and directness are communicated through this accepted form of eye contact (Asante & Davis, 1989). Eye contact has different interpretations among other cultural groups, however. Johnson (1971) stated that among African Americans, making eye contact with someone in authority is viewed as disrespectful. Among Asian groups, eye contact between strangers may be considered shameful. Prolonged eye contact may be interpreted as disrespectful in Latino cultures (Randall-David, 1989).

Facial expressions also are subject to various interpretations across cultures. Smiling or laughing is often used to mask other emotions in Asian cultures (Althen, 1988; Randall-David, 1989). Although it may seem incongruous to a service provider from another culture, it is not unlikely that an Asian family member may smile or laugh softly when describing an event that is confusing, embarrassing, or even sad—which would confuse the service provider who regards the same event as serious. In the author's experience in Indonesia, laughter often is used to cover embarrassment or as a response to a request that could not be fulfilled.

Many Anglo-European Americans show emotion through facial expressions. Smiling typically shows happiness or amusement; a set jaw and an intense stare may show anger; and rolling eyes may show disdain. Members of other groups, such as American Indians and Asians, may not communicate emotion to the observer through facial expressions unless the observer has a deep understanding of the person and the cultural norm (Althen, 1988). Smiling, a common expression for Anglo-Europeans, also is problematic in Indonesia, where bared teeth suggest aggression.

Proximity and Touching Cultures differ in the amount of social distance with which they are comfortable. Anglo-European Americans tend to maintain a distance of about 3 feet, or an arm's length, between themselves and others during conversations, unless they are very familiar with each other. Many Latinos, southern Europeans, Middle Easterners, and African Americans are comfortable with closer conversational distances, whereas many Asians prefer more space between the speaker and listener (Althen, 1988; Randall-David, 1989). The social distance that is preferred is usually easy to gauge by observing people's movement patterns in an interaction. When people back up, the other person is usually too close for comfort. When they move toward the other person, they are attempting to get closer and reduce the social distance.

The amount and the type of physical contact permissible is highly influenced by culture, but generalizations about touching are particularly dangerous because differences across cultures are confounded by differences in gender, age, religion, and personal preference. Although these same issues affect other forms of communication, one is far less likely to get into trouble for an inappropriate word or gesture than an inappropriate touch. Given that this is an area in which a cultural mediator or a guide is of special importance, some examples of different interpretations of touch are highlighted.

Among many Chinese and other Asian groups, hugging, back slapping, and handshaking are not typical and the service provider should avoid these gestures. In those cultures in which handshaking is used at a first introduction, it is often not so hearty as that used in the United States. Variations on handshaking such as the *wai* greeting (i.e., bringing the palms of the hand together and raising them to the chest or tip of the nose while lowering the head) practiced by people from India, Thailand, and other Asian groups or the elaborate handshaking seen among African Americans are greetings that may or may not be appropriate for a service provider to use. For example, the *wai* is a general form of greeting that is a signal of respect, whereas the elaborate handshake used by some in the African American community may be a sign of in-group membership that would be inappropriate to use until invited.

Among Muslims and some non-Muslim Middle Easterners, use of the left hand to touch another person, to reach for something, or to take or to pass food is inappropriate (Devine & Braganti, 1986). Because the left hand is associated with more personal bodily functions related to elimination, it is not used in other ways. Although service providers who are left handed need not give up writing in this situation, they may choose to limit the use of their left hand for other functions when they are with a traditional family who holds this belief. Shoes and the soles of one's feet also are considered to be unclean in certain cultures. As a result, stretching out one's legs causing the feet to point at someone or to touch someone is not appropriate. Certainly putting one's feet on the furniture would be inappropriate.

Service providers must be particularly aware of these differences when working with children. Many Americans show affection for children by patting them on the head. This is not an acceptable form of touch among many Asians, who believe the

head is the residence of the soul, or among some from India, who may believe that the head is so fragile that it should not be touched (Devine & Braganti, 1986). It is not uncommon for many people to sit with their hands clasped as they converse with others nor is it uncommon in early intervention programs to write objectives that focus on helping a child bring his or her hands to midline; however, in Guatemala, holding one's hands together is a sign of death. When an infant brings his or her hands together, the gesture is even more significant and is thought to portend death (Dresser, 1996).

As with the other aspects of nonverbal communication, no one can be expected to learn, know, or always behave in ways that are considered to be culturally appropriate for everyone in the situation. Nonverbal communication is also dynamic and varies depending on the individuals involved as well as cultural norms. It is, however, a sign of respect to learn the patterns of proximity and touch that prevail among those in one's own community and attempt to behave in ways that are not offensive.

Body Language   Positions and postures that are taken for granted by those who have been socialized in the United States may have different meanings for those from other countries or other cultures. Some Asians can view standing with one's hands on one's hips as extremely hostile. Many Muslims see sitting on the top of a desk or perching on the arm of a chair as rude. Sitting so that one's head is higher than the elders or chiefs in the room is interpreted as an affront by Samoans. Although there are a number of popular press books available about body language, service providers must remember that they are typically written from a Western perspective and may not accurately reflect how the same postures will be regarded by individuals from other cultures.

Gestures   Gestures can be used to supplement verbal communication or as symbols that substitute for verbal expression. Research on the cross-cultural interpretation of gestures suggests that members of different cultures claim recognition of 70%–100% of the gestures from other groups, but their rate of correct interpretation of these gestures was as low as 30% (Schneller, 1989). As a result, gestural language often contributes more to misunderstandings than to effective communication. This is a critical piece of information when one considers the extent to which individuals rely on gestures when they do not understand one another's language.

Different cultures use body movements to a different extent when communicating. Anglo-European Americans tend to use moderate gesturing to accompany their talk (Althen, 1988, p. 141). Although hand and arm movements are used for emphasis, Anglo-European Americans typically do not allow their elbows to go above their shoulders with the exception of waving greetings or goodbyes, raising a hand in a class, or voting by a show of hands (Althen, 1988). More expansive gestures are construed as too emotional and are carefully avoided by most Anglo-European Americans. Members of other cultures have different norms related to gestures: Some Latinos, Middle Easterners, and southern Europeans use large gestures with considerable arm waving when they communicate (Althen, 1988). Indonesians respect calmness and control in verbal communication and are often uncomfortable with the arm movement that is the norm for Anglo-European Americans. In addition to speaking with those who know the cultural community and its regional variations, it perhaps is most helpful to observe interactions among community members and to try to bring one's own communicative style into synchrony.

Nodding the head up and down is taken as a sign of understanding and agreement in mainstream culture in the United States. This same gesture is interpreted quite differently in many other cultures. Among Asian, American Indian, Middle Eastern, and Pacific Island groups, it often means, "I hear you speaking." It does not signal that the listener understands the message nor does it suggest that he or she agrees; however, because disagreeing would be impolite, head nodding is used. Individuals from India signal that they have heard what has been said by moving their head in a quick, horizontal, figure eight pattern (Althen, 1988).

Americans tend to beckon to people by pointing the index finger palm up and curling it toward the body. People from other cultures or countries (e.g., Middle East, Asia, India) use this gesture only when summoning animals (Devine & Braganti, 1986); it is never used with children or with adults. In Southeast Asia, people are summoned with the same gesture that people in the United States use to signal goodbye—holding the hand palm down and moving the fingers down and toward the palm (Dresser, 1996).

Finally, gestures that are common in the United States, such as bringing the thumb and index finger together to form a circle and holding it in the air to signify a job well done or the thumbs up sign to signal readiness or praise are obscene gestures among some Latino cultures. Because gestural language is so easily misunderstood, is specific to regions of the country, and sometimes is specific to one or more generations, it is important for service providers to periodically consult with others to determine what is and is not appropriate.

Listening to the Family's Perspective   A long-standing difficulty in communication between people who do not share a common language and worldview has been the tendency of the dominant group to describe the nondominant group in pejorative terms (Green, 1982). In an attempt to correct these faulty perceptions, anthropologists led by Franz Boas (1943) introduced another perspective. This new perspective suggested that the way to understand the thoughts of another group is to attempt to understand and analyze its experience in terms of its concepts rather than one's own. Perhaps the first element in developing effective communication for the service provider is to try to see the world from the family's point of view. For example, most service providers strongly believe in the concept of change. The very choice of the title *service provider* suggests that there is a belief that by entering into the situation with information, activities, or special expertise, positive change will occur. Thus, the service provider views an early intervention program for an infant with Down syndrome very positively, almost as a necessity. As illustrated on the cultural continua, however, not all cultures share the belief that they can influence change or even that change is a good thing. Instead, these cultures accept what is already established and place value on living harmoniously with what they have been given. In addition, families may not want to enroll their infants in early intervention programs, have physical malformations surgically corrected, or join support groups for families of children with disabilities. Using the service provider's concepts to analyze the situation, it might be said that the family is noncompliant or refusing intervention. Using the family's concepts, it would be said that intervention is not useful, and, in fact, it may interfere with achieving harmony in the situation.

Seeing the world from the family's point of view is not easy nor is it always reinforcing. It is difficult to consider that the approach that the service provider's culture values so highly is not valued by the family's culture. Service providers' attempts to prove that intervention is "the right thing to do" may leave families feeling harassed and wanting to distance themselves from the program. Likewise, when a family chooses not to participate or to follow the recommendations of professionals, service providers feel that they have failed. Cross-cultural understanding and competence can help defuse the situation. If the family members feel that the service provider is truly listening, honoring their right to make decisions, and respecting the decisions that they make, the family is far less likely to pull away and be lost to follow-up. If service providers are able to see the situation from the family's point of view, they need not feel that they have failed.

The service provider's role should be unilateral only in situations in which abuse or neglect are suspected and must be reported. Given information about all of the options and assistance in problem solving, the majority of families make decisions that are best for the child and the family. Although their decisions may be different from what the service provider had hoped for and may not correspond to the service provider's timeline, if the family members "own" a decision, then it will be one that they are likely to implement.

Acknowledging and Respecting Cultural Differences Rather than Minimizing Them

The concept of the United States as a melting pot was popularized in a play written by Israel Zangwill in 1909. Zangwill's conception of the country at that time was a fiery crucible in which people of all cultures were thrown and in which their differences were melted away, resulting in a fusion of strength and the coming of a "new superman" (cited in Tiedt & Tiedt, 1990). Now cultural differences are viewed as strengths rather than weaknesses, and the melting pot is no longer an accurate metaphor for the United States. Rather than melting away differences, the emphasis is on celebrating diversity and strengthening society through contact with other attitudes, values, beliefs, and ways of behaving. As a result, cultural differences are not ignored or assumed to blend together, but acknowledged, discussed, and valued.

People in the United States speak openly and publicly about many ideas and issues. Rules related to sexual intimacy are now portrayed on billboards, products for personal hygiene are advertised on prime-time television, and support groups are established for almost every imaginable condition or problem. However, discussions of cultural, racial, ethnic, and language diversity between members of different groups are rarely heard. According to Sam Chan (personal communication, May 10, 1991), a person's color is the first thing that we see and the last thing that we talk about. Effective cross-cultural communication includes the willingness to engage in discussions that explore differences openly and respectfully, interactions that dispel myths and open doors to understanding.

Communicating Attitudes Through Words

Attitudes about different groups of people and the ways in which they live and behave are communicated by the words that one uses to describe these people and their practices. Throughout history, in-groups have used pejorative terms to describe out-groups. Many groups, such as American Indians, were named by people outside of their own group (Helms, 1990). To overcome the negative connotations that have come to be associated with certain words and to increase the sense of group identity, the names of many cultural groups have changed over the years.

Perhaps the most obvious changes in name have been associated with African Americans as self-identity has recast vocabulary. As Neal and Allgood-Hill (1990) noted, *negro* was the word used by the Portuguese to describe the slaves who were brought to the United States, a term probably chosen because it meant "black" in Portuguese. Although early slaves had a preference for the term *African, negro* was the name used by the slave traders and owners. As the ties to and memories of Africa were lessened by time, many slaves chose to be called *colored*—a common appellation until the mid-1960s. With the birth of the black pride movement of the 1960s, *black* became the preferred term. In the 1990s, a number of prominent black Americans published a statement calling for *African American* to become the descriptor (Neal & Allgood-Hill, 1990).

These changes in the words used to describe a group are not unique to African Americans. For example, *Asian* has replaced *Oriental* (Tong, 1990); emphasis is growing on using more specific tribal affiliation instead of American Indian (LaDue, 1990); and *Latino* in some parts of the country has replaced *Hispanic*. (In the southwest, some young, Mexican Americans may prefer the term *Chicano*, but it may be considered an insult by older Mexican Americans who do not share the same political views.) Although the debate about names has not been settled, each of the changes represents increasing group identity and empowerment. Defining and describing individuals from any cultural, ethnic, linguistic, or racial group is similar to defining and describing families; that is, the words that are used should be those that the members prefer. As service providers, it is important to keep up with these changes and, as stated by Tiedt and Tiedt, "demonstrate our awareness of how thinking has changed by our own use of appropriate terms" (1990, p. 12).

General Characteristics of
Effective Cross-Cultural Communicators

In addition to the specific communicative behaviors that have been discussed for increasing one's competence in cross-cultural interactions, extensive literature is available on the characteristics found to be common among those who are successful in cross-cultural environments (Giles & Franklyn-Stokes, 1989). This literature is extremely complex, driven by a multiplicity of sometimes contradictory theories, and complicated by a stronger interest in sojourners' effectiveness outside the United States rather than their effectiveness in intercultural interactions at home. Even though different researchers and different studies have chosen varying theories, definitions, methodologies, and subjects, several characteristics seem to be shared by people who are effective cross-cultural communicators that are intuitively clear. Communication effectiveness is significantly improved when the service provider

- Respects individuals from other cultures

- Makes continued and sincere attempts to understand the world from others' points of view

- Is open to new learning

- Is flexible

- Has a sense of humor

- Tolerates ambiguity well

- Approaches others with a desire to learn

Working with Interpreters and Translators

Ideally, enough bilingual-bicultural service providers would be available to pair families with those who speak their language and understand their culture; however, most service systems are far from reaching that ideal. Until more service providers with these skills are available, interpreters and translators will be important resources in human services environments. In fact, in many instances, the service provider or translator may be the family's only link with the program. His or her effectiveness may determine the range of services that are offered as well as the family's interest in and understanding of the services. Interpreters and translators who are not well trained or who have a personal agenda in their interactions with families may impede the intervention process.

In this section, the terms *interpreter* and *translator* are used interchangeably; however, interpreting is often associated with oral communication and translation with written communication (Langdon, Siegel, Halog, & Sánchez-Boyce, 1994). In keeping with this book's emphasis on face-to-face interactions with families, this section concentrates on oral rather than written communication. The following paragraphs suggest strategies for using interpreters and translators more effectively and ways of interacting when a third party (i.e., the interpreter or the translator) is included on the intervention team.

Characteristics of Effective Interpreters Ideally, an interpreter should be someone who is 1) proficient in the language (including specific dialect) of the family as well as that of the service provider, 2) educated and experienced in cross-cultural communication and the principles and dynamics of serving as an interpreter, 3) educated in the appropriate professional field relevant to the specific family–service provider interaction, and 4) able to understand and appreciate the respective cultures of both parties and to convey the more subtle nuances of each with tact and sensitivity. "These interpreters are ideal because they not only translate the interaction but also bridge the culture gap" (Randall-David, 1989, p. 31). Aside from such ideal competencies, the interpreter should at the minimum have a basic understanding of the specific nature and purpose of the interaction with the family, the content areas to be addressed, and the relative significance of these content areas in the larger context. He or she should be able to translate information *accurately*, including important technical terms and the family's own words and true meaning, without omitting, adding, paraphrasing, or otherwise changing the intent or the substance of the message through personal interpretation. In other words, the interpreter should not gloss over details; present his or her own abbreviated summaries; spontaneously respond to the family's questions or comments (particularly those requiring technical knowledge); "soften" or edit information that he or she feels may be difficult for family members to accept; or offer his or her own opinions, interpretations, and advice.

Accurate translation further entails understanding the difference between literal "word-for-word" translation and context translation that correctly conveys the intent of the communication, particularly when selected English words or terms do not have suitable equivalents (Tinloy, Tan, & Leung, 1986). Interpreters also should know how to "guide" the service provider respectfully and assertively with regard to pacing, responding appropriately to family cues and significant verbal and nonverbal responses, and observing various do's and don'ts. Finally, interpreters should exhibit professionalism in their appearance, sensitivity, and demeanor; their understanding of the importance of honoring family confidentiality; and their obligation to maintain neutrality in their designated role. In other words, they must refrain from pushing the service provider's and/or their own agenda onto the family and from manipulating the service provider or the service agency to respond to the family's perceived needs or expectations in ways that are clinically inappropriate.

Another concern relates to the extent of the interpreter's skills in both languages. Many people have bilingual interpersonal competence that allows them to function in either language in daily life; however, their skills may not be adequate to understand or to explain issues that arise in intervention. Readers who have some competency in another language may recall times when, based on an excellent accent and quick, accurate response, their language competency was overestimated. It is easy to mistakenly assume that people who are fluent in daily life are fully bilingual.

Using Family Members as Interpreters: Cautions and Concerns Given the lack of fully qualified interpreters, intermediaries who are friends or other family members are often used to assist service providers in their interactions with families from different cultural and language backgrounds. Given the qualities described in the preceding paragraphs, the problems that may arise with continued reliance on intermediaries become more obvious. Even if the individuals are fully bilingual and proficient in the family's native language or specific dialect, communication difficulties and role conflicts may be exacerbated by their personal relationships with the family, their lack of direct training as interpreters, and their limited knowledge of the content of the material and the issues that are addressed in the translation.

The use of immediate family members and relatives as interpreters is particularly problematic. Parents, primary caregivers, or other significant family members are often reluctant and embarrassed to discuss intimate matters with members of the opposite sex or with younger or older family members. As interpreters, family members, in turn, may wish to censor what is disclosed either to shield the family or to keep information within the family, thus minimizing public shame or stigma. The tendency for parents of recent immigrants to rely on older siblings as their interpreters often creates significant psychological burdens for the children when they are involved in clinical interactions or formal meetings with professionals who are serving the family and the child with special needs. The role reversals, mutual resentments, and complex family dynamics that can emerge from this process should discourage service providers from using children, regardless of how mature they seem to be, as interpreters or translators.

Using Non–Family Members as Interpreters: Cautions and Concerns

When utilizing nonfamily members (whether interpreters from other agencies or bilingual staff), service providers must be particularly sensitive to the family members' rights to privacy and their choice of who should serve as an interpreter. Families may be concerned about confidentiality and/or resistant to working with an interpreter who is unacquainted with the family but from their same community. Problems also may arise when the interpreter has a different ethnic background; country or region of origin; immigration history (e.g., first-wave versus second-wave immigrant/refugee); and/or is of a different age, generation, social class, educational level, or gender. Apart from these characteristics, interpreters, like service providers, also present with varying levels of interpersonal skills, sensitivity, reliability, and overall competence and credibility, all of which have a major impact on establishing successful family–service provider relationships.

Interpreters and Stress

Unfortunately, the exceptionally "good" bilingual staff or experienced interpreters who are well trained; knowledgeable in various aspects of intervention; skilled; sensitive; reliable; and highly regarded by families, colleagues, and their respective ethnic communities are few in number and also extremely vulnerable to burnout. In their work with immigrant/refugee families who often have experienced trauma, profound loss, hardship, culture shock, and continuing struggles for survival in addition to coping with a child with special needs, interpreters may suffer from related stress, fatigue, and possible overidentification with the family. This is especially true if they share similar personal experiences. Interpreters also must cope with frequent client "transference" as well as potential "countertransference." This phenomenon occurs when the family focuses its feelings on the interpreter and develops a primary relationship or alliance with him or her in addition to, or instead of, the service provider. The interpreter, in turn, may fulfill his or her needs and wishes by reinforcing the family's dependency and experiencing reciprocal feelings and attachments. He or she also may feel compelled to establish a more personal, protective relationship with the family as an advocate and extended ethnic "family" member who is expected to attend to the welfare of "one of his or her own people" in need of special assistance. These individuals often may feel an accompanying sense of guilt associated with the prospect of ultimately "abandoning" their clients and community because very few, if any, bilingual individuals may be available to "replace" them.

Beyond client-related stresses and obligations, interpreters often face the added pressures and conflicts of working with various service providers who may be overwhelmed, demanding, difficult, impatient, frustrated, culturally insensitive (if not hostile), and generally unwilling or unable to develop closer relationships with English-language learners. These types of service providers may expect the interpreter to be available on very short notice and with little or no preparation for specific types of encounters with families. Interpreters also may be expected to provide their services without compensation, on a voluntary basis, or on their agency's time (Benhamida, 1988). High demand for their unique skills and pressing needs of the families for whom they interpret challenge the interpreters' existing work obligations and career advancement opportunities that require additional time, continuing education, and professional training, all of which must compete with the seemingly "obligatory" provision of hands-on services to families. Thus, while attending to families' needs and their own professional development and responsibilities, service providers must nurture mutually respectful relationships with interpreters and bilingual staff members.

Interpreter Preparation Prior to any interaction with a family that requires interpretation, time should be set aside for the preparation of the interpreter. This time should include a briefing in which the service provider identifies 1) the major goals and purposes of the contact or session with the family, 2) the important points to be made as well as potentially sensitive areas that will be discussed, 3) specific terms that will be used (the interpreter might review and share corresponding word/phrase equivalents or variations in the family's language), and 4) written documents that will be shown or referred to. The interpreter also may be invited to meet directly with the family before the session to exchange basic background information, establish rapport, and learn what the family wants to know or is hoping for in the meeting.

Guidelines for Working with an Interpreter Experts in the field have suggested a number of guidelines for service providers to follow when working with an interpreter (Hagen, 1989; Langdon et al., 1994; Randall-David, 1989; Schilling & Brannon, 1986):

- Learn proper protocols and forms of address (including a few greetings and social phrases) in the family's primary language, the names they wish to be called, and the correct pronunciation.

- Introduce yourself and the interpreter, describe your respective roles, and clarify mutual expectations and the purpose of the encounter.

- Learn basic words and sentences in the family's language and become familiar with special terminology they may use so you can selectively attend to them during interpreter–family exchanges.

- During the interaction, address your remarks and questions directly to the family (not the interpreter); look at and listen to family members as they speak, and observe their nonverbal communication.

- Avoid body language or gestures that may be offensive or misunderstood.

- Use a positive tone of voice and facial expressions that convey sincere respect and interest in the family. Address the family in a calm, unhurried manner.

- Speak clearly and somewhat more slowly but not more loudly.

- Limit your remarks and questions to a few sentences between translations and avoid giving too much information or long complex discussions of several topics in a single session.

- Avoid technical jargon, colloquialisms, idioms, slang, and abstractions.

- Avoid oversimplification and condensing important explanations.

- Give instructions in a clear, logical sequence; emphasize key words or points; and offer reasons for specific recommendations.

- Periodically check on the family's understanding and the accuracy of the translation by asking the family to repeat instructions or whatever has been communicated in their own words, with the interpreter facilitating, but avoid literally asking, "Do you understand?"

- When possible, reinforce verbal information with materials written in the family's language and visual aids or behavioral modeling, if appropriate. Before introducing written materials, tactfully determine the client's literacy level through the interpreter.

- Be patient, prepared, and plan for the additional time that will inevitably be required for careful interpretation.

Good interpreters are invaluable resources for human services agencies in which many of the service providers do not share families' languages and cultural backgrounds. Developing and maintaining positive relationships with individuals who can help bridge the gap between families and service providers is critically important for effective cross-cultural communication.

SUMMARY

This chapter has focused on the definition of cross-cultural competence and ways in which service providers can increase their effectiveness when working cross culturally. Implicit in the definition used in this book is the recognition that culture is not the only—and often not the most—salient variable when differences arise. Socio-economic status, educational experience, religion, place of birth, gender, age, and worldview all influence who we are. Throughout the chapter, particular emphasis was placed on understanding one's own culture and heritage, learning cultural information about the families in the service provider's community, and developing strategies to improve cross-cultural communication. This structure is based on a training approach that has been used successfully to prepare individuals for cross-cultural interactions. Although self-awareness is a beginning point, learning about other cultural perspectives and practicing new communication strategies can be addressed simultaneously. Service providers can work individually to enhance their knowledge and skill; however, people-oriented skills are better learned within a group. Having cross-cultural friends and colleagues who are willing to answer questions and who are able to provide feedback, and with whom one can practice, can only improve the learning experience.

Working with families through interpreters and translators requires a special set of skills. In addition to some philosophical issues and concerns that programs must address, service providers must learn and make time to practice the strategies that facilitate communication through a third person. Furthermore, intervention programs must invest in training interpreters if they are to adequately speak for families.

It would be wonderful if, with the wave of a magic wand, we could all possess the skills and attitudes that it takes to be cross-culturally effective. But, unfortunately, there are no shortcuts and there is no magic wand. Acquiring the skills is a lifelong process; however, desire, willingness to learn, and the potential outcomes for families and service providers alike make it a rewarding pursuit. Knowing oneself and the world more fully opens doors that can never again be closed. As Varawa said, "Culture is the garment that clothes the soul. We may never be able, or even want, to exchange our cloaks, but what matters is the perception of each other's realities" (1989, pp. 227–228).

REFERENCES

Abe, H., & Wiseman, R.L. (1983). A cross-cultural confirmation of the dimensions of intercultural effectiveness. *International Journal of Intercultural Relations, 7,* 53–67.

Althen, G. (1988). *American ways—A guide for foreigners in the United States.* Yarmouth, ME: Intercultural Press.

Angelou, M. (1993). *Wouldn't take nothing for my journey now.* New York: Random House.

Asante, M.K., & Davis, A. (1989). Encounters in the interracial workplace. In M.K. Asante & W.K. Gudykunst (Eds.), *Handbook of international and intercultural communication* (pp. 374–391). Beverly Hills: Sage Publications.

Barrera, I. (1994). Thoughts on the assessment of young children whose sociocultural background is unfamiliar to the assessor. *ZERO TO THREE, 14*(6), 9–13.

Barrera, I., & Corso, R.M. (with MacPherson, D.) (2003). *Skilled Dialogue: Strategies for responding to cultural diversity in early childhood.* Baltimore: Paul H. Brookes Publishing Co.

Barrera, I., & Kramer, L. (1997). From monologues to skilled dialogues: Teaching the process of crafting culturally competent early childhood environments. In P.J. Winton, J.A. McCollum, & C. Catlett (Eds.), *Reforming personnel preparation in early intervention: Issues, models, and practical strategies* (pp. 217–251). Baltimore: Paul H. Brookes Publishing Co.

Benedict, R. (1934). *Patterns of culture.* Boston: Houghton Mifflin.

Benhamida, L. (1988). *Interpreting in mental health settings for refugees and others: A guide for the professional interpreter.* Minneapolis: University of Minnesota Refugee Assistance Program, Mental Health Technical Assistance Center.

Boas, F. (1943). Recent anthropology. *Science, 98,* 411–413.

Brislin, R.W., Cushner, K., Cherrie, C., & Yong, M. (1986). *Intercultural interactions: A practical guide.* Beverly Hills: Sage Publications.

Chan, S.Q. (1990). Early intervention with culturally diverse families of infants and toddlers with disabilities. *Infants and Young Children, 3*(2), 78–87.

Cross, T.L., Bazron, B.J., Dennis, K.W., & Isaacs, M.R. (1989). *Toward a culturally competent system of care.* Washington, DC: CAASP Technical Assistance Center, Georgetown University Child Development Center.

Devine, E., & Braganti, N.L. (1986). *The travelers' guide to Asian customs and manners.* New York: St. Martin's Press.

Dresser, N. (1996). *Multicultural manners: New rules for etiquette in a changing society.* New York: John Wiley & Sons.

Giles, H., & Franklyn-Stokes, A. (1989). Communicator characteristics. In M.K. Asante & W.B. Gudykunst (Eds.), *Handbook of international and intercultural communication* (pp. 117–144). Beverly Hills: Sage Publications.

Green, J.W. (1982). *Cultural awareness in the human services.* Upper Saddle River, NJ: Prentice Hall.

Hagen, E. (1989). *Communicating effectively*

with Southeast Asian patients. Los Angeles: Immaculate Heart College Center.

Hall, E.T. (1976). *Beyond culture.* Garden City, NY: Anchor Books.

Hall, E.T. (1984). *The dance of life: The other dimension of time.* Garden City, NY: Anchor Books.

Hammer, M.R. (1989). Intercultural communication competence. In M.K. Asante & W.B. Gudykunst (Eds.), *Handbook of international and intercultural communication* (pp. 247–260). Beverly Hills: Sage Publications.

Hammond, J., & Morrison, J. (1996). *The stuff Americans are made of.* New York: Macmillan.

Hanson, M.J., Lynch, E.W., & Wayman, K.I. (1990). Honoring the cultural diversity of families when gathering data. *Topics in Early Childhood Special Education, 10*(1), 112–131.

Harry, B. (1992). Developing cultural self-awareness: The first step in values clarification for early service providers. *Topics in Early Childhood Special Education, 12*, 333–350.

Hecht, M.L., Andersen, P.A., & Ribeau, S.A. (1989). The cultural dimensions of nonverbal communication. In M.K. Asante & W.B. Gudykunst (Eds.), *Handbook of international and intercultural communication* (pp. 163–185). Beverly Hills: Sage Publications.

Helms, J.E. (1990). What's in a name change? *Focus, 4*(2), 1–2.

Johnson, D. (1971). Black kinesics: Some non-verbal communication patterns in black culture. *Florida Reporter, 9*, 1–2.

LaDue, R. (1990). An Indian by any other name or don't "kemo sabe" me, Tonto. *Focus, 4*(2), 10–11.

Langdon, H.W., Siegel, V., Halog, L., & Sánchez-Boyce, M. (1994). *The interpreter translator process in the educational setting.* (Available from Resources in Special Education, 650 Howe Avenue, Suite 300, Sacramento, CA 95825)

Lynch, E.W., & Hanson, M.J. (1993). Changing demographics: Implications for training in early intervention. *Infants and Young Children, 6*(1), 50–55.

McIntosh, P. (1988). *White privilege and male privilege: A personal account of coming to see correspondences through work in women's studies.* Wellesley, MA: Center for Research on Women, Wellesley College.

Mederos, F., & Woldeguiorguis, I. (2003). Beyond *cultural competence*: What child protection managers need to know and do. [Electronic Version]. *Child Welfare, 82*(2). Retrieved May 15, 2003, from EBSCO Host Databases.

National Center for Children in Poverty (2002). *Early childhood poverty: A statistical profile.* Retrieved March 2002 from http://www.nccp.rog/pub_ecp02.html

Neal, A., & Allgood-Hill, B.A. (1990). The labeling game. *Focus, 4*(2), 7–8.

Randall-David, E. (1989). *Strategies for working with culturally diverse communities and clients.* Washington, DC: Association for the Care of Children's Health.

Robertiello, R.C., & Hoguet, D. (1987). *The WASP mystique.* New York: Donald I. Fine.

Rorie, J.L., Paine, L.L., & Barger, M.K. (1996). Primary care for women—Cultural competence in primary care services. *Journal of Nurse-Midwifery, 41*(2), 92–100.

Ruben, B.D. (1989). The study of cross-cultural competence: Traditions and contemporary issues. *International Journal of Intercultural Relations, 13*, 229–240.

Samovar, L.A., & Porter, R.E. (1991). *Communication between cultures.* Belmont, CA: Wadsworth.

Schilling, B., & Brannon, E. (1986). *Cross-cultural counseling: A guide for nutrition and health counselors.* Washington, DC: U.S. Department of Agriculture/ & U.S. Department of Health and Human Services.

Schneller, R. (1989). Intercultural and intrapersonal processes and factors of misunderstanding: Implications for multicultural training. *International Journal of Intercultural Relations, 13*, 465–483.

Sowell, T. (1996). *Migrations and cultures: A world view.* New York: Basic Books.

Spitzberg, B.H. (1989). Issues in the development of theory of interpersonal competence in the intercultural context. *International Journal of Intercultural Relations, 13*, 241–268.

Spitzberg, B.H., & Cupach, W.R. (1984). *Interpersonal communication competence.* Beverly Hills: Sage Publications.

Storti, C. (1989). *The art of crossing cultures.* Yarmouth, ME: Intercultural Press.

Tiedt, P.L., & Tiedt, I.M. (1990). *Multicultural teaching: A handbook of activities, information, and resources* (3rd ed.). Needham Heights, MA: Allyn & Bacon.

Tinloy, M.T., Tan, A., & Leung, B. (1986). *Assessment of Chinese speaking limited English proficient students with special needs.* Sacramento, CA: Special Education Resource Network, Resource Service Center.

Tong, B.R. (1990). "Ornamental Orientals" and others: Ethnic labels in review. *Focus, 4*(2), 8–9.

Varawa, J. (1989). *Changes in latitude—An uncommon anthropology.* New York: Harper & Row.

Watson, B. (1993). Jaysho, moasi, dibeh, ayeshi, hasclishnih, beshlo, shush, gini. *Smithsonian, 24*(5), 34–43.

Wayman, K.I., Lynch, E.W., & Hanson, M.J. (1990). Home-based early childhood services: Cultural sensitivity in a family systems approach. *Topics in Early Childhood Special Education, 10*(4), 56–75.

A CULTURAL JOURNEY

Culture is unique to individuals, but the concept of culture is universal. All of us have a cultural, ethnic, racial, linguistic, and religious (or nonreligious) heritage that influences our current beliefs, values, and behaviors. To learn a little more about your own heritage, take this simple cultural journey.

Origins

1. When you think about your roots, what place(s) of origin do you identify for your family?

2. Have you ever heard any stories about how your family or your ancestors came to the place where you grew up or how they came to the United States? Briefly, what were the stories?

3. Are there any foods that you or someone else prepares that are traditional for your place of origin or some other aspect of your heritage? What are they? What is their significance?

4. Are there any celebrations, ceremonies, rituals, or holidays that your family continues to celebrate that reflect your place of origin or some other aspect of your heritage? What are they? How are they celebrated?

5. Do you or does anyone in your family speak a language other than English because of your origins? If so, what language(s)?

6. Do you recall any sociocultural factors in your family that made you different from your friends, classmates, neighbors, or others in your community? Consider, for example, your family's socioeconomic status, educational level, constellation, or worldview.

7. Can you think of one piece of advice that has been handed down through your family that reflects the values held by your ancestors? What is it? Does it reflect a cultural, religious, or individual value?

Beliefs, Biases, and Behaviors

1. Have you ever heard anyone make a negative comment about people from your place(s) of origin or about another aspect of your heritage? How did you handle it?

2. As you were growing up, do you remember discovering that your family did anything differently from other families because of your culture, religion, or ethnicity? What was it?

3. Have you ever been with someone in a work situation who did something because of his or her culture, religion, or ethnicity that seemed unusual to you? What was it? Why did it seem unusual?

4. Have you ever felt uncomfortable, upset, or surprised by something that you saw when you were traveling in another part of the United States or the world? If so, what was it?

5. How did what you saw in question 4 make you feel? Pick some descriptive words to explain your feelings. How did you react? In retrospect, how do you wish you would have reacted?

6. Have you ever done anything that you think was culturally inappropriate when you have been in another country or with someone from a different culture? In other words, have you ever done something that you think might have been upsetting or embarrassing to another person? What was it?

7. What did you try to do to improve the situation (from question 6)?

Imagine

Imagine that for a month out of this year you will become a member of another cultural or ethnic group.

1. Which group would you choose to be part of for that month? Why?

2. What is one value from that culture or ethnic group that attracts you to it?

3. Is there anything about that culture or ethnic group that concerns or frightens you?

4. Name one concrete way in which you think your life would be different if you were from that ethnic or cultural group.

PART II

CULTURAL PERSPECTIVES

Part II, Cultural Perspectives, is designed to give voice to many of the major cultural and ethnic groups that make up the population of the United States. The reader is introduced to the history, values, and beliefs of each group through knowledgeable professionals who are both well versed in that cultural group's perspectives and members or are closely associated with that group. These authors were selected not only for their knowledge of cultural issues but also for their experience working with families and children. They come from many different professional disciplines including education, medical anthropology, nursing, psychology, and social work. Each author also is an advocate for families in the broadest sense.

Each chapter in this section is organized to provide descriptive information on the values and beliefs of each culture or ethnic group with particular emphasis on issues related to the family, child rearing, and disability. Practical recommendations for interventionists are given at the end of each chapter, including an open-ended scenario called What Would You Do? Appendices are provided at the end of each chapter that contrast the primary beliefs, values, and practices of the group with those of the dominant culture. Appendices also describe each culture or ethnic group's significant holidays or events, outline major cultural courtesies and customs, and provide basic vocabulary words that may be useful for service providers.

The cultural groups that are identified in this volume do not reflect the entire range of cultural and ethnic groups in the United States. Rather, groups were selected because they represent a large segment of the population and/or because they reflect recent immigration patterns. It is likely that service providers will have the opportunity to work with members from each of these groups and others. Thus, the text is designed to provide basic information to make this work more effective and enjoyable for service providers as they work with children and families whose cultural backgrounds and perspectives may differ from their own.

CHAPTER 4

FAMILIES WITH ANGLO-EUROPEAN ROOTS

Marci J. Hanson

All men are created equal.

If at first you don't succeed, try, try again.

The early bird catches the worm.

No pain, no gain.

Where there's a will, there's a way.

The United States has been called a "Nation of Nations" (Marzio, 1976). It is a nation of immigrants; the first immigrants, nomadic ancestors of the American Indians, arrived more than 50,000 years ago (Kellogg, 1995). These peoples spread across the Americas and developed distinctly different cultural groups.

In what was to become the United States, the first or native Americans (later termed Indians by explorers) numbered perhaps 2–3 million in population when the earliest white settlers arrived (National Geographic Society, 1975). Though theories abound as to how the first Americans reached this continent centuries ago, several prominent perspectives are that the earliest peoples crossed the Bering Strait from Asia, arrived by boat from Polynesia, or migrated northward from the South American continent (Davis, 2003). However they arrived, these "natives" spread across the vast land base and their practices and lifestyle were adapted to the land. To the early Anglo-European settlers, the land undoubtedly represented an unlimited and relatively uninhabited resource. As they sought to settle and reshape the land, the fate of these native people was to be pushed aside and, in many cases, obliterated through warfare and disease.

The early white settlers, primarily from Western Europe and England, brought their values and life practices with them, which, along with their culture, were also shaped by the conditions they encountered in the new country—the vastness of the land, the seeming limitless natural resources, and the heterogeneity of the landscape. The values of independence, courage, fortitude, ambition, self-help, and hard work were all functional and needed for the task they defined as "taming" the wilderness and forging a new society from a vast, largely uninhabited and unsettled land. Americans have long revered these values and continue to do so into the 21st century. These values and the culture that evolved in America were continually fed and modified by the successive waves of immigrants.

Great migrations have occurred throughout history. Most were undertaken for the purpose of invasion or as a crusade; however, one of the greatest migrations, The Great Atlantic Migration, which brought more than 38 million Europeans to the United States between 1820 and 1920 (Degler, 1984), took place for a variety of other reasons. These included exploration and new resources and the need for the immigrants to escape devastating economic conditions and/or religious persecution. These Europeans brought with them the idea of finding new opportunity in a land rich with resources and promise. They also brought with them "the accumulated cultures of Western Europe, the inheritance of Arabic learning, the traditions and literatures of the classical world, the institutions, theologies, and philosophies of Judaism and Christianity, and the experience of a passage across a perilous ocean" (National Geographic Society, 1975, p. 24).

As mentioned in Chapter 2, the society to which these immigration efforts gave birth became known as a melting pot society, that is, a society that absorbed people from many different cultures and lands into the common but constantly changing whole of the society. Despite the overwhelming natural barriers of distance, mountains, and waterways, a common language was maintained. This feat was made easier as a result of the tremendous technological advances and the pursuit of information transfer (e.g., systems of transportation, such as steamboats and railroads; printed publications; communication systems, such as the telegraph and telephone) as the land was settled. Just as much as the Internet has united the world in recent years, these technological advances united the settlers in the North American continent. A united federation of states was established, a remarkable achievement in light of the diverse characteristics of the land. The country's continental mass alone (excluding Alaska and Hawaii) crossed nearly 25 degrees of latitude and nearly 58 degrees of longitude and reached from several hundred feet below sea level to almost 15,000 feet above sea level. It included grasslands, farmlands, mountains, everglades, swamps, prairies, deserts, tundra, and rain forests (National Geographic Society, 1975). Regardless of the regional uniqueness and differences, the states bound together to form a united federation—the United States of America. Although this unification of states, often with different goals and regional interests, has created tensions and even resulted in a devastating civil war, the states have remained unified and an even more centralized government has evolved.

BACKGROUND

Although the United States remains an entity with a definable national language, culture, and traditions, the complexion and goals of the society continue to be challenged, questioned, and changed as a result of the influx of newcomers into this society—newcomers who, particularly in the 1980s and 1990s, have non–Anglo-European roots. Both this promise of opportunity to a wide range of immigrants and the ability to accommodate change while adhering to core values have been hallmarks of America.

Geographic and Historical Origins

In the past century, a perspective more closely identified with cultural pluralism has slowly replaced the notion of a melting pot society. Yet, it is in the Anglo-European roots that the "dominant" or "mainstream" culture of the United States, as it is defined, is to be found.

Early Exploration   The first European immigrants or explorers were the Celts from northern Europe, and then the Vikings or Norsemen (Kellogg, 1995). The next European explorers came from southern Europe. Reports of a New World, rich in resources such as gold and spices, spurred the postmedieval interest in finding new lands and increased exploration efforts to the Americas. Governments and individuals eager to open new trading markets and to expand and claim the new land and the quest for passage from Europe to Asia fanned the flames of adventurism. England, France, Italy, the Netherlands, Portugal, and Spain all sent adventurers. The Spanish conquistadores violently overthrew native cultures in the South American continent and raised European expectations of potential riches in the new world. The early reports from voyages by Christopher Columbus and John Cabot, and later the expedition launched by Sir Frances Drake in 1577, led England to attempt to colonize the North American continent in the New World. The Spanish also established settlements in Mexico and land that later became part of the southern United States (i.e., Florida, New Mexico, California).

Early Settlements   The first permanent English settlement was in Jamestown, Virginia, in 1607. The famed Puritan settlement at Plymouth, Massachusetts, followed in 1620. By 1640, English, Dutch, French, Spanish, and Swedish colonies could be found along the coast of North America (Kellogg, 1995). Motivations for settlement in the Americas were primarily economic or religious, but military factors played a role in some cases as well as opportunities for trade and farming.

For the most part, by early accounts, the new colonists found what they sought: a land rich in natural resources and the freedom to pursue dreams. They displaced or lived peaceably alongside native Indians. They acquired land for themselves, which was difficult or impossible to do in the British Isles or Europe, and they acquired the freedom to pursue the political or religious practices of their choosing. Only slaves, brought in ships from Africa, were involuntary immigrants and were denied access to the opportunities and riches of the land.

Because the early settlers were able to acquire and own land, they expected participation in governing the land. They soon established forms of self-government from the proprietor lords. They fought disease, famine, and drought and clashed with American Indians to build and maintain their settlements.

The early settlers learned to hunt and to farm and eventually established some central, sustaining crops such as corn and tobacco (crops introduced to them by the native peoples). Trade with nations of origin also flourished for certain products, and Americans began to engage in some manufacturing.

Conflict with England and Declaration of Independence England, the protector and administrator of the original 13 colonies, also was the primary source for materials for the settlers. The taxation of the colonies for materials and goods became a central force in the colonists' desire to move to self-governance. Americans refused to submit to England's taxation and wanted their own assemblies and local governments. This move resulted in the establishment of the Continental Congress and, ultimately, the Revolutionary War.

The breaking of old political and economic ties brought the formation of a new nation. In the Declaration of Independence from England, adopted in 1776, the "Founding Fathers" articulated principles of government for the new country that were designed to guarantee freedoms to its citizens. It is important to note that these governing principles have deep roots in the western civilization of the Greeks and in English society. These statements of freedom laid the foundation for the dominant American culture and governmental structure that has endured to the present day. The focus on individual freedoms and self-governance represented in the American Constitution heralded unprecedented opportunities and individual rights for citizens in this country.

Industrial Revolution Following this political revolution, Americans were forced to increase their manufactured goods in order to provide supplies to their people. In this atmosphere, in the late 1700s, the American Industrial Revolution began. With plans for a spinning machine to make cloth smuggled out of Britain, the spinning mills of America were established, and the American fascination with "the machine," technology, and industry began and still exists.

Immigration Waves The country continued to grow both through new births and through a continued migration of people from other countries, primarily Europe. Of particular note is the large influx of Europeans to the United States in the 19th and early 20th centuries that came largely through the northeastern portion of the United States, particularly through New York. One way in which immigration during this period is described is by the geographic origins of the immigrants. The term *old immigrants* is used to describe those from northern and western Europe: England, France, Germany, the Low Countries, and Scandinavia; the term *new immigrants* refers to people from eastern and southern Europe, such as the Greeks, Italians, Polish, Russians, and Slavs (Degler, 1984). This influx of immigrants also was represented by waves (Freedgood, 1970). The first wave was largely composed of settlers from England, Ireland, and Germany. Two of the most massive immigrations included the Irish and the Germans. More than 1.25 million Irish immigrated in the 1840s and 1850s as a result of the potato famine; during this same period, approximately 4 million Germans came to this country to escape political unrest and economic depression (Chiswick, 1998). This was followed by the second wave, which brought many Scandinavians. In the 1870s to 1900s, approximately 1.5 million Danes, Norwegians, and Swedes immigrated to escape poverty and acquire farmland (Chiswick, 1998). The third major wave of Europeans in the late 1800s and early 1900s consisted of immigrants who hailed largely from Italy, Russia, and the Austro-Hungarian empire—those with Mediterranean and Slavic roots. In the 1880s to 1920s, 1 million Poles immigrated to escape poverty, cholera epidemics, and political repression; 2.5 million Jews from Eastern Europe immigrated due to religious persecution; and 4 million Austrians, Czechs, Hungarians, and Slovaks and 4.5 million Italians arrived to escape poverty and overpopulation conditions (Chiswick, 1998). Many of these newcomers did not speak English and were unskilled, unlike many of the immigrants in the previous waves. These latter waves of "peasant" immigrants produced tensions for the largely Anglo-Saxon population by creating a more heterogeneous society. In the mid-1800s the discovery of gold in California also sparked immigration from other non–Anglo-European groups such as the Chinese. The great spurt in immigration to the United States between the 1840s and 1914 (when World War I began) increased xenophobic fears about job competition. This led to immigration restrictions that brought an end to the flood of immigrants to America. The Immigration Act of 1924 not only slowed immigration but also imposed severe restrictions or quotas on groups such as Eastern Europeans and those from Mediterranean areas. The Act was designed to ensure that the cultural composition of the United States remained the same. The influence of this Act essentially remained until the passage of the Immigration Act of 1965, which liberalized the quota system. Kinship provisions allowed wives, husbands, and children to enter without being counted in the quotas. By the 1980s major immigration movements came from Mexico, Latin America and the Caribbean, and Asia. European and Canadian immigration figures fell to 13% (Chiswick, 1998). Though political unrest in other parts of the world has continued to fuel Anglo-European immigration to this country, as of 2004, the majority of immigrants have non–Anglo-European roots.

Westward Expansion   As the population of the United States grew, so, too, grew the desire to expand westward. The large transcontinental land mass allowed the population to continue its expansion across the continent. As settlers pushed westward, they engaged in more clashes with the American Indians who continued to move farther west to escape the settlements and pursue their own established way of life. Discoveries in the West, such as gold, silver, oil, rich land for farming, and new waterways, provided further incentives for massive migrations and settlements across the American continent. A new group of immigrants, the Chinese, also were brought to the United States to aid in the westward expansion. Although their labor was essential to miners and they built many of the railroads that linked the Atlantic to the Pacific, they were refused admittance to the mainstream of American society.

Specific Anglo-European Immigrant Groups   The many groups of immigrants to the United States over the years both adopted "American" ways and added their own unique contributions to the cultural practices of the nation. For example, in certain cities, groups such as the Irish and the Italians became active and highly influential in political life. All groups have influenced and enriched the cuisine, arts, music, literature, language, and folkways of the United States.

National census population figures (U.S. Bureau of the Census, 2000) showed the following groups of individuals in the United States that indicated Anglo-European ancestry (from greatest to least percentage of entire population): German (15.2%), Irish (10.9%), English (8.7%), Italian (5.6%), Polish (3.2%), French (3.0%), Scottish (1.7%), Dutch (1.6%), Norwegian (1.6%), Scotch-Irish (1.5%), Swedish (1.4%), French Canadian (.9%), Russian (.9%), Czech (.6%), Welsh (.6%), Danish (.5%), Hungarian (.5%), Greek (.4%), Portuguese (.4%), Slovak (.3%), Swiss (.3%), Ukrainian (.3%), and Lithuanian (.2%). An additional 7.3% of the population listed their ancestry as "American."

Several of these specific groups from Anglo and European roots are highlighted in the following paragraphs. They were selected for emphasis because of their numbers of immigrants and their maintenance of their group's cultural identity. The groups of Americans discussed here are representative of numerous peoples with Anglo and European roots who immigrated and continue to immigrate to this country. Some immigrants have maintained strong ties to their native lifestyles, languages, and practices; others have not. Their contributions to the mosaic of American culture are great.

Germans   Germans comprise the largest number of European immigrants to the United States (cited in Lassiter, 1995). At the beginning of the 21st century, Germans represented more than 15% of the population and numbered more than 42,885,000 (U.S. Bureau of the Census, 2000). Initial German immigration occurred primarily for religious, economic, and political reasons, and they were the largest first-generation group of immigrants between 1880 and 1920 (Lassiter, 1995). The early waves of German immigrants settled primarily in the states of the Carolinas, Minnesota, Missouri, Pennsylvania, Texas, and Wisconsin (Lassiter, 1995). Whereas the earlier settlers migrated to more rural areas, later waves of German immigrants sought the major cities.

German immigrants were often characterized as thorough, diligent, and industrious (Lassiter, 1995). The phrase *alles in ordnung* (all in order) often is used to describe German preferences and characteristics, enacted in child-rearing styles that emphasized structure, a focus on tasks and accomplishments rather than emotional expression, and strictness with little autonomy (Lassiter, 1995). Family life was deemed primarily nuclear and patriarchal. For women in some German enclaves such as the Pennsylvania Dutch communities, life was best described by the phrase *kinder, kirche, küche* (children, church, kitchen). A majority of German residents are Protestant, but many are Jewish, and almost a third are Roman Catholic (Lassiter, 1995).

Irish   The second largest immigrant group is the Irish. The Irish represent more than 5 million immigrants and nearly 40 million descendants. According to census reports (cited in Lassiter, 1995), large numbers of Irish people live in Alabama, the Carolinas, Louisiana, New York, and Texas. According to the most recent Census, more than 30.5 million Irish, or nearly 11% of the population, live in the United States (U.S. Bureau of the Census, 2000).

The early Irish immigrants in the 1700s were primarily Protestant and from northwestern Ireland. Subsequent groups were Catholic and experienced the full force of religious discrimination and intolerance when they arrived on these shores. The potato famine of 1845–1847 in Ireland killed more than 750,000 people from the mid-1840s to the early 1850s (Foster, 1988), and families were forced to leave or die.

Nearly 2 million Irish citizens immigrated to the United States by 1850, swelling their population to one tenth of the U.S. population.

Loyalty to their "own" and their families, conformity, and respectability characterized Irish immigrants. Family structures were typically patriarchal and nuclear; family welfare was often considered above the welfare of the individual. Children were taught to be polite, obedient, respectful, and subordinate (Lassiter, 1995).

English   The third-largest group of citizens that report ancestry outside the country are the English. Recent population figures indicate that more than 24.5 million individuals or 8.7% of the population identified their ancestry as English (U.S. Bureau of the Census, 2000). The earliest established settlements of Anglo-European populations were of English citizens. Of course, the primary language spoken in the country comes from these early settlers. Many of this country's political and legal roots are based on England's, as are the values and beliefs that will be subsequently discussed. Perhaps no other country or group of citizens has had such an enormous impact on the formation of this nation.

Italian   Another major immigrant group that continues to hold a strong cultural identity is the Italian community. At the beginning of the 21st century, Italians made up nearly 6% of the U.S. population and numbered approximately 14 million citizens (U.S. Bureau of the Census, 2000). A majority of Italians are Roman Catholics.

Traditionally, the Italian family clearly delineated the male–female roles, with fathers assuming more authoritative roles and mothers having a marked influence on the children (Lassiter, 1995). An extended family network often characterized families with roots in southern Italy; those with northern Italian roots were more likely nuclear in structure. Typically, children were raised to be supportive and loyal to the family, and swift discipline was used as well as love to control children's behavior (Lassiter, 1995).

Religious Origins

A primary force shaping the decisions of the early Anglo-European settlers to set out on the long and often treacherous journey to "the new land" was the hope for religious freedom. Persecution in their lands of origin stirred many to seek life in a new land. In the early settlements, the doctrine of Puritanism, or Reformed Protestantism, predominated. The influence of this religious force on the developing community was profound. Less distinction was made between church and state at that time, and religion permeated the structure of the original settlements; thus, the doctrine of Puritanism strongly influenced the education of the young. The Puritans' belief that children were born without the fear of God and with original sin drove their belief that children needed to undergo intense religious education through prayers, scripture reading, and instruction in the religious faith. The larger communal society shared the responsibility with each family for educating the young.

Over the years, as new immigrants came to what was to become the United States, many different religious sects (albeit primarily from Western religions) were introduced and flourished. As the nation was formed, religious freedom was guaranteed as a primary right. Although no national religion prevails and the government separates church and state, the influence of Western religion over the American culture has been great; indeed, the nation was founded "under God" and currencies bear the inscription "In God We Trust."

A wide range of religious preferences exists in the United States. Data from surveys provide the most current information on religion in the United States because the U.S. Census, unlike similar population surveys conducted in many countries, does not inquire about religion. The largest surveys of U.S. religious identification were the National Survey of Religious Identification (NSRI), conducted in 1990 on 113,000 Americans nationwide, and a follow-up study, the American Religious Identity Survey or ARIS, conducted in 2001 with a sample size of 50,000 Americans (Kosman, Mayer, & Keysar, 2001). The data reported in 2001 indicated the following 20 top religious affiliations or identifications and the percentage of the population that practices that faith: Christianity, 76.5% (52% Protestant, 24.5% Catholic); Nonreligious/Secular, 13.2%; Judaism, 1.3%; Islam, .5%; Buddhism, .5%; Agnostic; .5%; Atheist, .4%; Hinduism, .4%; Unitarian Universalist, .3%; and Wiccan/Pagan/Druid, .1%. Spiritualist Native American Religion, Bahai'i, New Age, Sikhism, Scientology, Humanist, Deity (Deist), Taoist, and Eckankar were each well under 1%. Of the major groups, those that have increased the most in the 10-year period between the NSRI and the ARIS are Nonreligious/Secular (+110%), Islam (+109%), Buddhism (+170%), and Hinduism (+237%). The largest denominations in 2001 were Catholic (24.5%), followed by Baptist (16.3%), Methodist (6.8%), Lutheran (4.6%), Presbyterian (2.7%), Pentecostal/Charismatic (2.1%), Episcopalian/Anglican (1.7%), Judaism (1.3%), Latter-day Saints/Mormon (1.3%), Churches of Christ (1.2%), Congregational/United Church of Christ (.7%), Jehovah's Witness (.6%), and Assemblies of God (.5%).

Although many different religions are practiced in the United States, they may not be distributed randomly across the population. Geographic area, ethnic heritage, and social class dictate location (Althen, 1988). For example, Catholics and Jews are found in larger proportions in eastern urban areas, and the fundamentalist Protestant groups have a larger representation in the South and Southwest (sometimes referred to as the "Bible Belt"). Furthermore, in some communities or regions, the majority of the population is represented by a particular religious group (e.g., Mormons in Utah, Lutherans in Minnesota, Quakers in Pennsylvania).

In summary, a majority of Americans report adhering to some religious belief. However, the religious practices are diverse and represent a wide range of denominations and belief systems.

WHAT ANGLO-EUROPEAN ANCESTRY REPRESENTS

As the previous discussion points out, the label *Anglo-European* is a term used to encompass a wide range of individuals whose ancestries span an entire continent and reflect vastly different cultural practices, languages spoken, values and beliefs, and histories. Indeed, many of these groups have experienced centuries of warfare with one another. Certainly, the English and the Irish and the English and the French, to name but several, have a long history of conflict between their nations. Furthermore, although immigrants from Spain are clearly European and typically from the white race, many may more closely identify with being Hispanic or Latino than with being European. Thus, the Anglo-European categorization is far from a unitary construct and not very useful for describing this large percentage of the U.S. population.

The reasons individuals from these many cultural groups immigrated to the United States varied widely from seeking riches and opportunity to escaping poverty, famine, and/or religious persecution. Furthermore, some groups or immigrant waves chose to quickly assimilate, whereas others continue to hold strong identification with their country and language of origin. Whereas most citizens of Anglo or European ancestry speak English in the United States, they also may speak their native tongue when at home or with elders. As with most groups, this is especially true with more recent immigrants.

Many white Americans of Anglo-European descent today claim they have "no culture" or that they are "just Americans," having assimilated to mainstream American values and practices. Because of the impact these groups have in terms of the timing of their immigration, the large influence on the legal and governmental structures in this country, and the large proportions they represent of the citizenry, the Anglo-European population as a whole has come to define the majority or dominant perspective in the United States. Thus, "mainstream" or "dominant culture" practices have been most closely associated with those of Anglo-European populations.

CONTEMPORARY LIFE

Three aspects of contemporary life for Anglo-Europeans are briefly examined in this chapter. These are 1) refinements in the definition of equal rights in the United States, 2) shifts in family patterns, and 3) changes in immigration patterns.

Equal Rights

Although citizens of the United States have always expressed pride in their guarantees of freedom of choice and opportunity, these freedoms have always been more readily available to white, male citizens than to other groups. Major challenges to a white, male-dominated society date back at least to the Civil War. Although the Emancipation Proclamation freed the slaves, full rights of citizenship, such as the right to vote and the right to own land, were not granted to African Americans even as free men and women. Women, too, did not share in the freedoms guaranteed in the Constitution. Not until 1920 did women throughout the United States gain the right to vote, when the 19th Amendment to the Constitution became law.

The next major push for equality began in the 1950s with people engaging in protests and court cases to demand equal access to education and freedom to participate equally in public life for African Americans. The Civil Rights Movement of the 1960s helped to reshape and redefine the meaning of freedom and equality in the United States. This tumultuous movement aided the birth of other movements, such as the disability rights movement and the women's rights movement, which further reexamined and redefined equal access for all citizens.

Family Patterns

For many years the term *family* in the United States was synonymous with a mother, father, and several children. A predominantly "nuclear" family unit was the norm. Today, a much broader definition of family applies. Family patterns reflect a variety of constellations including nonmarried adults, large extended family groups, homosexual and heterosexual partnerships, and blended families from remarriages. These variations have expanded the traditional two-parent, female–male family model.

Also changing familial patterns is the burgeoning employment rate for women. According to data from the Children's Defense Fund (2001), 65% of mothers with children younger than 6 years old and 78% of those with children ages 6–13 are in

the labor force. Of this group, 59% of those with infants younger than age 1 worked outside the home (Children's Defense Fund, 2001). Furthermore, based on 1999 data, more than 70% of single mothers had jobs (Children's Defense Fund, 2001). These factors have created continuing challenges for American families, among them, the intense need for accessible, affordable, quality child care options.

Immigration Patterns

The original great waves of immigrant groups entered the United States primarily from the Atlantic Coast. Since the 1970s, however, immigrant groups have settled predominantly in the West and have entered the United States from the Pacific and the South. Furthermore, these immigrants represent large numbers of people from areas not found previously in large immigrant waves, chiefly Asia, Southeast Asia, Mexico, and Central and South America. Throughout the United States's history, immigrants have tended to settle near their ports of entry, with other clusters of individuals from their cultural group, and/or where job opportunities are found (Chiswick, 1998).

VALUES

The cultural backgrounds and practices of immigrants from the British Isles and western Europe as well as the conditions and opportunities encountered in the new land shaped the major cultural values and practices of the American people. Some of these values and attributes include a focus on independence, freedom, assertiveness, equality, self-help, and self-directedness. Althen (1988), in his guide for foreigners in the United States, identified the following American values and assumptions: 1) individualism and privacy; 2) equality; 3) informality; 4) the future, change, and progress; 5) goodness of humanity; 6) time; 7) achievement, action, work, and materialism; and 8) directness and assertiveness. These eight values and assumptions are discussed next, followed by brief descriptions of values related to family life, religion, education/ schooling, and language origins in the Anglo-European American culture of the United States.

Individualism and Privacy

Americans traveling abroad may encounter someone who states that Americans have no culture; many Americans may share this view. Because the focus in American society is so strongly on the individual, it is often difficult to see the common or shared practices. Americans are taught to think for themselves and take personal responsibility for their actions, as in the adage, "You made your bed, so you must lie in it." Self-determination and self-reliance are highly valued. Some of the American folk heroes are people who overcame adversities and "pulled themselves up by their bootstraps." For example, politicians today still strive to point to humble roots and their climb to a higher status, much like heroes such as Abraham Lincoln. As Althen (1988) related, Americans revere those who do things the biggest, the best, or first—hence, the fascination with sports legends such as Jesse Owens, Jackie Robinson, and Babe Ruth; aviator heroes such as Charles Lindbergh and Amelia Earhart; and astronauts such as Neil Armstrong and Sally Ride.

From an early age, Americans are taught to make decisions and to be self-reliant. Young children often have their own rooms; separation from their parents for short periods of time is acceptable even for the very young; and early self-help skills, such as independent feeding and toilet training, are encouraged. Children are often given opportunities to make choices and decisions at an early age, and those decisions are respected.

Althen (1988) stated that the concept of privacy is closely related to the quest for individualism. Americans value time for themselves, private thoughts, and boundaries such as their own possessions. This value is reflected in family living practices in which children often have their own rooms. It is also reflected in topics of conversation; typically, Americans tend to avoid personal topics with others unless they are close friends, family, or professionals who are governed by rules regarding the protection of information (e.g., lawyers, psychologists, physicians).

Equality

The United States was founded on the principle that "all men are created equal." Clearly, not all citizens have had equal rights throughout the course of the country's history, but Americans nevertheless value this notion highly and strive toward this ideal. As such, signs of status may be less apparent than they are in some countries. Although the status of a person is often a factor in an interaction and may influence the way one dresses, the manner in which one is addressed, and how and with whom one speaks or sits, the signs of status or influence may be somewhat subtle. An underlying assumption is that no matter what the person's background, he or she has the potential for achievement and deserves respect.

Informality

Others may see the informal style practiced by Americans as disrespectful and "uncultured." Americans often greet others in an informal manner and may use first names even when addressing strangers. Casual dress, such as jeans and T-shirts, is common in most parts of the country for many occasions. Furthermore, many Americans use slang in discussions and in greetings, and their style is often friendly, informal, and open, even to strangers.

The Future, Change, and Progress

The United States, relative to most other world powers, has a short history. Perhaps this is a factor in why Americans place so little emphasis on their history and so much emphasis on the future. Change, newness, and progress are all highly valued. Americans believe that individuals as well as people working together can "make a difference" and that change is positive. Related to these notions is the assumption that social and physical environments are under human control or domination. This assumption has been borne out throughout American history, as early settlers cleared and reshaped the land in its "settlement."

The belief that individuals and groups are in control of their destinies is a powerful influence on the lives of most dominant-culture Americans; it is a notion that has proved to be a double-edged sword. On the positive side, it has given people self-confidence and made them feel that they can meet any challenge. On the negative side, it has made many mainstream Americans less tolerant of individuals and groups who are less successful. This belief also has fostered a use of force in interactions with the environment and other people that is evident in phrases such as "taming the wilderness," "winning the West," and "conquering space."

Goodness of Humanity

In general, Americans hold the belief that people are essentially good and that they are capable of self-improvement. This belief is consistent with the notion that with a futuristic outlook, change is possible. An emphasis on education—both formal and informal—throughout one's life is apparent, and many Americans strive toward self-improvement. Seminars and workshops aimed at self-help, self-reliance, and new skills are common and sought after. "How to" guides and self-help/support groups are in demand. Americans also generally believe that providing more knowledge can help turn people's lives around. Campaigns to provide more accurate information to remedy society's ills (e.g., smoking, drinking, abusing drugs) are used frequently. Rehabilitation is seen as both positive and possible. Providing individuals with the opportunity to improve their situations is valued, and those who do so are highly regarded.

Althen (1988) described Americans' support of volunteerism. Coupled with the belief in the ability of an individual or a collective group to make a difference, many Americans belong to service, charitable, or advocacy organizations designed to improve a societal concern. This focus on change and one's personal responsibility to the common good was underscored in John F. Kennedy's Presidential Inaugural Address (January 20, 1961): "My fellow Americans, ask not what your country can do for you—ask what you can do for your country."

Time

Efficiency and organization are valued in American life; time is seen as something that is used and must be saved. A primary demonstration of this assumption is the proliferation of fast-food restaurants in the United States. In these establishments, taste, presentation, and the experience of eating are secondary to the "best value" and the ease and speed with which the food is prepared and delivered. This focus on efficiency and the management of time goes hand-in-hand with the futuristic, change-oriented outlook.

Achievement, Action, Work, and Materialism

Americans can be characterized as achievement, action, and work oriented. The outgrowth or product of this work orientation often is the acquisition of material possessions, which has led to the view of Americans as materialistic. Americans are often seen as "on the go," even in their recreational activities. Attention is given to what a person "does," that is, what the person's job is. The person's income and/or status are often related to his or her type of job; monetary incentives are provided in many jobs for working longer, harder, or more efficiently.

Directness and Assertiveness

Americans often speak in a forthright manner, even about matters of grave concern. Typically, they are characterized as open, frank, and direct. Masking one's emotions is not a cultural norm; rather, Americans typically convey their feelings as well as express their thoughts on an issue. Certain topics, however, are usually not discussed so openly. These include topics that are considered personal, such as those dealing with body odors or sexual practices. Furthermore, less openness may be displayed when interacting with individuals with whom the speaker is not acquainted or with whom one does not want to risk an offense or confrontation. For example, a student may be less frank or open with a professor than with a peer, and a businessperson may be less open with a new business contact than with an established colleague. In such cases, a more indirect communication style may be used.

Family Life

The concept of *family* in the Anglo-European American United States typically refers to immediate family members such as the mother, father, and children. Other extended family members may or may not live close by and may or may not participate actively in the "nuclear family." These members are usually termed *relatives* as opposed to *family*. Although traditionally families often were characterized by a male head of the household, with male-dominated decision making, this pattern is less likely to be found in American homes today. Parents are more often equal partners in decision making, and women head many households. Furthermore, American culture is very child centered, and children have a great deal of say in events and in the practices of the family.

As previously stated, Anglo-European American families are diverse and represent many different constellations. Several characteristics that do differ from many other cultures are the age at which children leave the home and the care provided for older family members. After high school (or college), most young adults leave the primary home and establish their own residences. It is uncommon for individuals to return to the home permanently. With respect to older adults, typically they do not move into the homes of their children for care in their later years; rather, older members of the population maintain their own homes or live in long-term care facilities. This choice often is made by both parties, because adult children experience difficulties with their older parents moving into their home and the older parents, who value their own independence, feel awkward living with their children.

Religion

As was noted previously, the laws of the United States protect the individual's right to practice or not practice the religion of her or his choice. No one state religion is supported. Furthermore, the government is characterized by a separation of church and state. Although this doctrine has been debated throughout the history of the United States and continues to be questioned by some, this separation essentially remains. Questions such as whether prayer should be allowed in public schools and the content of textbooks regarding creation and evolution have produced disagreements.

Although religious practices are typically performed around life events or ceremonies, such as marriages and deaths, religious life often is not prominently displayed in American daily life. Rather, religious practices tend to remain separate from other aspects of life (Althen, 1988). Americans typically do not discuss their religious preferences or practices outside of their immediate circle of friends and families. Most Americans consider religious beliefs and practices a private matter.

Although many different religions are practiced in the United States, the country was founded under a Judeo-Christian belief system, and Christianity continues to be the religion practiced by the majority of people. (This focus is seen in the primary religious holidays that are celebrated, such as Christmas and Easter.) Although religious references are found in national holidays and practices such as inscriptions on national currency, "being religious" in America typically means going to church and practicing religious activities in the home.

Education and Schooling

Education is a major focus of American culture and is frequently discussed and debated. A major tenet is the right of all children to have access to education. Furthermore, it is believed that individuals should receive as much education as they can. Access to education is fundamental to the American assumptions of equal protection and equal opportunity for all citizens; it also underscores the value placed on literacy in American society. Thus, a publicly supported education is available to every child, and it is intended to meet the needs of all children regardless of their ability levels, socioeconomic status, or cultural/ethnic/linguistic background.

In most states, children are required to attend school until the age of 16, and it is estimated that one half of individuals between the ages of 18 and 25 are enrolled in a college, university, or technical training program (Lanier, 1996). Most children attend public schools that are tax supported; however, private schools, many of which are associated with a religious denomination, also are available. Since the 1990s, trends in education include increases in home schooling and year-round schooling.

Primarily, state and local governments make decisions regarding the public education system. Although the state typically provides funding and influences curriculum, assessment, and personnel practices, considerable local control is exercised. This local autonomy is typically valued and demanded. Although national standards for teachers and student performance have been proposed and discussed, they have not been implemented, and variation exists around the country and even within particular states.

The federal government has assumed an active role in certain educational policies. Given the concern with equal access to education and equal educational opportunities for all children, federal remedies have been implemented in cases where groups of children were denied these educational experiences. For instance, racial segregation and the lack of schooling for groups of children with disabilities resulted in legal consequences and the subsequent passage of federal laws ensuring equal educational opportunities for these individuals. The federal government provides considerable funding for these efforts as well as for other educational supports such as transportation services and facilities.

Parent participation is highly valued and expected in most educational systems. Parents are expected to volunteer and participate in school activities. Involvement is often sought through scheduled meetings and written materials, such as newsletters. Parent–teacher associations are available in most schools; in these associations, parents and school personnel meet to discuss budgets, curricula, school governance, and so forth. For Anglo-Europeans, the dominant cultural value is that these partnerships are important and valuable. Anglo-Europeans are usually well-educated about school policies and practices and are involved and confident about making demands on schools.

Public educational systems are seen as playing a major role in acculturation and citizenship. Schooling is essential to the American view of access to opportunity. Thus, schools are central to communities, and most children and families will pass through these systems.

Nancy is an administrative assistant at a small local business, and she is a single parent of Michael, now 7 years old. Michael's birth had been difficult and necessitated prolonged hospitalization. For these reasons, Nancy has worked closely with Michael's pediatrician and with his preschool and public school teachers to monitor his development.

Every Tuesday and Thursday after school, Michael attends a special tutorial session where he works on reading skills and computer use. Michael's teachers recommended the extra work to remediate his learning difficulties. The teachers feel that Michael may have learning disabilities, and they are tracking his school performance carefully. The tutorial sessions were designed to overcome these early difficulties. Michael's attention span is relatively short, and he has difficulty reading; however, he is motivated by the computer and likes it best when his lessons are in the form of a game on the computer. Nancy is highly supportive of the extra teaching sessions, even though it is financially difficult for her to pay for them. Nancy is relieved that she is receiving help; she welcomes the extra learning opportunities for Michael because they provide both extra practice and a quality activity for him while she is at work.

Language Origins

The Anglo-Saxon origins of this country established English as the primary language. Although the United States has absorbed a large number of immigrants throughout its history, English has remained the national language. Accents differ from region to region, and many local dialects have emerged, but the use of Standard American English is the norm throughout the country. Some Americans, however, may continue to speak their language of origin in their homes or with elders. Though more than 80% of U.S. households are English-only speaking, with demographic shifts in immigration patterns, more households are speaking other languages (e.g., Spanish, 10.7%; Indo-European, 3.8%; Asian and Pacific Island, 2.7%) (U.S. Bureau of the Census, 2000).

BELIEFS

The values discussed previously translate into belief systems that are reflected in the individual culture's philosophies regarding child rearing, medical and health care practices, death and dying, causation, and disabilities, to name a few. Each of these variables is discussed as it pertains to practices in the Anglo-European American culture.

Child Rearing

Traditionally, households were characterized as male dominated, and family roles were apportioned accordingly. Male members (i.e., husbands and fathers) were generally the "breadwinners" and responsible for things outside the home, such as the car and the yard; females (i.e., wives and mothers) typically were responsible for things inside the home, including child care and child rearing, cooking, cleaning, and other aspects of household management. As of 2004, as mentioned previously, more than half of the mothers of young children are employed in the labor force but still retain responsibility for household tasks. Although the traditional male/female family roles are still reflected in many homes, these distinctions are beginning to break down. Adult family members are more likely to share decision making and family-related tasks.

Children also participate actively in family life. American parents typically try to provide their children with a good quality of life, and children often participate in goal setting for the family or influence the family's allocation of resources. Parents often play with their children and believe in talking with them. The child-centeredness of families often translates into active schedules for children, including school, after-school activities, additional learning experiences, and an active social life. Young children often are involved in early education activities, and "preschool" experiences generally are valued. Beyond that, extra lessons for children may be sought, such as in music, dance, sports, or art.

Stemming from the Anglo-European emphases on individuality, achievement, and progress, developmental expectations for self-help and self-reliance are often high for children. Typically, infants are placed in their own beds from birth and may have their own rooms early on. Self-feeding and toileting are encouraged actively in the early years, and parents often separate from their children for short periods of time. Given that many mothers are employed outside of the home, many children are placed in child care and spend their days with caregivers other than their parents.

Children are often involved in decision making early on. For instance, during a visit to a store or a restaurant, parents may ask their children (even very young children) which toy or clothing they want or which food they wish to order. Many children also are expected to do their own chores around the house, such as keeping their room clean and setting the table. Later, in their teenage years, many hold part-time jobs. As children reach adolescence, they are expected to rebel and to discover their own identities. At the age of 18 or soon thereafter, it is accepted that they generally leave the family home and establish their own living situations.

Medical and Health Care

Americans' fascination with high technology is reflected in their medical and health care practices. Typically, medical treatments are focused on interventions through prescription drugs, surgery, and testing or diagnostic procedures using highly technical equipment. Preventive measures are emphasized, with information distributed through educational campaigns. Concern for good health focuses on prolonging life; health care practices are typically based on current scientific information on the subject. For example, foods are often selected on the basis of nutritional value or rejected on the basis of the food's association with carcinogenic effects as identified through scientific experimentation. Sources of health care and medical information typically are physicians and other health care providers trained in technical medical regimens.

Although more naturalistic and holistic approaches to medicine are gaining recognition, Western medicine, as practiced in the United States, has traditionally separated disorders of the mind and body and relied on scientific and technical information for diagnosis and treatment.

Jonathan was born prematurely at 25 weeks' gestational age to Susan and Roy. Susan's pregnancy was normal, but for unexplained reasons, she went into premature labor and was rushed to the hospital. When Jonathan was born, he was placed on oxygen and rushed to the neonatal intensive care unit. There, he lived in an incubator for nearly 3 months. His parents feared getting attached to him because they had been told that he had only a 50/50 chance of survival due to his medical and health complications. Yet, they did everything they could to get to know their baby and to ensure that he received the best medical treatment available. They were thankful to the many physicians and nurses who saved their baby's life and for the highly technical equipment and treatments that allowed Jonathan to live and grow. Susan expressed milk from her breasts daily and took it to her baby so that he could receive the very best nutrition. When Jonathan finally stabilized and was released home to his parents' care, the parents were loaned a baby monitor designed to alert the parents if he stopped breathing. A nurse specializing in the development of babies born prematurely also visited them regularly.

At 9 months, Jonathan was demonstrating some delays in development and his parents were referred to a local early intervention program, where he was assessed. In conjunction with the parents, the professional team at the early intervention program determined that Jonathan could benefit from receiving physical therapy services, consultations to the parents on specialized feeding techniques, early learning activities, and developmental monitoring.

Death and Dying

Practices and ceremonies related to death and dying are typically rooted in the religious beliefs and practices of the family. Given the diversity of religions found in the United States, these rituals vary from family to family. Therefore, practices related to the preparation and disposal of the body (i.e., cremation versus burial) and length of mourning, as well as practices surrounding the mourning period, may vary considerably. For instance, in the Jewish tradition, the burial services typically occur within 24 hours of the death and are simple (Lassiter, 1995). For American Irish Catholics, death may be considered a welcome release from suffering, and, hence, a celebration may be held. In some cases a wake is held during which the body is displayed in an open casket, and friends and family reminisce about the life of the deceased. For many families in the United States, funeral services are held in a church or a mortuary and are attended by family and friends. The degree of formality and elaboration depends on the family's preferences.

Although practices and preferences differ depending on the individual family members, their religion, the circumstances of the death, and the closeness of the relationship that the interventionist has with the family, a service provider may show respect during a period of grief in several ways. Sending a card expressing sympathy is nearly always appropriate, and some families are pleased to receive flowers that are then displayed at the funeral home or memorial service. Many families now request that contributions be made to a charity important to the family or the deceased. Other families welcome gifts of food that can be served to extended family members and friends who may visit in the days prior to or shortly after the burial or memorial services.

Causation

The emphasis on education and the futuristic, change-oriented outlook held by many Anglo-European Americans has led to the view of individuals as in charge of their own fate. Typically, adversity is seen as something that can be overcome with enough work, resources, and/or ingenuity. Many Americans have made heroes of such individuals as Helen Keller, who succeeded in life despite great restrictions or initial setbacks. Anglo-European Americans believe in the ability of individuals to better their circumstances through change or adaptation rather than to succumb to a preordained fate. The focus is much more on the here and now or future rather than on the past or historical explanations.

Disability

Anglo-Europeans tend to accept that disabilities cannot be ascribed to a single cause. They understand, for the most part, that some factors including genetic disorders, environmental agents (e.g., accidents, injuries, toxins), disease (e.g., viruses, severe bacterial infections), and prenatal and perinatal trauma could be prevented with better diagnostic care, health treatments, or improved living conditions, and some are likely a result of random events. Although social factors, such as the mother's caregiving style, have been blamed for some types of disabilities (e.g., autism) over the years, the more complete knowledge of disabilities has eliminated the claims for such causative factors in most cases.

Harriet and John are the parents of 3-year-old Caitlin. Caitlin was diagnosed at birth as having Down syndrome. The attending physician in the hospital informed Harriet and John of the diagnosis shortly after Caitlin's birth. She also told them that Caitlin suffered from a heart defect often found in children with Down syndrome and recommended open-heart surgery as soon as possible to correct the defect. John's mother and father were adamant about not performing surgery on baby Caitlin's heart to repair the birth defect. They thought it was "God's will" whether the baby lived or died.

Before release from the hospital, the physician also referred Harriet and John to the hospital social worker for support and assistance. The social worker met with the family and told them about a local parent group for families of children with Down syndrome and about an early intervention program in their community. Harriet and John elected to participate in both services. They were pleased to find the parent group because they were seeking a resource through which they could become acquainted with other parents of children with Down syndrome. In addition, they were eager to find out the latest scientific findings related to their daughter's disability and heart defect and to learn about other health and medical concerns that are common to children with Down syndrome so that they could prevent injury and best meet Caitlin's needs. The support of the parent group and pediatric specialists helped Harriet and John to overcome the pressure from their family regarding concerns about surgery. They were able to move forward with the medical intervention in order to help Caitlin survive and grow.

Caitlin was enrolled in early intervention when she was 3 months old. In the program, Caitlin received home- and center-based services from a transdisciplinary team of professionals that also worked with her child care program providers. Since the beginning, her parents were active participants in her educational activities. They worked closely with the early interventionists in the program to develop goals and objectives for Caitlin so that she could learn as much as possible and become as independent as possible.

At age 3, Caitlin is now "graduating" to a preschool in the public school system. Her parents are concerned that she be properly assessed and placed in a preschool program with children who are typically developing. They are seeking an educator or psychologist with special expertise in Down syndrome to conduct the assessment, and they are visiting preschool sites in the community to determine placement options. Their goals are for Caitlin to have friends, to enjoy her life, to be a productive citizen, and to live as independently as possible.

Services related to individuals with disabilities have increasingly focused on appropriate and available educational opportunities from birth and greater access to opportunities in American society, such as employment and independent living. Intervention is aimed at habilitation or rehabilitation or on environmental adaptations to accommodate the needs of the individual. The principles of normalization (Wolfensberger, 1972) and least restrictive environment (LRE) (the Individuals with Disabilities Education Act [IDEA] of 1990 [PL 101-476] and its Amendments of 1997 [PL 105-17]) have defined the goals of integrating individuals with disabilities into society in a culturally normative way and with access to educational services with typically developing peers. The disability rights movements of the last several decades, including a large body of federal legislation culminating in the Americans with Disabilities Act (ADA) of 1990 (PL 101-336), have led to legal protections and the right to equal access for people with disabilities.

SUMMARY

The history of the United States is a short one relative to other countries—a mere 200 years. In those two centuries, a federation (or united government) of states has been established, and the rights of its citizens have been defined and expanded to include citizens such as women, African Americans, and individuals with disabilities, who were initially denied equal participation. Furthermore, the vast land mass of the continental United States has been explored and changed by new settlers on the land, and the country has expanded beyond the unified land mass to include the states of Alaska and Hawaii.

The United States was founded in order to establish a new order, a new type of government. Although this new nation attracted settlers from many distant shores, the predominant customs, beliefs, language, and practices in the United States undeniably have their roots in the Anglo-European heritage. Yet, as new waves of settlers from Ireland and Europe arrived in the continental United States in the early 1900s, they were challenged and compared with the existing "Americans." Some were accepted; some were the target of intense discrimination and alarm. A major question was whether these immigrants would adopt the ways of the new world and "fit in" or remain separate. In 1980, the descendants of many of the immigrants of 1910, a peak period for immigration from Anglo-European points of origin, were interviewed. Many of those interviewed claimed that they were "just Americans," but a large percentage also indicated an ethnic identity (cited in Watkins, 1994, p. 2). Thus, these groups appear to have "melted" together culturally in the United States; however, for many, ethnic and cultural roots in their native lands also have been maintained.

Many American values and assumptions have been forged from this Anglo-European background. These values include 1) high regard for individualism and privacy; 2) the belief in equality of all individuals; 3) a tendency toward informality; 4) an orientation toward the future, change, and progress; 5) a belief in the goodness of humanity; 6) an emphasis on the importance of time; 7) a focus on achievement, action, work, and materialism; and 8) a directness and assertiveness in approach (Althen, 1988).

These values and assumptions have been translated into belief systems that reflect the individual culture's philosophies regarding child rearing, medical or health care practices, death and dying, causation, and disabilities, among other issues. Typically, Americans have high expectations for their child's development, and they foster early self-help and self-reliance skills in their youngsters. Education is highly valued and sought. The extended family networks found in the early years of the country are not as common in recent decades, and the primary focus in the American family typically is on nuclear family members. With respect to medical and health care practices, the American fascination with high technology is evident. Medical treatments typically focus on drugs; surgery; and sophisticated, technical diagnostic procedures. Education and intervention for individuals with disabilities have received a large amount of public attention. This has led to legal mandates ensuring free appropriate public education for children with disabilities and legal protections for all individuals with disabilities.

RECOMMENDATIONS FOR INTERVENTIONISTS

The complexion and goals of the United States continue to be challenged and defined. The growing number of immigrants to this country with non–Anglo-European roots will influence and shape these customs and practices, as have the contributions of immigrants throughout the nation's history.

LANGUAGE AND COMMUNICATION STYLE

Most Americans of Anglo-European roots speak directly and honestly and expect service providers to interact with them similarly. In cases of diagnosis of a disability or issues surrounding intervention, most Americans expect service providers to provide honest and factual answers to their questions and seek professional advice and/or information regarding appropriate intervention practices. Both parents and professionals are expected to speak their opinions in an open, direct style.

With respect to style of communication, Anglo-European Americans tend to look one another in the eye when speaking and prefer direct, face-to-face interactions. Professional greetings often involve shaking hands. Conversation is characterized by turn taking, wherein each person talks for a short while and allows time for others to respond. Personal topics and personal self-disclosure are typically avoided, as are argumentative or conflict-producing topics. Both professional and personal conversations typically are conducted in moderated tones of voice with a give-and-take exchange of information. This verbal exchange is encouraged as most Anglo-European Americans rely more heavily on verbal rather than non-verbal messages.

Different dialects and colloquial expressions are used in different regions of the country. Terms and vocabulary also may differ across ethnic, religious, and professional discipline groups; however, standard English is spoken and understood by most individuals. Service providers are well advised, however, to avoid professional jargon when interacting with families.

VIEW OF FAMILY INVOLVEMENT

Parent/family involvement in children's education has long been a tradition in Anglo-European families. Most parents expect to work as a partner with teachers and other professionals to establish goals for their children and to ensure that appropriate educational or intervention services are rendered. (Parents want to be informed and want to have a say in the process.) Many parents of children with special needs have taken active roles as policymakers and as teachers of their children. The Education for All Handicapped Children Act of 1975 (PL 94-142), which has been retitled as the Individuals with Disabilities Education Act (IDEA) of 1990 (PL 101-476) and subsequently amended as the Individuals with Disabilities Education Act (IDEA) Amendments of 1997 (PL 105-17), stipulate parent involvement in the education of young children with disabilities. Provisions of the amendments to the law related to infants and toddlers go further and require development of an individualized family service plan (IFSP) for children and their families participating in early intervention programs from birth through age 2 in states that offer services under this law. Recommended practices in early intervention services for young children who are at risk or who have disabilities reflect a family-focused or family-centered approach to delivering services. Parents are viewed as equal partners and decision makers in the intervention process.

INTERACTIONS WITH FAMILY MEMBERS

No one person or role in the family is considered the contact or dominant decision maker with respect to services for children. Although it is more common for mothers to be the primary caregiver, other family members (e.g., fathers, siblings, grandparents) may play active, pivotal roles as well. Typically, when asked, family members may specify the major contact(s) and the major "players" in the child's life.

ORGANIZATION AND SCHEDULING

Most Anglo-European families expect appointments to be scheduled and meetings to begin punctually. Many families have active and complex lifestyle patterns that necessitate careful scheduling. In American society, in which so many parents work outside of the home, flexible meeting times, places, and plans also must be considered (e.g., evening meetings with parents, meetings with the child's child care provider as part of the intervention effort).

RESPECT FOR INDIVIDUAL DIFFERENCES

Even within the cultural group with Anglo-European roots, many different subcultures are apparent. For example, individuals may strongly identify with being Irish, Italian, or Jewish, or they may strongly relate to their geographical area (e.g., westerners, southerners). Likewise, rural, urban, and suburban lifestyle differences hold a strong influence over families' life patterns. The family members' social and economic situation may dramatically affect their ability or desire to participate in intervention activities regardless of their ethnic identification. Thus, service providers must be respectful and sensitive to the wide range of families with whom they will work. This does not mean trying to become like the family members or mimicking their practices but rather, recognizing, allowing, and respecting the individual differences among families as well as within families across the various family members.

WHAT WOULD YOU DO?

Please return to the vignette on page 100 describing Harriet, John, and their 3-year-old daughter, Caitlin. Recall that Harriet and John were faced with the prospect of authorizing cardiac surgery for baby Caitlin because she was diagnosed with a cardiac defect at birth, a condition common to children with Down syndrome. John's mother and father vehemently opposed the surgery. John and

Harriet ultimately decided to have the surgery performed despite opposition from their family.

If John and Harriet had abided by the grandparents' wishes and decided not to have the surgery performed, how might you have reacted in a sensitive manner? Would you have taken any actions, and if so, what?

How would you feel about the parents making this decision?

REFERENCES

Althen, G. (1988). *American ways: A guide for foreigners in the United States.* Yarmouth, ME: Intercultural Press.

Americans with Disabilities Act (ADA) of 1990, PL 101-336, 42 U.S.C. §§ 12101 *et seq.*

Children's Defense Fund (2001, April). *Child care basics.* Retrieved March 15, 2004, from http://www.childrensdefense.org/early childhood/childcare/basics.asp

Chiswick, B.R. (1998). Immigration: The latest wave. In *The 1998 World Book Year Book: The annual supplement to The World Book Encyclopedia* (pp. 238–247). Chicago: World Book, Inc.

Davis, K.C. (2003). *Don't know much about history.* New York: Random House.

Degler, C.N. (1984). *Out of our past: The forces that shaped modern America* (3rd ed.). New York: Harper & Row.

Education for All Handicapped Children Act of 1975, PL 94-142, 20 U.S.C. §§ 1400 *et seq.*

Foster, R.F. (1988). *Modern Ireland: 1600–1972.* London: Penguin Books Ltd.

Freedgood, S. (1970). *The gateway states: New Jersey, New York.* New York: Time-Life Books.

Individuals with Disabilities Education Act (IDEA) Amendments of 1990, PL 101-476, 20 U.S.C. §§ 1400 *et seq.*

Individuals with Disabilities Education Act (IDEA) of 1997, PL 105-17, 20 U.S.C. §§ 1400 *et seq.*

Kellogg, W.O. (1995). *American history: The easy way* (2nd ed.). Hauppauge, NY: Barron's Educational Series.

Kennedy, J.F. (1961), January 20 [Inaugural address]. Also avaliable on-line; http://www.jfklibrary.org/j012061.htm.

Kosman, B.A., Mayer, E., & Keysar, A. (2001). *Religious Identification Survey.* New York: The Graduate Center of the City University of New York. Retrieved March 15, 2004, from http://www.gc.cuny.edu/studies/studies/aris_index.htm

Lanier, A.R. (Revised by C.W. Gay). (1996). *Living in the U.S.A.* (5th ed.). Yarmouth, ME: Intercultural Press.

Lassiter, S. (1995). *Multicultural clients: A professional handbook for health care providers and social workers.* Westport, CT: Greenwood Press.

Marzio, P.C. (Ed.). (1976). *A nation of nations: The people who came to America as seen through objects and documents exhibited at the Smithsonian Institution.* New York: Harper & Row.

National Geographic Society. (1975). *We Americans.* Washington, DC: Author.

Stewart, E.C., & Bennett, M.J. (1991). *American cultural patterns: A cross-cultural perspective* (Rev. ed.). Yarmouth, ME: Intercultural Press.

U.S. Bureau of the Census (2000). *Profile of general demographic characteristics: 2000.* Available on-line: http://censtats.census.gov/data/US/01000.pdf.

U.S. Department of Agriculture & U.S. Department of Health and Human Services. (1986). *Cross-cultural counseling: A guide for nutrition and health counselors.* Washington, DC: Author, Nutrition Education Committee for Maternal and Child Nutrition Publications.

Watkins, S.C. (Ed.). (1994). *After Ellis Island: Newcomers and natives in the 1910 census.* New York: Russell Sage Foundation.

Wolfensberger, W. (1972). *Normalization: The principle of normalization in human services.* Toronto, Ontario, Canada: National Institute on Mental Retardation.

APPENDIX A

CONTRASTING BELIEFS, VALUES, AND PRACTICES

Anglo-European	Other cultures
Personal control over the environment	Fate
Change	Tradition
Time dominates	Human interaction dominates
Human equality	Hierarchy/rank/status
Individualism/privacy	Group welfare
Self-help	Birthright inheritance
Competition	Cooperation
Future orientation	Past orientation
Action/goal/work orientation	"Being" orientation
Informality	Formality
Directness/openness/honesty	Indirectness/ritual/"face"
Practicality/efficiency	Idealism/theory
Materialism	Spiritualism/detachment

From U.S. Department of Agriculture & U.S. Department of Health and Human Services. (1986). *Cross-cultural counseling: A guide for nutrition and health counselors* (p. 3). Washington, DC: Author, Nutrition Education Committe for Maternal and Child Nutrition Publications; reprinted by permission.

APPENDIX B

CULTURAL COURTESIES AND CUSTOMS

The following practices represent some major characteristics of interactions.

- *The notion that all people are more or less equal.* It is customary to treat females and males with equal respect and to treat people providing daily services courteously (e.g., cab drivers, food servers, sales clerks).

- *People freely express their opinions.* Freedom of speech is a major characteristic of American life. Some topics are typically not openly discussed, however, particularly with strangers. These include topics related to sex, politics, religion, and personal characteristics such as body odors.

- *People are greeted openly, directly, and warmly.* Anglo-Europeans tend not to practice a lot of rituals in greetings. Typically, people greet one another openly and directly and get to the point of the interaction. Often, people will shake hands with strangers (particularly males). Eye contact is maintained throughout the interaction, and it is considered impolite not to look at the people to whom you are speaking.

- *A social distance of about an arm's length is typically maintained in interactions.* Most social interactions are conducted about an arm's length from the other person. People (males, in particular) do not expect to be touched except for greetings such as shaking hands. When people walk down the street together, they typically do not hold hands or put their arms around one another unless they are involved in a more intimate relationship.

- *Punctuality and responsibility in keeping appointments are valued.* Time is valued and most people expect punctuality. It is also considered rude to accept an invitation to someone's home and not show up or make an appointment with someone and not keep it.

See also Lanier (1996) and Stewart and Bennett (1991) for a more comprehensive discussion of customs and courtesies.

SIGNIFICANT CULTURAL EVENTS/HOLIDAYS/PRACTICES

New Year's Day

January 1

Holiday to celebrate the beginning of a new year

Martin Luther King, Jr.'s, Birthday*

January 15

Holiday to celebrate the life of Martin Luther King, Jr.

Valentine's Day

February 14

A commercialized holiday to honor one's sweetheart and others whom one holds dear

President's Day*

Mid-February

Holiday to commemorate George Washington's and Abraham Lincoln's birthdays

St. Patrick's Day

March 17

Holiday held in honor of the Catholic Saint Patrick, originally celebrated primarily by Irish Americans and now popularized and celebrated by many Americans. The holiday is marked by parades and by wearing green.

Passover

Typically in March or April

Jewish holiday commemorating the exodus of the Jews from Egypt

Palm Sunday

The Sunday before Easter

Christian holiday commemorating Jesus's entry into Jerusalem

Good Friday

The Friday before Easter

Christian holiday commemorating Jesus's crucifixion

Easter

First Sunday after the date of the first full moon that occurs on or after March 21

Christian holiday commemorating the resurrection of Jesus

Mother's Day

Second Sunday in May

Holiday to honor mothers

Memorial Day*

Typically around May 30

Holiday to honor the deceased members of the armed forces

*A legal holiday in most parts of the United States, and government businesses are usually closed. Some of these federal holidays are observed on alternative dates, usually Mondays (e.g., Memorial Day, Labor Day).

Father's Day

Third Sunday in June

Holiday to honor fathers

Independence Day*

July 4

Anniversary of the signing of the Declaration of Independence

Labor Day*

First Monday in September

Holiday in honor of laborers (i.e., working people)

Rosh Hashanah

Typically during first weeks of September

Jewish New Year

Yom Kippur

Typically in early September

Jewish Day of Atonement, day of fasting

Columbus Day*

October 12

Holiday commemorating the discovery of America by Christopher Columbus

Halloween

October 31

"The Eve of All Saints Day"—Originally a pagan celebration that has been popularized and is celebrated by children dressing in costumes and going to neighbors' houses to ask for candy and saying "trick or treat"

Veteran's Day*

November 11

Holiday to honor veterans of the armed forces

Thanksgiving Day*

Fourth Thursday in November

Holiday begun by the Pilgrims to give thanks to God for their survival

Chanukah

Typically in December

Eight-day Jewish holiday commemorating the victory of the Macabees over the Syrians in 165 B.C. and the rededication of the Temple of Jerusalem

Christmas

December 25

Christian holiday commemorating the birth of Jesus Christ

CHAPTER 5

FAMILIES WITH AMERICAN INDIAN ROOTS

Jennie R. Joe and Randi Suzanne Malach

We Indians are taught to take into consideration the less
fortunate members of our tribe. We believe that if you help
a pauper who does not have means, you will get a reward,
not from him, but from some other source. . . . Getting kind
thoughts from people who express their wishes for your
well-being means more than material things. . . .
My wife, for example, might go down the street and see
a man with both legs gone, holding a cup with some pencils.
She will give him something, but she won't take the pencils.
She would rather hear that man say "thank you."
As he says it, she might think, "This good
thought is for my little granddaughter."
—MR. OLD COYOTE
(AS QUOTED IN MOREY & GILLIAM, 1974)

The primary purpose of this chapter is to describe the historical background of American Indians and some of the more common experiences, cultural practices, and beliefs that may influence American Indians' communication and interaction with interventionists. The last section of the chapter discusses some of the communication protocols of which nonnative interventionists should be aware when working with American Indian families.

BACKGROUND

When Christopher Columbus landed in the Bahamas in 1492, the North American continent was home to more than 5 million natives (Hoxie, 1988). Columbus mistook the island for India and called its inhabitants Indians, and his misidentification of the land and its diverse population led to the people being labeled as American Indian peoples (Berkhofer, 1979; Peckham & Gibson, 1969).

The cultural and historic roots of tribal communities go back thousands of years to generations of ancestors, whose footprints in history are reflected in the evidence they left behind, including religious sites, mounds, and burial sites. These ancestors also left other examples of their accomplishments, such as fine pottery, woven clothing, masonry, basketry, ornaments, weapons, tools, and metallurgy with copper and gold. This material evidence clearly illustrates how these ancestors made use of the land and its resources. Indeed, indigenous groups such as the Mayans and Aztecs created great cities and monuments, and their accomplishments in the arts and sciences equaled and sometimes exceeded those of the Europeans.

The European Conquest: 1492–1800

The European conquest, a long period that began in 1492, devastated the Indian communities physically, politically, and economically. Although the Europeans tried to force the Indian people into adopting their values and beliefs, economic as well as cultural and religious, they were only partially successful. Instead, the net effect has been more of an "emulsion" of cultures rather than a smooth blending or mixing (Washburn, 1975).

This clash of cultures resulted in direct and indirect consequences for native people. Warfare brought direct destruction, but the most devastating impact resulted from communicable diseases the Europeans introduced. Most native people had no resistance to infectious diseases such as smallpox and diphtheria. Countless numbers of native people died during various epidemics. Thornton (1987) estimated that the native population of North America that numbered approximately 5 million in 1492 had dropped to about 600,000 by the late 1800s. Because many tribes were completely decimated by the epidemics, many of the details about the history and cultures of these tribes remain a mystery.

The tribal groups who survived the ravages of the epidemics were left with limited resources, and their social order was destroyed or fragmented. The cycles of epidemics cost many tribes their children, elders, and healthy warriors. The loss of the elders was especially devastating because they served as the key repository of cultural and historical knowledge. The depopulation of Indian tribes made way for further settling of the land by the Europeans (Axtell, 1981; Jennings, 1975).

The Europeans' perception of the natives, coupled with their ambitious drive to emigrate to North America, set the stage for the way the natives came to be treated at the hands of the Europeans. For example, the Spaniards quickly began to exploit the natives as a source of free labor to work the mines and/or to help build and support the missions; at the same time, the Spanish priests also tried to convert the natives to the Roman Catholic Church (Dobyns, 1988).

The Spanish and French influenced native tribes, as well. By the end of the 17th century, a strong blend of Hispanic and Indian cultures began emerging; however, early on, only a few Spanish–Indian marriages were approved by the church because most Spaniards viewed the Indians as a pagan and inferior race. The French, whose purposes in the New World were primarily economic, viewed the natives as valuable assets for helping them to achieve their goals. By the late 16th century, some French trappers and traders, for example, adopted Indian customs and lived among the natives. The French were able to expand and utilize this network of friendship to increase their fur trade, and many French traders and trappers were known to marry members of Indian tribes. French surnames remain common among many of the descendants of these marriages, although some French surnames were assigned to individuals by census takers who were unable to pronounce or write the traditional Indian names.

As the population of the English colonies expanded, those settling in the New World wanted little to do with the natives. Seeking religious freedom and/or a chance to improve their economic lot, most English colonists came to the Americas to build permanent settlements and to transplant their European way of life. They viewed the native people as pagan "savages" and as a barrier that had to be removed (Berkhofer, 1965). Because the native people were not Christians and, therefore, not "human" in the eyes of these English colonists, the invaders believed that their Christian faith and alliance to the king (who ruled by divine right) gave them the right to claim all of the land in the New World. This view of the natives as "savages" served as what they believed to be a justifiable excuse for removing the natives from their land, dispossessing them, and even killing them.

Assimilation and "Re-education": 1800–1900

During the 19th century, the American government continued its mission to assimilate American Indians, but this time the primary methods targeted Indian children. The official policy on education mandated formal schooling for all Indian children. The government often sanctioned or encouraged religious groups to send Indian children to distant boarding schools modeled after similar schools in Europe. The school environment discouraged any tribal or cultural practices (e.g., children were not allowed to speak their native languages), and the curriculum fostered the European lifestyle and values. The various government-sponsored classes aimed at the adult population in Indian communities espoused similar Eurocentric orientations.

In 1871, the U.S. Congress passed a law putting an end to treaty negotiations with tribes. This action signaled a new relationship between the U.S. government and the Indian tribes. Indian tribes were no longer accorded recognition as independent, sovereign nations. Thus, despite their drastic efforts to protect their ancestral lands, most tribes were caught in the web of conquest no matter where they lived. By the end of the 19th century, the Indian tribes, drastically reduced in population through disease and warfare, no longer posed a military threat to the Europeans. The final stages of the conquest concluded with relocation of many tribes to isolated and unproductive patchworks of land called "reservations." Although the

U.S. government justified reservations as "sanctuaries," such forced relocation not only broke the spirit of many once-proud Indian nations but also destined them to a life of poverty and hopelessness—conditions that persist today.

Lands set aside as communal or for reservations, however, did not remain the sole jurisdictions of the Indian tribes for long. The U.S. Congress enacted the Dawes Act in 1887, allotting to many eligible Indians approximately 160 acres of reservation land each. The sponsors of the legislation thought that such individual land owner-ship was essential to becoming civilized or to taking up the ways of mainstream American culture. Although this individual land ownership policy was intended to help assimilate North American Indians into mainstream society, the subdivision of land merely provided another way to take more of the land away from American In-dians because the unassigned land left after the allotment was made available to non–American Indians.

By the end of the 19th century, fewer than 250,000 American Indians remained in North America (Thornton, 1987). As a conquered people, many were left almost totally dependent on the federal government for their survival. In the ensuing years, the isolation of many reservations and villages provided a measure of protection from mainstream society, but the clash with the non–American Indian world has contin-ued, and the resulting experiences continue to shape the worldview and self-identity of most tribal groups today.

1900–Present

As conquered people, most American Indians became strangers in their own land. And, although they were indigenous to the Americas, American Indians were not automatically granted citizenship but had to prove themselves worthy of citizenship. During World War I, many American Indians volunteered to serve in the armed forces; in 1919, citizenship was awarded to those American Indians who had served in the war. Finally, in 1924, the Indian Citizenship Act granted all American Indians citizenship. Citizenship status, however, did not automatically guarantee American Indians the right to vote. At that time, state governments maintained the power to grant voting rights. Until after World War II, New Mexico and Arizona barred their Indian populations from voting, at which point they allowed them to vote only after the tribes sought legal recourse.

Shortly after the end of World War II, the federal policy favoring rapid assimila-tion of American Indians once again emerged as a congressional issue. A plan was presented in which federal trusteeship would be relinquished or terminated for tribes deemed by the Bureau of Indian Affairs (BIA) to be economically viable. This policy had a major impact on the 10 tribes recommended for termination: the Osages of Oklahoma, the Klamaths of Oregon, the Menominees of Wisconsin, the Flatheads of Montana, the Potawatomis of Kansas and Nebraska, the Chippewas of Turtle Moun-tain in Minnesota, the Six Nations of New York, and three small tribes in California. The aftermath of the termination policy for tribes released from federal trusteeship proved disastrous. Within a few years, tribes like the Menominee, who appeared to have a strong economic base, were left bankrupt and on the brink of losing their re-maining land base. Each year after termination, increasing numbers of Menominee families were forced to auction their homes or farmland to pay taxes and/or to apply for public welfare. Thus, the termination program increased poverty instead of eliminating it. In the 1970s, some of the terminated tribes began to lobby Congress to reverse their termination, and ultimately some were successful.

In addition to termination, the federal government initiated other programs to push American Indians into assimilation. One of these efforts included the relocation of many young American Indians into the cities. These young people were often relocated into the urban ghettos where they were purposefully settled so that they would not be living near another American Indian. Although the relocation worked for some, many found themselves isolated and ill-prepared to deal with the cultural shock of the impersonal urban lifestyles and returned home to the reservation.

By the late 1960s, participation of American Indians in sporadic outbreaks of public demonstrations and civil disobedience were reported by the media. The occupation of Alcatraz Island by a group Indian college students and the "fish-ins" organized by the Northwest Coast tribal groups are two examples of these protests. The purpose of the Alcatraz occupation was to ask for the return of federal surplus land to Indian tribes, whereas the fish-ins were staged by members of one Northwest Coast tribe to reaffirm their treaty rights to fish.

In the early 21st century, American Indian communities continue to foster their own tribal identity and to remain separate and distinct from one another. Their common experiences, forged during the colonization process and through the intertribal and pan-Indian alliances that have evolved in recent decades, however, have created agendas that are common to most tribes. These common agendas include the right to self-government, equal access to quality health care and education, and an appreciation and encouragement for fostering their tribal language and culture.

Religious Origins

Because religion was never a separate institution for American Indians, it is taken for granted that the origin of religion came with the emergence of mankind and/or the specific tribes. Within the traditional worldview of most tribes, the spiritual was perceived to be an integral part of everything. At the center of most of these traditional tribal religious beliefs is a deity that is referred to as the "Great Spirit," "Creator," "Grandfather," and so forth. Another core concept is the notion that all things (natural and supernatural) are interconnected because all of these elements have life.

Language Origins

It is estimated that in 1492, more than 1,000 separate American Indian languages were spoken (Driver, 1961; Washburn, 1975). In the early 21st century, eight different ancient language groupings are used to categorize most of the Indian languages in use. Iroquoian, Muskogean, Caddoan, and Athapaskan are examples of these major groupings.

The various tribal languages have also been greatly influenced by cultural contact with the Europeans. For example, in the Southwest, Spanish words have been incorporated into the different tribal languages for things that have been introduced into the tribes' cultures (e.g., words for currency, days of the week).

English is the most common second language found today in some American Indian communities (Malach, Segel, & Thomas, 1989). In fact, many of the younger generations do not speak or understand their tribal language at all. For these youth, English is their primary language.

CONTEMPORARY LIFE

Today, American Indians reside in every state and in most major cities of the United States. More than 500 federally recognized distinct tribal groups and villages are found in the United States, and they are often grouped regionally (e.g., Indians of the Northeast, Indians of the Southwest). Great diversity is still found among tribes as well as within each tribe and within extended families.

An American Indian family may consist of members with differing levels of acculturation and traditionalism. For example, the grandparents in one extended family may live on the reservation and predominantly speak the native language, whereas the younger generation may live in the city and speak predominantly English (Hoffman, 1981).

According to the 2000 Census, the population of American Indians and Alaska Natives in the United States reached 2.4 million people (U.S. Bureau of the Census, 2001). Despite the population growth since 1900, American Indians and Alaska Natives compose fewer than 1% of the total population. Compared with other minority populations, then, American Indians remain numerically "invisible." Despite efforts in the past to integrate American Indians and Alaska Natives into mainstream culture, many still prefer to maintain their unique cultures. In other words, they are willing to acculturate but are not always willing to assimilate into the majority culture. And contrary to the popular belief of the vanishing "First Americans," the population of American Indians continues to increase (Johnson, 1991; U.S. Bureau of the Census, 2001).

As discussed previously, American Indians are not a homogeneous group. Great diversity exists among tribes, beginning with the size of some of the American Indian groups. For example, tribes such as the Cherokees, the Navajos, the Sioux, and the Ojibiwas (Chippewas) have sizable populations in excess of 100,000 people. Other tribes such as the Cocopah, the Modoc, and the Chumush are very small, numbering fewer than 1,000 in each tribe. Some tribes also may not have a tribal land base, whereas others no longer reside on reservations because they have moved to cities. Other American Indians migrate back and forth between the city and the reservation, many leaving the reservation during times of economic hardship to seek work in cities or towns. The out-migration from the reservations, however, has increased since the 1950s; as of 2000, more than half of the Indian population resides in off-reservation communities or cities (Johnson, 1991; U.S. Bureau of the Census, 2001).

Although American Indians have experienced periods of intense pressure to assimilate, many continue to hold on to their tribal ways while adopting many non-Indian ways. The diversity among American Indians also continues to grow as a result of increasing numbers of intertribal marriages as well as intermarriage with people from non–American Indian cultures. For example, Olson and Wilson (1984) noted that only 105 of the 5,000-member Blackfeet tribe are full blood. The rest are of mixed blood.

With every new generation, increasing numbers of American Indians live in a bicultural world in which they have blended or selected values or mores of both cultures—their tribe's and the majority's culture (Joe & Miller, 1987). It is common to see a blending of traditional and nontraditional practices. For example, American Indian families may observe birthday celebrations or acknowledge the "tooth fairy" in addition to some of their traditional tribal customs such as conducting a "naming ceremony." An American Indian baby may start out in a traditional cradleboard and disposable diapers but is soon introduced to a baby walker and a stroller.

A continuum of acculturation exists within American Indian communities, ranging from individuals who hold fast to a traditional lifestyle to those who not only operate primarily within the dominant culture but also may identify more with the dominant culture (Northwest Indian Child Welfare Institute, 1987). Families may move about on this continuum, becoming more traditional at times (e.g., after the birth of a child) and less so at other times. Thus, although many American Indian families are integrated into mainstream society, many still maintain their traditional beliefs and customs to varying degrees. Oral history, songs and dances, and ceremonial activities are still part of the culture of most contemporary American Indians, and native languages are still used and taught in many tribal communities. These cultural phenomena are extremely important because varying levels of acculturation (including knowledge and experiences) affect the way American Indians respond to non-Indian service delivery systems and the professionals who help provide these services. Unfortunately, there are no set rules for identifying levels of acculturation.

Gaming, or legalized gambling, on Indian land has raised many issues for tribes across the United States. In 2001, Indian casinos were located in 28 states; however, only half of the existing tribes have casinos. Tribes such as the Navajo oppose gambling for religious reasons, and many tribes are either too small or located too far from major population centers to develop casinos or make a profit (Barlett & Steele, 2002). Gaming has brought increased prosperity for some and no benefit to others. In some cases, traditional values and practices have been directly threatened; in others, the new financial resources have strengthened tribal identity, traditions, and self-determination. In 1988, the U.S. Congress passed the Indian Gaming Regulatory Act (IGRA), which continues to govern Indian gaming—a business that generates from $7 billion (Twetten, 2000) to nearly $13 billion in annual revenues (Barlett & Steele, 2002). Tribes with profitable casinos have been able to improve infrastructure on tribal lands, provide employment opportunities, and ensure health care and education for their members. Many have also contributed generously to general community services in their region. Regardless of each tribe's situation and beliefs, gaming has raised a variety of complex issues for tribes with and without gaming.

In summary, the profile of many reservation communities today parallels that of developing countries. The population reflects a high proportion of young people: Approximately half are younger than age 20. Both high birth rates and high mortality rates characterize some tribes (Indian Health Service, 1998–1999). Poverty is endemic. The 2000 census indicated a median household income of $31,799 for American Indians in 1999, compared with $45,514 for non-Hispanic whites. Also in 1999, 25.9% of American Indians had household incomes below the poverty line (*American Indians*, 2002).

VALUES

Much of what is known about the value systems of American Indians emerges out of ethnographic studies, some of which date back to the colonial period. The aim of most early ethnographers, however, was not to focus on values but to capture the unique aspects of the culture and/or sometimes to capture anything and everything so that there would be a realistic picture of that tribal society before it vanished or changed. Thus, specific studies on values of American Indians have not been central in many of these observations (DuBray, 1985).

The few studies that have centered on the values of some tribes have focused on some common tribal values such as individual autonomy, the ability to endure deprivation, the importance of bravery, the proclivity for practical joking, and the belief in the existence and essence of a supernatural power (DuBray, 1985). On a broader scale, these values, or the different emphasis given to some of them by American Indians, do not appear to differ greatly from those of the mainstream society—until they are juxtaposed with non-Indian values. Table 5.1 and the text that follows present some of the differences in values between non-Indian culture and that of the Pueblo Indians of the Southwest (whose values are similar to those of other Indian tribes). With time and the ever-present pressure toward acculturation or assimilation, some of the traditional Indian values may no longer be held by some of the younger generation of American Indians, but they are still visible and upheld by others, especially the elders.

Table 5.1.　Value comparisons between American Pueblo Indians and non–American Indian cultures

Pueblo Indians	Non–American Indian
Harmony with nature	Mastery over nature
Present-time orientation orientation	Future-time
Cooperation	Competition
Anonymity	Individuality
Submissiveness	Aggressiveness
Work for present needs	Work to "get ahead"
Sharing wealth now	Saving wealth for self
Time is flexible	Time is inflexible

From Zintz, M. (1963). *Education across cultures* (p. 174). Dubuque, IA: William C. Brown; adapted by permission.

Harmony with Nature

The value of harmony with nature is still evident as many tribal communities continue to resist mining and mineral development on their land. These tribal groups continue to teach respect for the land and to forbid desecration of their ancestral lands. These groups also carry on various ceremonies and rituals to ensure harmony with, as well as protection of, the land (Mother Earth).

Cultural conflicts can arise when American Indian people must choose between land development that will possibly employ tribal members against the value of maintaining the cultural values that emphasize protecting and not destroying the land. In times of economic hardship, the decision about how to use the land is often based on survival; thus, land developers or mineral companies may be allowed on the reservations to set up commercial enterprises.

Time Orientation

Another value frequently cited as differing from that of the majority culture is the preference many American Indians have for a present-time orientation (Lewis & Ho, 1975); that is, one must attend to the needs of today and put less emphasis on the needs for tomorrow. Time is also viewed as a "rhythmic, circular pattern" (Ho, 1987, p. 71). In the past, rather than marking time by months or years, most tribes marked time based on the seasons, with daily routines gauged by the position of the sun or the moon.

Similarly, the milestones used to mark human development also were based on varying tribal customs. For example, the developmental milestones may not emphasize when a child starts talking but rather when the child has his or her "naming ceremony," takes the first step, laughs the "first laugh," and/or accomplishes the vision quest or other puberty ceremonies. In some instances, therefore, using a standard child development measurement form for a American Indian child may not be appropriate.

In most American Indian communities, health programs and nutrition supplement programs such as the Supplemental Nutrition Programs for Women, Infants, and Children (WIC) utilize various developmental tests to examine and follow the physical development of many young Indian children who are eligible for these public programs. Most Indian women who are seen for prenatal care are indoctrinated early about the need to bring their babies or other young children to the clinic for immunizations and/or scheduled well-baby visits. In addition, if American Indian women deliver in the hospital (and most do), the newborn is also given a routine assessment at birth and again at discharge. Most American Indian children with congenital abnormalities are therefore identified at an early age. More frequent follow-up is conducted with mothers of these newborns, and they are encouraged to note specific developmental milestones as the children age. In other cases, if the baby is at risk for, or is diagnosed with, developmental delays, referrals may be made to specialists for early intervention and therapy.

Family Roles and Relationships

In most American Indian families, the concept of family is defined broadly to include extended family members and fictive kin (i.e., non–family members incorporated into the family network) in addition to the immediate family (Malach et al., 1989).

A traditional American Indian family whose 2½-year-old daughter had a repaired cleft lip and chronic otitis media was referred for early intervention services by a community clinic pediatrician. The pediatrician was concerned about the child's speech and language as well as the child's behavior problems.

The early interventionist went to the home for the first visit in order to talk to the family and to obtain a social and medical history. She was told the mother and father lived with the mother's parents and an elderly aunt. During the first visit to the home, the four older children were very quiet. The aunt stayed in the kitchen, and the grandparents were in town shopping.

The early interventionist introduced herself and explained why she was there. She began to ask questions about the child's history. She was confused by the responses to questions regarding the child's development. The parents did not seem to remember when the child sat up or began walking. Although the physician stated that the child was using single words to name things, the parents said the child was not yet talking. The early interventionist also asked if the parents had any concerns about the child's behavior. The parents said "No." The early interventionist left after making an appointment to come back in a week.

The early interventionist went back to the clinic and asked a nurse who had been working in the community for 10 years if she would talk to her about this referral and about the home visit. She asked why the parents did not seem to know about developmental milestones. The nurse explained that in this particular American Indian tribe, the developmental milestones that are valued are different from those valued in the mainstream culture. In this family's tribal culture, events between the child's third and fourth birthday are considered important. For example, if the child does not talk as much as other children at that time, then the family becomes concerned.

Next, the early interventionist told the nurse about the pediatrician's concern about the child's behavior and the parents' lack of concern. The nurse explained that in more traditional Indian families, the responsibility for discipline often belongs to the elder aunt or grandmother. In American Indian culture, age and life experience are essential for child rearing. The parents are not considered to have the years of experience necessary to raise their children alone. In this family, the children were well behaved in the presence of elder family members; the parents had difficulty when they were out with the children and the elders were not around.

When the early interventionist went back the next week, she asked some different questions. She asked the parents to tell her about when their daughter first laughed. They told her about the event and celebratory party with enthusiasm. Then the early interventionist asked them who was responsible for disciplining the children and how it was done. She then asked what they did about discipline when an elder was not around. They stated they found disciplining their children difficult without an elder present. The early interventionist asked if they would like help. The mother indicated that they would, but that they could not take away the elder's role and responsibility. After discussion, they decided that the parents would talk with the elders about having the parents learn behavior management skills that they could use outside the home in situations when an elder was not around.

Other members of the family's tribe may be included as well. In many cases, extended family members rather than the biological parents may hold primary responsibility for the care of the children. Often, grandparents or other extended family members assume child-rearing responsibilities willingly so that parents of young children can be employed. Furthermore, parents may seek the advice and assistance of older family members and elders in the larger family network, given the value placed on age and life experiences. In interactions with interventionists, these extended family members may act as service coordinators for the child and family in obtaining needed services (Malach et al., 1989).

Group Orientation

Another cultural value of American Indians that has received considerable attention is group membership, with an emphasis on collaborative relationships with others rather than individualism. Group consensus is of major value in important decision making; usually sufficient time is allowed (even hours) to discuss and examine an issue until a consensus is reached.

This emphasis on group consensus can have interesting consequences. American Indian children are not likely to want to draw attention to themselves as individuals, for example, usually preferring to be part of a group. Educators often mistake this as passive behavior or interpret it to mean that American Indian children do not want to compete for top grades. Conversely, American Indian children who display the aggressive or individualistic behaviors common to the mainstream culture may be taunted or teased by their American Indian peers.

Acceptance

The general tendency of the non–American Indian culture to take charge and/or to manipulate nature to fit its needs has also frequently been contrasted with the Indian value of accepting natural and sometimes unnatural events as they are. This value of

accepting things as they are has often been described for Indians as "being-in-becoming" in contrast to the non–American Indian value of doing something about the situation (Kluckhohn & Strodtbeck, 1961). This acceptance of natural and unnatural events is representative of the American Indian belief that these events occur as part of the natural order of life and that one must learn to live with life and accept what comes, both the good and the bad (Coles, 1977). In some instances, non–American Indians have viewed this value of acceptance by Indians as an explanation for why American Indians do not want to impose themselves or their views on others when they are not asked (Good Track, 1973). Acceptance relates back to the traditional values of many tribes that called for respecting all living things and not interfering with the nature of life events without cause (Bopp, Bopp, Brown, & Lane, 1984).

Self-Reliance and Autonomy

Whether in the city or on the reservation, many American Indian parents still socialize their children based on their own cultural prerogatives. Some of these prerogatives may include teaching an American Indian child to be self-sufficient at an earlier age than that common to other cultures. Miller's (1979) comparison of certain tasks accomplished by white, African American, and American Indian children illustrates this point (see Table 5.2).

As Table 5.2 shows, most American Indian children assume responsibility for self at an earlier age than do children from other groups. This is because most American Indian children are reared in an adult-centered world, and as soon as they can master self-care skills, they are encouraged to do so. In fact, any imitation of acceptable adult behavior is encouraged and praised. For example, a young child who can help with chores around the home is praised for her or his willingness to take on responsibilities without being asked. Similarly, children are asked about their opinion in important family decisions.

Education

Prior to the European conquest and spread of European culture and practices, most American Indians educated their children informally at home with the help of relatives and/or formally by means of arranged apprenticeships. For example, a young tribal member who wanted to become a medicine person often sought out a teacher

Table 5.2.   Developmental milestones across cultures

Skills	Age accomplished in years		
	White	African American	American Indian
Dress self	3.7	4.0	2.8
Do regular chores	6.1	6.3	5.4
Go downtown alone	13.5	12.8	10.6
Left alone in evening	14.4	13.6	9.9
Take care of younger sibling	16.4	16.5	15.7

From Miller, D.L. (1979). *Mother's perception of Indian child development.* Unpublished research report (p. 10). San Francisco: Institute for Scientific Analysis; adapted by permission.

*Note: For all groups, it is likely that the age levels given have changed because of societal changes in the interim since this study was conducted.

or mentor, and the family arranged payment and the terms of the training program. In other instances, the clan or the society took on the responsibility for training and preparing the child for participation in the clan or the society's activities. Some of this training included learning the sacred songs, prayers, or dances. Children, therefore, were taught these and other skills to enable them to assume adult roles.

In addition to basic language and communication skills, boys and girls were taught about plants, herbs, animals, seasons, hunting, food preparation, child care, and religion. The whole family or community often shared kinship, values, and other moral teachings. Evening was often reserved for storytelling, and each story invariably had a lesson to impart.

The teaching philosophy of most American Indians also reinforced the value that each child was a distinct person taught to do or warned against doing certain things, not because these things were right or wrong, but because the act or failure to act was to his or her advantage or disadvantage in the afterlife. American Indians appealed to the child's pride and ambition and pointed out appropriate role models for emulation.

Most American Indians are not against formal education; however, when many young American Indian children enter the classroom, they frequently find themselves in alien environments without any familiar words, values, and lifestyles. As the classroom activities and language become increasingly different from those in their home environment, the students suffer a loss of confidence and self-esteem, a loss that is sometimes irreparable.

To lessen the impact of the foreign educational environment, many educators have advocated for bilingual and bicultural education programs. Bilingual teachers (and teacher aides) who can teach and write the native language of the children's cultural group are crucial as are new curriculum materials that incorporate oral history, legends, and language structures.

Humor

Humor is an essential part of most American Indian life. In fact, in some tribal communities one is expected to have a "joking" relationship with certain kin. Children come to understand these "joking" relationships at an early age as they in turn learn to tease their kin members.

Humor may also be used as a form of social control. For example, in some of the sacred dances, clown dancers often entertain the crowds with their antics and may reprimand a particular community member for behavior found displeasing to the rest of the community through teasing or shaming the individual or by acting out the individual's misdeeds. At other gatherings, it is common to hear jokes or humorous stories about animals such as the coyote, a crafty and popular trickster whose antics may be used by the tribe to explain unexplainable occurrences. Humorous events or characters are also found in art or in print. For example, one tribal newspaper in the Southwest periodically includes a cartoon series titled "Mutton Man" that depicts a hero with powers comparable to Superman, but the story line deals with issues confronted on the tribal reservation.

RELIGION AND BELIEFS

The belief in the interconnectedness of all things living and nonliving is central to many American Indian belief systems. The idea that human beings are but a small part of the larger fabric of the universe is a theme frequently heard in many tribal stories and legends (Neihardt, 1961). For example, among a number of North Central tribes, the four principles of the Medicine Wheel incorporate the four aspects of human nature: the physical, the mental, the emotional, and the spiritual (Bopp et al., 1984). The belief is that all four of these elements have to be in balance or in harmony for one to have good health. Many of the curative as well as preventive ceremonies, therefore, are aimed toward maintaining or regaining harmony.

Among some other tribes, similar ideas may be represented by references to the four cardinal directions, the four grandfathers, or the four winds—each direction symbolizing different concepts such as wisdom, growth, or generosity. The Hopis (a Pueblo tribe in northern Arizona) believe that the original spiritual "being" shared with the Hopi people certain rules of life and placed spiritual helpers, the Kachinas, near the tribe to protect and help them maintain that way of life. The Kachinas, therefore, help teach and guide the Hopis with their songs, prayers, and ceremonies (Titiev, 1972). Among the Apaches, the Mountain Spirits have a similar role to that of the Kachinas. Appropriate members of these respective tribes impersonate these deities during special ceremonies. In addition, the social structure of some Pueblo tribes of the Southwest have moieties (i.e., social groups in addition to one's clan relationship) whose ceremonial activities also function to ensure harmony and/or community welfare.

Many non–American Indians today continue to misunderstand the importance of the traditional beliefs that are a part of these ceremonies. They may fail to understand the ceremonies that are performed to bless a new baby, to offer prayers for rain, or to offer thanksgiving for a good harvest. American Indian children often participate in the rituals and ceremonies as soon as they are able to sing or dance. Special gifts may be made in a child's honor when she or he first dances or participates in an important ceremony. Family members and/or clan members may also honor a child by making appropriate clothing for him or her to wear during these occasions. A sacred pipe, for example, may be given to a young American Indian when he comes of age and is being indoctrinated into a special society. Most tribes hold strong beliefs about the proper preparation for someone who is to take on important responsibilities such as participating in the Sun Dance.

Child Rearing

In many American Indian families, the child-rearing activities may rest with family members other than parents. In many instances, the grandparents are responsible for the children. Aunts and uncles also are likely to be involved, especially if the family resides on the reservation and not in an urban area. American Indian families who live in the city tend to have nuclear households, whereas families on the reservation tend to include extended family members. In fact, in some tribes, the uncles instead of the parents may provide most of the discipline while grandparents provide most of the spiritual guidance and teaching.

The advent of cultural change (i.e., mainly the change from a subsistence lifestyle to that of a wage-labor lifestyle) and implementation of a number of government policies have disrupted this normal order of child rearing and family relationships for most tribes. The role and even the existence of extended family and nuclear family structures have also been changed drastically by various policies over the

An American Indian child with Down syndrome lived with his single teenage mother and grandmother. Members of the extended family lived nearby and were closely involved in decisions regarding the boy's rearing. The family received early intervention services for the first 2 years of the child's life. When the boy was 3 years old, he was ready to transition into a public school program. The mother believed that the public school would provide her son with a good program, and she was looking forward to a break from child care. She also wanted to take classes so that she could eventually get a good job.

The extended family did not support the decision to send this 3-year-old child to school. They believed it was the mother's responsibility to care for him. They believed the child was ill and that he had suffered enough because of his illness and should be kept at home and protected. They trusted the early interventionist who had been visiting the home weekly for 2 years, and wanted her to continue to see the child until he was at least 6 years old or when they decided he was ready for school. The family was upset that the early interventionist would not continue to provide services.

The early interventionist met with the family and explained that she would help them learn about the preschool programs available to them. She would also go with them to visit the programs and meet with the school staff. She would answer the family's questions and help them to make a list of questions they wanted to ask the schools. The family agreed and everything seemed to go smoothly for a while. The interventionist planned two follow-up visits after the child started in the chosen school program to make sure everything was going smoothly. The school reported the child had adjusted to the classroom and was doing well. The mother enrolled in a class at the local community college. Three weeks after school started, the mother called the early interventionist to say that the family was again questioning the decision. The early interventionist went to the home and met with the grandmother and aunt. They expressed their concerns and restated their cultural beliefs that the mother should be home caring for her child. At the end of the discussion, they told the early interventionist that they trusted her but not the school, and they wanted her to continue to visit the child at school and visit them at home every week. The early interventionist told them she could not do that weekly, but that she could visit twice a month.

For the next few months, the family continued to need support in their decision. After 2 months, the visits were extended to once a month. Efforts were made to help the family build a relationship with the teacher, school counselor, and other families who had children in special education. Four months after school started, the mother met another American Indian mother of an older child with Down syndrome, who shared many of her concerns and understood her situation. As the two families began to provide each other mutual support, the early interventionist extended the time between visits to 6 weeks. In the spring, she helped the family prepare for the individualized education program (IEP) meeting to plan for the next school year. She did not accompany them. After that meeting, she let the family know that she would not schedule regular visits but that they could call her if they wanted her help.

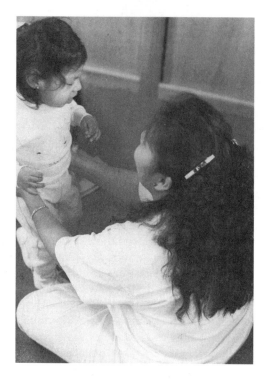

years. Social programs (e.g., Aid to Families with Dependent Children [AFDC]) have forced many American Indian families into nuclear households and/or forced the establishment of one-parent households. In other cases, young American Indian families who relocate to the cities in search of jobs often leave behind their much-needed family and extended family support networks.

Medical Care

The 2000 Census reports that 26.8% of American Indians/Alaska Natives lack health insurance (U.S. Bureau of the Census, 2001). This percentage is significantly higher than rates for African Americans (19.5%), Asian and Pacific Islanders (18.8%), and non-Hispanic whites (10.1%). For those living on reservations, the major health care service provider is either the federal Indian Health Service (IHS) or tribally managed health care facilities funded by IHS. The federal government has long played a role in the health care of most tribes. For example, the federal government became involved in the health of American Indians during the late 19th century, when efforts were taken to control smallpox or other infectious disease epidemics. A number of tribes also requested medical service as a part of their treaty agreements with the U.S. government. Depending on the size of the native community, medical care may be available to tribal members from IHS or IHS-funded hospitals, community health centers, or a health station. In addition to medical services, some of the IHS health delivery systems also include public health, mental health, and dental health. Health care provided by these health programs or hospitals is frequently free of charge to eligible American Indians, although cost of care may also be billed to Medicare, Medicaid, and private insurance for those who have insurance (Kaiser Family Foundation, 1996).

Some urban centers with sizable American Indian populations also have established some health resources, mostly primary health services. Sizable urban Indian health programs, however, tend to have more comprehensive services, including mental health, dental care, or other satellite health facilities.

Access to these health resources has greatly improved the health status of American Indians in a number of ways: Maternal and infant mortality has decreased dramatically as have deaths attributed to infectious diseases (Indian Health Service, 1998–1999). Health problems related to chronic diseases are on the increase (e.g., diabetes, heart disease), however. In an effort to address some of these problems, many Indian communities have initiated substance abuse treatment or prevention programs. In addition, most tribal communities also have established a cadre of community paraprofessional workers—the community health representatives.

Disability

The prevalence of disability varies from one Indian community to the next. Until the 1970s, various infectious diseases (e.g., meningitis, otitis media) were underlying causing of the most common disabilities in American Indian children. As of 2004, developmental delays rather than infectious diseases accounted for the majority of disabilities in American Indian children, with learning disabilities among the most commonly reported disabilities in American Indian school-age children. Between 1991 and 1996, accidents were the leading cause of death for American Indian children between the ages of 4 and 14 (IHS, 1996; 1998–1999). For this age group, respiratory system disease is the leading reason for hospitalization (IHS, 1998–1999).

Causation

Most American Indian belief systems incorporate the idea of multiple causes of illness and misfortune; some causes of illness, misfortunes, or disabilities may be attributed to supernatural or natural causes. The supernatural causes may link etiology to witchcraft, spirit loss, spirit intrusion, spells, and various other unnatural forces. In the natural category, the causes may be attributed to various disturbances of "balance" (i.e., disharmony) brought on by such actions as breaking a cultural taboo, acculturation, and/or accidents that are not instigated by witchcraft or through harmful wishes of others.

Indian families or parents who have children born with disabilities may be told by medical professionals that the disability is the result of a genetic disorder. The parents may not dispute this diagnosis because it explains *how* the condition occurred, but these parents may also turn to their cultural resources to find out *why* the disability occurred. This sociocultural explanation may be that a breach of a cultural taboo has occurred. To prevent the condition from worsening and/or to prevent future misfortune, the parents or family may turn to tribal healers or practitioners for assistance while at the same time continuing to take the child to physicians or to other specialists for treatment and follow-up care. Sometimes the family or parents may utilize their tribal healers to help enhance the treatment or therapy provided by the physician or by modern medicine.

When a family member has a disability or illness, traditional ceremonies are conducted to begin the healing process and to protect the individual and the rest of the family from further harm. For that reason, an American Indian family may want to complete traditional ceremonies before they become involved in a regimen recommended by physicians or other service providers. For example, when a child is born with a disability that is not immediately life threatening, the family may seek the consultation of a tribal healer before consenting to other interventions. Unfortunately, some families may not volunteer this information for fear that service providers might not respect their wishes.

The type of ceremonies used to help the child, the family, and the extended family will vary from one tribal group to the next. Sometimes various ceremonies or rituals are performed to ensure safe and healthy pregnancies and/or deliveries. In some tribes, the mother and child may have to observe a strict postpartum regimen. The child and mother may be sequestered until the appropriate number of days has passed and the newborn is formally introduced to the appropriate religious deities of the tribe as well as to other members of the community. Some of these rituals may require the mother to undergo certain purification ceremonies to prepare her to raise her child.

Death and Dying

Most American Indian groups view death and dying as a part of life's journey and the culmination of natural changes such as aging. In the cultural history of many tribes when life expectancy was low, those individuals who attained old age were considered special and were therefore honored and greatly respected. American Indians, like people in most societies, however, do not consider unexpected deaths, especially of children, to be typical. They might question why such an untimely death occurred and may attribute it to witchcraft.

Although the practice was more common in the past, members of various tribes still either bury prized belongings with the deceased or destroy these items. A number of reasons are given for this practice, including 1) to ensure that the deceased take their belongings with them to the other world, 2) to prevent the use of these items by others, and 3) to discourage the return of the deceased's spirit (returning to search for their belongings). For example, the family may destroy the cradleboard or the toys that belonged to the deceased child.

Among some Northern Plains tribes, notices about an individual's death are announced under the obituary section of the tribal newspaper section called "Walking On." In other words, even after death, individuals are still on a journey. In preparation for the continuing journey, most tribal funerary practices include dressing the deceased in their finest so that they do not appear impoverished in the next world.

Sometimes when a child dies, especially an infant, it is believed that the child will be reincarnated through the future birth of another child to the family. Because of high infant mortality, it was a common practice in some tribes not to name a newborn for a year or so for fear the newborn might die soon after birth. In other previous tribal practices, the name of an ill child might be changed to confuse malevolent spirits assumed to be causing harm or sickness. As a result of culture change, however, many of these practices are not observed today.

LANGUAGE

Because American Indian societies must live in a bicultural world, a number of formal institutions (e.g., Head Start) that serve American Indian children offer bicultural and sometimes bilingual education. Robert W. Rhodes, while discussing learning styles, noted that many young American Indian children "prefer a more holistic observational technique, whereas the Anglo process of categorization lends itself to a linear approach" (cited in Felciano, 1990, p. 1).

Foremost in these programs is the attention given to the continuation of the tribal languages. For example, the Navajo Nation's educational policy states

> The Navajo language is an essential element of the life, culture and identity of the Navajo people. The Navajo Nation recognizes the importance of preserving and perpetuating that language to the survival of the Nation. Instruction in the Navajo language shall be made available for all grade levels in all schools serving the Navajo Nation. Navajo language instruction shall include to the greatest extent practicable: thinking, speaking, comprehension, reading and writing skills and study of the formal grammar of the language. (Navajo Division of Education, 1985, p. 9)

According to Reyhner (1986), the Northern Utes of Utah also have a tribal resolution that declares the Ute language as the official language of their nation. The resolution, in part, states

> The Ute language is a living and vital language that has the ability to match any other in the world for expressiveness and beauty. Our language is capable of lexical expansion into modern conceptual fields such as the field of politics, economics, mathematics, and science. (Northern Ute Tribal Business Council, 1985, p. 16)

As mentioned previously, prior to the mid-1940s, the federal government did not favor cultural diversity and bilingual education for American Indians. Formal schooling was seen as an important vehicle for assimilating and detribalizing American Indians (Reyhner, 1986). To speed up the assimilation process, American Indian children were taken (sometimes forcibly) from their homes to boarding schools, in which they were forced to think and speak only in English. This process in the long run did not assimilate American Indian children; it only served to disrupt their culture (Reyhner, 1986).

Some English words have no equivalent in the native tribal language, and this creates difficulties. For example, an interventionist was asked to work with an American Indian family whose 6-month-old son was diagnosed with profound bilateral hearing loss (Malach, 1991). When the interventionist tried to explain the diagnosis to the family, the translator used the term *without ears* because there was no equivalent word for hearing loss. The elders in the family said that they did not see a need for intervention if the child could not hear at all, but the child's mother wanted some intervention because she said she wanted her son to learn to talk eventually. Her decision had to be supported by the aunts and grandparents, however. Because it was learned that there had been a translation problem, another attempt was made to explain the facts to the family using a different interpreter. The interventionist also brought an audiometer and demonstrated the different degrees of hearing loss. She also showed the family a videotape that illustrated the various types of therapeutic activities that would be prescribed for the child. The family finally understood about the hearing loss, but they wanted the intervention delayed until the child was taken to a traditional healer to prepare the child for the therapy sessions. In other words, the family wanted to ensure success with the intervention by seeking and receiving the appropriate blessing from the traditional healer.

Communication style differences may exist between professionals and families, and differences are noted between American Indians and others. Typically, professionals who are not American Indians ask many different questions and view eye contact as a sign of listening and respect. In contrast, some American Indian people are brought up to show respect for people of knowledge and authority by not asking direct questions and by not making eye contact. Also, within many American Indian cultures it is appropriate in certain situations to communicate an issue with a third person who assists in giving the information to the intended recipient. Sensitivity to differences in language and communication style will enable the interventionist to establish more supportive and effective exchanges with family members.

FAMILY PERSPECTIVES

Many individuals and institutions frequently touch the life of an American Indian family with a child with special needs. For some families, the contact may seem sensitive and caring, whereas for others the contact may seem insensitive and uncaring.

Sometimes the American Indian family and the interventionist will work together to help the child reach his or her potential. When this occurs, everyone benefits from the collaborative process. At other times, each may work at cross-purposes and thereby fail to bring about the expected results.

In American Indian communities, as in other communities, various formal and informal systems are involved in serving and protecting the well-being of community members. Families generally know how to gain access to or integrate these systems for their own well-being. Unfortunately, because of the growing complexity of U.S. health and human services systems, American Indian families may feel an overwhelming sense of powerlessness and hopelessness when trying to acquire services. These families require and need an interventionist not just to work with their child but also to provide advocacy and encouragement to help them navigate the various systems.

Many American Indian families distrust public agencies because of a history of negative experiences, including racism, discrimination, and/or cultural insensitivity. Many may have experienced the degrading and dehumanizing rituals of public agencies when they go to apply for, or to receive, public assistance. The workers in these institutions may treat them as if they were unworthy of the agency's time and money. Furthermore, American Indian families may not seek help for fear they will be refused and/or feel intimidated by the time-consuming procedures, documentation, and scheduling of appointments that may require them to visit four or more agencies for a single problem. It is critical that interventionists help coordinate and advocate for a more integrated and comprehensive community-based approach to working with families.

RECOMMENDATIONS FOR INTERVENTIONISTS

The following recommendations provide some general guidelines for interventionists working with American Indian families. These considerations are of particular value to interventionists from non–American Indian cultures.

RECOMMENDATIONS REGARDING INCLUSION OF FAMILY MEMBERS

- *Ask parents whom they want to include in meetings (e.g., individualized family service plan meetings, individualized education program meetings).* Do not assume that all American Indian parents want to include extended family members or that those family members will want to attend all the meetings. Explain to the parents that all family and fictive kin whom they choose to include are welcome. Some families may want to include extended family in meetings. Other families will meet with the professionals, and later the family will have their own meeting to discuss the information with other family members. During home visits, family members may actively participate, whereas in other homes they may watch or listen from another room.

- *When extended family members participate in a meeting, communication should be directed to the entire group, not just to the parents, interpreter, or spokesperson for the family.* This shows respect for the entire family.

- *Always show respect for and provide emotional support to the family.* This can be practiced by listening to the family's ideas, acknowledging their concerns and feelings, and including interested family members. This approach allows the family to be an integral part of the intervention plans.

RECOMMENDATIONS FOR IMPROVING COMMUNICATION AND INTERACTIONS

- *Take time to learn about the communication style of the American Indian families in the communities in which you are providing services.* Identify a contact person who is from the community and who can advise you and answer your questions. Be sensitive to the communication interaction styles. For example, an early interventionist who describes herself as a talkative and bubbly person found that in one American Indian community, she needed to be more reserved and quiet until the families felt more comfortable with her in their homes. She allowed periods of silence to occur and made an effort to talk more slowly.

- *When first establishing contact with a family, proceed at a pace that is comfortable for the family members.* Take some time at the beginning of each visit for "small talk." Ask how they are, comment on the weather, talk about road conditions, share an appropriate personal experience (e.g., you were glad to have rain for your own garden), or find things you have in common. This time provides an opportunity for the family to get to know you as a person, and it forms a foundation for developing rapport with the family.

- *Ask each family if they want assistance in explaining complicated information (e.g., the results of an evaluation) to other family members.* Explore with the family various options for doing this, such as meeting with other family members or together identifying an interpreter with whom they are comfortable and who can explain the technical information in their native language.

- *If the family members speak English as a second language, no matter how good their English language skills are, always offer the services of an interpreter.* Most people for whom English is a second language prefer to hear new, technical, or sensitive information in both their native language and English. Even if a family is comfortable talking in English during regular intervention visits, offer the services of an interpreter when a new evaluation or intervention needs to be explained.

- *Always discuss the choice of interpreter with each family.* You may think you have a great interpreter who speaks the language and comes from the same community; however, because the family knows the interpreter, they may be concerned about confidentiality and may talk less and be uncomfortable in his or her presence. In some situations, you may need the expertise of a particular interpreter who can translate specific technical terms or information. Explain to the family the reason you want to use that interpreter and review the information later after the interpreter is gone.

- *When you need to ask a lot of questions (e.g., when collecting information on the child's history), first explain to the family that you will be asking them questions, tell them about the types of questions, and inform them as to how the information will help you to serve their child.* Tell the family that it is okay for them to ask you for clarification by asking you questions at any time they do not understand your question or do not understand why you are asking it. Let them know that it is okay if they need to discuss a question with other family members before they answer. Ask them to tell you if they want to think about a question or to discuss it with other family members before they answer.

RECOMMENDATIONS REGARDING TRADITIONAL BELIEFS AND PRACTICES

- *Do not assume an American Indian family is or is not practicing its tribal religion and/or is consulting tribal healers.* You should ask the family to tell you if there are any scheduled evaluations or other interventions that might interfere with other activities the family has planned. Let them know that you wish to be respectful of their wishes or plans.

- *Unless the family volunteers, do not ask a lot of questions about these tribal ceremonies.* If you need to notify other co-workers about healing ceremonies that have been planned, ask the family's permission and how best to explain it. Some families may consider this information confidential.

- *If a child is wearing amulets or has certain markings on his or her body, do not remove them without discussing this first with the family.* These things may have been given to the child to protect him or her from harm. If they must be removed, then explain the reason why and allow the family members to decide who should remove them. If amulets are removed, give them to the family for safekeeping.

- *Do not be embarrassed to admit that you know little or nothing about the family's culture.* Let the family know that you respect their culture and ask them to let you know if you do or say something wrong. Sincere efforts to learn the culture are appreciated in most instances.

RECOMMENDATIONS REGARDING INTERVENTION PROCEDURES

- *When doing a home visit, always ask the family if it is a good time to visit before you step in the door.* If the family says "no," do not ask why. They may be attending to some religious ceremonies. Respect their privacy, and arrange for a re-visit.

- *Explain all time lines and time limitations to families.* Tell them the reasons why and the options. Families should be informed in the event that they need to make a decision by a certain date because of potential medical complications or financial arrangements. Discuss the options and consequences of each choice.

- *Explain medical and other procedures in detail and allow the family to discuss their concerns regarding these procedures.* Some may have strong taboos about certain interventions, such as transplants, amputations, and/or transfusions. When explaining procedures that involve internal organs, ask if models, diagrams, or pictures would be helpful to the family.

- *When using visual or intervention aids such as dolls or pictures, discuss with the family any cultural beliefs related to these that might make them feel uncomfortable.*

RECOMMENDATIONS REGARDING SERVICE COORDINATION

- *Whenever possible, the family should have the option to select a service coordinator whom they know and trust to assist them in obtaining services for their child with special needs.* When changes in staff occur, allow time for transition. Because relationships with individuals are so important, families often feel uncomfortable when they are assigned a new interventionist or service coordinator with no time for transition.

- *Families should be given opportunities to talk to other parents who have children with special needs.* This suggestion should be offered more than once. Some families have stated that when they were ready, they would have liked to know that the opportunity to talk to other parents was still available (Malach, 1991).

In working with American Indian families, interventionists must use strategies that are flexible enough to include extended family members if the family so desires and are open enough to incorporate relevant beliefs and values. If interventionists are not from a family's culture, they should identify a resource person who is knowledgeable about the community culture and language.

If there is one recommendation that stands out above all others, it is that interventionists must demonstrate that they respect the family. When interventionists show respect, all other shortcomings, such as not speaking the family's native language, become secondary.

WHAT WOULD YOU DO?

A physician refers American Indian parents to an early interventionist because their infant son was diagnosed with Down syndrome shortly after birth. The baby was born 3 weeks early and is now 2 months old.

The early interventionist who works in the community goes to the home and introduces herself. The family says that they know about her and are interested in getting help from her, but right now they need to do traditional "things" [curing ceremonies] to help their son. They tell the interventionist that they will contact her when their son is approximately 1 year old.

The early interventionist is concerned because as a professional she knows how important intervention can be during that first year. She has worked in the community long enough to respect the family's traditional cultural beliefs and practices, however. She feels torn because her professional values support her urge to find a way to get the family to start intervention sooner, yet her knowledge of the family's cultural beliefs support her inclination to wait until the family says they are ready.

If the early interventionist came to you for advice, what might you say?

REFERENCES

American Indians by the numbers from Census 2000 (2002). Retrieved December 3, 2002, from http://www.factmonster.com/spot/aihmcensus1.html

Axtell, J. (1981). *The European and the Indian: Essays in the ethnohistory of colonial North America.* New York: Oxford University Press.

Barlett, D.L., & Steele, J.B. (2002, December 16). Wheel of misfortune. *Time, 160*(25), 44–48.

Berkhofer, R.F., Jr. (1965). *Salvation and the savage: An analysis of Protestant mission and American Indian response, 1787–1862.* Lexington: University of Kentucky Press.

Berkhofer, R.F., Jr. (1979). *The white man's Indian: Images of the American Indians from Columbus to the present.* New York: Vintage Books.

Bopp, J., Bopp, M., Brown, L. & Lane, P. (1984). *The sacred tree.* Lethbridge, Alberta, Canada: Four Worlds Development Press.

Coles, R. (1977). *Children of crisis: Eskimos, Chicanos, Indians* (Vol. IV). Boston: Little Brown.

Dobyns, H.R. (1988). Indians in the colonial Spanish borderlands. In F. Hoxie (Ed.), *Indians in American history* (pp. 67–93). Arlington Heights, IL: Harlan Davidson.

Driver, H.E. (1961). *Indians of North America.* Chicago: University of Chicago Press.

DuBray, W.H. (1985). American Indian values: Critical factor in casework. *Social Casework, 66*(1), 30–37.

Felciano, R. (1990, Nov./Dec.). Bridging both worlds. *Children's Advocate, 18*(5). (Available from Action Alliance for Children, Oakland, CA, 510-444-7136).

Good Track, J.G. (1973). Native American noninterference. *Social Work, 18,* 30–34.

Ho, M.K. (1987). *Family therapy with ethnic minorities.* Beverly Hills: Sage Publications.

Hoffman, F. (Ed.). (1981). *The American Indian family: Strengths and stresses.* Isleta, NM: American Indian Social Research and Development Association.

Hoxie, F. (Ed.). (1988). *Indians in American history.* Arlington Heights, IL: Harlan Davidson.

Indian Health Service. (1996). *Trends in Indian health.* Washington, DC: U.S. Department of Health and Human Services.

Indian Health Service. (1998–1999). *Trends in Indian health.* Washington, DC: U.S. Department of Health and Human Services.

Jennings, F. (1975). *The invasion of America: Indians, colonialism, and the cant of conquest.* Chapel Hill: University of North Carolina Press.

Joe, J.R., & Miller, D.L. (1987). *American Indian cultural perspectives on disability.* Tucson: University of Arizona, Native American Research and Training Center.

Johnson, D. (1991). *1990 Census: National and state population counts for American Indians, Eskimos, and Aleuts.* Washington, DC: U.S. Department of Commerce, U.S. Bureau of the Census.

Kaiser Family Foundation. (1996). *The implications of changes in the health care environment for Native American health care.* Menlo Park, CA: Author.

Kluckhohn, F.R., & Strodtbeck. F.L. (1961). *Variation in value orientation.* Evanston, IL: Row Peterson.

Lewis, R.G., & Ho, M.K. (1975, September). Social work with Native Americans. *Social Work, 20*(5), 379–382.

Malach, R.S. (1991). *Case examples.* Unpublished manuscript. Bernalillo, NM: Southwest Communication Resources.

Malach, R.S., Segel, N., & Thomas, R. (1989). *Overcoming obstacles and improving outcomes: Early intervention service for Indian children with special needs.* Bernalillo, NM: Southwest Communication Resources.

Miller, D.L. (1979). *Mother's perception of Indian child development.* Unpublished Research report. San Francisco: Institute for Scientific Analysis.

Morey, S.M., & Gilliam, O.L. (1974). *Respect for life: Traditional upbringing of American Indian children.* Garden City, NJ: Waldorf Press.

Navajo Division of Education. (1985). *Navajo nation: Educational policies.* Window Rock, AZ: The Navajo Division of Education.

Neihardt, J.G. (1961). *Black Elk speaks.* Lincoln: University of Nebraska.

Northern Ute Tribal Business Council. (1985). Ute language policy. *Cultural Survival Quarterly, 9*(2), 1–3.

Northwest Indian Child Welfare Institute. (1987). *Cross-cultural skills in Indian child welfare: A guide for the non-Indian.* Portland, OR: Author.

Olson, J.S., & Wilson, R. (1984). *Native Americans in the twentieth century.* Chicago: University of Illinois Press.

Peckham, H., & Gibson, C. (Eds.). (1969). *Attitudes of colonial powers toward the American Indian.* Salt Lake City: University of Utah Press.

Reyhner, J. (1986). *Teaching the Indian child: A bilingual/multicultural approach.* Billings: Eastern Montana College.

Thornton, R. (1987). *American Indian holo-caust and survival: A population history since 1492*. Norman: University of Oklahoma Press.

Titiev, M. (1972). *The Hopi Indians of Old Oraibi: Change and continuity*. Ann Arbor: University of Michigan Press.

Twetten, D. (2000). Public Law 280 and the Indian gaming regulatory act: Could two wrongs ever be made into a right? *Journal of Criminal Law & Criminology, 90,* 1317–1353.

U.S. Bureau of the Census. (2001). *Census 2000 redistricting data: Summary file for states.* Washington, DC: U.S. Department of Commerce.

Washburn, W. (1975). *The Indian in America.* New York: Harper & Row.

Zintz, M. (1963). *Education across cultures.* Dubuque, IA: William C. Brown.

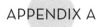

CONTRASTING BELIEFS, VALUES, AND PRACTICES

American Indian	Mainstream culture
Group life is primary	Individual is primary
Respects elders, experts, and those with spiritual powers	Respects youth, success, and high social status
Time and place viewed as being permanent, settled	Time and place always negotiable; plans for change
Introverted—avoids ridicule or criticism of others if possible	Extroverted—seeks analysis and criticism of situations
Pragmatic; accepts "what is"	Reformer; changes or "fixes" problems
Emphasizes responsibility for family and personal sphere	Emphasizes authority and responsibility for wide area of social life
Observes how others behave; emphasis is on how others behave, not on what they say	Eager to relate to others; emphasis on how others feel or think
Incorporates supportive nonfamily or other helpers into family network	Keeps networks of family, friends, acquaintances separate
Seeks harmony	Seeks progress

APPENDIX B

CULTURAL COURTESIES AND CUSTOMS

As previously mentioned, cultural diversity influences the variation of interaction customs. The following examples highlight some of the variation and the differing courtesies and customs interventionists may encounter among some American Indian groups.

- *Complimenting a family on their baby is acceptable, but it is deemed inappropriate by some families to give a lot of compliments and thereby draw attention to the child.* The child's family may believe that this behavior will bring harm to the child.

- *Cradle boards or swings are used by many American Indian families.* It is important to discuss with the family their wishes with respect to removing a child from the cradle board or other child-tending device for intervention activities.

- *Certain animals, dolls, and so forth may be considered bad luck or evil in certain American Indian tribes.* When the intervention therapy for a child requires toys or pictures, you should consult with the family to see if the toys or images selected are appropriate. For example, one American Indian family came from the reservation to keep a medical appointment, but when the interventionist suggested they eat lunch at the "Owl Café," the family became very upset. In this family's culture, owls are considered a sign of a bad omen or evil force.

- *Sometimes when a child is in the process of, or has completed, a healing ceremony, there may be markings or objects (considered sacred) placed on the child's body to protect and/or ensure healing.* If it is necessary to remove any of these objects, you should do this in consultation with the family. The family should be given the option to remove the objects, and when objects are removed, they should be returned to the family. In addition, if it is necessary to wash or cleanse an area on the child for certain procedures, and if the child has these sacred markings, the family again should be consulted and their wishes respected.

- *Because of distance and socioeconomic hardship, many American Indian families living in remote rural areas do not have telephones, so some of the home visits made by service providers may not be expected.* In these situations, it is customary to drive up and honk the horn to announce yourself. In the event that you were not expected, it is also customary that you wait until someone comes out to inquire about the purpose of the visit and with whom the visit is to be made.

- *It is always respectful to ask if it is convenient to visit and not assume that because an appointment was made for the home visit that the timing was good.* Sometimes no one may come to the door even though it appears that someone is home. This usually means the family is either busy or is not ready to receive a visitor. Ceremonial activities may be taking place, and it would be inappropriate for the family to leave the house or be interrupted.

- *During home visits, especially the first one, ask the family where they would like you to sit.* Do not assume a certain location is best. The family will feel more comfortable if you ask them.

- *It is not uncommon during home visits to have family members or other relatives coming and going; they may be participating in the discussion.* If confidential matters need to be discussed, it may be better to ask the family to come to the agency.

- *When conducting a home visit or carrying out therapeutic activities in the home, it is customary to address all those who are present.*

- *Often during home visits you may be offered food or coffee.* If you have just eaten, you may explain this and ask if you can take a little bit of the food with you or if you can have water instead of coffee. To refuse without explanation is considered rude.

- *Although it is not expected, it is also permissible to reciprocate and bring cookies or a small treat for the child or children if you wish to do so.*

- *As discussed elsewhere in this chapter, some families may follow the traditional tribal child-rearing practices, and therefore, grandparents, not parents, may have the primary parental role.* Other family members may serve as disciplinarians. In some homes, children with special needs may not be disciplined because it is believed that they have suffered so much already. These issues need to be discussed with the family so that the roles of the family and the interventionist are clear.

- *Rapport with a family sometimes happens immediately, but if it does not, it is important to be patient and to continue to be available and follow through on plans made with the family.* Once trust has developed, in most instances the service provider often becomes included in the family network.

SIGNIFICANT CULTURAL EVENTS/HOLIDAYS/PRACTICES

Great variation exists from tribe to tribe with respect to cultural events, particularly those related to child rearing, health, and healing practices. Within some tribes, a number of ceremonies can take place only at certain times. The ceremonial cycles may follow the seasons or be determined by the family's resources. In some ceremonial activities, the family must pay for the ceremony with money and gifts, whereas other ceremonies may require only gifts. In some instances, elders may schedule certain ceremonies with little prior notice. For example, a family may not know until the day of the ceremony that their child has been scheduled for the ceremony.

Because of the diversity among families and the continuum of acculturation within tribal groups and families, the interventionist should learn about the customs of his or her clients. If a tribe has a ceremony that prohibits interaction with outsiders for a week or two, it would be inappropriate for a service provider to schedule a home visit during this time. Such isolation, however, is not usually called for in most of the ceremonies, but it is important to ask prior to any home visit if a visit is convenient for the family.

Some cultural events that are common to many tribes include ceremonies related to the birth of a child, the celebration of the child's first smile or laugh, puberty, marriage, blessing of new homes, death, and/or the end of a mourning period. In addition to these more common ceremonies, healing ceremonies may take place during times of misfortune or illness; these also may occur prior to a significant intervention, such as surgery. Children with disabilities may undergo a number of healing ceremonies depending on the diagnosis and cultural orientation of the family.

Although most of these ceremonies are tribe specific, most American Indian families today also celebrate the national holidays, such as Christmas and Easter, and depending on the religious affiliation, religious holidays such as certain saints' days may be observed with tribal dancing or ceremonies. In some communities, the Fourth of July celebration may consist of a rodeo, traditional tribal dances, and carnival rides.

Within some American Indian communities, other events may not be culturally related but are nevertheless customary and may influence intervention activities. These may include hunting season, harvesting or planting, and "check day." The latter is usually when the public assistance check arrives, it is payday at work, and/or it is per capita distribution day. These days are usually busy for most American Indian families who live in rural communities because it may be the only time they go to town to shop or do a variety of other things, such as have the car fixed, do the laundry, take the children to the dentist, keep doctors' appointments, and so forth.

CHAPTER 6

FAMILIES WITH AFRICAN AMERICAN ROOTS

Winnie O. Willis

We are called to love ourselves—to love one another.
—EMILIE M. TOWNES (1998)

In order to survive, the ample soul needs refreshments
and reminders daily of its right to be and to be
wherever it finds itself.
—MAYA ANGELOU (1993)

If you're not alive and kicking, shame on you!
—LANGSTON HUGHES (1979)

African Americans and the richness of their culture have been a part of the United States since its founding. Although much of their history is only now being told, African Americans have contributed to every aspect of the country's development. Of all of the diverse groups that make up the United States, African Americans are unique in their history of immigration. Although some Africans entered the United States as free men and women, most were brought here against their will and were sold into slavery on colonial plantations. The long path to freedom and equality in the United States shaped the lives of the original African Americans and their descendants just as their cultural heritage and accomplishments have helped to shape the nation. This chapter highlights aspects of history, contemporary life, and the values and beliefs that are important for interventionists to know as they serve African American families.

BACKGROUND

The group of people referred to as African Americans originated from the continent of Africa. They come from several racial stocks and many Central and West African tribes, including Ashantis, Bantu, Efiks, Hausas, Ibos, Krus, Mandingo, Senegalese, and Yorubas (Bennett, 1966; Holloway & Vass, 1993).

Historical Origins

The following overview of African American history does not provide a myriad of detail about many of the historic events and the people who are important in African American history. Enough is included, however, for the reader to identify historical trends and events that have shaped the lives and the culture of all Americans, particularly African Americans. With a history of migration to this country unlike that of any other racial or ethnic group and through years of slavery and denial of basic "inalienable" rights, African Americans continue to survive, adapt, and even prosper within a cultural identity that has been shaped by Africa, the Caribbean, and America.

The 17th Century   By far, the majority of African American people spring from ancestors who came to America against their will as slaves. The transporting of slaves across the Atlantic from the West African coast is described as the "greatest migration in recorded history" (Bennett, 1966, p. 30). Of the millions of Africans forcibly removed from their homeland between the 15th and 19th centuries, it is estimated that 10 million came to the New World, including South and Central America, the West Indies, and North America (Curtain, 1969). Although the number of slaves brought to the Americas is debated (Stewart, 1996), the 4 million who came to North America are the genesis of today's African Americans.

By the beginning of the 18th century, 50,000–100,000 Africans each year were being moved across the Atlantic to Europe and the Americas. In fact, European and American economies were totally intertwined with and dependent on the slave trade. Although it appeared that the plantation system in America was the economic sector most heavily dependent on slavery, the mercantile system based in New England also could not have existed without slavery. African labor kept the rum, sugar, and molasses trade going; supported the industries that developed around tobacco, hemp, fishing, railroading, and distilling; and supplied the artisans (Genovese, 1974).

It is an important part of African American history to note, however, that some Africans who came to America were not slaves. The first recorded landing of Africans on American soil took place in 1619 (Stewart, 1996). Prominent historian Lerone Bennett stated that the first Africans' arrival in Jamestown, Virginia, occurred "one year before the Mayflower, 113 years before the birth of George Washington, and 244 years before the signing of the Emancipation Proclamation" (1966, p. 29). These Africans came to sell their services for a specified number of years as indentured servants, which also was common practice for whites who were looking for a new life. In the subsequent years, a small number of free men and women from the West Indies and Africa also immigrated to America.

The 18th and 19th Centuries   Whether slave or free, Africans were as integral a part of the building of pre– and post–Revolutionary America as the whites—and if bloodshed and sweat are weighed into the equation, some would say they were more so. Africans' contributions to trade, industry, and agriculture were significant and immeasurable; they distinguished themselves in the major wars of their new land as well. They fought side by side with whites in the American Revolution and the Civil War—in the hope that changes that took place would afford them the status proclaimed in the Declaration of Independence of being "created equal" with "certain inalienable rights."

Crispus Attucks, a former slave, was the first man to die during the Boston Massacre in 1770, the event that crystallized the colonies' commitment to severance from the British Empire. African American soldiers from all of the original 13 states fought bravely in most of the major battles of the Revolutionary War, and, as a result, approximately 100,000 slaves did receive their freedom (Bennett, 1966). Even this freedom was not easily won, however. It took an act of the Virginia legislature to ensure that slaves who enlisted and fought as substitutes for a free person would not be re-enslaved (Stewart, 1996).

During the Civil War, African Americans were originally barred from military service by the Lincoln administration; however, they finally were recruited and recognized, if not warmly accepted, when it became apparent that the confederacy would be a formidable opponent for the Union army. In spite of the Army Appropriation Bill passed by Congress in June 1864 requiring that African American soldiers receive pay, uniforms, and equipment equal to that of other soldiers, African Americans continued to be paid at a lower rate (Stewart, 1996). By the end of 1863, the year in which the Emancipation Proclamation was signed, some 50,000 African American soldiers were in the Union army. It was during that summer that they demonstrated the strength of their commitment to the cause and the skill and bravery with which they were willing to carry it out. African American men gained honor in fighting for freedom during the battles of Port Hudson, Milliken's Bend, and Fort Wagner. These battles were the first time white men saw skill and bravery in African American men, rather than the "kowtowing" of slavery (Bennett, 1966).

Neither the dreams inspired by the American Revolution nor the hopes built on the Emancipation Proclamation and the uniting of the states were to be easily realized. To most whites, blacks were tolerable as slaves, but as free people they were viewed as a threat to the way of life. What to do with them became the conundrum of the day: Too many African Americans were walking around free, some thought, and no plans for getting rid of them had been proposed. Years of racial hatred ensued, which saw the advent of contradictory social forces: on the positive side were the Reconstruction Era and the Freedmen's Bureau, while organizations such as the Ku Klux Klan continued to spread racial disharmony. The Reconstruction Era spanned from 1867 to 1877, during which time the South Carolina House of Representatives had an African American majority; and many postmasters, police officers, judges, and bishops were African American. The Freedmen's Bureau lasted from 1865 to 1870, during which time it gave aid and assistance to freed men and poor whites in the areas of medical care and education. The Ku Klux Klan, organized in 1866 as a white supremacy group devoted to committing atrocities against African Americans, and to whom the institutionalization of the practice of lynching can be credited, has continued to the present day. The Black Codes (1865–1866)—restrictive congressional regulations prohibiting African Americans' rights such as voting privileges, marriage with whites, and employment options—were harbingers of many years of systematic disenfranchisement of African Americans. In 1896, the U.S. Supreme Court wrote the doctrine of racial separation and classification into law (*Plessy v. Ferguson*, 1896). It gave states the sanction and the power to establish "separate but equal" accommodations and institutions for the races. Segregation had officially begun, and the spark ignited the kindling of the post–Civil War and Reconstruction Era racial discontent, which spread profusely across the nation.

Beginning in the 1890s and continuing through World War II, many African Americans migrated from the South to the North in search of greater opportunities; however, their migrations coincided with considerable crowding in northern and eastern cities occasioned by the influx of European immigrants (Leigh & Green, 1982). Although charity organizations with mostly affluent, white volunteers provided services to the newly arrived European immigrants, African Americans were viewed as "a group apart—a caste—physically present in American society but culturally distinctive because of appearance, origins, and the experience with slavery" (Leigh & Green, 1982, p. 95). Therefore, except for the settlement house movement of the 1880s, little was done to assist African Americans to obtain education, housing, and employment. As a result of the prejudice encountered in the North, many African Americans lived in burgeoning urban ghettos in slum conditions. The impact of prejudice, poverty, and urban ghettos continues to affect many African Americans disproportionately to the present day.

The 20th Century   By 1901, a body of legislation similar to the Black Codes that came to be known as the Jim Crow laws (legally enforced and sanctioned discrimination against African Americans) was in place. These laws came to form the fabric of how the races would relate to one another; it was clear that their relationships would be based on skin color and myths of white genetic superiority over African Americans. States expended considerable time and energy in implementing these Jim Crow laws that separated the races in schools, housing, jobs, public facilities, and services. The prohibition of *miscegenation*—the mingling of the races sexually—was seen by many as the real motivation behind the Jim Crow laws (Bennett, 1966). The culmination of Jim Crow, however, was seen in the systematic and extreme measures taken by states to deprive African Americans of the right to vote, which had been their right since the Emancipation Proclamation. "Grandfather" clauses, literacy tests, "white" primaries, and poll taxes were the most commonly used methods of disqualifying African American voters while maintaining sufficient loopholes for whites. From the turn of the century until the early 1940s, white Americans went about the business of pursuing the American Dream—getting an education, participating in meaningful work, marrying, and raising a family. With few exceptions, whether any dream at all was present in the African American community was of concern to African Americans only; because of the stranglehold of Jim Crow, African Americans could not partake of the vast resources and opportunities of that period.

Two major historical events became the catalysts for change. During World War II, after considerable pressure from organized African American groups, the military was officially desegregated. And, in 1954, the Supreme Court struck its most significant blow to the ignominious Jim Crow practices with the *Brown v. Board of Education* decision. The decision concluded that "separate but equal" had no place in the American system of education and stated that separate educational facilities were inherently unequal (Bremner, 1974). The legacy of the incredible wall of Jim Crow—the pervasive, deep-seated, and warped attitudes of whites toward African Americans—was not to be removed by a decree of the Supreme Court, however. Negative attitudes, instilled by years of institutionalized racism, fear, and contempt, are still evident. As the new millennium continues, reported events provide numerous examples of hatred and violence planned and executed for no other reason than racial hatred. They have evoked the surprise and consternation of those who witness them as well as those who are caught up in them. The resurgence of activity and membership in racist organizations such as the Ku Klux Klan and neo-Nazi groups, defamation of churches, and dramatic disparities in access and economics between African Americans and white Americans underscore the continued existence of racial and ethnic prejudice and hatred (Bullard, 1991; Southern Poverty Law Center, 2002; Tidwell, 1994).

African American heroes have existed throughout all of these years of adversity, however, and these individuals have distinguished themselves in politics, medicine, the arts, religion, education, and in the development of a social/community order. They have stoked the pride, the will to survive, and the determination to gain equal opportunity for their people during some of the darkest hours. African Americans from W.E.B. Dubois to Mary McLeod Bethune, Marcus Garvey to Gwendolyn Brooks, Duke Ellington to Kathleen Battle, Zora Neale Hurston to James Baldwin, Thurgood Marshall to Autherine Lucey, and Martin Luther King, Jr. to Maya Angelou have served as examples for the African American community as well as the world.

African American leadership organizations influenced the lives of these and other individuals, whose subsequent contributions to the viability of the organizations are undeniable. The National Association for the Advancement of Colored People (NAACP) was founded in 1909, and the Urban League was founded in 1910. The National Council of Negro Women began in 1935, the Congress of Racial Equality (CORE) in 1943, the United Negro College Fund (UNCF) in 1944, and the Southern Christian Leadership Conference (SCLC) in 1957. During the 1960s, new groups such as Operation Push and the Student NonViolent Coordinating Committee (SNCC) attained prominence as activist organizations.

Martin Luther King, Jr., after several years of involvement in the civil rights struggles of the late 1950s and the early 1960s, became the central charismatic leader around whom the committed activists of all races united. The civil rights workers who held the sit-ins, freedom rides, and voter registration drives and ordinary people of conscience coalesced as a dynamic, nonviolent force that could not be ignored. The efforts of years of action by people at the grass roots level came together under the banner of the movement for civil rights and racial equality. A spirit of readiness was in the air, and the galvanizing leadership of Martin Luther King, Jr. provided the necessary focus and cohesion.

Who, of a certain age, cannot remember the excitement, the hope, and the call to action engendered by the historic March on Washington in 1963? Because everyone was "there" by way of television, this event had a far wider impact than would have otherwise been possible. This nationwide visibility, as well as the televising of the civil unrest, peace demonstrations, and the violence attendant to the attempts of African Americans to gain admission to formerly segregated institutions, provided a large segment of the American population with a firsthand look at the pervasiveness of the problems of race relations in a society in which many people thought the problems no longer existed (Branch, 1988).

The Civil Rights Act of 1964 (PL 88-352), the Economic Opportunity Act of 1964 (PL 88-452), and the Voting Rights Act of 1965 (PL 89-110), as well as other landmark legislation affecting the quality of life for African Americans, were passed during the transition years between the Kennedy and Johnson administrations. During this time, there was a transition toward re-codifying the rights of poor people and people of color. These pieces of federal legislation gave the government the power to intervene in cases of discrimination within the individual states, without which school desegregation and other discrimination and criminal cases affecting African Americans could not have been settled.

Since the passage of civil rights legislation, African Americans have had more opportunities and greater influence (Smith, 1997). For example, in 1970 there were only 1,479 African American elected officials. By 1993 that number had grown to 7,984 (Horner, 1995). Education and opportunity have resulted in the emergence of a strong African American middle class. By 2000, 16.5% of African Americans older than 25 years of age had completed college compared with 26.1% of the white population and 43.9% of Asian/Pacific Islanders (U.S. Census Bureau, 2001). In 1999, 14.0% of African American households had annual incomes of $50,000 or more compared with 19.1% of white households. These gains have not been equally distributed, however. At the same time that the middle class was beginning to prosper, the lives of many African Americans were worsening (Smith, 1995). A study conducted by the *Wall Street Journal* examining reports filed with the Equal Employment Opportunity Commission found that during the recent recession, "African Americans were the only group to suffer a net job loss" (Jacob, 1994, p. 2). The same study found that African Americans were laid off at a rate of two to three times their proportion of the work force in some companies. Likewise, the income gap between African Americans and white Americans is still large; the average household income of African Americans in 1992 was $25,409 compared with $40,780 for white Americans (Horner, 1995). Since 1992, the gap has widened. In the *Money Income in the United States Report: 1999*, issued by the U.S. Census Bureau (2000), the median income of white non-Latinos was $44,366. For African Americans it was $27,910. These families then, are confronted with daily circumstances that contradict the intended effects of that legislation of the 1960s that has not reversed the effects of 350 years of inequality and racism, although they provided powerful legal incentives. We now know that several complementary strategies such as teaching tolerance, attacking intentional and institutional racism, and advocacy for social justice are needed.

Religious Origins

Early African religion was centered on the concept of a supreme God who created the Earth; this Creator had a life force that was present in all things. The worship of ancestors and the spirits of nature existed simultaneously. Ancestors were venerated and deified at their deaths, and it was believed that the ancestral spirit remained with the family as protector. The earliest ancestors were seen as having the greatest influence and power and, therefore, were most devoutly worshipped. The eldest family member conducted rituals of ancestor worship because that person had the closest connection to the ancestors. Religion and family were thus inextricably woven.

This link was best observed in the elaborate funerals provided to family members, in which the family was obligated to pay special attention to ritual in order to show respect for the spirit of the deceased. The worship of spirits of nature, such as the land, trees, and terrestrial bodies also was common. Ceremonies often included sacred objects made of wood, rock, or other minerals and ancestral bones. Sometimes worshipers sacrificed animals and prisoners to appease the gods. Ceremonies also included the drinking of specially prepared beer, wine, and other libations (Bennett, 1966; Franklin, 1967).

The influence of Islam and Christianity on the early African tribes has been greatly exaggerated, according to Franklin (1967). Neither religion ever supplanted tribal religious practices, although they clashed in a struggle for the souls of Africa. Islam offered opportunities for cultural and economic advancement. Christianity contained major contradictions for many Africans who questioned why the religion preached brotherhood and equality and yet did not condemn the brutality of the slave trade.

In the New Land, slaves were not allowed to practice their religion openly because religion, by its very nature, is collective, and any collective activity not supervised by the slave owner was thought to be seditious. Some slave owners did permit their slaves to hear the gospel as long as the central message was that which preached obedience of the servant to the master (e.g., Ephesians 6:5) (Bennett, 1966). Of course, slaves did, in secret, practice the religion they brought from Africa, and they sang openly. They sang the songs of hope, of joy, and of tears. Songs were a means of communicating with God and with one another in a collective experience, and a source of individual comfort. These spirituals, in their purity and intensity, continue to be the foundation of African American worship and a dynamic part of African Americans' proud heritage.

In 1787, Richard Allen and Absalom Jones established the first organized church for African Americans in Philadelphia after the Revolutionary War. It was called the Free African Society and out of it came the African Methodist Episcopal (AME) Church. At about the same time, the African Methodist Episcopal Zion (AMEZ) Church was established in New York City. Worth noting is that the establishment of these churches occurred approximately 75 years before the Emancipation Proclamation. During the early years of the entrenchment of Jim Crow, around the beginning of the 20th century, a surge occurred in the quality of the group life of African Americans because the church had become a vital and dynamic institution. The AME, AMEZ, and Baptist churches had increasing memberships and thereby increased financial bases and power. The churches were the places in which most African Americans saw and participated in leadership and organizational experiences (Bennett, 1966; Billingsley, 1974). According to Chambers,

> Since its inception, the black church has been more than a place to worship. It is where the community has gathered to lobby for freedom and equal rights, where African-Americans have joined together to celebrate their victories and mourn their losses . . . it is a symbol of hundreds of years of hopes and dreams. A living testament to the indomitable spirit of its people, the black church is not only a part of African-American history, it is a part of our collective American history. (1997, p. 42)

Language/Linguistic Origins

Many different languages were spoken in Africa, but there were commonalities. Although most were not written, Egyptian, Ethiopian, Berber, and a language of the Vai people in Liberia had written forms before white people ever came to the continent. It is believed that Swahili, the pan-African language, has been in written form since the 12th century (Maquet, 1972). Although new slaves were required to take on new names and to learn Pidgin English, many scholars have found evidence of the survival of "Africanisms" in the language of the United States, especially in the South. For example, the word *goober* is used for *peanut, gumbo* for *okra, tote* for *carry,* and *yam* for *sweet potato*. Many other African contributions to American English are a part of daily vocabulary, including *jazz* from the Bantu word *jaja,* meaning "to dance"; *jiffy,* from the Bantu word *tshipi* meaning "in just a moment"; *ruckus* from the Bantu word *lukashi,* meaning "applause, loud cheering, and shouts"; and some believe *okay* originates from the Mandingo *o-ke-len,* meaning "that be done" (Vass, as cited in Holloway & Vass, 1993).

The everyday spoken language used by many urban African Americans and known and spoken selectively by most African Americans is variously referred to as Ebonics, Black English, African American Vernacular English (AAVE), or African American Language (AAL) (Center for Applied Linguistics, 2000; Frieden, 1997; Pyle, 1997). Ebonics (a term coined in the 1970s combining the words *ebony* and *phonics*) is a language that many believe has its roots in the languages of Western and Central Africa (Pyle, 1997). The connection between AAL and African languages has been studied since the 1930s, and detailed analyses have been made of words and patterns of speech found in African languages that occur in the language of many African Americans (Holloway & Vass, 1993). Ebonics differs from mainstream American English (MAE) in its syntax, including the way verbs are used, the formation of plurals, and level of ambiguity or *double entendre*. According to LeMoine (personal communication, February 1995), Ebonics evolved during the period of slavery when slaves were prohibited from speaking their native languages. Because they were forced to use English rather than their African language, slaves developed a language that used an English lexicon built on the syntax (grammatical rules) of the Niger-Congo languages of Africa. As a result, in Ebonics, English vocabulary is used but the structure of the language differs from MAE. The persistence of Ebonics for more than 400 years can be attributed to the factors that help to preserve and maintain any language: the symbolic function it serves of uniting its speakers (Hannerz, 1969; Kochman, 1972; Labov, 1972; Mancini, 1980) and the bond that the language creates among its own members that is not shared by others (Tiedt & Tiedt, 1990).

Although political and educational issues surrounding the language used by many African Americans have surfaced over the years, the 1996 decision of the Oakland, California, School Board to recognize Ebonics as a separate language and request funding to teach African American students English as a Second Language (ESL) stirred national controversy. The goal of their decision is consistent with good educational practice—meet students respectfully where they are and give them the tools to succeed personally and academically. This goal is urgent in the case of many urban African American students whose standardized test scores and academic skills are considerably lower than their white classmates (Pyle, 1997; Smith, 1995). The decision was politicized and misrepresented, however, to suggest that teachers would speak Ebonics and students would be taught Ebonics. In fact, in programs such as those in the Oakland Unified School District and a few schools in Los Angeles, Ebonics is not spoken or taught by teachers but is recognized as a language, and children are not criticized for using their home language. Instead, it is used as a basis for beginning instruction in MAE (Pyle, 1997), and children learn to *code switch;* that is, they move back and forth between AAL and MAE depending on the situation.

CONTEMPORARY LIFE

Lerone Bennett described any person who came out of Africa as a "courageous individual" who was used to hard work and a well-organized social life (1966, p. 24). African history and values are so deeply rooted that many customs and traditions still exist today. With these influences and a history of struggle on American soil, African Americans have kept their faith; their sense of family, community, and country; and an abiding commitment to achievement, despite the disproportionate burden of health and social problems that exist in some segments of the African American community.

It is important to note that in contemporary America, black people are quite diverse in their values, lifestyles, and cultural preferences. The black community is a blending of people from different backgrounds and experiences because they are largely from three distinct ethnic groups: those born in America, those born in the Caribbean, and those born in Africa. Although the immigration of foreign-born blacks (3%) has an important impact on the community, it is only a small part of the explanation of diversity among blacks because there also are distinct social classes (Davis, 1993; Hill & Billingsley, 1993; McAdoo, 1997). World War II marked the beginning of increasing diversity along economic and educational lines among American-born blacks. This discussion focuses on American-born blacks who share a common history, identity, and culture (Landrine & Klonoff, 1996; Logan 2001). It presents several core African American characteristics and values. It does not address the varied or independent values that may be held by some members of the community. In addition, data on contemporary social, economic, and health disparities are provided.

Most African American families are doing well and thriving, with increasing numbers completing their education, entering the work force, and building strong, adaptive, and regenerative family units. The common bond is family and kinships (Billingsley, 1968; Logan, 2001). Most African Americans are ordinary people who are making it from day to day without fanfare (Gwaltney, 1980). Despite some gains, however, a disproportionate number of African Americans live in poverty or near poverty. Their circumstances highlight the need for national, state, and local policy changes, which would sustain a quality of life for all. The data also support the need for African Americans to work collectively to implement principles and concepts of enlightened self-development as proposed by Martin and Martin (1985; discussed in greater detail later in the chapter). The environments in which poor and low-income African American families live and raise their children are ones in which day-to-day survival is a struggle. Protecting themselves and their children from violence, locating affordable housing, trying to stay well, having access to medical care, providing food, and paying the rent are basic necessities that cannot be taken for granted.

African Americans comprised 12.3% (34.7 million) of the population of the United States (281 million) in 2000. Twenty-six percent of African Americans are younger than 18 years of age, and 7.8% are 65 years of age and older. African American populations are highly concentrated in the South (54.8%): More than 25% of each of the metropolitan areas of Atlanta, Baltimore, Washington, D.C., and Detroit are African American. Twenty-two percent of African Americans have attended some college; 14% percent have completed 4 or more years of college as compared with 29% of whites (U.S. Bureaus of the Census, 2000). The high school completion rate of 89% for blacks compared with 93% for whites and 62% for Hispanics may be undermined with the increase in standardized testing in most states. Student reading and math scores are used for "high stakes" decisions about student progress. Though gaps in math and reading scores have narrowed between blacks and whites overall, whites attained higher reading scores than blacks in 1999. Math score differences have spread at the critical transition grades of 8 and 12 (Children's Defense Fund, 2001).

Though unemployment for all groups had declined in 2000, blacks were twice as likely as whites to be unemployed (U.S. Bureau of the Census, 2000). This finding draws attention to the persisting black–white employment gap. According to the National Urban League (1995), the official unemployment rate for blacks tends to mask "hidden" unemployment. By their methodology, the official count underrepresented the magnitude of the problem by a factor of 1.75. Similar analysis of the 2000 data has not been published. The corporate mismanagement and the associated economic downturn characteristic of the early part of the 21st century have led to job losses for a large segment of the general population. This has stimulated new research and inquiry into the social and psychological sequalae of unemployment. Whether the results of this new research will lead to benefits for the long-term unemployed and especially for unemployed blacks remains to be seen. The percentage of African American males in the professional-managerial occupational groups was 17.7% in 2000, whereas the percentage of African American women in professional-managerial positions was 32%. This large gender difference favoring women is probably explained by the significant high school dropout rate among black male youths.

In terms of salaries, The Children's Defense Fund (2001) reported that in 2000, the weekly wage earned by African American men ($503) is one third less than that earned by white men ($669). In 1999, the median income for African American males was $17,675, which was 80% of the median income for whites and also less than the Hispanic median income. This is a decline of 17% since 1992. Of African American families with children younger than 18 years, 32.2% had incomes below 100% of the poverty level, which is 2.5 times more than the percentage of white families (13%) and slightly more than the percentage of Hispanic families (28.2%) living below 100% of the poverty level (U.S. Bureau of the Census, 2000). This may reflect that fewer blacks hold higher paying jobs, as well as possible wage inequity. A positive trend in economic events is seen in the increase in minority and women-owned businesses. The 1997 Economic Growth Survey found a 30% growth rate for these businesses as compared with a 7% growth rate for all U.S. firms. Of black-owned businesses, women owned a larger percentage than men. Black-owned businesses tended to be in the services and retail and trade sectors.

In 2000, the average life expectancy overall had increased. For African American men, it was 68.2 years as compared with 65.5 years in 1994; for women, it was 74.9 years as compared with 74 years in 1994. This is the highest life expectancy ever for both black men and women and continues a long-term upward trend for men. Similar to previous years, cancer, heart disease, and complications of diabetes and hypertension are the leading causes of death and illness for African Americans after age 25. African Americans are 34% more likely to die of cancer, 2 times more likely to die of diabetes, and have 42% (males) and 65% (females) higher age-adjusted death rates for heart disease than their white counterparts. Hypertension and stroke also contribute disproportionately to African American mortality and morbidity (Martin, Hamilton, Ventura, Menacker, & Park, 2002; Minino, Arias, Kochanek, Murphy, & Smith, 2002; U.S. Department of Health and Human Services, 2002). Although these health statistics are staggering, several new programs are targeted toward ethnically focused community-based or community-led interventions. Community-led interventions hold the greatest promise because they will more likely provide solutions that are appropriate for the community's human and environmental resources. Community-based interventions place strong emphasis on primary prevention, risk factor detection and treatment, and early identification and treatment (USDHHS, 2002).

U.S. Bureau of the Census figures for 1999 showed that 33% of African American children live in poverty compared with 13% of white children. This rate for African American children has declined significantly over a 6-year period. Although people are working more in general, the incomes of families below the poverty line declined by 4% since 1997 (Children's Defense Fund, 2001). In addition, 47.9% of African Americans live in a home in which the father is absent, and greater than half of these households are poor (U.S. Bureau of the Census, 2000).

The hard-earned social, economic, medical, and other forms of progress for African Americans that began in the 1950s and 1960s are not trends that can be taken for granted. Indeed, it is threatened daily. Resistance to affirmative action, to programs targeted for the poor, and to increased government spending is growing. Nationally, people seem impatient and resentful that the effects of centuries of segregation and discrimination did not disappear quietly and cheaply in a decade or two (Edelman, as cited in McAdoo, 1997, p. 326).

African Americans compose the majority of the population (53%) in large inner-city areas of the United States where crime, poor housing, unemployment, and lack of access to services are widespread (U.S. Bureau of the Census, 2000). Although lifestyles have improved for significant numbers of blacks that migrated north to these urban areas, the urban conditions that result from institutionalized racism in housing, job opportunities, and education are still prevalent. The high jobless rate among inner-city residents and the concentration of many African Americans in lower paying, dead-end jobs contributes to the inner-city social and environmental morass. In these areas, family instability and crime are pervasive (Darity & Myers, with Carson & Sabol, 1994; Henderson, 1994). Darity and Myers stated that young black men are becoming marginalized, that is, becoming "less and less useful for the functioning of the economy [with the] consequence . . . that the ability of the black community to reproduce healthy and productive members is hampered" (1994, p. 144).

These various risk factors pose a deadly threat to young African Americans. Whereas homicide is the second leading cause of death for young people between 15 and 24 years of age, it is the leading cause of death for blacks in this age group. (Motor vehicle death and injury also take a serious toll on this age group.)

Black males are 6–7 times more likely to be homicide victims than are white males. Death by homicide among black males 15–34 years of age was 84.9 per 100,000, compared with a rate of 13.0 per 100,000 for all people ages 15–34. The increase in homicide is associated with the explosion in drug trafficking. An associated tragedy is when one black youth is convicted and incarcerated for killing another black youth, creating a loss of two black males per incident for many homicides. Data from 2001 on the prevalence of incarceration points out another alarming and escalating experience for black families. Black males were more than twice as likely (16.6%) than Hispanic males (7.7%), and six times more likely than white males (2.6%) to be in prison.

African American infant mortality in 1999 was 14.6 per 1,000 births versus 5.8 per 1,000 white births, a ratio of 2.5:1. In spite of these continuing differences between races, black infant mortality has declined 55% since 1970 (Hoyer, Freedman, Strobino, & Guyer, 2001; U.S. Department of Health & Human Services, 2002). The 1999 low birth weight (LBW) rate for African Americans was 13.1% as compared with 6.6% for white infants, a ratio of nearly 2:1. The LBW rate for black infants shows no significant change, but for white infants the figure represents a 14% increase.

HIV and AIDS have increased among heterosexuals, and consequently, these conditions have increased in children as well. African American children accounted for more than 3 times the number of reported AIDS cases between 1981 and 2000 than did white children and 2.5 times the number reported for Hispanic children. New cases of pediatric AIDS have declined 76% during this period, however, primarily due to Zidovudine (ZDV) treatment during pregnancy (U.S. Department of Health and Human Services, 2002).

Death from nutritional deficiency in infancy is more than 10 times as likely for black infants as it is for white infants. Sudden infant death syndrome (SIDS) is twice as likely among black infants. Among children younger than age 6, one in eight has an elevated blood lead level (McAdoo & McAdoo, 1985).

These statistics show the particular vulnerability of African American individuals, which begins at infancy. Therefore, relevant interventions at that stage of family development could bring about life changes that would affect health throughout the life cycle. Moreover, these statistics have implications for service providers because they call attention to the heavy burden of "dis-ease" as well as actual diseases experienced by African Americans.

Even in families who have access to more resources, constant confrontation with discrimination often results in feelings of anger, distrust, and cynicism. These feelings may be expressed as a loss of empowerment or through destructiveness toward self, family, and/or community. Distrust of systems that have traditionally been at best irrelevant and at worst nonresponsive will influence the dynamics of contacts with service providers. These feelings may be demonstrated, as well, by failure to engage with care systems, such as not keeping appointments and not complying with prescribed regimens (Willis, 1999).

To be effective, intervention services must reflect an understanding of the family's ecological context and needs as a unit, not just the needs of the "client" individual (Allen & Majidi-Ahi, 1989). The most effective interventions will be developed around the strengths that African American families have and use routinely to take care of themselves, such as role flexibility, child-centeredness, extended family networks, and bicultural socialization (Hill & Billingsley, 1993; Logan, 2001). McAdoo (1997) identified additional African American family strengths on which interventions can be based. These are the family roles that legitimize being African American, provide a family code, give elasticity of boundaries, provide information, and mediate concrete situations.

Focusing on and linking care plans to these strengths will support the family's own mechanisms of fulfilling their obligation to meet their child's needs. Service providers need to recognize the difference between cultural/ethnic patterns and symptoms attributable to societal conditions, such as poverty and lack of environmental safety. Interventionists need to work within their service systems to ensure that discrimination is not occurring systematically rather than assuming that the family is pathological (Allen & Majidi-Ahi, 1989).

When the interventionists received the referral for Tanya, they were overwhelmed by the problems that they thought her family would present. The referral information included the following: Tanya was born at 36 weeks' gestation with myelomeningocele (i.e., a malformation of the spinal cord, usually in the lower back). She has had several surgeries to repair the opening but has not had to have a shunt implanted. At this point in her life (8 months adjusted age), she has spent more time in the hospital than at home; however, she is now medically stable and beginning to grow and gain weight. Her mother, Shareen, is 17 years old, single, and a high school dropout. She became involved in illegal drug use when she was 16 and continued to use drugs until she was admitted to a treatment program that would accept a pregnant teenager. Shareen is unemployed, unskilled, and does not have her own housing. Tanya's father was a street acquaintance of Shareen's; he has since disappeared.

The referral records for Tanya and her mother painted a very bleak picture; like many agency records, they described the weaknesses rather than the strengths and focused on dysfunction rather than resilience. The records did not include certain information about Shareen. Shareen was a bright student who had been doing well in high school until her father died unexpectedly of a heart attack. After his death, she became severely depressed and began to experiment with drugs. When she discovered that she was pregnant, she sought help from her mother, an aunt, and a school counselor with whom she had a strong relationship. During the drug treatment program, she began to study for the general equivalency diploma (GED) examination to complete high school, and she will be able to take the exam in 2 months. In anticipation of having her GED, Shareen has begun to explore community college options that would allow her to work and begin a degree program. She also is attracted to the local community college because there is cooperative child care on campus that would accept Tanya. The program also would give her a chance to learn more about parenting and child development. Currently, Shareen and Tanya are living with her mother and aunt, who are supportive and nurturing. Their home is comfortable, safe, and surrounded by family and friends who are available if needed. In addition to studying, caring for Tanya, and helping at home, Shareen works 20 hours per week in a local social service agency as a clerical assistant. Despite her medical problems, Tanya has become a happy, engaging baby; her prognosis is very good.

Clinical records often do not tell the whole story. This may be especially true when families of color are referred for services. This case example illustrates the differences between records and reality and how important it is to avoid stereotyping individuals and families.

VALUES

The deficit/deviance model that has been used against black families for too long is being replaced by awareness that African American families live their unique culture in a traditional manner. This way of being has historical roots that enable them to carry out their responsibilities to one another and to society in a way that has meaning for them. To have real value, assessments must be done in the context of the family system (Davis, 1993; Hill, 1993; McAdoo, 1997; Logan, 2001). Crawley discussed the importance of including an African-centered perspective among the choices available to families in the human services system and the fact that Eurocentric models have traditionally been unsuitable because they routinely see that which is fundamental to African American life and values as pathological (cited in Logan, 2001). She listed the seven foundation values of African-centered interventions: 1) *Umoja* (unity), 2) *Kujichagulia* (self-determination), 3) *Ujima* (collective work and responsibility), 4) *Ujamma* (cooperative economics), 5) *Nia* (purpose), 6) *Kuumbe* (creativity, fun), and 7) *Imani* (spirituality, faith). Self-help is a critical theme. These are the same principles that form the core of the Kwanzaa celebration.

Family

My family, my folks, my kin, and *my people* are terms used by African Americans to identify their blood relatives and to denote relationships with special friends or "cared for" individuals who are not related. Thus, family is a group of people who feel that they belong to each other, although they may or may not live in the same house (Billingsley, 1974). Values related to family are rooted in African traditions. Billingsley (1968) described the importance of marriage in West African society as a way to link lineages and villages. The family and kin relationships that resulted were governed by complex rules that guided interactions and ensured that physical necessities and support were available to all (Leigh & Green, 1982). Although slavery disrupted the traditions and family relationships that Africans had grown up with, it did not eliminate the value of kinship. In fact, kinship bonds became a major means of support for slaves. Because both men and women had to work on the plantations and tend to their own plots to supplement the food provided by their owners, young children were often cared for by older women or older children; often, the biological parents had little time with or direct involvement in the children's upbringing. Within the rigid constraints of plantation life, however, men established close, affectionate bonds with their wives and children and asserted their domestic authority to the extent possible. Women nurtured and socialized their children and took care of their husbands. Despite the facts that formal marriage among slaves was not recognized and family members were routinely separated from one another through sale to another plantation, family bonds and kinship ties remained strong (Leigh & Green, 1982). The stereotype that African American families were disorganized by slavery and that such disorganization persists is not supported by historical fact (Leigh & Green, 1982; Logan, 2001).

The fact that African American family members may or may not live together is of fundamental importance to service providers because it means that a demographic status such as "female, single head of household" does not, in many instances, credit the existence of this individual in a kinship group of people who care about each other and feel that they belong together. Although times have changed and African American lifestyles are undergoing tremendous evolution, the extended family is still viable for many. Extended family members, including distant relatives as well as social families, provide social and/or financial support (Hill, 1993; Taylor, 1994). Billingsley (1968) actually described 27 different combinations of family structure and composition for African Americans.

The family is the source and the reflection of the African American culture. The culture of a people is the way in which the individuals live their lives and the way they express their beings. African Americans value communication, both verbal and musical. Kochman, as cited by Genovese (1974), suggested that prestige associated with African American speech behavior relates to patterns of speaking that have been used successfully to manipulate and control situations—an art and a skill with high value in environments in which one has few other options. Genovese pointed out that "even today in the black urban ghettos verbal ability contributes at least as much as physical strength to individual prestige" (p. 432). In the African American culture, verbal communication includes making particular use of phraseology and rhythmic cadence of expression; it is reaching out, keeping the "lines open," and showing interest in what the other person thinks and feels.

Music is an integral part of African American life. It is experienced either interactively by attending to the words, singing, dancing, tapping, or bobbing to the rhythm; or it may be experienced passively as a part of the environment, like sunlight or wind, or as a part of life, like a heartbeat. However the individual prefers to experience music, it is a vital and living aspect of African American culture. Historically, music has been one of the active expressions of the struggle for equality, the expression of survival, the hope for future generations, religious fervor, and passion for life. This is illustrated by an excerpt from the Negro National Anthem written by James Weldon Johnson and regularly sung at the opening of important gatherings:

> Lift every voice and sing til earth and heaven ring
> Ring with the harmonies of liberty
> Let our rejoicing rise high as the listening skies
> Let it resound loud as the rolling sea.

For most African Americans, their national anthem is as necessary as the burning of sage at the beginning of significant meetings for some American Indians. It "prepares the hearts" for communication.

Because of the relatively continuous presence of words or music among African Americans, some people would characterize them as loud or shallow. Such pejorative terms reflect perceptions stemming from a different set of cultural values as well as a lack of understanding of African American values. The lessons are that both value systems have legitimacy and that recognizing differences opens the door to a better understanding among groups or between service providers and families.

African American families have been forced to keep their culture alive because information about the culture was either not available or was distorted in school or in the larger society (Billingsley, 1974). The American history that is taught in U.S.

schools has typically neglected the contributions of African Americans to the building of America. In addition, the African American influence on the manner in which all Americans live and work has typically been neglected. African American history and culture are increasingly being included in school curricula, a practice that extends what children learn in the family and community.

The family also has been the source of strength, resilience, and survival. The value of group effort for the common interest is taught as a more enduring strategy for the survival of the African American community than individual effort for private gain (Billingsley, 1974). Private gain is well respected, but there is an expectation among many African Americans that it will be shared in reasonable measure with the larger community. Martin and Martin (1985) presented African American self-development practices as an outgrowth of the extended family. These practices include

- Helping tradition, or the cross-generational struggle to survive and advance

- Extended family or obligation to a network of kin

- Mutual aid or the effort to pool resources for common benefit

- Social class (i.e., status group) cooperation toward the effort to downplay status differences in giving and receiving assistance

- Male–female equality or a de-emphasis on dominance of either sex

- Prosocial behavior or practices that promote cooperation, sharing, and caring

- Fictive kinship or caregiving and assistance among unrelated people

- Racial consciousness or keen awareness of history and the need to improve the social and political status of the group

- Religious consciousness or acts of charity and a way of life that reflects a closeness with God

These values exist as reinforcement for legitimizing the historical utility of the extended family as a means for self-development.

An important part of the message about survival that is instilled within the context of the family is the value of independence—the ability to stand on one's own feet, to have one's "own thing." This at first may seem to be in conflict with the group effort ethic, but it actually extends this ethic: the empowerment that comes when as many as are able can earn a living, meet their family's basic needs, and have a little bit left over to help others in the extended family. As the extended family circles widen and overlap, the entire community would theoretically be covered. In addition to contributions, it is common practice within African American families to make small loans with token or no interest to one another on a short-term basis. The ability "to get it from each other" is highly valued because underlying the exchange of funds is the strength that comes from self-reliance and the demonstration of trust among family members (Billingsley, 1992; McAdoo, 1997).

Moreover, the family provides socialization, guidance, and inspiration (Billingsley, 1974; Landrine & Klonoff, 1996). The primary socialization task of the African American family is instilling in its members a sense of who they are. This includes knowledge of the African heritage, the history of the American experience, and how the two sources have blended to produce the contemporary African American. According to Billingsley (1974), each is complex and varied but highly interrelated. The process is all about pride and the development of competent individuals. Billingsley further stated that the process of socialization enables the individual to develop an African American consciousness, which is an awareness of a common history, common heritage, and common predicament. The instilling of consciousness of self as a black person in a white-dominant culture is an important part of each child's socialization.

In general, whites have trouble relating to this because they have never experienced discrimination on the basis of the color of their skin. Many whites feel that African Americans are overly sensitive, imagining slights and offenses and tending to see racism where none exists. Many African Americans have tried to explain to whites in general, as well as to white friends and colleagues, that there is validity in this monitoring of racism. It is an adaptation and survival strategy. What can be called racism-barrier education is started early in the African American family's socialization process (McAdoo, 1997). A cornerstone in this process of racism-barrier education has to do with teaching the individual not to waste valuable energy on knee-jerk responses to "minor" incidents because there are more than enough seriously threatening ones to deal with. Although studies and polls show a decline in prejudice toward blacks (Pinckney, 1984; Smith & Sheatsley, 1984), there is strong public opposition to implementing social policies and structures to eliminate discrimination on the basis of race (Schuman, Steeh, & Bobo, 1985; Smith & Sheatsley, 1984). Prejudice and discrimination are the two components of racism. The institutional prejudice of the superiority of one group over other racial and ethnic groups supports the institutionalized differential treatment or negative treatment of certain groups in legislation, policies, and informal practices (Hill & Billingsley, 1993).

Most African Americans, even those who have acquired advanced education and attained a certain economic status, find it difficult to believe that others can see beyond their most salient characteristic—the color of their skin. Moreover, subordination of blacks is institutionalized in American society by the practice of racial stratification or ranking of groups in a hierarchy on the basis of racial/ethnic background. Even the continuing use of the word "minorities" for African Americans and other people of color communicates a negative connotation of a status of "less than." For these reasons, it is vital that interventionists understand that racism-barrier education is a fundamental building block in the socialization of African American children. McAdoo (1997) stated that this information assists the individual to anticipate, interpret, and manage complex experiences outside the home. Racism heads the list of experiences that undermine healthy growth and development in the United States. Children of parents who taught them about being African American and also about appropriate "racial coping" strategies had a greater sense of self-worth (Wilson, 1995).

Respect for Elders

Although changes in African American families, like changes in all families in the United States, have diluted the importance of older adults, many African American families continue to place a high value on respecting and obeying these individuals (Randall-David, 1989). Older adults are seen to have wisdom and hindsight. They have seen things "come around" and "go around," and they have witnessed a lot of what the younger generation calls history. In the South, titles of respect, such as

"Ma'am" or "Sir," are still widely used. Just as in the early African religions, the oldest family members also are believed to have a special status and an ability to communicate with God; therefore, they are routinely in charge of prayers. In addition to honoring the special status of older adults, there is a high value placed on obedience to parents as well as other older adults, including an older sibling. The learning of obedience and respect for older adults is the child's earliest contribution to family maintenance and cohesiveness.

Education and Schooling

The attainment of one's potential through the acquisition of education, life skills, and personal competence is a major goal and desired achievement among African Americans. The family nourishes and supports individual ability through a strong belief in education as the means to a better life. The promise of education is and has been a beacon for many African American families, and individuals who have attained high educational goals come not just from the so-called better, stronger families but also from families with a variety of statuses and fortunes. With regard to educational attainment, the difference between ordinary and extraordinary people is often opportunity—something that has not been consistently available to African Americans (Billingsley, 1974). Families often tell their children that times and situations may change, but a good education is something no one can take away. Education enables the individual to weather changing times.

African American churches have traditionally supported education as a valued pursuit, as evidenced by the large number of church-founded and church-sponsored colleges and universities. One example is Livingstone College, founded in 1879 in Salisbury, North Carolina. Most church-funded and church-sponsored black colleges are located in the South, are relatively small, and have a predominantly black student body.

In a classroom situation, particularly in the primary grades, African American students are likely to be less assertive than other students. They may be quieter or shyer than expected. They may be reluctant to raise their hands, may need more encouragement to take a chance to speak and give input, and may need more assistance toward independence in learning. Children's reluctance to speak up is generated by the fear of being judged negatively for a "wrong" response by their peers as well as by the teacher. African American children also are socialized to be "good" (i.e., to behave) and, consequently, run the risk of becoming nonparticipants or, worse yet, of becoming invisible. Either scenario leads to missed educational opportunities. The charter school movement has had an impact on the education of some African American children. Approximately 40 states and Puerto Rico have charter school laws (Children's Defense Fund, 2001). More than 500,000 students are enrolled in 2,000 charter schools (1% of total school enrollment). Charter schools receive a contract for funding from the state or local school board after they have documented their commitment to specified goals, objectives, procedures, governance, standards, and assessments. They have greater latitude to carry out their own plans for curriculum, calendar, schedule, budgeting, and hiring, however. They were created to enact an "alternative vision" of education. Nationwide, a higher proportion of black students are enrolled in charter schools. Sufficient data are not yet available to assess the effect of charter schools, but they will continue to be important in the debate on education reform (Children's Defense Fund, 2001).

Humor

In describing plantation life, Genovese said

> The songs, often made up on the spot, bristled with sharp wit, both malicious and gentle . . . but the songs also turned to satire . . . they [the slaves] turned their wit and incredible talent for improvisation into social criticism. (1974, pp. 317–318)

For many African Americans, humor continues to be a way of keeping the spirits up and a way of interpreting the reality of their world—the world "according to us." For example, Ralph Wiley wrote in his book *Why Black People Tend to Shout,* "Black people are too smart not to shout, especially when happiness comes in for a short visit before it has to go on down the road," adding, "Black people shout because they want the answers to questions that go unasked. Like, who knocked the nose and lips off the Sphinx?" (1991, pp. ii, 40).

The gift of people who are humorous may not always be in the raucous hilarity of the situation itself but as much in the act of telling the story or delivering the line. The world "according to us" is a good title for humor that African Americans use to reinterpret or find new meaning in situations acted out in the larger society. For example, they might strip the "fancy language" from a political speech and replace it with "plain talk" and say "here's what he really means" from the African American perspective. Ordinary conversations are often embellished with liberal sprinklings of metaphors and descriptors, whereas more gifted storytellers use body language and motion to illustrate or to emphasize points.

Service providers need to keep in mind that this kind of humor provides a healthy release of feelings and concerns. It does not mean that the humorist is making light of the situation or that he or she does not see its seriousness. In fact, satire and social criticism are extremely serious and sophisticated forms of humor that allow everyone involved to manipulate and interpret life events so that they are less threatening.

Religion

African Americans typically see religion as a confirmation of identity, of being God's children (Billingsley, 1974). African Americans may belong to one of several differ-ent organized religions, but more important than the particular denomination is the place of religion in the life of the family and the community. Religion has tradition-ally been the source of spiritual sustenance in the African American family, regard-less of whether the family regularly attends church (Randall-David, 1989). Most Af-rican Americans believe that it is important to sanctify life events such as marriages, births, and deaths in the church because it validates their meaning in the family and the community. Although organized churches are not as influential as they were in the past, the spiritual resources of the community have had a direct impact on the lives of most African American people (Billingsley, 1974). Children are taught at a young age that they must "believe in something" (i.e., have faith, spirituality) in order to have a good (i.e., meaningful) life.

Richardson (1994) reported that 78% of African Americans are "churched" as compared with 68% of other Americans. According to a Gallup survey conducted in 1984 and discussed by Hill (1993), 8 of 10 blacks are Protestants (with 55% Baptists and 13% Methodists), and only a small percentage (6%) are Catholic.

From its inception, the African American church has been the place in which community members learn the values and responsibilities of leadership and organi-zational skills; in the past, these experiences have not been available to African Americans in the larger society. The church is a complex organization that carries the responsibility for producing a weekly worship service, with all its component parts (e.g., choir, ushers, biblical and spiritual education). It also carries the responsibility for outreach; missionary programs; and community-based activities, such as visiting parishioners who are sick, providing food for those who are poor, and conducting educational and recreational programs. The older adults mentor young and inexpe-rienced people. Church also is where many children and young adults identify role models. The church also stresses the values of showing humaneness and sympathy for others and offering a helping hand when needed, among others. Many churches with black congregations provide a wide range of social and health services to their communities (not just to their members) to support family strengths and promote childhood and youth development. Model church programs assist young, black men and women to care for foster children, build housing, and lead community develop-ment efforts (Hill, 1993).

The Nation of Islam (black Muslims) is a religion as well as a social movement organization (Muhammad, as cited in Marsh, 1996). It started in the 1930s in De-troit. The prophet of the religion is Elijah Muhammad; the sacred texts used are the Islamic Qur'an (Koran) and the Christian Bible; the place of worship is the mosque. Muslims call their god Allah. Elijah Muhammad, the founder or prophet of the Na-tion of Islam, created an economic blueprint to stimulate self-help through collective business ownership. Members must adhere to a code of ethics, morality, and disci-pline. In 1952, Malcolm X joined the Nation, and in 1959, he became its national spokesperson. After the deaths of Malcolm X and Elijah Muhammad, Minister Louis Farrakhan became the most prominent leader. The legacy of the Nation of Islam to the African American community is most visible in their self-help philosophy and program. By way of their advocacy for economic independence, they have provided a model for black-owned businesses that provide jobs as well as supplies and services for the community. Through their role modeling of black pride, self-discipline, and responsibility to family and community, they help many young, disillusioned African Americans at high risk take charge of their lives (Davis, 1993; Marsh, 1996). Since September 11, 2001, the whole world has become more interested in the Muslim religion; because many native and immigrant Americans practice it, attention has been focused on whether the religion supports terrorism and therefore poses a threat to the interests of Western nations. American Muslims of all races (including blacks) have taken on the role of educating their neighbors, colleagues, and the community at large about their religious values, tenets, and beliefs.

Understanding the importance of religion, church, or spirituality to each of the African American families that they serve will allow service providers to include those values, beliefs, and networks in the provision of services. In some instances, with the family's permission, their minister or other church members may be important allies in the intervention (Randall-David, 1989). The informal support network provided through these channels may be far more valuable than referrals to a multitude of bureaucratic agencies.

BELIEFS

In spite of constant social change and an expected range of differences, a core of beliefs can still be identified for African Americans as a group. Change and circumstance may modify the actions taken as a result of these beliefs, but their utility and meaning remain the same.

Child Rearing

African Americans believe that children are the future. Children need to know that they are loved and that they belong, and they need adult protection and guidance. Children must be disciplined, and all responsible adults in the kinship circle of influence take part in the education and discipline of the child. Children must have a good education, good food, and a place to play. Once young children are able to speak and understand, they are expected to obey the family rules, to treat others as they want to be treated, and to do their schoolwork to the best of their ability. Although not all African Americans act on these beliefs because of their life circumstances, the core beliefs continue to be valued by many.

African Americans are firmly committed to developing the child's knowledge of his or her kinship and of who his or her people and family are. As the knowledge is instilled, so is a sense of curiosity and caring about family relationships. It is quite rewarding to see a child's first awareness that "Momma's sister" is "my aunt" or that Sandra is "my sister." As children place themselves within this circle of people they care about and who care about them, their experience of the meaning of family and their sense of belonging is heightened. Some African American families tend not to be especially verbal with the expression of love because they believe that actions, such as concerned care giving and attention to others' well-being, speak louder than words.

Setting limits or disciplining is part of the socialization process of the child and is seen in two ways: 1) as a means for the child to learn to be sensitive, and 2) as a way for the child to follow family rules outside of the home in order to avoid confrontation with authorities. According to Allen and Majidi-Ahi, "a final socialization issue, which exemplifies all that is distinct about the Black experience in America, is teaching children how to cope with racism" (1989, p. 157). The latter is seen as particularly critical for male children as a result of the high incidence of racially biased arrests of young African American males. In the first instance, it is believed that the building of self-respect derives from learning respect for the rights of others. This lesson starts early and at home. In fact, the permissive child-rearing practices common in many white, middle-class households in which discipline is seen as stifling creative expression would not be tolerated in most African American families (Darity & Myers, 1994).

Although less true than in the past, the African American community still maintains a belief that all responsible adults are expected to act *in loco parentis* for the children of the community. The presence of an adult has traditionally been enough to deter the young African American child from too much wrongdoing because the non-parent adult in whose presence the child is acting will usually comment on or correct the obvious problem behavior. Things have changed somewhat from the days when non–parent adults could "take a switch" to the child, but a considerable amount of behavioral observation and advice about appropriate punishment is alive and well in the African American community.

The belief in eating well, feeding one's family well, and having good food to offer one's guests is an abiding value in the African American family, although it is one that is difficult, if not impossible, for families living in poverty to maintain. Among middle-class families, the diet is generally rich in nutrients as a result of a particular preference for dark green leafy vegetables, red meat, and cheese. Potatoes, rice, and bread are staples, and a variety of fresh and dried fruits are liked and used. The primary dietary problems arise from the use of too much salt and a reliance on frying as a preferred method of cooking. Messages in the media may be modifying this behavior somewhat, but obesity, hypertension, diabetes, heart disease, and stroke—all of which are aggravated or improved by dietary practices—continue to exact significant morbidity and mortality. Children are generally switched from baby foods to some of the same foods that the rest of the family eats around 7–12 months of age. The same attitude about the importance of good and plentiful food for strength, stamina, and health prevails in the feeding of children. Mealtimes in some African American families may differ from those familiar to the service provider. Although a common mealtime is still preferred, prepared food may be "left on the stove" and available for family members to take when they are ready to eat.

Another belief about health for children has to do with the importance of play. Play is seen as important for both social (to have friends and fun) and physical (to have a strong body) well-being. In contrast with cultures that push children toward early adulthood, in African American families there is a belief that a child should be a child; and getting "grown" too soon is frowned on, especially if older family members live in the home or have influence in the family. A trend that is demanding a human services response is the increase in grandparents who must assume the care of children because the parents have lost or abdicated their right to do so. There is an increasing trend toward more families using out-of-home child care, either in family child care or center-based environments. Nearly 50% of black preschool children are in non-relative child day care arrangements. Moreover, 63% of all married women with children younger than age 6 are in the labor force. This represents a 140% increase since 1980, and a 332% increase since 1960. Part of the increase is related to the need for two salaries in the home as a result of the decline in real wages for families in the lower income brackets; part is also due to welfare reform of 1996, and part may be due to increas-

Andrew and Tamika are attorneys in Washington, D.C. Andrew is employed by a prestigious public policy organization; Tamika is a deputy prosecutor. Their one child, Jesse, is 3 years old. Jesse has visual impairments and has been involved in early intervention programs and services since his first year of life. He is active, mobile, and can see large print and pictures. Except for slight delays in gross motor functioning, Jesse is above average. His parents are eager to enroll him in a private preschool program that also provides extended child care, but the program director has said that she is concerned that the preschool environment is not safe for a child with Jesse's "handicaps."

Jesse's parents enlisted the help of the interventionists who had worked with Jesse since the early months of his life. Together, they talked with the program director at the preschool, showed her videotapes of Jesse's performance with his peers, and offered to provide follow-up consultation to her staff if it was needed. Through this parent–professional team approach, the private preschool director was convinced that Jesse could be accommodated in her program.

ing numbers of women choosing to get an education and join the workforce. Welfare reform in 1996 also created an increased need for child day care because mothers on public assistance are mandated to find jobs (Children's Defense Fund, 2001).

Medical Care

Medical and preventive health care, knowledge about treatment, and types of treatment that may be preferred vary widely within the African American community, particularly between middle- and upper-income families and families living in poverty. Most African Americans use a local private physician for basic health needs, and many are involved in work-related health plans that utilize health maintenance organizations as providers. For these families, access to health care is no different from any other mainstream U.S. family. For the large number of unemployed blacks, however, access to medical care is becoming more difficult than ever before. More than ever, health insurance (including public programs such as Medicaid) is the only key to the health care door.

Some African Americans, particularly those with strong ties to the rural south, may prefer holistic, natural approaches to health. An oral compendium of herbs, teas, roots, over-the-counter preparations, and foods that have preventive health and healing properties is available. Many families still rely on or have their own versions of mentholated petroleum jelly, castor and cod liver oil, sassafras tea, dried peaches and apricots, and "pot liquor." Some older people can discuss the variety of health uses of tallow, sulfur, and vinegar and water; and African American physicians of the "old school" may dispense advice and counsel based on knowledge of the individual and his or her family context as well as standard medical treatments. Logan (2001) presented a summary of the 1990 work of sociologist Harper. According to Harper, the care that blacks have always provided for the sick at home was never officially called "home care," "hospice care" was never attached to the care blacks provided for the dying at home, "respite care" was never used when blacks relieved each other from the rigors of caring and curing, and "volunteerism" was never applied to blacks who took care of each other in their homes and communities. These things were done because of the tradition of self-help in the black community, and because mainstream services were not available to African Americans.

High-technology medical care is viewed by some families lacking access to information as care that is used in trauma situations. This observation is based on the reality that violence and accidental death and injury are at the top of the list of leading causes of morbidity and mortality in the African American community (U.S. Department of Health and Human Services, 1985, 2000). Therefore, the experience with these events is reinforcing the perception of health care as trauma care. High-tech care also is encountered all too frequently in neonatal intensive care units because of the disproportionately high numbers of African American infants born with conditions such as low birth weight, prematurity, and the effects of risky health behaviors and lifestyles (Willis, 1999).

Although many healthy African Americans live in ways that support and stimulate good health, others, primarily living in the inner city and rural areas, lack opportunities for employment and live in poverty and for many, the societal institutions of mainstream America have not worked. For the families living in poverty, the range of health care provider options has become more limited with the complexities of third-party payers, the undermining of the safety-net providers, and the unrealized promise of Medicaid managed care. To further complicate the problem, access to care has become a maze. Likewise, the facts about the destructive nature of health problems prevalent among African Americans are not well known to these families. Publicly funded clinics and programs serve some who cannot pay or who can pay only a sliding or income-adjusted fee; however, there are significant numbers who have no health care access as a result of lack of knowledge, lack of money, lack of financial and motivational resources to receive care, or lifestyles and behaviors that prevent them from gaining access. Among these individuals, it is, however, common knowledge that a hospital emergency room can be used when one does not know of or does not have access to any other options. In fact, many poor, inner-city families use emergency rooms for all of their health care needs.

As a result of the increasing proportion of African American families who live in poverty or who are found among those who are working but poor, more families are compelled to wait for an illness to occur before seeking medical attention. Preventive health visits, including routine gynecological care for the women in the family, routine physical checkups for the entire family, and especially dental care, will not be sought. Even though visits for infants and children also may be less frequent, the family will usually ensure that children get the basics of whatever care they need. Even parents who may handle their own health in a cavalier manner by utilizing episodic care are motivated to get care for their child, although they may find the eligibility procedures drawn out, tedious, and sometimes even offensive.

The challenge to the society at large is to make the ineffective institutions work for people who are difficult to reach. The onus is on the larger society because fragmented, short-term demonstration programs are short lived and rarely become institutionalized. Although the short-term results may be promising, at the end nothing is left behind to meet the expectations raised by the quick-fix programs. The challenge to the service providers is to help make the system responsive to children and families and to work with the family by providing health education, support in seeking and using care, and assistance in maximizing the effects of treatment. An example of the previous point is a continuing practical problem related to medications. Many African Americans who lack access to information do not comply with medication regimens. They may not follow the directions for administration, may overmedicate, or may prematurely discontinue treatment when the pain is gone or when they are feeling better. Although misuse of antibiotics is a typical example, this behavior translates into all therapeutic interventions and regimens.

To counteract these problems and to encourage adherence to therapeutic programs in the home, the service provider should 1) make the initial teaching and take-home materials simple, uncluttered, and practical for home use; 2) ensure that at least two family members understand how the therapy is done; 3) ensure that the family can obtain the necessary equipment and materials; and 4) check on the progress and problems encountered by the family in order to make appropriate adjustments. These suggestions, although made in the context of working with African Americans of low socioeconomic status, are equally applicable to many families with whom service providers work.

Causation

According to Randall-David (1989), religion and beliefs about illness are intertwined among African Americans. Therefore, some African Americans may attribute the cause of illnesses to punishment for disobeying God; to the work of the devil; or, in some instances, to evil spirits. As with any diverse group of people, however, beliefs will vary from individual to individual and from family to family. Although some may take a fatalistic view of the world in terms of life and death, African Americans are typically amenable to doing things that can influence the course of their life.

Disability   Disability is often interpreted in one of two ways: 1) as bad luck or misfortune and, less so, 2) as the result of "sins of the fathers." The experience of most people with disabilities is by way of older adults. Until the 1970s, people with disabilities were not as visible in African American society as they were in the society at large. The young are taught not to stare at people with disabilities because it is rude. As has been shown in the larger society, this approach may have had the backlash of teaching individuals to "look right through" people with disabilities. This sets up a poor dynamic interaction between those with disabilities and those without. Attempts also are made to assist young children to view people with disabilities the same way as they view people without disabilities. For the most part, African Americans do not exhibit any particular prejudice toward people with disabilities. In fact, for people with mental retardation, African American families and communities were some of the first groups to incorporate these individuals into all aspects of their lives routinely.

Because many African Americans are practical people, neither of the previously mentioned attitudes about causation of disability has any real effect on how they interact with families who have a member with a disability or on how such families conduct the business of living. Initially, assigning blame or bad luck to a family member's actions may have to be acted out and assistance and counseling may need to be provided; however, this phase may be short relative to the subsequent phases that revolve around securing necessary health, medical, social, and educational services, and coping with the challenges of the person's developmental and maturational needs.

Ayisha is 18 years old and the mother of Charmaine, who is 18 months old and has Down syndrome and an accompanying heart defect. Ayisha has not yet completed high school and is due to deliver her second child in about 6 weeks. She and Charmaine live with Ayisha's parents, who are in their mid-thirties. Although they are providing support, they are not enthusiastic about having a second baby in the house and believe that Ayisha is not doing a very good job raising Charmaine or managing her own sexuality. Before the second pregnancy she also had resisted following through on appointments at the local family planning clinic to find an effective method of birth control. Ayisha says she cares a great deal about Charmaine and spends hours holding and rocking her; however, she has ignored all of the information that she has been given about Charmaine's heart condition, developmental delays, and overall prognosis.

Charmaine was referred to an early intervention program shortly after birth, and a staff member has made home visits about once a month. Ayisha frequently cancels scheduled home visits and says she "just hasn't gotten around to bringing Charmaine into the center-based program." During the home visits it is apparent that there is tension between Ayisha and her mother. It also is apparent that Ayisha has neither read the educational materials nor done any of the suggested parent intervention activities with Charmaine. Charmaine has become clingy, and Ayisha, in response, has become extremely protective. After months of feeling frustrated with Ayisha's lack of engagement in her child's therapy and encountering many of Ayisha's own developmental needs and her teenage parenthood issues, the interventionist decides to present the case in a team meeting with Ayisha as a member of the team. At the meeting a staff member described and encouraged Ayisha to consider a new pilot program that has just opened in their community for teen mothers. The program focuses on life skills development, parenting, GED preparation, and job training. Limited housing is available for teens who have unique or special family circumstances. After learning more about the program and being eager for more independence, Ayisha decides to apply to the program. The early intervention team supports her in her efforts by managing the initial stages of the interface between Ayisha and the staff of the teen program.

Timing and opportunity seem to have played a role in Ayisha's life. Although the interventionist implements the prescribed individualized family service plan, including support, information, and education, it is ultimately up to Ayisha to decide when and how she can use the assistance. Ayisha seems to see an opportunity to make a life change with the addition of a community-based, teen-focused program.

Death and Dying   African Americans' perspectives on death and dying are based on two facets: the traditional expectation and the current expectation. The traditional view of death dictated that no one "passed" except by old age, "bad" disease, or auto accidents. Homicide was relatively rare. People were familiar with the rituals of responding to the need for a funeral, for grieving, and for getting on with life. Although disease and automobile crashes meant premature death, they were not "unusual." The standard repertoire was designed to give the deceased a "good sendoff" and included the purchase of the best casket the family could afford and a funeral in the home church with stirring songs and eulogies. The mortician was usually rated on the basis of "how good" the deceased looked. If it rained on the day of the funeral, it meant that the deceased was a person of good heart and deeds. Phrases often spoken were "at peace," "no more suffering," and "God called him home." Cremation was and is still not considered.

The view of death in the black community is reflected in the statement "A child should not die before his parent." The incredible wave of homicide in recent years has severely strained the emotional resources of the urban black community. The traditional familiar repertoire does not comfort families in the way that it used to. The usual phrases spoken are inadequate for this occurrence and are being substituted with "What a waste!" "What went wrong?" and "Whose fault is it?" Even the ritual of death is being violently altered in these communities in which common celebrations and rituals are needed more than ever to hold the fabric of the community together in shared, predictable, and traditional cultural experiences. Churches and social organizations within and outside the black community recognize that this epidemic of horrifying child death has to be stopped. In spite of the portrayal of violence by African American youth in the media, there is no reason to believe that they want either to kill or to die.

When confronted with the death of the child with a disability or any member of a family, it would be appropriate for the service providers to consider what role she or he wants to play in the family's bereavement rituals. The decision probably will depend on the nature and the length of involvement with the family. Acknowledgments such as attendance at services and sending cards or flowers would all be well received by African American families. It may be best to confirm that one's attendance at the services is welcome, but generally "paying last respects" is seen as an honor to the life and family of the deceased. Service providers also have an important role in saving youth who are at risk and, as a result, need to acquire knowledge of the African American culture, youth risk behavior, model programs, and recommended practices for youth programming.

LANGUAGE ISSUES

As noted, African Americans may speak MAE and/or Ebonics or AAL. There is wide variation in the language(s) used depending on the speaker's education, region of residence in the United States, and situation. For many African Americans, the language that is used is often highly contextual, and they may choose to speak quite differently depending on the situation, the information to be communicated, and the listener. Among African Americans who have not been educated, those living in poverty, those who have remained in somewhat isolated coastal and island areas, and those who have recently immigrated to the United States from parts of the Caribbean, however, languages and dialects other than MAE are more prevalent.

Language for African Americans is another manner of identification because those who speak the same language or dialect share this. Personal identity and the attendant values underlie the thought process and shape verbal expression. Researchers in education have shown that African Americans have a preference for the aural mode of presentation in their learning (Shade, 1984); African Americans report that they learn better via the spoken word. Shade also described the importance of teaching African American children by incorporating movement and touch. She cited other researchers who have hypothesized that African Americans' distinctive

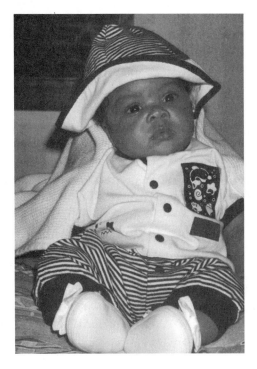body language and "kinetic" idiom have developed as a result of a preference for learning through interaction with the environment rather than learning through introspection. Pasteur and Toldson (cited in Shade, 1984) stated that the essence of African American culture is the development of somatic perception as a way of experiencing and expressing reality. A great deal of credence is given to gut feelings. Verbal as well as nonverbal communication are fine arts for African Americans because throughout their history they have had to communicate so much within the confines of a dominant "overseer." In contemporary life, an African American makes liberal use of the full body, not just facial expressions, to convey a variety of feelings. African Americans are high-context communicators who use shared experience, nonverbal cues and signals, and the situation itself as a large part of the communicative process. Interventionists need to be sensitive to this style of interaction and avoid overexplaining when they receive feedback from African American clients that is different from what they are used to.

Service providers also should look for cues that indicate a shutdown of communication or learning. These might include behaviors such as a completely bland face; the standard arms folded across the chest; totally intense, almost frantic involvement in the task being done, yet repeated inability to accomplish it (as a result of blocking out ongoing instructions and corrections that may be seen as harassing); or a range of expressions of exasperation, such as eye rolling, exhalations of air, and looking upward (as if looking toward heaven for divine intervention). Although some of these cues may be delivered reflexively, they also may be well planned to display dissatisfaction openly. Other families may be less expressive and will provide few, if any, clues to the fact that they do not find the intervention helpful, practical, or understandable. When working with African American families, service providers may want to seek advice and assistance from African American sercive providers or other team members to help them find ways in which the intervention might be modified to increase its likelihood of success.

SUMMARY

This chapter has reviewed the origins and the history of African Americans as they have influenced the values and beliefs of the mainstream American society. It has reviewed events that shaped their rich heritage on both the African and American soils—a heritage built on a strong sense of family, community, and kinship as well as a will to survive and to progress. In spite of historical obstacles and constraints, most

African American families are doing well within whatever societal milieu that they value and select. Other families are not making it, partly as a result of the inability of the major societal institutions to meet their complex needs. Whatever their level of education or attainment as viewed from the larger society, African Americans "act out their being" within a circle of kinship that reinforces their belonging, their roots, and their future.

RECOMMENDATIONS FOR INTERVENTIONISTS

- Capitalize on historical kinship bonds and mutual assistance patterns, and focus on family strengths rather than weaknesses in developing and implementing interventions. If extended family members are primary caregivers or are highly involved with the child and family, include them in the intervention.

- Use formal and informal support networks such as the church, neighbors, or friends whenever possible and acceptable to families to enhance the intervention effects or to reduce the need for formal interventions.

- Address family members formally, using titles and last names, until given permission to be more informal. This is a sign of respect.

- Determine families' attitudes and beliefs about health and medical care and work to include their preferences in appropriate intervention regimens.

- Become familiar with the resources in the African American community in your area and use those resources as partners in developing appropriate solutions.

- Adapt therapeutic interventions to the learning style and lifestyle of the family, and do periodic evaluations to determine their usefulness and progress or the need for redirection.

- Critically assess the effects of poverty on families and determine which issues are related to culture and which are related to socioeconomic status. Issues of personal discomfort, lifestyle change, insecurity, loss of personal power, self-esteem, trust, and fear must be taken into account by the service provider. To help understand this, consider the effects of significant economic or social decline in your own family by answering the following questions: How many months could your family weather unemployment without going under? What things would you have to do without if your monthly family income was cut by a third? In half? Where would you go if you had a problem with substance abuse? What would you do to protect your children from harm if they attended a school to which some of their schoolmates routinely brought a weapon?

- Recognize that poverty does not equate with dysfunction. Many impoverished families manage to provide strong, nurturing care for their children.

- Avoid stereotyping all African Americans on the basis of the behavior or lifestyles of a subset. Every racial/ethnic group has considerable variation within.

- Recognize that language is an important element of self-identity, and do not devalue a child or a family's home language. In working with children, learn some of the techniques used to teach second language learners and use those to help children add Mainstream American English to their repertoire.

- Recruit ethnically diverse staff members for your program *and include training and monitoring of cultural competence in your agency's staff development.*

WHAT WOULD YOU DO?

Robert (RJ, for Robert, Jr.) is a 7-year-old second grader who lives with his parents, his 3-year-old sister, Larissa, and his paternal grandmother. Robert, Sr., 27, is a bus driver, and Vernie, RJ's mother, age 24, is a hotel maid. His grandmother has diabetes and has lost her vision in one eye. RJ has worn glasses for about 1 year. Both parents work, so it is difficult for them to keep up with the grandmother's health needs and the care and attention that Robert and Larissa need. Larissa stays at home with her grandmother. So far things have worked out, but Vernie has just learned that she is pregnant. Vernie is concerned that RJ cannot read at grade level, and his teacher recently contacted her to report that he is easily distracted and "doesn't try." He fidgets and tries to distract other children, as well. His teacher has observed, however, that picture books will hold RJ's attention and that he loves to draw. He prints and copies well, and has even attempted to write his name in cursive. Vernie feels guilty that she doesn't really help RJ with his schoolwork, but she is often tired from her job and all of the work that she must do at home.

Using the list of Recommendations for Interventionists, how might RJ's teacher work with RJ's family to address RJ and the family's concerns and needs without alienating anyone?

REFERENCES

Allen, L., & Majidi-Ahi, S. (1989). Black American children. In J.T. Gibbs & L.N. Huang (Eds.), *Children of color* (pp. 148–178). San Francisco: Jossey-Bass.

Angelou, M. (1993). *Wouldn't take nothing for my journey now* (p. 79). New York: Random House.

Bennett, L., Jr. (1966). *Before the Mayflower.* Baltimore: Penguin Books.

Billingsley, A. (1968). *Black families in white America.* Englewood Cliffs, NJ: Prentice Hall.

Billingsley, A. (1974). *Black families in white America* (2nd ed.). Englewood Cliffs, NJ: Prentice Hall.

Billingsley, A. (1992). *Climbing Jacob's ladder.* New York: Simon & Schuster.

Branch, T. (1988). *Parting the waters—America in the King years 1954–63.* New York: Simon & Schuster.

Bremner, R.H. (1974). *Children and youth in America: A documentary history.* Cambridge, MA: Harvard University Press.

Brown v. Board of Education, 347 U.S. 483 1954).

Bullard, S. (Ed.). (1991). *The Ku Klux Klan: A history of racism and violence* (4th ed.). Montgomery, AL: The Southern Poverty Law Center.

Center for Applied Linguistics. (2002). Available on-line at http://www.cal.org

Chambers, V. (1997). Say amen, indeed. *American Way, 30*(4), 38–43, 102–105.

Children's Defense Fund. (2001). *The state of America's children yearbook 2001.* Washington, DC: Author.

Civil Rights Act of 1964, PL 88-352, 20 U.S.C. §§ 241 *et seq.*

Curtain, P.D. (1969). *Atlantic slave trade: A census.* Madison: University of Wisconsin Press.

Darity, W.A., & Myers, S.L., with Carson, E.D., & Sabol, W. (1994). *The black underclass—Critical essays on race and unwantedness.* New York: Garland Publishing.

Davis, R.A. (1993). *The black family in a changing black community.* New York: Garland Publishing.

Economic Opportunity Act of 1964, PL 88-452, 42 U.S.C. §§ 2701 *et seq.*

Franklin, J.H. (1967). *From slavery to freedom* (3rd ed.). New York: Vintage Books.

Frieden, L. (1997). *Leslie Frieden's Ebonics page* [on-line]. Retrieved from http://members.aol.com/LKFrieden/ebonics.html

Genovese, E.D. (1974). *Roll, Jordan, roll: The world slaves made.* New York: Pantheon Books.

Gwaltney, J.L. (Ed.). (1980). *Drylongso—A self-portrait of black America.* New York: Vintage Books.

Hannerz, U. (1969). *Soulside: Inquiries into ghetto culture and community.* New York: Columbia University Press.

Henderson, L.J. (1994). African Americans in the urban milieu: Conditions, trends, and development needs. In B.J. Tidwell (Ed.), *The state of Black America 1994* (pp. 11–29). New York: National Urban League.

Hill, R.B., & Billingsley, A. (1993). *Research on the African-American family—A holistic perspective.* Westport, CT: Auburn House.

Holloway, J., & Vass, W.K. (1993). *The African heritage of American English.* Bloomington: Indiana University Press.

Horner, H.L. (1995). *Black Americans: A statistical sourcebook.* Palo Alto, CA: Information Publications.

Hoyer, D.L., Freedman, M.A., Strobino, D.M., & Guyer, B. (2001). Annual summary of vital statistics 2000. *Pediatrics, 108,* 1241–1255.

Hughes, L. (1979). *Selected poems of Langston Hughes.* New York: Random House.

Jacob, J.E. (1994). Black America, 1993: An overview. In B.J. Tidwell (Ed.), *The state of Black America 1994* (pp. 1–9). New York: National Urban League.

Kochman, T.E. (1972). *Rappin' and stylin' out.* Urbana: University of Illinois Press.

Labov, W. (1972). *Language in the inner city: Studies in the Black English vernacular.* Philadelphia: The University of Pennsylvania Press.

Landrine, H., & Klonoff, E.A. (1996). *African American acculturation: Deconstructing race and reviving culture.* Thousand Oaks, CA: Sage Publications.

Leigh, J.W., & Green, J.W. (1982). The structure of the black community: The knowledge base for social services. In J.W. Green (Ed.), *Cultural awareness in the human services* (pp. 94–121). Englewood Cliffs, NJ: Prentice Hall.

Logan, S.L. (2001). *The black family: Strengths, self-help and positive change.* Boulder, CO: Westview Press.

Mancini, J.K. (1980). *Strategic styles: Coping in the inner city.* Hanover, NH: University Press of New England.

Maquet, J. (1972). *Civilizations of black Africa* (J. Rayfield, Trans.). New York: Oxford University Press.

Marsh, C.E. (1996). *From Black Muslims to Muslims—The resurrection, transformation, and change of the lost–found nation of Islam in*

America, 1930–1995 (2nd ed.). Lanham, MD: Scarecrow Press.

Martin, J.A., Hamilton, B.E., Ventura, S.J., Menacker, F., Park, M.M. (2002, February). *National vital statistics report: Deaths, final data for 2000.* Atlanta, GA: Centers for Disease Control and Prevention.

Martin, J.M., & Martin, M.P. (1985). *The helping tradition in the black family and community.* Washington, DC: National Association of Social Workers Press.

McAdoo, H.P. (1997). *Black families* (3rd ed.). Beverly Hills: Sage Publications.

McAdoo, H.P., & McAdoo, J.L. (Eds.). (1985). *Black children.* Beverly Hills: Sage Publications.

Minino, A.M., Arias, E., Kochanek, K.D., Murphy, S.L., Smith, B.L. (2002, September). *National vital statistics report: Deaths, final data for 2000.* Atlanta, GA: Centers for Disease Control and Prevention.

National Urban League. (1995). *The state of black America 1995.* New York: Author.

Pinckney, A. (1984). *The myth of black progress.* Cambridge, England: Cambridge University Press.

Plessy v. Ferguson, 163 U.S. 537 (U.S. Supreme Court, 1896).

Pyle, A. (1997, January 19). 95th Street school: Ebonics in real life. *Los Angeles Times,* pp. A1, A22.

Randall-David, E. (1989). *Strategies for working with culturally diverse communities and clients.* Washington, DC: Association for the Care of Children's Health.

Richardson, W.F. (1994). Mission to mandate: Self-development through the Black church. In B.J. Tidwell (Ed.), *The state of Black America 1994* (pp. 113–126). New York: National Urban League.

Schuman, H., Steeh, C., & Bobo, L. (1985). *Racial attitudes in America: Trends and interpretations.* Cambridge, MA: Harvard University Press.

Shade, B.J. (1984, August). *The perceptual process in teaching and learning: Cross-ethnic comparisons.* Paper presented at the annual meeting of the American Psychological Association, Toronto, Ontario, Canada.

Smith, T.M. (1995). *Findings from the condition of education 1994: The educational progress of Black students.* Washington, DC: National Center for Education Statistics, U.S. Department of Education.

Smith, T., & Sheatsley, P.B. (1984). American attitudes toward race relations. *Public Opinion Quarterly, 7,* 15–53.

Smith, V.E. (1997, March 17). The new generation gap. *Newsweek,* 52–60.

Southern Poverty Law Center. (2002, Fall). *Intelligence Report,* 107.

Stewart, J.C. (1996). *1001 things everyone should know about African American history.* New York: Doubleday.

Taylor, R. (1994). Black American families. In R. Taylor (Ed.), *Minority families in the United States: A multicultural perspective* (pp. 19–46). Englewood Cliffs, NJ: Prentice Hall.

Tidwell, B.J. (Ed.). (1994). *The state of Black America 1994.* New York: National Urban League.

Tiedt, P.L., & Tiedt, I.M. (1990). *Multicultural teaching* (3rd ed.). Needham Heights, MA: Allyn & Bacon.

Townes, E.M. (1998). *Breading the fine rain of death: African American health issues and a womanist ethic of care.* New York: Continuum.

U.S. Bureau of the Census. (2000). *Money income in the United States.* Retrieved May 7, 2001, from http://www.census.gov/hhes/www/income.html

U.S. Bureau of the Census. (2001). *Statistical abstract of the United States: 2001.* Washington, DC: Author.

U.S. Department of Health and Human Services. (1985). *Health status of minorities and low income groups* (DHHS Publication No. [HRSA] HRS-P-DV 85-1). Washington, DC: U.S. Government Printing Office.

U.S. Department of Health and Human Services. (2000). *Healthy people 2010: Understanding and improving health* (2nd ed.). Washington, DC: U.S. Government Printing Office.

U.S. Department of Health and Human Services. (2002). *Child health USA.* Washington, DC: Author.

Voting Rights Act of 1965, PL 89-110, 42 U.S.C. §§ 1973 *et seq.*

Wiley, R. (1991). *Why black people tend to shout.* New York: Carol Publishing Group.

Willis, W.O. (1999). Culturally competent nursing care during the perinatal period. *The Journal of Perinatal and Neonatal Nursing 13*(3), 4559.

Wilson, M.N. (1995). *African American family life: Its structural and ecological aspects.* San Francisco:Jossey-Bass.

CONTRASTING BELIEFS, VALUES, AND PRACTICES

African American	Mainstream culture
Collective orientation	Individual orientation
Kinship and extended family bonds	Nuclear and immediate family bonds
High-context communication	Low-context communication
Religious, spiritual orientation	More secular orientation
More authoritarian child-rearing practices	More permissive child-rearing practices
Greater respect for elderly and their role in the family	Less respect for the role of elderly in the family
More oriented to situation than time	More oriented to time than situation

APPENDIX B

CULTURAL COURTESIES AND CUSTOMS

In an African American home, it is not appropriate to

- Address the individual by his or her first name unless given permission. This is seen not as friendly, but as implying disrespect.

- Tell the family that they are "too touchy" about race.

- Make assumptions about the individual from knowledge of a particular demographic profile (e.g., single female, head of household, unwed mother). This has very little meaning in the absence of a direct professional assessment.

- Tell ethnic jokes about any group—not even your own. African Americans feel that were they not in the room, the joke would have been about them.

- Converse with co-workers about personal matters, such as husbands, vacations, boyfriends, new cars, and so forth, while providing care to African American clients. African Americans interpret this behavior as a lack of concern for them and their needs, as blatant disrespect, or that they are being put into the position of an "outsider."

- Assume that poverty equates with dysfunction.

APPENDIX C

SIGNIFICANT CULTURAL EVENTS/HOLIDAYS/PRACTICES

Kwanzaa

December 26–January 1

Started by Dr. Maulana Karenga in 1966. The purposes of the celebration are to reinforce African American identity (i.e., the bonds between African Americans and their communities), celebrate African American life and achievement, and inform society at large of the contributions of African Americans to human history. Kwanzaa emphasizes the core beliefs of Nguzo Saba (the seven principles of values): unity, faith, self-determination, cooperative economics (familyhood), collective work and responsibility, creativity, and purpose.

Martin Luther King, Jr.'s, Birthday and Human Relations Day

January 15

A national holiday celebrating Martin Luther King, Jr., and his contributions to the world community in the areas of civil rights and human rights.

VOCABULARY

Ebonics, African American Language (AAL), or African American Vernacular English (AAVE) differs from Mainstream American English (MAE) in several ways. The summary of difference presented below is based on descriptions provided by Genovese (1974), Pyle (1997), and Tiedt and Tiedt (1990).

Ebonics or AAL	MAE example	Ebonics or AAL example
The verb "be" is often used to indicate repeated or ongoing actions.	She works at the hospital.	She be working at the hospital.
The forms of the verb "to be" are often omitted.	Where are you?	Where you?
Multiple negatives are often used.	It won't do you any good.	It won't do you no good.
Consonants that occur at the end of words and suffixes tend not to be voiced.	I ate breakfast. It is finished.	I ate breakfas. It finish.
Plurals tend to be dropped or shortened.	Folks	Folk
The "d" sound is sometimes substituted for "th" in the initial position.	These Them Those	Dese Dem Dose
The "th" sound in the final or middle position in a word is often sounded as an "f," "t," or "v."	I am going with you. Lather the soap.	I go wit you [or] I go wif you. Laver the soap.
Gender is not differentiated.	He, she, and it are used to mean very specific and different things.	He, she, and it can be used to refer to the same person or thing.
Concepts and their meanings may vary.	Good = good	Bad = good

CHAPTER 7

FAMILIES WITH LATINO ROOTS

Maria E. Zuniga

No hay peor lucha que la que no se hace.
(There's no worse struggle than one that never begins.)

A todo se acostumbra el hombre, menos a no comer.
(Man can adjust to anything except not eating.)

Helping families to address the various issues they experience when coping with a family member with a disability demands knowledge and insight about the complexities of family life. When families come from culturally diverse backgrounds, the complexity is compounded. This chapter focuses on working with Latino families who have a family member with a disability. The core underpinnings of this chapter are the critical nature of individualizing for each Latino family system and carefully determining to what extent cultural themes are pertinent. The growing number of Latinos who are immigrants or who have come to this country under harsh and life-threatening conditions without legal documents is a dimension interventionists must consider in this individualization process.

BACKGROUND

The Latino population in the United States is characterized by its diversity. Latinos come from different Spanish-speaking countries, each of which has its own political history and unique immigration regulations. Particular settlement patterns and different acculturation rates also contribute to this diversity.

Geographic and Historical Origins

According to the U.S. Bureau of the Census (2001), 35.3 million people in the United States are Latino. This represents an increase of 57.6% from 22.4 million in 1990. This increase took demographers by surprise. Latinos have become the largest "minority" group in the nation, a change that has profound cultural and policy implications (Cohn & Fears, 2001). Latinos of Mexican origin compose the largest group. They increased from 13.5 million to 20.6 million (an increase of 52.6%), making up 58.4% of all Latinos in the United States. Puerto Ricans are the next largest group, increasing 24.9% between 1990 and 2000. Those of Cuban ancestry increased by 18.9% from approximately 1.0 million to 1.2 million. For those 10 million Latinos who designated themselves as "Other" on the 2000 Census forms, 1.7 million were Central American, 1.4 million were South American, and 765,000 were Dominican. Those who selected the Spanish/Hispanic/Latino box but did not provide more specific information on their grouping comprised 17.3%, or 6.1 million, of the total Hispanic group, second in size only to the Mexican origin group (U.S. Bureau of the Census, 2001).

In 2000, 43.5% of Latinos lived in the West and 32.8% lived in the South. About 14.9% lived in the Northeast and 8.9% lived in the Midwest. In the West, Latinos comprised 24.3% of the population. In the South they comprised 11.6% of the population, 9.8% in the Northeast, and 4.9% in the Midwest. Of note, half of all Latinos lived in one of two states: California and Texas. The seven states with Latino populations of 1 million or more included California, Texas, New York, Florida, Illinois, Arizona, and New Jersey. In 22 states, Latinos numbered between 100,000 and 499,000 (U.S. Bureau of the Census, 2001), yet in Colorado and New Mexico, Latinos numbered between 500,000 and 999,999. In New Mexico alone they composed 42.1% of the total state population.

An important phenomenon is the unusual and dramatic growth of the population of Latinos in states in which the Latino population has traditionally been quite small. For example, there has been dramatic emigration of Latinos to Georgia, North Carolina, Iowa, Arkansas, Minnesota, and Nebraska. In some of the counties of these states, Latinos represented between 6.0% and 24.9% of the county's total population

(U.S. Bureau of the Census, 2001). The issues of cultural competency for working with this new population will have major implications in these areas for human services, medical care, and school systems.

The population of Latinos from Central America varies: Salvadorans numbered 1.9% of the total Hispanic population. Nicaraguans made up 0.5% of Latinos. Costa Ricans numbered 0.2% of Latinos; and Hondurans were 0.6% of Latinos. Those from Guatemala were 1.1% of Latinos; with Panamanians composing 0.3% of all Latinos (U.S. Bureau of the Census, 2001).

The South American groups included 1,353,562 or 3.8% of all Latinos. The largest subgroup was from Colombia, numbering 470,684 and accounting for 1.3% of Latinos; Peruvians numbered 233,926 and accounted for 0.7% of Latinos; Ecuadorians numbered 260,559 and accounted for approximately 0.7% of Latinos. Those from the Dominican Republic located in the Caribbean numbered 764,945, or about 2.2% of Latinos.

Mexico   Mexico has a unique tie to the United States because it lost a significant mass of its territory to the United States in the Mexican War of 1848. These areas making up that mass include what are now Arizona, California, Colorado, Nevada, New Mexico, and parts of Oklahoma, Texas, Utah, and Wyoming. Mexico is one fifth the size of the United States, and shares its most extensive border with the United States as well as the largest port of entry in the world—San Ysidro, California. This port has one of the highest rates of crossings of undocumented people. Mexico has economic ties to the United States that have been the impetus for mass migrations to the United States, such as *Bracero* programs of the 1950s that recruited workers from Mexico to harvest U.S. crops. Yet, many Mexicans in the United States are not immigrants; they have lived in this country for generations in areas such as California and New Mexico, and their ancestors can be traced as far back as the 1700s.

The economic tide in Mexico has an impact on the rate of undocumented immigration. Mexico's economic woes have pushed Mexicans across its borders frequently. The devaluation of the peso in late 1994 contributed to further economic stress and increased migration. Census data estimate that about 3.5–4 million undocumented individuals reside in the United States (Fernandez & Robinson, 1994); and Mexico is believed to contribute to half of these residents. Given the increase of other Latino groups, the proportionate distribution of people of Mexican heritage has decreased from 60.4% of all Latinos in 1990 to 58.4% of all Latinos in 2000.

Puerto Rico   Puerto Ricans are the second largest Latino subgroup. The 2000 Census noted their increase to be 24.9%, from 2.7 million to 3.4 million. Although they increased in number between 1990 and 2000, given the increase in other Latino groups, their percent of the Latino population was reduced to 9.6%, down from 12.1% in 1990 (U.S. Bureau of the Census, 2001). Puerto Ricans have a political history that has resulted in them having U.S. citizen status so that their migration issues are distinct from Mexican Latinos. The U.S. invasion of Puerto Rico during the Spanish American War ended 400 years of Spanish rule. The United States retained Puerto Rico as an unincorporated territory and imposed its citizenship on Puerto Ricans (Montijo, 1985). The political issue that is coming to the fore for the Commonwealth of Puerto Rico is whether it should seek the status of a state, which could cause political polarization for many Puerto Ricans. In recent years, major political protests have been held against the use of one of their smaller islands, Vieques, as a bombing practice site by the U.S. military. This latest confrontation has contributed to further political conflicts among Puerto Ricans and between Puerto Ricans and Americans (*Orlando Sentinel*, 2001).

Puerto Ricans can migrate from the island of Puerto Rico with ease, contributing to the constant flux to and from the U.S. mainland. Many leave the island to seek economic advancement because poverty greatly affects their population. The major immigration movement began after World War II, when Puerto Ricans came to work in the industrial centers, in which there was a need for manufacturing, industrial, and service workers (Inclan, 1985). These employees settled in the eastern seaboard states: Connecticut, Massachusetts, New Jersey, and New York. By 1980, Chicago also had become a settlement area (Allen & Turner, 1988). On the West Coast, Puerto Ricans have settled primarily in San Francisco, although some are scattered in small numbers throughout Californian cities following military service on the West Coast.

The culture shock first encountered during the massive wave of immigration in the 1940s resulted in the establishment of barrios in which Puerto Rican culture and the Spanish language could be maintained. The experience of second-generation Puerto Ricans, however, was different; they were schooled in the United States, often living in urban slums and exposed to mainstream values. Yet, lack of educational and occupational opportunities, coupled with cultural insensitivity and racism, contributed to the many social problems that still plague this subgroup. In 1992, Puerto Rican families had the lowest median annual income—$20,000, compared with $24,000 for Mexican families and $31,000 for Cuban families. Puerto Ricans had the highest poverty rate among Latinos—32.5% in 1992 (Montgomery, 1994). In 1999, 22.8% of Latinos lived in poverty, compared with 7.7% of non-Latino whites. Puerto Ricans continued to have the highest poverty rates, with 25.8% living in poverty as compared with 24.1% for Latinos of Mexican origin, 17.3% for Cubans, and 16.7% for Central and South Americans (U.S. Bureau of the Census, 2001).

Cuba   The 2000 U.S. Census estimated the Cuban population to be 3.5 million (U.S. Bureau of the Census, 2001). The first wave of Cuban immigrants comprised refugees escaping the political upheaval that began in their country in 1959. Prior to this time, approximately 30,000 Cubans resided in the United States. In contrast to the Puerto Ricans, who experience a fluid migration to the United States, the Cuban subgroup is characterized by distinct waves of immigration that began with the Cuban Revolution and the reign of Fidel Castro in 1959. As Castro took over, many Cubans in the professional and upper classes fled Cuba on commercial flights; an estimated 248,070 fled the country at that time. After the Cuban Missile Crisis in 1962, another 55,916 fled in small boats, rafts, and any other available craft. Between 1965 and 1973, U.S. airlifts transported another 297,318 Cubans to the United States. In the last three stages, the largest group comprised those who came in the Mariel boatlift to Key West—about 124,789 Cubans (Szapocznik & Hernandez, 1988).

Cubans, in contrast to Puerto Ricans and Mexicans, have been recognized for their distinct economic success in the United States. The economic, social, and political know-how of the first waves of immigrants offered significant contributions to the Miami, Florida, economy and later spread to other areas such as New Jersey. A central outcome is that Miami has become a cultural and economic magnet for Latin Americans, bolstering the Latino culture in this area and offering a bicultural environment (Szapocznik & Hernandez, 1988). This does not mean that the stresses of acculturation and displacement have not had an impact on this group, however. For many first-wave Cuban immigrants, the belief that they would be able to return eventually to a free Cuba constrained some of the acculturation achievements. The most recent large immigrant wave from Cuba has been the *balseros,* who came in the summer of 1994, risking their lives in makeshift rafts. Unlike previous waves of refugees from Cuba, the *balseros* were subject to the "policy of interdiction," in which they were located in camps situated at U.S. military bases in Guantanamo or Panama (Puig, 2001; U.S. Seventh Coast Guard District, 1995). More than 34,000 refugees composed this group, with 2,833 being children younger than the age of 17 (Puig, 2001). This wave did not receive the government resettlement support granted to other waves; rather, support came from Miami's Cuban community, which orchestrated mechanisms wherein these immigrants, especially the children, could be brought to the United States at little if any cost to the taxpayers (Puig, 2001).

Similar to the other Latino cultures, Cuban culture before the revolution followed the Spanish tradition of designating the male the head of household and administrator of the family's funds. Women were expected to be obedient to their husbands. Becoming a mother enhanced a woman's status because it increased her reputation in society (Stoner, 1991).

Dominican Republic   2001 data documented the Dominican population of the United States to be approximately 765,000 (U.S. Bureau of the Census, 2001). Historically, the Dominican Republic had a small number of people emigrating to the United States until restrictions on emigration in their country were lifted after the 1961 murder of the dictator Trujillo Molina. Many have entered the United States legally; those who are undocumented have typically lost documented status because they overstayed their visa limits. The majority of undocumented Dominicans who are in the United States entered by flying in from Puerto Rico and passing as Puerto Ricans. As with many South Americans, Dominicans have typically worked as dishwashers in restaurants or as laborers, factory workers, and janitors. In New York City, approximately 40% of employed Dominican women work in the garment industry. Because of a lack of training in American ways or assimilation into American life, most of the upper- and middle-class immigrants have had to take lower status jobs than they had in their country. Many Dominicans appear to be black, which may constrain their acceptance into American society (Allen & Turner, 1988). For many Dominicans, as for those from Cuba and Puerto Rico, their racial heritage includes strong African roots, yet Spanish is the primary language.

Central America   More than 1 million Central American immigrants have arrived in the United States since 1820, with more than 90% arriving since 1981 as compared with 60% of the Mexican immigrants (*Migration News,* 1996). The 2000 Census reported 1.7 million individuals of Central American origin. There were 655,000 Salvadorans, or 1.9% of the total Hispanic population, 372,000 Guatemalans, or 1.1% of the Hispanic population, and 218,000 Hondurans, who made up 0.6% of Hispanics (U.S. Bureau of the Census, 2001). These immigrants are found dispersed in various parts of the United States. Some have settled in Florida, where usage of the Spanish language provides an important support; others have flocked to areas where relatives live or where enclaves of their compatriots have settled (e.g., New York, San Francisco, Los Angeles).

A primary reason for immigration in earlier times was the belief that there were better job and economic opportunities in the United States, which was particularly motivating to Costa Ricans and Hondurans. Before 1980, those from El Salvador settled in Los Angeles; San Francisco; and Washington, D.C. (Allen & Turner, 1988).

Since the late 1970s and early 1980s, as the wars in Central America have cost lives and freedom, legal and undocumented immigration of political refugees has steadily increased from war-torn countries such as El Salvador, Nicaragua, and Guatemala. Most Salvadorans consider themselves refugees. The Nicaraguans who fled political oppression during the Somoza and Sandinista regimes were classified as illegal immigrants because their appeals for refugee status were denied. Much disagreement occurred over who could be classified as refugees and who the (then named) U.S. Immigration and Naturalization Service viewed as illegal immigrants. This then became another major source of emotional challenge that overwhelmed these immigrants who had already suffered so much in their former country (Potocky-Tripodi, 1999).

The effects of trauma have affected large numbers of these immigrants. Many of these sojourners have been affected by the violence of the wars in their countries. Some women who traveled from Central American countries through Mexico without partners or family have told stories of months of submitting to sexual assaults and forced labor as payment to *coyotes* (i.e., illegal travel brokers who charge as much as $2,000 a person to help them cross the border) (Perez Foster, 2001). Typically, these stories of anguish are not shared with anyone, and this silence affects how the traumatized person functions in her new country. The experiences of war and conflict burden immigrants' emotional well-being, and, like the other subgroups, attending to the culture shock they encounter drains important energies.

South America   Immigration from South America occurred during the 19th and 20th centuries, with most occurring during the latter. Because of this long immigration history, there is a large number of people with Spanish ancestry who, over several generations, have become assimilated and who may feel a lack of ethnic identity (Allen & Turner, 1988). Immigration from this area increased during the 1960s, with the immigrants possessing high levels of education and income. Although South American professionals continued to emigrate during the 1970s, there also was an influx of people with less training. In addition, women experiencing frustration with the lack of professional independence they encountered in Latino society comprised many of these immigrants, outnumbering immigrant men. Many Argentinean and Chilean immigrants who were former political prisoners in their respective countries in the 1970s now live in the San Francisco and San Jose areas of California. Of the different South American groups, Colombian immigrants seemed to experience the most downward mobility as many professionals had to turn to driving taxicabs, working in factories, or working in other low-level jobs after their emigration (Allen & Turner, 1988).

Brazil   In comparison to other Latino countries, immigration from Brazil has been minimal, although Brazil contains half of the population of South America. During the 1960s, more than 2,300 immigrants were accepted; but because the Brazilian generals imposed restrictions on departure, the flow of immigrants has averaged 1,500 per year. In 1980, 17,640 Brazilians lived in the United States. There is a paucity of data on Brazil's immigrants, so it is often presumed that most people of Brazilian ancestry share characteristics with immigrants from the Spanish-speaking countries of South America. For example, until the 1970s, many of these immigrants tended to come from middle- and upper-class backgrounds. Some immigrants came initially as tourists, and many have been college students—in the 1980s, more than 2,500 individuals of Brazilian heritage resided in university centers (Allen & Turner,

1988). A major difference among immigrants from Mexico, Central and South America, and Brazil is that Brazilians speak Portuguese instead of Spanish.

An important caveat for the interventionist is to discern the country of origin of the family with whom he or she is working. For example, those from Central America who are middle or upper class often distinguish themselves from and have little in common with those who they consider low-status immigrants from Mexico or Puerto Rico (Allen & Turner, 1988).

Stages of Migration

Sluzki (1979) warned human services workers to be cognizant of the various stages of migration that Latino immigrants are experiencing because these stages may pose particular stresses and symptoms that can present problems. In illustration, these stages include the following:

1. *Preparatory stage.* How was the decision made to move? Were all members of the family involved in this process? Did they say goodbye to family and friends? Were there any rituals to mark this event, or was it characterized by emergency decisions to move without preparation—emotional or otherwise?

2. *Act of migration.* What was the process like—did it involve an atmosphere of fear, exploitation, or life endangerment? Were there tragedies wherein a family member had to be left behind; or did the migration entail robbery, rape, or other trauma?

3. *Period of overcompensation.* As recognition of the massive changes are realized, members may begin to doubt their own senses, values, and judgment. This is reinforced by incongruence between old and new realities. Families may choose to stay entrenched in their old culture with exaggeration of family rules or style.

4. *Period of decompensation.* This is a time during which conflicts, symptoms, problems, and crises arise for the family. Inverse role relations may appear when women are more able than men to find employment, contributing to reversal of traditional sex roles. This has an impact on the spousal system, in particular. Family violence may erupt during this time.

5. *Transgenerational impact.* With time, issues and conflicts arise among generations, especially as the young people become more acculturated than their older family members, especially their parents. Often, issues are related to conflicts about dating and contrasts in freedom between what the young generation sees around them and what their parents feel is appropriate given their own traditional backgrounds. Parental rules sometimes become more rigid with the immigration process.

For interventionists attending to the issues of a family member with special needs, their job is not to address these as would a family therapist. If the parents or the family are grief stricken by the birth of a child with a particular disability or lifelong illness, however, interventionists should know that this might activate buried grief related to the immigration process. For example, an unexpressed sense of loss that an immigrant Latino family may have experienced in leaving relatives behind in the country of origin may come to the fore in relation to the sorrow surrounding the birth of an infant with a disability. This compacted grief process may need to be addressed in family intervention.

In a similar vein, the increase of immigrants from countries with civil war histories could mean some of these people have been exposed to death and trauma and suffer from posttraumatic stress disorder (PTSD) (Perez Foster, 2001). Also, for those who have crossed into the United States without legal documents, the trauma of the crossing may imprint them with survivor guilt if they witness the death of family members or friends during their trek. Moreover, the increase in deaths that occur as immigrants cross treacherous mountains and deserts adds to their trauma experiences. Immigrants may be chased by border officials or be robbed or raped by border bandits. Sometimes the *coyotes* desert them without food or water in the middle of a desert or in rugged mountains. In recent years, immigrants being smuggled across the border in vehicles have been killed or seriously injured when the driver/smuggler loses control of the vehicle in a high-speed chase with police or border authorities. As Perez Foster (2001) noted, undocumented individuals have been subject to isolation, abuse, and economic exploitation. All of this has contributed to the enhancement of emotional distress. Cervantes, Snyder, and Padilla (1989) suggested that preoccupation with possible discovery and deportation for those undocumented may serve to augment symptoms of PTSD. This could complicate a family's abilities to respond effectively to caring for a family member with a disability.

The increase in deaths of these immigrant border crossers since 1995, when Operation Gatekeeper was mobilized to secure the U.S. border, has resulted in immigrants who carry the memory of traumatic experiences with them on a daily basis. In illustration, about 1,980 migrants have died during this time, including families and children (Sanchez, 2002). Journalist John Annerino (1999) was so affected by these deaths that he wrote a book chronicling the lives and struggles of people who continue to perish on what he termed "America's killing ground."

The constant anxiety that some individuals experience in anticipation that they or someone in their family will be apprehended by the border patrol can result in different degrees of PTSD, as well (Salcido, 1982). Thus, it may be appropriate to make a referral to a bicultural therapist or to a priest or a minister who may enable the immigrant family members to acknowledge and address the various grief or trauma themes they are experiencing.

When working with a family with a member with special needs, interventionists should consider attending to these familial needs so that the work and the emotional unveiling that must be addressed can be included in the arena of intervention focus. Often, this focus must entertain the religious belief system of the family so that the interventionist can better understand how the family perceives the person and his or her disability.

Religious Origins

As a result of the influence of the Spanish heritage, the majority of Roman Catholics in the world are Latinos. Thus, many of the Latino families that human services workers encounter will adhere to different forms of Catholicism, with unique aspects stemming from each of their home country's cultural and indigenous influences. It is important, however, that professionals realize that not all Latinos are Catholic. In reality, there is a growing influence of Protestant sects, both in Latino countries and in the United States. This diversity tends also to vary among the different Latino subgroups. Mexican Americans and Cubans have the most identification with Catholicism, whereas the Puerto Rican population tends to have a higher proportion of Protestants (Maldonado, 2000). Thus, an interventionist should determine to which religion a family adheres. Furthermore, the importance of assessing the extended family's or the grandparents' religious system is not to be overlooked because it may have implications for rituals or resources on which the immediate family may rely in dealing with the disability.

For families with Mexican heritage, the importance of Our Lady of Guadalupe as a patron saint and as the "Virgin Mother" of Mexico is a prominent feature in their practice of Catholicism. It is not uncommon for a parent to implore the Virgin Mary to intercede for him or her to cure a person of a disease or a disability. The use of *mandas* (i.e., a promise or offering in return for God's intervention) is another aspect of this intercession. For instance, a parent commits to carry out a tradition or a ritual in return for the intercession of a saint or the Virgin Mary. This may mean not cutting the child's hair until that parent can visit a shrine in Mexico, such as the Basilica of Our Lady of Guadalupe. Or it can mean dressing the afflicted child in robes similar to those of St. Martin de Porres, for example, as a bartering gesture (Smith-DeMateo, 1987). Still others may use a *milagro*, which is a small arm, leg, or heart made of bronze, silver, or gold that represents the person's affliction, and place it at a statue of a powerful saint as a plea for intervention. Egan's (1991) book is a helpful resource to elucidate the diverse Latino practices using *milagro* symbols. Sometimes families believe that the disability is the cross that has been sent to them as part of God's will and thus must be borne as part of the pain of the human condition. Others may respond with less acceptance, or they may believe they are being treated unjustly or that they are being punished for a previous wrongdoing. Each of the family members may have individual reactions.

For Cubans, too, religious beliefs and practices are not homogeneous, although the majority of Cubans are Catholic. In Latin America, especially in those countries where there is a significant African and/or Indian heritage (e.g., the Caribbean, Mexico, Central and South America), Christ, the Virgin Mary, and Catholic saints are fused with the deities and rituals of the Indian and the African populations (Rubinstein, 1976).

Puerto Ricans and Cubans, in particular, often practice Santeria, which is a syncretism of Catholic saints and African *orishas* or saints. During the time of the Spanish colonies, Yoruba slaves from Nigeria identified their saints with those of the Catholics, endowing the latter with the same supernatural powers of the African deities. This syncretism, although primarily practiced by illiterate Catholic masses in these countries, has also been taken on by some Anglo-European Catholics (Ortiz, 1973).

In Cuban culture, Santeria tends to promote and strengthen traditional family ties because the religion models a pantheon of saints and deities that interact as a "sacred family." The most influential of all African demigods are Chāngó and Obatālá, who are ascribed with miraculous powers. Reflections of this religion may be encountered in homes in which a Catholic statue such as Our Lady of Mercy stands next to a food offering to Ochún, the Santeria saint who is the patron of love, marriage, fertility, and gold (Gonzalez-Whippier, 1989).

Interventionists thus may find different manifestations of these religious belief systems related to a child's disability. For example, a *manda* made by Catholics to pay for a litany of masses, altars that are syncretisms of saints, and food offerings in Santeria to call on the powers of certain deities to help the child, or the placement of a glass of water or a Santeria idol under a child's bed may be used to protect the child.

These religious symbols represent the family's belief that a cure is possible or that a cure is in the hands of supreme powers. Interventionists must recognize these belief systems as part of the family's cultural context so that intervention efforts do not directly challenge or disregard the family's need to use a spiritual frame for comprehending the disability or to support a sense of hope.

Language/Linguistic Origins

In working with Latino families, comprehension of their attitudes and assessment of their situations also will demand knowledge of how their Spanish language affects their communication process. Spain's colonization of the New World imposed the Spanish language as the central political and economic communication mode. Thus, a major unifying factor for Latinos is their use of the Spanish language, albeit reflected uniquely in each country and region via indigenous idioms, vocabulary, or rates of speech. For example, the language of Puerto Ricans or Cubans is easy to detect because its pace is more rapid than that of Mexicans. Often, the Spanish spoken in the United States by the various subgroups mirrors English expressions used in various regions. For example, the Spanish spoken in Miami differs somewhat from the Spanish spoken in Los Angeles (Rubinstein, 1976). Mexican Americans classify this Spanish–English syncretism as *pochismos* or Americanized Spanish. In the last decade, this Anglicization of the Spanish language has been called *Spanglish*. For all Latino groups in the United States, the degree of fluency in Spanish will vary, especially with acculturation rates.

Third-generation, U.S.-born Mexican Americans often stop speaking Spanish, whereas their grandparents may only speak Spanish, resulting in communication estrangement in family systems. Commonly, Chicanos use Spanish for informal, in-group, familial, and personal interactions but use English for communicating with outsiders (Gomez, 1977). Awareness of this tendency to *code switch,* or shift from one language to another, should be understood as reflecting these interactional predispositions. An interventionist may misunderstand a family member's switching to Spanish with another member, deeming it as a way to hide data from the worker when it is often just tied to language predispositions.

When an interventionist does not speak Spanish and the family only speaks Spanish, translators must be utilized to ensure viable communication. Having the children in the family translate should be avoided if at all possible. When children act as translators and are placed in a superior position, the family structure shifts and parents may be hesitant to discuss emotion-laden content in front of their child. Equally important, this kind of translating places a great burden and pressure on a child to be accurate, or it may expose the child to the parents' pain, resulting in the child taking on the responsibility for the family's burden (Garcia-Preto, 1982; Mizio, 1974). When translators are used, Latino adults are preferable. The interventionist must be sensitive to the possibility of distortions that can result in this communication medium, however (Abad & Boyce, 1979).

If the interventionist is Spanish speaking but not of the family's culture, familiarity with that culture will enable an understanding of the nuances of communication used by each family (i.e., colloquialisms or nonverbal expressions). For example, among Cubans, the impact of African cultures on Cuban history and social institutions is reflected in language expressions. Many Cubans use such expressions as *mi negro(a)* (my black one) to manifest comradeship or familiar affection and love (Szapocznik & Hernandez, 1988).

Also, not all Spanish-speaking people are literate in the written form. For instance, many Mexican Americans, although they speak Spanish well, may have had no formal education to support reading and writing it in a viable way. In particular, an interventionist must be alert as to whether a monolingual Spanish-speaking parent is literate in Spanish. For example, health care workers have left medical regimens written in Spanish for parents to follow, not realizing that the parents could not read or write in Spanish. Often, parents are hesitant to reveal their lack of reading ability.

CONTEMPORARY LIFE

As a result of the large flow of immigrants of Latin descent, about one third of the Latino population in the United States in 1980 was foreign born. By 2000, 14.5 million or almost half of the nation's 28.4 million foreign-born had immigrated from Latin America (U.S. Bureau of the Census, 2002). Many suspect that these numbers have increased as a result of the amnesty process dating from 1986, which legalized thousands of undocumented immigrants; the continued legal immigration of Latinos; the increase of undocumented people from Mexico; and the high birth rate of Latinos. Those from Mexico comprised more than 25% of the foreign-born population and more than 50% of those from Latin America. In addition to Mexico, Cuba, the Dominican Republic, and El Salvador were among the United States's top 10 countries of foreign birth (U.S. Bureau of the Census, 2002).

Latino Foreign Born   The diversity among foreign-born Latinos varies by region of birth. Those born in Mexico tend to differ from other groups in education levels, employment, and other characteristics. Examination of education indices indicates that for those Latinos who were foreign-born, the proportion with a high school education or higher was 50% among the entire Latin American group. Within this group 80% of those who were 25 years and older and born in South America had a high school education or higher compared with 34% for those born in Mexico. For those 25–54 years, Latina women had a median labor force participation rate of 63%. This ranged from 74% for women from the Caribbean to 58% for women born in Mexico. Only 12% of Latin American–born workers were employed in managerial and professional specialty occupations; 71% were service or skilled workers, farm workers, or manual laborers. Whereas only 6% of Mexicans were employed in managerial and professional occupations, 83% of Mexican workers were service or skilled workers, or farm or manual laborers (U.S. Bureau of the Census, 2002).

The citizenship rates for foreign-born Latinos are relatively low. For example, in 2000, 28% of the foreign-born population from Latin America were naturalized citizens, whereas 52% from Europe and 47% from Asia were naturalized. Mexico had only a 20% naturalization rate as compared with Latinos from the Caribbean, who had a citizenship rate of 47% (U.S. Bureau of the Census, 2002).

Although these citizenship rates are low, the dramatic growth of the Latino population, including those who are native-born, has contributed to Latinos' evolving prominence on the political scene. The reality that Latinos are concentrated in the six states—California, Texas, Florida, New York, New Jersey, and Illinois—that cast two-thirds of the 270 electoral votes required to win the presidency gives their voting presence significant meaning. In illustration, Karl Rove, the political strategist who designed George W. Bush's re-election strategies, noted that President Bush would need 40% of the Latino vote in order to win a second term (Kammer, 2002). Voter registration forays into Latino communities become more aggressive as Latino leaders use their political power to bargain with politicians for policies that address Latino needs. It is noteworthy that in 2003, there were 1,520 Latino Democrats in elective office across the country. The Latino Democrats outnumbered their Latino Republican counterparts 13 to 1. Latino Democrats argue that the Republicans' recruitment of Latinos is a major challenge, particularly because Latinos align themselves with the Democrats' approaches to wages, health care, and working conditions. Republicans respond that the Catholic values of Latinos and their work ethic are factors that might enable Latinos to join the Republican party more easily (Kammer, 2002).

The youthfulness of the Latino population is reflected in the 2000 Census data. Nearly 35% of Latinos in the United States were younger than age 18, as compared with 23.5% of non-Latino whites. Within-group comparisons indicated that the Mexican-origin group had the highest proportion of its population younger than the age of 18 (38.4%), compared with the Cuban-origin population, who had the lowest percentage of individuals younger than age 18 (19.2%).

Conversely, only 5.3% of Latinos were age 65 and older, as compared with 14% of non-Latino whites. For those ages 25–44, 32.4% of Latinos fell in this range as compared with 39.5% of non-Latino whites. Last, 14.5% of Latinos were 45–64 years of age compared with 24.0% of non-Latino whites (U.S. Bureau of the Census, 2001). The proportion of within-group *ancianos* or the elderly (those 65 and older) ranged from 4.5% for the group including Mexicans and Central and South Americans to 21.0% for Cubans (U.S. Bureau of the Census, 2001).

Latinos tend to have larger family households than non-Latino whites. In 2000, just under 31% of family households consisted of five or more people. In contrast only 11.8% of white non-Latino family households were this size. Among Latino households, Mexican homes tended to have the largest numbers, with 35.5% having five

or more people. Small households with only two people were reflected in 21.7% of Latino households as compared with 46.0% in white non-Latino households. Cuban households tended to be the smallest, with 41.3% having only two people (U.S. Bureau of the Census, 2001).

Marriage statistics indicated that for the population ages 15 years and older, Latinos were more likely to have never been married than non-Latino whites, 33.2% compared with 24.5%, respectively. Of all the Latino groups, Cubans were least likely to have remained single, with 20.4% in this category (U.S. Bureau of the Census, 2001).

Although family violence for Latinos is not well-researched, a national survey found high rates of spousal abuse among Latinos, with one of every four Latino families surveyed experiencing one or more assaults against a spouse (Straus & Gelles, 1990). Although within-group rates are not readily evident, the mediating variable of substance abuse is a pivotal factor.

For those immigrants who have come from war-torn countries such as El Salvador, the impact of the civil violence may leave deep wounds that can become exacerbated with the stressors of immigration. For these immigrants, family violence may be a reality that they contend with alone, often due to lack of Spanish-speaking service providers or due to their fear of apprehension if they are undocumented. A paucity of resources exists for Latino immigrants coping with violence in their families (Connelly, 2000). In Portland, Oregon, however, a community group has recruited Latino immigrant women and men who perform skits or sociodrama to elaborate on the relationship of the historical violence they have experienced to the emotional trauma they often contend with as they adjust to new jobs and cultural situations.

The reality of undocumented status is a critical theme for many families with a member with a disability. The antipathy toward undocumented immigrants as well as the dramatic increase in border vigilance by the U.S. Border Patrol (Bender & Leane, 1997) may heighten the immigrant's distrust and resistance to formal interventions or general fear of any professional.

Acculturation Process

The process of migration is one of relocation to an unfamiliar context. The immigrant faces an environment in which the habits, values, and socialization processes from his or her country of origin are no longer applicable. Migration involves stressful experiences including culture shock, acculturative stress, and cultural fatigue. The conflicts characteristic of culture shock typically continue until the immigrant incorporates both his or her culture of origin and the host culture into an integral approach to his or her existence in the new society. This process is the acculturation process. It involves the conflict-ridden decision-making process in which the immigrant trades off his or her indigenous attitudes, values, and behaviors for those of the host group until she or he achieves a mixture of old and new that is deemed optimal (Salgado de Snyder, 1987). Some individuals resist this change process and underacculturate, which results in less adaptation to their new environment. Children who attend school or adults who obtain employment may be more exposed to acculturation pushes, which may result in uneven acculturation levels among family members, resulting in disagreement about values and behaviors. In this situation, the interventionist may not be able to intervene directly but may consider referring to therapists or to community agencies that can address these familial and acculturation strains.

Social Supports

An important factor in noting the immigrant status of a family is the designation of available support networks. The social support received from these networks helps to alleviate stress and contributes to the immigrants' adaptation. Thus, migration success is not only based on the learning of new sociocultural norms and behaviors, but it is also reliant on social support from co-nationals (i.e., immigrants from their country of origin) and the social acceptance of the host group (Boekestijn, 1984). De-Anda (1984) identified the various support roles co-nationals play as they help the new immigrant adapt to the new society's rules related to such daily needs as employment, housing, and shopping and to connect the immigrant to culturally driven supports or ethnic social networks.

Designation of ethnic social networks is important because it may be the only source of support during times of crisis. Ethnic networks are composed of coculturals with whom the immigrant may be more inclined to develop a more personal relationship. Immigrants can ask questions, discuss the beliefs and values of the host culture, and still obtain reaffirmation of the norms and values of the native culture in a supportive environment.

Ethnic networks may provide the brokering process wherein the new immigrant is taught about the resources, procedures, and mechanisms needed to survive. For a family who has a member with special needs, having this kind of network available may help to mitigate the stress, confusion, and pain related to addressing the issues of a disability. Especially for immigrant Latina women, ethnic networks that can offer confidante support are of particular value because these women may not have the natural familial or community networks that existed in their country of origin. If confidantes are not available, immigrant women may be in jeopardy of depression (Vega, Kolody, & Valle, 1988). In fact, research specific to Mexican mothers' adaptation to children's disabilities has indicated that the two most important coping strategies identified were seeking emotional support—particularly from extended family and friends—and seeking information about their child's disability from professionals or other resources such as parents (Shapiro & Tittle, 1990).

The interventionist needs to assess the family's natural support arena, including the presence of a religious system that may provide spiritual resources. Often, Latino immigrants may gravitate to a barrio church with a Latino congregation and Latino priests/ministers. Joan Koss-Chioino, a medical anthropologist, and Luis Vargas, a child psychologist (1999), reflected on how informal religious groups and individual religious healers take on even greater importance as ethnomedical healing systems when ethnic minority groups are adapting to their new but difficult or even hostile society. A reframing of Latinos' religiosity has been called *communitarian spirituality.* In this conceptualization, the focus may not be so related to healing per se, but on the support derived from building community (Diaz-Stevens, 1996). The interventionist may need to determine whether there are ethnomedical healing systems in the community in which their clients live that can be used as an emotional resource for a family stressed or grieving about a child with a disability, and if these resources are credible in that community. Although many communities may offer support groups for parents with children with such disabilities as cerebral palsy or Down syndrome, a paucity of Spanish-language support groups is available to Latino families. Interventionists should nonetheless discern if any do exist. In large metropolitan areas such as Los Angeles, regional centers, which are California's comprehensive service agencies for individuals with developmental disabilities, may be able to provide this information.

Aside from the stressors related to immigration, a critical stressor for many families is related to illegal immigrant status. Families in this situation may be hesitant to seek out resources for their family. Moreover, they may feel that service providers who come for help with the child may use the information about their illegal status to inform the U.S. Citizenship and Immigration Services. It is critical that the interventionist inform families that his or her job is not to call their illegal status into question. The interventionist may need to state very explicitly that she or he will not call

A bilingual, bicultural worker from a regional center in a Latino-populated area of Southern California was working with five Latina immigrant mothers, all of whom had a child with spina bifida; the children ranged in age from 6 months to 6 years. The mothers were from low socioeconomic levels and most were single. They were not used to talking about their feelings or expressing their needs directly. Their ages varied from 20 years to 38 years.

Common themes in their lives included their sense of isolation, lack of support, lack of transportation, and stresses related to acculturation and the diagnoses of their children. For the most part they felt overwhelmed; they also displayed a lack of confidence in their abilities to meet the needs of their children with disabilities.

The interventionist contacted various Latino and community resources to discern if a related support group was available in Spanish for these women. Despite the large Latino population, Spanish-speaking support groups were not common. The interventionist approached her agency director and advocated for the resources needed to begin a support group.

Initially, the support group met every 2 months. Talking about their needs and recognizing the generalized issues they all shared as immigrant parents of children with disabilities influenced the mothers' self-esteem in a positive way and enabled them to begin expressing themselves with more confidence. The effects were so dramatic that other Spanish-speaking mothers with infants with other diagnoses began to join.

The group asked to meet monthly. Apart from their mutual support processes, they requested speakers so they could be better informed about their infants. They also set the monthly agenda, depicting an empowerment theme that was critical to their sense of themselves as mothers. From this support group, two of the mothers with more English fluency participated in training other groups and learned to function as advocate volunteers for other Spanish-speaking parents of children with disabilities.

Interventionists may need to help Latino parents to empower themselves to be better equipped to advocate for their children. Support groups contribute to this process, enabling the interventionist to reach more of these needy parents and to facilitate the kinds of change that characterize group processes. Lack of support groups for Latino parents with children who have special needs is a dramatic void that must be addressed (Arias, 1990).

authorities. Moreover, the interventionist will need to know what resources can be used for illegal immigrants and which resources, if used, could jeopardize their legal immigration application at a later time. Helping the family to understand what options are available and which options could work against future legal application plans is an invaluable service to the family. This will help to heighten the trust level with the service provider while also undercutting the stress related to lack of information about this crucial area (Salcido, 1982). This theme of knowing what resources undocumented immigrants are eligible for was viewed as so important during the Clinton administration that public notice was given about eligibility for various medical and social resources (Bellisle, 1999).

Becoming familiar with eligibility issues is an important way to build the relationship with a family fearful of deportation and helps human service workers find the kinds of resources that will enable workers to do their jobs more effectively. For example, immigration legislation has deemed it necessary to allow women who are not documented to become eligible for income programs for themselves and their children if they have been or are in abusive or violent domestic scenarios (Zuniga, in press). The goal is to ensure that these immigrant women have a mechanism to survive financially in order to protect themselves and their children, rather than stay in an environment of domestic violence because the perpetrator is the only source of financial support. Again, interventionists who may be providing services for a child with a disability may not have the responsibility or expertise to be the social worker; however, awareness of resources—especially for undocumented families—may enable the family to seek out these benefits because the interventionist has been able to supply them with the necessary information. The end result is that the family may be able to participate in a more focused way on the needs of their child who is at risk or who has a disability if they have been able to address survival issues.

VALUES

The role of the Latino family as the central operating focus characterizes most of these subgroups (Bernal, 1982; Garcia-Preto, 1982; Zuniga, 1988b). The static traditional role configurations often ascribed to Latino families are being called into question, however (Vega, Hough, & Romero, 1983). The Latino family has traditionally been described as exhibiting male supremacy, maternal submissiveness, and strict gender-role delineations, for example, with child rearing veiwed as the exclusive domain of female members as fathers remain aloof. Latino social scientists have noted that Latino families are not static; they are typically in transition, so it is difficult to discern what a normative Latino family is like (Cafferty & Engstrom, 2000; Levine & Padilla, 1980; Montiel, 1975; Vega, 1980). Being foreign born or native born, regional differences, acculturation stages, upward class mobility, intermarriage rates, and other characteristics all produce a variation of Latino family configurations with a mix of structures, values, styles, and preferences.

One of the crucial themes to recognize is that class variations are misinterpreted just as often as are culture variations. Class phenomena may provide more insight about a family related to their worldview and experiences with freedom and self-identity. Abalos (1986) questioned whether the "passiveness or fatalism" often ascribed to Latinos is not more specifically an outgrowth of class dimensions. People who are poor and minimally educated may have a limited sense of options. They may have few experiences with self-empowerment as a result of the economic constraints under which they have lived. Moreover, their lack of political freedom, especially for those from South and Central American societies, may be a result of their accustomed stance of allowing those in power or those with status to make decisions for them. If an individual is poor, of lower status, and socialized to be powerless, she or he will be less prone to take the lead or be assertive in interpersonal interactions, especially with regard to decision making. Thus, the interventionist should discern how class realities affect a particular family system (Montijo, 1985). For example, an immigrant Mexican family from a middle-class milieu in Mexico City may be more similar in its values and behaviors to U.S. middle-class families than a U.S.-born Mexican family of low socioeconomic status.

This is not to say that there are not cultural frames around which the family organizes itself and functions; however, the traditional format is changing. Interventionists must individually assess each Latino family system to discern to what extent it follows these cultural formats. Ramirez and Arce (1981) noted that the concept of *machismo,* an absolute patriarchy of the father, is having less of an influence on the dynamics and structure of contemporary Mexican American families. Others found that the Mexican American family is often characterized by joint decision making and greater equality of male and female roles (Ybarra-Soriano, 1977). One significant contribution to these changes is the increasing influence of women's employment outside the home. Although Latina women have a lower employment rate compared with non–Latina Anglo-European Americans, Latina women often find work more easily than their spouses, albeit in low-paying jobs. This has enhanced the wife's position and supported her role in decision making (Chiswick & Hurst, 2000; Cromwell & Ruiz, 1979; Ybarra-Soriano, 1977).

Education and Schooling

In 2002, the U.S. Census indicated that the Latino population age 25 and older was less likely to have graduated from high school than non-Latino whites (57.0% compared with 88.4%). More than one fourth of Latinos had less than a ninth-grade education (27.3%), compared with 4.2% of non-Latino whites. The proportion of Latinos with a bachelor's degree or more was 10.6% as compared with 28.1% for non-Latino whites (U.S. Bureau of the Census, 2001).

Of Latino groups, Cubans 25 years and older were the most likely to have at least a high school education; namely, 73% of this group had a high school education as compared with 64.3% of Puerto Ricans and Central and South Americans (U.S. Bureau of the Census, 2001). In short, although Latinos' educational attainment in the United States has increased somewhat, they still fall behind non-Latino whites on this measure.

An overused stereotype is that Latinos, especially those of Mexican origin, do not value education. This misperception is easily attained from scenarios in which parents have their school-age children stay home to care for younger children and do not recognize the academic repercussions of this practice. Because many of these parents have no knowledge of the rules and procedures of U.S. education systems, they appear not to have strong educational values. Yet, one of the major reasons Latino families immigrate is to ensure a better education for their children. Because of language and cultural differences, however, they often find the school environment threatening, thus curtailing their participation in school activities such as parent–teacher associations (PTAs). Aggressive measures may need to be taken to include Latinos in typical school activities. For example, Spanish-speaking parents in Escondido, California, did not participate in PTA activities at a local high school. A concerned Anglo-European parent worked to help develop a translation system so that these parents could be educated about school policies and the protocol related to the PTA. First, they had their own Spanish-speaking PTA, and then they sent representatives to the larger school's PTA.

Similarly, it is important for school systems to reach out to these families in the high-context, relational modes highlighted by Harry (1992). As Harry discussed, the typical communication pattern, especially in special education arenas, is a low-context pattern, such as objective memos and letters that parents receive. That approach is incongruent with the high-context needs of Latino parents. This need for a more interpersonal approach is especially congruent when addressing the emotional elements associated with having a child with a disability.

Familialism

Examination of central tendencies in family life among the Latino subgroups denotes traits that are often attenuated by class, migration, and acculturation phenomena. Koss-Chioino and Vargas (1999) identified the impact of ancient history on present-day family structure and values that emanate from those ancient agrarian societies of the indigenous people of Latin America and from Spanish colonization. The importance of the extended family, and family hierarchy, wherein the oldest adult males dominate and within which power and position are delineated according to age and gender, is an outcomes of this mixed heritage. The legacy received from the Spanish culture contributes to viewing the man as the provider and the woman as the main person who takes care of the children. With immigration, the extended family role, along with the ethic of mutual obligations, becomes attenuated. The nuclear family is the basic unit for surviving; yet, the old traditions of interdependence continue and may intensify with the stressors Latino families encounter in their new country (Koss-Chioino & Vargas, 1999).

Latinos, as a whole, adhere to this collective sense, which often results in extended family configurations that offer valuable support services (Vega et al., 1983). Moreover, the godparent or *compadre* system offers support through additions to the family via marriage and the consequent use of godparents at baptism; at confirmation; and at the *quinceañeras*, the coming-out celebrations for 15-year-old girls.

Thus, many families may have these resources to call on for help in child care. Interventionists can discuss this area with families, particularly when there is a need for the parent to obtain some form of respite care when they have a child with a disability (i.e., care that helps temporarily relieve parents from demands for extensive attention and caregiving). Likewise, the parents may be asked to designate certain family members to be trained along with them in special medical regimens for the child; or a godmother (*comadre*) may be an additional resource to be trained.

Another tendency related to Latino families is that most Latino families remain two-parent families throughout their lives. The divorce rate (6.8%) for this population is lower than for the Anglo-European group (Montgomery, 1994). The fact that most Latinos are Catholic may influence this disinclination to divorce (Ho, 1987). Yet, in urban centers, the single-parent household is not uncommon for Latinos (Fitzpatrick, 1981) and appears to be growing. As Montgomery (1994) noted, the single head-of-household group grew from 26% to 30% from the 1980 to the 1990 census.

Another Spanish legacy is the emphasis on female virginity prior to marriage and female fidelity to her spouse thereafter. This purity is then reinforced by religious ideology. Consequently, childbearing patterns highlight the protection of girls and restriction of their freedom. Among Cubans, Bernal (1982) noted that sexuality, virginity, and *machismo* are difficult to address with most families. These issues also are awkward to address in other Latino subgroups. Bernal (1982) noted that when Cuban wives have to work outside the home, the power balance of the family is affected and may undercut the man's role. If the man is unable to obtain work, he loses face, self-esteem, and respect; marital and intergenerational difficulties likely will develop.

The collective and familial stance for Latinos also influences the worldview of these individuals. Research has found that Mexican American children have a more field-sensitive cognitive style than children of other ethnic groups. This field dependence implies a high sensitivity to nonverbal indicators of feelings and it is operationalized in the Latino cultural concept of *personalismo* (Ramirez & Price-Williams, 1974). This concept is predicated on warm, individualized attention and responsiveness in interpersonal interactions. This concept is coupled with interpersonal respect (Gomez, 1977) and supports the value stance of the various Latino groups.

To respect Latino values, the interventionist must consciously work at a humanistic orientation that first considers the interpersonal interaction versus the task-oriented style so readily adhered to by some human services professionals. The cultural practice of *platicando* must be incorporated into the interventionist's style of relating to Latino families. This involves friendly, informal, and leisurely chatting that establishes the *ambiente* or atmosphere in which the work will take place. The interventionist who can incorporate this style will be admired by the Latino family and may attract greater familial cooperation and trust. The trust of families also will be engendered when the interventionist is able to comprehend rather than reject the belief systems that these families espouse. Knowledge about differences in child-rearing practices, use of medical care, and views on what causes disabilities will help to support the interventionist's delivery of services.

BELIEFS

An important area in which there may be miscommunication between interventionists and Latino families centers around diverse or contrasting belief systems. In particular, one area of concern involves the beliefs around the roles and the developmental expectations surrounding family members, especially children.

Child Rearing

In Latino cultures, one marries for the purpose of having children. Children validate the marriage. The parent–child relationship has more importance than the marital relationship. Parents tend to be very nurturing toward their children and permissive and indulgent with young children. The attitude toward the young is to placate them, not to push for the achievement or developmental milestones that are often valued in Anglo families. This relaxed attitude toward the attainment of early skills may be related to a value thrust that supports a family member's interdependence with the family as opposed to the focus on the family member's independence and individuation (Roland, 1988).

The lack of push for independence can be carried to the extreme, however (e.g., children come to school not knowing how to button jackets, tie shoes, or cut food because everything has been done for them). More so, when a child has a disability,

special treatment from parents and extended family may include failing to discipline the child or making no demands on him or her, thus depriving the child of a much needed socialization format (Adkins & Young, 1976).

Juarez (1985) related the importance of recognizing different norms around child rearing that exist for many Latino families as compared with Anglo families. In illustration, Latinos may allow preschoolers to continue drinking from a baby bottle. Latino families find it acceptable for preteens to sit on the mother's lap. Moreover, it is typical in many Latino families for members to sit close to one another and to have direct physical contact regardless of age. Anglo professionals might view this closeness as symbiotic behavior and as unacceptable.

Torres-Matrullo (1982) noted that although positive emotions are encouraged among Latino women and children, emotions such as anger, aggression, and other negative feelings are not acceptable. Mothers may teach their sons to be dominant and independent, with the eldest son typically having more authority than younger male brothers (Kluckhohn & Strodtbeck, 1961). Siblings have close emotional ties, and parents discourage infighting (Goodman & Beman, 1971).

Research on the cognitive styles of Mexican American children has found that their field-dependent style may be attributed to various dimensions, including more traditional child-rearing practices in Mexican culture. These practices emphasize adherence to convention, respect for authority, and identity with the family (Romero, 1983). This traditional child rearing includes teaching children respect for their elders and should result in a child who is *bien educado,* or well educated. *Una persona bien educado* (a well-educated individual) is one who has been taught skills in human relationships and who understands the importance of interacting and relating to others with respect and dignity (Zuniga, 1988a). Thus, a person who calls a child *mal educado* is noting that the parents have not provided him or her with the education that is expected in Latino families.

An important aspect for children is the expectation that they will take up work roles within the family, whether this includes child care, helping with chores, or actually working with other family members. Often, this expectation of more responsibility for children may be economically related; for many poor families, the theme of survival may demand that all members participate for the good of the family.

Child-rearing practices differ depending on the particular Latino subgroup. It is important that interventionists recognize that factors such as class, region, and acculturation stage may contribute to formats for child rearing. Readings on children from culturally diverse families should be sought to strengthen interventionists' knowledge bases in this area (e.g., Gibbs & Huang [1989]; Koss-Chioino & Vargas [1999]; Powell, Yamamoto, Romero, & Morales [1983]), or knowledge specific to health (e.g., Giger & Davidhizar [1995]).

The interventionist must realize that cultures that value a collective style versus an individualistic style and a cooperative mode versus a competitive mode will result in the socialization of children who may have different goals and different learning processes from those raised in the majority Anglo-European culture. Although these differences contrast to the modes and styles of the majority cultural group, one must not assume that they are inferior or dysfunctional. For example, a family that does not focus on the developmental milestones referred to previously may not comprehend the interventionist's concern for teaching processes to a child with a disability to ensure that his or her development does not become too delayed. If a family does not follow through immediately on recommendations, the interventionist may need to consider the family's perspective. The interventionist will need to recognize that developmental goals may have to be addressed in alternative modes that enable the family to realize the need for these developmental processes.

Medical Care

One of the traits often ascribed to Latino families is their preference for natural healers. Again, economic issues may dictate what resources a family uses. Natural healers often are geographically accessible and affordable, and often families cannot afford or do not have access to Western resources. Mexicans will use *curanderos(as)* (natural faith healers), whereas Puerto Ricans will rely on spiritists because they value and believe in the religious/spiritual aspects that surround these healers. Although folk beliefs about medical and psychological interventions may be characteristic of the more traditional and less acculturated Latinos, there is evidence that even modern-day Chicanos are influenced by these beliefs and practices (Gomez, 1977).

For many Mexican-heritage people, as well as some other groups such as Puerto Ricans, medical folk beliefs include *mal ojo* (evil eye), *susto* (fright), and *mal puesto* (evil hex). *Mal ojo* is believed to be the result of excessive admiration or desire on the part of another. Mothers may isolate their children for fear of having one become victim of *mal ojo* (Gomez, 1977). *Susto* is a syndrome that is a result of an emotionally traumatic experience: A simple scare or witnessing an accident could result in *susto*. Symptoms of *susto* include restlessness during sleep, loss of appetite, disinterest in personal hygiene, loss of strength, weight loss, and introversion (Gomez, 1977). *Mal puesto* is an evil hex or illness willfully put on someone by a *curandero(a)* or a *brujo(a)* (witch). The hex may be given through food or one's photograph. Often the hex is motivated by jealousy or vengeance. When a child is born with a disability, this may be interpreted as a *mal puesto* by someone in the family's ecological context who is at odds with the parent or the family. For example, a Mexican mother perceived her child, born with mental retardation and with extreme facial distortions, as having that disability because her husband's family put a *mal ojo* on the child (G. Frederico, personal communication, October 10, 1990).

Parents may take a child with a disability to a *curandero(a)* to seek a *cura* (cure). Most Latino communities have healers or other specialists such as a *sobador* (person who heals through massage). It is not unusual, for example, for a family to seek a *sobador* for help with a child diagnosed with cerebral palsy. It is common for a family to refer to a healer for a second opinion. Families who live close to Mexico may make the effort to seek out healers who are available in border towns such as Tijuana. For example, a family may travel all the way from Los Angeles to obtain this type of second opinion (A. Dunn, personal communication, October 15, 1990). Families who are Puerto Rican may consult with their botanical shop to find herbal remedies or to obtain the services of a healer (Delgado, 1994).

Negroni-Rodriguez and Morales (2001) described how *espiritismo* among Puerto Ricans is based on the belief that everyone has spirits of protection, also that loved ones can be around in spirit even after they die and can offer protection and aid. The spiritist healers (*Espiritistas*) communicate with these spirits, and healing occurs with their prescribed folk healing. Delgado (1977, 1988) explained *spiritism* as a highly ritualized intervention that uses various paraphernalia to provide a healing environment. Statues or pictures of saints, flowers, cigars, and so forth may be a part of the assortment of resources needed to perform healing ceremonies. The principle is that multiple stages of spiritist practices offer various stages of intervention: 1) setting the atmosphere, 2) discovering the reason through a spirit medium for what is causing the physical or emotional discomfort, and 3) performing *despojas* (cleansing ceremonies) to take away the symptoms. These stages are similar to those that Western social workers are taught for interventions: 1) develop the relationship, 2) assess the individual and situation, and 3) offer a plan to dispel the problem (Hepworth & Larsen, 1990).

Interventionists must acknowledge these belief systems; this results in the act of "joining" the family in its desire to seek assistance for a family member with a disability. The issue of curative modes based on folk beliefs must be examined to ensure that the person's safety is protected and to minimize contraindicated interventions or medications, however. Direct but sensitive questioning about the folk modes, cures, procedures used, or medications offered should be carefully posed. The interventionist can frame the questioning in a positive manner to learn what the healer is providing, without putting the family on the defensive. Also, if prescriptions are similar, neighbors may offer their own medication prescriptions as a gesture to aid the family. Again, assessment needs to be indicated and made and educative input needs to be offered to protect the child (Smith-DeMateo, 1987). Herbal medicine is dispensed at storefronts that are located in the heart of many Puerto Rican communities. Delgado (1988) used various classifications for these shops, including the "commercial-orthodox" types that provide commercial products as well as a diverse assortment of herbal remedies that are difficult to find. These shops also offer referrals to local healers or may have a healer on the premises.

Causation and Disability

The belief in folk remedies is very much tied into religious beliefs for many Latinos. For instance, all these groups believe in the powers of good and evil, often reinforced by Catholic traditions. The Catholic belief that holy water can be used to ward off evil and to bless the person lends credence to indigenous themes about "warding off evil." The underlying principle is that illness or problems can occur as a result of the presence of evil in one's environment. Certainly the idea of the evil eye illustrates this theme and is a common belief among various Latino subgroups.

A curse put on the child by someone or the effects of an evil spirit can be interpreted as causing the birth of a child with a disability. Thus, amulets may be placed around the neck of the child to ward off evil. An interventionist may find a Cuban infant with a semiprecious black stone worn around the neck or the wrist. This is an *azabache* used to ward off evil and means that this parent may adhere to this type of folk belief system. If the stone shows chips, this is interpreted as demonstrating that the evil eye has been warded off (M. Sardinas, personal communication, September 15, 1990). Thus, the theme is that evil is a powerful force, and believers have to utilize the various means for contending with this force, often through symbolic rituals such as the use of amulets. However, there are pathways to address evil or to remedy its effects.

As noted previously, interpretations of what causes disabilities or birth defects for children may result from an array of influences: belief in a punishing God, folk beliefs about the power of evil, or beliefs that life is laden with tragedy and one accepts the good with the bad. Some families may adopt a fatalistic view that enables them to address a difficult situation with less emotional trauma; however, this kind of view may hinder the family's need to work aggressively in helping the child with his or her disability. A mother's family may argue that the disability was caused because the mother was not careful during her pregnancy. For example, one fairly acculturated Mexican American family felt that a child born with mental retardation was harmed during the pregnancy because of the mother's bowling.

Folk beliefs may play a role in the definition of many disabilities. For example, one such belief is that a pregnant woman must be careful when using scissors or sharp objects while pregnant or else the child can be born with a cleft palate. Another is that if the mother knits clothes for the child, she cannot wind the yarn into balls or the child will be born with the cord wrapped around his or her neck (Smith-DeMateo, 1987).

Interventionists will encounter variations in the interpretation of the disability. Education and social class may affect a family's belief system. Smith-DeMateo (1987) argued that often the higher the socioeconomic status, the more likely that a family member with a disability, especially mental retardation, will be kept hidden from society at large. Another view is that in folk cultures, disabilities such as mental retardation are more readily accepted. Thus, an immigrant family from a rural area in their country of origin may be more predisposed to accept a child with a disability and less likely to feel embarrassed by this "act of God." An additional perspective is that parents who are middle class and high in their biculturalism or ability to function well in their Mexican culture as well as the majority culture appear to have a more complex view of their child's behavior. This is important because the parents' concepts of development will influence the way they understand the behavior of their child (Gutierrez & Sameroff, 1990). The central principle is to view each family as an individual unit and to ascertain what meaning they ascribe to the illness or disability. Assumptions should not be made without first getting to know the family, because so many variables contribute to views on causation and disability, particularly related to children.

A mother had a 20-month-old infant who was diagnosed with Down syndrome. The mother was from a rural part of Mexico, had had 4 years of schooling there, and had attended English classes in the United States for 1 year. She had a brother and sister-in-law who lived in the area and who often offered their ideas on child care based on their experiences with their own four children.

The mother had noted that her infant had been restless and seemed to be uncomfortable. She felt the top of his head and noted that it was particularly soft. Sometimes parents who cannot ascribe a specific illness to a child who is fretful may say, *"Se ha caido la mollera,"* which implies that the child's fontanel has fallen, causing the discomfort. This mother had heard her brother describe the traditional Mexican interventions: one was to break an egg over the child's head; the other was to push on the roof of the child's mouth to address the problem. The mother held the child upside down and placed her hand in the child's mouth to push the *mollera* back up so as to bring relief to the child. Instead, the child began choking and almost stopped breathing. That same day the visiting nurse heard about this episode and made a referral to a worker who was bilingual. When the mother explained that she was concerned that the child had problems with his *mollera* and that she had been following her relative's prescriptions or interventions because he had more experience with children, the interventionist assessed the mother's other practices with the child. On reflection, the interventionist determined that this mother was not intending to be abusive and was only following a folk belief.

The interventionist provided important educational input regarding the danger of the manual intervention. An appointment with a physician was scheduled to identify the child's condition. The interventionist also had to work with this mother to explain about the special needs of her infant. She helped to focus the mother's folk beliefs so that they would not present a danger to the child. More important, she educated the mother about U.S. laws on child abuse and how sometimes authorities can confuse good intentions with bad. The interventionist acknowledged how important it was for this mother to have family support but underlined the special needs of her child and asked the mother to call for a consultation before proceeding with any interventions.

Death and Dying

The underpinning of Catholicism for many Latino Americans contributes to the reliance on religious beliefs and rituals for addressing death. The family and community follow extensive religious and demonstrative practices for supporting the family and facilitating the grieving process. The praying of the Rosary the evening before the Burial Mass and typical reception after both rituals at the home of the family ensures that grief is a communal event. Death and grief are viewed as "God's will" (Kuipers, 1995).

Some theorists posit that those from a Mesoamerican heritage, such as Mexicans and those from present-day El Salvador, Guatemala, and Honduras, have a dual perspective on death: They offer attention and respect to death in daily rituals while also using humor and indifference toward death. This is particularly notable with the Latino Catholic practice of using the 2nd of November as the Day of the Dead, which allows for annual religious ceremonies to grieve, to decorate and visit graves, or even to install family death altars. Yet, death is addressed lightly through the use of candied skulls to be eaten in Mexican culture or the extensive use of skeletons and death motifs in Mexican and Latin American art forms. This death duality is based on understanding death as intertwined with life and can be traced to Pre-Colombian, Mayan, and Aztec myths. These myths were based on the notion that the very existence of all things was ultimately dependent on death (Villarruel & Ortiz de Montellano, 1992). For those Latinos who are not Catholic, the rituals most likely are related to the particular religion they practice; however, they still have a communal aspect. Similarly, across the diverse Latino groups, black clothing is used for mourning by family members and those attending funeral rituals.

ISSUES OF LANGUAGE

Although the various groups referred to in this chapter are Spanish speaking, the interventionist needs to use caution in working with various immigrant groups because immigration trends in the last decade have produced some interesting differences in dialect. For example, in the early 1990s, Southern California received many immigrants from the state of Oaxaca in Mexico. Many came from very small towns in the interior where Indian dialects are prevalent. Thus, many of these immigrants are bilingual in their Indian dialect and Spanish, but they may feel more comfortable in their indigenous dialect. Even Spanish-speaking interventionists must be cautious in their communication, then, to ensure that they do not use idioms or concepts that immigrants may not comprehend. For example, the interventionist may ask if an individual uses an Indian language; she or he may then use this as a reminder to ask if the individual has understood the communication or to ask questions of the client to assess if comprehension has occurred. The interventionist may need to communicate the same idea or theme in various ways to ensure better comprehension.

Another theme related to communication is the field-dependent nature of Latinos. Latino people are very sensitive to interpersonal relations and may use nonverbal communication cues to assess their interaction with others, particularly in relation to an authority figure or in relation to someone with status. Thus, the interventionist must be conscious of her or his reactions to aspects of the individual's culture, for example, reactions to situations that are novel, curious, or even frightening to her or him. The interventionist's affect or body language may convey to the Latino client or family an image of a caring and respectful helper or someone who disrespects their style of coping and living.

SUMMARY

A variety of factors influences each Latino family system. The range of countries from which Latinos originate contributes to the differences that often are present. Discerning if an immigrant is a political refugee is important because it may imply emotional issues related to death or to the torture of family members as well as PTSD. Similarly, knowing if a family is not in the United States legally may offer insights on their reticence, distrust, or fear of apprehension with implications for how referrals can be used. An important consideration is that if someone who does not have legal documents experienced one or more traumatic events during his or her crossing, he or she also may be affected by PTSD, which can complicate his or her ability to address a family member's disability. Yet, the language commonality and the influence

A Latina mother from Central America gave birth to a girl with a stomach disorder that the teaching hospital had difficulty diagnosing. The infant could not eat normally and had to be tube fed. The mother's first two children, ages 4 and 2, were born healthy. The child with the disorder remained in the hospital more than 2 months; assessment indicated that the child would have long-term medical difficulties.

Because the child's discharge from the hospital was imminent, it was expected that the mother would visit frequently so that she could learn the complicated feeding procedures. The mother agreed to visitation schedules so that one of the staff could instruct her; however, she would typically miss two visits out of three. The staff believed that she was not bonding with the child because she was visiting with the child so infrequently.

A social worker was asked to work with this woman and to attend a staff meeting with the multidisciplinary team and the mother. Staff members spoke in English about the mother, noting that they believed child abuse issues might be occurring in view of her lack of participation. They described the mother as uncaring and unnurturing.

Review by the bilingual/bicultural social worker uncovered the following: 1) the mother, although she had lived in the United States for 5 years, had few friends and no relatives in the area, was a single parent, and had no one who could provide child care for her two other children and no money to pay for child care; and 2) she lived more than an hour's distance from the hospital in a rural area where bus transportation was infrequent and meant several bus transfers. The mother related to the social worker that lack of child care and money kept her from visiting her daughter. It was painful for her not to be able to see her daughter more often. Also, when she did come, the nurses acted very cold and she felt unwanted and disrespected by the staff members. Moreover, instructions were often given using highly formal Spanish with medical terminology that was difficult for her to follow, and she had made mistakes in trying to learn the complicated feeding instructions, which made her feel incompetent as a mother.

The interventionist explained these considerations to the staff. The staff asked why the mother had not told them of her problems. The mother answered in Spanish that no one had ever asked her. The social worker's intervention included educating the staff about this mother's embarrassment regarding her poverty and her lack of education and communication skills, as well as her reticence in interacting with professionals. Child care and transportation were obtained. Further monitoring revealed a loving and caring mother who was able to learn complicated procedures when they were demonstrated and explained clearly in lay terminology in Spanish.

of Spanish traditions, particularly around family life and expectations for children, offer some insight into the values and beliefs that may underlie how children are viewed and how disability may be addressed.

A critical theme is the influence of class on the Latino view of family life, gender roles, and roles of children. Moreover, class status also may influence the extent to which families rely on folk beliefs. Folk beliefs influence families' views of causation and disability. Care must be taken not to base services on assumptions of class, however. An immigrant may be poor now, but may come from a lifestyle that is middle or upper class in his or her country of origin. Latinos view class very similarly to others in the United States; for example, it is insulting to be called "low class" or to be assumed to be in a lower class group. Thus, it is critical that interventionists understand the theme of class in all its complexity. Every family and parent needs to be addressed as an individual in terms of his or her particular reactions and perspectives on the disabilities or illnesses that affect his or her child.

Moreover, assumptions cannot be made about a family's cultural stance. The interventionist is responsible for understanding the individuality of each family or parental system to determine the family's cultural traits. If families do, in fact, subscribe to the use of healers, the interventionist is cautioned to respect this fact while at the same time ensuring that there are no contraindicated interventions occurring that may harm the child.

Language themes will be particularly pertinent if a family is not English speaking. The interventionist must be careful in the selection of interpreters and recognize that communication can be foiled in the interpretation process. Last, interventionists must be conscious of and sensitive to how they use their role in order to ensure that they humanize their relationships and acknowledge the value placed in Latino cultures on interpersonal respect.

RECOMMENDATIONS FOR INTERVENTIONISTS

The importance of self-knowledge cannot be overstated. Interventionists' effectiveness with Latino families that have members with disabilities significantly depends on the extent to which the interventionists themselves are open to discerning how they handle ethnic, cultural, and racial differences. The following directives are offered to help the practitioner recognize these issues and also to consider the particular implications of the information offered in this chapter.

- *Examine your experiences with diversity, both culturally and racially.* Were you socialized to accept and appreciate cultural and racial differences? Did you have negative experiences in your socialization that now affect how you interact with a person of a different culture? Do you have a need to "hide" your prejudices or to rationalize them? Can you uncover these "-isms" and work on eradicating them? Can you make a commitment to unlearn prejudices or ingrained aspects of racism? These negative residues can only undermine your ability to be effective with client systems that are culturally diverse and can actually be harmful to clients (Lum, 2003).

- *Assess your typical style of interacting with people in general and clients in particular.* If you are always constrained by time, you may need to retune your timing mechanisms so that a Latino client does not receive the message that you are in a hurry and thus interpret this as your giving him or her less respect or concern. This is especially important in light of the Latino's sensitivity to interpersonal cues (Davis & Proctor, 1989).

- *If the family has recently immigrated, then assess their adaptation processes to discern if and where problems may be present.* Such problems could cloud the family's ability to focus on the needs of the identified infant or child (Perez Foster, 2001).

- *If the immigrant family is not legally documented, then go out of your way to delineate your role.* Highlight that it does not include informing the U.S. Citizenship and Immigration Service (ISCIS) or what is termed *La Migra*.

- *Given the reactions to illegal immigration, especially in states such as California, try to discern how you really feel about someone who is here without legal documents.* It will be important to monitor any resentment or antipathy toward "illegal aliens" because the client or family system will be especially sensitive to negative cues.

- *Out of respect for the immigrants' human status, professionals should avoid using the term* illegal aliens. Family service providers should instead use the term *undocumented immigrants* when referring to them, for example, on a referral slip or in consultation activities.

- *If the immigrant family is not in the United States legally, consider if and who might be suffering from PTSD.* This condition might be related to the trauma of crossing the border or the unrelenting fear of apprehension now that they are in the United States.

- *If the immigrant family members come from a rural region of their country of origin, then assess basic issues, such as whether they know about childproofing their home.* They may not recognize the need to have covers for electrical outlets because wiring in their previous country may have been structured differently.

- *Do not assume that a family or a parent is literate in English* or Spanish. Carefully assess this so that education inputs will be used appropriately.

- *For poor and immigrant families, assess their feelings about going to doctors' offices or large urban centers for examinations.* It may be necessary to accompany them and serve as a role model for them as they confront new situations such as using elevators or following expected protocol when entering a reception area in a doctor's office.

- *Assess whether the family has transportation for following through on a referral that you make.* They may gladly agree to all of your plans but may be embarrassed to inform you that they have no means of transportation. Or they may not know how to traverse freeways that you assume everyone can negotiate.

- *Learn about the class/economic backgrounds of families who are immigrants because their status in their country of origin may support a more Western view than you may realize.*

- *If a family comes from a Latino culture with which you are unfamiliar, such as El Salvador, do some research.* Assess what resources may exist in your community that can offer you consultation, readings, or perspectives so that you can become better informed.

- *In your city, identify the Latino community networks and agencies that exist so that you will know what is available for referral purposes and to whom you can call to support your work or to offer you consultation.* Attend Latino community celebrations as another avenue for you to gain respect for and knowledge of different Latino cultural rituals and practices

- *Keep abreast of changes in immigration policy.* Gaining access to such sites as the National Council of La Raza web site will give you current insights on immigrant rights and resource issues.

- *Check out which private agency(ies) provide services to undocumented immigrants so that you will have referral resources.* Often, organizations such as Catholic Charities or Episcopal Community Services provide such services.

- *Given the growing presence of Latinos, begin or continue to read about this population.* There are presently many publications, journals, and texts available. The *Hispanic Journal of the Behavioral Sciences* is an excellent resource that can be obtained from Sage Publications. For more leisurely reading on all Latino groups, a monthly periodical such as *Hispanic*, published in Washington, D.C., by Hispanic Publishing Corporation, can be quite informative.

In conclusion, it is important to realize that learning about cultural diversity is a lifelong process, just as enhancing one's competency as an interventionist is also lifelong. The variety of knowledge that interventionists are being asked to consider can be overwhelming. Do not react by shutting off emotionally; reframe your reaction so that you view this as an avenue for broadening your appreciation for how different cultures live, thus broadening your worldview.

WHAT WOULD YOU DO?

Carrie Johnson has just begun working with the Meza family to help their daughter, Alma, age 3. Carrie is a physical therapist with a nonprofit health clinic that serves a large percentage of Latino families. The Meza family is composed of Mr. and Mrs. Meza and their three children, including Alma; Berto, age 5; and Alicia, age 11. Mr. Meza works for a construction company and Mrs. Meza provides child care in her home to earn more money. Mr. and Mrs. Meza and Alicia were born in El Salvador and Alma and Berto were born in San Diego, California.

Although Mrs. Meza had typical pregnancies and health histories with Berto and Alicia, Mrs. Meza was sick repeatedly during her pregnancy with Alma. Her blood pressure became very low, and she had fainting spells; but because she had no medical insurance, she did not see a doctor until she delivered in a hospital emergency room. Alma was a low birth weight infant and had to have blood transfusions. Her mother was unclear about the medical diagnoses but related that Alma was jaundiced and stayed an extra 2 weeks in the neonatal intensive care unit. Mrs. Meza was not always able to follow through on the medical appointments for Alma because of limited funds and access to transportation. Now that the family lives closer to this health clinic, it has been easier for her to make her appointments, but she still misses about every other appointment. Alma is underweight, is not walking, and has been tentatively diagnosed with cerebral palsy.

Because Carrie is new to this family, most of the information she has about them is from the medical chart notes. Several of the notes indicate that Mrs. Meza may need to be referred to child protective services (CPS) because she has a history of failing to keep medical appointments. Mrs. Meza claims that personnel never clearly explained what was really wrong with Alma. It was hard for the clinic to obtain Spanish-speaking staff, and thus they had used inexperienced translators, including a janitor, when communicating with her. Because the baby seemed to lack physical strength and did not have the same development patterns of her other two children, she took the child to a *sabador* (a folk chiropractor) to see if that would help strengthen the child's muscles. One of the physicians who discovered this practice believed that the mother was not very bright and did not seem to understand the importance of medical appointments and following the exercise regimen that she had been given for the child. He also believed that her use of this *sabador*, whom he called "a quack," demonstrated poor judgment. When asking her (again through a translator) if she was following the regimen that had been given to her, the mother, usually flustered, would begin to argue with the translator.

The physical therapist who had been Carrie's predecessor had made a home visit, and she believed that poverty could be a factor in the mother's seemingly poor follow-through with Alma's physical needs. Alma and the other children were always clean, and milk and crackers were evident for the two children the mother was babysitting. But the mother initially would not answer the door, and the therapist questioned why she was being so resistant. Because the family had no telephone, the home visit was unannounced and this seemed to fluster the mother; she seemed very anxious during the visit.

One of the questions that has been raised is whether a referral to CPS might be in order to address the mother's apparent lack of cooperation and compliance with medical visits. Also, notes from the previous therapist question why this parent always seems to be anxious during appointments and was obviously very nervous during the home visit. The mother missed the appointment after the home visit but came into her next monthly appointment, again nervous. One of the Spanish-speaking nurses had been asked to speak to her and to relate the concern about Alma's care. The nurse had reported that Mrs. Meza swore that she tries her best to care for her child but that it is hard for her to understand all of what doctor says. Mrs. Meza also indicated that the directions on the exercise therapy regimen that she has in Spanish are hard to understand. Due to the civil unrest in her country she had not received much education and was not very literate. The mother explained further that because she now lives closer to the clinic (about a mile), she has to walk. There is no bus line to the clinic, and she has no other transportation. Also, if she cannot get babysitting coverage for the two children she cares for, she cannot leave home. Furthermore, although she tries not to use the main thoroughfare, that particular area is heavily patrolled by border patrol cars and she fears she will be apprehended. In tears, the mother admits she has lived in this country for 10 years without legal papers.

A consultation with the nurse who spoke to the mother in Spanish, the attending physician, and the physical therapist is undertaken to discuss the referral to CPS. The physician, who has only been practicing in this area for 9 months, indicates that he feels two referrals are probably needed: one to CPS to ensure medical care for Alma, and one to the authorities because he believes that the mother's behavior indicates she has broken the law if she is undocumented.

1. What are the responsibilities of the staff in relation to the report to the authorities?

2. Does this case, with the information that is now evident, warrant referral to CPS?

REFERENCES

Abad, V., & Boyce, E. (1979). Issues in psychiatric evaluations of Puerto Ricans: A sociocultural perspective. *Journal of Operational Psychiatry, 10*(1), 28–30.

Abalos, D.T. (1986). *Latinos in the United States: The sacred and the political.* Notre Dame, IN: University of Notre Dame Press.

Adkins, P., & Young, R. (1976). Cultural perceptions in the treatment of handicapped school children of Mexican-American parentage. *Journal of Research and Development in Education, 9*(4), 83–90.

Allen, J.P., & Turner, E.J. (1988). *We the people: An atlas of America's ethnic diversity.* New York: Macmillan.

Annerino, J. (1999). *Dead in their tracks: Crossing America's desert borderlands.* New York: Four Walls Eight Windows.

Arias, A.M. (1990, September). Casa Colina. *Hispanic: The magazine for and about Hispanics,* p. 60.

Bellisle, M. (1999, May 27). Policy on benefits is praised for clarity. *San Diego Union-Tribune,* p. A-3.

Bender, D., & Leane, B. (Eds.). (1997). *Illegal immigration: Opposing viewpoints.* San Diego, CA: Greenhaven Press.

Bernal, G. (1982). Cuban families. In M. McGoldrick, J. Pearce, & J. Giordano (Eds.), *Ethnicity and family therapy* (pp. 187–207). New York: Guilford Press.

Boekestijn, D. (1984, September). *Intercultural migration and the development of personal identity: The dilemma between identity maintenance and cultural adaptation.* Paper presented at the XXIII International Congress of Psychology, Acapulco, Mexico.

Cafferty, P.S.J., & Engstrom, D.W. (2000). *Hispanics in the United States: An Agenda for the twenty-first century.* New Brunswick, NJ: Transaction Publishers.

Cervantes, R., Snyder, S., & Padilla, A. (1989). Posttraumatic stress in immigrants from Central America and Mexico. *Hospital and Community Psychiatry, 40*(6), 615–619.

Chiswick, B.R., & Hurst, M.E. (2000). Hispanics and the American labor market. In P.S.J. Cafferty & D.W. Engstrom (Eds.), *Hispanics in the United States* (pp. 175–194). New Brunswick: Transaction.

Cohn, D., & Fears, D. (2001, March 7). Hispanics draw even with Blacks in new census. *The Washington Post,* p. A1.

Connelly, Lorena. (2000). Sociodrama: "Promotoras." In *Families Working Together Against Violence.* Workshop conducted at the Second Annual Power in Partnership Conference, University of Portland, Oregon.

Cromwell, R., & Ruiz, R.A. (1979). The myth of macho dominance in decision-making within Mexican and Chicano families. *Hispanic Journal of Behavioral Sciences, 1,* 355–373.

Davis, L., & Proctor, E. (1989). *Race, gender and class.* Upper Saddle River, NJ: Prentice Hall.

DeAnda, D. (1984). Bicultural socialization: Factors affecting the minority experience. *Social Work, 29,* 101–107.

Delgado, M. (1977). Puerto Rican spiritualism and the social work profession. *Social Casework, 58,* 451–458.

Delgado, M. (1988). Groups in Puerto Rican spiritism: Implications for clinicians. In C. Jacobs & D. Bowels (Eds.), *Ethnicity and race: Critical concepts in social work* (pp. 71–83). Silver Spring, MD: National Association of Social Workers.

Delgado, M. (1994). Hispanic natural support systems and the AODA field: A developmental framework for collaboration. *Journal of Multicultural Social Work, 2,* 11–37.

Diaz-Stevens, A.M. (1996, September). *Latino popular religiosity and communitarian spirituality, Program for the Analysis of Religion Among Latinos (PARAL), Occasional Paper No. 4.*

Egan, M. (1991). *Milagros: Votive offerings from the Americas.* Santa Fe, New Mexico, Museum of New Mexico Press.

Fernandez, E., & Robinson, G. (1994). *Illustrative ranges of the distribution of undocumented immigrants by state* (Bureau of the Census, Population Division, Working Paper 8.) Washington, DC: U.S. Government Printing Office.

Fitzpatrick, J. (1981). The Puerto Rican family. In C. Mindel & R. Habenstein (Eds.), *Ethnic families in America* (pp. 189–214). New York: Elsevier.

Garcia-Preto, N. (1982). Puerto Rican families. In M. McGoldrick, J. Pearce, & J. Giordano (Eds.), *Ethnicity and family therapy* (pp. 164–186). New York: Guilford Press.

Gibbs, J.T., & Huang, L.N. (Eds.). (1989). *Children of color: Psychological interventions with minority youth.* San Francisco: Jossey-Bass.

Giger, J.N., & Davidhizar, R.E. (1995). *Transcultural nursing: Assessment and intervention.* St. Louis: Mosby.

Gomez, E. (1977). *Chicano culture and mental*

health: Trees in search of a forest. San Antonio, TX: Our Lady of the Lake University of San Antonio.

Gonzalez-Whippier, M. (1989). Santeria, the religion. New York: Harmony Books.

Goodman, M.E., & Beman, A. (1971). Child's-eye-views of life in an urban barrio. In N. Wagner & M. Haug (Eds.), Chicanos: Social and psychological perspectives (pp. 109–122). St. Louis: Mosby.

Gutierrez, J., & Sameroff, A. (1990). Determinants of complexity in Mexican-American and Anglo-American mothers' conceptions of child development. Child Development, 61, 384–894.

Harry, B. (1992). An ethnographic study of cross-cultural communication with Puerto Rican–American families in the special education system. American Educational Research Journal, 29(3), 471–494.

Hepworth, D., & Larsen, J. (1990). Direct social work practice: Theory and skills. Belmont, CA: Wadsworth.

Ho, M.K. (1987). Family therapy with ethnic minorities. Beverly Hills: Sage Publications.

Inclan, J. (1985). Variations in value orientations in mental health work with Puerto Ricans. Psychotherapy, 22, 324–334.

Juarez, R. (1985). Core issues in psychotherapy with the Hispanic child. Psychotherapy, 22, 441–448.

Kammer, J. (2002, October 7). Engineer pays "debt of gratitude" by courting Hispanics for Bush. San Diego Union-Tribune, pp. A1, A10.

Kluckhohn, F., & Strodtbeck, F. (1961). Variations in value orientations. Evanston, IL: Row & Peterson.

Koss-Chioino, J.D., & Vargas, L.A. (1999). Working with Latino youth: Culture, development, and context. San Francisco: Jossey-Bass.

Kuipers, J. (1995). Mexican Americans. In J. Giger & R. Davidhizar (Eds.), Transcultural nursing, assessment and intervention. St. Louis: Mosby.

Levine, E., & Padilla, A. (1980). Crossing cultures in therapy: Pluralistic counseling for the Hispanic. Belmont, CA: Wadsworth Group.

Lum, D. (Ed) (2003). Culturally competent practice: A framework for understanding diverse groups and justice issues. Belmont, CA: Wadsworth Group.

Maldonado, D. (2000). The changing religious practice of Hispanics. In P.S.J. Cafferty & D.W. Engstrom (Eds), Hispanics in the United States: An agenda for the twenty-first century (pp. 97–121). New Brunswick, NJ: Transaction Publishers.

Migration News. (May, 1996). Central American immigrants (Vol. 3).

Mizio, E. (1974). Impact of external systems on the Puerto Rican family. Social Casework, 55(1), 76–83.

Montgomery, P.A. (1994). The Hispanic population in the United States: March 1993 (U.S. Bureau of the Census, Current Population Reports, Series P29-475). Washington, DC: U.S. Government Printing Office.

Montiel, M. (1975). The Chicano family: A review of research. Social Work, 18(2), 22–31.

Montijo, J. (1985). Therapeutic relationships with the poor: A Puerto Rican perspective. Psychotherapy, 22, 436–440.

Negroni-Rodriquez, L. & Morales, J. (2001). Individual and family assessment skills with Latino/Hispanic Americans. In R. Fong and S. Furuto (Eds.), Culturally competent practice: Skills, interventions, and evaluations (pp. 132–146). Boston: Allyn & Bacon.

Ortiz, F. (1973). Los Negros brujos [The Negro witches]. Miami, FL: New House Publishing.

Orlando Sentinel. (2001, June 15). Navy officials, GOP lawmakers fume at Bush Vieques decision. San Diego Union Tribune, p. A2.

Perez Foster, R.M. (2001). When immigration is trauma: Guidelines for the individual and family clinician. American Journal of Orthopsychiatry, 71, 153–170.

Potocky-Tripodi, M. (1999). Refugee children: How are they faring economically as adults? In P. Ewalt, E. Freeman, A. Fortune, D. Poole, & S. Witkin (Eds.), Multicultural issues in social work: Practice and research (pp. 622–633). Washington, DC: National Association of Social Workers.

Powell, G., Yamamoto, J., Romero, A., & Morales, A. (Eds.). (1983). The psychosocial development of minority group children. New York: Brunner/Mazel.

Puig, M. (2001). Organizations and community intervention: Skills with Hispanic Americans. In R. Fong & S. Furuto (Eds.), Culturally competent practice: Skills, interventions, and evaluations (pp. 269–284). Boston: Allyn & Bacon.

Ramirez, M., & Price-Williams, D. (1974). Cognitive styles in children: Two Mexican communities. InterAmerican Journal of Psychology, 8, 93–101.

Ramirez, O., & Arce, C.H. (1981). The contemporary Chicano family: An empirically based review. In A. Baron, Jr. (Ed.), Explorations in Chicano psychology (pp. 3–28). New York: Praeger.

Roland, A. (1988). *In search of self in India and Japan: Towards a cross-cultural psychology.* NJ: Princeton University Press.

Romero, A. (1983). The Mexican American child: A sociological approach to research. In G. Powell, J. Yamamoto, A. Romero, & A. Morales (Eds.), *The psychosocial development of minority group children* (pp. 538–572). New York: Brunner/Mazel.

Rubinstein, D. (1976). Beyond the cultural barriers: Observations on emotional disorders among Cuban immigrants. *International Journal of Mental Health, 5*(2), 69–79.

Salcido, R.M. (1982). Use of services in Los Angeles County by undocumented families: Their perceptions of stress and sources of support. *California Sociologist, 5*(2), 119–131.

Salgado de Snyder, N. (1987). *Mexican immigrant women* (Spanish Speaking Mental Health Research Center, Occasional Paper. 22). Los Angeles: University of California at Los Angeles.

Sanchez, L. (2002, June 24). Memorializing border crossers. *San Diego Union-Tribune,* pp. B2, B4.

Shapiro, J., & Tittle, K. (1990, April). Maternal adaptation to child disability in a Hispanic population. *Family Relations, 39,* 179–185.

Sluzki, C. (1979). Migration and family conflict. *Family Process, 18,* 379–390.

Smith-DeMateo, R. (1987, February). *Multicultural considerations: Working with families of developmentally disabled and high risk children: The Hispanic perspective.* Paper presented at the Conference of the National Center for Clinical Infant Programs, Los Angeles.

Stoner, K.L. (1991). *From the house to the streets: The Cuban woman's movement for legal reform.* Durham, NC: Duke University Press.

Straus, M., & Gelles, R. (1990). *Physical violence in American families: Risk factors and adaptations to violence in 8,145 families.* New Brunswick, NJ: Transaction Publishers.

Szapocznik, J., & Hernandez, R. (1988). The Cuban American family. In C. Mindel, R. Habenstein, & R. Wright, Jr. (Eds.), *Ethnic families in America* (3rd ed., pp. 160–172). New York: Elsevier.

Torres-Matrullo, C. (1982). Cognitive therapy of depression in the Puerto Rican female. In R.M. Becerra, M. Karno, & J. Escobar (Eds.), *Mental health and Hispanic Americans: Clinical perspectives* (pp. 101–113). New York: Grune & Stratton.

U.S. Bureau of the Census. (2001, May). Census 2000 brief: The Hispanic population. Washington, DC: U.S. Government Printing Office.

U.S. Bureau of the Census (2002, January). Coming from the Americas: A profile of the nation's foreign-born population from Latin America (2000 update). *Census brief: Current population survey.* Washington, DC: U.S. Government Printing Office.

U.S. Seventh Coast Guard District. (1995). *Cuban rescue statistics.* Author.

Vega, W. (1980). Mental health research and North American Hispanic populations: A review and critique of the literature and a proposed research strategy. In R. Valle & W. Vega (Eds.), *Hispanic natural support systems* (No. 620047; pp. 3–14). Sacramento: State of California Department of Mental Health.

Vega, W., Hough, R., & Romero, A. (1983). Family life patterns of Mexican Americans. In G. Powell, J. Yamamoto, A. Romero, & A. Morales (Eds.), *The psychosocial development of minority group children* (pp. 194–215). New York: Brunner/Mazel.

Vega, W., Kolody, B., & Valle, R. (1988). The relationship of marital status, confidante support, and depression among Mexican immigrant women. *Journal of Marriage and the Family, 50,* 391–403.

Villarruel, A., & Ortiz de Montellano, B. (1992). Culture and pain: A Mesoamerican perspective. *Advances in Nursing Science, 15*(1), 21–32.

Ybarra-Soriano, L. (1977). *Conjugal role relationships in the Chicano family.* Unpublished doctoral dissertation, Department of Sociology, University of California, Berkeley.

Zuniga, M. (1988a). Chicano self-concept: A proactive stance. In C. Jacobs & D. Bowles (Eds.), *Ethnicity and race: Critical concepts in social work* (pp. 71–83). Silver Spring, MD: National Association of Social Workers.

Zuniga, M. (1988b). Clinical interventions with Chicanas. *Psychotherapy, 25,* 288–293.

Zuniga, M. (in press). Latino immigrants: Challenges and resources. *Journal of Immigration.*

CONTRASTING BELIEFS, VALUES, AND PRACTICES

Latino	Mainstream culture
Collective orientation	Individual orientation
Interdependence	Independence
Collective, group identity	Individual identity
Cooperation	Competition
Saving face	Being direct
Relaxed with time	Time sensitive
Emphasis on interpersonal relations	Emphasis on task orientation
Spiritual/magical belief orientation	Rational/empirical orientation
More recent agrarian influence	More urbanized/industrialized mode
Tendency toward more patriarchal family structure	Tendency toward more democratic family structure
More relaxed toward child development	Strong expectations regarding child development
More overt respect for the elderly	Less value/respect toward the elderly
Extended family system more pronounced	Nuclear family system more pronounced
Death more ritualized	Death less ritualized

APPENDIX B

CULTURAL COURTESIES AND CUSTOMS

It is inappropriate for the interventionist to

- Speak to the wife before the husband when both are present
- Not ask whether the father is in agreement with the recommendations or plans, even if he is not at the session or meeting
- Decline a beverage or food offering
- Begin on work or tasks immediately, before any informal and relaxed exchange with the client has taken place
- Use a tone of voice that is harsh and authoritarian
- Show impatience or act hurried
- Sit in a slouched or extremely relaxed manner
- Use teasing to break the ice
- Laugh at a cultural artifact or ritual or dismiss its importance to the family

APPENDIX C

SIGNIFICANT CULTURAL EVENTS/HOLIDAYS/PRACTICES

Dia de los Reyes

January 6

Holiday in Latino countries commemorating the visit of the Magi or three kings to the Christ child, in which children leave their shoes out and the shoes are filled with treats.

Nuestra Señora de la Caridad del Cobre

Eve of September 8

Celebration by those from Cuba and the Caribbean honoring the patron saint of Cuba and Ochún Santeria. After the mass, the statue of this saint is paraded in the church and those present wave handkerchiefs in the air (Gonzales-Whippier, 1989).

Feast of St. Francis of Assisi or Orunla, the syncretized Santeria deity

October 4

Coconuts are brought to the house of the babalawo who is the high priest of Santeria. The coconuts are *derechos* (rights) that the children bring as offerings.

Dia de los Muertos (Day of the Dead, All Souls Day for Catholics)

November 1 for all children who have died; November 2 for all adults who have died

Holiday celebrated by Mexicans and many Latinos that contains aspects of Indian ancestor worship coupled with Catholic prayer rites for the deceased. Mexican families may build altars to commemorate the dead. Statues, pictures of the dead, food offerings, decoration of skeletons, candied skulls with the names of the deceased, candles, and so forth are placed on the altars.

Feast of Our Lady of Guadelupe

December 12

In parish churches in Mexican communities, a mass of extensive celebration, often with parades, commemorates the apparition of Our Lady to Juan Diego, an Indian peasant in the 1500s who lived in what is now Mexico City.

Noche Buena

December 24

Holiday celebrated by preparing foodstuffs for the holiday, such as tamales for Mexicans, then attending midnight mass.

APPENDIX D

VOCABULARY

English	Spanish	Pronunciation
Mother	Madre	Mah-thray
Father	Padre	Pah-thray
Family	Familia	Fah-mee-lēah
Hello	Buenos días	Bway-nōs dee-ahs
Good-bye	Adiós	Ah-dee-ōs
Thank you very much	Muchas gracias	Moo-chas grră-sē-ahs
Please	Por favor	Poŏr fah-bore
With your permission	Con su permiso	Cone su pear-mi-so
Pardon	Perdón	Pear-don
It was a pleasure meeting you	Un placer	Uhn-pla-sare

CHAPTER 8

FAMILIES WITH ASIAN ROOTS

Sam Chan and Evelyn Lee

When you drink water, think of where it came from.
—CHINESE SAYING

You can fall down seven times; but you'll stand up
after the eighth.
—KOREAN SAYING

Don't choose a straight path, and don't reject a winding one.
Choose a path your ancestors have trod.
—CAMBODIAN SAYING

Birds have nests. People have roots.
—VIETNAMESE CHILDREN'S SAYING

Asian Americans and Pacific Islanders (AAPIs) are the fastest growing racial/ethnic group in the United States. From 1990 to 2000, the AAPI population increased by 72% to a total of 12 million (4.3% of the U.S. population), whereas the general population only increased by 13% (U.S. Bureau of the Census, 2000). By the year 2050, the AAPI population is projected to reach 40 million, or 10% of the total U.S. population (Aponte & Crouch, 1995; Day, 1995). Immigration accounts for nearly 75% of this population explosion (O'Hare, 1992). Two factors were responsible for more than 90% of foreign-born AAPIs entering the United States: 1) the landmark Immigration and Nationality Act Amendments of 1965, which abolished discrimination based on national origin; and 2) the withdrawal of the United States from Vietnam in 1975 (Hing, 1992). Given the continuing unstable economic conditions and volatile political climates of selected Asian countries, Asian immigration levels in the United States are projected to remain high for many years.

In addition to being the fastest growing racial/ethnic group, the AAPI population also exhibits many unique characteristics:

- *AAPIs are the most culturally diverse minority in terms of countries of origin.* The term *Asian American Pacific Islander* includes members of more than 60 different ethnic groups who originate from Asia, the Pacific Rim, and the Pacific Islands. The vast majority of Asian immigrants have come from three major geographic regions: East Asia (China, Japan, and Korea); Southeast Asia (Burma, Cambodia, Indonesia, Laos, Malaysia, the Philippines, Singapore, Thailand, and Vietnam); and South Asia (India, Pakistan, Sri Lanka, Bangladesh, Bhutan, and Nepal; see Chapter 12). Each immigrant group has been highly affected by the unique cultural and/or linguistic characteristics and historical, sociopolitical, and economic conditions of their respective countries of origin. Time of arrival and varying modes of adaptation to the United States host society have further shaped the unique experiences, lifestyles, and ethnic identities of Asian immigrants (Booth, Crouter, & Landale, 1996; Karnow & Yoshihara, 1992; Sodowsky, Kwong-Liem, & Pannu, 1995; Uba, 1994). According to the 2000 Census, the five largest Asian subgroups (both foreign-born and born in the United States) in order of percentage of the total AAPI population are Chinese (23.7%), Pilipino (18.1%), Asian Indian (16.4%), Vietnamese (11.0%), and Korean (10.5%).

- *A high percentage of Asian Americans are foreign born, although most Pacific Islanders are not.* It is estimated that more than 65% of the AAPI population in the United States is foreign-born. More than 25% of the U.S. foreign-born population is from Asia. Since 1975, more than 200,000 Asian immigrants have been admitted annually to the United States, accounting for nearly half of all legal immigrants (Min, 1995a; U.S. General Accounting Office, 1990). In 2000, 7.2 million of the nation's foreign-born residents were born in Asia, up from 5.0 million in 1990 (U.S. Bureau of the Census, 2000). The countries of origin contributing to the nation's largest Asian-born populations were China, India, Korea, the Philippines, and Vietnam.

- *AAPIs are younger on average than most other population groups.* In 1999, children younger than 18 comprised 29% of the AAPI population, whereas people ages 65 and older constituted only 7% of the AAPI population; this is in contrast to 24%

This chapter is dedicated to the eternal spirit and joyful energy of my co-author and friend, Evelyn Lee. She will be fondly remembered by all of those whom she healed, inspired, enlightened, and advocated for in her lifetime.

and 14%, respectively, for non-Hispanic Whites (U.S. Bureau of the Census, 2000). Significant growth also is projected among Southeast Asian immigrant/ refugee populations as a result of high fertility rates. The birth rate for Southeast Asian women ages 14–40 years is 4.2 children, double the average national birth rate. Southeast Asian American women of childbearing age also constitute a larger proportion of Southeast Asian Americans relative to the proportion of all women of childbearing age in the total U.S. population (Martin, 2001).

- *AAPIs reside mainly in states along the east and west coasts and in Hawaii.* In 1999, 53% of AAPIs resided in the west, 20% resided in southern states, 18% in northeastern states, and 9% in the midwest. The states with the highest AAPI populations were California (4.0 million); New York (1.02 million); Hawaii (0.754 million), and Texas (0.577 million) (U.S. Bureau of the Census, 2000).

- *AAPIs often live in large urban cities and counties.* Fifty-four percent of AAPIs live in just six metropolitan areas: Los Angeles, New York, San Francisco, Honolulu, Washington, D.C./Baltimore, and Chicago.

- *Research indicates a bimodal income distribution among the AAPI population.* The AAPI population had the highest median household income of all of the nation's racial groups ($46,637); yet, many AAPI people lived below the poverty line (in 1998, the AAPI population living below the poverty line was 12.5% as compared with 8.2% for non-Hispanic whites). In AAPI inter-group comparisons, Southeast Asian refugees and Pacific Islanders have been found to be the most impoverished groups (U.S. Bureau of the Census, 1999).

- *Research indicates a bimodal distribution in educational attainment among AAPI groups.* In 1999, 42% of AAPIs ages 25 and older had at least a bachelor's degree, compared with 28% of non-Hispanic Whites (U.S. Bureau of Census, 2000). Among AAPI groups, south Asian Indians have the highest proportion of members with at least a bachelor's degree (58%); whereas Cambodians, Laotians, Hmong, and Tongans have the lowest proportions of members (each 6% or less) with bachelor's degrees (Shinagawa & Jang, 1998).

- *AAPIs often intermarry with members of other ethnic groups.* In 1990, 31.2% of all married AAPI men and 40.4% of all married AAPI women were married to a person of a different race or ethnic group. Among women, Japanese and Pilipino wives were the most likely to be intermarried (51.9% and 40.2%, respectively) (Shinagawa & Jang, 1998). The 2000 census revealed a relatively large mixed-race population. Of the 6.8 million people who reported more than one race, nearly 13% said they are "White and Asian" (U.S. Bureau of the Census, 2000).

- *Profound inter- and intraethnic differences exist among AAPIs.* These differences are reflected in subpopulation sizes, regional concentrations, preferred residential locations, migration and settlement experiences, degree of acculturation, age, generation, gender, education level, occupational skills, socioeconomic status, languages, religions, ethnic identities, and cultural values and beliefs (Fong & Mokuau, 1994; Lee, 1996a; Min, 1995a; Uba, 1994). Moreover, the complex cultures of individuals and families within given groups vary considerably and change over time. Such diversity and complexity obviously defies generalizations that can be applied to all of the constituent ethnic groups. A deeper understanding of the roots of Chinese, Korean, and Southeast Asian Americans is necessary to more effectively serve their growing needs, however.

Despite their rapid growth and increasing visibility and diversity, AAPI have remained one of the most poorly understood ethnic minorities. Throughout their respective histories of experience in the United States, Asian immigrants have been persistently confronted with racism, prejudice, and stereotypic perceptions. Contemporary Asian Americans may find themselves celebrated as America's "model minority" because of their generally high level of educational and occupational achievement, yet, they also have been victimized by increasing hate crimes and violence fueled by waves of anti-immigrant sentiment (Min, 1995c; National Asian Pacific American Legal Consortium [NAPALC], 1995). Successive groups of Asians in America and their ancestors have been considered both threatening and "enigmatic." Just as earlier immigrants were seen as a monolithic race originating from the "mysterious East," ethnic distinctions among recent Asian immigrants are still blurred, and they continue to be perceived as "strangers from a different shore" (Takaki, 1989). This perception serves to disguise the reality of unique customs, traditions, values, beliefs, and familial systems based on political and religious foundations that are thousands of years old (Shon & Ja, 1983).

Acknowledgment and appreciation of such rich histories is critical in the delivery of human services to increasingly diverse Asian immigrant populations. In particular, an understanding of the distinct historical, social, and political experiences of those who are served significantly enhances the effectiveness of early intervention programs. Viewing children and families within an ecological context further entails specific knowledge of traditional values, beliefs, and practices pertaining to religion, family, child rearing, education, health, mental health, disability, death, and dying; language characteristics and communication styles; and cultural orientations and behaviors related to service utilization (Chan, 1986).

This chapter addresses these topics in relation to the following selected Asian American ethnic groups: Chinese, Koreans, and Southeast Asians (specifically Cambodians, Laotians, and Vietnamese). Collectively, these groups represent approximately half of the total Asian Pacific American population. In contrast to other immigrants, such as South Asian Indians (see Chapter 12) and Pilipinos (see Chapter 9) (who are generally proficient in English), the most recent Chinese and Korean immigrants as well as Southeast Asian refugees are predominantly non–English speaking. They also have typically concentrated their economic resources and primary social and cultural institutions within their respective ethnic communities or enclaves. These particular Asian immigrant and refugee populations consequently pose significant challenges with respect to the delivery of accessible as well as culturally and linguistically appropriate services. As families with infants and young children continue to increase in number, they may face conditions of poverty and the profound effects of acculturation stress. Their corresponding service needs most likely will exceed available resources.

CHINESE AMERICANS

The Chinese American community remains the largest Asian subgroup in the United States, with the population growing 48% from 1.6 million in 1990 to nearly 2.5 million in 2000 (U.S. Bureau of the Census, 2000). Chinese Americans reflect the extreme heterogeneity of the larger Asian American population. Some Chinese families have been in the United States for six generations, whereas others have arrived within the past week. They are characterized by significant linguistic, social, and political differences. They primarily originate from many different provinces in the People's Republic of China, Hong Kong, Taiwan, and numerous Southeast Asian countries. In sum, 2.5 million Chinese Americans join the collective "family" of more than 1.3 billion Chinese in the People's Republic and an estimated 30 million "overseas Chinese" people in 110 countries; together they constitute more than one fifth of the world's people (Farley & Tempest, 1996; Park, 2003).

Geographic and Historical Origins

As the mother country, "China is as much an idea as it is a place; to be Chinese is to share a particular cultural identity" (Major, 1989, p. 1). This identity is tied to a common heritage in which every person of Chinese ancestry is a cultural heir to one of the world's oldest living civilizations—one that originated on the northern China plain more than 4,000 years ago and spread throughout the "Middle Kingdom." This region was viewed as the center of the world from which the influence of Chinese people and culture extended. The realm of the Middle Kingdom was called *tianxia* (all under heaven). Beyond precise geographical or political definition, *tianxia* represented the cultural and moral world of Chinese civilization—that is, the essence of being Chinese (Porter, 1983).

The realm of the Middle Kingdom was finally extended to the United States in 1820. The Chinese were the first of the early Asian immigrants and, in the late 1840s, began voluntarily departing China (primarily from the Guangdong province in Southeast China) by the tens of thousands. The discovery of gold in California served as the catalyst for emigration from a country plagued by overcrowding, droughts, widespread famine, economic depression, and ongoing civil wars. Chinese laborers, as sojourners, originally expected to amass their fortune in America or *Gam Saan* (Gold Mountain) and then return home to their families in 3–5 years and retire in prosperity (Sung, 1971). Yet, the vast majority of them did not find any gold and were forced to remain in America and struggle for survival.

Their survival was threatened as the labor market diminished and economic competition fueled anti-Chinese sentiment. Despite their profound contributions in constructing the transcontinental railroad and as service, factory, and farm laborers, Chinese immigrants experienced economic exploitation and racial antagonism, which forced the Chinese to remain strangers to white Americans. Escalating hostility toward the "heathen Chinese" culminated in the passage of the Chinese Exclusion Act of 1882, which barred Chinese laborers and their relatives (including their wives) from entering the United States; the Act was later broadened to include all people of the Chinese race. This was the first time in U.S. history that a federal law was enacted to specifically ban a designated ethnic, racial, or nationality group from entering the country. Thus, the "Chinese invasion" and the "Chinese problem" were addressed by legislating the disappearance of the Chinese presence in America. The experience of the Chinese in the 19th century signaled the beginning of a pattern to be repeated for subsequent Asian groups (Takaki, 1989). In fact, within 40 years of the Chinese Exclusion Act, *all* Asian immigration was banned.

The Chinese Exclusion Act was not repealed until 1943, when China became an American ally at the beginning of World War II. During the 6 decades in which the act remained in force, more Chinese left than entered the United States. While the Chinese population declined, the remaining immigrants survived in the face of antimiscegenation laws, special taxes directed against them, institutionalized racism,

persistent humiliation, racial violence, loss of property, loss of livelihood, and sometimes loss of life. Those who decided to stay or who could not return to their homeland needed to change their status from laborers, who were targets of deportation,
to businessmen, who were exempt from deportation. Chinatowns became the basis
for this conversion, which was accomplished by drawing on traditional structures
such as clans and family associations to organize an urban economic community
built on the service industries (Chen, 1981; Huang & Ying, 1989). Chinatowns also
emerged in many rural areas. Thus, the Chinese continued to create their own colonies or communities that served to perpetuate tradition and adherence to Chinese culture. As a result of immigration laws that continued to prohibit Chinese women from
entering the United States, however, Chinatowns essentially were bachelor societies.
The extremely low proportion of Chinese women further contributed to a steady decline in the Chinese population and delayed the growth of a second generation of
Chinese Americans. This condition also had a profound impact on the development
of family life among the early Chinese immigrants (Lee, 1996b; Wong, 1995).

Despite the repeal of the Chinese Exclusion Act in 1943, a national origins quota
system was imposed whereby a token quota of only 105 Chinese (50% of whom
were required to be professionals) were allowed into the United States each year.
Subsequent immigration policy reforms and laws enabled Chinese wives and children of U.S. citizens to enter the country. Consequently, the vast majority of Chinese
immigrants from 1943 to 1965 were female. In 1965, the landmark Immigration and
Nationality Act Amendments abolished the national origins system. With its emphasis on family reunification, this act granted each country a quota of 20,000 immigrants per year (Chan, 1991; Wong, 1995). Immediate family members were ex-
empted from the quota, and preferred immigrant status was given to educated,
professional, and skilled workers.

While marking a radical change in U.S. immigration policy, the 1965 Immigration Act resulted in the "second wave" of Asian immigration, which produced massive increases as well as changes in the Asian American population. Within 15 years,
Chinese and Pilipinos surpassed Japanese as the largest Asian American ethnic
groups, and nearly two thirds of all Asian Americans were foreign born. In contrast
to the earlier immigrants, who were primarily farmers and laborers with rural origins,
the second wave of newcomers included significant numbers of urban professionals,
who have been considered the most highly skilled of any immigrant group the
United States has ever had. Unlike the pre-1965 immigrants who came over as individuals and sojourners, most of the new immigrants arrived as families and as settlers
seeking permanent U.S. residency (Takaki, 1989; Wong, 1995).

The majority of second-wave Chinese immigrants have settled in two states, California and New York, where they have revitalized Chinatowns and transformed the
Chinese American communities into predominantly immigrant communities once
again. As *San Yi Man* (new immigrants), they come primarily from urban areas in
China and include Mandarin as well as Cantonese speakers. Most were initially refugees from the People's Republic of China and usually emigrated from a second point
of departure such as Hong Kong or Taiwan. After normalization of relations between
China and the United States in 1979, the People's Republic of China was allowed to
have its own quota; this was followed by dramatic increases in the number of family members reuniting with relatives in the United States (Takaki, 1989). During this
same time period (between 1978 and 1980), ethnic Chinese who had constituted the
business class in Southeast Asia became targets for discrimination under the new

Communist regimes; they thus joined the "third wave" of Southeast Asian refugees as "boat people" and came to the United States in large numbers. A significant number of them were survivors of hunger, rape, incarceration, torture, and forced migration (Lee, 1996b).

The *San Yi Man* have dramatically contributed to the current diversity of the Chinese American immigrant population, which ranges from monolingual, less-educated, and semi-skilled individuals to middle-class and affluent, highly educated city and suburban residents. They have immigrated to be reunited with families; to pursue their education as foreign students; to establish themselves in business, industry, and professions; and/or to seek refuge from repressive governmental policies, political conflict, and instability in their respective countries of origin. For most new Chinese immigrants, "America is not *Gam Saan,* a place to work temporarily, but a new home in which they hope to find greater economic opportunities for themselves and educational advantages for their children" (Takaki, 1989, p. 423). Although adapting to American society, they are part of the 150-year-old history of Chinese in the United States that has been "characterized by episodes of prejudice and discrimination, of racism, xenophobia, and exclusion, and more recently, of varying degrees of acceptance or tolerance" (Wong, 1995, p. 58).

Religious Origins

Throughout the past 2,000 years, Chinese culture has been principally influenced by the doctrines and philosophies of Confucianism, Taoism, and Buddhism. Collectively referred to as the "three teachings" of Confucius, Lao Tzu, and Buddha Gautama, they serve as the religious-philosophical systems that undergird all facets of Chinese life. Confucianism, Taoism, and Buddhism thus significantly contribute to the commonalities evident in the worldviews, ethics, social norms, values, folk beliefs, and lifestyles of Chinese and many other Asian people. Each has its unique emphasis; however, together they have evolved into a complementary system of blended teachings that enable Asians to integrate into and be guided by complex mixes of corresponding thoughts and faiths (Leung, 1988).

Confucianism   "For nearly 2,000 years—from shortly before the birth of Christ to the early 20th century—Confucianism was the single most important force in Chinese life" (Bosrock, 1994, p. 45). Confucius (551–479 B.C.) expounded no systematic doctrine but rather he expressed a philosophy about humanity, spoke about man in society, and prescribed a way of life. He believed his mission was not to reform but to rectify his wayward times by trying to restore the ethical, benevolent government of the past—the Way of the Ancients. "The origin of social harmony and good government lay in the cultivation of individual virtues and the observance of reciprocal social obligations that were the moral fabric of society" (Porter, 1983, p. 96). Confucius's ideal was the "perfect gentleman" who behaved in a princely way and was characterized by the "five virtues": 1) *ren* or *jen,* benevolence and humanism (the cardinal principle or primary virtue of Confucianism and the essential quality of humanity), 2) *yi,* righteousness or morality, 3) *li,* proper conduct, 4) *zhi* or *chih,* wisdom or understanding, and 5) *xin,* trustworthiness.

The embodiment of these five virtues is *xiao*—filial piety—that is, the duties owed to one's parents and ancestors (Major, 1989). Filial piety consists of unquestioning loyalty and obedience to parents and concern for and understanding of their needs and wishes. It also includes reverence for ancestors whose spirits must be appeased. Filial piety further extends to relations with all authority figures and defines a social hierarchy of allegiance and reciprocal moral obligations characterized by the "five relations": 1) king/justice, subject/loyalty; 2) father/love, son/filiality; 3) elder brother/brotherly love, younger brother/reverence; 4) husband/initiative, wife/obedience; and 5) friends/mutual faith.

Confucius thus offered prescriptions for regulating "proper" human relationships, which served to maintain the social order. He believed human nature was at best neutral, but anyone could be "made good" by cultivating virtues through study and self-discipline. Such endeavors would, in turn, lead to proper conduct, both in personal and public life. His goal was not religious salvation but rather the full realization *in this life* of the human potential for wisdom and virtue (Major, 1989).

Taoism Unlike Confucianism, Taoism (pronounced DOW-ism) was not associated with any definitive historical figure, although Lao Tzu (who was born about 604 B.C.) is viewed as the legendary patriarch. He advocated the cultivation of inner strength, selflessness, spontaneity, and harmony with nature and man, rather than Confucius's group-oriented propriety and codes of conduct. In fact, society is the antithesis of *Tao*, which literally means the "way" or "path"—the ultimate reality that is eternal and enigmatic. Taoist philosophy stressed the need to transcend artificial man-made human culture (i.e., society) and to avoid worldly entanglements because there is no valid way of making judgments in a world in which everything is relative. Lao Tzu espoused that the truth is infinite; the mind is finite. Taoism thus encouraged the practice of training, asceticism, meditation, and discipline in the pursuit of good health and long life. The tenets of the Taoist life include the following: to know nature, to be natural (i.e., live a natural life), and to avoid interfering with nature. Lao Tzu also explained natural and social phenomena by incorporating the ancient theory of the cyclical counterbalancing forces of yang (the creative, forward, dominating, and manifest force represented by the male and heaven) and yin (the receptive, recessive, submissive, and hidden background force represented by the female and the earth). Everything in reality is not only regarded as generated from the interactions between these two forces, but everything also is composed of both yin and yang.

Taoism was ultimately transformed from an elitist philosophy to an elaborate religion. Taoism further evolved into superstition, magic, divination, and sorcery. Its rituals and mystical practices were compatible with animism, and, although closely associated with the alchemical search for immortality, popular Taoism continues to be widely accepted by the masses, with millions of adherents (Bosrock, 1994; C.-Y. Cheng, 1987; Leung, 1988; Major, 1989; Porter, 1983).

Buddhism Buddhism was founded by Prince Siddharta Gautama (560–480 B.C.) and entered China as an alien religion from India long after Confucianism and Taoism were already established as mature traditions. Although Buddhism later profoundly influenced Confucianism, it also was radically transformed in the process (Porter, 1983).

Original Buddhist doctrine is summarized in the following "four noble truths":

1. All life is suffering.

2. Suffering is caused by desire or attachment to the world.

3. Suffering can be extinguished and attachment to all things (including the self) can be overcome by eliminating desire.

4. To eliminate desire, one must live a virtuous life by following the Middle Way and the Eightfold Noble Path.

The Middle Way is a way of life that avoids both the uncontrolled satisfaction of human desires and the extreme forms of self-denial. The Eightfold Noble Path consists of 1) right views (knowledge of the truth), 2) right resolve (to resist evil), 3) right speech (saying nothing to hurt others), 4) right action (respecting life, morality, and property), 5) right livelihood (working at a job that does not injure others), 6) right effort (trying to rid one's mind of evil), 7) right attention (controlling thoughts and feelings), and 8) right meditation (practicing proper forms of concentration). Buddhism asks all of its adherents to follow this path, which is the basis for the monastic life of the *bonzes* (i.e., priests or monks). Buddha also urged his followers to practice the virtues of kindness and compassion, meekness and nonviolence, charity, and reflection and contemplation (Bosrock, 1994).

Buddha's teachings claimed that the world has no reality; it is an illusion that only seems real because people want it to be. Attachment to the illusion of reality inevitably produces suffering and leads to an endless cycle of rebirths governed by the law of *karma* (whereby an individual's position and fate in this life are the consequence of his or her actions in previous lives). The only escape from the cycle of birth, aging, sickness, and death is Buddhahood or enlightenment in *dharma* (the doctrine of the life of Buddha). The Buddhist's goal is to be released from the "wheel of life" or circle of reincarnation in order to reach *nirvana* (a state of perfect peace, happiness, or complete redemption wherein the world and all sufferings are transcended) and one's soul is merged into the cosmic unity—the only true reality (Lopez, 2001; Major, 1989; Te, 1989a).

Such beliefs obviously challenged the "Chinese attitude," which was much more instinctively down to earth and practical than the South Asian Indian view. Whereas Buddhists denied the world, the Chinese affirmed it (Porter, 1983). Consequently, Chinese Buddhism had to accommodate itself to Chinese cultural imperatives by adopting the basic philosophy that filial piety is the highest morality; however, Buddhism was soon to influence a reinterpretation of Confucianism. Ultimately, Mahayana Buddhism (described in more detail in the Southeast Asian Americans section of this chapter) became the dominant form of spiritualism in China. More specifically, the Chan (Zen in Japan) sect was most widely practiced and, with its emphasis on meditation and rigorous self-discipline, became almost indistinguishable from philosophical Taoism. Buddhism spread from China to Korea to Japan and Southeast Asia; it has had a profound long-term influence on these cultures (Major, 1989).

Ancestor Worship   The "three teachings" of Confucianism, Taoism, and Buddhism are further complemented by ancestor worship, which is considered the universal religion of China and the foundation for popular religion. Ancestor worship serves as the central link between the world of man and the world of the spirits. This practice, which assumes that the living can communicate with the dead, is rooted in the belief that the natural and supernatural are enmeshed in the same world (Lassiter, 1995). Ancestor worship is characterized by the following three basic assumptions:

1. All living people owe their fortunes or misfortunes to their ancestors; if a family worships the spirit of its ancestors, it will be rewarded with good fortune.

2.   All departed ancestors, like other gods and spirits, have needs that are the same as the living.

3.   Departed ancestors continue, as in life, to assist their relatives in this world, just as their descendants can assist them.

These assumptions contribute to corresponding beliefs and practices. Individual achievements and successes are viewed as evidence of one's ancestors' high moral worth and good deeds. Departed ancestors should be provided with offerings of food and various possessions (often in the form of life-size paper models of clothing, furniture, horses, servants, and so forth). A social tie remains between departed ancestors and living descendants; that is, one's condition may be improved by the spiritual efforts of departed ancestors, and the spiritual welfare of departed ancestors may likewise be enhanced by the worldly actions of living descendants. Belief in the mutual dependence and interaction between the living and the dead thus reinforces efforts (including a variety of traditional rituals) to maintain a positive and close relationship with one's departed ancestors as well as living kinsmen. The souls of ancestors stand apart from other spirits or gods who may be worshiped in a more neutral and distant fashion. Thus, "the worst imaginable plight for any Chinese is, while alive, to be without known parents and relatives, and when dead, to be without living descendants" (Hsu, 1981, p. 252).

Complementarity and Polytheism   Indigenous Chinese religion cannot be abstracted from its historical context. Although Neo-Confucianism, Christianity, and Islam have also been somewhat influential, the basic Chinese philosophical/religious orientation has remained rooted in the secular world and has been relatively consistent throughout the past 2,000 years. Adherence to the three teachings reflects a polytheistic orientation that stresses complementarity rather than conflict among Confucianism, Taoism, and Buddhism. Many Chinese temples, for example, were built expressly to house Confucius, Lao Tzu, and Buddha together; moreover, a person might typically pray at a Confucian temple before taking the civil service examinations, call a Taoist doctor to cure an illness, and invite a Buddhist priest to chant at a funeral (Major, 1989).

Confucianism, Taoism, Buddhism, and ancestor worship are "eclectic rather than dogmatic, humanistic rather than theological, and communal rather than personal" (Bosrock, 1994, p. 44). They have been embraced by a collectivistic Chinese society in which human relationships are inclusive rather than exclusive. Polytheism encourages a belief in many gods and emphasizes the coexistence of all supernatural beings. Many Chinese will indicate that they have no particular religion or that because all religions are essentially beneficial to people, they all are equally good. This orientation dramatically contrasts with the monotheistic orientation of most Western societies, with their individualistic religions that emphasize a direct link between the one and only God and the individual human soul; Westerner's corresponding belief in individual self-reliance pervades nearly every aspect of life.

Thus, the American tendency to exclude and the Chinese tendency to include represent fundamental differences in religious orientations as well as many other values and belief systems (Hsu, 1981). These contrasts and more specific relationships between traditional religious and/or philosophical beliefs and disability and service utilization are discussed subsequently in this chapter.

Language/Linguistic Origins

No single Chinese language exists, but rather, Chinese people speak a multiplicity of dialects. In contrast to regional American English dialects, the major Chinese dialects have evolved into distinctly different spoken languages that are mutually unintelligible. The national language or common speech of the People's Republic of China is *Putonghua* (Mandarin), which is spoken by more than 70% of the people. Mandarin includes various northern Chinese dialects and is spoken in the north, northwest, west, and southwest regions of China. The *Wu* dialects (e.g., Shanghainese) are spoken in the east. The most widely differentiated dialects (e.g., Cantonese, Min, Hakka) are spoken in the southeast. In past decades, most Chinese American immigrants were from Cantonese-speaking provinces of Southeast China and Hong Kong. Another popular dialect among immigrants is Taishanese, a Cantonese-related dialect from the Taishan province in the People's Republic of China. Taiwanese immigrants typically speak Taiwanese, Fukienese, and Mandarin. Cantonese (and a rarer dialect, Chiuchow) is typically spoken among ethnic Chinese immigrants and refugees from Vietnam and other Southeast Asian countries (Lee, 1996b; Tinloy, Tan, & Leung, 1986). In practical terms, the complexity of Chinese dialects may pose significant challenges in working with monolingual Chinese-speaking families. For example, an English-speaking interventionist may not know how to assess the primary dialect of the family or have the right interpreters available to match the dialect. A Mandarin-speaking provider from Taiwan may not be able to communicate with a Cantonese-speaking client from Hong Kong.

The various dialects of Chinese also have many monosyllabic words. Each monosyllabic word or each syllable of a compound word has a distinctive pitch, referred to as a tone. Mandarin has 4 basic tones, whereas Cantonese has 10 tones. Tones do not refer to individual speaker expression and have nothing to do with the mood or the personality of the speaker. Instead, they convey different meanings for the syllables to which they are assigned. For example, depending on which tones are used, the Cantonese word *mai* may mean either "buy" or "sell"; for the Mandarin word *ma*, there are at least four possible meanings (e.g., "mother," "hemp," "horse," "scold") corresponding to four different tones. Moreover, there are many Chinese homonyms, that is, words that have the same sounds and tones, yet still have multiple meanings (Tinloy et al., 1986).

Apart from tonal pronunciation, the linguistic structure of Chinese differs significantly from English. Intonations tend to rise at the end of a sentence in the Chinese language, which is in contrast with English, in which they tend to fall. The Chinese language has no digraphs (e.g., because there is no "th" sound, a word like "some*th*ing" might be pronounced as "somesing"). It also uses no gender pronouns, tenses, plural endings, or verb conjugations; thus gender, time, and quantity are denoted by word additions rather than through the modification of words as in English (Chin, 1983). Words are thus very context-bound, wherein "the meaning of the whole determines the meaning of the parts" (L.L. Cheng, 1987, p. 33). Sequencing of sentence parts (e.g., subject, verb, object) also is different in the two languages.

Remarkably, all dialects of spoken Chinese share the same written language, which has been revered and respected for preserving Chinese culture and history while playing a critical role in binding the diverse people of China together. The Chinese written language also has served to cement ties between neighboring countries such as Korea and Vietnam, both of which used classical Chinese as their written language for official government documents and important works of literature (Major, 1989). The majority of Chinese from Hong Kong, Taiwan, and Southeast Asian countries practice the "traditional," or classical, writing style. The People's Republic of China developed the "simplified" writing style (Lee, 1996b). The written language consists of approximately 50,000 ideograms, or characters, that represent an object or idea; there also are more than 100,000 combined compounds (thousands of individual characters change meaning when used with other characters). Fewer than 6,000 characters are in common use, however. Reading fluency requires knowledge of 3,000–4,000 characters (Bosrock, 1994).

Because the Chinese written language has no alphabet, the transliteration of Chinese ideograms into English is purely phonetic. The official system of the People's Republic developed in 1958 to simulate Chinese words using the English alphabet is called *pinyin*. Older systems are still in use, however, and thus account for the multiple spellings of Chinese words rendered in English (e.g., Peking and Beijing [pinyin], Mao Tse-tung and Mao Zedong, Canton and Guangzhou) (Bosrock, 1994).

Contemporary Life

As previously noted, the number of Chinese immigrants and/or refugees from China (including Taiwan), Hong Kong, and various Southeast Asian countries dramatically increased throughout the late 1970s and 1980s. A major event that contributed to increased Chinese emigration in the early 1990s was the 1997 formal conversion of Hong Kong (by agreement between Great Britain and China) to a Special Administrative Region (SAR) of China. On July 1, 1997, Britain's 99-year lease of the New Territories (extending from Kowloon to the Chinese border) expired, and Hong Kong reverted to Chinese sovereignty. To ensure Hong Kong's smooth transition to its new status as an SAR, the agreement originally provided a "one country, two systems" guarantee from China that Hong Kong's unique political, legal, economic, and social systems would remain unchanged for another 50 years. Despite such an assurance, large numbers of Hong Kong immigrants (particularly businesspeople and professionals) left prior to 1997 to settle in the United States and Canada (primarily in the provinces of Ontario and British Columbia). Fears of the ultimate "Communist takeover" by a potentially unstable and repressive Chinese government were greatly exacerbated following the brutal suppression of the prodemocracy movement in the People's Republic in June 1989 and the continuing challenges to human rights and political freedom. Since the actual British handover, however, the earlier predicted Hong Kong "exodus" of even more people and businesses has not occurred.

A related phenomenon has been the creation of a new breed of wealthier transpacific families dubbed "astronauts" or "frequent flyers." They typically set up and travel between two households: one for their children in the United States and one in Asia for the adults who continue to work in countries such as Taiwan even after they have received their green cards. Such families have increased in number as a result of the Pacific Rim economic boom as well as the difficulty in finding suitable employment in the United States. After the September 11, 2001, terrorist attacks and the resulting economic downturn in the United States, more Chinese people have returned home to pursue a better life. In addition to the newer immigrants, this phenomenon also applies to many Chinese American families who have been long-term residents (Lee, 1996b).

Another interesting phenomenon is the increase in adoption of Chinese infants and toddlers by American parents. China's "one-child" policy and the value placed on sons to carry the family name has led to large numbers of girls being abandoned or given up for adoption. As a consequence of this condition, the rising trend to adopt orphans from China reached a record of 5,053 in the year 2000; almost all of these children were girls; one fourth were adopted by families from New York State.

Population distribution and immigrant settlement patterns in the United States indicate that the vast majority of Chinese Americans are continuing to reside in the western and northeastern regions of the United States, particularly in the west and east coast cities and metropolitan areas of San Francisco/Oakland, Los Angeles, and New York (U.S. Bureau of the Census, 2000). Chinese, like many other Asian American populations, are generally electing to locate in communities in which other Chinese reside and are thus accelerating the growth of urban as well as suburban Chinatowns. Throughout this process, the new immigrant communities have become bimodal; they are essentially divided between unskilled working classes and entrepreneurial, professional, upper-middle classes, with relatively few classes in between (Wong, 1995). Recent immigrants often experience initial occupational downgrading and periods of underemployment; however, many eventually become successful and join the ranks of suburban Chinese professionals.

In contrast, a great many Chinese immigrants with limited formal education and English language skills belong to a colonized labor force of low-wage laborers employed as service workers and operatives in urban Chinatowns. Their condition is illustrated by the fact that, except for Southeast Asian refugees, the Chinese have the highest number of people living below the poverty level of all Asian American groups in the United States (U.S. Bureau of the Census, 1994). Furthermore, the annual influx of thousands of new immigrants to the Chinatowns in major metropolitan areas has exacerbated longstanding inner city problems and placed even greater strain on community resources and services (Wong, 1995).

KOREAN AMERICANS

With a population of 1 million people, Korean Americans are the fifth-largest Asian group, representing 10.5% of the AAPI population. The Korean American population grew 135% from 1980 to 1990, and another 35% from 1990 to 2000 (U.S. Bureau of the Census, 2000).

Geographic and Historical Origins

Traditionally known as *Choson* (Land of the Morning Calm), Korea is a peninsula stretching southward from the Asian mainland (Manchuria) for 600 miles. China and the former Soviet Union border on the north. To the south, the Korea Strait separates Korea from Japan. Historically, this location has had the advantage of providing easy access to adjacent cultures and the disadvantage of vulnerability as a target of invasion from neighboring countries. Thus, Korea served as a land bridge through which continental culture and religion were transmitted to Japan from China; however, for centuries, Korea also was plagued by attack from outside forces; foreign domination; and exploitation by China, Manchuria, and Japan (Park & Song, 1982).

The Korean peninsula was controlled by a series of powerful dynasties including the Silla Dynasty (A.D. 57–935); the Koryo Dynasty (A.D. 935–1392), from which the country's name *Korea* is derived; and the Yi Dynasty (A.D. 1392–1910). These dynasties directed the political and cultural development of the region as well as the defense needed to protect against outside invasions. Toward this end, Korea virtually closed itself off from the outside world during the later years of the Yi Dynasty and thus became known to Westerners as the "Hermit Kingdom" (Park & Song, 1982).

As the first step in its imperialistic expansionist movement, Japan overtook and formally annexed Korea in 1910. During the subsequent 35-year period of colonization, Japan attempted to eradicate the Korean culture and language through educational, economic, and political means. In response to such domination, however, the Korean people adhered even more tenaciously to their own prevailing cultural values and traditions; they developed a fierce national pride and determination to seek independence (Park & Song, 1982).

Korea was finally liberated from Japan in 1945, at the end of World War II; however, to disarm the Japanese, Soviet troops occupied the northern part of Korea and United Nations troops (predominantly U.S. forces) occupied the south. According to the Yalta agreement, the country was divided along the 38th parallel into "political zones" in which the respective governments of the Democratic People's Republic (North Korea) and the Republic of Korea (South Korea) were ultimately established. The ensuing Korean War (1950–1953) was one of the bloodiest wars in history and brought total devastation to the entire country. Millions of Koreans died, and the majority of the population became homeless refugees within their own national boundaries. Shaped by centuries of hardship, adversity, and cataclysmic sociopolitical upheaval, however, the Korean national character (i.e., pride, pragmatism, stubborn determination, endurance, and the will to survive and overcome) prevailed and enabled the Korean people to rebuild their country. South Korea has since emerged as one of Asia's most influential nation, with a leading world economy (Kim, 1996; Park & Song, 1982).

Throughout their long history of both external and internal turmoil (including mass destruction of their land and their people), Koreans have maintained remarkably homogeneous cultural traditions against great odds. The continuing need to unite for defensive purposes and strong adherence to traditional values were factors that promoted the development and maintenance of Korean cultural distinctiveness, particularly among the first generation of Korean immigrants to America. "The struggle of early Korean immigrants in the United States during the first half of the century reveals their immense pride in and dedication to the Korean people, Korean culture and the Korean Independence Movement" (Yu & Kim, 1983, p. 149).

Koreans have emigrated to the United States in three distinct waves, described next.

First Wave   The first wave of immigration consisted of farm laborers and their families (numbering approximately 7,000 in all) who were recruited to work in the sugar plantations of Hawaii to augment the dwindling labor force of Chinese and Japanese farm workers (Patterson & Kim, 1986). These first Korean immigrants arrived between 1903 and 1905. Unlike the original Chinese and Japanese immigrants, they had diverse occupational backgrounds and most were from urban rather than rural areas. Hawaii represented a haven from the harsh and exploitative Japanese imperial government that was controlling Korea at that time and from conditions of poverty, famine, and drought. Hawaii also provided Korean immigrants with opportunities for work (primarily for unmarried males). Hawaii, and later the U.S. mainland, also promised a better life for many young Korean "picture brides" who arrived between 1910 and 1924. These approximately 1,000 Asian-born women were brought to the United States to become the wives of single men living in Hawaii and the United States and were selected on the basis of their photographs and written descriptions of their family history.

During this period, approximately 900 additional Korean immigrants came to the United States; this group consisted primarily of students, intellectuals, and political exiles who formed the core of Korean community leadership in America during the pre–World War II period (Yu, 1983). Thus, the first wave of Korean immigrants was a relatively small and isolated minority but they retained a strong sense of ethnic identity and solidarity. As a people without a country who could not become American citizens, they organized their family life and communities around the nationalist movement for Korean independence from Japanese colonial rule (Min, 1995b; Takaki, 1989). These efforts continued from 1924 until the end of World War II, during which time there was no further emigration from Korea as a result of the 1924 Immigration Act, which completely barred Asian immigration.

Second Wave   The second wave consisted of Koreans who entered the United States between 1945 and 1964. Nearly one third of these new immigrants were students, many of whom became permanent residents. After the outbreak and ending of the Korean War (1950–1953), the majority of immigrants consisted of Korean wives of U.S. servicemen (war brides) and war orphans (predominantly girls younger than 4 years of age) who were adopted by non–Korean American parents. Unlike the earlier first-wave arrivals, approximately three quarters of these interim immigrants were young women and children who were dependents of American citizens. They were dispersed throughout the country and remained isolated from the mainstream activities of the Korean community (Hurh & Kim, 1984; Yu, 1983). During this postwar period, then, the larger Korean population was characterized by rapid dispersion and assimilation. Second-generation Korean Americans could not relate to their parents' nationalism and saw their future in America, not Korea. They thus left their parents' communities and intermarried at a rate higher than that of all other Asians until the mid-1960s. "With the loss of a unifying theme and the desertion of the second generation, the Korean community stagnated until revitalized in the 1970's by renewed immigration from Korea" (Yu, 1983, p. 27).

Third Wave   The third wave of Korean immigration began with the landmark Immigration Act of 1965, which resulted in the phenomenal growth of Korean immigrants as well as other Asian groups. Between 1970 and 1990, more than 30,000 Koreans were admitted to the United States each year, accounting for a tenfold increase in the Korean American population, from less than 100,000 to nearly 1 million (Min, 1995b). Prior to this time, the relatively small size of the Korean American population and its widespread geographic dispersion contributed to Koreans' status as a hidden minority. The new wave of Korean immigration, however, led to the dramatic emergence of Koreans as a highly visible group in selected communities throughout America (Takaki, 1989). As one of the fastest growing Asian ethnic groups, Korean Americans have become increasingly distinct from Chinese and

Japanese Americans. This change in recognition is important to most Korean Americans because of their ethnic pride and identity and in light of their ancestors' historic conflicts and intense struggles with China and Japan. In fact, Koreans typically view it as an insult to be misidentified as Chinese or Japanese, a sensibility rarely appreciated by most Americans (Kim, 1996).

Religious Origins

One of the earliest religions of Korea was shamanism or spirit worship. As a system of beliefs about the supernatural world, shamanism originated in the tribal communities of ancient Korea and continues to be practiced in the rural areas and by many older Koreans. Shamanism is concerned with the relationship among people, spirits, and the universe. A great number of spirits are the objects of religious worship, and each has a specific function. Moreover, a person's life, death, happiness, misfortune, and all other events are dependent on the spirits. Spirits, which are immortal, must be worshiped and well served to prevent misfortune and to bring good fortune (Mun, 1979).

Animism, the basic principle of shamanism, is a belief that all forms of life and things in the universe maintain their existence by virtue of *anima* (i.e., soul). Inanimate objects and natural phenomena are attributed the qualities of conscious life and an innate soul or spirit (Bosrock, 1994). The universe is composed of the heavenly world, the earthly world, and the underworld, wherein everything is interrelated by shamanistic laws of cause and effect. Therefore, nothing is accidental (Mun, 1979). Shamans serve as intermediaries with the spirit world and are believed to have the power to prevent, diagnose, and treat (or cure) illness; bring good luck and predict change in a person's fortune and/or misfortune; and ensure passage from this world to the next (Young-Kwon, 1978).

The previously described three teachings of Confucianism, Taoism, and Buddhism flowed into the peninsula from China in the first century and were embraced by the Korean people. Taoism laid the groundwork for Korea's earliest belief systems and was later blended into Buddhist premises and teachings. Buddhism underwent profound transformation in ways suited to the Korean people; it served the people's spiritual needs and had the biggest impact on individual religious life and art. Of the three teachings, however, Confucianism exerted the principal influence.

Confucianism provided the foundation for the development of Korea's educational, social, and political systems. The initial impact of Confucianism in Korea was the establishment of higher learning. Confucianism then continued to strongly influence the ruling class and provided the state with capable government officials. During the Yi Dynasty, Korea became the center of Confucian learning; Confucianism reached its theoretical and philosophical peak while becoming an integral part of the general public's daily lives (Yum, 1987). In having provided all-embracing values and an ideology for the Korean people, Confucianism thus serves as a key to understanding Korean culture (MacMahon, 1977).

The introduction of Christianity to Korea marked the beginning of a major social and cultural transition period. The abolishment of laws forbidding Christian missionaries from entering Korea resulted in a rapid expansion of missionary activity in the late 1800s. The missionaries promoted modern education and the Western work ethic and encouraged thousands of Koreans who had converted to Christianity to emigrate to America. Significantly, 40% of all first-wave Korean immigrants were Christians (Takaki, 1989). As they established communities in the United States, their churches became forums for promoting Korean nationalism while also perpetuating traditional Korean values. Unlike other Asians, recent Korean immigrants are predominantly Christian, usually Protestants (Lassiter, 1995). Between 70% and 80% of Koreans in America (as compared with less than 50% in Korea) are affiliated with Christian churches. As both an acculturation agent and a resource for preserving cultural and ethnic identity, the church continues to be the most important institution in the community.

Language/Linguistic Origins

The Korean language reflects centuries of Chinese cultural influence. Approximately 50% of the Korean vocabulary is derived from Chinese. Therefore, many words have the same meaning in Chinese and Korean but are pronounced differently. Korean, unlike Chinese, is not a tonal language. It consists of a single phonetic alphabet, *hangul,* with 24 phonetic symbols or characters representing different sounds that are combined to form words. Interestingly, the shapes of some *hangul* letters were originally designed to mirror the corresponding shapes of the tongue during articulation. Koreans take great pride in their language because it was invented in 1443, centuries before phonetics became a systematic discipline. In fact, Koreans celebrate the date when *hangul* was proclaimed the Korean vernacular script, which is probably the only linguistic holiday observed in the world (C.S. Lee, 1988; Wang, 1983).

Several Korean dialects are spoken, but unlike the major Chinese dialects, they are mutually understandable. Korean morphemes, or meaning units, also are predominantly polysyllabic (in contrast to generally monosyllabic Chinese words). Yet another distinction between the languages is the very elaborate Korean inflectional system (based on suffixes); Chinese has essentially no morphological inflections (Wang, 1983).

Thus, although the Korean vocabulary reflects significant Chinese influence, the language structure is different. Given the additional historical influence of Japan, however, the Korean and Japanese languages are genetically related and have many common grammatical features. The most important one is that they are "verb-final" languages; that is, for the vast majority of sentences, the verb always occurs at the sentence-final position (Li, 1983). This particular feature has great communicative significance wherein sentence-final verbs may indicate the attitude of the speaker in relation to the anticipated response of the listener. The speaker will typically state the subject and object while observing the listener's reaction, then adjust the verb to accommodate the listener. The speaker also may add a negative at the end, thereby reversing the entire meaning of the sentence, but preserving the human relationship (Weisz, Rothbaum, & Blackburn, 1984). Therefore, the language is designed to maximize interpersonal harmony and reinforce traditional values derived from the three teachings. Confucian values, in particular, are also evident in the "honorific" system of the Korean language in which different verbs and nouns will be used in addressing or speaking with individuals of varying social status or rank, thus reflecting the hierarchical nature of the society (C.S. Lee, 1988). In fact, the highly stratified social classes of the past relied on each person to observe his or her *boon-soo* (i.e., knowing and accepting one's status or place) in order to preserve the status quo (Kim, 1996).

Contemporary Life

The third wave of Korean immigration has occurred within the context of rapid in-dustrialization and economic modernization in South Korea. The concurrent popu-lation explosion emerged as one of the most urgent domestic problems confronting South Korean society. In fact, South Korea's population density is the third highest in the world (Kim, 1987). Corresponding over-urbanization in cities such as Seoul created overcrowding, air pollution, unemployment, underemployment, and wide-spread exploitation of cheap labor; there also was extreme competition for college entrance and an oversupply of highly educated people as well as major human rights restrictions and curtailment of political freedoms. These conditions and the prospects for greater economic and educational opportunities in the United States were among the primary premigration push factors contributing to the large-scale Korean emi-gration process since the late 1970s (Kim, 1987). Since the early 1990s, however, economic, political, and social conditions have improved in South Korea. South Ko-reans also have been well informed of the significant adjustment difficulties of Ko-rean immigrants in the United States. Consequently, the influx of Korean immigrants continues to decline. The most recent immigrants also tend to be lower in socio-economic status than the earlier Korean professional immigrants (Min, 1995b).

The largest proportion of Korean immigrants in the United States (more than one third) have settled in California, particularly in the Los Angeles and Orange County areas. About one fourth of all Koreans who live in the United States reside in the five-county region of Los Angeles. New York and Illinois, and the respective metropolitan areas of New York City and Chicago, have the second- and third-largest Korean American populations. With the exception of "Koreatown" in Los Angeles, Korean newcomers have generally settled in and around urban population centers and shown a tendency toward rapid suburbanization and residential/geographic dis-persal. In fact, relative to other recent Asian immigrants, Koreans are the most widely dispersed and have established the highest level of suburban residence of all American ethnic groups (Lassiter, 1995; Min, 1995b). Beginning in January 2003, hundreds of Korean American organizations celebrated their 100th anniversary of the Korean immigration to the United States.

This distinctive pattern of geographic mobility and dispersal reflects, in part, Ko-rean adaptability to a new life environment and prior experience with the rapidly changing urban-industrial structure of Korea. One of the most important contribut-ing factors, however, is the relatively high educational level and occupational prepa-ration of Korean immigrants. A large percentage of college graduates and profes-sionals embark on new ventures and are not bound to any particular locality once they overcome limitations of language and familiarity with American social customs. They are typically willing to move to wherever education, employment, and business opportunities beckon them (Kim, 1996). During the initial adjustment period, how-ever, Korean immigrants typically experience downward occupational mobility.

An overwhelming majority of the third-wave Korean immigrants (post-1965) held professional or other white-collar positions in Korea. More than one third have bachelor's and graduate degrees, and half have high school diplomas with some col-lege education. Such high educational achievement (among the highest of all ethnic groups in the United States) has not translated into higher status or higher paying oc-cupations, however. Severely hampered by their limited English proficiency and dif-ferences in Korean and American job market requirements, most college graduates educated in Korea are initially grossly underemployed. They typically have taken low-paying jobs as cooks, waiters/waitresses, gas station attendants, and other kinds of laborers. to have an alternative to such blue-collar occupations, approximately half of Korean immigrant workers in major urban centers such as Los Angeles have turned to self-employment (Min, 1995b). Korean Americans, in fact, have the highest rate of self-employment relative to all other Asian American groups, and the most common source of income for Korean immigrants is the self-owned business (Yu, 1983).

Although Korean small businesses have penetrated predominantly white suburbs, shopping centers, and rural towns, a great many are located in inner-city sections or large metropolitan areas among predominantly low-income African American and Latino communities. Korean-owned green groceries, delicatessens, liquor and convenience stores, markets, dry cleaning and garment businesses, trade businesses dealing in Korean-imported merchandise, gas stations, restaurants, fast-food franchises, manicure salons, and many other small businesses have proliferated in such communities. During the 1990s they became targets of volatile conflict, however (Min, 1995b).

The conflicts occurred in all major Korean communities in the nation but were most severe in New York and Los Angeles. Many African American boycotts (each lasting 2 months or longer) were staged against Korean merchants in New York City. Intergroup race relations also had deteriorated in Los Angeles following separate incidents in which two African Americans were shot to death by Korean merchants. In the 1992 Los Angeles riots or civil unrest (the worst in American history), thousands of Korean-owned stores located in South Central Los Angeles and Koreatown were burned, vandalized, and/or looted by predominantly African American and Latino rioters, resulting in more than $3 million in property damage (Min, 1995b).

High rates of self-employment, economic segregation, and long hours necessary to sustain labor-intensive small businesses have had far-reaching effects on Korean immigrants. Beyond the previously described interethnic relations problems, associated physical/emotional stress and trauma also have exacerbated major family and generational conflicts (Min, 1995b). For example, the vast majority (more than 90%) of first-generation Korean American parents list Korean as their primary spoken language and actively encourage their children to learn it; however, despite these efforts, the children are mainly English speaking, and the differentiated language pattern between generations complicates family life (Yu, 1983). Typical immigrant family parent–child conflicts thus arise from loss of parental authority and respect caused by basic communication problems, acculturation clashes, unrealistic expectations, and limited availability of many parents and family members who work long hours and cannot provide adequate guidance and support for their children. The problems are more serious for school-age children who are Korean-born immigrants—the "1.5" generation. These children gradually lose their Korean language skills during the period of several years that may be required to attain English proficiency; as a result they may fail to develop a positive self-identity within either the Korean or American culture. Like other Asian immigrant youth experiencing similar identity crises, they have come to be referred to as a lost generation that adjusts by rejecting traditional values in favor of a peer subculture, which may include youth gangs (Kim, 1980; Lee & Cynn, 1991; Min, 1995b).

Like their predecessors (or first-wave immigrants to America), adult Korean immigrants in the 1990s are profoundly proud of their natural heritage, rich culture, language, and distinctive history spanning nearly 5,000 years (Yu & Kim, 1983). The

70%–80% of the Korean population who are foreign-born, married, and living as nuclear families share investment in teaching their children to become proud Koreans as well as successful Americans. Although cultural homogeneity and economic segregation have helped Korean immigrants maintain high levels of ethnic identity and attachment, these factors have hindered Koreans' assimilation into mainstream society (Min, 1995b). Many immigrants indicate that the first generation must be sacrificed in order to ensure their children's future of upward social mobility. Propelled by the values of hard work and education, parents must struggle in order for their children to attend college and become professionals as they themselves had been in Korea (Takaki, 1989). Yet, the resulting family pressures, stresses, and persistent generational conflicts pose major challenges to family stability.

Korea was once the lead country for interracial adoptions for American parents. The tide of American families adopting Korean orphans has slowed down gradually since 1993. In 1999 and 2000, there were 2,008 and 1,794 adoptions, respectively. Another trend affecting the Korean American community is their hope for a constructive U.S. policy that would encourage peace on the Korean peninsula, leading to an early reunion of families separated by the Korean War. Such hope, however, has diminished given the increasingly strained international relations between the United States and North Korea.

SOUTHEAST ASIAN AMERICANS

The 2000 U.S. Bureau of the Census indicated that there were 206,052 Cambodian Americans, 198,203 Laotian Americans, and 1.12 million Vietnamese Americans. Vietnamese represent 11% of the total AAPI population and are the fourth largest AAPI group; they grew 125% from 1980 to 1990 and 89% from 1990 to 2000, making them the second fastest growing AAPI group after South Asian Indians. (U.S. Bureau of the Census, 2000). It is estimated that approximately 25% of the refugees from Vietnam and 15% of those from Cambodia are ethnic Chinese. More than 80% of the Southeast Asian American population entered the country as refugees and arrived after 1980 (Rumbaut, 1995).

Geographic and Historical Origins

The geographically dispersed region of Southeast Asia consists of many countries, including several island nations. The term "Southeast Asian" has often been confused or used interchangeably with "Indochinese"; however, Indochina refers only to those countries situated on the Indochinese peninsula, located between China and India. Southeast Asia consists of Burma, Malaysia, and Singapore (former British colonies); Cambodia, Laos, and Vietnam (formerly French colonies); and Thailand (the only Southeast Asian country that has never been colonized by Western powers) (Te, 1989a).

This section focuses specifically on the refugee populations from Cambodia, Laos, and Vietnam. They are designated by the geopolitical term "Southeast Asian refugee." In the years following the end of the Vietnam War in 1975 and the civil wars in Cambodia and Laos, more than 1 million Southeast Asian refugees arrived in the United States (Rumbaut, 1995). Although people from other Southeast Asian countries also have been given refugee status since 1975, they constitute less than 0.5% of the total population. Thus, discussion of Southeast Asian refugees usually centers on people from the three nations of Cambodia, Laos, and Vietnam (Gordon, 1987).

Unlike the majority of foreign-born Asian Americans, most Southeast Asian Americans share the experience of being *refugees* (those who left their homelands for survival) rather than *emigrants* (those who left their countries by conscious choice). Significant historical, cultural, and linguistic differences can be found—as well as many distinct subcultural and ethnic minority groups—among the people from Cambodia, Laos, and Vietnam. The following sections highlight the respective backgrounds of these major Southeast Asian refugee populations and illustrate their extreme diversity.

Cambodia

Bordered by Laos, Vietnam, Thailand, and the Gulf of Siam, Cambodia is a country of flat delta terrain with few plateaus and mountains. Cambodia is the European name for the country known as *Kambuja* or *Kampuchea*. Its predominant ethnic group is the Khmer people, who are a racial mix of indigenous tribal people and invaders from India and Indonesia. Their civilization dates back almost 2,000 years, to the Kingdom of Funan. Cambodia's long history has been punctuated by persistent political and military struggles, civil wars, and threats from neighboring states. However, the Angkor period (A.D. 800–1430) was the "Golden Age" in which monuments were built in the city of Angkor Wat. This city is considered one of the Seven Wonders of the World and a national symbol of an advanced and civilized Khmer empire that extended over a vast area, including much of present-day Laos, Thailand, and Vietnam. The post-Khmer period was marked by constant warfare with Thailand and Vietnam and the decline of the empire. After years of Thai dominance, Cambodia became a French protectorate in 1863, and remained under French rule until 1954. At that time, then "King" Norodom Sihanouk negotiated Cambodia's complete independence from France; he subsequently established a monarchy, which he controlled for 16 "peaceful" years (Chhim, 1989).

During this period, Sihanouk played off Chinese, Soviet, and American interests. Although brutally suppressing tiny groups of Communist Khmer Rouge in the countryside, he later allowed North Vietnamese Communist troops to establish sanctuaries and move supplies inside Cambodia's borders. In 1970, Sihanouk was deposed by General Lon Nol, who established the Khmer Republic. While officially recognizing Lon Nol's new government, the United States then extended the Vietnam War into eastern Cambodia by saturation bombing North Vietnamese supply lines and storage facilities with the aim of stopping the flow of supplies and personnel from North to South Vietnam along the Ho Chi Minh Trail. However, backed and trained by the well-entrenched North Vietnamese Army, Khmer Rouge forces waged a full-scale war. The Khmer Rouge were Cambodia's Communist underground and Maoist-inspired government led by Pol Pot. By the end of 1971, an estimated 2 million of the country's estimated 7 million population had been displaced, and 20% of its property had been destroyed (Chhim, 1989). Finally, in April 1975, while the North Vietnamese stormed Saigon, Khmer Rouge forces marched into the capital of Phnom Penh and immediately started clearing the entire city of its 2.5 million inhabitants.

The new regime officially renamed the country Kampuchea, declared the Year Zero, and embarked on a campaign to rid Cambodia of all Western influences. Pol Pot instituted a brutal program to evacuate the cities and relocate the urban population to rural labor camps in massive numbers, and to eradicate all Cambodians affiliated with the American-supported Lon Nol government (Takaki, 1989).

All healthy, educated, and professional people were sought out and executed. Teachers, doctors, and soldiers were killed or had to disguise their identity in order to survive. A systematic program of thought control by the Khmer Rouge followed. Children were separated from their parents, put into children's camps, and made to inform on their parents [who were put in forced labor camps]. The Khmer Rouge maintained control [in the camps] by mass public torture, execution, and disembowelment of all dissidents or suspected dissidents. Family members, neighbors, and co-workers were forced to watch without showing any emotion; any outpouring of emotion was punished by similar brutality (McKenzie-Pollock, 1996, p. 309).

The Khmer Rouge era (from mid-1975 to 1978) was thus infamous for unprecedented atrocities in which 3 million people (more than half of Cambodia's population) were decimated through torture, execution, disease, starvation, and exhaustion from forced marches and compulsory labor (Dresser, 1996; Union of Pan Asian Communities, 1980).

A once relatively prosperous country went into collapse as the Pol Pot regime dismantled the old social order by destroying infrastructure, large segments of the middle and upper middle classes, and major economic and social systems. Famine and disease became endemic, and the human devastation and bloodbath intensified with the Vietnamese invasion in 1978 (Dresser, 1996; McKenzie-Pollock, 1996). Hundreds of thousands of "land refugees" fled on foot through the dense jungles infiltrated by guerrillas and Communist soldiers to the camps on the Thai/Cambodian border. Having completed the long, dangerous journey through a mine-studded border region where many died or lost limbs, they arrived malnourished, sick, diseased, weak, and depressed. Brutalized by the Khmer Rouge, at least half of these survivors had experienced the death of a family member (Huang, 1989). As victims of the most horrible genocidal war known to modern history, they left the "killing fields" behind, but the killing fields did not leave them (Takaki, 1989).

Cambodian refugees subsequently spent anywhere from 1 to 18 years awaiting resettlement in a third country while living in the austere, overcrowded, and often unsafe conditions of the refugee camps in Thailand. During that time, according to Dresser,

> The Vietnamese Communists took over [Cambodia] and drove out the Khmer Rouge, who withdrew to Thai sanctuaries. Later, a U.N.-backed government was formed, and, finally in 1993, the Cambodians held multiparty elections. For the second time in the country's history, Norodom Sihanouk resumed leadership, this time as King. The country is now [once again] called Cambodia. (1996, p. 254)

A complex interplay of social forces that include pre-revolutionary cultural patterns, communist/socialist influences, and the effects of a reintroduced market economy and democracy characterize Cambodian society in the 21st century. The country remains heavily dependent on foreign assistance. Pervasive social problems include growing landlessness, lack of effective health care, and overexploitation of natural resources. A new generation of Cambodian young adults who did not live through Pol Pot's nightmare is emerging to address these problems. It remains to be seen how they will choose to reshape society in the aftermath of 30 years of war (Ledgewood, 2003).

Laos

As the only "landlocked" country in Southeast Asia, Laos is wedged between Thailand and Vietnam and bordered by Burma and China to the north and Cambodia to the south. Mountains and forests cover more than half of the country. Among the nearly 70 different ethnic groups in Laos, the majority are "lowland Lao"; other major ethnic groups include the "highland Lao" or Hmong (which means "free," and who also are known as Meo and Miao, the Lao of the mountaintops) and the Mien (which means "people"). Laotians first migrated from China and created the ancient kingdom of *Lan Xang* (Kingdom of a Million Elephants) in 1353. After centuries of continued wars and conquests by neighboring countries such as Burma, Cambodia, and Thailand (then Siam), the French ultimately colonized Laos in 1893. After World War II (following a 4-year period of Japanese invasion and occupation), the French retook their French Indochinese territories (Cambodia, Laos, and Vietnam); however, Laotian nationalists led by the Pathet Lao began their struggle to overthrow French colonialism. The 1954 Geneva Accord finally established Laos as an independent state (Luangpraseut, 1989; Takaki, 1989).

Throughout the next 20 years, Laos's political history was one of prolonged civil strife and struggle among opposing forces seeking control of the country. This internal conflict merged with developments in Vietnam. By the 1960s, the Vietnam War had been extended into Laos. North Vietnam supported the Pathet Lao in order to protect the Ho Chi Minh Trail (which ran through Laos as a supply line to the south), while the United States gave assistance to the Royal Lao and the Hmong and Mien in the highlands to interrupt the movement of troops and military supplies. Shortly after Cambodia and South Vietnam fell into Communist hands in the spring of 1975, the Royal Lao Government also collapsed. As the Pathet Lao took power and established the Lao People's Democratic Republic, they began a campaign of bloody repression and reprisal, one in which the Mien and Hmong tribespeople (who had been recruited and trained as guerilla soldiers to conduct American military operations in Laos and fight America's "secret war") were targeted for destruction as "tools of the CIA" or "lackeys of American imperialism" (Takaki, 1989). Thousands were killed in vicious military attacks, thousands more retreated further into the mountains to face starvation, and others were taken to "re-education centers" from which they never returned. No one knows how many more refugees died or were killed as they fled on foot across Laos to the Mekong River, in which many more drowned trying to swim across to the Thai border. The long Indochinese war and subsequent brutal campaigns of retribution thus decimated the people of Laos. The Hmong, in particular, lost nearly one third of their population; in almost all families at least one or two members were killed. In many cases, only the women and children survived (Kourmarn, 1980; Tou-Fou, 1981). Ultimately, nearly half a million refugees fled the country, including tribal people as well as the wealthy and educated upper classes. Among them, some 140,000 ethnic Laotian, 20,000 Mien, and 125,000 Hmong have settled in the United States (Dresser, 1996).

Vietnam

Because of its strategic location for trade and military activities, Vietnam has been called "a crossroads of the Asian world." It lies on the eastern coast of the Indochinese peninsula and is bordered on the north by China, on the west by Cambodia and

Laos, and on the south and east by the South China Sea (with 1,200 miles of coast-line). The northern part of the country is a mountainous region surrounding the Red River Delta; the central region consists of a long series of small coastal plains and a range of high mountains; the southern part is a flat area formed by the Mekong Delta—the most productive agricultural area in Vietnam, where tropical monsoon conditions of heavy rainfall and a hot climate create ideal conditions for growing rice (Rutledge, 1987; Te, 1989a, 1989b).

The Vietnamese people most commonly are thought to have originated from a mixture of the Viet tribes from southern China and the inhabitants of the Red River Delta, originally from Indonesia. Whereas the Vietnamese represent approximately 85% of the total population, there are more than 50 different ethnic/linguistic minorities in Vietnam (Bosrock, 1994). They include ethnic Chinese, more than 30 mountain tribes (aboriginal people referred to by the French term *montagnards*), the Chams (who live primarily in the lowlands of the southern part of central Vietnam), the Cambodians or Khmers, and other smaller ethnic groups (Malays, Indians, Pakistanis, and French). Most of these ethnic groups left Vietnam in 1975 (Rutledge, 1987; Te, 1989a, 1989b).

Vietnam has a recorded history of more than 2,000 years and an additional 2,000 years of unrecorded history based on oral legends. The history of the Vietnamese people is characterized by a profound sense of national identity, long-term strength, and resistance, all of which have enabled them to survive as a nation despite centuries of foreign domination. China first ruled over Vietnam for approximately 1,000 years (from 111 B.C. to A.D. 938). Numerous rebellions ultimately led to the overthrow of Chinese rule and a subsequent 900-year period of independence. This era of independence came to an end when the French conquered Vietnam and colonized the country from 1883 until 1954. During this period, French influence dominated Vietnamese culture; French became the second language of the Vietnamese, and the country experienced major changes and growth in medicine, architecture, government, and education. The Vietnamese people also suffered severe hardships as well as the imposition of European social and economic systems on traditional cultural institutions and lifestyles, however. Thus, the longer the French remained in control, the fiercer the resistance became.

As previously noted, the Japanese drove the European colonial forces out of Indochina during World War II. While the Japanese occupied Vietnam, Ho Chi Minh, a veteran Communist leader, organized an independence movement known as the Vietminh. The purpose of the Vietminh was to fight the Japanese and to oppose French rule. When the war ended, the French, determined to resume their rule over Vietnam, reoccupied the South; however, the Vietminh seized power in the North, established the Democratic Republic of Vietnam, and allowed 1 million people to go south (Chung, 1996). Even though the country was divided, the Vietnamese culture maintained its homogeneity; Vietnamese in both the northern and southern areas of the country were opposed to French rule. Thus, attempts to reinstate a French colonial regime by force resulted in open rebellion. In 1954, after 8 years of fighting, the Vietnamese defeated the French in the decisive battle of Dien Bien Phu. As a result of the ensuing Geneva Accord, Vietnam was divided into two separate states along the 17th parallel, known as the DMZ (Demilitarized Zone). Ho Chi Minh was named leader of North Vietnam, with a Communist government based in Hanoi; in the South, Emperor Bao Dai and later Premier Ngo Dinh Diem served as Chiefs of State in what was called the Republic of Vietnam, with a non-Communist regime based in

Saigon (Dresser, 1996). The agreement called for a cessation of fighting, national elections, and a reunification of the country by 1956.

Both governments, however, claimed exclusive right to rule all of Vietnam, and civil war erupted. As hostilities between the North and the South escalated, China and the Soviet Union provided aid to North Vietnam while the United States assisted the South Vietnamese government. By 1960, a full-scale war was under way within Vietnam. U.S. military involvement continued to expand and reached a peak in 1969, when the number of American troops in Vietnam had risen to more than 500,000. The Vietnam War gave rise to increasingly widespread and sometimes violent domestic protest in the United States by those who viewed the war as immoral; they engaged in bitter debate with others who believed that America had a responsibility to combat the spread of Communism in Southeast Asia. Several years of peace talks culminated in 1973 with the Treaty of Paris, in which a cease-fire agreement was signed and stipulated the withdrawal of all U.S. troops from Vietnam. Two years later, North Vietnam launched a major offensive and, on April 30, 1975, the South Vietnamese government fell, the city of Saigon was overrun by northern troops, and the entire country was reunited under the Communist regime (Rutledge, 1987; Te, 1989b) in what came to be called "Black April."

The cost of the prolonged, nearly 20-year conflict was high for all involved. With the exception of the Civil War in the United States a century earlier, the Vietnam War became the most divisive event in U.S. history. Of the 2.2 million American soldiers who served in Vietnam, more than 58,000 died there or were missing in action (Rumbaut, 1995, pp. 234, 235). It defined an entire generation of young people in the 1960s, polarized the American electorate into "hawks" and "doves," and was viewed by many Americans as the first war that the United States ever lost. The war also cost the United States hundreds of billions of dollars.

If the war divided America, it devastated Vietnam as well as Cambodia and Laos. As a tragedy of epic proportions, it was considered the "war that nobody won" and left these three countries among the poorest in the world. In South Vietnam alone, half of the total forest area and 10% of the agricultural land were partially destroyed. An estimated 4 million Vietnamese military personnel and civilians on both sides were killed or wounded (Rumbaut, 1995). Many more millions of people were uprooted and forced to flee as refugees. Ultimately, more than 1 million Vietnamese left the country to seek asylum in other Asian or Western countries. This was the first time in the 4,000-year history of Vietnam that an exodus of such magnitude had taken place (Te, 1989b).

"Black April" of 1975 was the beginning of mass evacuations of Vietnamese from Saigon. More than 200,000 "first-wave" refugees were airlifted out of South Vietnam, resettling primarily in the United States and France. These Vietnamese were predominantly well-educated, urban, middle-class professionals, government officials, military personnel, and religious leaders who spoke English (and French) and who had been closely associated with the Americans and the former South Vietnamese regime. In 1975, the United States resettled approximately 130,000 Vietnamese refugees, the majority of whom were initially placed in reception centers or processing camps located at Camp Pendleton in California, Fort Chafee in Arkansas, Elgin Air Force Base in Florida, and Fort Indiantown Gap in Pennsylvania. Basic adjustment to a new American lifestyle and "survival skills" training occurred within the camps. Sponsors were then found (a necessary condition of resettlement), and the refugees were dispersed throughout the country. The U.S. policy in 1975 was to disperse the Vietnamese geographically so that a sudden inpouring of refugees would not overwhelm a given local or state government. This dispersal policy also was predicated on the belief that more rapid adaptation to American society would occur if the Vietnamese were not concentrated in one place, where they might form ethnic enclaves (Rutledge, 1987). Within a few years, however, many Vietnamese began to relocate and gather in communities that were concentrated in southern California metropolitan areas (e.g., Los Angeles, Orange, and San Diego counties), where Mutual Assistance Associations (MAAs) were formed (Rumbaut, 1995; Takaki, 1989).

The second-wave refugees were typically the immediate families or other relatives of first-wave refugees and entered the United States between the fall of 1975 and the fall of 1978. They included individuals who were at high risk in Vietnam because they had fought in the South Vietnamese army or, like their predecessors, had been associated with the U.S. or South Vietnamese government. Many had originally fled to other countries or were in refugee or displacement camps in Asia awaiting sponsorship and money to join their families in the United States. These second-wave refugees were relatively quickly resettled with their families (Keiter, 1990).

The third wave of refugees occurred between 1978 and 1980. This period saw the exodus of several hundred thousand "boat people" from Vietnam, consisting primarily of ethnic Chinese who faced persecution and were forced to leave the country (Chung, 1996). Other Vietnamese, in anticipation of being sent to "reeducation centers" or "new economic zones," also began to flee. Moreover, many parents, resigned to the belief that their children had no future in Vietnam, arranged for their children's escape while they remained behind (Huang, 1989). Together, these third-wave refugees

> Boarded crowded, leaky boats, risking their lives at sea where storms threatened to drown them and pirates waited to rob them and rape the women. Pirates attacked two thirds of the boats, each boat an average of more than two times. (Takaki, 1989, p. 452)

Approximately half of these refugees died trying to escape. The boat people who did survive typically landed in countries such as Thailand, Malaysia, and the Philippines, where they were given temporary asylum in prison-like holding centers (Lassiter, 1995).

The third-wave refugees also included "land refugees" from Vietnam, Cambodia, and Laos who had languished in the desperate conditions of refugee camps for extended periods of time. Relative to the refugees who had gone before them, the conditions and methods of flight of the third-wave refugees were much harsher. Many survived starvation, disease, robbery, rape, and extortion on a daily basis for many years. They came to the United States as fishermen, farmers, and working-class people from small coastal cities, rural areas, and villages, having had little prior contact with Americans and virtually no experience with Western culture. Their adjustment difficulties and culture shock were thus much greater (Huang, 1989). Moreover, although their stories of transition into urban American communities elicited sympathy and compassion among some, others viewed these "foreigners" with resentment, hostility, and contempt (Attorney General's Asian and Pacific Islander Advisory Committee, 1988). These negative attitudes were, in part, a result of the refugees' relative cultural/linguistic insularity from the larger community, contrasting lifestyles, perceived dependence on welfare, and/or continuing threat to existing norms and practices among local workers.

In the United States, the rescue of Southeast Asian refugees was initially thought to be a one-time crisis intervention or short-term process following the Communist takeover in 1975. The subsequent flow of hundreds of thousands of third-wave refugees "prompted the passage of the historic Refugee Act of 1980, which, for the first time, defined who could be admitted to the United States as a 'refugee,' and further established the framework under which the federal refugee assistance program operates" (Le, 1993, p. 169). In response to the international resettlement crisis created when "first asylum" countries refused to accept more refugees into their already swollen camps, the United States began to absorb significant numbers of the refugee camp populations under the family reunification provisions of the Refugee Act of 1980; however, many thousands of refugees still remained in the camps awaiting resettlement (Rumbaut, 1995).

The Orderly Departure Program (ODP), which was initiated in 1979, further allowed the controlled emigration of thousands of Vietnamese nationals directly to the United States. They included primarily former reeducation camp internees or political prisoners and Amerasian children and youth. By the end of 1992, more than 300,000 Vietnamese had immigrated to the United States through the ODP as well as the subsequent Amerasian Homecoming Act. Meanwhile, by the early 1990s, refugee flows from Laos and Cambodia had virtually ended, with the focus shifting to the voluntary repatriation of refugees still in camps in Thailand and elsewhere (Rumbaut, 1995).

Under an international program introduced in 1989 known as the Comprehensive Plan of Action, refugee camps across Southeast Asia were scheduled to close by June 1996, and the detention centers in Hong Kong were to be cleared by June 1997, before China resumed control of the territory. Most of the Vietnamese detainees in Hong Kong were deemed economic migrants, not political refugees, and were either voluntarily or forcibly repatriated (Dizon, 1996). Several thousand Hmong refugees were among the last to leave the Thai camps to be resettled in the United States ("Final Group of Hmong Refugees," 1996). The closing of the camps, in effect, closed one of the final unfinished chapters of the Vietnam War and marked the end of an era in which 2 million refugees fled Vietnam, Laos, and Cambodia. Their exodus—which peaked in 1980 but has continued ever since—(Rumbaut, 1995) resulted in more than 1 million people participating in the largest refugee resettlement program in U.S. history.

Religious Origins

Among the religious or moral systems that have most profoundly influenced Southeast Asian cultures, Buddhism is predominant. Buddhism has two branches: Mahayana (Great Vehicle), which flourishes in Vietnam as well as China, Japan, and Korea; and Hinayana (Little Vehicle) or Theravada, which flourishes in Cambodia and Laos as well as in Burma, Thailand, and Sri Lanka. Each branch is based on the same Buddhist doctrines that were previously described in this chapter; they do not require a belief in a god but insist on the responsibility of each individual for his or her behavior. The ascetic life necessary to follow the doctrines of Buddhism is extremely strict; most people are unable to adhere fully to it. Mahayana Buddhism offers *nirvana* to more people. Theravada Buddhism is stricter; in fact, historically, nearly all young Cambodian and Laotian males went to the local *wat,* or temple, for at least 3 months to spend time as a member of the *sangha* (monastic order) to learn to become a novice monk (Te, 1989a).

Religious life in Cambodia and Laos is given an added dimension by Brahmanism or Hinduism with its associated South Asian Indian philosophy; deities; and traditional worship of Brahma, the supreme being, who is simultaneously the Creator, the Preserver, and the Destroyer. The Khmer and Laotian people also have been significantly influenced by animism and spirit worship. This is the belief that spiritual and supernatural powers are present throughout the universe, and all natural phenomena and things (animate and inanimate) possess an innate soul. It is believed that these powers can and will change the destinies of human beings if the *Phi* (spirits, ghosts, demons, and other supernatural beings) are not satisfied (Chhim, 1989; Luangpraseut, 1989).

The various beliefs and rites of Brahmanism and animism are often mixed. They are at the core of the Lao *su-kwan* (*su* meaning "to invite," *kwan* meaning "the soul") ceremony or *Baci*. This ceremony typically is performed to help ward off sickness or danger during transitional periods in life and rites of passage (e.g., marriage, pregnancy, birth of a child) or on other occasions such as when someone is ill or is recovering from serious illness or about to undergo surgery, the death of a person, a return home from a long journey, a change of status or dwelling, or a reunion of family or friends. The purpose of the *Baci* is to contact the body spirits (or "thirty-two souls"), protect them, and bind them to the person who needs help, because these body spirits are likely to leave his or her body on these occasions. Each of these mobile souls that preside over the body has its own organ of residence. The King soul is believed to "live" in one's head (this is the main reason why some Southeast Asians do not wish their head to be touched or even pointed at by another person). A community or family elder or Buddhist monk is invited to perform the rite by chanting from a religious text to call the spirits or souls into the person receiving the *Baci*. Then the elder or monk and other participants will tie white string or pieces of yarn around the wrist of the person to bind the spirits to his or her body (the tied knot symbolizing the effective return of the absent soul). These are then worn for at least 3 days (Dresser, 1996; Luangpraseut, 1989). It is common to see pregnant women and infants wearing such strings with special knots. Children also may wear cords or protective charms (amulets and talismans made out of medicinal substances, animal bones, stones, or metal) around their neck, wrists, or waist; in some instances, a shaman or magic expert may have chanted a secret phrase (*mon*) on certain charms given to the sick to hasten their recovery. Among the Cambodians, pieces of soft metal are engraved with Pali (a Buddhist language) or Sanskrit (sacred sayings in an Ancient Indic language), rolled into tubes, and threaded onto chains that are worn around children's necks. These materials are deeply revered and, generally, should not be directly removed by care providers outside the family without first seeking the family's permission or offering an explanation (Chung, 1996; Ratliff, 1994).

The Hmong practice animism as well as ancestor worship.

> Hmong religion cannot be separated from the Hmong kinship network and the commonality of the Hmong ancestral sites. Two dominant features have an impact on the Hmong way of life: the relationship between ancestors and their descendants and the relationship between religion and social structure. (Chung, 1996, p. 88)

Hmong religious ceremonies (e.g., the trance or *ua neeb*) are intended to renew social groupings, strengthen lineage solidarity, and provide inspiration for new members to fulfill their obligation to the living, the dead, and the unborn (Chung, 1996; Quincy,

1988). The Hmong typically do not practice prayers and have no temples, images, or priests. Instead, shamans act as healers and protect the community (Dresser, 1996).

The Mien also believe in animism, but unlike the Hmong, most of the Mien religious and magical rituals have been borrowed from the Chinese. Mien priests, literate in Chinese, read and chant the lyrics of rituals that have been recorded in hand-sewn books. During important religious rites, painting representations of the 3 Pure Beings and 15 other deities are displayed. Shamans or priests conduct ceremonies involving divination, placating spirits, and recalling the souls of the ailing. Many rituals for ancestor worship also are observed (Dresser, 1996).

Although the majority of Vietnamese are Buddhists, a mixture of Buddhism, Confucianism, and Taoism have shaped their culture and lifestyle. Like the Chinese, many Vietnamese have adhered to the three teachings and practiced syncretism or a blending of beliefs. Animism also has been a strong influence on Vietnamese belief systems. The belief in spirits has led many Vietnamese to worship a host of deities (e.g., the Earth God, the Luck God, the Fortune God) and to observe astrology, fortune telling, omens, and natural signs. The calendar system is marked by a 12-year cycle of different animals that have natural and supernatural qualities. South Vietnam fell in 1975, the year of the Cat, which is considered an especially ill-fated year, whereas 1976 was the year of the Dragon and brought new hope. These beliefs are especially prevalent among rural populations of Vietnam and among many urban people of all classes, most of whom will not fail to consult a horoscope before an important event, transaction, or special occasion (Pan Asian Parent Education Project, 1982; Te, 1989a).

Ancestor worship is yet another very common practice among Vietnamese and underlies all other religions. An ancestral altar is typically placed in the main room of Vietnamese households, where rites to honor the death of each ancestor can be performed on various occasions. This ceremony and form of worship serve to reinforce the enduring sense of respect and high esteem for the elderly.

Apart from other minor religions or religious sects unique to the Vietnamese, about 10% of the southern Vietnamese and many of those living in the United States are Catholic. European missionaries introduced Christianity in the form of Roman Catholicism to the Vietnamese people in the late 16th century. Catholicism subsequently flourished, was suppressed, then was reinstated and fostered during the period of French colonialism, resulting in an Asian Catholic population second only to that of the Pilipinos (Chung, 1996) (see Chapter 9). Until 1975, the Catholic Church was a well-organized religious, educational, and political force in Vietnamese society. Although a relatively small percentage of the Vietnamese population was Roman Catholic, the religion significantly influenced the culture because many Vietnamese received their education in Catholic schools, and Catholics filled key positions in the government, the army, and the police force. Almost one third of the first wave of Vietnamese refugees who came to America were practicing Roman Catholics (Rutledge, 1987; Te, 1989b).

Language/Linguistic Origins

Khmer or Cambodian is the official language of Cambodia and is the mother tongue of the Khmer people (approximately 85% of the country's population). Khmer is the major language of the Mon-Khmer family and includes multiple regional dialects that are spoken throughout the country; minority languages also are spoken, such as Cham, Chinese, and hundreds of hill tribe languages (Chhim, 1989).

Khmer is a monosyllabic language in which there are many polysyllabic loan words and derivatives from Sanskrit (owing to historical ties to Indian culture); to a much lesser extent, Khmer also has words borrowed from Chinese, Thai, and Vietnamese. Unlike the Chinese, Lao, Thai, and Vietnamese languages, Khmer is a nontonal language (i.e., variations in pitch do not change the meaning of the words). In fact, Khmer has a monotone but staccato quality, with a rising inflection at the end of each sentence. Like Lao and Vietnamese, however, Khmer is an uninflected language (i.e., there are no plural, possessive, or past tense endings).

The Khmer written language consists of an alphabet that originated in southern India. It contains a total of 66 consonant and vowel symbols. Efforts to Romanize Khmer writing during French colonial rule were unsuccessful, largely because of resistance from religious circles. Moreover, exact transliteration of Khmer and English sounds is extremely difficult, if not impossible; therefore, any Romanization of written Khmer by Westerners could be only an approximation. The Khmer script is written from left to right and from top to bottom. Similar to Lao writing, it has a decorative and artistic appearance (Chhim, 1989).

Lao is the national and official language of Laos, but approximately 20 million people in Southeast Asia speak it as well (this includes approximately 18 million Lao speakers in northeast Thailand and other neighboring countries). Many minority languages are spoken in Laos, such as Hmong, Mien, Thai-Dam, and other hill tribe languages. Lao is a monosyllabic, tonal language, but like Khmer, it has a substantial number of polysyllabic words borrowed from Sanskrit.

Lao writing is also based on Sanskrit but appears different from Cambodian script. It consists of 50 consonant and vowel symbols and four tone marks. The same consonant sound occurring in different words with different pitches will often be represented by different symbols. Lao script is written from left to right (Te, 1989a). The appeal of the aesthetic Lao written language is complemented by the beauty and poetic quality of the spoken language. For example, the Lao equivalent of "thank you" literally means "from the heart" (Luangpraseut, 1989).

Vietnamese is the national language of more than 56 million speakers in Vietnam and more than 1 million Vietnamese immigrants living overseas. It is not mutually intelligible with any other language spoken in Asia. Vietnamese is diversified into three main regional dialects (i.e., northern, central, and southern), which differ slightly in pronunciation and vocabulary, but not in grammar (they are thus intelligible across regions). The Vietnamese language is characterized by its tonal system, monosyllabic nature, and vocabulary that contains a great many loan words of Chinese origin. Moreover, similar to Chinese, Khmer, and Lao, Vietnamese is an uninflected language; the concepts of plural, past tense, and so forth are expressed by context or by a separate word (Te, 1989a).

As of 2004, the current and only writing system used by the Vietnamese was based on the Roman alphabet. European missionaries devised the Vietnamese alphabet in the 16th century in order to translate the Bible into the vernacular, but the Vietnamese educated classes rejected it and continued to use the demotic writing system based on Chinese characters. The Vietnamese alphabet did not become the national writing system until after World War I. The alphabet consists of approximately 32 consonant (single and compound) and vowel letters and 5 tone marks. A highly consistent correlation exists between the sounds and the letters (Te, 1989a; Wei, 1983).

Southeast Asian refugees thus bring to the language-learning experience distinct linguistic variables that directly influence their ability to develop proficiency in English. The precise nature of various Southeast Asian languages and their effect on English language acquisition has been examined since the early 1980s; a few detailed treatments of specific Southeast Asian language systems (particularly Vietnamese) and their relationship to English have been published (e.g., Dien, Te, & Wei, 1986; Li, 1983; Te, 1989b; Walker, 1985). In addition to the unique characteristics of Southeast Asian languages, however, corresponding nonverbal communication patterns, relevant cultural characteristics, traditional values, and contemporary sociopolitical experiences further combine to exert strong influences on second-language acquisition and overall adaptation and adjustment to the dominant culture of the United States. These additional factors are addressed in subsequent sections of this chapter.

Contemporary Life

The end of the Cold War in 1989 and a subsequent series of remarkable events in Cambodia and Vietnam have resulted in fundamental changes in international relations. They, in turn, transformed the nature of Southeast Asian refugee resettlement in the United States. In this post–Cold War context, the U.N. High Commissioner for Refugees proclaimed the 1990s the "decade of repatriation." Most of the Orderly Departure Program family reunification cases have been leaving Vietnam as emigrants, not as refugees. Moreover, the refugee flows from Laos and Cambodia to the United States have been sharply reduced and virtually terminated.

> For some first-generation [Southeast Asian] adults exiled in America, the new developments in their homelands may open the possibility of return or of establishing business and other linkages between their native and adoptive countries. Bilateral relations are also likely to affect future immigration flows as well as entrepreneurial opportunities and the very nature of institutional life within established refugee communities. [However,] a sizable and rapidly growing second generation of young Vietnamese, Laotian, and Cambodian Americans are now rooted in communities throughout the United States. [They are part of a new era] in which the legacy of war may recede in practical importance. Theirs is an American future. (Rumbaut, 1995, pp. 238–239, 265)

Southeast Asian Americans are located in every state in the nation, primarily as a result of the initial resettlement efforts that were directed by federal policy toward widespread geographic dispersion; however, larger concentrations of refugees in selected cities and states have resulted from secondary migration. These concentrations have been spurred by opportunities for better training and jobs, a familiar climate, and the tendency of the second- and third-wave refugees to locate in well-established ethnic communities with existing social networks and community support systems (Chung, 1996). Nearly half of the Southeast Asian American population thus resides in California. Of the three major refugee nationality groups, residential concentration in California is most characteristic of the Vietnamese. The largest concentration of Vietnamese in the United States is found in Orange County, with its hub in the communities of Garden Grove, Santa Ana, and Westminster (referred to as "Little Saigon"). Texas has the next-largest Vietnamese (as well as total Southeast Asian) population, with sizable communities in Houston, Dallas, and along the gulf coast (Rumbaut, 1995).

In addition to California, Cambodians are concentrated on the opposite coast in Washington, D.C., and Massachusetts (as well as other eastern states such as New York,

Pennsylvania, Rhode Island, and Virginia). The Lao people are the most dispersed, but their largest populations are in the midwest. The Hmong are the most concentrated; more than half have settled in California in the San Joaquin Valley (in the cities of Fresno, Merced, and Tulare). Uncertain of their welfare eligibility because of the federal and state welfare reform legislation, however, thousands of Hmong people have left the area. They continue to relocate in other major Hmong urban population centers in Oregon and the Midwest (e.g., Michigan, Minnesota, Wisconsin) (Arax, 1996).

As of 2004, the age composition of the resident refugee population revealed a disproportionately large share of young people. Nearly one third of the population consisted of children who were school age or younger (Le, 1993); in fact, compared with fewer than half of all American households, more than 67% of the Vietnamese, 80% of the Lao and Cambodian, and 90% of the Hmong households consist of families with minor children. Moreover, the percentage of young children will continue to increase given the extremely high birth rate among Southeast Asian refugees (particularly Hmong women) and the relatively larger proportion of Southeast Asian American women of childbearing age (Rumbaut & Weeks, 1986). For the Hmong and Cambodian populations, childbearing also tends to begin early in adolescence and continue into the upper end of a woman's reproductive life (often past 40 years). The corresponding dramatically higher percentages of births to Southeast Asian American women younger than 17 and older than 40 years (relative to the general population) further contribute to a greater incidence of high-risk pregnancies and low birth weight (LBW) infants with special needs (Lin-Fu, 1987).

Relative to larger Asian American ethnic groups with much longer histories in the United States, the research literature on Southeast Asian Americans is very extensive. Although they may have become an "overdocumented" population in comparison to other Asian immigrants, continuing efforts to monitor and address the complex economic, psychological, and social adjustment of Southeast Asian refugees to the United States have yielded highly significant findings. The third-wave refugees, in particular, had very low levels of education, literacy, and extremely limited or no English language proficiency (Haines, 1989). Annual surveys have consistently shown that in their first few years of residence, Southeast Asian refugees manifested low labor force participation, high unemployment, low wages among those who are employed, and a high use of government cash assistance programs (U.S. Office of Refugee Resettlement, 1992). These characteristics (which are precisely the opposite for Asian Americans as a whole) are most dramatically illustrated by the Mien and Hmong, whose rate of unemployment has reached as much as 90%. Although the relatively high welfare dependency rates for Southeast Asian refugees ranged from 25% to 50% for the Vietnamese, Laotians, and Cambodians, nearly 70% of the Hmong population has received public assistance. This is, by far, the highest rate for any immigrant group in the country and is unprecedented in U.S. history (Rumbaut, 1995). The additional factors of large families and disproportionately high numbers of dependent children have contributed to overcrowded living conditions and extremely high rates of poverty among all Southeast Asian American ethnic groups; in fact, their respective poverty rates were two to five times higher than the poverty rate of the total U.S. population (Rumbaut, 1995).

The significant economic difficulties of many Southeast Asian refugees are compounded by major health and mental health problems (Chen et al., 1993; Uba, 1994;

Zane, Takeuchi, & Young, 1994). Large numbers of Southeast Asians display parasitism, anemia, malnutrition, growth retardation in children, tuberculosis, hepatitis, and genetic blood disorders such as thalassemia (Chen et al., 1993; Lassiter, 1995; Lin-Fu, 1988). Decades of war, trauma, torture, starvation, personal loss (vividly detailed by Uba, 1994), and the profound psychological impact of the refugee experience also have contributed to the high incidence of acute and chronic mental disorders among Southeast Asian refugees (Chen et al., 1993; Le, 1993; Rumbaut, 1985, 1995). Depression, anxiety, psychosomatic illnesses, and posttraumatic stress disorder (PTSD) (which may persist as long as 20 years after the refugee experience) are among the more common mental health problems (Leung & Boehnlein, 1996). Yet, more severe, even fatal, conditions and outcomes have included reactive psychoses, hysterical conversion symptoms (e.g., psychosomatic blindness among Cambodian women), "sudden nocturnal death syndrome" occurring in Hmong men, and suicide (Bliatout, 1981; DeAngelis, 1990; Lin & Masuda, 1981).

Southeast Asian refugees also have had to cope with the sheer need to survive and adapt to a host culture. They have typically encountered barriers of poverty, prejudice and racism, pervasive uncertainty, and culture shock (Lin & Masuda, 1981). They have experienced the severe disintegration of traditional family structures, role hierarchies, and social support systems as well as persistent cultural conflicts and challenges to long-held beliefs, values, and socialization practices. Consequently, the process of survival and acculturation has often produced chronic family dysfunction (including domestic violence, divorce, and intergenerational alienation) and major youth adjustment problems and acute identity crises, which may be expressed as self-destructive, antisocial, school dropout, and acting-out behaviors (Huang, 1989; Le, 1983; E. Lee, 1988; Uba, 1994). With the increasing number of American-born Southeast Asian children reaching adolescence and young adulthood, inter-generational conflicts and communication breakdowns within families are increasing.

These economic, health, and psychosocial status indicators tend to overshadow the relatively successful adjustments and achievements of many Southeast Asian Americans, particularly those among the earlier refugee populations. The Southeast Asian American profile has been characterized by impressive educational attainment, rapid movement into various professional fields, and aggressive growth in entrepreneurship. Thus, as originally noted in the introduction to the section, Southeast Asian Americans are extremely diverse; they include, as Takaki described, "preliterate tribesmen from the mountains as well as college-educated professionals from the cities, welfare families as well as wealthy businessmen, and super achieving university students as well as members of youth gangs" (1989, p. 470). Between these stereotypical extremes is a very heterogeneous group made up of people whose future "will likely be as diverse as their past, and will be reached by multiple paths" (Rumbaut, 1995, p. 265).

VALUES

Cultural values are the core conceptions of what is desirable within the individual and the larger society of a given group of people (Gollnick & Chinn, 1990). Cultural values are thus a major factor in contributing to a sense of identity and characteristic ways of perceiving, thinking, feeling, and behaving. Central to an understanding of cultural values is a major dimension of cultural variation: individualism versus collectivism. Individualism is a cultural pattern found in most northern and western re-gions of Europe and in North America, whereas collectivism—an emphasis on group needs over individual needs—is most common in Africa, Asia, Latin America, and the Pacific (Triandis, 1995).

The traditional collectivist values of Chinese, Koreans, Cambodians, Laotians, and Vietnamese, in particular, are rooted in the "three teachings," which were previ-ously described in this chapter within the doctrines and philosophies of Confucian-ism, Taoism, and Buddhism. The corresponding predominant values pertaining to family, harmony, education, and selected virtues are detailed next.

Family

According to Confucian principles, the family is the basic unit or backbone of soci-ety. While guiding and protecting the individual, the family serves as the tie between the individual and society and is a model for society as a whole (Major, 1989; Te, 1989a). In fact, "all (traditional) values are determined by reference to the mainte-nance, continuity and functions of the family group" (Union of Pan Asian Commu-

nities, 1980, p. 10). As the central focus of the individual's life, the family engenders primary loyalty, mutual obligation, coop-eration, interdependence, and reciprocity. Because individuals have an ingrained pro-found sense of responsibility and duty to the family, individual members thus en-gage in sustained efforts to promote the welfare, harmony, and reputation of their family. Throughout this process, each indi-vidual views him- or herself as an integral part of the totality of the family and the larger social structure and experiences a social/psychological dependence on oth-ers. This family-centered orientation and its attendant values contrast sharply with the more individualistic values of competi-tion, autonomy, independence, and self-reliance in the context of a society with significantly less well-defined, more highly varied, and often ambiguous social/familial roles and expectations (Chan, 1986; Mo-kuau, 1991).

The values of family and filial piety include reverence for elders, ancestors, and the past. An individual is viewed as the product of all generations of the family from the beginning of time. Individual behaviors therefore reflect on one's ancestors as well as entire culture. While striving to defend the family's honor and enhance its reputation, individuals must properly observe historical events and maintain family traditions. This orientation toward living with the past differs markedly from the individualistic cultural preoccupation with the future and living for tomorrow (Chan, 1986).

Harmony

Among Asian cultural groups, the practice of *syncretism* or blending of beliefs (e.g., those prescribed by the "three teachings") reflects a basic philosophical and pragmatic orientation. The keynote of existence is to reconcile divergent forces, principles, and points of view in an effort to maintain harmony. The individual must strive to achieve intrapsychic harmony, interpersonal harmony, and harmony with nature as well as time. This orientation is manifested in characteristic "situation centeredness." In interpersonal relationships, the individual thus mobilizes his or her thoughts and actions to conform to social reality (Chan, 1986). The "middle-position" virtue is valued by seeking oneness with the group and being in step—neither ahead nor behind—with others (Ho, 1987). In accordance with Confucian and Taoist teachings, one avoids direct confrontation, conforms to the rules of propriety, and "gives face" or recognition and respect to others. These guiding principles translate into verbal, social, and emotional restraint and the consistent use of politeness, tact, and gentleness in interpersonal relations. Preservation of harmony is thus a primary value characteristic of "heart-oriented" (versus "mind-oriented") cultures and further reinforces a pervasive humanistic (versus materialistic) orientation among traditional Asian people (Chao, 1992; Pan Asian Parent Education Project, 1982; Uba, 1994).

Education

"The reverence and status conferred on teachers and the social significance of scholarship have firmly established the value of education in . . . Asian countries" (Leung, 1988, p. 91). This value is embodied in the Chinese proverb: "If you are planning for a year, sow rice; if you are planning for a decade, plant trees; if you are planning for a lifetime, educate people." Children are ingrained with a lifelong respect for knowledge, wisdom, intelligence, and love of learning. Confucian teachings emphasize the moral aspect of education as well as the belief that the development of the human character varies according to experience. Parents thus assume primary responsibility for ensuring that their children receive appropriate guidance. Throughout this process, securing a good education for their children becomes paramount. According to Kim, Koreans, in particular, place a very high value on academic credentials (*hak-bul*):

> Parents' self-esteem is intimately tied to the academic success or failure of their children. The fiercely competitive nature of the Korean educational system has made successful education of children an all-consuming enterprise for most families, requiring much time, energy, and money, with the mother assigned to this task full-time. (1996, p. 286)

Therefore, families literally may follow the teachings of Mencius (the Chinese philosopher): "A good mother is ready to move three times to give children a good education" (Min, 1995b, p. 224).

The children, in turn, fulfill their responsibility and obligation to the family primarily through successful academic achievement—the greatest tribute one can bestow on one's parents and family (Leung, 1988). By excelling in school, the child brings honor to the family while preparing for future educational and occupational successes that will further enhance the family's social status and ensure its economic well-being, as well as that of the individual and his or her own family or the next generation (Serafica, 1990).

Selected Virtues

The primary values of family, harmony, and education are further supported by highly valued virtues or character traits among Asian groups. The Vietnamese people, for example, place great value on the trait called *t'anh can cu*, which includes the combined characteristics of thrift, industriousness, patience, determination, endurance, tolerance, and accommodation. This quality has contributed to the profound strength and resiliency demonstrated by the Vietnamese and other Southeast Asian people throughout their respective histories of war, disruption, and loss (Union of Pan Asian Communities, 1980). When similarly expressed among Chinese, Korean, and other Asian groups, these characteristics translate into the ability to persevere without complaint, to "suffer in silence." Such character traits are reinforced within the context of a fatalistic orientation in which life is presumed to be essentially unalterable and unpredictable. An individual thus feels a need to resign to external conditions and events over which he or she presumably has little or no control. If human suffering is viewed as part of the natural order, then acceptance of one's fate, maintenance of inner strength, and emotional self-restraint also are considered to be necessary expressions of dignity (Chan, 1986).

Other major virtues include assumption of responsibility, hard work, self-sacrifice on all levels (i.e., spiritual, emotional, material, and physical), modesty, and humility (which is often expressed through self-denigration). Again, these virtues are consistent with a collectivist orientation wherein individual achievements are valued in terms of their contribution to the group status and welfare, and needs for corresponding personal recognition are transcended.

The previously described traditional cultural orientations and values derive from religious and philosophical foundations that are thousands of years old. Therefore, they have been promoted throughout successive generations and may continue to have a profound influence on the socialization of Asian American children in more traditionally oriented families. Despite their enduring and historically adaptive nature, however, traditional Asian values have undergone significant transformation within the contemporary Asian American experience. One can obviously anticipate wide individual variation in the extent to which traditional values are maintained or increasingly challenged, shifted, and blended, while alternative, contrasting values are incorporated as part of the acculturation process. The complex acculturation patterns of Asian immigrants and refugees also are influenced by factors such as class and regional differences in countries of origin, premigration experience, time of arrival, proximity to same-ethnic communities, age, gender, education, language proficiency, and socioeconomic status (Leung, 1988; Okamura, Heras, & Wong-Kerberg, 1995; Uba, 1994). Awareness and appreciation of such complexity is critical in determining the relative influence of traditional values among Asian American families.

BELIEFS

Traditional values translate into belief systems that are further reflected in child rearing, medical or health care, views about the causation and meaning of disability, and death and dying. Each of these areas is discussed with relevance to corresponding practices among selected Asian cultures.

Child Rearing

The respective traditional child-rearing beliefs and practices of Chinese, Korean, Cambodian, Laotian, and Vietnamese families have been detailed in various publications (Chung, 1996; Greenfield & Cocking, 1994; Hamner & Turner, 1996; Ho, 1987; Lassiter, 1995; McGoldrick, Giordano, & Pearce, 1996; Morrow, 1989; Pan Asian Parent Education Project, 1982; Uba, 1994; Yu & Kim, 1983). Examination of this literature reveals obvious cultural variation among these ethnic groups, although relatively few empirical studies have been conducted of inter- and intraethnic differences in parental behaviors, beliefs, and values that influence child rearing among Asian American families (Fillmore, 1994; Kelley & Tseng, 1992; Sigel, 1988; Uba, 1994). As is the case with traditional cultural orientations and values, however, many similarities exist among selected Asian groups with respect to family structure, dynamics, and socialization patterns. These shared characteristics as well as culture-specific practices are described in this section.

Family Structure

As previously indicated, the family and its structure and function serve as the most basic social institution among Asian people. Sustained throughout the centuries by the "three teachings," the primary reference groups are the immediate family (i.e., husband; wife; unmarried children; and, typically, sons' wives and children) and the extended family (i.e., immediate family and close relatives sharing the same family name as well as ancestors, and, in the case of the Hmong, all members of the "clan" living in the same community) (Chung, 1996). The immediate family is characterized by well-defined, highly interdependent roles within a cohesive patriarchal vertical structure. This structure derives from the Confucian doctrine of filial piety that establishes a social hierarchy based on the "five relationships" and the "three obediences" (whereby a woman is instructed to obey her father as a daughter, her husband as a wife, and her eldest son as a widow). Traditionally, sons (particularly the all-important eldest son) are more valued than daughters because they are "born facing *in*"; they are the ones who symbolically carry on the family name and also are responsible for caring for the parents when they become old. Daughters have a devalued status because they are "born facing *out*" and viewed as children who are raised to join another family when they marry (Uba, 1994). Each family member has a particular designation and is referred to by corresponding honorific kinship terms and forms of address that indicate his or her relative position and role within the family structure. Distinguished on the basis of generation, age, and gender, the hierarchy of authority and reverence begins at the highest level with grandparents (usually paternal), and then proceeds to father, mother, oldest son ("big brother"), middle daughter, and youngest son (in a boy/girl/boy family). This Confucian hierarchy is observed by the Chinese, Koreans, and Vietnamese, whereas traditional practices among Lao families dictate that married couples initially live in the bride's parental household (typically for 2 to 3 years), and the youngest son (or daughter) typically inherits the house site after the parents' death (Luangpraseut, 1989).

Marital Roles

Within the immediate family, traditional marital roles have been characterized by the husband serving as the principal provider and family representative in the public domain; that is, the father serves as the "secretary of state" or "minister of foreign affairs" (Dung, 1984). The wife serves as the "minister of the interior" and is primarily responsible for what happens inside the house, which includes monitoring the family's emotional well-being, raising and educating the children, and taking care of financial matters (Dung, 1984). According to the Korean maxim, the woman's most important role is to be a wise wife and a good mother (Pan Asian Parent Education Project, 1982). She thus derives her status through her role as a wife, mother, or daughter-in-law. Moreover, within the ostensible power structure, the traditional Vietnamese saying applies—"the husband is king and his wife is his slave" (Thuy, 1980). In fact, a wife is almost considered a nonperson until she produces a son; she acquires increasingly greater power as she becomes the mother of a son, then a mother-in-law (Kim, 1985). Although the father is the acknowledged authority figure and head of the family, in the eyes of the children, the mother has the same status. She acquires profound psychological power over them and is seen as "the embodiment of love and the spirit of self-denial and sacrifice" (Te, 1989b, p. 69). She also has the power of the purse. Thus, "while the husband thinks he is the master of the house, the wife knows she is" (Kim, 1985, p. 345).

Parental Roles/Responsibilities

Among many Asian families, the strongest family ties are between parent and child rather than between spouses. Parental roles and responsibilities supersede the marital relationship. Parents are thus readily prepared to sacrifice personal needs in serving the interests of their children and in providing for the welfare and security of the family as a whole. In turn, the parent assumes the right to demand unquestioning obedience and loyalty from the child. The role of the parent is to define the law; the duty of the child is to listen and obey. Strict parental authority translates into parental accountability and responsibility for the child's behavior, which is considered a direct reflection of the parents' ability to provide proper guidance.

Infancy

Children are viewed as extensions of their parents. They continue the family lineage, bring status to the family name by virtue of their achievements, and literally give meaning to their parents' lives. The newborn child is thus treasured as a "gift from the gods." Depending on selected spiritual/religious orientations, birth also signifies the reincarnation of a soul into a new body (Quincy, 1988). Given the infant's relative vulnerability, a number of corresponding traditional customs have been practiced. In ancient China, parents often dressed infant boys like girls and put silver dog collars on them in the belief that this would protect the child from evil spirits. Parents later continued to give children pets' names for nicknames because it was believed that animals had a better chance of surviving than human infants and would not be harmed by evil spirits. The Hmong people have traditionally guarded against malevolent spirits by not naming children until they are approximately 2 years of age and giving them numbers instead of first names when they are infants; children also are never called "number one" because the spirits might not look for "number two" until they have found "number one" (National Indochinese Clearinghouse, 1980; Olness, 1986). Vietnamese parents traditionally avoid praising the infant and may become anxious if others make complimentary comments regarding the infant's health or appearance for fear that a lurking evil spirit may overhear and attempt to steal the baby away. Similarly, infants are dressed in old clothes until their 1-month birthday celebration to avoid making the spirits jealous, thus causing the baby to become ill (Pan Asian Parent Education Project, 1982). If an infant does become ill, a Cambodian parent may temporarily change the infant's name to confuse the spirits (Hollingsworth, Brown, & Brooten, 1980).

Infants initially are perceived as being relatively helpless and not responsible for their actions. Parents are thus very tolerant and permissive (by Anglo-European American standards) and immediately gratify the infant's early dependency needs. Mother–infant interaction is characterized by an emphasis on close physical contact rather than active vocal stimulation; infants are carried much of the time, even during naps, or kept nearby and picked up immediately if they cry. Korean infants are customarily wrapped in a shawl or blanket, strapped around the mother's (or grandmother's) back, and carried piggyback (Yu & Kim, 1983). Infants are rarely, if ever, left to sleep alone and typically sleep in the same room or bed with their parents and other siblings until school age or older. There is an absence of rigid schedules, and parents have later age expectations with respect to selected developmental milestones such as weaning; infants are usually breastfed on demand and may continue to nurse up to 2 years of age or older.

In contrast, toilet training may be introduced when the infant is as young as 3–4 months old, when the mother becomes sensitive to his or her schedule. It begins by placing the baby on the toilet after selected feedings; the mother's awareness of the infant's schedule helps her recognize how the baby typically signals elimination through facial expressions, behaviors, or noises, which the mother may imitate or initiate (Pan Asian Parent Education Project, 1982). Despite this early onset of toilet training, however, no strict demands or pressures are placed on the child. In fact, although this toilet training practice is common among traditional Korean families, there are no words for toilet training in the Korean language (Yu & Kim, 1983).

Throughout infancy and the toddler period, parents (particularly the mother), older siblings, grandparents, and other members of the extended family, if available, provide the child with a very nurturing, indulgent, secure, and predictable environment. Children are conditioned from infancy to respond to multiple caregivers and authority figures and learn to see the world in terms of a network of relationships. This experience serves as the foundation for the development of very strong family attachments and subsequent reciprocity.

Early Childhood and School Age

The preschool period represents a transitional phase wherein the child moves from a period of affection and indulgence (infancy to the late toddler stage when he or she is not expected to "know any better") to a period of discipline and education as the child approaches school age and is expected to assume increasingly greater responsibility for his or her own behavior. Parental expectations for earlier acquisition of personal-social and self-help skills (e.g., grooming, dressing, completing chores) are evident.

On reaching school age, the child is increasingly expected to be independent within the context of the family and home environment. Asians facilitate this process, in part, by including the child in adult affairs and activities such as weddings, funerals, and social and business functions. The child thus shares the same world with his or her parents and receives early exposure to socially appropriate patterns and proper codes of public behavior, which he or she quickly learns through participation, observation, and imitation. At this time, the father typically assumes a more active role in the child's social and moral development. The immediate parent–child relationship becomes more formal, and adult demands are more rigidly enforced. In contrast to the repeated indulgence experienced during earlier years, the child is now subjected to markedly increased discipline (Morrow, 1989).

As the child matures and acquires younger siblings, he or she must further assume selected child-rearing responsibilities that augment those of his or her parents. Older siblings are routinely delegated the responsibility of caring for younger siblings

and are expected to model adult-like behaviors, thereby setting good examples. The eldest son, in particular, is entrusted with the greatest responsibility as the leader among his siblings who must provide them with guidance and support. Like the parent, the older sibling also is periodically expected to sacrifice personal needs in favor of younger siblings. These roles are formalized to the extent that children in the family are addressed by kinship terms that indicate whether they are older or younger and that may further specify their ordinal position in the family. The "reciprocity" inherent in sibling relationships is clearly illustrated in the classic parental response to sibling arguments: The older sibling is generally scolded for not setting a good example, and the younger sibling is chastised for failing to respect his or her older brother or sister.

Socialization Strategies

Children learn to view their role within the family and society in terms of reciprocal relationships and obligations. They must readily acquire a sense of moral obligation and primary loyalty to the family. This translates into behaviors that serve to maintain and enhance the family name, honor, and face. Herein lies the "pride and shame" principle whereby individual behavior reflects on the entire family. On the one hand, highly valued individual achievements such as academic or occupational success serve to promote the family welfare and are a source of shared pride among family members. On the other hand, dysfunctional, antisocial, or otherwise negatively valued behavior exhibited by a family member contributes toward a collective family experience of profound shame (Sodowsky, Kwong-Liem, & Pannu, 1995).

Observance of specific roles, relationships, and codes of conduct results in a persistent awareness of the effects of one's behavior on others. In contrast to the more egocentric individualistic orientation, Asian children are socialized to think and act in proper relation to others and must learn to transcend their personal concerns. They are obliged to be sensitive to the social environment. The parent effectively controls the child by modeling appropriate behaviors and by appealing to the child's sense of duty or obligation. Parents also may periodically evoke fear of personal ridicule or the prospect of family shame as a consequence of misbehavior (Uba, 1994).

Behaviors that are punished include disobedience, aggression (particularly sibling directed), and failure to fulfill one's primary responsibilities. Primary forms of discipline include name-calling; teasing; and the use of verbal reprimands including harsh criticism, scolding, and shaming to engender a sense of potential family disgrace. The child is reminded that his or her negative behaviors reflect poorly on the entire family and the family name. The child can absolve him- or herself of this "loss of face" by actively displaying changes in behavior. It is not sufficient for children to ask for forgiveness and verbally promise to do better. Actions speak louder than words (Tinloy et al., 1986). Parents may respond to more serious transgressions by either threatening or actually engaging in temporary removal ("banishment") of the child from the family household and/or isolating the child from the family social life. On occasion, the use of physical punishment (e.g., spanking; paddling with a stick on the legs, arms, and buttocks) is considered acceptable (Ho, 1990). While assuming primary responsibility for teaching the child to behave properly, the mother serves as the main disciplinarian for daily problems. The father assumes the role of implementing harsher punishment for more serious misbehavior.

Child rearing is based on the assumption of a child's inherent predilection for good; however, the development of positive character requires proper training during early childhood. Subsequent emphasis is placed on formal education and high standards of academic achievement—the child's primary means of fulfilling his or her family responsibility and obligation. Whereas the family sacrifices and mobilizes its resources to provide an environment conducive to academic achievement, the child, in turn, is expected to work hard and receive high grades. Effort is often viewed as more essential in contributing to success than is innate ability (Stevenson & Lee, 1990). Within this context, overt rewards, contingent praise, and personal credit are generally not given for positive achievements or behaviors because they are expected (Uba, 1994). Although parents may occasionally tell their children that they are proud of them, acknowledgment of accomplishments may be more often manifested in the form of exhortations to "do better," to strive for even higher levels of achievement. A mother may also express family pride by preparing a special meal, or a father may ask a child to take on a special task that shows the family's confidence in his or her abilities. These indirect forms of acknowledgment extend to extrafamilial relationships whereby public discussion of the child's accomplishments with others outside the family is considered arrogant and inappropriate. In fact, unsolicited recognition and compliments are often politely dismissed, may cause silent embarrassment, or are negated by immediate counter-discussion of the child's other faults and by self-deprecating remarks. The virtues of humility and modesty are thus modeled in such behaviors (Chan, 1986; Morrow, 1989; Tinloy et al., 1986).

In general, Asian parents who adhere to more traditional child-rearing values and practices are relatively controlling, restrictive, and protective of their children. Children are taught to suppress aggressive behavior, overt expressions of negative emotions, and personal grievances; they must inhibit strong feelings and exercise self-control in order to maintain family harmony. Parents and children typically avoid frank discussion or highly verbal communication, particularly in the area of sexuality. Sexuality is suppressed in cultures in which physical contact between members of the opposite sex is minimized and public displays of affection are rare and embarrassing. The communication pattern also is one way: parent to child (the parent

speaks, and the child listens). The father is particularly distant in this respect and generally neither invites confidences nor initiates "talks" with his children. The mother–child relationship is closer and more verbal. Father–mother interaction is often characterized by indirect communications, inferences, and unstated feelings (Uba, 1994).

The protective and controlling orientation of Asian parents also may be manifested in a basic distrust of outsiders. In an attempt to control outside influences, parents often restrict the child's social interaction by allowing access to only selected role models (e.g., family, close friends); this may include the child's peer group and playmates. Independent peer interaction and autonomous social behavior (including ultimately leaving the family to reside outside the home) typically occur at much later ages relative to Anglo-European American norms (Uba, 1994). Although Asian parents tend to promote family interdependence, however, they may simultaneously encourage the development of individual independence *outside* the family. Whereas the primary collectivist value system reinforces deference to the group, it also supports personal control and self-improvement in the accomplishment of internal goals. This is the element of independence that is conducive to success and achievement in the larger society, which, in turn, enhances the family welfare and fulfills filial obligations. Thus, although traditional values continue to influence child-rearing practices significantly, immigrant/refugee families may adopt bicultural socialization strategies that enable children to function effectively in their respective ethnic subcultures and the mainstream culture of the society at large (Harrison, Wilson, Pine, Chan, & Buriel, 1990; Lin & Fu, 1990).

Medical Care

Chinese and Korean immigrants and Southeast Asian refugee groups vary considerably with regard to health beliefs and health care practices. Many families utilize a pluralistic system of care that includes a blending of traditional Chinese medicine and various folk medicine practices with Western medicine (Kraut, 1990). An examination of the more common traditional Asian health orientations and healing cultures of the respective ethnic groups is thus warranted.

Health Beliefs   During centuries of isolation from the rest of the world, ancient Chinese scholars developed a distinctive and extremely well-organized system of medicine that continues to dominate medical thinking in China. This unique system has further influenced the medical concepts adopted by the people of Korea and Southeast Asia.

Fundamental to traditional Chinese medicine is the philosophy of Taoism, the cosmic forces of *yin* and *yang,* and the "five elements." Tao signifies "the way" or the harmony between heaven and earth; following the Tao enables one to be in accord with the fundamental laws of nature and the universe. The basic dualism of the universe is represented by the interaction of yin and yang, which can be used to classify everything, whether it is concrete or abstract, physical or moral. Yin is the passive or negative female force that includes the moon, earth, water, evil, poverty, and sadness and produces cold, darkness, emptiness, contraction, and downward movement. In contrast, *yang* is the active or positive male force that includes the sun, heaven, fire, goodness, wealth, and joy and produces warmth, light, fullness, expansion, and upward movement (Chung, 1996; Lee, 1989; Tom, 1989). *Yin* and *yang* are not regarded as conflicting principles, but as mutually necessary complementary forces, as indicated in the symbol of the Tao. Each penetrates the other's hemisphere, and together they are resolved in an all-embracing circle.

> Intimately associated with *yin* and *yang* are the Five Elements. It was believed that all things are composed of five elements: metal, wood, water, fire, and earth. The proportions of these elements are determined by the mutual influence of *yin* and *yang.* (Tom, 1989, pp. 71–72)

Chinese concepts of health and disease are thus closely related to these principles.

> Since man and the universe have been composed of these same elements, man is subject to the same forces that govern the universe. If man remains in harmony with the Tao, and *yin* and *yang* and the Five Elements are in proper balance, he can enjoy good health and longevity. Imbalance, however, results in illness and death. (Tom, 1989, p. 72)

The traditional classification system of Chinese medicine divides body parts between the *yang*-related surface organs as well as selected internal organs (e.g., gall bladder, stomach, large and small intestines, bladder) and the *yin*-related visceral organs. Chinese physiology considers the five viscera (i.e., heart, lungs, spleen, liver, and kidneys) to be the main organs corresponding to the "five elements." *Qi* or *Ch'i* (life force energy), *Jing* (essence), and *Shen* (spirit) are the "three treasures" that, together with blood and body fluids, comprise the "fundamental substances" that flow through the body pathways (meridians). Illness and disease are interpreted as a state of imbalance in yin and yang. Internal and external factors that contribute to illness correspond to one of three categories: environment, emotion, and way of life. The environmental or climatic factor of illness includes the "pernicious influences" of wind, cold, heat, dampness, and dryness. The "seven emotions" include joy, anger, hate, jealousy, sorrow, worry, and fear. "Way of life" includes diet, sexual activity, physical activity, and other factors (Chen et al., 1993; Chung, 1996; Spector, 1991).

The hot–cold classification of various diseases provides a means of both diagnosing and treating selected illnesses and medical conditions. For example, excessive "heat" or *yang* illnesses are generated from within the body itself and include such conditions as constipation, hypertension, rashes, pimples, cold sores, fever, ear infection, and blurry vision. "Cold" or *yin* maladies are caused by intrusion of cold or "bad wind" into any part of the body and may contribute to conditions such as diarrhea, anemia, coughing, headaches, muscle aches, poor appetite, weight loss, weakness, miscarriage, and infectious illnesses, such as colds, the flu, and measles, as well as other diseases (e.g., cancer) (Chen et al., 1993; Lassiter, 1995; Muecke, 1983a). Wind is presumed to enter the body during periods of vulnerability such as during surgery and during and after childbirth. *Yin* illnesses also may be produced by loss of blood (which has the quality of heat and *yang*). Improper diet is yet another cause of imbalance. It is believed that most foods have hot or cold properties and, when digested, turn into air that is either *yin* or *yang*. Thus, selected cold foods (e.g., fruits and/or vegetables such as melon, bean sprouts, spinach, cabbage, seaweed, fruit juices, and ricewater) are prescribed for hot illnesses; hot foods (e.g., chicken, beef, pork, fried food, beans, nuts, cereal, black pepper, ginger and other spices, alcohol, coffee) are prescribed for cold illnesses (Chen et al., 1993; Wong, 1985).

Among internal factors believed to contribute to illness are excesses of the "seven emotions." As previously indicated, among most Asian cultures there is great value placed on the ability to control emotions and subjugate them to reason. When selected emotions are not openly expressed and accumulate in intensity within the body, however, they result in blockage of *Ch'i* and malfunction of the organs, thus producing physical illness (Koss-Chioino, 1995). A related Korean illness is called *hwa-byung*; in the folk tradition, *Hwa* refers to "anger" and "fire," whereas *byung* means "sickness." Thus, individuals suffering from repressed or suppressed anger of long duration may manifest somatic symptoms such as loss of appetite, indigestion, epigastric pain, alternating diarrhea and constipation, dyspnea, hypertension, palpitation, headaches, dizziness, and fatigue. Interestingly, similar kinds of multiple somatic symptoms have been found among Chinese with *frigophobia* (i.e., morbid fear of cold weather) who believe that their problems stem from a disturbance of *yin–yang* balance and the element of fire. Most people with frigophobia are men, in contrast to *hwa-byung,* which is primarily a condition of women (Lin, 1983).

These beliefs reflect an orientation in which there is often no clear differentiation between psychological and physical problems. Psychological stresses are seen as capable of producing both, and psychological disturbance is often expressed through somatic symptoms (Lin, Carter, & Kleinman, 1985). This tendency toward somatization corresponds with the holistic philosophy of Chinese medicine that does not separate mental illness from physical illness. Health maintenance thus entails ensuring harmony between the *yin* and *yang* forces of the body, mind, and emotions. Illness is an affliction of the *whole* person—a generalized lack of well-being (Do, 1988; Lassiter, 1995).

In addition to the more metaphysical causes of illness associated with traditional Chinese medicine, Asian folk medicine may further attribute illness to supernatural causes such as soul loss. As described in a previous section, many Southeast Asian groups believe that the body is inhabited by more than one soul (the numbers vary according to different ethnic groups). These souls inhabit various organs and parts of the body, the primary one being the head. Good health requires that all souls be present within the body and in harmony. When one or more souls are lost from the body, a wide range of symptoms—from physical illness to emotional and mental problems—may occur. The Lao soul-calling ceremony (*Baci*) described previously is a means by which illness can be prevented or health restored. Apart from soul loss, illness also is believed to be caused by a malevolent spirit or from an offense against good spirits or deities (Lew, 1989).

Health Practices   Many Southeast Asian groups believe in the supernatural etiology of illness (particularly mental illness). Corresponding treatment can include soul calling, exorcism, ritualistic offerings, chanting or recitation of sacred prayers, and other spiritual healing ceremonies such as sprinkling the person with holy water. The treatment is typically performed by or in consultation with priests, shamans, spiritual masters, or sorcerers (Bliatout, Ben, Bliatout, & Lee, 1985; Egawa & Tashima, 1982; Kemp, 1985). A traditional healers is called the *Kru Khmer* (he who knows) for Cambodians and the *Maw Dyaa* for Laotians; these healers serve as conduits or channelers for gifted spirits or shamans from the past and have the power to contact the spirit world for advice about physical and psychological problems (particularly when people are experiencing significant emotional distress and are unable to identify the source of their physical ailment). Hmong people prefer to see living shamans who are believed to have direct healing powers; these shamans use divination to diagnose the "patient's" problem and then perform a trance ceremony to cure him or her (Chung, 1996; Dresser, 1996).

A variety of diagnostic and treatment methods exist for illnesses resulting from perceived metaphysical causes within the context of traditional Chinese medical theory as well as Ayurvedic medicine, which originated in India and followed Indian cultural influences into Cambodia and Laos. With respect to diagnostic procedures, the best physician is viewed as one who intrudes on the body the least (Muecke, 1983b). The physician or traditional healer typically employs four methods of making a diagnosis: inspection (of appearance, facial color, tongue, secretions, and excretions), listening and smelling (sounds and odors of the body), inquiring (asking questions of the patient), and touching (pulse taking and abdominal palpation) (Chen et al., 1993; Chung, 1996). The pulse is taken from 12 different positions along the radial pulse of both wrists; each position is closely linked with the meridians and internal organs. Pulse diagnosis is considered the best method and is used to indicate the condition of the humors and vital organs (Egawa & Tashima, 1982; Tom, 1989). Combining the "four examinations" enables the traditional practitioner to perceive "a total body landscape of harmony and disharmony that transcends purely physical categories of description" (Chen et al., 1993, p. 746).

In contrast, for the diagnosis of illness and disease, Western medical practice often relies on comprehensive individual histories and extensive laboratory tests as well as symptomatology. According to traditional Chinese medicine practice, a good clinician should be able to make a diagnosis based on a brief history and examination alone. Many traditionally oriented Asians may thus perceive American physicians as too dependent on ostensibly irrelevant questions, unnecessary physical examination, and excessive and invasive tests, such as X-rays and blood sampling, the latter being particularly problematic for those who believe venipuncture (through insertion of the needle) will upset the "hot–cold" balance of the body, result in soul loss, and/or that the body cannot reproduce lost blood (Chen et al., 1993; Dresser, 1996; Muecke, 1983b; Spector, 1991).

Among the more widely used traditional treatment methods are herbal medications, a great many of which are based on sound pharmacological principles. Some of these same medications also were traditionally used in Western medicine, including iodine from seaweed, ephedrine from a native herb, calcium from the velvet of a deer horn, and a fine clay used in diarrhea drugs. Ongoing research continues to document the proven effectiveness and specific pharmacology of various herbal medicines (Chen et al., 1993). However, some of the more popular exotic remedies such as ginseng and angelica root or dried sea horse, snake, and rhinoceros horn appear to have questionable, if any, pharmacological properties (Tom, 1989).

Aside from the specific effects and relative efficacy of various herbs and medications, the way in which they are obtained and ingested significantly contrasts with Western prescription medication. "Patients boil herbs in the prescribed amount of water for the designated time to achieve proper concentrations of broth. Usually a single dose of the correct herb is sufficient. In contrast, Western medicines are [typically] given in many pills over a period of time [and at prescribed intervals]" (Chen et al., 1993, p. 747). Moreover, in terms of "hot−cold" therapy, Western medications are generally classified as "hot" and, with their many chemical agents, are perceived as very potent compared with the more natural herbal medicines, most of which are "cool." Concern about side effects may lead some Asian patients to adjust the dosage of various prescriptions downward or to stop taking them altogether if there has been no quick relief of symptoms (which Asians expect). They also may have difficulty understanding or appreciating why it is necessary to continue using selected prescription medications (e.g., antibiotics) well after specific symptoms have abated. Such expectations and orientations reflect a traditional focus on disease symptoms rather than underlying causes. Thus, there is a tendency to self-medicate and independently manage both prescribed and over-the-counter medication as well as to utilize more traditional herbal medication simultaneously or alternatively (Muecke, 1983a, 1983b).

Additional treatment methods for a variety of illnesses and conditions include therapeutic massage, acupressure, and acupuncture (practiced for more than four thousand years). Moxibustion (i.e., heating "moxa" or crushed wormwood, mugwort leaves, and other herbs on the skin) is used to treat abdominal pain, cramping, diarrhea, and other ailments such as ulcers and hernias and is often used in conjunction with acupuncture. The herbs, which may be formed into a cigar-shaped cylinder or a small pellet, are usually slowly smoldered near or on the abdominal wall, the chest, the back, or at the site of the acupuncture (if performed) after the needle has been withdrawn. In the Chinese practice of moxibustion, a slice of ginger or a pinch of salt is placed on the skin (over the identified acupuncture point) before the moxa is applied; the skin is not in contact with the moxa and no lesion results. Yet, for some Cambodians and other Southeast Asians, the intervention is exorcistic, and the negative spiritual forces believed to be causing the illness are driven out by actually blistering the skin. On an infant or young child, the resulting first-, second-, or even third-degree burns can thus be misinterpreted as cigarette burns (Chen et al., 1993; Ratliff, 1994).

Dermabrasion, which derives from "hot−cold" therapy, is yet another traditional practice that is self-care in nature and one of the most common treatments among Southeast Asians. Considered a massage treatment, various dermabrasive techniques entail abrading the skin in selected areas of the face (i.e., forehead and bridge of the nose), but is performed more commonly along selected muscle groupings of the body including the neck, the chest (over the ribs), the back, inside the upper arm, the shoulder, the abdomen, or the legs. These areas are locations for meridians used in acupuncture and acupressure. Dermabrasion is generally done to treat "wind illnesses" such as fever, chills, muscle ache, headache, and symptoms of a cold or a respiratory infection. The most popular form of dermabrasion is coining or *cao gio* (scratch wind). The practice involves first covering the affected area with a medicated ointment such as Tiger Balm and then gently rubbing the area with the edge of a coin (or spoon), downward and away from the head, until dark marks that look like bruises can be seen. This procedure allows the "toxic wind" to be brought to the body surface and released; supposedly, the sicker the affected person, the darker the marks will be. Other dermabrasive techniques include pinching and cupping, which, similar to coining, have been detailed in other publications (Chow, 1976; Ratliff, 1994). These practices all typically produce welts and superficial bruises that may last a few days and can be easily mistaken as signs of physical abuse (Masterson, 1988; Nguyen, Nguyen, & Nguyen, 1987; Stauffer, 1991). Various health professionals have indicated that these "treatment bruises" may mimic the lesions of inflicted trauma but are *not* harmful. There is no medical reason to discourage what are considered to be well-intended, emotionally nurturant folk practices (Chao, 1992; Muecke, 1983b; Yeatman & Dang, 1980). To the extent that individuals practicing these folk practices may be stigmatized by the host society, the opportunity for cross-cultural education and awareness should be made available.

As noted in the previous section, appropriate diet is important not only for treating illness but also for the purpose of health maintenance, disease prevention, and prenatal and postnatal care. For Asian women who believe in the hot–cold system, prescribed dietary practices during pregnancy and after giving birth are strictly followed. The traditional prenatal as well as the restorative postpartum diets include selected hot–cold foods and exclude others. During the first trimester of pregnancy, the woman's diet consists of "hot" foods such as eggs, meat, and black pepper and ginger. In the second trimester, she eats "cold" foods such as squash; melons; fruit; and foods high in fat, protein (e.g., bean curd), sugar, and carbohydrates. Herb tea with special roots becomes part of the daily meal as a nutritional supplement. In the last trimester, or "hot period," hot foods are limited, and hot medications such as iron supplements are avoided to prevent indigestion and rashes or sores on the newborn's skin. Throughout the entire pregnancy, explicit taboos and dietary restrictions dictate the exclusion of foods, such as shellfish, rabbit, and lamb. During the "cold" period (i.e., 1 month postpartum), women may abstain from vegetables, fruits, and juices. Chinese women eat simmered chicken with special herbs and soup consisting of pig's feet or knuckles, sweet black vinegar, black beans, ginger, and hard-boiled eggs. Cambodian women receive special meals of salty eggs and rice soup with pork. Drinking herb-steeped wine or eating a dish of "chicken whiskey" (i.e., rice wine, chicken, lichen, and ginger) also may be encouraged. These foods and drinks are intended to assist in the involution of the uterus, help get rid of gas, improve circulation, chase the "bad blood" away, and regulate menstrual flow. In Cambodia and other Southeast Asian countries, the postpartum mother is placed on a slatted bed with a heat source underneath it, then, turned to different sides of her body by an attendant. This practice of "mother roasting" serves to further replace the heat lost during childbirth. To protect against postpartum illness, women also are advised to not go outdoors, drink cold water, wash their hair, or take a shower during this period (Chow, 1976; Chung, 1996; Dresser, 1996; Lee, 1989).

Disability

Among the various Asian ethnic groups, the most severe disabilities (e.g., those associated with developmental disabilities, physical/sensory impairments, and serious emotional disturbance) are traditionally viewed with considerable stigma. Such stigma is created, in part, by traditional attributions linking specific disabilities to various causes.

Causation   Many of the traditional beliefs and attributions regarding the etiology of disabilities mirror the previously described health beliefs about varying causes of illness. The more naturalistic or metaphysical explanations often focus on the mother's presumed failure to follow prescribed dietary and other health care practices during pregnancy and/or the postpartum period. These are illustrated by various case examples of families who have sought assistance for their children with developmental special needs. One mother, a recent Chinese immigrant and parent of a child with Down syndrome, attributed her daughter's hypotonia to her failure to drink adequate amounts of beef bone soup during pregnancy. Another Chinese mother believed that her son's epilepsy was a result of her having eaten lamb (a forbidden meat) during pregnancy; in fact, one of the Chinese colloquialisms for epilepsy is synonymous with the name for a disease in lambs that results in seizures (Lim-Yee, 1995). A Vietnamese mother was concerned about having eaten shellfish during her pregnancy with her son as a possible cause of his mental retardation and hyperactivity. While escaping from Vietnam as a "boat person," another mother had fallen overboard into the sea and suffered from exposure shortly after giving birth to her son; she later attributed his multiple disabilities to the excessive "cold wind" that entered her body after his birth.

Aside from these individual attributions, it is noteworthy that some traditional beliefs regarding dietary and nutritional practices may actually contribute to increased perinatal risk. For example, some expectant mothers at risk may fail to take prescribed prenatal vitamins and supplements because they believe or have been warned that excessive iron intake will harden the fetus's bones, thus contributing to a potentially difficult labor and delivery (Lim-Yee, 1995). A related belief (particularly among the Hmong and Mien women) is that weight gain must be restricted to produce a small infant and an easy delivery (Doutrich & Metje, 1988); however, this belief also may derive from the practical consideration that in remote rural areas, where adequate obstetrical care is not available during delivery, a large baby can pose a serious threat to a pregnant woman with a small pelvis.

Mothers also may believe that they directly contributed to their children's disabilities by violating certain taboos during pregnancy. For example, one mother (who was ethnic Chinese-Vietnamese) worked throughout her pregnancy as a seamstress and thus frequently used scissors; she felt that this caused her daughter's unique congenital hand anomaly, which was characterized by fused fingers and a split thumb. This attribution is consistent with the traditional belief that women should avoid using scissors, knives, and other sharp objects during pregnancy for fear of causing a miscarriage or birth defects; ironically, although this belief is widely held among the hill tribeswomen of Cambodia and Laos, the incidence of congenital anomalies (e.g., cleft lip) among their children is exceptionally high because of inbreeding (Lee, 1989). Another mother (Chinese from Hong Kong) of a child with a cleft palate and other congenital facial anomalies assumed that these were related to her having seen horror films and pictures of evil gods during the initial stages of her pregnancy. A very tragic "case" involved a Hmong woman who believed she caused her infant son's hydrocephaly by taking medication for kidney stones during her pregnancy. Her profound distress resulted in her shooting the baby in the head, then killing both herself and her husband. She said in a suicide note that she did not want her son to grow up "deformed" and "brain-damaged" (Silver, 1996). Yet another mother (Korean) of a child with autism attributed his inconsolable crying to her having attended a funeral when she was pregnant; she also indicated that his condition was compounded by her frequent mood swings and temper outbursts during pregnancy. This latter belief reflects an expectation among many Asian cultures that the prospective mother must engage in the "prenatal education" of her growing fetus, or "womb rearing" as it is referred to by the Chinese; more specifically, the expectant mother must counsel her unborn child in physical, intellectual, and moral principles and must speak and act at all times as a proper role model—as if the child were listening, observing, and learning (Hollingsworth et al., 1980; Masterson, 1990).

Among other types of causal explanations for disability in a child is the more popular belief that it represents a divine punishment for sins or moral transgressions committed by the parents or their ancestors (Groce & Zola, 1993). For example, a Chinese father reported that his persistent gambling and involvement in an extramarital affair at the time of his wife's pregnancy caused his son to experience neonatal distress and subsequent cerebral palsy. A Cambodian father attributed his daughter's clubfoot to an incident when he and his pregnant wife were escaping as refu-gees through the jungles of Thailand; in an attempt to hunt and kill a bird with a rock, he instead only wounded its claw and leg. In yet another case, a Korean mother of a boy with autism believed her son's disability was linked to her father who drank excessively (Chan, 1986). Such attributions often contribute to a prolonged sense of guilt, self-blame, and a fatalistic orientation toward stoically accepting one's situation. Parents may consequently fail to proactively seek formal assistance and intervention for their child and/or employ religious practices to amend their personal or family member's past wrongdoing.

Spiritual attributions also are employed when demons, ghosts, or evil spirits are believed to be involved in causing disability. For example, a Korean mother of two boys with mental retardation claimed that the spirit of a dead horse that had entered her sons' bodies during her respective pregnancies caused their "sickness." She, in turn, sought the cure for their affliction by resorting to daily prayer and meditation. Another mother (Chinese) insisted that her daughter with severe developmental delays was possessed by a ghost and would regularly bring her to a monk who sang chants, gave offerings to appease the spirits, and provided the mother with a "lucky charm" made from special herbs to hang around the child's neck. In cases of children with epilepsy, family members are known to seek the help of shamans, priests, or spiritual masters to perform healing rituals and exorcisms (Chan, 1986). Expectant mothers (particularly Southeast Asians) will avoid standing and/or sitting near doorways because of beliefs in the threat of errant spirits roaming the household (Lee, 1989). The Chinese further believe that a pregnant woman should remain in the house and avoid events such as funerals and weddings. Her attendance at a funeral may invite the spirit of the deceased to enter her womb; her presence at weddings might bring bad luck to the newlyweds and the family (Char, 1981).

Nature and Meaning of a Disability   Traditional assumptions regarding the etiology of various disabilities typically are accompanied by corresponding views concerning their respective nature and meaning. Among many Asian languages, a number of different terms are used to describe characteristics associated with conditions such as mental retardation or mental illness. These terms often are highly varied, and

Nhia, a 2½-year-old Hmong girl, was the youngest of 12 children in her family. She had a cleft lip and submucous cleft palate, vision impairments, chronic respiratory problems, and profound deafness. Nhia was enrolled in a center-based program, but the early interventionist working with her conducted several initial home visits. These visits typically involved nearly the entire family because the older children often stayed home from school, and extended family members were present as well. A Hmong social worker who served as an interpreter accompanied the early interventionist on each visit.

The family's primary concern was whether Nhia would ever be able to talk. They were informed about the effects of deafness on developing speech and that Nhia's ultimate ability to speak should not be ruled out. In the meantime, the recommendation was to develop her language in school through the use of total communication (i.e., the combination of sign and speech). Nhia's parents and family were receptive to this approach when they understood that it also could facilitate Nhia's learning to read and write and her overall progress in school.

In a subsequent home visit, the early interventionist planned an activity wherein she modeled interacting with Nhia using sign language and speech to teach her common foods that she ate (the first words that her parents wanted her to learn). The interventionist also incorporated a "fun" warm-up activity in which she taught family members how to initialize their respective names by using corresponding alphabet signs. At one point during the session, as the various signs were being demonstrated, Nhia's father and some of the other adult males abruptly left the room. The social worker also indicated that she needed to leave soon for another appointment. The interventionist, although sensing the tension and apparent embarrassment among some family members, encouraged everyone to continue to follow her modeling the alphabet signs. She assumed that the novelty of using one's hands, face, and body for communication may have been creating discomfort.

When the interventionist later contacted the social worker to determine what had happened in the home visit, she was informed that the family members (and the social worker herself) were uneasy with some of the aspects of signing that involved sustained eye contact and frequent touching of the head and face, which are cultural taboos. Moreover, some of the handshapes for the various alphabet signs (particularly the sign for the letter "T," thumb placed between the curled index and middle fingers) had distinct sexual connotations and/or mimicked obscene gestures.

What follow-up strategies might the early interventionist use when next meeting with Nhia's parents/family?

How can she best address the parents' concerns while continuing to teach them and Nhia total communication strategies?

(*Source:* Maley, 1996.)

do not necessarily connote the same meaning or refer to more precise clinical descriptions and definitions characteristic of Western terminology. For instance, mental retardation may be equated with learning disabilities or emotional disturbance, which, in turn, may be narrowly defined in terms of extreme deviance involving overtly aggressive, antisocial, acting-out behavior.

Parents, however, may be highly tolerant of deviant behavior in young children and reluctant to admit their perceived inability to cope with problems by seeking professional help. A sense of parental inadequacy is particularly acute if the school-age children are exhibiting persistent learning and/or psychosocial difficulties at school. Such problems are traditionally attributed to laziness and oppositional behavior on the part of the child, as well as the presumed inability or failure of the parents to provide proper training. Given such training and sufficient parental resolve, these children may be expected to ultimately outgrow their difficulties.

Each of these traditional views pertaining to the causes and nature of various disabilities typically create family embarrassment, shame, and stigma (Uba, 1994). Even if provided with objective information about the child's disability, parents must still cope with the prospect that their affected child will be unable to fulfill expectations of academic or occupational achievement that gives the family a "good name" (Groce & Zola, 1993). Their subsequent reactions may vary considerably and are influenced by a number of unique family and child characteristics, as well as relative experience in receiving information and/or assistance from professionals (Chan, 1986).

Death and Dying

Traditional beliefs about death and dying among Chinese, Koreans, Cambodians, Laotians, and Vietnamese are interrelated with various spiritual and/or religious orientations that were detailed in previous sections. For example, the Buddhist's goal is to be released from the "wheel of life" or circle of reincarnation and reach *nirvana*; however, before attaining this goal, one must attempt to reincarnate into a better person. The individual's mind should thus be calm, hopeful, and clear at the time of death. Consequently, a dying person or their family members may refuse medication that could alter consciousness (Tien-Hyatt, 1987).

Discussions about death in the presence of someone with a terminal condition are taboo among most traditional Asian cultures. If there is a belief that a "death date" is predestined, then talking out loud about death will tempt fate. Moreover, a holistic belief in the unity of mind and body, and their reciprocal interaction implies that the body reacts poorly to "bad news" received by the mind. Candid information about fatal illnesses, diseases, health conditions, or poor prognoses of any kind should be avoided because this kind of truth telling may seem like a death sentence. Physicians and health care providers may be advised to share such information privately with family members only. The dying individual also may prefer to let family members make key medical decisions on his or her behalf because of the assumption that they know and understand what is needed and wanted. For older individuals, this practice is an expression of "filial piety" or reciprocity in which parents expect their children to care for them in their dotage (Monmaney, 1995; Steelman, 1994). Apart from frank discussions of death, the symbols of death also are shunned. Many hospitals serving large populations of Chinese, for example, have incorporated changes whereby they assign no Chinese patients to rooms with a number 4, nor do they place Chinese patients in blue and white rooms, and physicians do not write prescriptions in red ink—all of which are associated with death (Dresser, 1996).

Animism and the belief in spirits also contribute to a number of practices and observances related to death and dying. The Mien specifically believe that each human being has three spirits: one that is reborn (or reincarnated through another person), a second that stays with the family, and a third that becomes a ghost or "bad" spirit. Like the Hmong, the Mien believe that the dying are passing on to another life and will need their body whole to survive. Therefore, they will rarely agree to a biopsy, autopsy, or removal of any organ such as the brain, lungs, heart, or tongue. Otherwise, the next generation could be born with these parts missing. They also commonly believe that it is better to die at home because the spirit of a family member who dies in a hospital is thought to be lost without a home (Steelman, 1994).

Some Chinese recognize errant or bad spirits to be "hungry ghosts" who had no descendants, did not have a proper burial, died a bad death, or were neglected after death. They are dangerous because they can repossess the spirits of children and adults and cause illness or misfortune; they also are known for crashing weddings and other happy celebrations. The Hungry Ghost Festival or "Fourteenth Day of the Seventh Moon" is thus a celebration in which the gates of the underworld are opened and the hungry ghosts are allowed to wander about looking for sustenance. Feasts are then prepared for them so they can be properly fed, cared for, appeased, and then sent back to purgatory or hell (Tom, 1989; Watson, 1988).

Closely linked to animism is ancestor worship, which is also based on a belief in the interdependence and interaction between the living and the dead. It requires efforts (including a variety of traditional rituals) to maintain a positive and close relationship with one's departed ancestors. Among many Chinese and Vietnamese, the practice of ancestor worship presumes that there is a literal connection between the grave and the soul. If the dead are buried and properly honored, they become benevolent and bring good fortune. Tom (1989) provided a highly detailed account of various Chinese funeral customs. For traditional burials, white clothing is worn as a sign of mourning. The mourners also may wear five different kinds of clothing to identify their relationship to the deceased and thereby define the appropriate severity of mourning. Visitors who come to pay their last respects present gifts of incense, paper offerings, cut flowers, or money enclosed in a white envelope. On entering the funeral hall, each visitor receives a piece of candy and *li-see* (a red paper packet containing a 5-cent coin). The candy is eaten to "sweeten" the sorrow and to counteract the bitterness of death. The li-see symbolizes "good luck and happiness," and the coin is to be spent as soon as possible to buy something sweet. For some ethnic groups, the older the deceased, the longer and more elaborate the funeral ceremony will be (Lassiter, 1995; Tom, 1989).

Commemoration rituals follow funerals and burials; cleaning the grave or tomb; and caring for the souls of departed ancestors by offering up food, incense, and burying paper money and other simulated possessions. The 1-year anniversary typically is celebrated with a huge gathering and feast. In some cases, the body (initially buried in a coffin) is exhumed after 7 years, cremated, and the remains placed in an urn that is reburied in a tomb. Chinese and Vietnamese who practice Buddhism, as well as Cambodians and Laotians, prefer cremation instead of burial and keep the ashes in beautiful urns placed in ancestral altars. All of these practices serve to bridge the land of the living with the nether world of the dead (Geissler, 1994; Watson, 1988).

ISSUES OF LANGUAGE

Culture is communication and vice versa. Effective intercultural interactions are primarily a function of the success of the communication process between culturally different people. Cultural competence is defined as the ability to establish interpersonal relationships with people from a different culture by developing understanding through effective exchange of both verbal and nonverbal levels of behavior (Hall, 1976). Throughout this process, it becomes increasingly apparent that "the message perceived is not always the message intended" (Te, 1989a).

Intercultural communication difficulties are not simply a matter of different languages but of different thought patterns, values, and communication styles. The previously detailed "language/linguistic origins" of Chinese, Korean, Cambodian, Lao, and Vietnamese revealed considerable diversity among these respective languages and contrasted with the English language. Moreover, the psycholinguistic characteristics of these languages (how they influence thought) and the corresponding verbal/nonverbal communication patterns serve to reinforce the previously described traditional cultural values. Consistent with a primary orientation toward situation centeredness, each of these Asian languages is very context bound. In fact, Asian cultures are among the highest-context cultures in the world; that is, within these cultures, most of the meaningful information is either in the physical context or internalized in the person who receives the information, whereas relatively little is contained in the verbally transmitted part of the message (Hall, 1976). The speaker or the sender's true intent often is camouflaged in the context of the situation. The receiver must have knowledge of shaded meanings, nonverbal cues, and subtle affect in order to correctly interpret the speaker's intent without specific reference to what he or she means. This style contrasts dramatically with the low-context Eurocentric cultures in which information is conveyed primarily though the verbal code and communication is more precise, explicit, and straightforward.

The languages of high-context Asian cultures also reflect a collectivist orientation, which places the highest value on human relationships and the preservation of harmony and face. This value takes precedence over pure task efficiency and getting to the "business" end of goal attainment; the more important aim is to achieve mutually satisfactory and face-saving outcomes. The principal goal of communication is to promote unity and harmony. This is facilitated, in part, by characteristic communication patterns and styles that employ formality and honorific language systems; special terms of address and polite behaviors convey respect for authority, status, and position. More specifically, personal characteristics such as age, sex, education, occupation, social status, family background, and marital or parental status may each serve to dictate what is communicated between individuals and in what manner. Respective individual attributes and the nature of a given relationship may traditionally determine language style and/or structure and behaviors, such as who will bow the lowest, initiate communication, change subjects, speak more loudly or softly (or not at all), look away when eyes meet, and be most accommodating (Chan, 1995). Individuals from low-context cultures may perceive such formalism as excessive and unnecessary; however, observing the rules of propriety is considered an essential aspect of harmonious social interaction.

Preservation of group harmony also is enhanced by indirect communication styles that are significantly more intuitive and contemplative than low-context, direct, open communication styles. In the interest of preserving face, Asian people exhibit a characteristic reluctance to contradict, criticize, disappoint, or otherwise cause unease or discomfort in another. An indirect style of responding is adopted whereby the use of the word "yes" and ostensibly affirmative head nodding can actually mean "no"; that is, the listener may tell the speaker what he or she thinks the speaker wants to hear, rather than giving an absolutely truthful answer that might be offensive. The listener also may be noncommittal or hesitant in response to a direct question when reluctant to do something that is not fully understood or is disagreeable, and/or when saying "no" is to be avoided. Unfortunately, such behavior is frequently misinterpreted or evaluated by low-context cultures as evasive, devious, and dishonest. Individuals who are socialized to be sensitive to subtle culture-specific cues and nuances thus take pride in their ability to "know" intuitively (without benefit of words) what others are thinking and feeling (Crystal, 1989). Koreans refer to this ability as *nun-chi* (reading the eyes)—an affective sense by which one can quickly and accurately pick up external cues to assess another's genuine attitudes and emotional reactions to a given topic, proposal, or situation that arises in an ongoing dialogue. This process enables the parties engaged in conversation to understand what is going on without being told, to detect whether others are really pleased or satisfied, and to choose a course of action that is both nonoffensive and appropriate (Gudykunst & Ting-Toomey, 1988; Kim, 1996; Yum, 1987). Early on, children are taught to observe nonverbal cues that guide behaviors in social interactions; moreover, they are scolded (e.g., "Have you no eyes!") and feel ashamed if they lack ability to meet someone's needs that were not articulated.

Nonverbal communication thus conveys significantly more information in high-context Asian cultures, wherein silence is particularly valued. Again, the significant contrast between communication styles (Asian versus European American) is illustrated by the perception of a recent Southeast Asian refugee: "In America, you value freedom of speech; in Vietnam, we value freedom of silence" (Chu, 1990, p. 2). Others have noted that in most cultures throughout the world, individuals start talking when they have to; Asians, instead, tend to stop talking when they have to. The relative importance of silence among Asian cultures is further evidenced by proverbs such as the following: "Keep your mouth shut, your eyes open," and "He who knows, talks not; he who talks, knows not." Native-born Chinese perceived being silent as opposed to being verbal as a primary control strategy in conversation, for example (Wiemann, Chen, & Giles, 1986). On the one hand, maintaining silence in a conversation may serve as an expression of interest and respect. On the other hand, if silence follows consistent verbal responses and affective acknowledgment on the part of a listener, it may indicate disagreement or negative reactions, such as anger (e.g., the "silent treatment"). In fact, a typical practice among many Asian people is the refusal to speak any further in conversation if they cannot personally accept the speaker's attitude, opinion, or way of thinking about particular issues or subjects. A related aspect of silence is the state of mind referred to by the Chinese as *wu-wei*. It describes one who is alert but not tense, deliberately nonactive without being passive, relaxed but concentrated. In this state, one continues to "express" thoughts without words. Thus, as suggested in the proverb, "Think three times before you act," doing or saying nothing at the right time can be an appropriate action.

Eye contact and facial expressions serve as additional examples of contrasting styles. Direct and/or sustained eye-to-eye contact with relative strangers may be interpreted as a sign of hostility or considered impolite and even shameful (between male and female, it may have sexual connotations). Similarly, direct eye contact with an elder or person in authority or a family member of higher status is considered disrespectful. Affective expressions also have differing connotations. In general, the value placed on control of emotional expression contributes to a demeanor among selected Asian groups that is often interpreted by Eurocentric individuals as "flat," "stoic," "enigmatic," or even "inscrutable." Koreans, for example, in keeping with the national character of the "Land of the Morning Calm," may present with a demeanor referred to as *myu-po-jung* (lack of facial expression). Casual smiling and direct eye contact when greeting or interacting with strangers is considered inappropriate. Furthermore, although friends and family may be greeted by a smile, the greeting may not be verbalized. Koreans as well as many Southeast Asian groups also may smile when embarrassed. Smiling, rather than verbal comments (e.g., "I'm sorry"), serves as an expression of apology for minor offenses. Smiling also can be an expression of deference to an authority figure who scolds a child or criticizes an adult; it indicates acceptance of guilt, sincere acknowledgment of fault or the mistake committed, and that one is neither offended nor harbors any ill feeling or resentment toward the interlocutor (as opposed to an expression of disrespect or nonverbal challenge to authority). Such smiling may even occur when falsely accused of wrongdoing or when submitting to an unjust situation. Smiling (or blushing) is also considered a proper nonverbal response to a compliment. The person who delivers the compliment should not expect a "thank you" in return. A verbal response of gratitude on the part of the recipient would suggest a lack of modesty. The recipient may deny the compliment if a verbal response seems to be expected, saying that he or she does not deserve it (Te, 1989a). Smiling can signal acceptance of a desirable offer, invitation, or proposal, rather than responding with an eager "yes," which might appear overenthusiastic and less humble. Smiling may further be used to mask difficult feelings and emotions (e.g., pain, distress, discomfort, anger, disapproval, disappointment) or to avoid conflict when insulted, threatened, or otherwise provoked. These multiple, context-bound meanings and interpretations obviously suggest that "not all people smile in the same language" (Te, 1989a, p. 54).

Various gestures and body language also have differing meanings. The American gesture for waving "good-bye" (particularly to a child) actually approximates the gesture for "come here" used by Southeast Asians (i.e., slowly waving all fingers, closed and in unison with palm down, facing inward). Furthermore, the American gesture for "come here" (using the pointing finger with hand raised and palm inward) is a hostile, aggressive gesture among Southeast Asians or is the manner in which one beckons dogs, lower animals, or an "inferior" person. Similarly, the crossing of the index and middle fingers as a gesture for "good luck," the "V" sign to indicate "peace", the "OK" sign (with curled thumb and forefinger), or the thumbs up sign all potentially constitute obscene gestures with sexual connotations for Southeast Asians, as well as many other ethnic/national groups (Axtell, 1991).

With regard to acceptable interpersonal space, Asians typically prefer to maintain greater distance from those they are talking to than the average American comfort zone of 12 inches to an arm's length. Physical touching or body contact between men and women also is avoided in public; however, public handholding between same-sex members (both men and women) is commonly practiced and considered socially acceptable among many Asian cultures. In general, these significant contrasts in nonverbal behaviors and patterns of communication serve to illustrate how understanding specific cultural values and contexts is critical in facilitating successful intercultural interactions. Because communication is a vital tool in assessment and treatment, interventionists need to have a keen sense of awareness of their communication styles and how to manage the intercultural differences in communicating with traditional Asian clients.

SUMMARY

The dramatically accelerated growth of the AAPI population is largely attributable to the continuing waves of Asian immigrants and refugees since the 1960s. In contrast to the earliest Asian immigrants who were primarily farmers and laborers, the relative newcomers (since passage of the Immigration and Nationality Act Amendments of 1965, PL 89-236) include significant numbers of Chinese and Korean professionals and people considered to be the most highly educated and skilled of any immigrant group in U.S. history. The withdrawal of the United States from Vietnam in 1975 further led to the mass exodus of hundreds of thousands of Southeast Asian refugees seeking sanctuary in America. Over time, this population has become increasingly diverse, including preliterate rural tribespeople as well as college-educated urban professionals.

Such diversity among the more recent Asian immigrants and refugees has contributed to the formation of bipolar, ethnic communities that are divided between the two extremes of unskilled, working, or "welfare" classes (with the highest rates of poverty) and successful, professional, entrepreneurial upper middle classes. Apart from highly varied educational and socioeconomic backgrounds, the heterogeneity of AAPI ethnic groups is further reflected in their diverse cultural/linguistic characteristics and the unique historical, sociopolitical, and economic conditions of their respective countries of origin. Despite such diversity as well as rapid growth and increasing visibility, however, the new Asian immigrants and refugees have been persistently confronted with stereotypic, undifferentiated, and often hostile perceptions.

These perceptions serve to disguise the reality of distinct lifestyles, customs, traditions, social norms, values, and folk beliefs with ancient religious and philosophical origins. In particular, the Chinese, Korean, and Vietnamese cultures are rooted in some of the world's oldest civilizations (more than 4,000 years old) and have been principally influenced by the doctrines and philosophies of Confucianism, Taoism, and Buddhism—the "three teachings." Together with ancestor worship, shamanism (including animism and spirit worship), and Christianity, the "three teachings" have evolved into a complementary system of blended beliefs. The practice of syncretism or polytheism has enabled Asians to integrate complex mixes of corresponding thoughts and faiths that provide both practical and spiritual guidance. These beliefs have further shaped the traditional collectivist values that are common to the various Asian cultures and have been preserved with pride and dedication throughout the centuries.

The predominant Asian values pertaining to family, harmony, education, and selected virtues offer fundamental guidelines for living. The family, for example, is the basic unit of society and the central focus of the individual's life. Harmony is the keynote of existence. Successful academic achievement is the greatest tribute one can bestow on one's parents and family. Virtues such as patience, perseverance, self-sacrifice, maintenance of inner strength, self-restraint, modesty, and humility are each considered necessary expressions of dignity that promote group welfare.

These values have contributed to the profound strength and resiliency demonstrated by Asian people throughout their respective histories of severe hardship, war, disruption, and loss. They have been maintained for many generations and continue to influence the contemporary socialization experiences of Asian American children. Despite their enduring and historically adaptive nature, however, these collectivist values contrast sharply with the more Eurocentric individualistic values and have been transformed in the process of acculturation. Therefore, the relative influence of traditional values among Asian immigrant/refugee families must be considered in the context of complex economic, psychological, and social adjustment patterns and factors such as class and regional differences in countries of origin, premigration/migration experiences, time of arrival, proximity to same-ethnic communities, age, gender, education, language proficiency, and socioeconomic status.

Although traditional values indeed have been transformed, the extent to which they have historically influenced child-rearing beliefs and practices among Asian cultures is readily apparent. As the most basic social institution, the family is characterized by well-defined, highly interdependent roles within a cohesive patriarchal vertical structure—one that derives from the Confucian doctrine of filial piety. The respective marital and parental roles and/or responsibilities typically entail significant personal sacrifice and accountability in return for the right to assume strict authority over and unquestioning obedience and loyalty from the child. Children, in turn, are viewed as extensions of their parents. They are treasured, protected, and readily indulged within a very nurturing, secure, and predictable social environment (involving both immediate and extended family members) throughout infancy and the toddler period. As they approach and enter school age, children experience accelerated movement toward independence training and direct participation in the adult world. Therefore, the child assumes increasingly greater responsibilities as an older sibling and learns to view his or her role in the family and society in terms of specific relationships, obligations, and codes of conduct. In general, more traditional child-rearing beliefs and practices promote family interdependence and deference to the needs of the group. They also support personal control, self-improvement, and the development of individual independence outside the family—all of which are conducive to successful achievement in the larger society, thereby enhancing the family welfare and fulfilling filial obligations.

Traditional child-rearing beliefs and practices are complemented by various health beliefs and health care practices that have endured for many centuries. Among Chinese and Korean immigrants and Southeast Asian refugees, the more common traditional health orientations include a blending of traditional Chinese medicine and folk medicine practices. Related fundamental concepts include maintaining balance between the cosmic forces of yin and yang, the "five elements," and internal body organs. Lack of clear differentiation between mental illness (or psychological problems) and physical illness is yet another aspect of the holistic philosophy of Chinese medicine. In addition to natural or metaphysical explanations of health and/or illness, supernatural beliefs and spiritual healing practices also are prevalent, particularly among the Southeast Asian refugee populations. The contrasts between traditional Asian health care practices and those of Western medicine include significantly less invasive diagnostic and treatment procedures; use of herbal medication versus prescription medications; and the use of therapeutic massage, acupressure, acupuncture, moxibustion, and dermabrasion. The importance of understanding these traditional health care practices is underscored by the fact that many

Asian families utilize a "pluralistic" system of care that blends folk medicine with Western medicine. Thus, the relative compatibility of various health orientations often becomes a central issue in the care of infants and children with disabilities and developmental special needs. Furthermore, many of the traditional beliefs and attributions regarding the etiology of various disabilities directly reflect traditional health beliefs about the varying causes of illness.

A final area of focus encompasses issues regarding language characteristics and communication styles among the various Asian ethnic groups. The previously detailed "language/linguistic origins" of Chinese, Korean, Cambodian, Laotian, and Vietnamese revealed considerable diversity among these respective languages as well as contrast with the English language. Moreover, corresponding psycholinguistic characteristics and verbal/nonverbal communication patterns serve to reinforce traditional cultural orientations and values. Asian languages, for example, are situation centered or context bound; thus, they often are dependent on the receiver's ability to correctly interpret the speaker's intent without specific reference to what he or she means. Consistent with the primary value of preserving harmony and face in human relationships, Asian languages employ relatively formal rules of propriety and communication patterns that promote harmonious social interaction. These include indirect communication styles; reluctance to criticize or contradict overtly; and ability to "read" others' genuine attitudes, opinions, or feelings through nonverbal cues. A significant amount of information is thus conveyed through nonverbal forms of communication, including silence (and the timing of verbal exchanges), facial expressions (e.g., smiling), eye contact, body movements and gestures, posture and positioning, and interpersonal space. Relative to more Eurocentric cultures, the subtle and often distinctly different (if not entirely opposite) meaning of such nonverbal communication may create significant communication barriers and conflicts—well beyond basic language differences. Thus, the primary challenge in achieving the goal of successful intercultural communication is to address the fact that the message perceived is not always the message intended.

RECOMMENDATIONS FOR INTERVENTIONISTS

The effectiveness of programs and providers serving multicultural populations "rests heavily upon the sensitivity, understanding, and respect paid to the specific cultural, [linguistic], familial, and individual diversity involved" (Anderson & Schrag-Fenichel, 1989, p. 18). Therefore, early interventionists must develop cultural competence. This process requires several tasks, which include 1) clarification and awareness of one's own values, assumptions, and biases; 2) gathering and analyzing ethnographic information regarding the cultural community within which each family resides; 3) determining the degree to which the family operates transculturally; and 4) examining each family's orientation to specific child-rearing issues (Hanson, Lynch, & Wayman, 1990). Understanding recent immigrant/refugee families further entails acquisition of culture-specific knowledge of traditional values, beliefs, and practices pertaining to family, religion, child rearing, education, health, mental health, and disability, as well as language characteristics and communication styles (Lowenthal, 1996). These topics have been addressed throughout this chapter in relation to selected Asian American ethnic groups. Ethnic or cultural competence, however, also requires learning and refining skills necessary to engage in successful intercultural interactions and corresponding behavioral (as well as attitudinal) changes on the part of individual service providers. Culturally competent programs for young children and their families must similarly incorporate administrative strategies, policies, program designs, and services that are increasingly responsive to culturally diverse client populations (Hanson & Lynch, 1992; Roberts, 1990; Shu-Minutoli, 1995; Taylor, 1995). In 2000, cultural competence standards for four racial/ethnic groups were published (Center for Mental Health Services, 2000). The following recommendations, therefore, address practical considerations in responding to various cultural orientations and behaviors related to service utilization by Asian American families.

OUTREACH

Critical to the process of providing services to selected Asian American families and clients is a recognition of the "trust" factor and the degree to which traditional family-centered and ethnic community orientations contribute toward a tendency to view "outsiders" with a degree of suspicion (Sue, 1981). "Helping" professionals and various human services agencies must be aware of the proper entry points to Asian communities. More specifically, certain formal and informal communication networks and established social relationships within various Asian communities play a major role in determining how a family in need will initially view an available public service. Trust typically begins when contact with a particular agency or helping professional has been initiated or affirmed by friends, relatives, or respected authorities (Leung, 1988). In some Asian communities (e.g., the Hmong), identified community leaders are usually consulted in relation to health or other matters involving external resources; their counsel, approval, and recommendations are often sought first (Keiter, 1990).

Thus, third parties or indigenous intermediaries who have credibility within the family or the ethnic community may assume a major role in providing initial support, reassurance, and needed information about available services and their value, thereby facilitating the family's successful entry into a system. Providers and agencies need to identify such community gatekeepers, acknowledge their potential liaison role, and establish working relationships with them. The information source through which a family learns about a particular service, the nature of corresponding word-of-mouth communications, and initial encounters or first experiences all profoundly contribute to the agency's reputation within the community and its ultimate acceptability (Chan, 1985).

WORKING WITH INTERPRETERS

To the extent that the previously described intermediaries are bilingual, they may be relied on as interpreters (and/or translators) for non–English-speaking, limited–English-speaking, or English-language-learning families during initial contacts as well as during subsequent client/family interactions. In many instances, families may prefer or assume that English-speaking family members, relatives, friends, advocates, indigenous community representatives, or bilingual staff from other agencies will accompany them on the first visit and continue to be available to serve as interpreters; issues of trust, moral support, dependency, personal relationships, and a collectivist or group orientation may reinforce this preference. Lack of available and appropriate bilingual/bicultural personnel or access to "outside" interpreters also may be a practical agency constraint that further necessitates this arrangement.

Whether utilizing intermediaries as interpreters or selecting others, a number of important considerations warrant attention (see Chapter 3), particularly given the variety of problems associated with using both skilled and unskilled interpreters (Lee, 1997; Uba, 1994). Comprehensive guidelines for selecting, preparing, and training interpreters (particularly for parent meetings and developmental and psychoeducational assessments) have been developed (Chan & Valverde, 1996; Langdon, Siegel, Cima, & Sanchez-Boyce, 1994) and further specified in relation to selected Asian groups (e.g., Dien et al. [1986] for Vietnamese-speaking children and/or families; Tinloy et al. [1986] for Chinese-speaking children and/or families). A training manual and curriculum on mental health training for interpreters of Southeast Asian languages offers excellent guidelines in the training of intepreters (Lochnicht, 1995).

INITIAL EXPECTATIONS/ORIENTATIONS

Once contact has been established with agencies and/or providers, more traditionally oriented Asian American families will likely expect an initial formality characterized by well-defined roles and clear communication regarding what is being requested of them and what specific services can be offered. Professionals are viewed as authority figures who are directive; employ structured, practical problem-solving approaches; and provide specific advice, "answers," and recommendations (Behring & Gelinas, 1996; Kim, 1985). Providers who are relatively non-directive, maintain a neutral or nonjudgmental demeanor, and fail to promptly offer practical assistance may be perceived as disinterested, uncaring, or even incompetent (Uba, 1994). The professional is presumed to have expertise and the ability to offer assistance that uniquely supplements family resources and can address more immediate areas of need. The establishment of credibility and the provision (or "giving") of services that yield direct benefits from the outset are thus likely to facilitate client follow-through and maintenance of the professional–client relationship (Sue & Zane, 1987). These considerations are especially significant for those recent immigrant/refugee families who may have very high expectations of "American" services and who have been referred for formal assistance after having exclusively drawn on, and possibly exhausted, family resources and coping strategies in response to the child's needs.

Throughout the initial process of developing client/family relationships, providers also should be cognizant of traditional parental orientations toward schools and professionals entrusted with the education and related care of children with special needs. Filial piety defines a social hierarchy of allegiance that proceeds downward from "king" to "teacher" to "father." Parents are expected to respect and honor teachers and professional specialists by assuming a corresponding "dependent" orientation of deference, noninterference, and delegation of authority and responsibility (Chan, 1986; Cheng, 1987; Uba, 1994). Therefore, many Asian families (particularly recent immigrants) are often unfamiliar with and confused by legislative mandates and policies that emphasize parental rights, responsibilities, and entitlements. They also may initially be uncomfortable with agency/provider philosophies and "recommended practices" that require collaborative, family-focused identification of needs and subsequent interventions. In fact, these concepts and expectations may be both alien and threatening, particularly if formal requests for parent participation are interpreted as indications that the child's difficulties have exceeded the professionals' teaching or intervention capabilities, and the parents are presumably being held accountable.

FACE SAVING AND THE COUNSELING PROCESS

Whether parents are requested to meet with professionals or have initiated efforts to obtain assistance, their ultimate public disclosure of child- or family-related difficulties is often extremely difficult. Such disclosure could be considered a betrayal of family loyalty or trust, an act of weakness, and/or a form of disgracing the family's honor and reputation. This belief is reinforced by a more general reticence to burden others with problems that the parent or family should presumably be able to resolve. Moreover, sharing personal problems and concerns with an authority figure (even though such an individual is an identified helping professional) may be construed as an act of disrespect. This perception particularly affects counseling transactions with mental health professionals whose roles and expectations are conceptually foreign to many traditionally oriented Asian American families (Chan, 1986; Ho, 1987; Locke, 1992; Uba, 1994).

The concept of face saving (e.g., *chae-myun* among Koreans) is very important in nearly all relationships. Maintaining face protects the dignity, honor, and self-respect of the individual and the family. One must anticipate that a family member or key informant will be reluctant to initially reveal "vital" information if this will cause loss of face (Kim, 1996). The helping professional is cautioned against venturing into a frank discussion of specific problem areas too quickly. Although the family may expect initial formality, the professional is encouraged to spend time establishing personal rapport and to allow for discussion of information that may be tangential or even unrelated to the referring problems or perceived needs. Asian parents typically place great value on professional sensitivity to the family's face-saving needs and positive regard for indirect approaches to typically stigmatic difficulties. Consequently, problems often need to be reframed and approached in a circular fashion while establishing mutual trust, respect, and movement toward a more personalized relationship. This may be manifested in the professional's attention to small but important details that show continued interest and concern for the family's comfort, general health, and well-being. In fact, this expression of empathy, sympathy, and compassion (referred to as *jeong* by Koreans) enables the professional to "humanize" his or her relationship with the family and to gain their confidence (Kim, 1996). The importance of this dynamic is further illustrated by a Vietnamese phrase, "A good doctor is a good mother." Similarly, the literal translation of "psychologist" in Chinese and Vietnamese is "expert of the inner heart" (Chao, 1992).

Providers also may need to demonstrate flexibility and accommodation by being willing to meet at variable times in more informal, culturally familiar surroundings. They may further be expected to provide direct assistance, accompany families in contacts with other agencies and/or professionals, and assume multiple provider roles (including serving as a proactive child and family advocate) (Chan, 1986; Lee, 1996a). Unfortunately, agency fiscal constraints and/or the professional's designated roles and responsibilities may prohibit or limit such involvement. Nonetheless, the professional can still communicate genuine regard for the family's welfare effectively and cultivate personalized relationships while observing agency guidelines and/or policies and recognizing reasonable boundaries in satisfying the family's dependency needs. The counseling process thus can be conceptualized within a "cultural-developmental" framework involving various phases and appropriate timing of selected interventions (Serafica, 1990).

COMMUNICATION STYLES AND ASSERTIVENESS

Mainstream providers and agencies are often frustrated by the subtleties and slower paced processes that typically accompany successful relationship building with many Asian immigrant/refugee families. More ethnocentric providers may interpret culturally appropriate behavior patterns as indicative of inhibition, passivity, submissiveness, excessive dependency, deceptiveness, or resistance. Such value judgments can then accelerate efforts to pressure the parents or the family members into greater self-disclosure, independent decision making, and definitive action. The resulting provide–family conflicts and alienation often strengthen provider preferences for clients who are ostensibly more sophisticated and cooperative and who demonstrate initiative.

Service providers may thus directly contribute to deteriorating relationships by failing to acknowledge certain behavior patterns as manifestations of deference to authority. When interacting with professionals, Asian American family members may convey respect for authority by engaging in prescribed behaviors such as repeated head nodding, avoiding direct eye contact and affective expression, refraining from asking questions or interrupting for clarification or making their needs and/or desires explicit, and withholding critical comments (Uba, 1994). Conveying respect and adhering to traditional virtues such as patience, reserve, and "holding back" can result in a persistent reluctance to seek explanations of services and policies or to clarify specific verbal communications and agency/provider explanations. Moreover, limited–English-proficient or non–English-speaking Asian American family members who are unfamiliar with the system are most likely to demonstrate such reticence although they remain in great need of relevant information. This tendency is particularly apparent in the area of self-advocacy and Asian American parents' orientation toward pursuing their legal rights and service entitlements for their children with special needs. In contrast to the belief that "the squeaky wheel gets the grease," Asians may be more inclined to abide by proverbs such as "the nail that raises its head is hammered down," or "the taller the tree, the more wind it attracts" (i.e., too much attention invites trouble).

Traditional Asian American parents may postpone indicating their choice of alternatives or following through on multiple recommendations that are presented to them. The perceived ambiguity of the professional–family relationship exacerbates parental anxiety and fear of committing a social error in behavior or speech that will invoke a "loss of face." When given options, parents may tend to select those that they presume the professional values the most. To save face, parents will conservatively avoid "second guessing" the professional and selecting what may be the "wrong" choice or course of action. As mentioned previously, a value is traditionally placed on private preparation before public action. The professional therefore must be patient and allow for sufficient time and input to facilitate family decision making. Throughout this process, he or she must recognize the family as the primary social unit, observe protocols, and respect the traditional hierarchical roles of immediate or extended family members in collectively providing input, making decisions, and addressing their own needs.

RECIPROCITY

Successful professional–family relationships are often characterized by the traditional Asian American parent's ensuing sense of moral obligation and reciprocity. As particularly embodied in the Korean concept of *unhae*, such reciprocity applies to "favors" that are graciously given and willingly returned. A twofold obligation thus arises from interchanges in which those in "superior" positions grant assistance to those who require and depend on their services; the recipients, in turn, owe a debt of gratitude that can be repaid when a fitting occasion arises.

In the absence of opportunities to respond reciprocally to the professional's own needs for assistance or to provide direct monetary repayment, family members may display their gratitude through personalized gift giving, invitations to dinner or family celebrations (e.g., weddings, graduations), and other expressions of appreciation. Such reciprocity is the basis of a relationship or bond of friendship that persists well after the initial "debt" has been paid. Thus, a professional's refusal to accept a family's offer of gifts, favors, or invitations to participate in more personal social interactions may be construed as rejection and failure to give face (Behring & Gelinas, 1996). Considerable tact, forethought, and sensitivity must be employed in such situations.

ALTERNATIVE SERVICE DELIVERY AND TRAINING MODELS

The previously detailed cultural orientations and behavior may have a significant impact on service utilization by many Asian American families. Among the most frequently cited service utilization barriers in the literature are difficulty communicating with professionals, lack of practical information about needed services, and insufficient awareness and/or understanding of how to gain access to the "system" (Chan, 1978; Rogow, 1985; Smith & Ryan, 1987; Sue, 1993; Uba, 1994; Yao, 1988). Such barriers are often experienced by a great many parents and/or families of children with disabilities, irrespective of ethnic background; however, they are exacerbated by the cultural/linguistic characteristics of recent immigrants and refugee families. According to *Mental Health: A Report of the Surgeon General* (U.S. Surgeon General, 1999), AAPI groups are less likely than whites and members of other ethnic groups to seek mental health services. When they receive services, linguistically and culturally competent services are not usually available.

Throughout continuing efforts to promote greater client/family access to needed services within selected Asian American communities, a number of alternative service delivery models have been developed (Lee, 2002). While delivering culturally and linguistically appropriate services, many related programs have linked Asian American families to more comprehensive service networks. Such programs have promoted interagency service coordination, resource sharing, effective utilization of indigenous community-based providers, and a "critical mass" of bilingual/bicultural multidisciplinary professionals and staff who can serve many of the major Asian ethnic groups in a given community. Most of these programs have been located in urban areas with high concentrations of various Asian American populations (e.g., Chan, 1992; Cleveland, 1987). A document addresses how to build systems of care for children and youth, and many recommendations are applicable to AAPI communities (Pries, 2002). Each of these alternative service delivery models and approaches are integrally related to issues of training. As Asian American communities continue to undergo accelerated growth, the number of available bilingual/bicultural providers to serve their respective needs has become increasingly inadequate. Given critically deficient resources and the acute shortages of personnel, education and training programs for non– or English-language-learning parents, in partnership with professionals, have been an essential means of promoting access to needed services as well as increased parental involvement and advocacy in the formulation of policies and development of programs for children with disabilities (Sileo, Sileo, & Prater, 1996). A series of model parent education and training projects serving Chinese, Korean, and Vietnamese populations has been successfully developed and implemented (Chan, 1990). The projects have incorporated education of trainers and parent–professional collaboration strategies designed to enhance the impact of relatively short-term "demonstration" projects. The hallmark of the projects' success has been the subsequent organization of formal parent groups among the various Asian American parent participants.

Selected parent trainers have assumed instrumental leadership roles in guiding the establishment and incorporation of parent organizations serving Chinese, Korean, and Vietnamese families with children with disabilities. These organizations are engaged in pioneering efforts to provide mutual support, education/training, and advocacy for their respective members and communities (Chan, 1990, p. 86).

Parent leaders also have emerged as representatives who serve on various local, statewide, and national advisory and policymaking bodies charged with prioritizing needs and developing corresponding plans, programs, and services.

Related efforts to augment resources for Asian American and other culturally diverse populations include systematic student recruitment and preservice training initiatives (e.g., Keiter, 1990) and comprehensive education and training programs designed to promote cultural competence among advocates, early interventionists, and providers of services for young children with disabilities (Chen, Brekken, & Chan, 1997). The commitment of resources to effective service delivery and training models thus entails sustained collective endeavor on multiple fronts. Throughout this complex and challenging process, everyone who serves Asian American families is called on to demonstrate flexibility, versatility, and sensitivity in responding to their diverse nationalities, immigrant histories, cultural orientations, language characteristics, life experiences, and unique personal circumstances.

WHAT WOULD YOU DO?

Ming, a 5-year-old Chinese boy, was diagnosed with autism. His parents were originally referred to the Asian Family Services Center (AFSC) for parent education/support and speech and language therapy. As recent immigrants from China, Ming's parents were very receptive to receiving services from AFSC (an agency with a well-established reputation for effectively serving local Chinese-speaking families with children who have developmental special needs). Ming's mother, who worked as a teacher's aide in a local public school in Chinatown, had also independently obtained additional speech and language services for her son. This included private speech therapy for which she was paying $110 per session.

As had been the case with many other immigrant Chinese families with children with developmental disabilities, Ming's parents focused primarily on his speech and language delays and articulation difficulties. Although well informed of the various diagnostic characteristics of autism and their associated conditions, the parents were most concerned about Ming's ability to acquire more age-appropriate, functional speech. In fact, to further supplement the services they were receiving from AFSC and the private speech therapy, Ming's father returned to China with his son; there Ming received an 8-week series of acupuncture treatments from a specialist who was known by reputation for his expertise in treating children with speech disorders. As part of the procedure, Ming's head was shaved and various meridian points had been drawn on his scalp to assist his parents in subsequently administering the daily treatments themselves. For a follow-up treatment, Ming and his mother recently made another trip to China to revisit the acupuncturist for a 2-week period. On this occasion, Ming received acupuncture treatments with electrical stimulation. His mother purchased the relatively expensive electrical device required to generate the current in order to continue providing these advanced treatments at home; however, she has not been able to use it for lack of a special adapter that was needed to run the machine from an AC electrical outlet.

Ming's parents obviously have gone to great lengths to address his speech and language delays. They are highly invested in fulfilling their parental "obligations" and doing everything possible to treat his autistic disorder by way of multiple and costly speech intervention strategies. The AFSC developmental specialist who has been working with the family is concerned about their limited financial resources and the extent to which they seem to be focusing exclusively on Ming's speech problems. The acupuncture treatments have not yielded any dramatic improvements in Ming's speech/language functioning. Moreover, his multiple problem behaviors and social skill impairments characteristic of autism are becoming increasingly stigmatic as he grows older. (*Source:* N. Lim-Yee, personal communication, 2003.)

What are the key considerations that must be addressed in guiding Ming's parents at this point in time?

What are your views regarding the use of such alternative (and often expensive) treatments in the quest for a "cure" and/or remediation of this increasingly prevalent disorder?

REFERENCES

Anderson, P.P., & Schrag-Fenichel, R. (1989). *Serving culturally diverse families of infants and toddlers with disabilities.* Washington, DC: National Center for Clinical Infant Programs.

Aponte, J.F., & Crouch, R.T. (1995). The changing ethnic profile of the United States. In J.F. Aponte, R.Y. Rivers, & J. Wohl (Eds.), *Psychological interventions and cultural diversity* (pp. 1–18). Boston: Allyn & Bacon.

Arax, M. (1996, November 10). Hmong seek better life in exodus from state. *Los Angeles Times*, pp. A1, A29.

Attorney General's Asian and Pacific Islander Advisory Committee. (1988). *Final report.* Sacramento, CA: Office of the Attorney General.

Axtell, R.E. (1991). *Gestures: The do's and taboos of body language around the world.* New York: John Wiley & Sons.

Behring, S.T., & Gelinas, R.T. (1996). School consultation with Asian American children and families. *California School Psychologist, 1,* 13–20.

Bliatout, B.T. (1981). *Hmong sudden unexpected nocturnal death syndrome: A cultural study.* Portland, OR: Sparkle Publishing Enterprises.

Bliatout, B.T., Ben, R., Bliatout, H.Y., & Lee, D.T.-T. (1985). Mental health and prevention activities targeted to Southeast Asian refugees. In T.C. Owan (Ed.), *Southeast Asian mental health: Treatment, prevention, services, training, and research* (pp. 183–207). Washington, DC: National Institute of Mental Health.

Booth, A., Crouter, A.C., & Landale, N. (1996). *Immigration and the family: Research and policy on U.S. immigrants.* Mahwah, NJ: Lawrence Erlbaum Associates.

Bosrock, M.M. (1994). *Put your best foot forward: Asia.* St. Paul, MN: International Education Systems.

Brigham Young University. (1996). *Culturegram.* Provo, UT: Brigham Young University, David M. Kennedy Center for International Studies, Publication Services.

Center for Mental Health Services. (2000). *Cultural competence standards in managed mental health care services: Four underserved/underrepresented racial/ethnic groups.* Rockville, MD: Substance Abuse and Mental Health Services Administration, U.S. Department of Health and Human Services.

Chan, S. (1978). *Services for the developmentally disabled: A study of Asian families within a regional center system.* Unpublished doctoral dissertation, University of California–Los Angeles.

Chan, S. (1985, April). *Reaching out to Asian parents.* Paper presented at the Annual Convention of the Council for Exceptional Children, Anaheim, CA.

Chan, S. (1986). Parents of exceptional Asian children. In M.K. Kitano & P.C. Chinn (Eds.), *Exceptional Asian children and youth* (pp. 36–53). Reston, VA: Council for Exceptional Children.

Chan, S. (1990). Early intervention with culturally diverse families of infants and toddlers with disabilities. *Infants and Young Children, 3,* 78–87.

Chan, S. (1991). *Asian Americans: An interpretive history.* Boston: Twayne Publisher.

Chan, S. (1992, April). *Service delivery models.* Paper presented at the "Research on Ethnically Diverse Families with Retarded, Developmentally Disabled, and Physically Disabled Members" workshop, MRDD Branch of the National Institute of Child Health and Human Development, Rockville, MD.

Chan, S. (1995). Freedom of silence. Understanding the world's highest context cultures. In *Access silent Asia: The Asian deaf experience, conference proceedings* (pp. 13–18). DeKalb: Northern Illinois University Research and Training Center on Traditionally Underserved Persons Who Are Deaf.

Chan, S., & Valverde, A. (1996). Working with the interpreter: Basic steps and considerations. In *Project CRAFT, Training manual for instructors.* Northridge: California State University, Department of Special Education.

Chao, C.M. (1992). The inner heart: Therapy with Southeast Asian families. In L.A. Vargas & J.D. Koss-Chioino (Eds.), *Working with culture: Psychotherapeutic interventions with ethnic minority children and adolescents* (pp. 157–181). San Francisco: Jossey-Bass.

Char, T.Y. (1981). The Chinese family. In A.L. Clark (Ed.), *Culture and childrearing* (pp. 140–164). Philadelphia: F.A. Davis.

Chen, A., Ng, P., Sam, P., Ng, D., Abe, D., Ott, R., Lim, W., Chan, S., & Wong, W. (1993). Special health problems of Asian and Pacific Islanders. In R. Matzen & R. Lang (Eds.), *Clinical preventive medicine* (pp. 739–761). St. Louis: Mosby.

Chen, D., Brekken, L.J., & Chan, S. (1997). Project CRAFT: Culturally responsive and family focused training. *Infants and Young Children, 10,* 61–73.

Chen, J. (1981). *The Chinese of America: From the beginning to the present.* New York: Harper & Row.

Cheng, C.-Y. (1987). Chinese philosophy and contemporary human communication theory. In D.L. Kincaid (Ed.), *Communication theory: Eastern and Western perspectives* (pp. 23–43). San Diego: Academic Press.

Cheng, L.L. (1987). *Assessing Asian language performance: Guidelines for evaluating limited English-proficient students.* Rockville, MD: Aspen.

Chhim, S.-H. (1989). *Introduction to Cambodian culture.* San Diego: San Diego State University, Multifunctional Resource Center.

Chin, J.L. (1983). Diagnostic considerations in working with Asian-Americans. *American Journal of Orthopsychiatry, 53,* 100–109.

Chow, E. (1976). Cultural health traditions: Asian perspectives. In M.F. Branch & P.P. Paxton (Eds.), *Providing safe nursing care for ethnic people of color* (pp. 99–114). New York: Appleton-Century-Crofts.

Chu, T.L. (1990, April). *Working with Vietnamese families.* Paper presented at the Harbor Regional Center Conference, Towards Competence in Intercultural Interaction, Torrance, CA.

Chung, E.L. (1996). Asian Americans. In M.C. Julia (Ed.), *Multicultural awareness in the health care professions* (pp. 77–110). Boston: Allyn & Bacon.

Cleveland, J.O. (Ed.). (1987). *Service delivery models for outreach/prevention/intervention for Southeast Asian refugee infants, children, and their families, conference proceedings.* San Diego: San Diego—Imperial Counties Developmental Services.

Crystal, D. (1989, September). Asian Americans and the myth of the model minority. *Social Casework, 70,* 405–413.

Day, J.C. (1995). *Population projections of the United States, by age, sex, race, and Hispanic origin: 1993 to 2050.* Washington, DC: U.S. Bureau of the Census, Population Division.

DeAngelis, T. (1990, July). Cambodians' sight loss tied to seeing atrocities. *APA Monitor, 21,* 36–37.

Devine, E., & Braganti, N.L. (1986). *The traveler's guide to Asian customs and manners.* New York: St. Martin's Press.

Dien, T.T., Te, H.D., & Wei, T.T.D. (1986). *Assessment of Vietnamese speaking limited English proficient students with special needs.* Sacramento: California State Department of Education, Office of Special Education, Personnel Development Unit.

Dizon, L. (1996, June 26). For thousands of refugees, return to Vietnam looms. *Los Angeles Times,* pp. A1, A9.

Do, H.K. (1988). *Health and illness beliefs and practices of Korean Americans.* Unpublished doctoral dissertation, Boston University, School of Nursing.

Doutrich, D., & Metje, L. (1988). *Cultural factors and components of prenatal care for the Hmong and Yiu-Mien.* Unpublished master's thesis, Oregon Health Sciences University, Portland.

Dresser, N. (1996). *Multicultural manners: New rules of etiquette for a changing society.* New York: John Wiley & Sons.

Dung, T.N. (1984). Understanding Asian families: A Vietnamese perspective. *Children Today, 13,* 10–12.

Egawa, J., & Tashima, N. (1982). *Indigenous healers in Southeast Asian refugee communities.* San Francisco: Pacific Asian Mental Health Research Project.

Farley, M., & Tempest, R. (1996, October 17). What does it mean to be Chinese? *Los Angeles Times,* pp. A1, A6.

Fillmore, L.W. (1994). Cultural change and adaptation: A critique of four articles. *Journal of Applied Developmental Psychology, 15,* 341–343.

Final group of Hmong refugees to fly to United States. (1996, July 26). *Asian Week,* p. 8.

Fong, R., & Mokuau, N. (1994). Not simply "Asian American": Periodical literature review on Asian and Pacific Islanders. *Social Work, 30,* 298–305.

Geissler, E.M. (1994). *Pocket guide to cultural assessment.* St. Louis: Mosby.

Gollnick, D.M., & Chinn, P.C. (1990). *Multicultural education in a pluralistic society.* Columbus, OH: Charles E. Merrill.

Gordon, L.W. (1987). Southeast Asian refugee migration to the United States. In J.T. Fawcett & B.V. Carino (Eds.), *Pacific bridges: The new immigration from Asia and the Pacific Islands* (pp. 153–173). New York: Center for Migration Studies.

Greenfield, P.M., & Cocking, R.R. (1994). *Cross-cultural roots of minority child development.* Mahwah, NJ: Lawrence Erlbaum Associates.

Groce, N.E., & Zola, I.K. (1993). Multiculturalism, chronic illness, and disability. *Pediatrics, 91,* 1048–1055.

Gudykunst, W.B., & Ting-Toomey, S. (1988). *Culture and interpersonal communication.* Beverly Hills: Sage Publications.

Haines, D.W. (Ed.). (1989). *Refugees as immigrants: Cambodians, Laotians, and Vietnamese in America.* Totowa, NJ: Rowman & Littlefield.

Hall, E. (1976). *Beyond culture.* Garden City, NY: Anchor.

Hamner, T.J., & Turner, P.H. (1996). *Parenting in contemporary society*. Boston: Allyn & Bacon.

Hanson, M.J., & Lynch, E.W. (1992). Family diversity: Implications for policy and practice. *Teaching Early Childhood Special Education, 12*, 283–306.

Hanson, M.J., Lynch, E.W., & Wayman, K.I. (1990). Honoring the cultural diversity of families when gathering data. *Topics in Early Childhood Special Education, 10*, 112–131.

Harrison, A.O., Wilson, M.N., Pine, C.J., Chan, S.Q., & Buriel, R. (1990). Family ecologies of ethnic minority children. *Child Development, 61*, 347–362.

Hing, B.O. (1992). *Making and remaking Asian America through immigration policy*. Stanford, CA: Stanford University Press.

Ho, C.K. (1990). An analysis of domestic violence in Asian American communities: A multicultural approach to counseling. *Women and Therapy, 9*, 129–150.

Ho, M.K. (1987). *Family therapy with ethnic minorities*. Beverly Hills: Sage Publications.

Hollingsworth, A.O., Brown, L.P., & Brooten, D.A. (1980, November). Indochina moves to Main Street: The refugees and childbearing: What to expect. *RN*, 45–48.

Hsu, F.L.K. (1981). *Americans and Chinese: Passages to differences*. Honolulu: University of Hawaii Press.

Huang, L.N. (1989). Southeast Asian refugee children and adolescents. In J.T. Gibbs & L.N. Huang (Eds.), *Children of color: Psychological interventions with minority youth* (pp. 278–321). San Francisco: Jossey-Bass.

Huang, L.N., & Ying, Y.-W. (1989). Chinese American children and adolescents. In J.T. Gibbs & L.N. Huang (Eds.), *Children of color: Psychological interventions with minority youth* (pp. 30–66). San Francisco: Jossey-Bass.

Hurh, W.M., & Kim, K.C. (1984). *Korean immigrants in America*. Cranbury, NJ: Associated University Press.

Immigration and Nationality Act Amendments of 1965, PL 89-236, 79 Stat. 9118 U.S.C. §§1151–1152.

Karnow, S., & Yoshihara, N. (1992). *Asian Americans in transition*. New York: The Asia Society.

Keiter, J. (1990). *The recruitment and retention of minority trainees in University Affiliated Programs—Asian-Americans*. In M.L. Kuehn, (Ed.) Madison: University of Wisconsin.

Kelley, M., & Tseng, H. (1992). Cultural differences in child rearing. *Journal of Cross-Cultural Psychology, 23*, 444–455.

Kemp, C. (1985). Cambodian refugee health care beliefs and practices. *Journal of Community Mental Health Nursing, 2*, 41–52.

Kim, B.-L.C. (1980). *The Korean-American child at school and at home* (Project Report). Washington, DC: U.S. Department of Health, Education and Welfare (ACYF).

Kim, B.-L.C. (1996). Korean families. In M. McGoldrick, J. Giordano, & J.K. Pearce (Eds.), *Ethnicity and family therapy* (pp. 281–294). New York: Guilford Press.

Kim, I. (1987). Korea and East Asia: Premigration factors and U.S. immigration policy. In J.T. Fawcett & B.V. Carino (Eds.), *Pacific bridges: The new immigration from Asia and the Pacific Islands* (pp. 327–345). New York: Center for Migration Studies.

Kim, S.C. (1985). Family therapy for Asian Americans: A strategic-structural framework. *Psychotherapy, 22*, 342–348.

Koss-Chioino, J.D. (1995). Traditional and folk approaches among ethnic minorities. In J.F. Aponte, R.Y. Rivers, & J. Wohl (Eds.), *Psychological interventions and cultural diversity* (pp. 145–163). Boston: Allyn & Bacon.

Kourmarn, Y.S. (1980). Hmongs of Laos: 1896–1978. *Indochinese refugee education guides: General information series #16: Glimpses of Hmong history and culture*. Washington, DC: National Indochinese Clearinghouse.

Kraut, A.M. (1990). Healers and strangers: Immigrant attitudes toward the physician in America—A relationship in historical perspective. *Journal of the American Medical Association, 263*(13), 1807–1811.

Langdon, H., Siegel, V., Cima, L., & Sanchez-Boyce, M. (1994). *The interpreter/ translator in the school setting: A resource manual*. Sacramento, CA: Resources in Special Education (RISE).

Lassiter, S.M. (1995). *Multicultural clients: A professional handbook for health care providers and social workers*. Westport, CT: Greenwood Press.

Le, D.D. (1983). Mental health and Vietnamese children. In G.J. Powell (Ed.), *The psychosocial development of minority group children* (pp. 373–384). New York: Brunner/Mazel.

Le, N. (1993). The case of Southeast Asian refugees: Policy for a community "at-risk." In LEAP Asian Pacific American Public Policy Institute & UCLA Asian American Studies Center (Eds.), *The state of Asian Pacific America: A public policy report* (pp. 167–188). Los Angeles: Editors.

Ledgewood, J. (2003). *Cambodian recent history and contemporary society: An introductory course*. Northern Illinois University: Department of Anthropology and Center for

Southeast Asian Studies.

Lee, C.S. (1988). *Korea—Land of the morning calm.* New York: Universe Press.

Lee, E. (1988). Cultural factors in working with Southeast Asian refugee adolescents. *Journal of Adolescence, 11,* 167–179.

Lee, E. (1996a). Asian American families: An overview. In M. McGoldrick, J. Giordano, & J.K. Pearce (Eds.), *Ethnicity and family therapy* (pp. 227–248). New York: Guilford Press.

Lee, E. (1996b). Chinese families. In M. McGoldrick, J. Giordano, & J.K. Pearce (Eds.), *Ethnicity and family therapy* (pp. 249–267). New York: Guilford Press.

Lee, E. (1997). *Working with Asian Americans: A guide for clinicians.* New York: Guilford Press.

Lee, E. (2002). *Meeting the mental health needs of Asian and Pacific Islander Americans.* Alexandria, VA: National Technical Assistance Center for State Mental Health Planning.

Lee, J.C., & Cynn, V.E.H. (1991). Issues in counseling 1.5 generation Korean Americans. In C. Lee & B. Richardson (Eds.), *Multicultural issues in counseling: New approaches to diversity* (pp. 127–140). Alexandria, VA: American Association for Counseling and Development.

Lee, R.V. (1989). Understanding Southeast Asian mothers-to-be. *Childbirth Educator (American Baby), 8,* 32–39.

Leung, E.K. (1988). Cultural and acculturational commonalities and diversities among Asian Americans: Identification and programming considerations. In A.A. Oritz & B.A. Ramiriz (Eds.), *Schools and the culturally diverse exceptional student: Promising practices and future directions* (pp. 86–95). Reston, VA: Council for Exceptional Children.

Leung, P.K., & Boehnlein, J. (1996). Vietnamese families. In M. McGoldrick, J. Giordano, & J.K. Pearce (Eds.), *Ethnicity and family therapy* (pp. 295–306). New York: Guilford Press.

Lew, L.S. (1989, May). *Understanding the Southeast Asian health care consumer: Bridges and barriers.* Paper presented at the National Symposium on Genetic Services for the Medically Underserved, Washington, DC.

Li, C. (1983). The basic grammatical structures of selected Asian languages and English. In M. Chu-Chang (Ed.), *Asian- and Pacific-American perspectives in bilingual education: Comparative research* (pp. 3–30). New York: Teachers College Press.

Lim-Yee, N. (1995). Having a child with special needs: Parental reactions, cultural differences, and Chinese families. *Social Work Perspectives, 5,* 52–57.

Lin, C.C., & Fu, V.R. (1990). A comparison of child-rearing practices among Chinese, immigrant Chinese, and Caucasian-American parents. *Child Development, 61,* 429–433.

Lin, E.H., Carter, W., & Kleinman, A. (1985). An exploration of somatization among Asian refugees and immigrants in primary care. *American Journal of Public Health, 75,* 1080–1084.

Lin, K.-M. (1983). Hwa-Byung: A Korean culture-based syndrome? *American Journal of Psychiatry, 140,* 105–107.

Lin, K.-M., & Masuda, M. (1981). Impact of the refugee experience: Mental health issues of the Southeast Asians. In Special Service for Groups (Ed.), *Bridging cultures: Southeast Asian refugees in America* (pp. 32–52). Los Angeles: Asian American Mental Health Training Center.

Lin-Fu, J.S. (1987). Meeting the needs of Southeast Asian refugees in maternal and child health and primary care programs. In J.O. Cleveland (Ed.), *Service delivery models for outreach/prevention for Southeast Asian refugee infants, children, and their families, conference proceedings* (Appendix E). CA: San Diego—Imperial Counties Developmental Services.

Lin-Fu, J.S. (1988). Population characteristics and health care needs of Asian Pacific Americans. *Public Health Reports, 103,* 18–27.

Lochnicht, M.B. (1995). *Building bridges: Mental health training for interpreters of Southeast Asian languages.* Seattle, WA: Asian Counseling and Referral Services.

Locke, D.C. (1992). *Increasing multicultural understanding: A comprehensive model.* Beverly Hills: Sage Publications.

Lopez, D.S. (2001). *The story of Buddhism: A concise guide to its history and teachings.* San Francisco: Harper SanFrancisco.

Lowenthal, B. (1996). Training early interventionists to work with culturally diverse families. *Infant-Toddler Intervention, 6,* 145–152.

Luangpraseut, K. (1989). *Laos culturally speaking.* CA: San Diego State University, Multifunctional Resource Center.

MacMahon, H. (1977). *"Confucianism" the Korean way.* Seoul: Samsung.

Major, J.S. (1989). *The land and people of China.* New York: J.B. Lippincott.

Maley, V. (1996, March). *Parents and professionals can bridge the communication gap.* Presentation at the Project CRAFT Instructor

Training Workshop, Costa Mesa, CA.

Martin, J.A (2001). Births: Final data for 2001. *National Vital Statistics Report 51*(2). Washington DC: Population Reference Bureau (AmeriStat).

Masterson, L.C.-C. (1988, Summer). Chinese folk medicine and child abuse. *California Regional Centers Journal,* pp. 23–26.

Masterson, L. C.-C. (1990, May). *Working with Chinese families.* Paper presented at the Lanterman Regional Center Conference, Enhancing Multicultural Awareness: Serving Immigrant Families, Los Angeles.

McGoldrick, M., Giordano, J., & Pearce, J.K. (Eds.). (1996). *Ethnicity and family therapy.* New York: Guilford Press.

McKenzie-Pollock, L. (1996). Cambodian families. In M. McGoldrick, J. Giordano, & J.K. Pearce (Eds.), *Ethnicity and family therapy* (pp. 307–315). New York: Guilford Press.

Min, P.G. (1995a). An overview of Asian Americans. In P.G. Min (Ed.), *Asian Americans: Contemporary trends and issues* (pp. 10–37). Beverly Hills: Sage Publications.

Min, P.G. (1995b). Korean Americans. In P.G. Min (Ed.), *Asian Americans: Contemporary trends and issues* (pp. 199–230). Beverly Hills: Sage Publications.

Min, P.G. (1995c). Major issues relating to Asian American experiences. In P.G. Min (Ed.), *Asian Americans: Contemporary trends and issues* (pp. 38–57). Beverly Hills: Sage Publications.

Mokuau, N. (Ed.). (1991). *Handbook of social services for Asian and Pacific Islanders.* Westport, CT: Greenwood Press.

Monmaney, T. (1995, September 14). Ethnicities' medical views vary. *Los Angeles Times,* pp. B1, B3.

Morrow, R.D. (1989). Southeast Asian child rearing practices: Implications for child and youth care workers. *Child & Youth Care Quarterly, 18,* 273–287.

Muecke, M.A. (1983a). Caring for the Southeast Asian refugee. *American Journal of Public Health, 73,* 431–438.

Muecke, M.A. (1983b). In search of healers— Southeast Asian refugees in the American health care system. *Western Journal of Medicine, 139,* 835–840.

Mun, S.H. (1979). Shamanism in Korea. In Y.C. Shin (Ed.), *Korean thoughts* (pp. 17–36). Seoul, Korea: International Cultural Foundation.

National Asian Pacific American Legal Consortium (NAPALC). (1995). *Audit of violence against Asian Pacific Americans.* Washington, DC: Author.

National Indochinese Clearinghouse. (1980).

Glimpses of Hmong history and culture, *Indochinese refugee education guides: General information series #16.* Washington, DC: Author.

Nguyen, N., Nguyen, P.H., & Nguyen, L.H. (1987). *Coin treatment in Vietnamese families: Traditional medical practice vs. child abuse.* Unpublished paper.

O'Hare, W.P. (1992). America's minorities— The demographics of diversity. *Population Bulletin, 47,* 1–47.

Okamura, A., Heras, P., & Wong-Kerberg, L. (1995). Asian, Pacific Island, and Filipino Americans and sexual child abuse. In L.A. Fontes (Ed.), *Sexual abuse in nine North American cultures: Treatment and prevention* (pp. 67–96). Beverly Hills: Sage Publications.

Olness, K.N. (1986). On "Reflections on caring for Indochinese children and youths." *Developmental and Behavioral Pediatrics, 7,* 129–130.

Pan Asian Parent Education Project. (1982). *Pan Asian child rearing practices: Filipino, Japanese, Korean, Samoan, Vietnamese.* San Diego: Union of Pan Asian Communities.

Park, K. (2003). *The world almanac and book of facts 2003.* New York: World Almanac Educational Group.

Park, S.J., & Song, K.S. (1982). The Korean community. In Pan Asian Parent Education Project, *Pan Asian child rearing practices: Filipino, Japanese, Korean, Samoan, Vietnamese* (pp. 51–76). San Diego: Union of Pan Asian Communities.

Patterson, W., & Kim, H.-C. (1986). *The Koreans in America.* Minneapolis: Lerner Publications.

Porter, J. (1983). *All under heaven: The Chinese world.* New York: Pantheon Books.

Pries, S.A. (2002). *Building systems of care: A primer.* Washington, DC: National Technical Assistance Center for Children's Mental Health, Georgetown University Child Development Center.

Quincy, K. (1988). *Hmong: History of a people.* Cheney: Eastern Washington State University Press.

Ratliff, S.S. (1994). Health and healing. In the Southeast Asian Regional Community Health Project (SEARCH), *The training guidebook.* Columbus: Ohio Commission on Minority Health.

Roberts, R.N. (1990). *Workbook for developing culturally competent programs for children with special needs.* Washington, DC: Georgetown University Child Development Center.

Rogow, S.M. (1985, April). *Where service begins: Working with parents to provide early in-*

tervention, considerations for the culturally different. Paper presented at the annual convention of the Council for Exceptional Children, Anaheim, CA.

Rumbaut, R.G. (1985). Mental health and the refugee experience: A comparative study of Southeast Asian refugees. In T.C. Owan (Ed.), *Southeast Asian mental health: Treatment, prevention, services, training, and research* (pp. 433–486). Washington, DC: National Institute of Mental Health.

Rumbaut, R.G. (1995). Vietnamese, Laotian, and Cambodian Americans. In P.G. Min (Ed.), *Asian Americans: Contemporary trends and issues* (pp. 232–270). Beverly Hills: Sage Publications.

Rumbaut, R.G., & Weeks, J.R. (1986). Fertility and adaptation: Indochinese refugees in the United States. *International Migration Review, 20*(2), 428–466.

Rutledge, P. (1987). *The Vietnamese in America.* Minneapolis: Lerner Publication Co.

Serafica, F.C. (1990). Counseling Asian American parents: A cultural-developmental framework. In F.C. Serafica, A.I. Schwebel, R.K. Russel, P.D. Isaac, & L.J. Meyers (Eds.), *Mental health of ethnic minorities* (pp. 222–244). New York: Praeger.

Shinagawa, L.H., & Jang, M. (1998). *Atlas of American diversity.* Walnut Creek, CA: Alta Mira Press.

Shon, S.P., & Ja, D.Y. (1983). Asian families. In M. McGoldrick, J. Giordano, J.K. Pearce, (Eds.), *Ethnicity and family therapy* (pp. 208–228). New York: Guilford Press.

Shu-Minutoli, K. (1995). Family support: Diversity, disability, and delivery. In E.E. Garcia & B. McLaughlin (Eds.), *Meeting the challenge of linguistic and cultural diversity in early childhood education* (Yearbook in early childhood education, Vol. 6) (pp. 125–140). New York: Teachers College Press.

Sigel, I.E. (1988). Commentary: Cross-cultural studies of parental influence on children's achievement. *Human Development, 31,* 384–390.

Sileo, T.W., Sileo, A.P., & Prater, M.A. (1996). Parent and professional partnerships in special education: Multicultural considerations. *Intervention in School and Clinic, 31,* 145–153.

Silver, B. (1996, August 13). Mom shoots son, kills husband, self. *Daily Breeze,* p. A7.

Smith, M.J., & Ryan, A.S. (1987). Chinese-American families of children with developmental disabilities: An exploratory study of reactions to service providers. *Mental Retardation, 25,* 345–350.

Sodowsky, G.R., Kwong-Liem K.K., & Pannu, R. (1995). Ethnic identity of Asians in the United States. In J.G. Ponterotto, J.M. Casas, L.A. Suzuki, & C.M. Alexander (Eds.), *Handbook of multicultural counseling* (pp. 123–154). Beverly Hills: Sage Publications.

Spector, R.E. (1991). *Cultural diversity in health and illness.* New York: Appleton-Century-Crofts.

Stauffer, R.Y. (1991). Vietnamese Americans. In J.N. Giger & R.E. Davidhizar (Eds.), *Transcultural nursing: Assessment and intervention* (pp. 403–434). St. Louis: Mosby.

Steelman, J. (1994). *Death: A difficult subject.* Sacramento, CA: Josie Steelman Interpreting Services.

Stevenson, H.W., & Lee, S. (1990). Contexts of achievement: A study of American, Chinese, and Japanese children. *Monographs of the Society for Research in Child Development, 55* (1–2, Serial No. 221).

Sue, D. (1981). Cultural and historical perspectives in counseling Asian Americans. In D. Sue (Ed.), *Counseling the culturally different: Theory and practice* (pp. 113–140). New York: John Wiley & Sons.

Sue, S. (1993). The changing Asian-American population: Mental health policy. In LEAP Asian Pacific American Public Policy Institute & UCLA Asian American Studies Center (Eds.), *The state of Asian Pacific America: A public policy report* (pp. 79–94). Los Angeles: Editors.

Sue, S., & Zane, N. (1987). The role of culture and cultural techniques in psychotherapy. *American Psychologist, 42,* 37–45.

Sung, B.L. (1971). *The story of the Chinese in America.* New York: Collier.

Takaki, R. (1989). *Strangers from a different shore: A history of Asian Americans.* Boston: Little, Brown.

Taylor, T.D. (1995). *Promoting cultural diversity and cultural competency: Self-assessment checklist for personnel providing services and supports in early intervention and early childhood settings.* Washington, DC: Georgetown University Child Development Center.

Te, H.D. (1989a). *The Indochinese and their cultures.* San Diego: San Diego State University, Multifunctional Resource Center.

Te, H.D. (1989b). *Introduction to Vietnamese culture.* San Diego: San Diego State University, Multifunctional Resource Center.

Thuy, V.G. (1980). *Getting to know the Vietnamese and their culture.* New York: Frederick Unser Publishing.

Tien-Hyatt, J.L. (1987). Keying in on the

unique care needs of Asian clients. *Nursing and Health Care, 8,* 268–271.

Tinloy, M.T., Tan, A., & Leung, B. (1986). *Assessment of Chinese speaking limited English proficient students with special needs.* Sacramento, CA: Special Education Resource Network, Resource Service Center.

Tom, K.S. (1989). *Echoes from old China.* Honolulu: University of Hawaii Press.

Tou-Fou, V. (1981). The Hmong of Laos. In Special Service for Groups (Ed.), *Bridging cultures: Southeast Asian refugees in America* (pp. 73–82). Los Angeles: Asian American Mental Health Training Center.

Triandis, H.C. (1995). *Individualism and collectivism.* Boulder, CO: Westview Press.

Uba, L. (1994). *Asian Americans: Personality patterns, identity, and mental health.* New York: Guilford Press.

Union of Pan Asian Communities. (1980). *Understanding the Pan Asian client: Book II.* San Diego: Author.

U.S. Bureau of the Census. (1994). *1990 census of population, general social and economic characteristics, the United States.* Washington, DC: U.S. Government Printing Office.

U.S. Bureau of the Census. (1996). *Children ever born by parity, race, age, marital status, and nativity of women: April 1990.* Washington, DC: U.S. Government Printing Office.

U.S. Bureau of the Census. (1999). *Household income at record high: Poverty declines in 1998.* Washington, DC: Census Bureau Reports.

U.S. Bureau of the Census. (2000). *The Asian and Pacific Islander population in the United States.* Washington, DC: Census Bureau Reports.

U.S. General Accounting Office. (1990). *Asian Americans: A status report.* Washington, DC: Human Resources Division.

U.S. Office of Refugee Resettlement. (1992). *Annual report.* Washington, DC: U.S. Department of Health and Human Services.

U.S. Surgeon General. (1999). *Mental health: A report of the Surgeon General.* Washington DC: U.S. Government Printing Office.

Walker, C.L. (1985). Learning English: The Southeast Asian refugee experience. *Topics in Language Disorders, 5,* 53–65.

Wang, W.S.-Y. (1983). Speech and script relations in some Asian languages. In M. Chu-Chang (Ed.), *Asian and Pacific-American perspectives in bilingual education: Comparative research* (pp. 56–72). New York: Teachers College Press.

Watson, J.L. (1988). *Death ritual in late imperial and modern China.* Berkeley: University of California Press.

Wei, T.T.D. (1983). The Vietnamese refugee child: Understanding cultural differences. In D.R. Omark & J.G. Erickson (Eds.), *The bilingual exceptional child* (pp. 197–212). San Diego: College-Hill Press.

Weisz, J.R., Rothbaum, F.M., & Blackburn, T.C. (1984). Standing out and standing in: The psychology of control in America and Japan. *American Psychologist, 39,* 955–969.

Wiemann, J., Chen, V., & Giles, H. (1986, November). *Beliefs about talk and silence in a cultural context.* Paper presented at the Speech Communication Association Convention, Chicago.

Wong, C. (1985, April-June). Yin and yang of nutrition. *Perinatal Nutrition Newsletter, California Department of Health Services,* 1.

Wong, M.G. (1995). Chinese Americans. In P.G. Min (Ed.), *Asian Americans: Contemporary trends and issues* (pp. 58–94). Beverly Hills: Sage Publications.

Yao, E.L. (1988). Working effectively with Asian immigrant parents. *Phi Delta Kappan, 70,* 223–225.

Yeatman, G.W., & Dang, V.V. (1980). *Cao gio* (coin rubbing): Vietnamese attitudes toward health care. *Journal of the American Medical Association, 244,* 2748–2749.

Young-Kwon, K. (1978). *A handbook of Korea.* Seoul: Korean Overseas Information Services.

Yu, E.-Y. (1983). Korean communities in America: Past, present, and future. *Amerasia Journal, 10,* 23–51.

Yu, K.H., & Kim, L.I.C. (1983). The growth and development of Korean-American children. In G.J. Powell (Ed.), *The psychosocial development of minority group children* (pp. 147–158). New York: Brunner/Mazel.

Yum, J.-O. (1987). Korean philosophy and communication. In D.L. Kincaid (Ed.), *Communication theory: Eastern and Western perspectives* (pp. 71–86). San Diego: Academic Press.

Zane, N.W.S., Takeuchi, D.T., & Young, K.N.J. (Eds.). (1994). *Confronting critical health issues of Asian and Pacific Islander Americans.* Beverly Hills: Sage Publications.

CONTRASTING BELIEFS, VALUES, AND PRACTICES

Traditional Asian	**Mainstream culture**

Civilization

Traditional Asian	Mainstream culture
Agricultural	Industrial
• Harmony with nature	• Mastery over nature

Religion

Traditional Asian	Mainstream culture
Polytheistic, spiritualistic	Monotheistic
• Humanistic	• Christian

Philosophy

Traditional Asian	Mainstream culture
Heart-oriented	Mind-oriented
• Contemplative, circular thinking	• Analytic, linear thinking
• Fatalism	• Personal control over environment and one's fate
• Stoicism, patience	• Optimism, eagerness to take action
• Tradition, living with the past	• Change, future orientation
• Being (person orientation)	• Doing (task orientation)
• Self-denial, self-discipline	• Self-assertiveness, self-gratification
• Spiritualism, detachment	• Materialism

Social Orientation

Traditional Asian	Mainstream culture
Collectivist (we)	Individual (I)
• Group welfare, public consciousness	• Self-actualization, privacy
• Mutual interdependence	• Independence, self-reliance, individual autonomy
• Hierarchy, role rigidity, status defined by ascription (birthright inheritance, family name, age, sex)	• Equality, role flexibility, status defined by achievement
• Conformity	• Challenge or question authority
• Cooperation, nonconfrontation, and reconciliation	• Competition, aggressiveness

Traditional Asian	**Mainstream culture**

Family

Family-centered	Individual-centered

• Family as primary unit	• Individual as primary unit
• Family solidarity, responsibility, and harmony	• Individual pursuit of happiness, fulfillment, and self-expression
• Continued dependence on family is fostered	• Early independence is encouraged
• Hierarchical family roles, ascribed status	• Variable roles, achieved status
• Parent–child (parental) bond is stressed	• Husband–wife (marital) bond is stressed
• Parent provides authority and expects unquestioning obedience, submission to structure	• Parent provides guidance, support, and explanations and encourages curiosity and critical/independent thinking
• Family makes decisions for the child	• Child is given many choices
• Children are extension of parents	• Children are individuals
• Parents ask: "What can you do to help me?"	• Parents ask: "What can I do to help you?"
• Older children are responsible for the siblings' actions	• Each child is responsible for his or her own actions

Communication

Indirect	Direct
• Implicit, nonverbal	• Explicit, verbal
• Formal	• Informal
• Goal oriented	• Spontaneous
• Emotionally controlled	• Emotionally expressive
• Self-effacing, modest	• Self-promoting, egocentric

Note: "Traditional Asian" values must be viewed within a historical context. Significant differences in values obviously exist among contemporary Asian Americans, who represent a highly diverse population. Similarly, "dominant culture" values should not be equated with "American values" as if they were "homogeneous, clearly defined, static, and synonymous with middle-class, Euro-American attitudes and beliefs. [Moreover,] American values are not necessarily the opposite of Asian values (Uba, 1994, p. 14). The respective values presented above, however, serve to illustrate the distinct historical contrasts between traditional Asian and dominant cultural orientations that continue to be prevalent among various ethnic subgroups.

APPENDIX B

CULTURAL COURTESIES AND CUSTOMS

The following behaviors and expectations should be considered when interacting with certain Asian American populations. Failure to recognize and respect culturally appropriate customs, gestures, and so forth and/or acting in a contrary manner may risk offending clients and families who adhere to traditional social practices.

Greetings

- Greet family members in order of age, beginning with the oldest and typically the male members first. In a case in which there is an older woman and a younger man, greet the woman first unless the man is the father in the family receiving services.

- Use *Mr.*, *Mrs.*, *Miss*, or other appropriate title with the family name (surname) for Chinese and Koreans and with the individual's first (given) name for Cambodians, Laotians, and Vietnamese.

Nationalities	Example	Formal greeting
Chinese	Tien (surname) Chang-Lin (given)	Dr. Tien
Korean	Kim (surname) Bok-Lim (given)	Mrs. Kim
Cambodian	Pok (surname) Than (given)	Mr. Than
Laotian	Luangpraseut (surname) Kamchong (given)	Mr. Kamchong
Vietnamese	Nguyen (surname) Van Hai (given)	Mr. Hai

After marriage, Chinese, Korean, and Vietnamese women typically keep their own family name and do not combine it with their husbands' family name (e.g., if a Miss Lee marries a Mr. Chen, she may be referred to as Mrs. Lee).

- Women typically do not shake hands with men. Younger people do not shake hands with an elder or significantly older person. Although a handshake between men is often acceptable, an initial slight bow before shaking hands or waiting for the other man to extend his hand first may be more appropriate. To show respect when shaking hands with Korean men, support your right forearm with your left hand. The traditional Lao greeting or *wai* consists of bowing one's head—the higher the hands are placed, the more respect is shown; however, the tips of the fingers should never be above eye level.

- Kissing, hugging, slapping a person on the back, or putting one's arm around another's shoulders is considered inappropriate. In general, direct physical contact (particularly between men and women) should be avoided.

Nonverbal Communication

- Avoid prolonged gazing or expecting direct/sustained eye contact with individuals who are relative strangers and in formal interactions.

- Touching the head (including a child's) is often considered threatening or offensive by Cambodians, Lao, and certain Buddhists because of the spiritual belief that it is the most sacred part of the body.

- Waving arms to elicit attention and pointing or beckoning with an index finger are considered to be signs of contempt. Instead, point with an open hand and indicate "come here" by waving the fingers of one hand closed together with the palm down, facing inward.

- Winking or batting one's eyes at another is impolite.

- When sitting, if one's legs are crossed, the soles and toes of the feet should point downward or away from the other person. In very formal situations, keep both feet on the floor and place hands in the lap or keep them visible.

- Emotional restraint, formality, reserve, tact, and politeness are essential. Avoid engaging in demonstrative behavior and talking or laughing loudly.

Conversation

- In an initial encounter or first meeting, refrain from asking personal questions of the other party too quickly, but be prepared for people to ask personal questions of you (e.g., "Where are you from?", "How old are you?", "Are you married?", "How many children do you have?").

- Avoid talking about politics, either regarding the United States or regarding people's native countries.

Private Homes

- Removing one's shoes before entering a house is considered appropriate for many Asian groups.

- Expect to be offered food or drinks, and partake of such hospitality.

- Refrain from complimenting household decorations; if a guest comments or offers compliments about a particular household object, the host may feel compelled to give it to him or her as a gift.

Gift Giving

- Gifts are offered and received with both hands (as is the case with politely handing something to another person or receiving other objects).

- Gifts are typically not opened in the presence of the giver(s).

SIGNIFICANT CULTURAL EVENTS/HOLIDAYS/PRACTICES

HOLIDAYS

Lunar New Year's Day

Celebrated by most Asians on the first day of the first month of the lunar calendar; usually falls between January 19 and February 20

Vietnamese New Year's Day

Known as Tet and celebrated throughout the country for a period of several days, (dates vary from year to year)

Cambodian and Laotian New Year's Day

In the fifth month of the lunar calendar; usually falls in mid-April, just after harvest time

Hmong New Year's Day

Follows the thirteenth day of the Hmong twelfth moon when the moon is the darkest; usually falls near the end of November or beginning of December. The Hmong living in the United States have adapted their New Year's Day to coincide with Christmas.

More detailed information regarding specific customs and practices associated with the Lunar New Year as well as other native holidays celebrated by Chinese, Koreans, and Southeast Asians is provided by Brigham Young University (1996), Devine and Braganti (1986), Dresser (1996), Te (1989a), and Tom (1989).

AGES, BIRTHDATES, AND BIRTHDAYS

Among the Chinese and Vietnamese, age is traditionally counted from the time of conception and thereafter according to the lunar calendar. A child is thus considered approximately 1 year old at birth. He or she then becomes 2 years old on New Year's Day of the lunar calendar, even if born as late as the last day of the preceding lunar year. New Year's Day is especially meaningful, therefore, because it serves as the common birthday for the entire nation; everyone becomes 1 year older at that time.

Personal birthdays are typically not celebrated except 1 month after the birth of an infant son and on the first anniversary of his birth. The Chinese celebrate these two birthday occasions by hosting a "red egg and ginger" party for relatives and friends. At these times, red-tinted hard-boiled eggs and sliced pickled ginger (red is the color of good luck and these foods symbolize new birth) are served with a feast or dinner. In the initial celebration at age 1 month, the infant son is traditionally given a first name, and an elder, grandparent, or his mother shaves his head. He is then dressed in a red gown and carried to the temple by his father wherein the gods and spirits of ancestors are notified of the birth of a son. Special offerings of foods, including red eggs and ginger, are also made at that time. Southeast Asian babies are similarly officially named at 1 month of age. Elders, temple monks, and other learned people are consulted on the baby's name, especially if it is a boy. They consider the precise moment when the child was born in accordance with the lunar calendar, the season, the wind, and the elements. The name must also reflect the personality and characteristics of the child and must not duplicate names of relatives. For the Hmong, the newborn infant is not officially recognized into the human race until it is 3 days old and a shaman can come to invite the soul to be reincarnated into the baby's body (Chung, 1996).

OTHER CUSTOMS/BELIEFS

The Hmong also have taboos regarding infants and children. A baby's feet should not be tickled or he or she will grow up to be a thief. If a child is fed chicken gizzards, he or she will grow up lacking in intelligence (Arax, 1996).

Whereas red is the color of good luck, white is the color of mourning and represents death; it is the color typically worn at funerals. Thus, when entering a hospital for the first time, seeing white sheets and doctors and nurses in white may suggest that those who stay there are going to die.

The Chinese also believe that a pregnant woman should avoid events such as funerals and weddings. Her attendance at a funeral may invite the spirit of the deceased to enter her womb; her presence at weddings might bring bad luck to the newlyweds and the family (Char, 1981).

Another belief among Chinese and Koreans (as well as Japanese) is that the number *four* is unlucky; when translated, it sounds like the word "death." The number *four* in combination with other numbers also translates into threatening phrases, and may lead to avoidance of various homes/businesses with corresponding addresses as well as unlucky dates on which to schedule surgery or other major events. The number *seven* is related to the notion that ghosts return 7 days after death.

For the Chinese, other numbers are associated with positive meanings: *one* for guaranteed; *two* for *easy*; *three* for *life*; *six* for *happiness*; *eight* for *prosperity* (and good luck); and *nine* for *long life* (Dresser, 1996).

APPENDIX D

VOCABULARY

| | Chinese | | | |
English	Cantonese	Mandarin	Korean	Vietnamese
Hello	Nay-ho	Nee-how	Ahn-nyong-ha-say-yo (In person)	Chao quiong (Mr.)/ba (Mrs.)
Good-bye	Joy-geen	Zai-jen	Ahn-nyong-hee-ga-say-yo (Person leaving) Ahn-nyong-hee-gye-say-yo (Person staying)	Xing chao
Yes	Heigh	Suhr	Yeh	Vang
No	Mm-heigh	Boo-suhr	Ah-nee yo	Khong
Please	Ching-nay	Ching-nee	Jeh-song hahm-nee-dah	Xing
Thank you	Doh-jeh	Sheh-sheh	Kahm-sah-hahm-nee dah	Kam on
Father	Ba-ba	Fu-cheen	Ah buh ji	Cha
Mother	Ma-ma	Mu-cheen	Un muh ni	Meh
Family	Gah-ting	Ja-ting	Gah jok	Gia-dinh

CHAPTER 9

FAMILIES WITH PILIPINO ROOTS

Rosa Milagros Santos and Sam Chan

Ang sakit ng kalingkingan damdam ng buong katawan
(When the little finger hurts, the whole body hurts.)
—PILIPINO SAYING

Ang hindi lumingon sa pinanggalingan,
di makararating sa paroroonan
(One who does not look back at where he came from
will not get to where he is going.)
—PILIPINO SAYING

Pag may tiyaga, may nilaga
(Patience will yield results.)
—PILIPINO SAYING

Huli man daw at magaling, ay naihahabol din
(Worthwhile things even when presented late
can still be included.)
—PILIPINO SAYING

With approximately 52,000 admissions per year between 1989 and 2000, Pilipinos are the second-largest Asian immigrant group to the United States and the third largest of all legal immigrant groups (U.S. Bureau of the Census, 2002a).

> To understand why the Philippines is [one of the largest contributors] to U.S. immigration, it is important to take into account the country's long colonial experience with the United States. Although decolonization occurred several decades ago, the formal severing of political ties does not sunder overnight the social, cultural, and economic links that bind former colonies and mother countries and generate population movements between them. The Americanization of Filipino culture is pervasive and a major factor in the integration of Filipinos to the United States. (Cariño, 1987, pp. 308, 310)

BACKGROUND

Although Pilipinos may have a decidedly Western orientation and share a heritage of many significant ideas and values rooted in Euro-Christian ethics, their traditional social and cultural characteristics contrast sharply with those of mainstream America.

The reader will note the spelling *Pilipino* throughout this chapter. The term *Pilipino* came into use during the Pilipino American ethnic consciousness and identity movement of the late 1960s. It was argued that Filipino was a remnant of the colonized mentality because the pre-Hispanic Tagalog language did not contain an "F" sound. Others, however, have noted that there is an "F" sound in some indigenous languages. Furthermore, some members of the second and later generations who have always called themselves "Filipino" feel that the "P" label emphasizes post-1965 immigrants and not American-born Filipinos. Thus, the use of "P" or "F" is a matter of individual preference but also reflects the long-standing national identity and ethnic pride debate on whether "to 'P' or not to 'P'" (Agbayani-Siewert & Revilla, 1995; Cordova, 1983).

Understanding the Pilipino American character is complex. The differences among Pilipinos in terms of history, language, familial and other forms of affiliation, religion, education, and individual experiences can be great. Although this chapter provides some general insights into families with Pilipino roots, great caution and consideration must be taken to prevent perpetuating stereotypes. Although many Pilipino Americans have a shared history and common cultural experiences, other factors not related to being Pilipino may have a more decided influence on their self-identities.

Geographic and Historical Origins

Although the Philippines is located geographically in Asia, according to Gochenour,

> There is a general sense of being neither this nor that, of sharing something of the Pacific islands, of being heavily influenced by Spanish and American cultures, and of perceiving only a remote historical relationship with the major cultures of Asia. (1990, p. 42)

Further examination of the unique history of the Philippines and of Pilipino emigration to the United States illustrates how this country has been a "Pacific Bridge" between many cultures. The Republic of the Philippines is an archipelago approximately 1,500 miles long, bounded on the north by Taiwan and on the south by Indonesia. In terms of area, the Philippines is slightly larger than the state of Arizona (Central Intelligence Agency, 2003). It is a nation of 7,107 islands, divided into 14 regions, 73 provinces, and 60 cities. The climate is tropical year-round with two distinct seasons: wet or rainy (June–October) and dry (November–May). Most of the islands consist of alluvial plains, valleys, hills, mountains, and irregular shoreline patterns. The country is divided into three major geographic island groups: 1) Luzon, the largest and one of the most northern islands (where Manila, the capital city is located); 2) the Visayas or central islands; and 3) Mindanao, the southernmost island (About the Phillippines, 2003).

The Philippines is one of the most ethnically diverse countries in Asia. Its rich, complex, and multicultural history has led others to misinterpret and depict Pilipinos as a people who are "without a culture" (V. Malabonga, personal communication, November 12, 2002).

> Not dominated by Confucian philosophy, oral in tradition, coming from societies that have matriarchal structures and bilateral kinship systems, intersected and invaded by seafarers, traders, military, missionaries, and colonizers, Filipinos of America are seldom accurately situated in history or culture and are therefore often misinterpreted. We share cultural affinities with people from Mexico, Central and South America, Cuba, and Puerto Rico because of Spain. We share shamanic and animistic traditions with indigenous peoples throughout the world. We share cultural patterns of communication with Japanese, Chinese, Vietnamese, and Koreans. An archipelago of Malayan people, our braiding of cultures and phenotypes creates affinities with Pacific Island people, who clearly are recipients of the African diaspora. A century of American contact provides Filipinos with a familiarity, if only in distorted images, of America and European American values. (Root, 1997, p xiii)

Historians and other social scientists have found evidence of thriving communities in what is now the Philippines, with strong cultural, trading, and economic bases, centuries before the arrival of the Spaniards in the early 16th century (Posadas, 1999). Anthropological findings in the Philippines suggest the presence of inhabitants as early as 24,000 B.C. (Jocano, 2001). Although there is a general belief that *Aetas* or *Negritos* were the original migrants to the Philippines (Bautista, 2002), anthropologists have rejected this theory (Jocano, 2001). In fact, more recent research findings suggest that other groups preceded the presence of Negritos and Aetas in the Philippines (Jocano, 2001). Evidence of the presence of Malays, Indonesians, East Indians, Arabs, Chinese, and other Eastern Asians inhabiting the islands have been dated 5,000–6,000 years prior to the 21st century (Bautista, 2002). Much of this migration was brought about by trade links with the country's Asian neighbors. The entry of various traders and settlers contributed to the enduring Hindu, Confucian, and Islamic influences that have profoundly affected the Pilipino culture and way of living. It has been purported that most Pilipinos are of Malay stock (Bautista, 2002; Gochenour, 1990; Winter, 1988). Noted anthropologists such as F. Landa Jocano dispute the attribution of Pilipino culture to the Malays, however. Jocano contended that, "Filipinos are products of evolutions and movements of people" (as cited in Bautista, 2002, p. 16). Malaysians and Indonesians formed cultural groups at the same time as Pilipinos and therefore could not have been the dominant culture or race. Finally, many contemporary Pilipinos trace their ancestry to other ethnic groups and nationalities including Chinese, Americans, Spaniards, East Indians, and Arabs.

History of Colonialism

In 1521, Ferdinand Magellan led a Spanish expedition to make the official European discovery of the archipelago that was later named the "Las Islas Filipinas" in honor of the Spanish prince who became Phillip II, King of Spain (Root, 1997; Winter, 1988). The Europeans imported "colonialism," the idea of owning a territory thousands of miles from home, inhabited by people culturally and racially different from themselves. Although "the Spaniards were never able to consolidate political control over the entire archipelago, with Muslims and indigenous [groups effectively] resisting the colonizers" (*A Brief History of the Philippines*, 2002), they established their control over many parts of the Philippines for 400 years. The imposition of a feudal system found many Pilipinos, who were then referred to as "indios" or natives, being reduced to landless peasant sharecroppers. The Catholic Church owned vast tracts of land and controlled the educational system (Karnow, 1989). Missionaries, government officials, and representatives of the Spanish empire thus imprinted on the Pilipino culture and consciousness some of its most enduring characteristics. Most of the population was converted to Hispanic Catholicism, and the visible aspects of culture (e.g., personal names, vocabulary, urban architecture, fine arts, dress, cuisine, customs) were profoundly influenced or modified (Harper & Fullerton, 1994; Posadas, 1999). Centuries of Spanish rule also imposed a severe colonial mentality, leaving Pilipinos with

> A legacy of attitudes that are firmly embedded in society: an equation of light skin with beauty and status, the identification of foreign with authority and indigenous with inferiority, and a conception of officialdom as a system serving its own ends, not those of the people. (Gochenour, 1990, p. 6)

From the beginning, Spaniards faced multiple and recurrent revolts led by Pilipinos. One of the early revolts recorded in history is the famous battle of Mactan led by Lapu-Lapu, the local chieftain who is purported to have slain Magellan in a bloody encounter between the Spanish colonizers and Pilipino soldiers (Posadas, 1999). Toward the end of the 19th century, reformers such as the martyred Dr. Jose M. Rizal, Andres Bonifacio, and many other Pilipino heroes continued laying down the foundation for independence, which eventually led to the Philippine Revolution at the close of the 19th century and the ultimate establishment of the first Philippine republican government (also the first of its kind in Asia). This government was short-lived, however. In the context of the Spanish-American War, American military forces arrived in Manila in 1898, first siding as allies of the Pilipinos against the Spanish. Although the Pilipinos were promised independence in return for their support in land battles against the Spanish, they were ultimately betrayed. Following the Spanish defeat, the Philippines was ceded to the United States at the Treaty of Paris for $20 million, together with Cuba and Puerto Rico. The Philippines became America's first and only colony (Harper & Fullerton, 1994). American leaders claimed that while they had not entered the war to gain territory, they did not believe that the Philippines was ready for independence (Winter, 1988). In later explaining how he had made the decision to approve the annexation of the Philippines, President William McKinley said he had gone down on his knees to pray for "light and guidance" from the "ruler of nations" and had been told by God that it was America's duty to "educate, uplift, and Christianize" the Pilipinos (despite the fact that Pilipinos had had educational, religious, and governmental systems established for centuries). He echoed the sentiments of American Protestant clergy leaders who sought to fulfill the "manifest destiny" of the Christian Republic through the conquest of Asia (Harper & Fullerton, 1994; Takaki, 1989).

The people of this new American possession were seen by their guardians as backward natives to be "civilized" by Americans seeking to carry the "white man's burden" (Takaki, 1989). Thus, the goal of annexation was based on an ideology of racial and religious supremacy that was further justified in terms of corresponding commercial and military gains. In response to this betrayal and seizure, Pilipinos continued their struggle for independence—this time against the United States. The ensuing Philippine-American War (1899–1902) was waged by the United States to overcome the so-called "Philippine Insurrection" (Bautista, 2002, p. 63). This bitter and bloody campaign required two thirds of the U.S. Army and resulted in the deaths of nearly 1 million Pilipinos (Bautista, 2002; Gochenour, 1990; Harper & Fullerton, 1994; Winter, 1988).

One form of colonialism replaced another. Americans, in the presumed spirit of white paternalism and benevolence, saw themselves as bestowers of education, religion, public health, development, and democracy to their "little brown brothers" (Bautista, 2002; Gochenour, 1990). In fact, the American educational system was adopted, and English (which children were required to speak in school) was made the official language (Kang, 1996). Thirty years later, the Philippines became self-governing, and the Tydings-McDuffie Act of 1934 promised complete independence by 1946. The country remained a territorial possession of the United States, however, which retained control over its economy and military forces.

World War II came abruptly to the Philippines. The Japanese attacked Manila within a few hours after Pearl Harbor and took over the country 5 months later. A million Pilipinos perished during the war, which also devastated the country and its economy. However, the ultimate Japanese surrender and close of World War II in 1945 brought the return of the exiled Philippine Commonwealth Government to Manila. With U.S. financial aid, it undertook the enormous task of reconstruction and rehabilitation. Moreover, the United States kept its promise and, on July 4, 1946, the Philippines was finally granted its long-sought independence and proclaimed the Republic of the Philippines (Harper & Fullerton, 1994; Winter, 1988).

A long history of external domination and influence remains potent in Pilipino life and thought. None of the attitudinal legacies of the Spanish were removed by 4 decades of U.S. rule. Yet, the pervasive Americanization of Pilipino culture also occurred as evidenced by the fact that, years after independence, Pilipino school children were still learning the American Pledge of Allegiance, and their education focused more on the United States than on neighboring countries in the Pacific. Two successive colonial eras led to the popular saying: The Pilipino character is a product of "350 years in a convent and 50 years in Hollywood" (Harper & Fullerton, 1994, p. 1). Contemporary Pilipino culture is thus a composite of foreign and indigenous elements, a mixture of Malay, Madrid, and Madison Avenue. "Neither history nor geography permitted the Filipinos time to consolidate their parochial and isolated strands into a culture integrated enough to repel outside pressures and influence" (Gochenour, 1990, p. 5). Throughout centuries of colonialism, Pilipinos have nevertheless avoided becoming "carbon copies" of their colonizers. They have pursued a dual historical path of understanding, accommodating to, placating, or opposing the overwhelming power foreigners have exercised in their lives while simultaneously preserving what is essentially Pilipino in themselves (Gochenour, 1990).

Waves of Immigration

Sufficient evidence now exists that Pilipinos have settled in various parts of the United States, including California and Louisiana as early as 1763, via passage in Spanish galleons that traveled between Acapulco and Manila (Posadas, 1999; Tamayo-Lott, 1997). Spaniards referred to these Pilipino people as indios, and later as Manilamen. However, there is also documentation of Pilipinos arriving in California in 1587 on the Spanish galleon, *Nuestra Señora de Buena Esperanza* (Bautista, 2002). They were part of a landing party that surveyed the area off the coast of Morro Bay. Several members of the landing party, including one of the eight Pilipino members of the crew, were wounded or killed in an altercation with the native Indians. This prompted the remaining crew to retreat. Thus, Bautista noted that the Pilipinos' "first presence in the United States was considered a visit, not a settlement" (2002, p. 108).

Similar to other Asian immigrants, Pilipinos have come to the United States in successive waves, and their patterns of immigration have reflected American economic and political policies. However, unlike the Chinese, Japanese, and Koreans, Pilipino migrants came from a territory of the United States. Despite the restrictions placed on the immigration of workers from other parts of Asia, Pilipinos migrated freely to the United States, protected by their colonial status as U.S. "nationals." Beginning in 1903, an early, relatively small group of Pilipino immigrants was thought to consist of *pensionados*—or students—who matriculated at major U.S. universities and returned to the Philippines to become social, political, and economic leaders (Agbayani-Siewert & Revilla, 1995; Posadas, 1999).

The indios and pensionados preceded the "first wave" of Pilipino immigrants who were brought into the United States in response to massive recruiting campaigns in the early 1900s by agricultural interests (particularly the sugar industry) primarily in Alaska, California, Hawaii, and Seattle. These immigrants consisted mainly of young, single, male contract laborers, Sakadas and Manongs, from the Ilocos region, which was experiencing growing poverty. Between 1906 and 1934, approximately 120,000 Pilipinos came to Hawaii and the west coast. Pilipinos were hired in large numbers to fill the void of cheap labor when Oriental exclusion policies and the passage of the Immigration Act of 1924 completely halted Chinese, Japanese, Korean, and Asian Indian immigration. While Pilipinos in Hawaii worked sugar plantations, the West Coast Pinoys (a term used by Pilipinos to distinguish themselves from Pilipinos living in the Philippines) were concentrated in three general types of work: agricultural "stoop" labor (particularly on large California farms), domestic and personal services, and the fishing and canning industries that extended from California to the Pacific Northwest and Alaska (Okamura & Agbayani, 1991; Posadas, 1999; Takaki, 1989; Tamayo-Lott, 1997; Winter, 1988).

Although enjoying protected status as U.S. nationals, Pilipinos were not immune from the racial discrimination that other Asian groups had traditionally experienced. Anti-Pilipino sentiment grew in proportion to their increasing numbers, and, as the Great Depression engulfed the nation, fear and hatred mounted. White-nativist reactions against Pilipinos were fueled by intensifying economic competition between white workers and Pilipino laborers. This ethnic hostility erupted into racial violence, including vigilante activity and a series of widely publicized race riots in California farming towns in 1929 and 1930. The extreme anti-Pilipino violence was further rooted in fears of sexual relationships developing between Pilipinos and whites. The refusal of Pilipino men to accept the color bar in their relationships with white women triggered resentment, anxieties, and underlying fear of their "threat to white racial purity." California's antimiscegenation law that prohibited marriage between whites and "Negroes, mulattoes, or Mongolians" thus was amended in 1933 to add people of the Malay race to the restricted category (12 other states had similar laws). Increasingly viewed as social "undesirables" with "offensive personality traits and behavior" (Okamura & Agbayani, 1991), Pilipinos nonetheless competed (sometimes all too successfully) for jobs and for white women (Posadas, 1986/1987). The exclusionist movement, led by organized labor, claimed that Pilipinos were biologically unassimilable, did not "belong," and should not be permitted to emigrate to the United States. However, the Pilipino "problem" had no easy solution. A repatriation scheme at the height of the Depression failed, and national immigration restriction and West Coast antimiscegenation laws promised only limited control.

Finally, in 1934, the Tydings-McDuffie Act closed the door to Pilipino immigration by reclassifying all Philippine-born Pilipinos as aliens and limiting their immigration to 50 people per year (Agbayani-Siewert & Revilla, 1995). Although ostensibly passed in order to establish the Philippines as a commonwealth and to provide independence in 10 years, some believe that the real purpose of the act was Pilipino exclusion. A year later, Congress responded to the demands of exclusionists and passed the Repatriation Act; this law offered Pilipinos free one-way transportation to the Philippines on the condition that they forfeit their right of reentry to the United States. Thus, originally allowed to enter the United States to serve as "cheap labor," Pilipino migrants had completed their "period of service to American capital" and were no longer wanted because of their labor militancy or needed because of the availability of Mexican labor (Takaki, 1989, p. 333). But most of the Pilipino sojourners (who originally did not see America as a place to bring families and to settle) did not return to the Philippines. Racial prejudice, social isolation, and persecution minimized the old-timers' (or first-generation Manongs) chances for acculturation and resulted in their retention of traditional Pilipino culture as they struggled for survival in America (Santos, 1983). Their "real" story was later chronicled with great detail and sensitivity in the writings of Carlos Bulosan (1911–1956), who drew deeply from his own experiences and those of fellow Pilipinos to give his compatriots a voice.

Following the passage of the Tydings-McDuffie Act in 1934, emigration from the Philippines to the United States dropped to a mere trickle. The "second wave" of Pilipino immigrants occurred between 1946 and 1964. During World War II, thousands of Pilipino nationals were "permitted" to serve in the armed forces or to work in defense factories. Through their often-heroic deeds, contributions, and profound sacrifices to the war effort (more than half of the 200,000 Pilipinos who served in World War II were killed), Pilipinos proved their loyalty to the United States, despite years of discrimination and violence. A corresponding positive change in American attitudes toward Pilipinos resulted in new policies, laws, and rulings that gave resident Pilipinos the right to own property and to become citizens and declared antimiscegenation laws unconstitutional. The passage of the War Brides Act of 1946 allowed those who had served in the U.S. armed forces in the Philippines and who had married there—including resident Pilipino servicemen—to bring their wives, children, and dependents to the United States. As military "push and pull" forces contributed to this second wave of Pilipino immigration, new employment opportunities opened up in areas such as aircraft, electronics, and chemical industries. The newer immigrants, unlike the first wave of Pilipino immigrants during the pre-World War II era who were largely agricultural laborers, were beginning to find jobs as clerks and accountants as well as in many other fields formerly closed to them (Winter, 1988).

The third wave of Pilipino immigrants began with the 1965 U.S. immigration reform, which eliminated the restrictive national-origins quota system and dramatically increased the number of immigrants admitted from Asia as a whole. The new law favored the entry of people employed as professionals and also the relatives of people already living in the United States. With regard to the former group, one major consequence of the 1965 amendments has been the "brain drain" from the Philippines—the emigration of individuals with professional and technical qualifications. In 1970, for example, nearly half of all Pilipino immigrants were professionals (including scientists, engineers, attorneys, accountants, teachers, physicians, nurses, and pharmacists). Facilitated by an educational system that reflects American modes of learning, programs, practices, and priorities, the country was producing college graduates much faster than a primarily agriculturally based economy could absorb them (Morales, 1974; Pernia, 1976). Some have argued that this professional emigration represents lost educational investment; the Philippines bears the cost of educating this highly skilled labor but does not directly benefit from it (Cariño, 1987). While the brain drain from the Philippines has been considerably reduced since the 1970s, large numbers of highly educated young adults and professionals have continued to emigrate to the United States in search of better employment opportunities. In fact, nearly half of the Pilipino immigrants to the United States from 1985 to 1990 were college graduates (Agbayani-Siewert & Revilla, 1995).

The U.S. military presence in the Philippines has been yet another contributing factor to the mass exodus of Pilipinos. Since 1970, nearly 200,000 Pilipino women have immigrated to the United States as wives of U.S. citizens and servicemen stationed in the Philippines (Liu, Ong, & Rosenstein, 1991). Since the U.S. air and naval bases in the Philippines were closed in January 1992, immigration through intermarriage has significantly declined (Agbayani-Siewert & Revilla, 1995).

The "third wave," made up of post-1965 Pilipino "newcomers," include immigrants dating to the present time; however, a fourth wave of emigrants fled the Philippines as political exiles and refugees during the martial law era from 1972 to 1982. During this period, Ferdinand E. Marcos (originally elected president of the Philippines in 1965) began to rule by decree after the Congress was dissolved, the constitution was revoked, and opposition leaders were arrested. Under a new constitution, Marcos retained absolute power to act as both president and prime minister for an unlimited time. Among those who ultimately left the Philippines to live in self-imposed exile in the United States was former senator Benigno Aquino, Jr., leader of the increasingly popular "People's Power" party and Marcos's most important political opponent (Winter, 1988). Aquino's momentous return to the Philippines on August 21, 1983, and his immediate assassination on deplaning at the Manila airport accelerated the anti-Marcos movement from one that had long been supported and promoted by Pilipino American activists and fourth-wave political exiles/refugees. These groups were instrumental in alerting the American public to the mounting atrocities committed by the Marcos regime and years of dictatorial abuse and misrule. Thus, when Corazon "Cory" Aquino, the slain senator's widow, announced her candidacy for president in a "snap election" (which Marcos had hastily called to appease U.S. supporters), she effectively unleashed the "People's Power" movement (Bello & Reyes, 1986/1987). Marcos' subsequent "official" victory was a result of massive election fraud, which resulted in the United States switching its support to Cory Aquino. A rapid but remarkably peaceful revolution and transition of power followed the change in U.S. policy. After 20 years of rule, Marcos was finally ousted, with him and his family being shuttled to Hawaii by the American government. Immediately after his departure, Cory Aquino was installed as the first woman president of the Philippines in March 1986. Marcos later died in exile in Hawaii.

The "people's victory" and President Aquino's new leadership offered the promise of democratic reform. After assuming the presidency, Cory Aquino immediately restored the rights of free speech and a free press, released 500 political prisoners (including Communist party leaders), replaced the constitution as well as numerous political leaders who were Marcos loyalists, and retired more than half of the country's generals. However, insurgency and recurring threats of military coups persisted throughout her presidency; in fact, she survived six coup attempts to unseat her. In 1992, the "age of Aquino" peacefully transitioned to the election of a new president, retired general Fidel Ramos, one of the leaders during the "People's Power" revolution (Harper & Fullerton, 1994). Ramos was followed by actor-turned-politician Joseph E. Estrada in 1998 (Posadas, 1999). In 2001, three years into his presidency, Estrada was ousted by a "People's Power II" amidst allegations of widespread corruption. He was later arrested and charged for allegedly engaging in illegal gambling schemes, bribery, and misuse of power. In January 2001 (at the same time that George W. Bush was inaugurated the 43rd President of the United States), duly elected Vice-President Gloria Macapagal-Arroyo was sworn into power as the Philippines' second female President. Macapagal-Arroyo is the daughter of former President Diosdado Macapagal (1961–1965).

The restoration of democracy in the Philippines since the mid-1980s has been severely challenged by continued political unrest and instability. The country continues to be plagued by severe and persistent social and economic problems: runaway population growth and increasing density and scarcity of land; rampant inflation, unemployment, and widespread poverty; and huge foreign debt and domination by foreign capital (Cariño, 1987; Steinberg, 1994). These "push" conditions have contributed to the "Philippine diaspora," a term used to describe large-scale migration of Pilipinos to the United States and other countries (Posadas, 1999; San Juan, 1998).

After September 11, 2001, the ongoing relationship between the Philippines and the United States is once again characterized by the presence of American military troops assisting the Philippine military in Mindanao. This is in response to reported links between members of Muslim rebel groups in the southern island to an international terrorist network. At the time this book was published in 2004, the effects of the United States's efforts to change its immigration and naturalization laws had yet to be realized. Thus, while the future of the Philippines remains uncertain, continued mass emigration to the United States and other countries is inevitable.

Religious Origins

The Philippines is the only nation in Asia that is predominantly Christian. As a result of being ruled by Spain for more than 400 years, approximately 85% of the Pilipino population in the Philippines is Roman Catholic (Winter, 1988). "During centuries of Spanish colonialism, Catholicism was the only acceptable faith, and its teachings, vocabulary, and practices left an indelible stamp upon Filipino consciousness" (Gochenour, 1990, p. 34). The American occupation also brought Protestantism to the

Philippines. Today, Pilipinos exhibit a growing interest in various evangelical and charismatic movements. Thus, whereas 3% of the population is Protestant, 6% belong to indigenous Christian cults, including the Iglesia Filipina Independiente (the Philippine Independent [or Aglipayan] Church) and the Iglesia ni Kristo (Church of Christ), an independent offshoot of the Catholic church (Brigham Young University [BYU], 1986; Gochenour, 1990; Steinberg, 1994). "The country has many other sects, cults, and revivalist movements, usually centered on a charismatic leader offering followers, who are typically poor and underprivileged, a sense of fraternity and promises of a new utopia" (Harper & Fullerton, 1994, p. 61).

As a result of contact with Arab and other Muslim traders who frequented the southern part of the archipelagos during the 14th and 15th centuries, Islam was a growing presence in the Philippines before the arrival of the Spanish. However, "the further spread and influence of Islam were cut short by the conquest and colonization of the Philippines" (Bautista, 2002, p. 18). Today, Islam is a significant minority religion that is predominant in much of the southern island of Mindanao. Approximately 5% of the Pilipinos are Muslims (also called Moros). The historical tension and continuing hostility between Christians and Muslims has been intractable. Faction groups have maintained a separatist movement and a guerilla war of national liberation against the Philippine government that alternates between explosiveness and quiescence (BYU, 1986; Gochenour, 1990; Steinberg, 1994).

A relatively small percentage of the Philippine population (who are predominantly ethnic Chinese) follow Buddhism and Taoism. Their temples are found in cities with large Chinese populations, such as Manila and Cebu. Buddhism has been blended with Catholicism to some extent as is evidenced by various icons and festivals that are characterized by elements of both religions. In remote areas, rural indigenous tribespeople maintain many aspects of their traditional religions, folk beliefs, and practices that preceded Spanish colonial rule and include ancestor worship, animism, and shamanism. Certain "mystical" places on various islands also are known for their sacred, supernatural power and reputation for witchcraft and sorcery; they are reportedly inhabited by numerous esoteric sects and hermits (Harper & Fullerton, 1994).

A great many Pilipinos may be followers of Roman Catholicism, but they are typically not dogmatic and still may practice ancient rituals. In fact, Pilipino people are known to blend folk beliefs with Christian practices imposed on them through a history of conquest and colonialism. Similar to many other Asian ethnic groups, Pilipinos thus may assume a polytheistic orientation in which Christianity, Islam, and Buddhism intermingle with the local traditions of peasant belief (Steinberg, 1994).

Language/Linguistic Origins

Throughout the 7,107-island archipelagos, Pilipinos speak 154 languages (Filipino Family, 2002). The three most common languages are Tagalog (central and southern Luzon); Ilocano (northern Luzon); and Cebuano (southern islands) (BYU, 1986; Roseberry-McKibbin, 1997). Linguistically, Pilipino languages are historically related; they derive from "Original Indonesian" as a subfamily of the Austronesian or Malayo-Polynesian languages and share most of their basic grammatical features (Harper & Fullerton, 1994; Li, 1983; Roseberry-McKibbin, 1997). Despite their similarities in grammar and pronunciation, centuries of isolation have produced distinct and mutually unintelligible native languages (Gochenour, 1990).

For a period of time during the Marcos regime, a popular movement existed to establish and mandate the use of a national language called "Pilipino." Pilipino is primarily Tagalog, the language spoken by a minority of people in the Manila region. It is highly structured grammatically and has a rich vocabulary, with words invented or borrowed from Spanish, English, and other native dialects. More than half of the population understand Pilipino (Harper & Fullerton, 1994). Because of its main basis in Tagalog, however, Pilipino has never gained full acceptance by speakers of other languages, although it is a required subject of study in schools throughout the islands and is used as a language of business along with English and Chinese (BYU, 1986; Gochenour, 1990).

With so many languages, English has in many cases, served as a unifying language. In fact, the Philippines has the third-largest English-speaking population in the world, after the United States and the United Kingdom (BYU, 1986). Since the arrival of the first American teachers in the early 1900s (referred to as the Thomasites, named for the ship that brought them from the United States to the Philippines), English has been taught in the majority of the schools. It is also considered the de facto national language of business, commerce, law, government, and often the mass media and popular entertainment. It is the language of the elite who have status, wealth, and authority. The power of English and its selective usage is exemplified in the Pilipino home environment, particularly in middle- and upper-class homes. Members of a Pilipino family may speak to one another in their particular language, with an added sprinkling of English words. For example, in many daily conversations, English and Tagalog may be combined (referred to as Taglish) such as, "Hoy, don't go over there, baka madapa ka. Be careful!" ("Hey, don't go over there, you might trip and fall. Be careful!"). Parents sometimes use English when disciplining their children; for example, a father, when admonishing a child, may summon up a tone of authority by employing a few English words or shifting entirely into English. Similarly, educated Pilipino friends may typically converse in their language but gradually shift into English if the subject becomes technical or especially serious. This shifting may be related to vocabulary, but it also reflects the way some Pilipinos may feel about the language. "Things may be easier to say in English, or the use of English may serve to emphasize the importance of the topic. The speakers may feel that they can be more precise in English or that English is less personal and not as potentially threatening" (Gochenour, 1990, p. 38); however, other factors may also influence language shifting such as one's fluency in any of the languages.

English in the Philippines often contains a mixture of indigenous language elements. A Pilipino individual's first language significantly influences his or her accent, intonation, vocabulary, syntax, and idiomatic expressions when he or she speaks English (Santos, 1983). The phonological systems of the various languages also are a factor. For example, because Tagalog distinguishes more vowel sounds than do other languages, some Pilipinos may find it easier to make the distinction in English between, say, "bit" and "bet" than would someone who speaks a Philippine language other than Tagalog. In addition, several English sounds are not found in Philippine languages, such as /f/ which is often substituted with /p/ (face—pays), /th/ with /d/ (that—dat), or /a/ with /o/ (Paul—Poll) (Roseberry-McKibbin, 1997).

Indigenous Philippine languages are prepositional, verb-initial (i.e., basic sentences have their verbs in the sentence-initial position), and regularly stress the next-to-last syllable in most words (Li, 1983). Like many other Asian languages, they also have a single word for the gender pronouns "he" and "she." Apart from grammatical and phonological characteristics, it is noteworthy that Chabacano (a local language spoken in the area around the city of Zamboanga in Mindanao) is heavily mixed with Spanish. Other Pilipinos know a fair number of Spanish words that have entered their particular regional languages, and many Pilipino people and places have Spanish names. As a functional language, however, Spanish is clearly peripheral, and a relatively small number of Pilipinos (primarily Spanish-Pilipino *mestizos*) speak it fluently (particularly because it was used exclusively by the wealthy, land-owning families during the period of Spanish rule, and no more than 10% of the population ever spoke it). In fact, despite nearly four centuries of Spanish dominion, the Philippines is one of the few former colonies of Spain in which Spanish did not become the national language (Gochenour, 1990; Harper & Fullerton, 1994; Winter, 1988).

The Philippines is regarded as the only nation in Asia that is predominantly English speaking, and Pilipinos often are assumed to be fully proficient in the English language, with "90% of Filipino-American students . . . designated as Fluent English Proficient" (Roseberry-McKibbin, 1997, p. 5). Roseberry-McKibbin warned, however, of a significant range of proficiency, in English and Tagalog or other languages, experienced by Pilipino Americans born in the United States and those who immigrated to the United States. Nevertheless, the following discussion serves to illustrate the reality of an extremely multilingual country in which English is a second language. It also offers cautions and considerations regarding the dynamics of communication with English-speaking Pilipinos.

CONTEMPORARY LIFE

Pilipino Americans are the third-fastest growing ethnic group in the United States, with a population of 2.4 million in 2001, approximately half of whom were born in the Philippines (U.S. Bureau of the Census, 2002a). These figures often do not include undocumented immigrants, overstaying tourists and students, and Pilipinos serving in the U.S. Navy (San Juan, 1998). Root described Pilipino Americans as "immigrants—now citizens, American born, immigrant spouses awaiting eligibility for green cards, mixed-heritage Filipinos, students or workers on visas, tago ng tago (undocumented), and transnationals moving between the Philippines and the United States" (1997, p. xiv).

According to The National Data Book (2001), well over two thirds of the Pilipino American population is concentrated in the west coast (67.7%) of the United States, with the rest living in the south (13.2%), northeast (10.9%), and midwest (8.2%). The Pilipino American population is primarily urban, with the greatest concentrations in cities and metropolitan areas such as Los Angeles/Long Beach; San Francisco/Oakland; Honolulu; New York; Chicago; Washington, D.C.; Seattle; San Diego; and Stockton and San Jose, California (U.S. Bureau of the Census, 1993). The 2000 data on the Asian population living in the United States reflect a similar geographic pattern, with most living in New York, Los Angeles, Chicago, Houston, Philadelphia, Phoenix, San Diego, Dallas, San Antonio, and Detroit (U.S. Bureau of the Census, 2002b).

Although Pilipino Americans are highly concentrated in the west coast, they have not established easily recognized ethnic enclaves comparable to the Chinese, Korean, and selected Southeast Asian populations. Gudykunst (2001) wrote that prior to the post-1965 immigrants, more distinct Pilipino enclaves existed that promoted and supported Pilipino resources, such as stores that sold Philippine products and community groups that held various activities brought from the homeland (e.g., beauty pageants, picnics). In more recent years, no consistent pattern of residential clustering has emerged. It has been argued that generally, Pilipinos tend to assimilate into the American mainstream quickly, primarily because they are typically of well-educated and professional backgrounds, have good command of the English language, and are familiar with American culture through the U.S. influence on the Philippines. However, Cimmarusti pointed out that "the stereotype that Filipinos are well assimilated into American culture has colluded with aspects of the Filipino culture that, in my opinion have been both misunderstood and misapplied and have lead to making Filipinos an invisible Asian minority" (1996, p. 206). As a result of prior and ongoing emigration to the United States, as mentioned previously, half of the Pilipino American population is foreign born. Further reflecting their substantial immigrant numbers is the fact that more than 70% of Pilipinos (ages 5 years and older) speak a language other than English at home (U.S. Bureau of the Census, 1993). However, the vast majority of Pilipinos age 15 years and older are American citizens, and various sources of social support for Pilipinos are available, including organizations and groups based on one's linguistic group, birthplace in the homeland, religious affiliation, and high school and college or university alumni associations (Gudykunst, 2001; Posadas, 1999).

With regard to employment and socioeconomic status, Pilipino Americans are among the highest ranked Asian American groups. A majority of Pilipinos are employed in technical, sales, and administrative support work and as managers and professionals (Posadas, 1999; Lott, 1997). The educational attainment of Pilipino Americans is relatively high. Foreign-born Pilipinos are much more highly educated than their U.S.-born counterparts and are the most highly educated Asian ethnic group (Agbayani-Siewert & Revilla, 1995; Lott, 1997). This "in part reflects the immigration of Filipino health professionals, particularly nurses" (Lott, 1997, p. 17). Pilipinos also are unique among Asian Americans in having a greater proportion of female than male high school and college graduates. These characteristics are consistent with the fact that the Pilipino immigrant population includes more women and more people with generally superior educational qualifications and occupational experience than those of the population of the Philippines (Cariño, Fawcett, Gardner, & Arnold, 1990).

The preceding review of social, economic, and educational characteristics of the Pilipino American population indicates that they compare very favorably with other Asian American groups as well as with national medians and rates. If adjustments are made for factors such as years of work experience, education, and generation, however, then the per capita income (versus family income) for Pilipino Americans is considerably less than their U.S.-born counterparts and most other Asian groups. This is, in part, a result of Pilipino American families having larger families and a greater number of workers per household (Lott, 1997). Pilipino Americans also are underrepresented in professional and managerial positions and must confront persistent conditions of underemployment and "glass ceilings" (Agbayani-Siewert & Revilla, 1995; Suzuki, 1989). A particularly well-known and well-documented aspect of this phenomenon is that many Pilipino medical and health care professionals remain unlicensed and work in jobs that are either totally unrelated to their training and education or considerably below their former positions in the Philippines (Takaki, 1989). In addition to this pattern of occupational downgrading, there also are substantial differences in socioeconomic status among Pilipinos in the various states. Pilipinos in Hawaii, for example, are one of the most economically disadvantaged and have the lowest educational attainment of any of the major ethnic groups (Okamura & Agbayani, 1991).

Third- or fourth-wave, post-1965 Pilipino immigrants are thus vulnerable to related social and psychological problems. The experience of downward occupational mobility, for example, results in considerable loss of self-esteem, disappointment, frustration, and possible depression. Many Pilipino professionals who come to the United States in search of better economic opportunities are often shocked to learn that their previous education and employment experiences are not legitimately valued or even recognized; they must confront the feeling of failure on being rejected for positions they thought they were qualified to hold (Okamura & Agbayani, 1991; Posadas, 1999). Many miss the psychological benefits of higher status, social privileges, and greater respect and recognition that they enjoyed in the Philippines, even though the financial compensation for their work was inadequate. Pilipino immigrants from the upper echelons of Philippine society may have to confront the American reality that specific family names associated with high social status in their native country are common Spanish surnames that may translate into "second-class" citizenship (Santos, 1983).

The problems associated with loss of ascribed status, social dislocation, and employment discrimination are often compounded by family stress and generational conflicts. The cultural discontinuities experienced by most immigrant families may also contribute to a weakening of extended family ties, loss of parental authority and credibility, and increasing youth alienation. The continuing clashes and reconciliation between Pilipino values brought from the "home" country and those of the "host" society are discussed in detail in the following section.

VALUES

Traditional Pilipino values pertaining to family, authority, and harmony reflect collectivist values characteristic of many Asian cultures. However, descriptions of "surface" versus "core" values indicate contrast, complexity, and possible stereotypic portrayals of the Pilipino character in literature. The authors thus caution readers that the values described in this chapter are based on anecdotal information, observations, theories, and derivations from linguistic analyses of words for Pilipino values. Moreover, traditional Pilipino customs serve multiple functions in the lives of Pilipino Americans by "simultaneously preserving, reinterpreting, and reinventing Philippine cultural elements into the redefined varied identity that is [Pilipino] American" (Posadas, 1999, p. 45). A more detailed examination of the values, customs, and beliefs of Pilipinos within the context of modern American society follows.

Family

With regard to the Pilipino focus on family life, Gouchenour stated, "To understand Pilipino Americans is to accept the complete centrality of the family and that means the extended family, including several generations" (1990, p. 18). Posadas noted, "Deeply rooted in culture and religion, Filipino values and customs emphasize respect for, loyalty to, and dependence upon the family" (1999, p. 45).

In 1990, the average Pilipino American family was composed of four individuals. The majority (78%) were headed by married couples, whereas approximately

16% were headed by females (Lott, 1997). However, these numbers must be considered within the context of how most Pilipinos define *family*. For the majority of Pilipinos, family includes extended family members from both the father's and the mother's sides (Cimmarusti, 1996; Salvador, Omizo, & Kim, 1997). Cimmarusti noted that Pilipino families tend to expand with marriage and baptism by "adding" godparents or wedding sponsors (described in more detail later in the chapter). For many immigrants, literal physical distance from their family members does not necessarily diminish the influence they may have on how they live their lives in the new country. For example, it is not uncommon for family members living in the home country to impart advice to those living in the new country, especially when making life-changing decisions. Often, family members living in the new country may seek advice from family living "at home" before making decisions regarding finances, marriage, and other things of this nature.

> No other single aspect of life is likely to be as important, lasting or influential on choices and decisions from childhood to old age. . . . [The typical Pilipino individual] exists first and foremost as a member of a family and looks to the family . . . [a] reliable protection against the uncertainties of life. (Gochenour, 1990, p. 18)

For Pilipino Americans, reliance on the family for love, support, and refuge has historically been as much an economic necessity as it is a cultural tradition. For some Pilipino Americans, the extended family also serves as a safety net and welfare system. However, the Pilipino relationship to family is not just a practical trade-off of autonomy for social security. It transcends socioeconomic, educational, and regional differences and is part of an orientation or way of perceiving the place of the individual in the social context (Cimmarusti, 1996; Gochenour, 1990; Santos, 1983). For many Pilipinos, the family is the source of one's personal identity and of emotional and material support; it also is the focus of one's primary duty and commitment (Cimmarusti, 1996; Posadas, 1999; Salvador et al., 1997).

Concern for the welfare of the family is expressed in the honor and respect bestowed on parents and older relatives, the care provided to children, and the individual sacrifices that are made on behalf of family members (Okamura & Agbayani, 1991). A primary focus on the needs of family members may translate into behaviors such as considerable sharing of material things. Pilipinos living in the United States will routinely send money, clothes, household goods, and other items as well as bring many gifts on personal visits to extended family members "left behind" in the Philippines. (In fact, the vast majority of Pilipino Americans [particularly the most recent immigrants] send large sums of money back home to their kin; these "remittance dollars" add up to billions a year and are the biggest source of hard currency in the Philippines [Schoenberger, 1994].)

The sense of family obligation begins early on when children are raised and enculturated to bear in mind the sacrifices their parents have made to give them a "better" life. Thus, they experience a lifelong debt of gratitude or *utang na loob* ("profound indebtedness"), which serves to further strengthen binding relationships of love, loyalty, respect, and obedience (Posadas, 1999). This value "rests on the premise that doing good begets reward, and if someone does you a kindness [sic], then you are obliged to repay the kindness" (Cimmarusti, 1996, p. 210). Repayment comes in many forms, ranging from giving gifts or favors to being included in the family as a godparent (Cimmarusti, 1996). "The failure to repay this moral obligation is considered extremely shameful and disrespectful" (Salvador et al., 1997, p. 205).

Authority

"Traditional Pilipino families and other social systems are usually highly authoritarian. Age, power, prestige, and wealth are the chief sources of authority" (Santos, 1983, p. 140). However, others argue that this authority does not "imply blind authoritarianism" (Cimmarusti, 1996, p. 207). Within the family, age determines a hierarchical system of authority that flows downward from oldest to youngest. Outside the family, other factors such as social class, professional status or official government affiliation, and ecclesiastical positions may supersede age as determining factors in the locus of authority.

The relationship between those in authority and those subject to it is further permeated by a debt of gratitude. Authority figures enjoy many privileges and prerogatives, such as obedience, respect, adulation, and gifts in the form of money, material items, and personal services. These gifts are given to seek or return favors or to acknowledge a person's position of authority (Cimmarusti, 1996; Santos, 1983). Those in authority must, in turn, ensure that this reciprocity is created in a socially acceptable manner; one that conveys mutual respect and achieves the overall objective of maintaining group harmony. The appearance of subservience to parents, elders, leaders, and officials may also be interpreted as deference in return for support and assistance (Harper & Fullerton, 1994).

Throughout this ongoing exchange process, the accent is on the personalized aspect of the relationship. *Tiwala* (trust) is a key element of camaraderie. Pilipinos perceive authority to be ultimately personal and thus subject to influence, affiliation, and patronage. The corresponding presumption is that whatever the law or the rules might say, someone in authority is making decisions based on personal motivations. The authority that allows some avenue of communication is presumably more trustworthy. In essence, within the larger social context, authority typically may be viewed as something to be dealt with personally as best one can by alternately placating it, keeping it at a distance, or using it to one's advantage when possible.

Among family and friends, Pilipinos may seek consensus prior to taking any action. The preference is for decision making within the group or for solicitation of advice from someone senior. When personal decisions must be made, the individual often feels a need to have further confirmation. The Pilipinos' tendency to enlist the opinions of others is again consistent with a more collectivist orientation and primary affiliation with the groups or contexts in which they live; these include family, neighbors, the *barkada* (peers), work associates, and other larger loyalties and identifications. Pilipinos are defined by—and linked to—the identity of groups to which they belong and their shared past experiences (Gochenour, 1990; Posadas, 1999). This also translates into a communal spirit (*bayanihan*) that enables Pilipino Americans to come together and help each other (Harper & Fullerton, 1994; Posadas, 1999).

Harmony

Group identity or the value of community life is reinforced through the creation and maintenance of sustained, secure interpersonal relationships and a system of support and cooperation among group members (Burgonio-Watson, 1997). The goal of preserving harmony between individuals, among family members, and among the groups and divisions of society is embodied in the sense of *kapwa*, which permeates and guides the daily lives and behaviors of Pilipinos (Salvador et al., 1997). Enriquez defined *kapwa* as "a recognition of shared identity, an inner self shared with others" (cited in Salvador et al., 1997, p. 202). This recognition of equivalence with others ("Hindi ako iba sa aking kapwa" [I am no different from my fellow man], Salvador et al., 1997, p. 202) serves as the basis for the values around developing and maintaining harmonious relationships with others. These values have continued to be reported in the literature since the 1960s.

Several well-known studies conducted at that time focused on the concepts of *pakikisama, hiya, amor propio,* and *utang na loob. Pakikisama* (group solidarity) represents both a value and a goal that consists of maintaining good feelings in all personal interactions and getting along with others at all costs (Salvador et al., 1997). Achieving smooth interpersonal relationships may take precedence over clear communication and the accomplishment of a particular task. To avoid open displays of conflict and stressful confrontations, Pilipinos may yield to group opinion (even if it contradicts their own desires), lavish extravagant praise on one another, use metaphorical language rather than frank terms, hide negative feelings or depressed spirits beneath a pleasant demeanor, smile when things go wrong, avoid saying "no," and refrain from expressing anger or losing their temper (Cimmarusti, 1996; Guthrie, 1968; Harper & Fullerton, 1994).

Pakikisama also is pursued by showing sensitivity to *hiya* and *amor propio. Hiya,* although commonly translated as "shame," has been further described as a feeling of "inferiority, embarrassment, shyness, and alienation which is experienced as acutely distressing" (Guthrie, 1968, p. 62). It is integrally related to the concept of "face" and a preoccupation with how one appears in the eyes of others. *Hiya* is inculcated as a necessary part of a child's development and used as a means to shape approved or desired behaviors (Llamanzares, 1999). Thus, an individual's capacity for appropriate behavior with authority figures is a reflection of one's family and upbringing and the fear of "losing face" (Pan Asian Parent Education Project, 1982). Salvador and colleagues noted that *hiya* "is one of the more powerful sanctions operating to maintain the overall system of social relationships" (1997, p. 204).

This profound concern for "face" further derives from the value of *amor propio* (self-pride). Although literally translated as "self-respect" or "self-esteem," *amor propio* has been characterized as "the high degree of sensitivity that makes a person intolerant to criticism and causes him to have an easily wounded pride" (Union of Pan Asian Communities [UPAC], 1980, p. 42). Pilipinos learn to withstand a "loss of face" in some situations, particularly when they perceive themselves to be at fault, but it is devastating to be publicly criticized, insulted, belittled, or humiliated, or to lose one's self-respect. It thus becomes essential to behave in ways that will ensure that everyone's "face" and *amor propio* are not threatened (Cimmarusti, 1996; Gochenour, 1990; Posadas, 1999; Salvador et al., 1997).

The previously described value of *utang na loob* also is an integral aspect of maintaining group harmony and relationships that require the balancing of obligations and debts. *Utang na loob* binds the individuals involved more closely, in contrast to the typically Western orientation in which the discharge of a personal obligation tends to liberate or release the individual to go on being him- or herself (Gochenour, 1990). As one of the most important facets in the lives of Pilipino Americans, group acceptance is contingent on loyalty and devotion. The services of friendship are thus always reciprocal and safeguarded by these value systems (Posadas, 1999; UPAC, 1980).

Alternative Concepts and Other Values

Critics of the 1960s values studies maintain that concepts such as *pakikisama, hiya, amor propio,* and *utang na loob* have been inappropriately generalized from vernacular terms associated with specific behaviors and situations into all-pervading, organizing values and trait complexes (Lawless, 1969). They have been perceived as a central core of fundamental culture traits that create and define an almost stereotypic Pilipino character and have been accepted as valid by scholars, foreigners, and Pilipinos in general (Okamura & Agbayani, 1991). As one of the most outspoken critics of studies of Philippine values, Enriquez argued that most of these studies (which were presented in English) employ "the colonizer's perspective and colonial language," rather than making use of indigenous concepts available in native Philippine languages. Thus, "the organization and logic of the value system" from a Pilipino perspective is lacking. He further contended that the four values described in the literature represent only "surface values" that derive their significance from the "core" value of *kapwa* (shared identity) (1987, p. 30).

Studies of Pilipino values have focused on significantly less abstract concepts. A Philippine Senate–commissioned task force conducted one of the most comprehensive studies of Pilipino character traits and values in 1988. The study identified the following major strengths of the Pilipino character: *pakikipagkapwa-tao* (having a regard for the dignity and being of others), family orientation, joy and humor, flexibility, adaptability and creativity, hard work and industry, faith and religiosity, and ability to survive (Licuanan, 1988). Each of these characteristics was summarized by Okamura and Agbayani (1991) and has been consistently identified by Church (1986) in a review of other studies on Pilipino personality values or ideals.

Pakikipagkapwa-tao is manifested among Pilipinos in their basic sense of justice and fairness and concern for others' well-being. Pilipinos recognize the essential humanity of all people and regard others with respect and empathy. This orientation instills a heightened sensitivity to the nature and quality of interpersonal relationships, which are the principal source of security and happiness. The related family orientation and interdependence among Pilipinos was previously detailed.

Pilipinos' sense of joy and humor is evident in their optimistic approach to life and its travails. The ability to laugh at themselves and their predicament is an important coping mechanism that contributes to emotional balance and a capacity to survive. This characteristic is complemented by Pilipino flexibility, adaptability, and creativity, which are manifested in the ability to adjust to circumstances and prevailing physical and social environments that are often difficult. Pilipinos have a high tolerance for ambiguity, which enables them to respond calmly to uncertainty or lack of information. As resourceful, creative, fast learners, Pilipinos often improvise and make productive and innovative use of whatever is available. These qualities have been repeatedly demonstrated in their capacity to adapt to living in any part of the world and in their ability to accept change (Okamura & Agbayani, 1991).

The related capacity for hard work and industry among Pilipinos is widely recognized. Pilipinos are universally regarded as excellent workers who perform well whether the job involves physical labor and tasks or highly sophisticated technical functions. This propensity for hard work, which often includes a highly competitive spirit, is driven by the desire for economic security and advancement for oneself and one's family. This achievement orientation is further accompanied by typically high aspirations and great personal sacrifices.

Each of these characteristics strengthens a Pilipino individual's ability to survive and endure despite difficult times and often little resources. Moreover, these characteristics cluster around distinctly religious beliefs and a deep faith in God. This faith is evident in Pilipinos' ability to accept reality (including failure and defeat) in terms of God's will and to adopt a philosophical/religious attitude that cushions them from disappointments. Pilipino faith is related to the concept of *bahala na* ("It's up to God" or "Leave it to God"), which has tended to be incorrectly equated with an expression of fatalism and a passive acceptance or resignation to fate. *Bahala na* can instead be viewed more positively as determination in the face of uncertainty or stressful, problematic conditions. This faith helps individuals relax, especially if one strongly believes that ultimately everything is in God's hands. Although it is an indication of an acceptance of the nature of things, including one's own inherent limitations, *bahala na* operates psychologically to elevate one's courage and conviction to persist in the face of adversity and to improve one's situation (Enriquez, 1987; Okamura & Agbayani, 1991); in essence, it serves as a healthy coping mechanism.

Apart from the more fundamental Pilipino personality characteristics and values are those related to physical appearance. As briefly noted at the outset of the chapter, centuries of Spanish and American colonial rule reinforced the Pilipino tendency to equate light complexion with high social status. "White" meant everything associated with the ruling classes: worth, beauty, desirability, and power. The lighter skinned Pilipino usually has either Chinese or Spanish blood in the family line; having Spanish ancestors is likely to be a point of pride (Gochenour, 1990). Similarly, for many Pilipino Americans, white Americans constitute a very powerful reference group. Many may not only equate light complexion with being beautiful or handsome, but also may think that to be American is to be white. This perception or value is often transmitted to the children, unfortunately, and may contribute to feelings of inferiority and second-class status. Corresponding negative self-concepts based on skin color are further reinforced by the realization that other "brown" ethnic groups and people of color do not enjoy the same social and economic status as their white counterparts (Santos, 1983).

Furthermore, status is integrally linked to education (Posadas, 1999). Pilipinos view education as a "passport to good jobs, economic security, social acceptance, and as a way out of a cycle of poverty and lower-class status, not only for their children, but for the whole family" (Santos, 1983, p. 146). Education, then, is not an individual but a family concern and is considered to be an economic investment toward which family members must contribute significant effort and often personal sacrifice. It is not uncommon for an older child to take a job to help support a younger sibling to obtain higher education (Posadas, 1999). This practice reflects the value of *utang na loob*, in which the debt of gratitude incurred to the whole family ensures the graduate's contribution to the family welfare, which takes precedence over individual economic and social mobility (Santos, 1983). Thus, degrees, diplomas, certificates, good grades, and academic honors are much sought-after symbols. Such achievements are typically recognized with great pride and significant attention by extended family, friends, and the larger community. In 1990, "Filipino Americans were second only to Indian Americans in the percentage of high school graduates" (Blair & Qian, 1998). However, there is a growing concern within the community reflected in the 1997 dropout figures (46%) and dismal test scores (50% at or below the 50th percentile in reading scores) of Pilipino American high school students (Posadas, 1999). The underachievement of Pilipino American students highlights the disparity between the value placed by the community on education and the reality faced by the youth growing up as Pilipino Americans in the United States.

The preceding review of traditional Pilipino values reveals complexity as well as contrast among such values and those corresponding to more individualistic, Eurocentric cultural orientations. There also are apparent contrasts between various Pilipino values and observed behaviors among Pilipinos. These contrasts can be expected between immigrant and American-born Pilipinos and among those of varying social class, generation, and degree of acculturation. Thus, as is similar to other Asian ethnic groups, awareness and appreciation of such contrasts and complexity are critical to determining the relative influence of traditional values among Pilipino families.

BELIEFS

Pilipino American values have clearly influenced beliefs and practices pertaining to family structure and functioning, child rearing, medical care, disability, and death and dying. Diversity in beliefs and practices among Pilipino Americans may be related to a variety of factors. Level of acculturation, economic status, access to services, discrimination, underemployment, loss of support due to distance from family and friends "left behind," and intergenerational tensions are but a few of the daily challenges that contemporary Pilipino Americans struggle with to "make it" in America. Pilipino individuals' beliefs and practices are constantly challenged as the contrast between the values of Pilipino parents and of their children being raised in the United States becomes more and more stark. Posadas noted that "some Filipino immigrants do find themselves caught between cultures over questions that might not even be asked in the Philippines" (1999, p. 120). Factors pertaining to family, child rearing, and health are thus considered in terms of variations in beliefs and practices.

Family Structure

The complete centrality of family life and the importance of family loyalty, obligation, and interdependence have been previously described. These values are supported by family structures and kinship ties that value the equality between men and women. This translates into a bilateral extended kinship system wherein the lineage of both mother and father are given equal importance. Thus, for example, names may be inherited through the male line or both the father's and mother's family name; often, the mother's maiden name is used as the child's middle name (Posadas, 1999).

Although expanded through bilateral lineage, the extended family system is further enlarged by the *compadrazgo* system, or ritual co-parenthood, a legacy of Spanish colonial Catholicism (Posadas, 1999). As mentioned, in addition to blood and marriage relatives, each Pilipino gains relatives by incorporating godparents in rituals and ceremonies. Close friends or relatives of the natural parent are called on to serve as a godparent (known as *ninong* or *ninang* to the child) and assumes a surrogate parental relationship to the child by virtue of acting as a sponsor at the religious rites of baptism, confirmation, and, later, marriage. The relationship of the godparent to the child's parents is that of a *compadre* or *comadre*. Godparents assume more active roles as benefactors who may be expected to participate in their godchild's socialization, oversee his or her religious education, aid the child in times of financial need, contribute to the cost of the child's education, and assist in finding him or her

Tony, a 5-year-old Pilipino boy with autism, was receiving in-home intensive tutoring, speech therapy, and behavior intervention through a well-known program based at the University of California, Los Angeles (UCLA). At the time of his referral to the regional center for service coordination, the immediate need and priority was to identify and place Tony in an appropriate preschool program.

In presenting Tony's early developmental history to the counselor, Tony's mother, Cora (who had separated from her husband, Roy, when Tony was about 3 years old), described how difficult Tony was to care for. Her oldest daughter (15 years old) was very helpful and assumed a major caregiving role whenever Cora needed to work the late-afternoon/early-evening shift. Tony's *ninang* or godmother was also available to care for him regularly in her home. Despite the availability of such family supports and resources, however, Cora was often overwhelmed by Tony's persistent attention impairments, behavior problems, tantrums, and hyperactivity. Prior to having learned of the UCLA program for children with autism, Cora had been unable to find any professional resources that were effective in helping her to better manage Tony's problems. In fact, his *ninang* suggested that Cora consider taking Tony to a faith healer after a psychologist was unsuccessful in remediating his tantrums and oppositional behavior. Tony's *ninang* recalled a young child she had known who cried inconsolably and seemed to live in his own world. She was convinced that a faith healer succeeded in driving the evil spirit (which was presumably contributing to the child's condition) from his body. Cora was reluctant to act on this suggestion and felt that her personal spiritual faith would ultimately enable her to find help. Moreover, Tony's isolated special talents (e.g., ability to write his name and identify nearly every major auto company/make/model) were a sign that he also had a "gift from God."

Thus, when Cora was finally able to find the UCLA project and witness the immediate benefits of the home intervention program, she became very attached to the staff and was profoundly grateful for their help. Her loyalty and debt of gratitude to the UCLA team contributed toward a major decision-making dilemma, however. The team felt that despite Tony's significant difficulties in social skills and pragmatic language, he should be placed in a general kindergarten program and that all efforts should be made to prepare him for a full inclusion experience. In a subsequent individualized education program (IEP) meeting, Tony was declared eligible for public preschool services, but the district's school psychologist insisted that Tony's level of functioning warranted special education placement.

After visiting and observing several public school programs (with the regional center counselor and the UCLA team leader), Cora continued to feel caught in the middle between UCLA (who maintained that the special education classes were inappropriate) and the school district personnel (who continued to challenge the full inclusion recommendation). Cora was unsure as to the regional center counselor's position and neither wished to offend the UCLA team nor to disagree with the school district.

Consequently, Cora enrolled Tony in her own church summer preschool program but was told by the director after Tony's first day that he was just not "fitting in." He was allowed to continue attending 2 days per week but received a minimum of individualized attention from an untrained aide. The counselor was disturbed by this turn of events and felt that Tony "lost out" on a full summer's educational programming, whereas Cora had to personally cover the expense of an inadequate preschool program.

At this juncture, what specific recommendations or guidance should the regional center counselor provide to Cora, and what would be her likely response?

employment (Affonso, 1978). Depending on their level of comfort and acceptance within the family, others may be viewed as surrogate parents to adult family members. Thus, other social institutions and relationships also become incorporated into the extended family system. The *compadrazgo* system extends and binds family ties, loyalties, obligations, reciprocity, and interdependence among people in the community (Agbayani-Siewert & Revilla, 1995; Posadas, 1999). Through this expanded network of kinship relationships, Pilipinos are likely to consider 100 or more living individuals as "relatives" (Pan Asian Parent Education Project, 1982; Santos, 1983; Yap, 1982). Finally, it is not unusual to find adult children (often unmarried); extended family members such as grandparents, aunts, uncles, or cousins; and other related members (e.g., boarders, roomers, foster children) living in the same house and assuming vital roles (Almirol, 1982; Pan Asian Parent Education Project; Posadas; Santos). In 1990, this type of household arrangement was reported in up to 31% of all Pilipino American homes (Posadas, 1999).

Marital and Parental Roles/Expectations

Pilipinos often believe that young people should not marry before they have completed some kind of educational preparation for a career so that they will be economically self-sufficient. They also should be sufficiently mature to assume the responsibilities of raising a family. Once married, Pilipinos are expected to start their families within a year or so. The birth of a child fixes the ties between the married couple's respective families. Although the bond of marriage is considered permanent, especially among Catholic families, divorce and separation is not uncommon. In 1990, reports of divorce and separation among foreign-born Pilipino Americans was 4.8% for men and 6.9% for women, significantly less than their American-born counterparts (9.2% for men and 11.9% for women) (Posadas, 1999).

Researchers note that egalitarian roles and relationships between Pilipino men and women are reflected in family decision-making processes. As noted, family authority is often based on respect for age, regardless of gender. However, the changing status and roles within Pilipino American families brought about by unemployment or underemployment, language proficiency, and overall level of acculturation, may also have an impact on who becomes the authority figure within the family. Family decisions are often made after a consensus has been reached to ensure that the ultimate decision will be representative of and acted on by all family members. Family disagreements are avoided, if possible; when disagreements do occur, they are kept strictly within the family (Cimmarusti, 1996; Posadas, 1999).

With regard to parenting, fathers may be ostensibly perceived as the main authority figure in the Pilipino nuclear family; however, the mother has considerable authority and influence. She generally controls the finances, may work full time (even with many children at home), and usually earns as much as or more than half the family income. Women enjoy high status in the family. Bilateral lineage attests to this higher status of Pilipinas compared with women in more patriarchal Asian countries. The long-accepted phenomenon of the "working mother" in the Philippines thus does not pose a drastic role change as it does for other recent Asian immigrant families in the United States (Pan Asian Parent Education Project, 1982).

Children are the center of the parents' concerns. They are viewed as an extension of the family and recipients of the family's good fortune. Many adults do not strictly adhere to the Confucian expectation of unquestioning child obedience. Parents are expected to persuade a child to accept their point of view, rather than impose their authority on the child without consideration for the child's preferences or wishes. The child, in turn, is expected to show proper respect and obedience, to compromise, and to maintain good relationships with all other family members (Pan Asian Parent Education Project, 1982).

Child Rearing

Formal studies of Pilipino child-rearing beliefs and practices have shown considerable consistency in their findings (Church, 1986). Moreover, the specific socialization patterns and "training" for desirable childhood traits and behaviors (particularly during infancy/toddlerhood and early childhood) are highly consistent with other Asian cultural groups. Pilipino child-rearing beliefs and practices are reinforced within a family structure and extended family system, however, with characteristic similarities and differences relative to mainstream American and other Asian cultures.

Infancy/Toddlerhood   Among Pilipino Americans, the birth of children is often an expected and desired outcome of marriage; however, considerations such as economic status, job security, marital bliss, religious beliefs, and access to child care are taken into account when deciding on when to have children. The newborn child's vulnerability contributes to the use of folk practices by many Pilipino mothers, such as keeping garlic and salt near the baby to protect him or her from evil spirits, pinning religious medals on a baby's clothing to offer the protection of angels, wrapping a 50-cent coin on the baby's umbilicus with a belly band to make it heal faster, and avoiding exposing the infant to the bright colors to prevent strabismus. A baby's clothes are loose and comfortable and preferably white in color to symbolize the purity God gives to every newborn (Affonso, 1978). Many of these practices may be more prevalent in the Philippines than in the United States as acculturation into

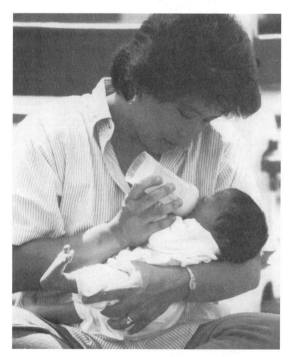

the mainstream American way of life has a huge impact on the degree to which parents protect and care for their infants and toddlers.

For some Pilipino families, newborns are kept at home until 3 or 4 weeks of age; the first trip is usually to the doctor and the second to the priest for a blessing or conditional baptism. With the economic realities and lifestyles typical in the United States, however, some families may not be able to afford to stay at home with their children for a long period of time. Formal Christian baptism often occurs when the baby is 1–3 months old. For many families, a child's baptismal party is often second in importance to the marriage feast.

Infancy is characterized by indulgence; constant attention; and few, if any, demands on the child. Compared with their European American and Puerto Rican counterparts, expectations for Pilipino American children in terms of the attainment of milestones (e.g., use of training cup, utensils, weaning, and sleeping by themselves) occur at a significantly later age (Carlson & Harwood, 1999/2000). The child is frequently cuddled and carried, and crying is attended to quickly by feeding, holding, and other consoling tactics. This practice is made possible or easier by the presence of extended family, often grandparents, who can assume significant caregiving roles (Posadas, 1999).

The emphasis on dependency and physical closeness is further manifested in mothers breastfeeding on demand until a child is 36 months old, on average, and children typically co-sleeping with parents until the average age of 39 months old (Carlson & Harwood, 1999/2000). For the Pilipino child, the process of toilet training is yet another occasion for familial helpfulness and closeness because it involves imitation of and assistance from other family members. Interestingly, Pilipino children are expected to be day toilet trained at a young age (at approximately 20 months), significantly younger than their European-American and Puerto Rican counterparts are expected to be day toilet trained (Carlson & Harwood, 1999/2000). In general, however, throughout infancy and the toddler period, child rearing is characterized by significant indulgence, protectiveness, gradual training for responsibility, and minimal adult anxiety about early performance (Church, 1986).

Early Childhood   A shift from a highly indulgent to a more authoritarian parental stance occurs as the child approaches school age, which is when Pilipinos believe that children develop *isip,* or a mind of their own. Particularly after the Pilipino child is weaned, older brothers, sisters, and other relatives become substitutes

for the parents' constant attention. Older siblings, referred to as *kuya* (older brother) or *ate* (older sister), are expected to help with household chores and to care for younger siblings (Cimmarusti, 1996). The younger child, in turn, must learn to conform to family expectations of respect for elders and obedience to authority, adults, parents, older siblings, and other substitute caregivers.

Discipline in Pilipino American homes varies greatly depending on various factors, including education and acculturation of the parents and their children. In extreme situations, children may be sent "home" to the Philippines to remove them from seemingly dangerous situations such as gang involvement (Posadas, 1999). Verbal threats or reprimands are common, often appealing to the child's developing sense of *kapwa* and their obligation and duty to the family. Children also may be reminded of their *utang na loob* to the family and *hiya* or lack thereof (*"Walang hiya kang bata ka!"* "Child, you have no shame!"). Given the multiple demands on each parent, it is not unusual for mothers and fathers to work separate shifts to enable at least one parent to be at home with the children. The main parental disciplinarian may thus vary depending on who assumes the primary caregiver role.

Some of the behaviors that are more severely punished or condemned are sibling-directed aggression, as well as hostility toward kinship group members. Teasing serves as a means of limit setting and controlling or suppressing anger and hostility; it also is an outlet for anger and an acceptable substitute for overt aggression and direct criticism. Children are encouraged to subordinate their personal interests and competitive behaviors for the sake of cooperation and maintaining family harmony and smooth interpersonal relationships. Cimmarusti, however, noted that children "can assert their individuality in a first generation Filipino-American family when it is quite clear that the actions in no way challenge or question the importance of the family" (1996, p. 209).

Medical Care

As is the case among other Asian immigrant groups, considerable intracultural diversity exists among Pilipino Americans with regard to health beliefs and health practices. Centuries of colonialism and the Americanization of Pilipino culture have obviously infused the science of Western medicine and contributed to the training of thousands of Pilipino health care professionals. Access to modern medical technology and to Pilipino American medical providers may have affected the health practices of Pilipino Americans. Just as the larger contemporary Pilipino culture is a composite of foreign and indigenous elements, however, health orientations and healing practices also may incorporate traditional Pilipino folk medicine. The various aspects of such folk medicine warrant review.

Health Beliefs

"Diseases are traditionally conceptualized as either natural or supernatural in origin. In practice, however, people seem to make no clear-cut distinction between the two" (Montepio, 1986–1987, p. 152). Explanations of illness (particularly chronic, debilitating illnesses) are typically multicausal.

> Among the natural forces believed to affect health are overwork, overexposure to natural elements, overeating, insufficient nutrition, lack of sleep, too much worry, unsanitary environment, and imbalance of hot and cold elements. Supernatural ailments are those that result from the displeasure of environmental spirits, souls of the dead and evil people, or from punishment for transgression against God, against fellow human beings, or against nature. (Montepio, 1986–1987, p. 152)

The particular belief in *usog* or *tuyaw* is widespread in the Philippines. Individuals afflicted with various illnesses or conditions that are not readily treated by conventional medicines may have had contact with a person who possessed a power similar to the Spanish *mal de ojo* (evil eye). The Pilipino counterpart appears more powerful because "it can be transmitted through the eyes and also the hands, fingers, words (as through a greeting), or in extreme cases, through physical proximity to a possessed person who had been exposed to the sun's heat" (Montepio, 1986/1987, p. 155).

Health Practices   Health practices are rooted in deeply ingrained values and beliefs. Spiritual healing is sometimes the first or ongoing recourse for Pilipino American families. "Filipinos are deeply spiritual people . . . . it does not matter whether one is attached to a religious institution or not" (Burgonio-Watson, 1997, p. 326). Catholic families may seek the assistance of a priest, request special prayers (e.g., lighting candles at church), or go on a pilgrimage to religious sites to pray for a miracle cure. It is not uncommon for families to blend spiritually based practices with a more modern approach to health care.

Studies of health practices among Pilipino Americans suggest that people originally from rural areas in the Philippines are more knowledgeable regarding home remedies, traditional healing techniques, and supernatural ailments, whereas those from urban areas rely more on Western medical intervention and over-the-counter drugs. In both rural and urban areas, however, a variety of indigenous folk practices and modern health care systems are utilized simultaneously (Montepio, 1986/1987; Vance, 1991).

Among the more traditional forms of self-medication are certain Chinese oils or ointments, which serve as "cure-alls" in relaxing, heating, and comforting the muscles or providing relief for dizziness, colds, headaches, sore throats, and so forth. Other self-medication may include the use of folk healing techniques consistent with the Chinese hot/cold classification system of diseases and the concept of wind illnesses (see Chapter 8). For example, a technique called *ventosa* is used for treating joint pains believed to be caused by the presence of "bad air." This technique consists of wrapping a coin with cotton, wetting the tip with alcohol, lighting it, and placing the coin on the aching joint area, then immediately covering it with a small glass or cup. The fire is extinguished as soon as it is covered, creating a vacuum that will suck the "bad" air out of the joint (Montepio, 1986/1987).

Faith Healers, Folk Healers, and Herbalists   Some Pilipino American families (depending on their religious beliefs and level of acculturation) may return to the Philippines to utilize the help of faith healers, folk healers, or herbalists. In serious illnesses, some Pilipino and Pilipino American families may seek the help of a local "folk healer" who may utilize a variety of treatments including the use of herbs and roots (McKenzie & Chrisman, 1977). It is important to note that the use of herbs to cure illnesses may be passed down to generations through a source other than folk healers. Although folk healers are presumed to possess a God-given gift, their relative popularity and prestige in the community depends a great deal on their interpersonal relationships with their patients. People in rural areas are accustomed to friendly and accommodating folk healers and expect the same treatment from physicians. If these expectations are not met, they avoid Western health centers or switch doctors. Moreover, when healers are viewed with trust and respect, they often are expected to perform "instantaneous" healing. If there is no immediate improvement in an illness or related symptoms, individuals may change doctors (Montepio, 1986/1987).

The various types of healers common throughout the Philippines include midwives, masseurs, and specialists for supernaturally caused ailments. Although these types of healers each have native labels, no traditional word exists for "faith healers," the newest and increasingly popular genre of Philippine folk healers. The Philippines is considered the world's faith healing center. In fact, there are as many as 15,000 faith healers found in the Philippines, and most are devout Christians (Harper & Fullerton, 1994). Faith healers do not attempt to identify or diagnose a disease, which is in contrast to the traditional concern for identifying the cause of illness (which could, presumably, be supernatural). Their orientation is holistic and uniform and incorporates the belief in concurrent physical, emotional, and spiritual healing. Regardless of the individual's specific affliction, the same techniques are employed (Montepio, 1986/1987).

In a regular session, the faith healer's techniques include blessing the body with holy water, laying on of hands, and anointing with oil. The technique of laying on of hands is a very important aspect of faith healing and is practiced by several other groups such as the Pentecostal-Charismatics and the Cuban American *santeros*. In laying on of hands, it appears as though the healer is attempting to transfer the healing energy from his or her hands to the individual's body through the forehead. The healer also anoints the individual by wetting his or her fingers with consecrated oil and making the sign of the cross on the forehead, on each eye, and on the chin of the person. If certain body parts need healing, they will be directly anointed. The person, in turn, typically attests to the sense of warmth or flow of energy that seems to enter his or her body and provides instant well-being (Montepio, 1986/1987).

These healing techniques are enhanced by ritualized prayer, chanting, and the creation of an "atmosphere" that reinforces the individual's faith. During healing sessions, the faith healer, for example, typically wears a white dress of soft, flowing material, creating an ephemeral quality; white (worn by the Virgin Mary) is the symbol of purity and is associated with environmental ghosts and spirits (Montepio, 1986/1987).

One of the most dramatic forms of faith healing that has attracted significant international attention is "psychic surgery." According to Harper and Fullerton, psychic surgery "involves the painless insertion of the healer's fingers into the individual's body, removal of tissues, tumors, growths, or foreign matter, and closing the incision without a scar" (1994, p. 62). Numerous Western scientists have investigated tales of "miracle cures" produced by psychic surgeons and found evidence of fakery; however, they also have reportedly witnessed incredible feats of healing (Harper & Fullerton, 1994).

Whether in the Philippines or the United States, faith healing and more traditional folk healing practices typically are utilized simultaneously with modern medicine. In fact, folk healers may serve as indigenous allies whose work can complement modern health practitioners and who can provide the psychological, emotional, and spiritual well-being necessary to the healing process.

> The healer never advises against going to doctors or hospitals. In several cases, spiritual healing is used only after these doctors have diagnosed a disease as incurable. Even after a patient feels that he has been healed by [traditional healers], he still goes back to his doctor to establish that he is actually cured. Western medicine is thus used to validate the efficacy of spiritual healing. (Montepio, 1986/1987, pp. 159–160)

Disability

Similar to many other Asian ethnic groups, Pilipinos may view the more severe disabilities with considerable stigma. In fact, according to selected Pilipino American professionals working in the field of developmental disabilities, this profound stigma partially explains the paucity of Pilipino literature pertaining to disability issues (Fuentes, 1990; Soldevilla, 1989). Such stigma derives, in part, from traditional attributions linking specific disabilities to various causes.

Causation

Many of the traditional beliefs regarding the etiology of disabilities (particularly physical conditions) are consistent with the previously described health beliefs about varying causes of illness. Naturalistic explanations might focus on the mother's failure to follow prescribed dietary practices during pregnancy. For example, excessive intake of sweet foods is believed to contribute to an obese baby. There also are foods that some Pilipinos believe should be excluded from the prenatal diet: squid (because it might get tangled in the woman's body and cause the umbilical cord to wrap around the fetus' neck), crab (because it might cause clubbed fingers and toes), dark foods such as prunes and black coffee (because they might result in a dark-skinned baby), and taro root (because it is believed to cause the baby to have eczema or skin problems). Another common belief is that all of the pregnant woman's food cravings should be immediately satisfied or the baby could be born prematurely or have a birthmark (Affonso, 1978; Pan Asian Parent Education Project, 1982). Other traditional practices during pregnancy include avoidance of explicit taboos such as sitting on steps or standing in a doorway (this could cause the baby's head to be blocked during passage through the birth canal), arguing with relatives (this may result in complications or miscarriage), and walking over a rope (which could result in a delayed expulsion of the placenta) (Lassiter, 1995).

Religious beliefs also are employed to account for various disabilities. A Pilipino's deep faith in God and belief in *bahala na* may reinforce a fatalistic orientation whereby a disability is accepted as God's will. Disability in a child, however, also may represent a divine punishment for sins or moral transgressions against God that were committed by the parents or their ancestors. This spiritual attribution contributes to a shared sense of *hiya* (shame) that affects the entire family; it may further negatively affect siblings' chances of finding desirable marital partners because of presumed hereditary "taint" and the strong belief in "bad blood" (*na sa dugo*) or a familial disorder (Fuentes, 1990; Rita, 1996). Apart from spiritual attributions, an older child or an adult with a so-called "hidden" disability (e.g., cognitive impairments, emotional disturbance) without ostensible physical origins may be viewed as having a weak will or a frail character (Araneta, 1993).

Disabilities also may be associated with supernatural ailments that are attributed to spiritual causes. Infants who are chronically irritable and engage in prolonged, inconsolable crying are presumed to be troubled by evil spirits (Pan Asian Parent Education Project, 1982). Similarly, children with serious emotional disturbances or disabilities such as autism as well as epilepsy are often traditionally described as being "possessed," the victims of angry or evil spirits (Church, 1986).

Nature and Meaning of a Disability   As indicated in Chapter 8, the respective terms related to specific disabilities are highly varied among Asian groups. Similarly, Pilipino conceptions of selected disabilities vary according to their expression (e.g., mental, emotional, physical) and presumed etiology. Education, religion, and acculturation into mainstream American society will also factor in the way Pilipino Americans conceptualize disabilities. These differing conceptions further suggest corresponding intervention modalities.

Although the types of "outside" assistance and intervention resources that are sought may vary considerably, the family typically remains centrally involved in the primary care of the child with a disability. As the most reliable source of protection and support for the child with a disability, the family also is the focus of siblings' pri-

Becky, a 5-year-old Pilipino girl with mild mental retardation, was referred for regional center service coordination when she began attending kindergarten. Becky was diagnosed at 1 year of age as having a genetic disorder, Prader-Willi syndrome, characterized by overeating, extreme obesity, behavior problems, and mental retardation. However, she had not received any subsequent early intervention or special education services.

In the Philippines, Becky's father, Macario, had been a physician and her mother, Lorenza, had been a teacher. Since having immigrated to the United States approximately 10 years ago, Macario had worked as a lab assistant and Lorenza as a travel agent. They have two older children who are excelling in school and of whom they are very proud. Becky, however, is a source of constant stress for the family with her traits related to her disorder.

The counselor, at the time of her meeting with Becky's family, discussed resources such as respite care and behavioral intervention programs that could be made available to assist them. Macario and Lorenza indicated their appreciation and said they would consider utilizing such help. Lorenza, however, noted that her mother and older sister would soon be arriving from the Philippines to live with them for an indefinite period. She felt that the responsibility of caring for Becky could thus be shared with other family members, and outside resources would not have to be utilized. The counselor asked more questions, however, and learned that Lorenza's mother and sister would probably not be arriving for another 6 months. The counselor also learned that these relatives had not seen Becky since she was an infant and were relatively unaware of the severity of her condition.

Macario indicated that he had considered placing Becky outside the home. A Pilipino co-worker told him that her sister-in-law owned a group home and cared for children with mental retardation. He seemed encouraged by the fact that there were Pilipino care providers in the community but was reluctant to pursue such resources and make contact with them on his own. However, although Lorenza would not directly offer her opinion or concerns about placing Becky, she seemed interested in continuing to keep Becky at home.

While addressing these dynamics and dilemmas, how might the counselor advise the parents to pursue the next course of action for Becky's care?

mary duty and commitment. Parents thus expect their older sons and daughters to continue to provide the primary care for a family member with a disability. In fact, the long-standing tradition of family and small-group orientation has contributed to a proliferation of Pilipino American care providers who have established small group homes or community-based residential facilities serving individuals with developmental disabilities. These providers caring for children may naturally view their "clients" as family members and fully include them in daily living activities and socialization experiences that incorporate many aspects of Pilipino American culture and traditional lifestyle (Marquez, 1991; Soldevilla, 1989).

Death and Dying

Beliefs about death and dying among Pilipinos are interrelated with the various religious orientations that were described in the previous section. The principal denominations that account for nearly 95% of the Philippine population are Catholicism, Protestantism, and Islam. Beliefs about death and dying correspond to each of these major religions that have been extensively detailed in theological literature. In interviews with Pilipino Americans in Hawaii, Shimabukuro, Daniels, and D'Andrea (1999) reported that Pilipino Americans' mourning rituals tend to be a mix of religious and animistic beliefs. They found that the animistic beliefs tend to be downplayed, however, especially when individuals from other ethnic groups are present.

Although the vast majority of native Pilipinos are Roman Catholic, their funerary customs differ somewhat from those of the West. Essentially, the "grieving process" is less private and mournful. Wakes are well attended, and the mood may be anything but somber. Though families and friends come together to comfort each other and pray for the deceased (Shimabukuro et al., 1999), they accompany expressions of fond remembrance with eating, drinking, card games, and music. Pilipinos also often celebrate the first year anniversary of the death of the loved one. It is acceptable among Pilipino Americans to "stay connected" with their deceased love ones. This may be manifested in their prayers, stories, and even in their dreams.

ISSUES OF LANGUAGE

The receiver-oriented and relatively indirect style of most Asian languages is characteristic of communication patterns among Pilipino immigrants. Length of stay in the United States, education, language proficiency, and acculturation may heavily influence the way Pilipino Americans communicate with each other and with non–Pilipino Americans. In many cases, communication patterns are integrally related to primary Pilipino American values such as family, authority, interpersonal harmony, concern for others' well-being, and the importance of "saving face." Similar to other Asian ethnic groups, Pilipinos typically employ formality and honorific language that conveys proper respect for authority, status, and positions by terms of address and titles. For example, a physician or a lawyer will continue to be addressed as "Dr. Cruz" or "Attorney Ramos" by clients, friends, and colleagues well after more personalized and informal relationships have been established (in contrast to the American tendency to move more rapidly toward a first-name basis) (Santos, 1983).

Respect for authority and concern for "face-saving" further reinforce the frequent use of euphemisms, third parties, and agreement when the opposite is meant (Santos, 1983). Pilipinos often will go to great lengths to avoid making a direct appeal when they have encountered a problem or wish to convey an important request. They instead prefer to introduce a go-between, whose status or position within the family may help abate further conflicts and assure the resolution of issues in contention (Cimmarusti, 1996; Gochenour, 1990). In counseling terms, this has been referred to as triangulation (Cimmarusti, 1996). It is important to note however, that these behaviors and those that are described in the succeeding paragraphs, may be more prevalent when Pilipinos deal with fellow Pilipinos but are not as common when Pilipinos are dealing with individuals from other ethnic groups.

In their wish to be accommodating, some Pilipino Americans may find it impolite or embarrassing to decline social invitations or to respond directly to other requests that might elicit a negative answer or contrary opinion. Although apparently concurring in some manner (through failure to express or defend an alternative point of view) or ostensibly indicating agreement, they may actually be privately opposed to the issue or question at hand. They generally will make an ambiguous statement rather than say "No," or say "Yes," but mean "No," "Maybe," or "I don't know." They find it hard to reject or disagree, especially when conversing with someone considered superior. When they feel the truth will offend or embarrass, they answer indirectly. The purpose of an evasive reply is not to deceive but to please or avoid confrontation (Harper & Fullerton, 1994). Thus, as a result of values such as *pakikisama* and *amor propio,* mistakes will go unmentioned, questions unasked, and issues unsettled (Pan Asian Parent Education Project, 1982). This communication style obviously may challenge a more Eurocentric orientation that values frankness, directness, honesty, and sincerity (Cimmarusti, 1996; Gochenour, 1990).

Consistent with other high-context cultures, Pilipinos have a highly developed sensitivity to the nonverbal aspects of communication (Gochenour, 1990). Pilipinos are considerably less dependent on spoken words than are European Americans; they watch their listeners carefully and identify body language cues to assess what the person is feeling. The essence of this more intuitive and affective sense that guides nonverbal communication is captured in the phrase "talking with one's eyes" (Pan Asian Parent Education Project, 1982). Pilipino sensitivity to context thus "extends from a keen awareness of appropriate speech and behavior in a given situation to a well-developed instinct for what is implied and not stated" (Gochenour, 1990, p. 61). This sensitivity is further complemented by a high tolerance for ambiguity that enables Pilipinos to respond calmly to uncertainty or lack of information. Again, however, this orientation may conflict with the characteristically Eurocentric utilitarian emphasis on forthrightness and achieving results in the least amount of time (Gochenour, 1990).

When Pilipinos converse with each other, the use of English can affect sensitivities. If, for example, in an ordinary transaction between two Pilipinos, one of them addresses the other in English, it may be viewed as an attempt to show off and "put down" the other. This is more common among new immigrants or first generation Pilipino Americans. This view may not hold true for second or later generation Pilipino Americans who may speak English as their primary language. In fact, in a longitudinal study of Asian American high school students, Pilipino American students reported the lowest use of a native language (not English) at home compared with their Chinese, Korean, Japanese, and other Southeast Asian counterparts (Blair & Qian, 1998).

Some Pilipinos' tendency to equate facility in English with social class and intelligence may foster self-consciousness and insecurity in dialogues with native English-speaking Americans. Many Pilipino immigrants pride themselves on being English speakers. Once in the United States, however, they may find their own version of English to be unacceptable and a cause for embarrassment (Santos, 1983). Furthermore, when speaking to Pilipino immigrants who appear to be fluent in English, Americans usually presume that their English language comprehension is extensive, which may not be always the case. This expectation obviously strains Pilipino American interactions, "tension which the American is certain to feel much less than the Filipino, who is typically his or her own harshest critic" (Gochenour, 1990, p. 40). Such sensitivity needs to be considered when communicating with Pilipinos whose English comprehension is better than their expressive English and who may be insulted when addressed in childlike English (Harper & Fullerton, 1994).

Many Pilipino immigrants may also experience tension among generations brought about by their proficiency and fluency in the English language and Philippine languages that the older generations may speak (Tseng & Fuligni, 2000). It is not unusual for Pilipino families to speak one or more languages in the home. In a study of the quality of relationship between immigrant parents and their adolescent children, Tseng and Fuligni (2000) found that Filipino adolescents who communicated with their parents in their native language were more likely to discuss their concerns and issues with them than those who communicated in English. Researchers suggest that the choice families make to maintain their native language may be equated to retention of their values and cultural beliefs (Tseng & Fuligni, 2000). Thus, it is not surprising to find that in a survey of Pilipinos who have immigrated over the last 20 years, 54% expressed interest in their children learning both English and Tagalog (Garza & Scott, 1996).

SUMMARY

Pilipinos are the largest and fastest growing Asian ethnic group in the United States. Half of the Pilipino American population is foreign born. Originating from a nation of 7,107 islands and the most ethnically diverse country in Asia, Pilipinos have been in the United States since 1587, and in successive waves have immigrated to the United States since the late 1800s. The more recent waves of Pilipino immigrants

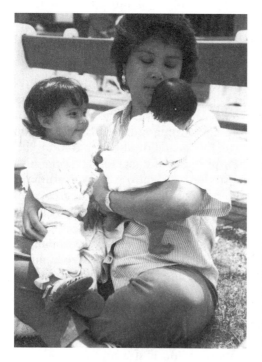

(post-1965 and in 1972) have included large numbers of highly educated young adults and professionals in search of better employment and economic opportunities. Unfortunately, these individuals typically must confront persistent conditions of occupational downgrading and under-employment. The problems associated with loss of ascribed status, social dislocation, and employment discrimination often are compounded by family stresses and generational conflicts. Alienated Pilipino youth increasingly challenge their elders' traditional values (Posadas, 1999).

Four hundred years of Spanish colonial rule left an indelible impression on the Pilipino culture and consciousness, forming some of its most enduring characteristics. After the Philippines became a colony of the United States, one form of colonialism was replaced by another, and 40 years of U.S. rule further contributed to the pervasive American influence on Pilipino culture. Pilipinos thus may have a decidedly Western orientation and share a heritage heavily influenced by Hispanic Catholicism and Euro-Christian ethics. However, their indigenous Malay roots and historical Hindu, Confucian, and Islamic influences have further shaped a sense of identity and traditional values that reflect other Asian cultures but also are uniquely Pilipino American.

Although commonalities in values, beliefs and practices are described, varying individual, regional, societal, and environmental factors are highly likely to create significant differences among Pilipino Americans. The diverse experiences of Pilipinos in the United States throughout history and current economic, social, and political climate all contribute to the way Pilipino Americans live their lives. Such factors must always be considered in understanding families with Pilipino roots.

For many Pilipino Americans, value is placed on the centrality of the family (and the importance of family interdependence, loyalty, and obligation), hierarchical and highly authoritarian social systems, and preservation of interpersonal harmony. The associated concepts of *pakikisama* (achieving smooth interpersonal relationships), *hiya* (shame), *amor propio* (self-respect), and *utang na loob* (debt of gratitude) have been variously perceived as fundamental cultural traits versus surface values that derive their significance from the core value of *kapwa* (shared identity). The Pilipino character has further been defined in terms of basic strengths: regard for the dignity of others; family orientation; joy and humor; flexibility, adaptability, and creativity; hard work and industry; faith and religiosity; and ability to survive, which is reinforced by the concept of *bahala na*. Education also is highly valued as a means of upward mobility; it is integrally linked to status and enhancement of family welfare and reputation.

The Pilipino American family structure and extended family system serves as a vehicle for transmitting basic values through specific socialization and child-rearing beliefs and practices. Pilipino American families are often defined by a bilateral extended kinship system (including *compadres* and many other surrogate parents and "relatives" from various social institutions). Within the immediate nuclear family, marital and parental roles are characterized by a commitment to marriage as a permanent bond, relatively egalitarian roles, status, a balance of power between men and women, and the expectation of reciprocity between parent and child in meeting mutual needs and maintaining good relationships. Specific Pilipino American child-rearing practices employed from infancy throughout early childhood may reflect the broad range of practices found among other Asian American cultural groups.

Although Pilipino American culture has been infused with the science of Western medicine, popular health beliefs and practices have also incorporated traditional Pilipino folk medicine. Folk orientations conceptualize disease (as well as disabilities) in terms of either natural or supernatural origins. Diseases or illnesses originating from natural causes typically are treated through the use of self-medication or other techniques derived from the hot/cold classification and wind illness concepts of Chinese medicine. "Faith healers" are a genre of folk healers who may be utilized regardless of the presumed etiology of various illnesses. Folk health beliefs and practices further extend to conceptualizations of the causes as well as the nature and meaning of specific disabilities (whether mental, physical, or emotional). An important consideration for early interventionists and those providing services for children with special needs is that families may simultaneously utilize traditional folk healing practices in conjunction with modern medicine and health care resources. In fact, Western medicine is often used to validate the efficacy of spiritual healing. The profound impact of a child with a disability on the family also must be considered in terms of the feelings of shame and stigma it may engender in families. This shared experience will typically result in coping strategies that draw heavily on spiritual faith and parental expectations that all family members will make personal sacrifices to participate in the primary care and support of the child with a disability.

Characteristic Pilipino American communication patterns are a final area of focus. They are integrally related to primary values such as family, authority, interpersonal harmony, concern for others' well-being, and the importance of "face." Thus, similar to other Asian groups, Pilipinos traditionally employ formality and honorific language (in conveying respect for authority, status, and position), and indirect communication styles. Furthermore, they have a highly developed sensitivity to the nonverbal aspects of communication.

The Pilipino American population is complex, with contrasts in cultural orientations relative to the blending of Eurocentric and more indigenous collectivist values, as well as contrasts between immigrant and American-born Pilipinos and among those of varying social class, generation, and degree of acculturation. Thus, as is the case with other Asian ethnic groups, awareness and appreciation of such contrasts are essential in determining the relative influence of traditional cultural factors among Pilipino families.

RECOMMENDATIONS FOR INTERVENTIONISTS

The following recommendations correspond to selected elements of service utilization that were highlighted in this chapter. They address practical considerations in responding to various cultural orientations, values, and behaviors that may be demonstrated by some Pilipino American families.

OUTREACH

The first step in reaching out to Pilipino American families is to learn who they are within the context of American society. Understanding their level of acculturation into mainstream American culture is a step towards unraveling the many facets that may contribute to utilization of early intervention services by Pilipino Americans.

The previously described "trust" factor and importance of "proper" entry points to Asian communities similarly applies to many Pilipino American families. Pilipinos traditionally operate within a "circle of loyalty" that begins with the immediate family, proceeds to the extended family kinship system (including *compadres*), and finally reaches authority figures (Morales, 1990). Thus, in seeking direct services or assistance for a child with a disability, the family typically may utilize intermediaries or third parties (who are often extended family members) to make initial contact with appropriate providers or agencies. This practice serves to convey respect for the providers, who are viewed as authority figures and, as such, are not directly approached to request assistance. It also enables a family to filter information and learn more about the personal and professional qualities of the provider(s) through the perspectives of a trusted go-between. Early interventionists should be receptive to this practice and avoid rigid insistence on initial direct contact with the identified child and his or her family members to the exclusion of designated intermediaries. Restrictive agency policies and relevant client/family confidentiality issues must be examined in this light.

INITIAL EXPECTATIONS/ORIENTATIONS

The ascribed credibility of professionals is based on their presumed expertise and ability to offer practical assistance in the form of direct benefits or services. In the context of the Pilipino American value system, professionals are often expected to assume an authoritarian and directive role, giving explanations and advice and recommending specific courses of action. Although assuming an authoritarian and somewhat paternalistic role, the interventionist also is expected to be personable and subject to influence and affiliation. He or she must be sensitive to the family's desire for acceptance and an appropriate level of emotional closeness (Okamura & Agbayani, 1991). This type of relationship allows for the ultimate expression of *utang na loob* and reciprocity that preserves the family's "face" and dignity.

FACE SAVING AND THE COUNSELING PROCESS

Although typically demonstrating a heightened sensitivity to the nature and quality of interpersonal relationships, Pilipinos are particularly concerned about "face"
and how one appears in the eyes of others. The profound stigma associated with
various disabilities and the corresponding sense of family shame or *hiya* may create significant apprehension about public loss of face, particularly when seeking
special services. Yet, at the same time, traditional families will maintain a deep religious faith and the *bahala na* spirit; this orientation promotes a high tolerance
for ambiguity that enables them to respond calmly to uncertainty or lack of information and to remain determined in the face of stressful, problematic conditions.

Early interventionists must be sensitive to the face-saving needs of families
by using caution in frankly discussing specific problem areas too prematurely.
They also must respect and incorporate the family's religious, spiritual, and philosophical beliefs as adaptive coping strategies, rather than dismiss them as defenses, denial, fatalism, and/or lack of initiative and motivation to pursue prescribed courses of action actively. Respect for the family's need to engage in
collective decision-making processes also is necessary. Sufficient time must be
allowed for the family to seek advice, confirmation, and group consensus before
making important decisions.

COMMUNICATION STYLES

Consistent with the value of *pakikisama*, achieving smooth interpersonal relationships often takes precedence over clear and forthright communication. Characteristic Pilipino communication patterns thus include formality and honorific language,
indirectness, and heightened sensitivity to the nonverbal aspects of communication. Concern for interpersonal harmony may reinforce verbal and nonverbal behaviors that serve to mask, if not contradict, genuine intent, thoughts, opinions,
or feelings that could threaten another's "face" and *amor propio*.

Early interventionists are advised to exercise significant patience and tolerance in responding to such communication styles. They also should suspend culturally biased judgments regarding the presumed honesty and integrity of Pilipinos who seem to avoid frank and direct modes of expression. Although some
degree of frustration is expected, the process of learning the subtleties of Pilipino
American communication styles is facilitated by fully appreciating the core values
that support them.

WHAT WOULD YOU DO?

Fernando is 7 years old and has cerebral palsy. His parents were born in the
Philippines but have lived in the United States since they were teens. Fernando's
family is affluent and has adapted to the American way of life in many ways, but
they have worked hard to maintain the values of their native Pilipino culture.
Among the values Fernando's parents hold dear is *utang na loob*, a sense of

indebtedness and desire to "repay" those in authority or those who have done a favor for the family.

They see you, Fernando's teacher, as an authority figure and as someone whom they respect and want to repay for all of your work with their son. Just before the end of the school year, Fernando's mother left a large package for you when she picked him up for an appointment. When you opened the box, you found a note of thanks and gratitude along with a microwave oven.

What is the ethical dilemma?

What might you do to resolve this dilemma in a way that gives face to all involved?

REFERENCES

A brief history of the Philippines from a Filipino perspective. (n.d.). Retrieved September 25, 2002, from http://www.tribo.org

Affonso, D. (1978). The Filipino American. In A.L. Clark (Ed.), *Culture, childbearing, health professionals* (pp. 128–153). Philadelphia: F.A. Davis.

Agbayani-Siewert, P., & Revilla, L. (1995). Filipino Americans. In P.G. Min (Ed.), *Asian Americans: Contemporary trends and issues* (pp. 134–168). Beverly Hills: Sage Publications.

Almirol, E.B. (1982). Rights and obligations in Filipino American families. *Journal of Comparative Family Studies, 13,* 291–306.

Araneta, E.G. (1993). Psychiatric care of Pilipino Americans. In A. Gaw (Ed.), *Culture, ethnicity, and mental illness* (pp. 377–411). Washington, DC: American Psychiatric Association.

Bautista, V. (2002). *The Filipino Americans (1763–present): Their history, culture and traditions* (2nd ed.). Naperville, IL: Bookhaus Publishers.

Bello, M., & Reyes, V. (1986–1987). Filipino Americans and the Marcos overthrow: The transformation of political consciousness. *Amerasia Journal, 13,* 73–83.

Blair, S.L., & Qian, Z. (1998). Family and Asian students' educational performance: A consideration of diversity. *Journal of Family Issues, 19,* 355–374.

Bosrock, M.M. (1994). *Put your best foot forward: Asia.* St. Paul, MN: International Education Systems.

Brigham Young University (BYU). (1986). *Culturegram: Republic of the Philippines.* Provo, UT: David M. Kennedy Center for International Studies, Publication Services.

Burgonio-Watson, T.B. (1997). Filipino spirituality: An immigrant's perspective. In M.P.P. Root (Ed.), *Filipino Americans: Transformation and identity* (pp. 324–332). Beverly Hills: Sage Publications.

Cariño, B.V. (1987). The Philippines and Southeast Asia: Historical roots and contemporary linkages. In J.T. Fawcett & B.V. Cariño (Eds.), *Pacific bridges: The new immigration from Asia and the Pacific Islands* (pp. 305–325). New York: Center for Migration Studies.

Cariño, B.V., Fawcett, J.T., Gardner, R.W., & Arnold, F. (1990). *The new Pilipino immigrants to the United States: Increasing diversity and change.* Honolulu, HI: East-West Population Institute, East-West Center.

Carlson, V.J. & Harwood, R.L. (1999/2000). Understanding and negotiating cultural differences concerning early developmental competence: The six raisin solution. *ZERO TO THREE, 20,* 19–24.

Central Intelligence Agency (2003). *CIA—The world factbook—Philippines.* Retrieved September 25, 2002 from http://www.cia.gov/cia/publications/factbook/geos/rp.html

Church, A.T. (1986). *Filipino personality: A review of research and writings.* Manila: De La Salle University Press.

Cimmarusti, R.A. (1996). Exploring aspects of Filipino-American families. *Journal of Marital and Family Therapy, 22,* 205–217.

Cordova, F. (1983). *Filipinos: Forgotten Asian Americans.* Dubuque, IA: Kendall/Hunt.

Devine, E., & Braganti, N.L. (1986). *The traveler's guide to Asian customs and manners.* New York: St. Martin's Press.

Enriquez, V.G. (1987, November). Filipino values: Toward a new interpretation. *Tasibol,* pp. 29–34.

Enriquez, V.G. (1992). *From colonial to liberation psychology: The Philippine experience.* Quezon City, Philippines: University of the Philippines Press.

Filipino family. Retrieved October 2, 2002 from http://www.seasite.niu.edu

Fuentes, N. (1990, May). *Working with Pilipino families.* Paper presented at the Lanterman Regional Center Conference, Enhancing Multicultural Awareness: Serving Immigrant Families, Los Angeles.

Garza, E., & Scott, C.M. (1996, November). *Language perceptions and practices of Filipino-American immigrants.* Paper presented at the annual meeting of the American Speech-Language-Hearing Association, Seattle, WA.

Gochenour, T. (1990). *Considering Filipinos.* Yarmouth, ME: Intercultural Press.

Gudykunst, W.B. (2001). *Asian American ethnicity and communication.* Thousand Oaks, CA: Sage Publications.

Guthrie, G.M. (1968). *The Philippine temperament: Six perspectives on the Philippines.* Manila: Bookmark.

Harper, P., & Fullerton, L. (1994). *Philippines handbook.* Emeryville, CA: Publishers Group West.

Jocano, F.L. (2001). *Filipino prehistory: Rediscovering precolonial heritage.* Quezon City, Philippines: PUNLAD Research House.

Kang, K.C. (1996, January 26). Filipinos happy with life in U.S., but lack united voice. *Los Angeles Times,* pp. A1, A20.

Karnow, S. (1989). *In our image: America's empire in the Philippines.* New York: Random House.

Lassiter, S.M. (1995). *Multicultural clients: A professional handbook for health care providers and social workers.* Westport, CT: Greenwood Press.

Lawless, R. (1969). *An evaluation of Philippine culture-personality research.* Quezon City: University of the Philippines Press.

Li, C. (1983). The basic grammatical structures of selected Asian languages and English. In M. Chu-Chang (Ed.), *Asian- and Pacific-American perspectives in bilingual education: Comparative research* (pp. 3–30). New York: Teachers College Press.

Licuanan, P.B. (1988, April 27). *A moral recovery program: Building a people—building a nation.* Report submitted to Senator Letician Romas-Shahani, Manila.

Liu, J., Ong, P., & Rosenstein, C. (1991). Filipino immigration to the United States. *International Migration Review, 25,* 487–513.

Llamanzares, C.V. (1999). Rearing children: Filipino parenting styles. *Philippine Journal of Nursing, 69,* 7–11.

Lott, J.T. (1997). Demographic changes transforming the Filipino American community. In M.P.P. Root (Ed.), *Filipino Americans: Transformation and identity* (pp. 11–20). Beverly Hills: Sage Publications.

Marquez, E. (1991, April). *Pilipino care providers.* Paper presented at the San Gabriel/Pomona Regional Center Conference, Enhancing Multicultural Awareness, Baldwin Park, CA.

McKenzie, J.L., & Chrisman, N.J. (1977). Healing, herbs, gods, and magic: Folk health beliefs among Filipino-Americans. *Nursing Outlook, 25,* 326–329.

Montepio, S.N. (1986/1987). Folk medicine in the Filipino American experience. *Amerasia Journal, 13,* 151–162.

Morales, R. (1990, April). *Considerations in serving Pilipino clients.* Paper presented at the Harbor Regional Center Conference, Toward Competence in Intercultural Interaction, Torrance, CA.

Morales, R.F. (1974). *Makibaka: The Pilipino-American struggle.* Mountain View, CA: Mountain View Press.

The Official Government Portal of the Republic of the Philippines web site. *About the Philippines.* Retrieved March 3, 2003, from http://www.gov.ph/aboutphil/default.asp

Okamura, J.Y., & Agbayani, A. (1991). Filipino Americans. In N. Mokuau (Ed.), *Handbook of social services for Asian and Pacific Islanders* (pp. 97–115). Westport, CT: Greenwood Publishing Corporation.

Pan Asian Parent Education Project (PAPEP). (1982). *Pan Asian childrearing practices: Filipino, Japanese, Korean, Samoan, Vietnamese.* San Diego: Union of Pan Asian Communities.

Pernia, E.M. (1976). The question of the brain drain from the Philippines. *International Migration Review, 10,* 63–72.

Posadas, B.M. (1986/1987). At a crossroad: Filipino American history and the old-timers' generation. *Amerasia Journal, 13,* 85–97.

Posadas, B.M. (1999). *The new Americans series: The Filipino Americans.* Westport, CT: Greenwood Press.

Rita, E.S. (1996). Pilipino families. In M. McGoldrick, J. Giordano, & J.K. Pearce (Eds.), *Ethnicity and family therapy* (pp. 324–330). New York: Guilford Press.

Roces, A., & Rocees, G. (1985). *Culture shock! Philippines.* Singapore: Time Books International.

Root, M.P.P. (1997). *Filipino Americans: Transformation and identity.* Thousand Oaks, CA: Sage Publications.

Roseberry-McKibbin, C. (1997). Understanding Filipino families: A foundation for effective service delivery. *American Journal of Speech-Language Pathology, 6,* 5–14.

Salvador, D.S., Omizo, M.M., & Kim, B.S.K. (1997). Bayanihan: Providing effective counseling strategies with children of Filipino ancestry. *Journal of Multicultural Counseling and Development, 25,* 201–209.

San Juan, E., Jr. (1998). *From exile to diaspora: Versions of the Filipino experience in the United States.* Boulder, CO: Westview Press.

Santos, R.A. (1983). The social and emotional development of Filipino-American children. In G.J. Powell (Ed.), *The psychosocial development of minority group children* (pp. 131–146). New York: Brunner/Mazel.

Shimabukuro, K.P., Daniels, J., & D'Andrea, M. (1999). Addressing spiritual issues from a cultural perspective: The case of the grieving Filipino boy. *Journal of Multicultural Counseling and Development, 27,* 221–239.

Schoenberger, K. (1994, August 1). Living off expatriate labor. *Los Angeles Times,* pp. A1, A16–A17.

Soldevilla, E. (1989, September). *Serving Pilipino clients.* Paper presented at the North Los Angeles County Regional Center Conference, Cross-Cultural Issues in a Multicultural Society of Personal and Professional Aspects, Los Angeles.

Steinberg, D.J. (1994). *The Philippines: A singular and plural place.* Boulder, CO: Westview Press.

Suzuki, B.H. (1989, November/December). Asian Americans as the "model minority"—Outdoing whites or media hype? *Change,* 13–19.

Takaki, R. (1989). *Strangers from a different shore: A history of Asian Americans.* Boston: Little, Brown.

Tamayo-Lott, J. (1997). Demographic changes transforming Filipino American community. In M.P.P. Root (Ed.), *Filipino Americans: Transformation and identity* (pp. 11–20). Thousand Oaks, CA: Sage Publications.

The National Data Book (121st ed.). (2001). *Statistical abstract of the U.S.: 2001.* Author.

Tseng, V., & Fuligni, A.J. (2000). Parent-adolescent language use and relationships among immigrant families with East Asian, Filipino, and Latin American backgrounds. *Journal of Marriage and the Family, 62,* 465–476.

Union of Pan Asian Communities (UPAC). (1980). *Understanding the Pan Asian client: Book II.* San Diego: Author.

U.S. Bureau of the Census. (1993). *1990 census of population, Asian and Pacific Islanders in the United States* [Electronic version]. Washington, DC: U.S. Government Printing Office.

U.S. Bureau of the Census. (2002a). *A profile of the nation's foreign-born population from Asia* (2000 Update) [Electronic version]. Washington, DC: U.S. Government Printing Office.

U.S. Bureau of the Census. (2002b). *The Asian population: 2000* [Electronic version]. Washington, DC: U.S. Government Printing Office.

Vance, A.R. (1991). Filipino Americans. In J.N. Giger & R.E. Davidhizar (Eds.), *Transcultural nursing: Assessment and intervention* (pp. 279–401). St. Louis, MO: Mosby.

Winter, F.H. (1988). *The Filipinos in America.* Minneapolis, MN: Lerner Publications.

Yap, J. (1982, May). *The Filipino American family.* The Asian American Journey, *5,* 15–17.

APPENDIX A

CONTRASTING BELIEFS, VALUES, AND PRACTICES

Although Pilipino-Americans may appear to have a Western orientation and share a heritage heavily influenced by Hispanic Catholicism and Euro-Christian ethics, their sense of identity is uniquely Pilipino. Many of their traditional beliefs, values, and practices reflect the collectivist orientation of other Asian cultures. Thus, Appendix A in Chapter 8 may be more applicable to traditional Pilipinos, with the following exceptions regarding religion and family:

Pilipino	**Traditional Asian**
Monotheistic (e.g., Christian-Roman Catholic)	Polytheistic, spiritualistic
Bilateral kinship system	Patrilineal kinship system
Roles between men and women are more egalitarian	Men tend to dominate women
Parents use persuasion and model concepts of compromise, mutual respect, and maintenance of smooth interpersonal relationships	Demand unquestioning obedience and absolute submission to authority

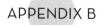

CULTURAL COURTESIES AND CUSTOMS

The following behaviors and expectations are representative of customs in the Philippines. Although Pilipino Americans constitute a highly diverse population characterized by many levels of acculturation, there remains a need to demonstrate sensitivity to the families and clients who value traditional social practices. (Much of the information provided in this section was obtained from Bosrock [1994], Devine & Braganti [1986], and Roces & Roces [1985].)

Greetings

English greetings are customary. On first and subsequent meetings, the appropriate greeting is a handshake both between same-sex adults and men and women. In most informal situations, the handshake is friendly and casual. Pilipinos may also greet each other by making eye contact, then quickly raising their eyebrows to signify recognition.

Special terms such as *lolo* and *lola* are used (particularly among relatives) when greeting older people. Even greater honor is shown by placing one's hand on your or the other person's forehead while saying *mano po*, which is a time-honored gesture of respect. Here are some other ways to show respect:

- Show respect for elders by greeting (and saying goodbye) to the oldest person first.

- When visiting a family's home, expect children to leave shortly after they greet you. They often do not remain when a guest is visiting.

Nonverbal Behavior and Communication

- Beckoning someone with an index finger may be interpreted as a sign of contempt. Instead, extend your arm and hand, palm down, and make a scratching motion with your fingers.

- Holding hands in public between individuals of the same gender is acceptable; this gesture often has no sexual implications.

- Never show anger or criticize someone in public. People are expected to control their emotions and avoid direct confrontation.

- Some Pilipinos may smile or laugh when upset or embarrassed.

- "Yes" is signified by a jerk of the head upward. "No" may be signified by a jerk of the head down.

- Prolonged eye contact or staring may be uncomfortable for some.

- Pilipinos may touch someone's elbow lightly to attract his or her attention.

- To point at an object or a person, some Pilipinos may shift their eyes toward the person or purse their lips and point with their mouth.

- In social situations, Pilipinos extend their hands and stoop when passing in front or between two people.

Conversation

- In an initial encounter, be prepared for people to ask personal questions of you (e.g., whether you are married, whether you have children). Such questions are typically intended to be an expression of interest in the person and a way of showing concern or pleasure at seeing a person or of sharing in the other's condition or good fortune (as opposed to simply being inappropriately nosy or intrusive). In fact, the question "Where are you going?" is a direct translation of a common Pilipino greeting, *Saan ka pupunta?* This may often mean in effect no more than a "Hi." A typical response that is given might be, "Just around the corner" or "Just taking a walk." The importance of the interaction is the exchange of friendly responses rather than the exchange of content and information per se (Gochenour, 1990).

- Do not immediately assume that Pilipino immigrants who appear to be fluent in English have extensive English language comprehension. You may need to speak somewhat more slowly and carefully to avoid misunderstandings. However, you should also be wary of offending truly English-proficient Pilipinos who speak with an "accent" by speaking to them in an overly simplistic manner. You should further refrain from correcting certain word pronunciations, grammar, and so forth, and/or fixating on selected English words or phrases that may be initially difficult to understand. As noted previously, English-speaking Pilipino immigrants typically have a high degree of self-consciousness about their relative English language proficiency. The importance of preserving their "face" should outweigh the need to comprehend literally all of their speech during an initial encounter.

- In conversations or meetings with a family, questions are typically first directed to the adults. If elders are participating, it is very important not to disagree publicly with them.

Private Homes

- Removing your shoes before entering a house is considered appropriate to some Pilipinos.

- Expect to be offered food or drinks, and partake of such hospitality.

- If served a meal, you may be given a fork and spoon, but not a knife. The spoon is to be held in your right hand and the fork in your left. Push food onto the spoon with the fork, and eat from the spoon.

Gift Giving

- Food and other personal gifts often serve as small tokens of appreciation. Such gifts may pose significant dilemmas for interventionists employed by agencies that enforce policies prohibiting the acceptance of gifts of this nature.

APPENDIX C

SIGNIFICANT CULTURAL EVENTS/HOLIDAYS/PRACTICES

Pilipino Americans typically celebrate the same holidays observed in the United States (e.g., Thanksgiving, Christmas, New Year's Day, Easter, Memorial Day, and Labor Day) in the home with family and friends. Other holidays they may celebrate include:

- Holy Week—week before Easter
- Holy or Maundy Thursday—3 days before Easter
- Good Friday—2 days before Easter
- Philippine Independence Day—June 12
- Philippine-American Friendship Day—July 4
- All Saints' Day—November 1
- Rizal Day—December 30 (anniversary of the death of Dr. Jose P. Rizal, a Philippine national hero)

Special Household Celebrations

Birthdays, anniversaries, baptisms, confirmations, graduations, and arrival and departures of guests and relatives are among the special occasions that typically are celebrated at home. The celebrants customarily spare no expense in setting a lavish display of food and drink for their guests and friends.

These celebrations provide opportunities to display one's hospitality. Often, tables are loaded with several entrees, desserts, and other delicacies served buffet style. Usually an extraordinary amount of food is prepared. This is not viewed as extravagant, but as a gesture of generosity. Extra food is usually given to guests to take home with them.

These celebrations tend to be very adult centered. Even children's birthdays may often become occasions for parents to invite their adult relatives and friends, with children, to the festivities. The birthday celebrant is not the "star of the show" as is customary at American birthday parties. However, with increasing acculturation, "many Filipino-American families are now incorporating some of the more child-centered aspects of birthdays and other celebrations" (Santos, 1983, p. 137).

Note: The traditional rituals and practices associated with newborns and baptisms are described in the Beliefs and Child Rearing section of this chapter.

VOCABULARY

English	Tagalog	Pronunciation
Hello (How are you?)	Kumusta po kayo	Koo-moos-ta pó kī-yo
Goodbye	Paalam na po	Pa-ah-lahm na pó
Yes	Oo	O-o
	Opo	Oh pó
No	Hindi	Heen-dée
Please	Paki	Pah-key
Thank you	Salamat	Sah-láh-maht
Father	Tatay	Tah-tī
Mother	Nanay	Nah-nī
Older sister	Ate	Ah-te
Older brother	Kuya	Koo-yah
Sibling	Kapatid	Kah-pah-teed
Family	Pamilya	Pah-ḿeel-ya

CHAPTER 10

FAMILIES WITH NATIVE HAWAIIAN AND SAMOAN ROOTS

Noreen Mokuau and Pemerika Tauili'ili

He hi`i alo ua milimili `ia i ke alo, ua ha`awe `ia ma ke kua,
ua lei `ia ma ka`ā`ā`ī.
(A beloved one, fondled in the arms, carried on the back,
whose arms have gone about the neck as a lei.)
NATIVE HAWAI'IAN
—PUKUI 1983

O tama a tagata e fafaga i upu, ao tama a manu e fafaga i
fuga o la'au.
(Human children are fed with words, but animal children
are fed with flowers.)
—SAMOAN SAYING

The Pacific Ocean encompasses approximately 64 million square miles (Quigg, 1987), with the central area being divided into three major geographical areas known as Melanesia, Micronesia, and Polynesia. Fiji, New Guinea, New Caledonia, and the Solomon Islands make up the major land areas of Melanesia; the Federated States of Micronesia, the Northern Mariana Islands, the Marshall Islands, Guam, and Palau form Micronesia; and New Zealand, Tonga, Tahiti, Samoa, and Hawai'i make up the major island geography of Polynesia. This chapter describes the two Pacific Island groups with the highest population census in the United States: Native Hawaiians and Samoans. The descriptive information on background origins, contemporary life, values, beliefs, and language provides the context from which to examine appropriate and effective intervention with these cultures. Such a context provides a generalized profile of Native Hawaiians and Samoans, and, therefore, it is important to note that diversity within each group may not always be fully expressed.

BACKGROUND

The origin and migration of Native Hawaiians and Samoans to the islands of Hawai'i and Samoa vary according to different accounts (Nordyke, 1989) because there is no written information to document the geographical movements of these peoples. Data from archeological, botanical, and linguistic studies does trace the probable origin of Polynesians to southern Asia, however (Nordyke, 1989).

Geographic Origins

Buck (1981) suggested that the ancestors of the Polynesian people came from the Himalayas, moved through the Malay archipelago, and then migrated east into the Pacific. The Polynesians, strong seafaring voyagers, hypothetically traveled through either the Micronesian chain or the Melanesian islands, eventually reaching the Polynesian islands of Hawai'i and Samoa. Native Hawaiians settled in Hawai'i approximately 2,000 years ago (Blaisdell, 1989), and Samoans settled in Samoa approximately 1,000 years before that (Nordyke, 1989). In the years considered "precontact," or before Western contact, Native Hawaiians and Samoans developed unique cultural systems that flourished. While living in isolation from the rest of the world, Native Hawaiians and Samoans cultivated a relationship with the land that contributed to a thriving, prosperous people who maintained clearly demarcated systems of spirituality, education, economics, and politics.

Historical Origins

The robust cultural systems that Native Hawaiians and Samoans developed underwent significant change with the advent of Western influence. The first documented contact between Europeans and Samoans occurred in 1722, with the arrival of the Dutch navigator Jacob Roggeveen. Soon thereafter, in the 1830s, Christian missionaries and the London Missionary Society converted the Samoan people to their teachings (Brigham Young University [BYU], 1977). The London Missionary Society, in particular, had a profound religious and educational impact on Samoan lives as it reduced the influence of traditional spirit lore and ancient mythology (Holmes, 1974). The United States, England, and Germany asserted their influence over Samoan culture through administration and occupation throughout the major portion of the

20th century. In 1900, Samoa was divided into two parts: American Samoa, which was administered by the United States, and Western Samoa, which was administered by a German and then a New Zealand administration. In the 21st century, American Samoa is still affiliated with the United States as a territory, and Western Samoa, although now an independent nation, still maintains ties with New Zealand as well as with the United States. The influence of these foreign countries has had an effect on Samoan cultural subsystems such as religion, education, economics, and politics. However, a policy agreement between the U.S. Department of Interior and American Samoa in 1951 upholds an honoring of cultural norms and traditions. Professor Lowell Holmes, an anthropologist who conducted field research in American Samoa in 1954, 1962–1963, and 1974, captured the sentiment in the agreement:

> The customs of the Samoans not in conflict with the laws of the United States concerning American Samoa shall be preserved. The village, county, and district councils consisting of the hereditary chiefs and their talking chiefs shall retain their own form or forms of meeting together to discuss affairs of the village, county or district according to their own Samoan custom. (Holmes, 1974, p. 16)

Native Hawaiians were introduced to Western culture with the arrival of the English ships led by Captain James Cook in 1778. By 1820, missionaries of the American Board of Commissioners for Foreign Missions began the conversion of these islands to Christianity and the transformation of "the nation of half-naked savages. ...eating raw fish, fighting among themselves...and abandoned to sensuality" (Hopkins, 1862, p. 194). Throughout the 19th century, visitors from the United States, England, Germany, Spain, Portugal, and other countries influenced massive changes not only in the religious practices but also in the political and socioeconomic practices of Native Hawaiian people. The coming of Westerners had a nearly fatal impact on the Native Hawaiian population, causing a dramatic decline of the number of pureblood Native Hawaiians by the 20th century (Nordyke, 1989). Demographic estimates indicate that the Native Hawaiian population at the time of Captain Cook's arrival was between 800,000 and 1,000,000; yet, by 1893, slightly more than 100 years after that first Western contact, the Native Hawaiian population decreased to 40,000 (Stannard, 1989). This depopulation is primarily attributed to diseases to which the Native Hawaiians had no immunity, such as chickenpox, measles, and venereal diseases. Significant in this period of depopulation was the overthrow of the Native Hawaiian monarchy by the United States in 1893.

The decline of the pure blood Native Hawaiian population through high mortality rates and poor health status continues (Blaisdell, 1993; Look & Braun, 1995). Furthermore, high rates of interracial marriage contribute to a decline of pureblood Native Hawaiians. Increases in the population of interracial children and families reflect a variety of Asian cultures such as Japanese, Chinese, and Pilipino, as well as a blending of other Pacific Islander Caucasian, black, Hispanic, and American Indian populations. When Hawai'i assumed statehood in 1959, Native Hawaiians were only one group among the culturally diverse populations of the islands; and they, along with other residents, experienced the attendant privileges and problems of association with the United States.

Religious Origins

Western contact has shaped the prevailing religious systems in both Hawai'i and Samoa. In Hawai'i, in addition to Catholic and Protestant denominations, there are sects with origins in Eastern religions. In American Samoa, the principal denominations are the Christian Congregational Church, the Roman Catholic Church, the Methodist Church, and the Church of Jesus Christ of Latter-Day Saints (Mormon) (BYU, 1977). Missionaries from Great Britain introduced the Christian religion to the Samoan islands, and missionaries from the United States introduced the Mormon religion. The church assumes a very powerful role in the lives of the Samoan people, with each village having a church, strict observation of the Sabbath, and the practice of prayer hours.

Prior to Western contact, Native Hawaiians and Samoans held similar views of spirituality in terms of the belief that people, the natural environment, and the transcendent realm were all connected. In general, they believed in the reciprocity of humankind and the environment such that their caring for the land would contribute to the land providing sustenance to the people. Furthermore, elements of the natural environment were believed to be imbued with spiritual power, often characterized as ancestral guardians.

In Samoan culture of the 21st century, the Christian and Mormon teachings are prevalent. The early missionaries who brought Christianity to the Samoan islands almost succeeded in ridding Samoa of precontact views on spirituality. There are no native gods or idols except in the written language, in which the goddess Nafanua, the god Tagaloa and others are only briefly described. In the oratory chiefly language, reference is made to important precontact spiritual events called *taeao*, but very often the

Alisi was born in American Samoa and emigrated to Hawai'i several years ago with her first husband, a Samoan pastor. Shortly after moving from Hawai'i to California in 1997, Alisi's husband died suddenly. She relied heavily on the church network for support for her and her 2-year-old son. Alisi, now 38 years old, is remarried and has a second child.

Despite having lived in Hawai'i for 5 years, Alisi is limited in her awareness and knowledge of Western ideas. The information that she does have has been gained primarily from watching television and is, therefore, quite biased and distorted. She lives in a predominantly Samoan community, associates almost exclusively with other Samoans who attend her church, and participates actively in Samoan cultural events such as weddings and funerals.

One of the conflicts between Alisi's Samoan culture and Western ideas has brought her to family court, where she has been accused of physically abusing both of her children. When the children have not responded quickly to her demands, she has used rulers and belts as a method of discipline. When asked to explain such harsh treatment, Alisi has said, "I didn't want to spoil the child."

To be successful, the family court workers who are working with Alisi will have to intervene in a culturally appropriate way. Because Alisi is relatively traditional in her values and views of the world, it would be helpful to emphasize the family, the pastor, and the church network. Some of the following intervention strategies might be useful: 1) involve the entire family when exploring alternative ways of child rearing and discipline, 2) invite the family's pastor to participate in some of the sessions, and 3) schedule group discussions with others from the Samoan community who have been in a similar situation.

talking chief will downplay their significance. Despite the dominance of Christianity, however, communication with the spirits of ancestors and those of the underworld is a practice that does emerge in Samoan culture when Western medicinal remedies fail.

Although Christian doctrines are widespread, in Native Hawaiian culture it is evident that appreciation and practice of precontact views of spirituality is growing. In recent research, Native Hawaiian participants define spirituality as *pono* (perfect order) and emphasize the balance of relationships in their lives, with particular reference to balance among the family, others, the environment, and the spiritual realm (Mokuau, Reid & Napalapalai, 2002; Oneha, 2001) Practicing spirituality includes many activities, such as caring for the land (*malama `āina*), holding family healing sessions (*ho`oponopono*), and engaging in traditional forms of martial arts (*lua*) and dance (*hula*). The increased willingness among Native Hawaiians to "relearn" and practice spiritual beliefs associated with their relationships with nature and ancestral guardians, however, does not preclude their subscription to Western religions. For many Native Hawaiians, it appears possible to blend the two.

Language Origins

Native Hawaiian and Samoan cultures are predicated on oral traditions and languages that come from a common stock and are linguistically similar; however, with the arrival of Westerners, the native language was minimized, and Native Hawaiians predominantly wrote and spoke English. The missionaries, however, transformed the native language in the 1820s into written and more or less permanent form (Wise & Judd, 1981). The native language shows an alphabet with 12 letters, with 5 vowels (*a, e, i, o, u*) and 7 consonants (*h, k, l, m, n, p, w*). Every word in the Hawaiian language ends in a vowel and no two consonants occur without a vowel between them (Wise & Judd, 1981). The Native Hawaiian language has a musical quality because of the arrangement of vowels and the absence of harsh consonants. Today, few Native Hawaiians are bilingual, with fluency in both the English and Hawaiian languages. Since the advent of Western contact, Samoans have retained their spoken language while resorting to writing in English. The overwhelming majority of Samoans are bilingual. Samoans in American Samoa speak Samoan both in the workplace and in the home, whereas Samoans in the United States speak Samoan primarily in the home. Similar to the Hawaiian language, the Samoan language has 5 vowels (*a, e, i, o, u*); however, it is different from the Hawaiian language in that it contains 12 consonants (*f, g, l, m, n, p, s, t, v, h, k, r*). Every consonant is followed by a vowel or two (e.g., *fa`afetai*: thank you; *tu`u*: leave it alone), or perhaps three vowels (e.g., *paaa*: bone dried). The break between two vowels is believed to have been a "t" or "k" because those consonants are interchangeable. The Samoan language has words that are foreign to the Samoan culture that can include the letters *h, k,* and *r* (e.g., *Konekeresi*: Congress; *ratio*: radio). The Samoan language, similar to any living language, is dynamic and undergoes changes that result from outside influences.

CONTEMPORARY LIFE IN THE UNITED STATES

The 2000 U.S. Census counted 874,000 Pacific Islanders residing in the United States, with the two largest groups being Native Hawaiians (401,000) and Samoans (133,000) (U.S. Bureau of the Census, 2001b). For the first time, the 2000 U.S. Census collected multiracial information and recorded responses from people who identified with "one race" or with "more than one race." Of all racial groups in the United States, the Pacific Islander population had a much higher proportion of respondents reporting more than one race, and it was the only population in which the number of people reporting two or more races was higher than the number reporting a single race (U.S. Bureau of the Census, 2001b). Sixty-five percent of Native Hawaiians and sixty-eight percent of Samoans reported multiracial backgrounds. Native Hawaiians and Samoans live primarily in the states of Hawai'i and California. Native Hawaiians are indigenous to the islands of Hawai'i but compose only 20% of the total state population of 1,211,537 (Office of Hawaiian Affairs, 2002; U.S. Bureau of the Census, 2001b). Of the 57,000 people residing in the Territory of American Samoa, approximately 90% are of Samoan ancestry (U.S. Bureau of the Census, 2001a).

Many Native Hawaiians in contemporary life have intensified efforts to reclaim an indigenous land base that would serve as a foundation for Native Hawaiian sovereignty. Inherent in these efforts is the importance of cultural revitalization and cultural identity. One leader among the sovereignty movement, Dr. Kekuni Blaisdell, suggested that more Native Hawaiians are ready to "assert their heritage rather than hide it" (as cited in Hosek, 1993, p. A6). Another leader, Ms. Mililani Trask, expressed that "every Hawaiian in his heart would like to be independent" (as cited in Reinhold, 1992, p. B3). Sovereignty efforts have resulted in the Apology Resolution (1993) in which the United States government acknowledged and apologized for the illegal overthrow of the Native Hawaiian government in 1893. Sovereignty efforts have also led to the Hawaiian Federal Recognition Bill (2003), which proposes that Hawaiians be formally recognized as the indigenous people of Hawai'i. In seeking to affirm the indigenous status of Hawaiians and their political relationship with the United States, advocates say this bill will help Hawaiians to achieve parity, with more than 550 Native American and Alaska Native tribes already recognized by the federal government. Many Hawaiians support the Hawaiian Federal Recognition Bill, whereas many others oppose it. Critics argue that the bill lays the foundation for a nation-within-a-nation model of self-governance and thus undermines the intent of self-determination, transfers "wardship" status of Native Hawaiians from the state to the federal government, and minimizes political and legal autonomy of the native people (Kelly, 2002, pp. 5–6). Despite such conflict among Native Hawaiian groups, sovereignty is a topic that will continue to be prominent in the 21st century.

A concern for many Samoans in contemporary life relates to the cultural adjustments inherent in immigrating to the United States. The migration of Samoans to California and Hawai'i from American Samoa has occurred as recently as the 1950s (Mokuau & Chang, 1991). Three major reasons for the migration include 1) the transfer of naval base personnel with the closing of the United States Naval Base in American Samoa in 1951, 2) increased opportunities for education and employment in the United States, and 3) the increase in population and the concomitant lack of employment and economic opportunities in American Samoa (State of California, Department of Mental Health, 1981). In particular, many Samoan young people, both male and female, are recruited into the military each year. To many individuals, the military is viewed as an opportunity to improve one's life and broaden one's horizon. As is true of many newly arriving immigrant populations, Samoans have tended to settle in communities in which there are established ethnic enclaves. Still, immigration to the United States leaves many Samoans feeling disenfranchised (Iyechad,

1992). One common area of conflict encompasses familial and social support. "Samoans often take extended family and church obligations more seriously than they do career advancement or accumulation of capital which commonly define 'success' in America" (Alailima, 1996, p. 89). The absence of large kinship and social networks in the United States contributes to a loss of many cultural norms, such as the use of celebrations to honor Samoan ways (e.g., births, weddings, funerals). Some hypothesize that such losses are related to increasing substance abuse and crime among Samoans, both in Hawai'i and in California (Young & Galea'i, 1999). Furthermore, many Samoans in the United States experience economic problems stemming from sending money to their relatives in American Samoa—in total, more than $1 million annually is sent to relatives in American Samoa in the form of remittances (Alailima, 1996). Sharing the wealth—evident in the continuous flow of money, food, fine mats, and other goods between families in the islands and in the United States—may create economic pressures for many Samoans. This practice solidifies kinship ties, however (Liki, 1999). Pressures of cultural adjustment have mobilized many Samoans to strengthen and use institutions in the United States such as the church and civic associations to facilitate cultural preservation.

Issues of sovereignty and cultural adjustment highlight the need for interventionists working with Native Hawaiian and Samoan families to recognize the importance of cultural "reclaiming" and preservation. In light of a history of oppression and cultural change, contemporary Native Hawaiians and Samoans struggle with cultural preservation as a basic way to maintain identity and integrity. Service providers who support the empowerment of these people will acknowledge their struggle, understand the impact it has on contemporary problems, and help Native Hawaiians and Samoans to participate in the formulation of their own solutions.

VALUES

Values represent what is deemed to be important in life and thereby serve as an index and a guide to the way people define themselves and the world in which they live. Any exploration of values must take into account two key considerations: 1) Values may change in definition and form over time, and 2) people may vary in their perception of and adherence to the same set of values. Since the early 18th century, the values of precontact Native Hawaiian and Samoan cultures have been altered significantly and, to a large extent, have deteriorated with the infusion of Western languages, religions, lifestyle practices, and behavioral norms. Contemporary efforts of cultural revitalization, as exhibited by the Native Hawaiians' sovereignty movement or Samoans' strengthening of the church and civic associations, are viewed as essential steps in the resurgence of traditional cultural values and practices.

The values that exist in the 21st century have relative worth for different people. For Native Hawaiians and Samoans, the degree of acculturation to the majority American culture influences their profile of values. Samoans, who have a relatively short history of residence in the United States, have had fewer opportunities for acculturation than have Native Hawaiians; thus, their maintenance of cultural values is stronger. Within each of these Pacific Islander groups, intragroup variation exists in the promotion of values because of differences in geographical residence, age, gender, socioeconomic status, and so forth. The following section highlights major val-

ues of both Native Hawaiian and Samoan cultures, including relationships, spirituality and religion, and education. The usefulness of this information is contingent on
the interventionist's understanding of the uniqueness of the individual in the context
of these cultural values, however.

Native Hawaiian Values

Most major values of Native Hawaiian culture appear to be derivatives of values associated with relationships, particularly as they reflect the relationship of the individual to the family, the community, the land, and the spiritual world. The fundamental unit in Native Hawaiian culture is the *'ohana* (family), or relatives by blood,
marriage, and adoption (Handy & Pukui, 1977). Emphasis is placed on the needs of
the family unit rather than on the needs of any individual family member.

Family and Spirituality   In traditional times, the family unit functioned as
part of a larger geographical region, and the importance of relationships within the
general community was acknowledged. Handy and Pukui (1977) suggested that implicit in the value of familial relationships is the recognition of the value of the `āina
(land) as a source of food and nourishment. The relationship of the family and the
land is more than just a physical linkage, however; it is perceived as a spiritual bond
between family members and nature. This spiritual bond is amplified as living family members recognize and interact with deceased ancestors who are represented in
nature.

> One . . . hears that old Hawaiians are sometimes observed talking to plants and
> trees before picking their flowers—asking before taking—and that they often
> leave offerings when they take something of significance. . . . Many Hawaiians
> also believe that they have ancestral spirits (`aumākua) who dwell in animal or
> other nature forms. . . And they think of their ancestral spirits, and the nature
> forms they inhabit, as family members. (Dudley, 1990, pp. 1–2)

The spiritual bond also extends to future generations of family members. Traditional
values related to relationships and spirituality are evident among Native Hawaiians
today. As in historical times, the emphasis on genealogy and familial relationships is
depicted in a continuum of past, present, and future generations. For some Native
Hawaiians, the construction of genealogy is a practice that promotes spirituality because it locates oneself within a family tree and affirms the familial and cultural identity (Mokuau, Reid, & Napalapalai, 2002). Furthermore, traditional values continue
to be manifested in actions that demonstrate people's reciprocal relationship with
and caring for the land (*mālama `āina*). For example, ecosystem development in Na-
tive Hawaiian communities is emerging as a viable strategy in which to enhance economic sufficiency and cultural promotion (Mokuau & Matsuoka, 1995). Illustrative
projects emphasize traditional cultural practices of fishing and farming, in which
people receive nourishment and economic support from their work and, at the same
time, observe and respect the traditional norms in their use of the land. The planting
of one crop, taro, occurs ceremonially according to both prayer and planetary cycles.

As discussed previously, many Native Hawaiians appear to believe in a natural
blending of Native Hawaiian spirituality and Western religion. Although differences
may exist between Hawaiian spirituality and Christianity, many Native Hawaiians
perceive common tenets that emphasize love, compassion, and a reverence for a
higher power (Mokuau, Lukela, Obra, & Voeller 1997; Mokuau, Reid, & Napalapalai,

Kekoa, a 7-year-old child of Native Hawaiian, Japanese, Chinese, and Irish ancestry, resides with his mother, aunt, and grandparents in rural O'ahu, Hawai'i. Kekoa's mother, Nalani, is a young, single parent who is busy trying to complete requirements for her associate of arts degree from a local community college, working part-time as a waitress, and assuming her parenting responsibilities. One additional activity that Nalani is dedicated to is her education in *hula halau*. After studying this for 10 years, Nalani has learned a lot about Native Hawaiian culture and has a strong sense of her cultural identity. Despite such a busy schedule, Nalani and Kekoa share a close and loving relationship. Kekoa's grandparents and aunt, who often serve as additional caregivers, support this relationship.

Even though the home environment has its special challenges, Kekoa seems to thrive there; however, the school environment is different. Kekoa often engages in behaviors that are disruptive to class, such as talking when the teacher is talking. He occasionally gets into fights when he is teased for being "a dumb Hawaiian." His grades reveal below standard performance. Such behaviors and school performance prompted an assessment by the counselor, during which Kekoa was assessed as having special education needs, and, in particular, he was diagnosed as "hard of hearing."

For the interventionist, several areas might be considered. Kekoa needs to receive developmentally appropriate education to accommodate his hearing disorder. The involvement of Nalani and, if necessary, her parents are essential and twofold. They need to understand the nature of, and resolution to, the diagnosis, and they need to help Kekoa understand his special needs and ensure a smooth transition.

Nalani is also considering enrolling Kekoa in a Hawaiian language immersion program to strengthen his understanding and identification with Native Hawaiian culture. Her desire for Kekoa to take language lessons in Native Hawaiian as well as to support Kekoa's development will contribute to increased quality time between mother and son.

2002). One example of Christian ways mixed with precontact spiritual beliefs in practice might be a Christian minister who teaches about Jesus Christ, yet still invokes the help of his ancestral guardian spirit (Kanahele, 1986).

Education and Schooling   Education, like relationships and spirituality, was highly valued in traditional Native Hawaiian culture. In traditional times, respected elders transmitted knowledge embracing all aspects of life through the spoken word. Native Hawaiians believed that all children should be recipients of instruction and should have opportunities to observe and learn. In contemporary times, although education is still valued among Native Hawaiians, educational opportunities and attainment have eroded. Economic and social factors such as low income, high rates of teenage pregnancy, and high rates of child abuse and neglect have a negative impact on "school readiness" (Ho`owaiwai Na Kamali`i, 2002). Moreover, reports indicate that Native Hawaiian students in elementary and secondary schools in Hawai'i are not at parity with other students, both nationally and in Hawai'i, and they consistently score below the norm on standardized tests (Ho`owaiwai Na Kamali`i, 2002). When comparing the University of Hawaii degree completion rates in 2000 for Native Hawaiians with other major ethnic groups in Hawai'i, Native Hawaiians have rates comparable with Pilipinos (both groups have approximately 12%) but lower than Caucasians and Japanese (both have approximately 20%) (Office of Hawaiian Affairs, 2002).

Implications Service providers working with Native Hawaiian people may draw several implications from this emphasis on the value of relationships, spirituality, and education. First and foremost, interventionists should focus on the family system rather than just the individual. For example, the goals or objectives identified

as part of the intervention should advance the needs and the desires of the family over the aspirations of one family member. Second, the high value placed on relationships suggests that interventionists must define and address interpersonal interactions among Native Hawaiian people in culturally appropriate ways. For example, acknowledging and working with a *haku* (family elder or leader) may facilitate linkages and coordination of family meetings. Third, interventionists must consider the Native Hawaiian value placed on spiritual relationships. Communion with the land and with spiritual ancestors is critical for many Native Hawaiians; the interventionist must be sensitive to such values and not impose typical Western judgments that assume such beliefs and practices are "bizarre" or "crazy." In fact, values of spiritual relationships might even be incorporated proactively into the intervention plan (Mokuau, 1990). Finally, education remains an important element in the ability of individuals to define themselves, and interventionists who facilitate educational opportunities for Native Hawaiians should demonstrate an ultimate respect for the integrity of Native Hawaiian people.

Samoan Values

In a general sense, the major values held by Native Hawaiian and Samoan cultures are similar. "Dominant values . . . in Samoan culture focus on the family, communal relationships, and the church" (Mokuau & Chang, 1991).

Family and Religion The Samoan way of life is organized around the `aiga (family), which is a hierarchical system comprising nuclear and extended families. The structure is determined by rank or chiefly status as well as by age and gender. For example, a *matai* (village chief) is responsible for the welfare of all related families in a village, and each household may have its own chief. The females are subordinate to the males, and the young always defer to the old. The family's goal is the well-being of all of its members, and a "family" may be as large as an entire village. A Samoan individual carries the sacredness (*pa`ia*) of his or her `aiga, and whatever that person does is reflected on the whole family and vice versa (Liki, 1999). The values inherent in such a system include reciprocity, cooperation, and interdependence. A Samoan phrase that reflects the structure, responsibilities, and values of the family is *"E leai se isi e tu faa-mauga"* ("No one stands like a mountain"). This phrase emphasizes the value system that people are interconnected and dependent on one another, should not stand alone, and should always consider how one's actions will affect others.

The church is a highly valued institution in Samoan culture—one that is in direct contact with the family system. The church affirms the structure and responsibilities of the family and, in turn, is supported by contributions from the families. The largest Samoan church congregations in Hawai'i, the London Missionary Society (LMS), are Samoan-speaking and can generate enough income to purchase their own church property and buildings (Alailima, 1996). Alailima suggested that the LMS theology helps to stabilize families in perpetuating Samoan language, identity, and customs. For example, church-based activities are facilitated by parents who only speak Samoan to their children. Religious practices in the LMS and other religious denominations are strictly adhered to and include participation in prayer hours in the morning and the evening, church attendance on the Sabbath day (Brigham Young University, 1977), and observance of rituals. The third Sunday in October is Children Sunday or White Sunday, in which children attired in new white clothes recite Bible verses and sing songs before the entire congregation. In past years, this was the only time that children received new clothes. In present day, this is the one special occasion in which children are honored with a special meal, often of their favorite foods, eaten before adults, and served by their parents and other adults.

Education and Schooling   The institution of education, similar to that of religion, is highly valued by Samoan people and represents a major reason for their immigration from American Samoa to the United States. Their completion rates of high school are lower than the rates for the total United States population (71% versus 75%), and their completion rates of college are extremely low (8% versus 20%) (U.S. Bureau of the Census, 1993). Whereas most Samoans complete high school, they are not necessarily encouraged by families to pursue college (Brewer, 1987). Several issues arise when Samoan students are in American schools. One issue relates to the difference between Samoan culture, which values obedience, and American culture, which rewards individuality, and the subsequent confusion experienced by the Samoan student (Alailima, 1996). If and when the student is able to successfully adapt to the creative, individualistic style of learning, problems can be expected in the home because immigrant parents may fear they are losing control of their child.

Another issue in education pertains to the difference between Samoan culture, which places a greater value on family obligations than education, and American culture, which emphasizes completion of school. Samoans who subscribe to traditional values of family priority will miss school occasionally and sometimes drop out permanently to stay at home to care for someone or to seek menial work to provide economic support (Brewer, 1987). Another educational issue is the lack of bilingual teachers for an immigrant population and the importance of language supports for quality education. The challenges to learning are exacerbated for those students who are not fluent in the English language and who have teachers who communicate solely in English.

Implications   Several implications for intervention emerge from this discussion of values. Similar to the situation with Native Hawaiians, the focus for the Samoan population should be on the extended family system rather than on the individual. Yet, realistically, it would be extremely difficult for the interventionist to work with these large groups of people making up the family system. Conferring with and involving individuals in the extended family system who have authority, such as the chiefs, however, may be appropriate and helpful in resolving family problems. Using a few phrases from the Samoan language establishes lines of communication much faster. For example, it is helpful to use a common greeting such as *talofa* (hello). Or, it is helpful to note the language distinctions for different people; for example, in greeting a high chief, pastor, elderly female, or chief's wife, the translation of "How are you?" is "*O a mai lau Susuga?*", but in greeting a talking chief, the translation is "*O a mai lau tofa?*" and when greeting anyone else, the proper address is "*O a mai oe?*"

Another implication relates to the hierarchical nature of the family system and the appropriate ways to initiate and maintain discussions in the process of intervention. Interventionists need to be knowledgeable of the family lineage and to recognize the members who exercise family authority and thereby acknowledge through appropriate greetings these individuals of authority. To further any discussion, it also is important for interventionists to recognize the rituals of culturally appropriate behavior, such as 1) presenting a posture of interest and concern for the welfare of the family; 2) not delving into personal issues or difficulties too soon in the intervention process; and 3) maintaining all conversations from a sitting position, never standing. Finally, because Samoans place a high status on the church and the pastor, in many cases, involving the pastor in the intervention would be culturally appropriate.

BELIEFS

The following section highlights beliefs and behavioral norms of Native Hawaiian and Samoan people that may be especially relevant to service providers.

Beliefs involving children, disability and causation, health and healing, and death and dying are in some ways manifested in the behavioral norms of Native Hawaiians and Samoans. It is important to note, however, that like values, beliefs and the strength of these beliefs may change over time and individuals' perceptions of them may differ.

Native Hawaiian Beliefs

Children   The worth of children in Native Hawaiian culture is captured in the saying, "A house without children is a house without life" (Young, 1980, p. 12). Young further described the Hawaiians' commitment to their children, "In any Hawaiian community children are everywhere. In virtually every home children are coddled, showered with attention, and fondled. Seldom is an infant left alone when crying. There is much contact, touching, and caressing" (1980, p. 12).

The care of children is promoted in the strongly interdependent traditional family system, and many people have child-rearing responsibilities. Although parents hold primary responsibility for their children, grandparents and other Native Hawaiian elders also contribute to the physical, emotional, and spiritual care of the children. In this respect, child care is an extended family and community responsibility. In traditional times, the *hiapo* (firstborn child) was permanently given to the grand-

parents, and on other occasions, infants who were not the first born were sometimes given to other relatives who asked for them (Pukui, Haertig, Lee, & McDermott, 1979). This process of informal adoption, *hānai*, was common. As a result of the closeness of the family unit, the giving of the child did not necessarily mean parent–child separation. Rather, it meant that the child grew up in a household in which he or she could count on the support of the grandparents, parents, and other family seniors. Some accounts suggest that the informal adoption process still occurs among Native Hawaiian families today. Thus, it is not uncommon for children to have strong relationships with parents and grandparents and to have many family members taking care of their welfare (Korbin, 1990).

The emphasis on familial networking is evidenced in the work of one organization, the Queen Lili`uokalani Children's Center, which has as its mission the caring of orphaned Native Hawaiian children and their families. When a child is without one or both parents, the center's first approach is to preserve the family by placing that child with a relative. The pioneering position of this organization is observed in their vision for the future that emphasizes not only the family but also the welfare of the community (Queen Lili`uokalani Children's Center, 1997). An undergirding belief is that the welfare of the child is related to the welfare of the entire community.

Disability and Causation   Little information exists on children's disabilities in traditional Native Hawaiian culture, either in the period before Western contact or immediately thereafter. It is not clear whether the unavailability of information is a result of the low numbers of disabilities in historical times, people's preference to emphasize only the healthy children, or a preference to not distinguish children with disabilities from those without disabilities. A noted authority on Native Hawaiian culture, Mary Kawena Pukui, when discussing infants born with congenital abnormalities, recalled that children with club feet were accepted and that massage efforts were used to correct the malformed foot (Pukui et al., 1979). Pukui also recalled that atypical infants or miscarried fetuses that resembled things of nature such as fishes or lizards were "returned" to the ocean or another body of water. The pre-Christian belief was that the child looked like and was a form of the family ancestral spirits and must be returned to these ancestor gods. This type of historical belief assumes importance for intervention because it affirms the value of spirituality and the need to consider spiritual variables when working with Native Hawaiians who subscribe to traditional values. In line with such historical beliefs, a qualitative study indicated that Pacific Island parents of children with disabilities viewed their experiences as being a punishment or gift from God or other spiritual entities and engaged in prayer as a form of coping (Nishimoto, 1999). People from these cultures have a sense that life events are directly related to the working of the spiritual world, and although these individuals are not totally helpless to these events, some things are beyond the control of the individual. Congenital abnormalities and infant mortality rates are higher for Native Hawaiians than they are for other ethnic groups in Hawai'i (Bell, Nordyke, & O'Hagan, 1989; Office of Hawaiian Affairs, 2002), and an understanding of the importance of spirituality may play an important role in intervention.

Health and Healing   In historical times, medical care often was left to *kahuna lapa'au* (medical experts) who used prayers, physical massage, and medicinal plants and herbs (Blaisdell, 1989). In contemporary times, much credibility is attributed to individuals of such status, and interventionists should consider appropriate referral and linkages with kahuna lapa'au. Pukui, Haertig, and Lee suggested that to denigrate the client's belief in the *kahuna man* or in the "prayer lady" may only reinforce resistance to accepting treatment at a medical clinic or a hospital (1972, p. 165). Although systematic findings about the utilization of health care services are lacking, the limited evidence reviewed suggests that Native Hawaiians receive fewer health care services than other ethnic groups in Hawai'i (Blaisdell-Brennan & Goebert, 2001; Tsark, Blaisdell & Aluli, 1998), even though they experience substantially higher rates of health problems (Johnson, Oyama, & Le Marchand, 1998). Underutilization of services might stem from many reasons, including lack of geographical accessibility, lack of medical insurance, high cost of services, cultural biases of health care workers, and cultural inappropriateness of the programs. Attention to these areas will facilitate Native Hawaiians' use of medical clinics and hospitals in the future.

Death and Dying   Native Hawaiian spirituality and Christian beliefs also are evident in matters pertaining to death and dying. Braun and Nichols reported that some Native Hawaiians accept death as a part of life and see "an 'openness' between this life and the next" (1996, p. 261). Some Native Hawaiians believe in different realms of being and the ability of spirits and people to communicate between realms. Specifically, `aumākua (family ancestors who have become gods) watch over descendants; they judge and punish as well as serve as protectors (Pukui et al., 1979). The `aumākua and people converse about many of the things that affect daily living. In qualitative studies on Native Hawaiian spirituality, participants affirmed the importance of `aumākua but also revealed strong reverence for the Christian God (Mokuau et al., 1997; Mokuau, Reid, & Napalapalai, 2002). Focus group participants indicated that God is always present in their lives and implied that the events of their lives are always possible through God's grace.

Interventionists working with Native Hawaiian families who have lost a child or other member to death can best provide support by focusing on the family. Attending funeral services, providing care for young children, and bringing food to the family are specific activities that demonstrate support. Although the pain from the death of a child can never be diminished, for those Native Hawaiians who maintain a strong sense of native spirituality or religious conviction, the loss is mediated by the awareness that the child is in a place where there is purity and peace. Furthermore, that child is not considered "lost" to the family, but within the embrace of the "spiritual" or ancestral family. Interventionists who acknowledge the appearance, or apparition, of the deceased to family members are acting appropriately and demonstrating respect for traditional beliefs about relationships after death.

Samoan Beliefs

Children   "Samoan culture views children as an asset and source of pride" (BYU, 1977, p. 6). Biological parents are responsible for the discipline and training of their children. Often, however, the chief of the family may function in a parental role and may exercise as much authority as the biological parents (Markoff & Bond, 1980). Many grandparents are brought to live with their children's families, and they are the ones who supervise the grandchildren while the parents are working. Older siblings of very young children also assist in their care.

Samoans believe that the firstborn belongs to the father's family, the next child belongs to the mother's family, and other children born afterward belong to the village consisting of both paternal and maternal families. Three types of adoption occur in Samoa: 1) through the husband's family line (*Tamafai e auala i le faiavaga*), 2) through the wife's family line (*Tamafai e auala i le nofo tane*), and 3) through cheif (*matai*) titles that are not necessarily blood related. (*Tamafai e auala i le gafa*). These are formal adoptions intended to separate the child from the real parent(s), and very often the child assumes the family name of the adopted parents. In contrast, informal adoptions also occur in which the child is raised in a household of grandparents and other family members and maintains some contact with his or her biological parents.

In line with the highly interdependent nature of the family structure, children are taught the importance of mutual sharing. Thus, this belief in sharing may be manifested in children leaving the home for indefinite lengths of time to visit with uncles and aunts or with married brothers or sisters (State of California, Department of Mental Health, 1981). Children also are taught to behave properly and to respect their elders. Illustrations of proper and respectful behavior include sitting down while addressing an older person and not interrupting an adult conversation. The Samoans' emphasis on interdependence and proper behavior in the family system encourages the use of social control as a form of child rearing. In Samoan culture, social control and discipline tend to be overt and direct and often involve physical punishment. "Punitive measures are regularly employed by age three, when children first begin to be involved in the work of the household, and continue through mid-adolescence" (Markoff & Bond, 1980, p. 187).

Disability and Causation   Information on children's disabilities is not documented in Samoan literature and is not a subject discussed in everyday conversation.

Considering the value of children in Samoan culture and the Samoan family's commitment to the church, however, the belief that emerges is that the child with a disability is the result of a poor relationship with God within the family. Newborns are viewed as special gifts from God. In the case of a child with a disability, it is believed that God must be displeased with the family. Abnormalities in Samoa are viewed as the manifestation of some wrong committed by the parents or because the mother passed through a wrong place during pregnancy, or of a higher spiritual power. In such cases, parents will blame themselves or their partner for a child's disability. They believe that they personally exercise very little control over their own destinies and that it is the supernatural powers that cause life events. One qualitative study suggested that Samoan parents of children with disabilities, like other Pacific Island parents, experience pervasive embarrassment and guilt because of their belief that the disability is attributed to the wrongful behavior of ancestral or living family members (Nishimoto, 1999). Some families who hold such beliefs will try their best to hide their infants and children from public exposure because of fear of public scrutiny and ridicule. In American Samoa, however, the development of new programs to assist people with disabilities has mediated negative perceptions and encouraged people's compassion and sensitivity. The following example depicts a situation of acceptance and support in which a community assumes responsibility for one individual with disabilities:

> Tigaina is a person with disabilities living in a small island community whom everyone knows and loves. He addresses people with appropriate cultural protocol and greets everyone with a smile. When hanging out at his favorite place, the bank, people often give him money as they exit the bank. One day, one of the authors observed Tigaina giving a handful of wrinkled dollars to a bank secretary, and the author later learned from the secretary that she banks his money for him.

Interventionists working with Samoan families must be sensitive to complex feelings such as guilt and blame experienced by parents and extended family, examine the religious connotations of having a child with a developmental disability, and promote a community's acceptance of and support for this population.

Health and Healing   The use of Western medical facilities is linked with Samoans' religious beliefs. In general, Samoans believe that God works through hospital care or medication and if family members of the ill person and health workers perform a right or ritual before God, then healing will occur. Their preference, however, is to use traditional healing individuals or to seek advice from relatives or their pastors. "Samoans have an iron-clad faith in their local or herbal remedies and their bush doctors" (Fiatoa & Palafox, 1980, p. 254). One such remedy involves a massage called a *fofo*, which is administered with leaves, roots, and fruits. This massage is used for every conceivable childhood illness, from rashes to spine malformations (Fiatoa & Palafox, 1980).

Death and Dying   Before being exposed to Christianity, Samoans believed that people's spirits after death proceed to the *Fafa o Saualii*, which is a big hole in the ocean at the eastern end of the biggest Samoan island, Savai'i. After death, the chiefs were believed to take one path to the *Fafa o Saualii*, whereas everyone else followed another. If a person died a natural death, he or she would proceed to the *Fafa* and, thus, cause no anxiety for the living; however, those who did not experience a natural death did not go to the *Fafa* and were believed to return in different forms to haunt the living.

One person who has spiritual power and can mediate with the haunting spirits is the Samoan bush doctor, or a *Taulasea*. The *Taulasea*, in addition to intervening with haunting spirits, has an ability to treat illnesses. One of the authors of this chapter observed a family member talking to a sick person he believed to be possessed, begging the spirit to come out and forgive the sick person. To establish communication with the spirit, typically, appropriate medicinal plant parts are either applied over the infected area or are given orally.

Family members are immediately notified when a person is seriously ill. In the case of a chief, some of the more valuable Samoan mats are brought out and laid on the body. Showing valuable possessions is a reflection of the respect and care that survivors have for the deceased. When people—family members and others—view these possessions, they will believe that the deceased is loved and respected by his family. This is the time for close relatives to be on their best behavior, not only as an expression of love and affection but also so that the dying chief may bless or forgive them. The following example depicts a blessing bestowed on a dying individual.

> The aunt, on her deathbed, instructed Ofisa to open his mouth as she breathed into it and uttered a blessing that the boy did not understand. Now, as an adult, Afamasaga Ofisa is a Samoan high chief who is well-versed and well-known for Samoan oration. He composes songs, speeches, and hosts a talk show on public television about Samoan customs and traditions.

If a chief's sickness lasts a long time, family members are questioned about wrongful deeds that they might have committed against him. One by one, family members confess in the presence of the chief some misconduct they may have committed that brought on the illness. If guilty, the member is entreated to remove the misdeed or curse, perhaps with a plea to the gods, so the chief might recover.

With the death of most individuals, the body is prepared for burial simply and within a few hours; however, when the deceased is of high rank, many customs are observed. In contemporary times, funerals of high chiefs have become increasingly complex and elaborate. The chief's relatives as well as the wife's family donate many fine mats of value, pigs, cattle, whole carcasses, and money. These materials of value are later distributed to chiefs in the village council, to the chiefs in the district, and to representatives of traditional sections of Samoa.

Funerals of high chiefs start with loud mourning and wailing by the family. A council of chiefs prepares the grave and plants coconut fronds on both sides of the road as far as the boundaries of the council jurisdiction. At the early dawn of the burial, younger chiefs, using appropriate language, announce a special declaration, or *manu*, of the sacredness of the event. No one works the land or fishes the ocean, and people attend to customary observances of the chief's funeral. Following the *manu*, the council, primarily the talking chiefs, performs a sacred ritual. Each of these chiefs, carrying a piece of coconut frond reverently over his forearm, shouts, *"Tulouna le lagi!"* ("Reverent is the heavens!") with a salutation to the deceased chief. They go around the house where the chief is laid in state, continuing to call, *"Tulouna le lagi!"* This act signifies that the *lagi* ("total event") is open. Other talking chiefs from different parts of Samoa can now make the same observances, thereby demonstrating their respect and announcing their presence. The involvement of these other chiefs is referred to as the pathway for paying respect to the *lagi* or *auala*. People who observe and perform the *auala* to the *lagi* will be rewarded when fine mats and other valuable properties are distributed at the end of the funeral.

ISSUES OF LANGUAGE

As noted previously, few Native Hawaiians are adept at speaking the Hawaiian language, whereas the majority of Samoans are bilingual. Eight percent of Native Hawaiians speak a native language at home, compared with sixty-four percent of Samoans residing in the United States (U.S. Bureau of the Census, 1993). Interventionists must practice caution when working with bilingual and native speaking Samoan clients because language can prove to be a barrier to assessment and intervention. Some possible difficulties include 1) Samoan words that have multiple English meanings, and 2) English words for which there is no equivalent Samoan word (Fiatoa & Palafox, 1980). Examples of words with multiple meanings are *lima* (hand, five) and *malamalama* (light, understanding). Examples of English words with no directly equivalent Samoan words are *vegetables* (*la`au aina*, plants that are eaten), *fertilizers* (*fa`alelei ele`ele*, to improve the earth), *dinner* (*taumafataga o le po*, the evening meal), and *nutrition* (*mea`ai paleni*, balanced meal). The use of interpreters may be helpful, but, as is typical in any translation of language, meanings may be interpreted inaccurately.

Language is an important aspect of culture, and a reclaiming of the native language by many Native Hawaiian people today is inherent in self-determining acts. Although the 1990 U.S. census noted only a small percentage of Native Hawaiians speaking their native language, appreciation for and acquisition of the mother tongue is on the increase since the 1980s. In Hawai'i, language immersion schools opened in 1984 with an intent of providing education within the traditional language, culture, and perspective of the Native Hawaiian people (Kamehameha Schools/Bishop Estate, 1993). Although academic content is considered important, "most parents felt that it really was the Hawaiian language which many of them didn't speak themselves to be by far the most important facet of the immersion program" (Kamehameha Schools/Bishop Estate, 1993, p. 154). Eleven students educated entirely in Hawaiian graduated in 1999, and in the 1999–2000 school year, approximately 2,000 students were enrolled in immersion programs in Hawai`i from preschool through high school (Aha Punana Leo, 2002).

The pronunciation of both the Native Hawaiian and Samoan languages are important in conveying the right message. Kahananui (1989) underscored the idea that in the Native Hawaiian language, agreement on the analysis of language sounds may be lacking *by language specialists*; however, she offered several broad guidelines. First, diction is important because the manner in which one pronounces some words may mean different things. Each vowel has two sounds, so emphasizing the vowel sounds in some words will change the meaning of the word (e.g., *nānā* means "look" when the vowel is emphasized, but *nana* means "for him/belongs to him" when a vowel is not emphasized) (Kahananui, 1989, p. xii). Second, diphthongs, or the combination of vowels, also affect pronunciation (e.g., *ao* is like *ow* in *how*, whereas *au* is like *ou* in *out*) (Kahananui, 1989, p. xiii).

Similar to the Native Hawaiian language, the Samoan vowels have two sounds—the long and the short. One word with the same spelling may have more than one meaning, depending on the type of vowel sounds used. For example, the Samoan word *manava* can mean different things depending on the sound of the first vowel *a*. When the vowel is emphasized, or has a long sound, *manava* means "breath" or "the work is finished." When the vowel is not emphasized, *manava* means "stomach."

Nonverbal communication is important to both Pacific Island cultures. Traditionally, both cultures have relied on oral traditions, particularly chants and songs, to document their lineage, values, and beliefs. Although the "spoken word" can have various levels of power, so can the "unspoken word." In Native Hawaiian culture, for example, paralinguistics is reflected in guttural sounds indicating agreement or musical sounds indicating greetings. Examples in Samoan culture include the biting of one's teeth, which indicates anger and frustration, or the movement of the shoulders, which indicates confusion or ambivalence. As the specific nuances of nonverbal language are sometimes difficult to ascertain, the interventionist must thoughtfully consider the combined messages of verbal and nonverbal communication.

SUMMARY

Broadly examined, culturally sensitive intervention refers to a helping transaction that is predicated on an understanding of the individual in the context of his or her culture. For Native Hawaiians and Samoans, culturally sensitive intervention specifically refers to knowledge of the influence of historical variables on the current values, beliefs, and lifestyle practices of these people. Native Hawaiians have experienced more than 200 years of dramatic social changes, which have raised questions about the survival of this population as a distinctive people. In a similar time period, Samoans also have been exposed to Western influence but not to the same devastating degree as Native Hawaiians. In the Samoan islands, the majority of the population is still Samoan; in Hawai'i, the majority of the population is non–Native Hawaiian. Samoan culture today is in a great state of transition; however, the comfort for Samoans is the awareness that *fa'a Samoa* (the Samoan way) still predominates in the Samoan islands. For Native Hawaiians, that comfort is less tangible, although a resurgence of the culture is being experienced on many different levels, including the sovereignty movement, the "reknowing" of Native Hawaiian spirituality, and the language resurgence.

A few recommendations are offered to facilitate culturally sensitive practices when providing services to Native Hawaiians and Samoans. These recommendations are appropriate for interventionists working with those people maintaining a close connection with traditional values and beliefs and may be less appropriate for more acculturated individuals.

- Focus attention on the family system rather than the individual as the vehicle for intervention. Inherent in this focus on the family is the acknowledgment of the status and responsibilities of different members and knowledge of the interpersonal dynamics of family members. Furthermore, the goals and processes of intervention should address the needs of the collective unit.

- Give consideration to traditional values and beliefs about spirituality, particularly as they relate to healing. These values and beliefs should be respected and worked with rather than rejected (Territory of American Samoa, 1990). Traditional healers may provide consultative information, work directly in collaboration with Western interventionists, or, on some occasions, be used as referrals.

- Promote the use of bicultural and bilingual assistants with these populations. Encourage the training and development of Native Hawaiian and Samoan individuals to work with their people, as well as the training and development of other culturally diverse people to work with them. Content for training may include knowledge of historical variables, general values and beliefs, problem areas, coping patterns, and healing styles.

Intervention can only be effective when those providing services are aware of the richness of cultural diversity and committed to enhancing the quality of life through an understanding and a promotion of that richness. Since Western contact began, Native Hawaiians and Samoans have experienced tremendous cultural changes and losses; however, despite such losses, the resiliency of the people is clearly evident. Saleebey (1997) stated that resilience is an important characteristic of the strengths' perspective that inherently acknowledges people's strongpoints rather than their limitations. Interventionists who acknowledge the strengths of a culture and the resilience of a people not only to *survive*—but also to *thrive*—despite strife and loss are truly interested in the empowerment of people. The usefulness of these recommendations for Native Hawaiians and Samoans will only be apparent when interventionists refuse to *impose* Western values and beliefs and instead start to *infuse* culturally appropriate values and beliefs into the practice situation.

WHAT WOULD YOU DO?

Sia and Mataio were born and married in American Samoa and moved to California so that Mataio could pursue a college education. Their bilingual skills helped them in their transition from island home to the United States. They lived in a community where they were near extended family and other Samoan people.

Shortly after moving, Sia gave birth to a son who had difficulties with verbal and nonverbal communication and showed a restricted range of social activities. Although Sia initially tried to deny that her son had disabilities, a physician's diagnosis of autism spectrum disorder confirmed her fears. After hearing the diagnosis, Mataio and Sia experienced concerns about their son's future and uncertainty about what his needs would be and how they would provide care. They wanted to seek help and guidance from people in their church network; however, their embarrassment and guilt were obstacles to their reaching out. Sia thought that her son's disabilities were her fault, caused by her failure to behave properly with extended family prior to their moving to California from American Samoa. She anguished over her wrongdoing. Mataio, while concerned and involved, was very busy trying to manage his job to support his family and pursue his education. A part of him reluctantly believed that Sia was at fault for their son's disabilities.

How can you recognize Sia's and Mataio's cultural appraisal of the cause of their son's disability and still find the appropriate cultural resolution that leads to quality care for their son?

REFERENCES

Aha Punana Leo. (2002). *E ola ka Ōlelo Hawai`i*. Retrieved May 3, 2003, from http://www.ahapunanaleo.org/OL.htm

Alailima, F.C. (1996). The Samoans of Hawai'i. In B.L. Hormann & A.W. Lind (Eds.), *Ethnic sources in Hawai'i* (pp. 88–94). New York: McGraw-Hill.

Apology Resolution of 1993, PL-103–150, 107 Stat. 1510 (November 23, 1993).

Bell, B., Nordyke, E., & O'Hagan, P. (1989). Fertility and maternal and child health. *Social Process in Hawai'i, 32,* 87–103.

Blaisdell, K. (1989). Historical and cultural aspects of Native Hawaiian health. *Social Process in Hawai'i, 32,* 1–21.

Blaisdell, K. (1993). The health status of Kānaka Maoli (Indigenous Hawaiians). *Asian American and Pacific Islander Journal of Health, 1*(2), 116–160.

Blaisdell-Brennan, H.K., & Goebert, D. (2001). Health care utilization among women on O`ahu: Implications for Native Hawaiian women. Pacific Health Dialog. *Journal of Community Health and Clinical Medicine for the Pacific, 8,* 274–279.

Braun, K.L., & Nichols, R. (1996). Cultural issues in death and dying. *Hawai'i Medical Journal, 55,* 260–264.

Brewer, N. (1987, July 13). Samoans suffer dashed dreams. *Honolulu Star Bulletin,* p. A1.

Brigham Young University (BYU). (1977). *People of Samoa.* Provo, UT: Brigham Young University, Language and Intercultural Research Center.

Buck, P.H. (1981). Polynesian migrations. In E.S.C. Handy, K.P. Emory, E.H. Bryan, P.H. Buck, & J.H. Wise (Eds.), *Ancient Hawaiian civilizations* (pp. 23–34). Rutland, VT: Charles E. Tuttle Company.

Dudley, M. (1990). *Man, gods, and nature.* Honolulu, HI: Nā Kāne O Ka Malo Press.

Fiatoa, L., & Palafox, N. (1980). The Samoans. In N. Palafox & A. Warren (Eds.), *Cross cultural caring* (pp. 250–271). Honolulu: University of Hawai'i, School of Medicine.

Handy, E.S.C., & Pukui, M.K. (1977). *The Polynesian family system in Ka'u, Hawai'i.* Rutland, VT: Charles E. Tuttle Company.

Hawaiian Federal Recognition Bill of 2003, S. 344, 108th Cong. (February 11, 2003).

Holmes, L.D. (1974). *Samoan village.* New York: Holt, Rinehart & Winston.

Ho`owaiwai Na Kamali`i. (2002). Retrieved February 18, 2004, from http://uhfamily.Hawaii.edu/publications/HNKReport/HNKIndex.asp

Hopkins, M. (1862). *Hawai'i: The past, present, and future of its island kingdom.* London: Longman, Green, Longman, and Roberts.

Hosek, L. (1993, January 4). Hawaiians are pressed to assert their heritage. *Honolulu Star Bulletin,* pp. A1, A6.

Iyechad, G.L. (1992, March 8). Many Samoans here find adjustments difficult and stereotypes binding. *Honolulu Star Bulletin,* pp. F1, F5.

Johnson, D.B., Oyama, N., & Le Marchand, L. (1998). Papa Ola Lokahi Hawaiian health update: Mortality, morbidity and behavioral risks. Pacific Health Dialog. *Journal of Community Health and Clinical Medicine for the Pacific, 5,* 297–314.

Kahananui, D.M. (1989). *E Pāpā Ōlelo Kākou: Hawaiian Level One.* Honolulu, HI: Kamehameha Schools Press.

Kamehameha Schools/Bishop Estate. (1993). *Native Hawaiian educational assessment 1993.* Honolulu, HI: Author.

Kanahele, G. (1986). *Kū Kanaka: Stand tall.* Honolulu, HI: University of Hawaii Press and Waiaha Foundation.

Kelly, A.K. (2002, Jan. 30). A field guide to the Akaka bill(s). *Honolulu Weekly, 12*(5), 5–6.

Korbin, J.E. (1990). Hana `ino: Child maltreatment in a Hawaiian-American community. *Pacific Studies, 13*(3), 7–22.

Liki, A. (1999). Encountering the 'remittance-dependence' image of Pacific Islanders: The case of Samoans at home and abroad. In *Tātou, tusi, tala: Let's write stories—An anthology of Samoan writings, 1,* 99–113.

Look, M.A., & Braun, K.L. (1995). *A mortality study of the Hawaiian people: 1910–1990.* Honolulu: The Queen's Health Systems.

Markoff, R., & Bond, J. (1980). The Samoans. In J. McDermott, Jr., W.-S. Tseng, & T. Maretzki (Eds.), *People and cultures of Hawai'i* (pp. 184–199). Honolulu: University of Hawai'i, School of Medicine and University Press of Hawai'i.

Mokuau, N. (1990). A family-centered approach in Native Hawaiian culture. *Families in Society: The Journal of Contemporary Human Services, 7,* 607–613.

Mokuau, N., & Chang, N. (1991). Samoans. In N. Mokuau (Ed.), *Handbook of social services for Asian and Pacific Islanders* (pp. 155–170). Westport, CT: Greenwood Press.

Mokuau, N., Lukela, D., Obra, A., & Voeller, M. (1997). *Native Hawaiian spirituality: A perspective on connections.* Honolulu: University of Hawai'i School of Social Work.

Mokuau, N., & Matsuoka, J. (1995). Turbulence among a native people: Social work practice with Hawaiians. *Social Work, 40,* 465–472.

Mokuau, N., Reid, N., & Napalapalai, N. (2002). *Ho`omana (Spirituality): Views of Native Hawaiian women.* Honolulu: University of Hawai'i School of Social Work.

Nishimoto, P.A. (1999). *Exploring the role of family appraisal and coping with caregiver stress: The experience of caring for children with cleft lip and palate.* Unpublished doctoral dissertation, University of Hawai'i.

Nordyke, E. (1989). *The peopling of Hawai'i.* Honolulu: University of Hawai'i Press.

Office of Hawaiian Affairs. (2002). *Native Hawaiian data book.* Honolulu, HI: Author.

Oneha, M.F.M. (2001). Ka mauli o ka `āina a he mauli kānaka: An ethnographic study from a Hawaiian sense of place. Pacific Health Dialog. *Journal of Community Health and Clinical Medicine for the Pacific, 8,* 299–311.

Pukui, M.K. (1983). *`Olelo No`eau, Hawaiian proverbs and poetical sayings.* Honolulu, HI: Bishop Museum Press.

Pukui, M.K., Haertig, E.W., & Lee, C.A. (1972). *Nānā i ke kumu (Look to the source) (Vol. I.)* Honolulu, HI: Hui Hānai.

Pukui, M.K., Haertig, E.W., Lee, C.A., & McDermott, J. (1979). *Nānā i ke kumu (Look to the source) (Vol. II.)* Honolulu, HI: Hui Hānai.

Queen Lili`uokalani Children's Center. (1997). *Annual report.* Honolulu, HI: Author.

Quigg, A. (1987). *History of the Pacific Islands studies program at the University of Hawai'i: 1950–1986.* Honolulu: University of Hawai'i, Pacific Islands Studies Program.

Reinhold, R. (1992, Nov. 17). Talk of sovereignty disturbs Hawai'i. *San Francisco Daily Journal,* p. B3.

Saleebey, D. (1997). *The strengths perspective in social work practice.* New York: Longman.

Stannard, D.E. (1989). *Before the horror: The population of Hawai'i on the eve of Western contact.* Honolulu: University of Hawai'i, Social Science Research Institute.

State of California, Department of Mental Health. (1981). *Samoans in America.* Oakland: Author.

Territory of American Samoa. (1990). *Mental health plan 1989–1991.* Pago Pago, American Samoa: Author.

Tsark, J.U., Blaisdell, R.K. & Aluli, N.E. (1998). Guest editorials. Pacific Health Dialog, *Journal of Community Health and Clinical Medicine for the Pacific, 8,* 228–229.

U.S. Bureau of the Census. (1993). *We, the American. . . . Pacific Islanders.* Washington, DC: U.S. Department of Commerce.

U.S. Bureau of the Census. (2001a). *Census Bureau releases Census 2000 population counts for American Samoa.* Washington, DC: U.S. Department of Commerce.

U.S. Bureau of the Census. (2001b). *The Native Hawaiian and Other Pacific Islander population: 2000.* Washington, DC: U.S. Department of Commerce.

Wise, J.H., & Judd, H.P. (1981). The Hawaiian language. In E.S.C. Handy, K.P. Emory, E.H. Bryan, P.H. Buck, & J.H. Wise (Eds.), *Ancient Hawaiian civilizations* (pp. 159–164). Rutland, VT: Charles E. Tuttle Company.

Young, B. (1980). The Hawaiians. In J. McDermott, Jr., W.-S. Tseng, & T. Maretzki (Eds.), *People and cultures of Hawai'i* (pp. 5–24). Honolulu: University of Hawaii, School of Medicine and University Press of Hawaii.

Young, K., & Galea`i, K.E. (1999). Samoans in California: A perspective on drug use and other health issues. In N. Mokuau (Ed.), *Responding to Pacific Islanders: Culturally competent perspectives for substance abuse prevention* (pp. 117–136). Washington, DC: U.S. Department of Health and Human Services.

APPENDIX A

CONTRASTING BELIEFS, VALUES, AND PRACTICES

Beliefs, values, and practices	Native Hawaiian	Samoan	Mainstream culture
Unit of focus	Extended family	Extended family	Individual
Family system	Hierarchical	Hierarchical	Egalitarian
Religious/spiritual	Combination of traditional and Christianity	Christianity	Christianity
Language	English	Combination of Samoan and English	English
Interpersonal styles	Cooperative styles	Cooperative styles	Competitive styles
Child rearing	Verbal and physical discipline	Physical discipline	Verbal discipline
Healing styles	Combination of Western and traditional medicine	Combination of Western and traditional medicine	Western medicine

CULTURAL COURTESIES AND CUSTOMS

The following courtesies and customs represent some major characteristics of interactions in Native Hawaiian and Samoan homes.

Native Hawaiian

- It is inappropriate to touch a child on the top of the head because this area is considered sacred.

- Bestowing of a name on a child (*inoa*) is very important and often reflects conditions of birth or family lineage. Sometimes, names for a child are given in a dream to a member of—or someone close to—the family.

Samoan

- It is inappropriate to walk past an elder or person with status (e.g., pastor) without a show of physical deference such as bowing the head and body and downcasting the eyes.

- It is inappropriate for a child or adult to stretch his or her legs toward others when sitting in a *fale* (traditional Samoan home). If someone wishes to stretch, he or she should cover the legs with a mat or a *lavalava* (cloth).

- It is inappropriate to eat or drink while standing or walking. It is also inappropriate to talk while standing.

SIGNIFICANT CULTURAL EVENTS/HOLIDAYS/PRACTICES

NATIVE HAWAIIAN

Prince Kuhio Day

March 26

Holiday honoring the Hawaiian "citizen" Prince Kuhio, who fought for the rights of Native Hawaiians in the early 1900s.

King Kamehameha Day

June 11

Holiday celebrating the birthday of the first king of Hawai'i

Aloha Week

September

Week of festivities, including Hawaiian pageantry, canoe races, parades, hula dances, and a variety of other forms of entertainment

SAMOAN

Flag Day

April 17

Holiday celebrating the date when American Samoa became a territory of the United States

White Sunday

Third Sunday of October

Religious celebration for children when they perform before the congregation and are accorded special rights and privileges

Funerals

Throughout the year

Significant events in Samoan culture are recognized with the exchange of gifts and the presentation of fine meals

VOCABULARY

English	Hawaiian	Pronunciation	Samoan	Pronunciation
Family	ʻOhana	o-HA-nuh	ʻaiga	eye-ing-a
Father	Makua	mah-khuah	Tama	tah-mah
	Kane	Khah-neh		
Mother	Makuahine	mah-khuah-hine	Tina	ti-NAA
Child	Keiki	keh-kee	Tamaititi	tah-mah-ee-ti-ti
Hello	Aloha	ahh-loh-ha	Talofa	tah-LOH-fah
Good-bye	Aloha	ahh-loh-ha	Tofa soifua	toh-FAH soh-ee-FU-ah
Please	ʻOluʻolu	o-lu o-lu	Faʻamolemole	FAH-a-mohlay-MOH-lay
Thank you	Mahalo	ma-HAA-lo	Faʻafetai	FAH-a-fay-tai tele lava
Disability	Hiki ʻole	hee-kee o-le	Le atoa le ola	Le-ahtor-le-ohler

CHAPTER 11

FAMILIES WITH MIDDLE EASTERN ROOTS

Virginia-Shirin Sharifzadeh

رضاء الله من رضاء الوالدين

(To satisfy God is to satisfy parents.)
—ARABIC SAYING

درس معلم ار بود زمزمه محبتی   جمعه به مکتب آورد طفل گریز پای را

(A whisper of love in the teacher's instruction can bring
to school the reluctant student on a holiday.)
—IRANIAN SAYING

لم ده س داگری له ده س نه روی

(You shall receive with the same hand with which you give.)
—(KURDISH SCRIPT) ARABIC, IRANIAN, KURDISH, AND TURKISH SAYING

INTRODUCTION

The Middle East is a region of the world comprising some 17 nations, situated between the continents of Asia, Africa, and Europe. As the seat of the earliest civilizations and the birthplace of major monotheistic religions, the Middle East has always played a prominent role in the history of humankind.

Geographic Origins

Opinions differ regarding the exact boundaries of the Middle East. Generally, however, the Middle East refers to the area in Asia and Africa composed of the political states of Lebanon, Syria, Israel, Palestine (an established sovereign state in place of the Occupied Territories), Bahrain, Egypt, Iran, Iraq, Jordan, Kuwait, Oman, Qatar, Saudi Arabia, Sudan, Turkey, the United Arab Emirates, and Yemen. In addition, the *Middle East* is used as a cultural designation for a society and civilization found not only in that region but also to some degree in a number of adjacent countries such as Afghanistan, Algeria, Cyprus, Libya, Morocco, Pakistan, and Tunisia (Fisher, 1969). Also, Middle Eastern religions, languages, and values are strongly shared by the Central Asian countries of Kazakhstan, Kyrgyzstan, Tajikistan, Turkmenistan, and Uzbekistan, as well as the Transcaucasian countries of Armenia, Azerbaijan, and Georgia.

The geographic location of the Middle East has made it one of the world's greatest human junctions, with exposure to cultural influences from several directions. As a convenient land bridge between Africa and Eurasia and between the Mediterranean world and the Asian world of India and the Far East, it has hosted nations, tribes, traders, armies, and pilgrims, who along the way discovered the wealth of the area and the civilization of its people.

With the exception of the tropical climate, the Middle East represents all varieties of climates and physical environments, ranging from the severely cold alpine climate in the mountainous regions of Northwest Iran to the hot and arid deserts in the central regions of Iran and Saudi Arabia. In between these two extreme climates, countries in the Middle East enjoy a range of subtropical and semitropical environments, which enable them to produce many different agricultural crops and products. There is, therefore, wide variety in the food traditions of the Middle Eastern countries.

In countries to the east of the region such as Afghanistan and Iran, rice is the staple food and tea is the predominant drink of the people. In most other countries in the Middle East, however, bread is the staple food, and people generally drink coffee.

Current Statistics

Although immigrants from the Middle East have lived in the United States since 1875, the greatest period of immigration from this area to the United States has occurred since the late 1970s. By the official account of the 2000 U.S. Census, 1.25 million people of Arab ancestry were present in the United States at that time; however, most believe the actual number far exceeds this figure and may near 3 million (Salah, 2002). According to Salah, this is due, in part, to the fact that people of Middle Eastern origin are classified as "white." The "white" classification has historically served the purpose of denying the Arab immigrants the status of a minority group, hence, limiting their power and influence. At the same time, however, "white" classification has not protected members of Middle Eastern communities from racial profiling and discrimination (Salah, 2002).

Similarly, the 2000 Census puts the number of immigrants of Iranian ancestry at 338,266, a figure that seems unrealistic considering the visibly large Iranian communities in all the major cosmopolitan cities of the United States. A careful census study by Bozorgmehr and Sabagh (1988) estimated the Iranian population of the United States in 1986 to be 245,000–341,000. The 2000 Census figures do not seem to accurately reflect changes in this population after 17 years. A 2003 study detailing the relative size of the Iranian American community in each congressional district suggests that the Iranian population in the United States is most probably three times more than indicated in the Census 2000 figures. The study attributes some of this discrepancy to the confusion between race and ethnicity inherent in the 2000 Census questions (Fata & Rafi, 2003).

Likewise, the reported numbers for immigrants of Turkish (117,575) and Afghan (85,414) ancestries seem lower than their actual numbers (U.S. Bureau of the Census, 2003). These low figures may also reflect unwillingness on the part of the immigrants from the Middle East to reveal their countries of origin in the light of prevailing societal prejudices. The 2000 Census also reported as foreign-born 82,355 people of Assyrian/ Chaldean/Syriatic origin; 385,488 people of Armenian ancestry; and 109,719 Israelis.

Within these major categories of immigrants from the Middle East are wide varieties of ethnicities and religions. One large ethnic group that is generally concealed within these major categories is the Kurds, who represent large minorities in Iran, Iraq, Turkey, and Syria. An individual from an Arab country, Iran, or Turkey can have multiple ethnic identities, such as Armenian/Arab, Turkish/Kurd, and Assyrian/ Iranian. He or she may be Muslim, Christian, Jewish, Zoroastrian, Bahai, or of another religion.

A large percentage of immigrants from the Middle East are highly educated. For example, the 1990 records of the U.S. Bureau of the Census (1994) ranked Iranian immigrants in third place after Indians and Taiwanese in terms of educational attainment. These records suggest that 57% of Iranians 25 or older residing in the United States had at least a tertiary education (Torbat, 2002).

Most of the immigrants from the Middle East are concentrated in a few cosmopolitan regions of the United States. The report by the Immigration and Naturalization Service (2000) indicated that immigrants from the Middle Eastern countries are mostly concentrated in California, Florida, Illinois, Massachusetts, Michigan, New Jersey, New York, Ohio, and Texas. California has been the most preferred state since 1976. Los Angeles, specifically, is a microcosm of the Middle East. This preference may be related to the location of family members who had emigrated earlier as well as job opportunities and climate.

Today, children with fresh roots in the Middle East occupy many seats in American classrooms. Service providers developing programs for young children and their families can profit by understanding the cultural patterns that shape the behavior of their clients from the Middle East. Interventionists can be more effective if they can anticipate the perspectives and behaviors of the families with whom they are working and plan accordingly. This chapter addresses some general beliefs and practices shared by a majority of people with roots in the Middle East.

Emigration to the United States

In 1875, Christian tradesmen from the Syrian province of the Ottoman Empire were probably the first Arabs to come to the United States seeking opportunities (Thernstrom, Orlov, & Handlin, 1980). In the period between 1890 and 1930, large groups of Armenians fled the persecution of the Turkish government and sought refuge in the United States.

During the 20 years that followed the Armenian exodus, no large-scale emigrations to the United States from any country in the Middle East took place. However, with new developments in transportation technology and new possibilities in cultural and educational exchanges, more and more people from different countries in the Middle East arrived in the United States as visitors or as students.

The establishment of the State of Israel in 1948 led to the development of new conflicts and, hence, a new exodus from the Middle East. Palestinians whose lands were lost under the newly established Jewish state became refugees in different countries and account for much of the post–World War II Arab emigration to the United States (Thernstrom et al., 1980). In addition to Palestinians, many Jewish people emigrated from Israel to the United States; among them were some Middle Eastern Jews who had first resided in Israel but then moved westward.

The two major Arab–Israeli wars in 1967 and in 1973, the continued Arab–Israeli conflict, the Lebanese Civil War that started in 1975 and lasted for approximately 15 years, and the political instability of many regimes in the region have resulted in a continuous flow of Arab immigrants from the Middle East to the United States. Political events that began in the mid-1970s also have led to the migration of large groups of Iranians, Afghans, and Iraqis to the United States. The largest number of Kurdish refugees in the United States arrived from Iraq in 1975, following a failed uprising that resulted in their severe persecution.

Two events in 1978 led to additional migrations: 1) the beginning of the Iranian Revolution and 2) the occupation of Afghanistan by the Soviet Union. The Iranian Revolution brought dramatic changes in the political and social structure of Iran. These changes led large groups of Iranians, among them many religious minorities, to emigrate to the United States. Many followers of Judaism, Christianity, Zoroastrianism, and the Bahai faith gradually left Iran, and some emigrated to the United States.

The occupation of Afghanistan by the Soviet Union led to the migration of large groups of rural, nomadic, and urban Afghans from Afghanistan. Many Afghans who had higher education or better economic means moved westward, and some took refuge in the United States. In Afghanistan, the end of the Soviet occupation was replaced by a deadly civil war that lasted for more than a decade and gave rise to the Taliban, an Islamic fundamentalist group of an extremist nature. Curbing Afghan women's already limited freedom and showing intolerance for any manifestation of human rights, the Taliban became one of the most detested governments in the world. This resulted in a continuous flow of Afghani citizens into many host countries including the United States (Immigration and Naturalization Service, 1996). Emigration from Afghanistan, however, may be slowing down as a result of dramatic changes in the Afghanistan government by a U.S.-led military operation against the Taliban in 2002. Although it is too soon to report on Afghani immigrants in the United States, Afghani refugees from neighboring countries have returned to Afghanistan in large numbers (Nawa, 2002).

Simin and Farhad, an Iranian couple whose first child, Arya, was diagnosed at birth in Iran as having serious disabilities, immigrated to the United States in the hope that their son's situation could be dramatically improved by advanced medical intervention. The couple spent a great deal of time and money going to different doctors and hospitals. As time went on, however, it became clear that Arya would have severe mental and physical disabilities for the rest of his life.

As Simin struggled to confront the reality of her son's disabilities, overwhelming feelings of responsibility and guilt overtook her. Her reaction to those feelings was to become overly protective of her son and to devote all of her time to his care. Farhad reacted by pulling away and becoming disengaged from his wife and son. This reaction was reinforced by Simin's total preoccupation with Arya and her neglect of Farhad and by Farhad's need to work long hours in his business to earn enough money to cover the high costs of Arya's health care.

The relationship between Arya's parents continued to deteriorate, and Farhad left his wife and son. Simin and Arya moved into her male cousin's home, who took it on himself to take full care of his relatives. During this time, Simin learned about the importance of early intervention and enrolled Arya in an early childhood education program. Through the support of her cousin, the interventionists, and another Iranian parent whom she met in the program, Simin began to regain her own equilibrium, and Arya made small but significant gains. Farhad continued to maintain contact with Simin's cousin and agreed to meet the father of the other Iranian child in the early intervention program. After Farhad had many long talks with the other father and observed the other child, he also began seeing Arya and Simin again; ultimately, Farhad and Simin were reunited.

Throughout this process, the interventionists listened carefully to Simin and her cousin. They recognized the cultural issues that made the acceptance of her son with a disability especially difficult and introduced Simin to another Iranian parent when Simin indicated that she was interested. They worked with her to identify goals for Arya and worked diligently with her to accomplish them. When Farhad returned to the family, the interventionists welcomed him to the program and acknowledged his role as the head of the household. Farhad and Simin went on to have another child who is developing typically.

The Iran–Iraq war, which began in 1980 and lasted until 1988, resulted in a continuous flow of Iranian emigrants to the United States, making the Iranians the largest group of immigrants from the Middle East since the late 1970s. Although the end of the Iran–Iraq war has brought a substantial decrease in the number of Iranian emigrations, Iranians continue to be the largest group of immigrants from the Middle East fleeing the social and economic conditions brought about by the Islamic Fundamentalist Government of Iran (Immigration and Naturalization Service, 1996). The Iran–Iraq war also encouraged large groups of Iraqis of Arab and Kurdish origin to flee the repressive Iraqi regime and the hardship brought about by the economic sanctions against Iraq.

The occupation of Kuwait by Iraq in 1990 and the subsequent Persian Gulf War in 1991 also resulted in a new surge of emigration from the region. In the aftermath of the Persian Gulf War, Saddam Hussein killed thousands of Iraqi Kurds and Shi'as to avenge their cooperation with American forces. This resulted in massive emigration of Iraqi Kurds and Shi'as, who took refuge in the neighboring countries, and some may have come to the United States. Additional blending of people who share the Middle Eastern cultural values took place in the adjacent regions of Transcaucasia and Central Asia. The disintegration of the Soviet Union in 1991 spurred wars between the two big and newly independent states of Azerbaijan and Armenia. This resulted in a large exodus of Azerbaijanis into the neighboring countries and some emigration to the United States in 1993 and 1994 (Immigration and Naturalization Service, 1996). Political instability in other Central Asian countries has brought to the United States and other Western countries some immigrants from these newly independent states, most notably Uzbekistan (Immigration and Naturalization Service, 1996). The flow of emigrants from the Middle East to the United States slowed down dramatically following the terrorist attack against the United States on September 11, 2001. Strict visa laws and harsh treatment of Middle Eastern immigrants already in the United States have kept many people waiting to become U.S. citizens. Still, the Middle Eastern population of the United States will continue to rise as a result of birth rates and as families bring members who were initially left behind in their home countries.

Like most immigrants to this country, however, Middle Eastern immigrants cherish the democratic principles of the United States and aspire to belong to this nation. They represent a multitude of ethnicities, languages, and religions contributing to the colorful fabric of society.

Contemporary Life

Today, the Middle East is a troubled and a troubling part of the world. Many nations of the Middle East suffer from regional conflicts, wars, totalitarian regimes, and economic depression. In the wake of such strife, radical fundamentalism seeks its grounds and legitimacy. The September 11, 2001, attacks on the United States by a group of radical Muslim fundamentalists, which claimed thousands of innocent lives, are painful reminders that these troubles have left the borders of the Middle East and are now spreading around the world.

In addressing general beliefs and practices in the Middle East, it is important to remember that the term *Middle East* refers to one of the most diverse and complex combinations of geographic, historical, religious, linguistic, and racial places on earth. Any discussion of the Middle East, its history and people, should, therefore, give careful consideration to these differences and the complex issues surrounding Middle Eastern cultures and politics. Sadly, information about Middle Eastern cultures, politics, and societies has historically been absent or grossly misrepresented in the United States. Since the end of World War II and the escalation of political conflict over the newly established State of Israel, the media in the United States have portrayed Arab and Muslim nations of the Middle East unfavorably (Madani, 2000). Often, they have portrayed this complex region of the world and its people in simplistic ways, reducing it to such stereotypes as a barren land of deserts, with oil as its only resource, used primarily by Muslim Arabs representing *Islamic fundamentalism* to cause *terrorism* in the world. For the average American, the Middle East is where "bad guys," mostly Muslims, come from. This image of "us," (i.e., the West and Israel) versus "them," (i.e., the Arabs and Muslims), or "good guys" versus "bad guys," is dominant in the psyche of much of the American public, much like the perceptions of the "cowboys" versus "Indians" a few decades ago.

The Middle Eastern population of the United States, particularly those of Arab and Muslim origins, have lived in the shadow of negative stereotypes spread by sensational movies and exaggerated reports in which they are often portrayed as villains (Suleiman, 2001). Such issues as the status of women, the role of fathers, and marital and family relations are frequently discussed out of the general context and used to denigrate entire nations and cultures (Aswad & Bilge, 1996).

With the exception of Ancient Egypt, little or no information is provided in the school curricula about the rich ancient civilizations of the Middle East and their contribution to science and technology, mathematics, arts and music, architecture, and medicine. The lack of information taught in schools is even greater regarding the rich and tolerant Islamic civilization of the High Middle Ages and its contributions to world civilization (Menocal, 2002). Instead, discussions and talks about the Middle East have often been reserved to modern-day conflicts and wars that have brought this region to the forefront of political news. These discussions have frequently omitted a balanced picture of the root causes of troubles in the region, the most prominent of which is Palestinian–Israeli conflict. As a political ally of Israel, the United States, until recently, was seen as largely indifferent to the plight of Palestinians under the Israeli occupation. Valid or not, the general perception among most Muslim and Arab nations is that for the average American, the worth of a Palestinian life is not equal to that of an Israeli citizen. Also omitted from these discussions is the perspective that religious fundamentalism is not limited to Islam but is alive and well in all the religions of this world, including Christianity, Judaism, and Hinduism. Indeed, in the Middle East, the greatest divide is not between the people of Israel and Palestine or between the Jews and Muslims, but between the radical fundamentalists and the people who seek peaceful resolutions on both sides of this conflict. The Jewish fundamentalist faction of the Israeli government and the Hamas movement of the Palestinian resistance have a lot in common. Both seek the total destruction of the other and both resort to violence to achieve their goal. Indeed, it is not a far-fetched conclusion to say that those who opt for violent solutions to problems belong to the same culture and legitimize each other no matter which religion or society they represent.

In the minds of the Middle Eastern nations, the United States and its Western allies are partly responsible for the region's troubles. Since the fall of the Ottoman Empire, Western and other governments have played a significant role in stirring regional conflicts and maintaining and strengthening totalitarian governments of the Middle East, fueling resentment. A few cases in point are the CIA-led coup in Iran in 1953 (Byrne, 2000), the selling of arms to Saddam Hussein during the Iran–Iraq war, and the CIA's role in the creation of the fundamentalist group of Taliban in Afghanistan (Blum, 1999). Against the interests of Middle Eastern nations, Western governments have consistently ignored human rights by supporting dictatorial regimes of the region for financial and strategic gains.

Since September 11, 2001, immigrants and Americans of Middle Eastern origin, and particularly of Arab and Muslim backgrounds, have seen the erosion of their civil rights (Moore, 2002). With the passage of the USA Patriot Act of 2002 (PL 107-56), many have been experiencing discrimination and racial profiling at the hands of U.S. government agencies and other institutions (Feldman, 2002). Immigrants in many Muslim communities in the United States live in fear of arbitrary arrests and long detentions without charge (Feldman, 2002). Passage of new immigration laws has curbed immigration and visits by people from the Middle East (Cainkar, 2002). According to some sources, in the name of war against terrorism, the U.S. government has sidestepped such fundamental principles as attorney–client privilege (Feldman, 2002) and has not ruled out torture as a viable means to gain information (Economist of London, 2003).

According to the Council on American-Islamic Relations, since September 11, 2001, institutional racism has affected 60,000 Arab and Muslim immigrants (Cainkar, 2002). Christian Arabs, who constitute 1.5 million of the population (Cainkar, 2003), have not been immune to this treatment. This atmosphere of suspicion and fear has many unintended consequences for the Middle Eastern families residing in the United States. Fear of being deported or incarcerated for even minor violations has caused many families to keep a low profile, avoiding unnecessary contacts with governmental agencies. Under these circumstances, children's well-being will be compromised. Parents may refrain from receiving official visitors at home, filling out questionnaires, or being interviewed. Accurate information may be difficult to obtain from families fearing deportation.

Service providers need to be aware of the emotional and psychological burden created for the Middle Eastern families in this climate of political hostilities. They need to reach out to them with sensitivity and understanding. The success of an intervention program will depend on the degree of trust established between the Middle Eastern family and the service provider.

The isolation of Middle Eastern families from the mainstream of the society has negative consequences not only for the family but also for general society and beyond. Middle Eastern immigrants of the United States are valuable sources of knowledge and insight about the Middle East. The need to gather firsthand knowledge about the people, the history, and politics of this complex region has gained urgency in recent years.

It appears that in the post–9/11 atmosphere, to achieve peace and harmony for Israel, Palestine, and the world, a balanced view of the Middle East and its people, cultures, and political scene is no longer a luxury reserved for university scholars but a necessity required of every conscientious citizen of the world.

Historical Origins

The Middle East is the seat of humankind's earliest civilizations. The valleys of the Indus, the Tigris-Euphrates, and the Nile—blessed with a warm climate, fertile soil, native animals and plants, water available for controlled irrigation, and varied mineral resources—were most favorable for the propagation of human life and for the growth of an organized society (Fisher, 1969).

Unlike China or India, where civilizations have seen a unity of culture, language and religion from the ancient to the modern, Middle Eastern civilizations began and evolved in a number of different ways. Although they gradually moved toward one another, significant differences continue to exist in the cultures, beliefs, and customs within this region (Lewis, 1995).

The Sumerian people, an Asiatic type of Mediterranean race, arrived at one of the mouths of the Tigris-Euphrates rivers before 4000 B.C. Hence, the Sumerian city-states evolved, with society divided into technological-social classes, nobility, priests, traders, farmers, and artisans—divisions that have persisted as constant factors in all of the Middle Eastern civilizations (Fisher, 1969). The Semites (probably coming from the desert) and the Hamites (coming from East and North Africa) established similar civilizations at the same time along the Nile and the Tigris-Euphrates.

During the second millennium B.C., Indo-Europeans from Eastern Europe and western Asia began a wave of southward movement. In their transition to an organized life on the Middle Eastern pattern of greater specialization and division of labor, these migrants added something in religion, the art of writing, metallurgical skills, political organization, transportation, irrigation, and astronomy (Fisher, 1969).

From the beginning of the first millennium B.C., significant empires began to rise and fall in the Middle East, each trying to unite the area under one cultural and political system. Before the rise of Islam, the most significant of these empires included the Assyrian, the Babylonian, the Egyptian, the Persian, the Greek, and the Roman. The vision of cultural unity, however, may have been more closely achieved with the spread of Islam. With the establishment of the Arab empire, in the seventh century, the long conflict between the Persian and Byzantine empires ended and the entire region from Central Asia to the Mediterranean was unified under a single imperial and commercial system (Lewis, 1995).

Religious Origins

The Middle East is the birthplace of several major monotheistic religions in the world. Religion has always played and continues to play an important role in the formation of cultural, social, and political structures in this region. In the tradition of Middle Eastern societies, religious identity serves as a point around which historical memories, social customs, and political loyalties tend to cluster.

People from the Middle East do not consider religion to be a strictly private and personal matter; therefore, they are not usually offended by questions such as "What is your religion?" The same people, however, may be perplexed if asked the question "What is your race?" Because of the significance of religion in the Middle East and the fact that Middle Eastern people rarely identify themselves in terms of race or racial origin, one must be especially sensitive to the role that religion has played in shaping the values and customs of the people in the region.

The earliest known system of belief among different people in the Middle East was the honoring of a hierarchy or a multiplicity of gods associated with natural forces. The first monotheistic religions in the Middle East emerged during the first millennium B.C. in Iran and Palestine. In Iran, Ahura Mazda (the "Wise Lord") came to be worshipped as the supreme god under the guidance of the prophet, Zoroaster. Zoroastrians believed that forces of good were in constant battle with the forces of evil and the good would win if men and women showed virtues and ritual purity. Ahura Mazda, they believed, would send a savior (Saoshyant), born of a virgin, who would eventually defeat the evil. The teaching of Zoroaster was kept in the sacred book *Avesta*. Zoroastrianism became the dominant religion in Persia for centuries and influenced many religions (Lewis, 1995).

In Palestine, the Jews, or Hebrews, came to believe in Yahweh as the creator of the universe. Believing themselves to be chosen by this god to hold the truth about creation, they grew from a tribal cult to a universal ethical monotheism that was reflected in the successive books of the Hebrew Bible.

The conquests of Alexander the Great in the first millennium and the establishment of the Greek cities spread Greek polytheism in the Middle East. Monotheism thus remained limited and contained for many centuries until the Roman Empire adopted Christianity as the official religion in the fourth century A.D. Problems arose over the nature of Christ and His relationship with God, however. The earliest Christians, therefore, branched off into the Melkites, the Monophysites, and the Nestorians.

The Rise of Islam   The rise of Islam in the seventh century and the formation of the Empire of Caliphs, stretching from Spain and Morocco to central Asia, marked a new period in the religious and political history of the Middle East. Muslims (Moslems) believed that God had given His final revelation to the Prophet Muhammad, whom they believed to be the last in a succession of prophets including Moses and Jesus. The *Qur'an* (Koran), the holy book containing Muhammad's revelations, was believed to be the full expression of the divine will for human life.

Prophet Muhammad was born in or about 571 A.D. in Mecca, an oasis town in the Arabian Peninsula. His family belonged to the nomadic tribe of Quraysh, a tribe of traders who raised sheep, goats, and camels. It is said that members of the tribe had some connections to Ka'ba, the town's sanctuary where images of local gods were kept.

When he was a young man, Muhammad looked after the trading business of a wealthy widow named Khadija, whom he later married. It is a largely held belief that on his long and solitary trading journeys between the Arabian Peninsula and the Fertile Crescent, Muhammad met Jewish Rabbis, Christian monks, and Arab soothsayers predicting the coming of a prophet (Hourani, 1991). By the account of those who later wrote his life, this was a time when "a world was waiting for a guide and a man searching for a vocation" (Hourani, 1991, p. 15).

According to the tradition, Muhammad's call to prophecy came as Muhammad was approaching his 40th year. One night, as he slept in solitude on Mount Hira, Angel Gabriel appeared to him, giving him a message from the God and asking him to recite the following:

> Recite: In the name of thy Lord who created, Created man of a blood clot.
>
> Recite: And thy lord is the most bountiful, who taught man by the pen, taught man what he knew not,
>
> No, indeed: surely man waxes insolent, for he thinks himself self-sufficient.
> Surely unto thy Lord is the returning. (Qur'an 96:1–8)

Those who were very close to him, including his wife, Khadija, accepted Muhammad's claim to this first message. From this time on he began communicating to the people of his birthplace a series of messages urging them to give up their idolatrous beliefs and to worship a single universal god. As the number of converts increased, so did the pressures and persecutions from the holders of the old traditions. In 622 A.D., approximately 13 years after the first Call, Muhammad and his followers were forced to leave Mecca and migrate to the small town of Yathrib, from which people welcomed Muhammad and his followers. This migration or *Hijra*, as it is called in Arabic, is regarded by Muslims as the decisive moment in Muhammad's apostolate. The year of *Hijra* was subsequently used as the beginning of the Arabian year when a Muslim calendar was established. Yathrib later became known simply as Madina (Medina)—the City (Lewis, 1995).

In Madina, Muhammad began to rise as a religious and political figure whose authority radiated throughout the oasis and the surrounding desert regions. Before long, Madina entered into war with the Pagan rulers of Mecca, including Muhammad's own tribe, Quraysh. After 8 years of struggle, Muhammad conquered Mecca and established the Islamic faith in place of the old idol worship of his fellow towns-men. The *haram,* the house of the pagan worship, which was believed to have been built by Abraham, changed hands and became the destination of Muslim pilgrimage, albeit with a changed meaning (Hourani, 1991).

During this period of expanding power and struggle, until his death in 632 A.D., Muhammad brought a series of messages directed to the whole of pagan Arabia and, by implication, to the whole world (Hourani, 1991). These messages defined the rit-ual observances of religion, social morality, rules of social peace, property, marriage, and inheritance. Muhammad had managed to bring peace among the rival tribes and to preside over the spiritual, social, and political affairs of a wide area in the Arabian Peninsula.

Muslims believe that the purpose of Muhammad's prophetic mission was to fin-ish the task that the previous monotheistic religions had left unfinished. At his death, they believe, Muhammad had completed the revelation of God's purpose for hu-mankind. According to Muslim faith, he was the last—or the Seal—of the prophets and there would be no prophets after him (Lewis, 1995).

Within little more than a century following his death, the Prophet's successors, called the caliphs, had established the Muslim Empire of the Caliphs, extending far into Asia, Africa, and Europe. In this empire, Islam was the state religion and the Arabic language replaced the local languages as the principal medium of public life. According to Bernard Lewis (1995), the people of the embattled regions often em-braced Islam rapidly, in numbers, and rallied around the new Arab leaders because the new masters were less demanding, more tolerant, and more welcoming than the old. In fact, the *Qur'an* explicitly states: "There is no compulsion in religion" (2:256). Those who professed a monotheistic religion recognized by Islam were allowed to practice their religions under the new conditions imposed by the Islamic state (Lewis, 1995). Generally, the conquered peoples were offered inducements such as lower taxations.

As an empire and a civilization, Islam lasted for centuries and became extremely sophisticated in the high Middle Ages. The Islamic world of this period was interna-tional, multiracial, polyethnic, and intercontinental (Lewis, 1995). Positioned histor-ically between antiquity and modernity, it shared the Hellenistic and Judeo-Christian heritage with Europe and was enriched by remote lands and cultures. In Lewis's words, "The Islamic Civilization of the Middle Ages, at its peak, presented a proud spectacle—in many ways, the apex of human civilization achievement to that date" (1995, p. 269).

As a religion, Islam underwent major changes and split into different branches. The main body of Muslims, who were later called Sunnis, believed that the Prophet had transmitted his temporal authority to a line of caliphs. The three most prominent of these caliphs—in order of succession—were AbuBakr, Omar, and Othman.

The major split in Islam took place over the position of the fourth caliph, Ali, the cousin and son-in-law of Muhammad, who was murdered and succeeded by Mua-wiya, the governor of Syria. Ali's supporters, known as "Partisans of Ali" (Shi'a`Ali), developed the doctrine that Ali was not only the temporal ruler of the community but also the Imam, the only authoritative interpreter of the *Qur'an.* Shi'as also be-lieved that the office of Imam could be designated only to members of his and the Prophet's family. The Shi'as, however, differed among themselves over the issue of the line of transmission. Hence developed the branches known as the *Twelvers,* or simply the *Shi'as,* the *Zaidas,* and the *Seveners* (also known as Isma'ilis).

Judaism, Christianity, and Islam all underwent new kinds of divisions from the 16th century onward. The opening to the modern Western world in the 19th century also may have played a role in such developments.

The Pillars of Islam

In his "pilgrimage of farewell" in Mecca, just before his death, Prophet Muhammad addressed his faithful followers: "Know that every Muslim is a Muslim's brother, and that the Muslims are brethren" (Hourani, 1991, p. 147).

Believers of the Muslim faith lived under the authority of the Word of God, revealed to the Prophet Muhammad in the Arabic language. The faithful belonged to a community of Muslims (*Umma*). To maintain the sense of belonging to a community, certain rituals had to be performed by all Muslims capable of performing them. Of these rituals, five were known as the "Pillars of Islam." They formed the foundations of religious practice and created a link both between those who performed them and successive generations (Hourani, 1991).

The first Pillar is the *Shahada*. It is the testimony that "there is no god but God and Muhammad is God's Prophet." This is a testimony by which a person becomes a Muslim and it is repeated in the daily ritual prayers. It is through this testimony that Muslims distinguish themselves from believers of other faiths: "That there is only one God, that He has revealed His Will to mankind through a line of prophets in whom the line culminates and ends" (Hourani, 1991, p. 148).

The second Pillar is *Salat*—or saying of the daily prayers. *Salat* should be performed five times per day: at dawn, noon, mid-day, dusk, and in the early part of the night. In traditional Muslim communities around the world, the time of these prayers are announced by a public call (*adhan*) made by a *muezzin*, a caller to prayer, from atop a mosque's tower or minaret. Before each prayer, a Muslim performs the ritual of *wudu* or washing of the hands, toes, face, and the crown of the head. Facing in the direction of Mecca and reciting the unchanging prayer, the worshipper proclaims the greatness of God and the lowliness of man in His presence, while engaging in motions of bowing, kneeling, and prostrating him- or herself to the ground. Following the prayer, the worshipper might engage in supplications or individual petitions (*du'a*) (Hourani, 1991).

Individual prayers can be performed in public or private and in any location considered clean. The noontime prayer on Fridays (*Jooma*), however, should be held in a particular mosque (*Jami*), which has a pulpit (*minbar*) and is followed by the sermon (*khotba*) of a preacher (*Khatib*). Like Jews and Christians, Muslims set aside a day of the week for communal prayer. Unlike the Jewish and Christian Sabbath, however, Muslim Friday (*Jooma*) is a day of heightened public activity in the market and elsewhere (Lewis, 1995).

The third Pillar of the Muslim religion is *zakat*. It is an obligation on those whose income exceeds a certain amount to make donations for the poor, the needy, the relief of debtors, the liberation of slaves, and the welfare of the homeless.

The fourth Pillar or *sawn* is the obligation to fast in the month of Ramadan. Ramadan is the Arabic month during which the Prophet received his first revelations. Muslims older than the age of 10 are to abstain from eating, drinking, and sexual intercourse from dawn to dusk. Exceptions were made for those who were physically weak, those with unsound mind, those performing heavy labor, soldiers at war, and travelers. Fasting in the month of Ramadan is regarded as a solemn act of repentance for sins—a denial of self for the sake of God (Hourani, 1991). Muslims who fast should begin the day with a statement of intentions and end it with special prayers. Ramadan is a month during which Muslims draw nearer to each other. Breaking fast (*Iftar*), which happens daily at dusk, is usually done in the company of friends and family or even with a whole village or city, and extends into the nighttime hours. The affluent families may provide food for the less fortunate throughout the month of Ramadan.

Hajj, the fifth Pillar, is the Arabic word for pilgrimage. Every Muslim should, in principle, make a visit to Mecca, the House of God, at least once in his or her lifetime. To do so in a meaningful way, this pilgrimage should take place along with other Muslims at a special time of the year during the Arabic month of *Dhu'l-Hijja*. *Hajj* is the central event of the year and perhaps a whole lifetime; it is a reflection of the unity of Muslims with each other (Hourani, 1991). Muslims travel in whatever form and means from lands near and far and gather in numbers often reaching several million.

Before approaching Mecca, the pilgrim purifies him- or herself by ablutions. All pilgrims put on an *Ihram*, a white garment made of a single cloth. The pilgrim then proclaims his or her intention to make the pilgrimage by a kind of act of consecration: "Here am I, O my God, here am I; no partner hast Thou, here am I; verily the praise and the grace are Thine, and the empire" (Hourani, 1991, p. 150).

Arriving in Mecca, the pilgrim enters the *Haram al Sharif*, a sacred area within which various sites and buildings have holy associations. At the heart of the *Haram* stands the *Ka'ba*, the rectangular building that Muhammad had made into the center of Muslim devotion after purging it of idols. The pilgrims go around the *Ka'ba* seven times, touching and kissing a black stone, which is embedded in one of its walls. On the eighth day of the month, the pilgrims go out of the city toward the East to visit the hill of Arafat. In an essential act of pilgrimage, they remain there for a while before returning to Mecca. On their way back to Mecca, at Mina, the pilgrims end this period of dedication with two more symbolic acts: the casting of stones at a pillar signifying the devil, and the sacrifice of an animal. At this point, the *Hajj*, which began with putting on the *Ihram*, ends with taking it off, and the Pilgrims return to their ordinary lives.

Muslim believers all over the world celebrate the departure and the return of the pilgrims each year and perform the act of animal sacrifice in their households simultaneously with the pilgrims at Mina. According to Hourani (1991), the *Hajj* is an act of obedience to God's commands as expressed in the *Qur'an*. Historically, the simultaneous performance of the rituals of *Hajj* brought Muslims together and created a sense of community, strengthening the Muslims' duty to look after each other and to protect and expand the scope of the community.

Other Islamic Rules   Along with these positive commandments or pillars, Islam has a series of negative commandments or sins. Many constitute basic rules of social coexistence, such as prohibition of murder and robbery. Others have specific religious connotations. They include the bans on pork, alcohol, fornication, and charging or accepting interest on borrowed money. The ban on pork is shared with Judaism. The ban on alcohol, however, is unique to Islam, Hinduism in some countries, and some Christian denominations (Lewis, 1995).

Jihad and Martyrdom   The need to protect and to expand the scope of the community also found expression in another important ritual of Islamic faith. Although not a Pillar, *Jihad* is regarded as an obligation almost equal to a pillar. The literal meaning of the word *Jihad* in Arabic is *striving*. As a religious ritual endorsed by the Qur'an, *Jihad* was defined as " . . . war against those who threatened the community . . . " (Hourani, 1991, p. 151). In its strictest definition, it is a "holy war" against the infidel. In its most benign form, Muslim theologians interpret it as the duty to strive in the path of God in a spiritual and moral sense (Lewis, 1995). Unlike the five pillars of Islam, however, *Jihad* was not an individual obligation of all Muslims but a community's obligation to provide a sufficient number of fighters (Hourani, 1991).

According to Lewis (1995), the idea of holy war in the Middle East is not limited to Islam. The Christian Byzantines, he suggested, had used it against the Persians. The Christian crusaders were involved in *Jihad* of their own. These, however, were limited in scope compared with the Muslim *Jihad,* which is perceived as an unlimited religious obligation. In the course of history, *Jihad* went through different changes and acquired different meaning by different Muslim communities. At times, different Muslim sects have used it against each other. In the early days of Islam, however, *Jihad* unleashed a tremendous force resulting in great territorial expansion of Arab Muslims. After the fall of the Islamic Empire and the beginning of the counter attacks from Western Europe, particularly during the crusades, *Jihad* came to be regarded as a defense mechanism rather than expansionism (Hourani, 1991). Lewis (1995) suggested that, from early on, Muslim theologians were wary of the misuse of *Jihad* for such purposes as looting and enslavement and insisted that *Jihad* could only be true if used for a pious motivation.

According to Lewis (1995), it is a misconception that Islamic religion was spread by conquest. In fact, although the expansion of Islam was made possible by the parallel processes of conquest and colonization, the Islamic conquerors, Lewis suggested, were not attempting to impose the Islamic faith by force. Today, *Jihad* is used by different groups of Muslims to justify different ends. For example, while in Palestine and Lebanon, groups have used *Jihad* to mobilize their nations against the Israeli occupation, the Al'Qaeda members led by Osama bin Laden have used it to wage a "Holy War" against all who contradict the most puritan concept of Islam. In the postrevolutionary Iran, *Jihad* was used to mobilize forces against the Iraqi invasion. It has also been used to oppress the voices of dissent, Muslim or otherwise, within the country as well as to mobilize the nation toward the development of the country.

Closely related to the concept of *Jihad* is the concept of *martyrdom*. The *Qur'an* promises that those who are killed in the path of God will go to heaven. In the early days of Islam, those who fought in the *Jihad* were promised the fruit of their victories in this world and the pleasures of Paradise in the next. Though in principle, a martyr or *Shahid* in Arabic achieves this status in a war against the infidels, this term is commonly used for the victims of conflicts even among Muslim nations. Thus, the Iranian soldiers who were killed during the Iran–Iraq war were called *Shahids.*

Contrary to the practice of martyrdom, suicide is explicitly banned in Islam. This distinction, however, has become blurred by the emergence of a category of Islamic fighters commonly referred to in the West as "suicide bombers." After the Palestinian uprising or *intifada,* suicide bombing became a prevalent means for the Palestinians to resist the Israeli occupation and expansion of settlements in their lands. The extremist group Al'Qaeda, however, adopted this method to create a universal network with the intent of terrorizing nations. In the eyes of religious extremists, however, these acts are neither suicides nor terrorism but are legitimized under *Jihad* against their perceived enemies.

The Present Situation

With few exceptions, all of the religious beliefs mentioned continue to have adherents in the Middle East. The most widespread of all of the religions in the Middle East is Islam in its Sunni form. Its followers number in the majority in Egypt, Turkey, Syria, Jordan, Saudi Arabia, South Yemen, Oman, most of the Persian Gulf states, Afghanistan, Pakistan, all countries in Central Asia, and countries in North Africa. It also is present in all of the other countries of the region. The Sunni form of Islam is also the dominant religion in many Asian countries including—but not limited to—Indonesia, Malaysia, and Bangladesh.

Shi'a'ism in its "Twelvers" form is followed by most Iranians, the Azerbaijanis of eastern Transcaucasia, and a majority of people in Iraq. It also is widespread in the Persian Gulf, Saudi Arabia, eastern Turkey, and southern and eastern Lebanon. *Zaydis Shi'a'ism* is followed in northern Yemen. Other *Shi'a* branches have followers in small communities in Syria, Yemen, Lebanon, Israel, and western Iran.

Followers of the Eastern Orthodox Church are found mostly in Lebanon, Syria, Jordan, Israel, Cyprus, and the Transcaucasian countries of Armenia and Georgia; Armenian Apostolic and Georgian Orthodox are, however, the majority in the latter two countries. The Nestorian Church has its followers among Assyrians in northern Iraq and western Iran and several other countries. Armenian Monophysites are found mainly in Syria, Lebanon, and Iran. There also are Coptic Catholics in Egypt; Maronite Christians in Lebanon; Greek Catholics in Lebanon, Syria, Jordan, and Israel; Chaldean Catholics in Iraq and Iran; Syrian Catholics in Syria and elsewhere; and Armenian Catholics in Lebanon and elsewhere.

The Jewish population of the Middle East is mostly concentrated in Israel. Many Israeli Jews, however, have immigrated to Israel from western, central, and eastern Europe and are referred to as *Ashkenazis*. The Jewish people from the Mediterranean or the Middle East are known as *Sephardis*. Of the latter Jewish communities in the Middle East that still exist, the communities in Turkey and Iran are the largest. Jewish populations also live in Uzbekistan and Georgia.

Iran also has the world's largest, albeit shrinking, communities of Zoroastrians and Bahais. (For more information on religions in the Middle East, refer to *The Cambridge Encyclopedia of the Middle East and North Africa* [Mostyn & Hourani, 1988]. Also, see *The Europa World Yearbook* [1996] for information on Central Asian and Transcaucasian countries.)

Language Origins

Unlike Europe, where almost all languages derive from the common Indo-European language family, Middle Eastern languages are divided among three very different language families: the Hamito-Semitic, the Indo-European, and the Altaic. Language is one of the primary ways by which people from the Middle East differentiate themselves and define their national identities and/or political allegiances.

The most widely spoken language in the Middle East is Arabic. A sister language to Hebrew, it belongs to the Semitic subdivision of the Hamito-Semitic language family. There is a distinction between written and colloquial Arabic. Written Arabic, which is the religious and literary language throughout the Arab world, does not vary and serves as a bond among all Arabs. It is a spoken form of standard Arabic that is used as a *lingua franca* and the principal instrument of commerce, culture, and government. At the regional level, however, Arabic has a number of dialects that may be so different as to preclude communication unless standard Arabic is used.

Globally, Arabic ranks as the sixth most-common first language. It is the chief language in 18 countries in the Middle East and North Africa, with the exception of Iran, Turkey, Israel, and Central Asian countries. The significance of the Arabic language, however, far surpasses its rank because most non-Arab Muslims also revere it as the language of scripture and Revelation, not subject to substitution or translation.

The Arabic alphabet consists of 29 letters, all of which, except the first, are consonants. They are written from right to left. The most approved word order in Arabic grammar is verb–subject–object; however, the subject may also be put first.

Turkish, Persian (Farsi), and Kurdish are three other widely spoken languages in the Middle East and adjacent regions. The Turkish group of languages belongs to the Altaic language family. Turkish is the predominant language in Turkey. Variations of the Turkic group of languages are spoken in most of the countries in Central Asia. Also, related to Turkish language is Azeri, mainly spoken in Azerbaijan, which also is spoken by almost one third of Iranians (mostly called Azeri Turks from the Iranian province of Azerbaijan), as well as by groups in Afghanistan and Cyprus. Modern Turkish used in Turkey employs a modified form of the Roman alphabet, consisting of 29 letters. The most frequent word order in modern Turkish is subject–object–verb.

Persian (also known as Farsi) belongs to the Indo-European language family. It is the third most widely spoken language in the Middle East. The overwhelming majority of all Persian speakers are in Iran, where Persian is the official language. Persian also is spoken in western Afghanistan in a dialect known as Dari, the Central Asian country of Tajikistan, Bahrain, and small communities around the Persian Gulf. The Persian language (along with *Shi'a'ism*) is a major component of Iran's distinctive national identity and helps to differentiate the country from its neighbors. Modern Persian also is written from right to left and uses a modified Arabic script, which makes it appear the same as Arabic. The two languages, however, are completely different. Nevertheless, the two languages have borrowed many words from each other. The word order in Persian is subject–object–verb.

Related to Persian and also widely spoken is Kurdish, which is the language of large Kurdish populations of Iran, Iraq, Turkey, and Syria. Hebrew (the official language of Israel), Armenian, Assyrian, and Greek are other major languages spoken by large groups in the Middle East and adjacent regions. (For more information on Middle Eastern languages, refer to *The Cambridge Encyclopedia of the Middle East and North Africa* [Mostyn & Hourani, 1988]. Also, see *The Europa World Yearbook* [1996] for information on Central Asian and Transcaucasian countries.)

Middle Eastern languages are known for their poetic richness. According to Menocal (2002), the pre-Islamic Arab–Bedouin cultures had a great love for the language and idolized poetry of sentimental and delicate nature called the "odes." In poetry competitions held in Mecca, the winning poem would be embroidered in gold and hung in the "the House of God." The idol of poetry survived the coming of Islam and even flourished with time. In time, the poetic nature of Arabic language influenced many other languages, and poetry became the preferred literary genre of most Middle Eastern cultures. The power of poetry, however, goes beyond literature. Poetry and rhymes are used in the everyday lives of ordinary people. One of the most pleasurable pastimes of the Middle Eastern people, regardless of ethnicity, religion, and language, is to read poetry during the gatherings of friends and family. Some of the most well-known poets of all time come from the Middle East. Among those better known in the West are the Persian poets Omar Khayyam, Hafez, and Rumi. The works of the contemporary Arab/Lebanese poet Khalil Gibran have been translated into many languages and revered by many.

CONTEMPORARY LIFE

Values

In spite of the great variation in language, religion, and social and political systems, most Middle Eastern societies share many similar values pertaining to family interactions and child-rearing practices; however, it is important to recognize that considerable differences exist across groups within any culture. This is certainly true among Middle Eastern people. Educated people who have come from urban areas often do not share many of the values and practices of those who came from more traditional rural areas. Factors such as the level of education, type of work, availability of time and space, degree of religious faith, and degree of exposure to a Western way of life are important determinants in shaping the family values and child-rearing practices among many Middle Eastern families.

Most Middle Eastern families in the United States come from educated backgrounds, and almost all of the Middle Eastern people who came to live in the United States before the 1980s can speak English (Sabagh & Bozorgmehr, 1987; Thernstrom et al., 1980). Although the knowledge of English and the educational level of the more recent immigrants have been lower than their predecessors, a great majority of them have at least a high school degree (Bozorgmehr & Sabagh, 1989; Thernstrom et al., 1980). Whereas a knowledge of English and higher educational background can facilitate better communication between Middle Eastern families and non–Middle Eastern interventionists, overt and subtle cultural differences continue to interfere with the clarity and the efficacy of intervention in many instances.

Role of the Family

Family in its extended form is the most important institution in the Middle East. It is very common for three generations of a family to live together in the same house. Other family members may live as close as a few blocks away or as far away as another city. Physical remoteness, however, rarely affects the loyalty to the extended family.

In most cultures in the Middle East, the individual's first and foremost loyalty is to his or her family, clan, or kin. Family interactions and dynamics, in turn, are shaped by the religious rules and a patriarchal family structure. Religious rules provide the strongest guidelines in shaping the relationships within the family. This contrasts with many industrialized Western societies in which secular rules coming from formal institutions often govern the nature of interaction even within the family.

The extended family performs important functions in the Middle Eastern societies. It provides many of the services that are performed by formal organizations in the West. For example, it is within the network of the extended family that the children, the elders, and those with disabilities are often nurtured and protected. In addition to being a source of guidance and support, the family also is where most recreation and entertainment take place.

   In most Middle Eastern cultures, members often cite the collective achievement of the family as a source of pride and identity. It is very common to cite the achievements of ancestors, uncles, aunts, or even distant cousins and take extreme pride in them. Identification with the family's achievements is generally as important and sometimes even more important than identification with one's personal achievements. This interconnectedness of achievement and pride within the family contrasts sharply with the mainstream American values of individual achievement and independence.

   Strong family ties and the need to interact with family members often persist among Middle Eastern individuals and families who emigrate to the United States. Whenever possible, Middle Eastern families or individuals in the United States try to bring relatives from their homelands to stay with them over long periods of time. The emphasis, in much of the West, on the nuclear family is not easily understood or appreciated by the newly arrived immigrants. It often is hard for many Middle Eastern families to relate to the multitude of social organizations that are devised to replace the functions of the extended family. Even when they understand the purpose and function of these support organizations, some people may still view them as unfamiliar or impersonal. In their preference for familial and informal networks, many may try to establish quasi-extended families. The clustering together of people of the same religions, languages, or nationalities from the Middle East, in addition to other purposes, also may have the function of filling the psychological vacuum created by the absence of the extended family.

   In summary, Middle Eastern families in the United States bring with them a deep-rooted and strong belief in the informal support system provided by the extended family in their homelands. This contrasts with the emphasis placed on the role of formal organizations as sources of support to the family in the United States. Whereas time may be a factor in bridging this gap, differences in attitude and values are likely to persist. An interventionist working with a Middle Eastern family may greatly facilitate communication by trying to establish a more informal relationship with the family.

Family Size

In the tradition of most Middle Eastern societies, all men and women must have children, and not having children is a reason for great unhappiness. The motive behind many marriages in the Middle East for having children is often as strong and many times even stronger than that of love and intimacy. The desire for many children and a strong preference for male children are often characteristic among followers of Judeo-Christian faiths in the Middle East, particularly among Muslims. Islam strongly endorses procreation. "Wealth and children are the ornaments of this life," says the *Qur'an* (Sura 18). In Egypt, for example, prior to the modern age, a wife's worth in the eyes of her husband and even her acquaintances depended on fruitfulness and the preservation of her children (Lane, 1963). This attitude was not limited to Egypt and has not completely vanished in the Middle East. Part of the great desire for large families, however, stemmed from the high infant mortality rate, which often left parents with few or no children in spite of many births (Prothro & Diab, 1974).

The birth of a boy has always been a reason for great celebration in a traditional Middle Eastern family. One possible reason could be the loss of men to wars, leaving villages and towns populated only by women. Professional and lay midwives in villages all over the Middle East can tell stories of occasions when they have received gold jewelry for helping deliver a boy and sour faces for delivering a girl.

In addition to the joy of having children, in most Middle Eastern cultures, children are needed to support the parents in their old age. Many Iranians believe that children are like canes in the hands of the old parents. In the eyes of Middle Eastern cultures, once children arrive, parents must put aside their individual interests and fully attend to the needs of their offspring. Negligence and lack of love and care toward children is severely scorned in these societies. Yet, among many traditional or uneducated families, a good part of the responsibilities for child rearing also may be placed on God's shoulders. Thus, the definition of care and attention varies greatly from society to society in the Middle East. Many lower income families or traditional families have more children than they can possibly attend to by modern or middle-class definitions of child rearing. Having many children, however, usually is justified by a strong belief that God will protect them and provide for them. One commonly hears the saying, "He who gave teeth will also give bread" from Muslims in Iran.

Most Middle Eastern societies have strict laws against abortion; however, birth control and abortion are available in large cities. Abortion is generally performed illegally by physicians in their private clinics and is mostly available to affluent women in less-religious families. This does not mean that women of more traditional background or lesser means do not seek abortion, however. Rural and traditional women in the Middle East will try to get rid of an unwanted pregnancy through a variety of means that they believe will cause a miscarriage. Unsuccessful abortion attempts in many rural areas in Iran, where no immediate medical care is available, commonly result in the mother's death or damage to the fetus.

Pregnancy and Childbirth

Pregnancy and childbirth are generally regarded strictly as a women's affair in most Middle Eastern cultures. Men view themselves as responsible for providing the material necessities and for making major arrangements but do not engage in day-to-day caregiving procedures during pregnancy or following the birth of the child. This attitude is manifested in different degrees depending on the family's educational background and degree of traditional beliefs, however.

Women in many rural areas in the Middle East often go through pregnancy without being seen by a doctor. This is in great part because in most rural areas in many Middle Eastern countries, medical care and facilities are not readily available. A pregnant woman's likelihood of making regular prenatal visits to a doctor also may be hindered by religious beliefs. For example, in many traditional Muslim families, men do not like their wives to be seen by a male specialist. Women themselves usually prefer to be seen by a female obstetrician/gynecologist.

Most women in rural areas who do not have easy access to medical services are provided with a natural system of care by older, experienced women. These older women, who could be regarded as the equivalents of midwives, often use the pregnant woman's external signs, such as changes in the expression of the eyes, the paling of the skin, the shape of and changes in the navel, or the location and kinds of pains, to assess the pregnant woman's condition. To reduce pain or discomfort, they usually use herbal medicine. The same women often help with the delivery of children in rural houses. In instances when they face abnormal situations, such as unfamiliar signs or sequences, they often urge the pregnant woman to seek the help of a medical doctor.

In many rural areas around the Middle East, children are born in families' homes with the help of such midwives or experienced women. A study on the health status of some immigrants in the United States, however, shows that childbirth at home among Iraqi women is a common practice. This was found to be independent of economic factors (Young, 1987). Although the study did not indicate the reasons, one reason could well be the unwillingness of traditional Muslim women to be exposed to strange environments. It also is important to remember that many immigrants have fresh roots in the rural regions of their countries.

Among most urban, middle-class people, the procedures for childbirth are very similar to what occurs in the West. Deliveries take place in hospitals. Men, however, are not generally present in the labor room during delivery. In the tradition of most Middle Eastern cultures, it is not socially acceptable for men to watch women during delivery. One commonly held belief is that a man will lose his sexual attraction to his wife if he watches her during delivery.

Once at home, the mother usually becomes the primary caregiver of the baby. During this period, the father may take more responsibilities for the older siblings; however, members of the extended family usually come to help the mother. The extended family typically provides the Middle Eastern woman with a network of support and relieves the mother from the burden of attending to every aspect of infant care or child rearing by herself.

In most Muslim cultures, these social norms have been strongly influenced by the religious belief that assigns separate roles for men and women. For example, women's roles are generally perceived as childbearing, child rearing, and homemaking. Men perceive themselves as "breadwinners" and moral authorities who are charged with dealing with the affairs of the outside world. Although separation of men and women is much more emphasized in the Muslim religion, this pattern of pre- and postnatal care is not limited to Muslim groups. Most societies from the Middle East, regardless of religious background, follow similar patterns. For example, practices such as Lamaze that engage both men and women in the process of pregnancy and childbirth are not common. Many traditional Middle Eastern men living in the United States may resist taking part in activities that they regard as belonging to women.

Feeding and Health Care

Whenever possible, Middle Eastern women prefer to breastfeed their infants. Although Islam allows women to refrain from breastfeeding their infants if they wish, they rarely choose to exercise this right. Weaning from the breast may vary depending on the child's readiness to accept solid food or on the mother's circumstances. Powdered formulas are regularly used to substitute for mother's milk. Middle Eastern mothers, in general, feed their infants on a very flexible schedule. Feeding is usually in response to the infant's demand. The child may be eating solid food (rice purée) or even drinking water or light tea from a cup before weaning occurs. The strict feeding schedules commonly advocated in the United States are not common in the Middle East.

Traditional approaches to medicine are viewed as keys to solving most minor health problems of infants from Middle Eastern families. In Iran, for example, a mother may calm an infant's stomach pain by using fig syrup or mint essence. Light tea sweetened by rock sugar also is commonly used for stomach pain. Many Iranian women use rice water instead of milk when their infants have diarrhea. Herbal mixtures are commonly used to soothe an infant's rashes. For young children, fruit juices such as sweet lemon juice may be used to cure the flu. Cooked turnips, starch, or quince seeds are regularly used to relieve congested lungs; some pediatricians in Iran put children with chickenpox on a strict diet of watermelon.

The use of traditional medicine is different from region to region and is often rooted in the experiential knowledge that passes across generations. Similar to the Chinese concept of yin and yang, Iranians believe that food can be classified into "hot" and "cold" categories and that people also can have hot and cold natures. *Garmi* (hot) food, they believe, thickens the blood and speeds the metabolism, whereas *sardi* (cold) food dilutes the blood and slows the metabolism. Dates, figs, and grapes are examples of fruits with hot (*garmi*) properties; plums, peaches, and oranges are among fruits with cold (*sardi*) properties (Batmanglij, 1986). A dietary balance of hot and cold food is believed to be essential to good health. This firm belief in hot and cold character and the healing qualities of different foods is shared by all groups of people in Iran, including many Iranian pediatricians. An Iranian mother who lives in the United States and who is the author of an Iranian cookbook wrote:

> My son, like many other five-year-olds, sometimes eats too many dates or chocolates. Because he has a hot nature—something I learned very early in his life!—too much of this hot food does not agree with him at all. Drinking watermelon or grapefruit juice, or nectar from other cold fruits quickly helps restore his balance—and his smile. (Batmanglij, 1986, p. 2)

Middle Eastern parents, especially in the colder climates, like to have their young children well covered and warmly dressed. Many mothers believe that children can catch a cold even with a breeze. They are particularly careful to cover their baby's head and ears. This may seem to be overdressing in the eyes of an American interventionist; however, he or she should know that parents may perceive overdressing as a way of preventing problems that may put them in need of medical care. One Iranian mother in the United States firmly believed that there were more ear infections among children in the United States than in Iran; she attributed this to the common use of hats for children in Iran. Although this is merely an opinion, it attests to the rationale behind many practices that may seem strange to the Western interventionist.

Proximity and Physical Contact

Proximity to and physical contact with infants are very prevalent among Middle Eastern families. In general, Middle Eastern mothers stay closer to their infants, have more physical contact with their infants, and are less concerned than Western mothers about the individuation process.

Infants may have a separate bed, although not usually a separate room. Infants in many rural areas in the Middle East sleep in small wooden cradles. Infants may share a room with other siblings or may even sleep on the mother's bed. A mother will often cradle her baby and sing a lullaby to put him or her to sleep or to comfort crying. Iranian mothers, for example, often cradle their infants on their legs while stretched out on the floor or on the bed; with their hands free, the mothers usually perform other tasks. As with feeding, Middle Eastern mothers generally do not follow a fixed schedule when putting their infants to sleep. This may contrast with the practice in some Western societies in which infants are put to bed at regular times and are expected to go to sleep without much cradling or assistance from the mother.

Middle Eastern mothers also are much more permissive than their Western counterparts in allowing their infants and young children to be kissed, held, or hugged. Babies are generally included in social activities of the family; they are regularly picked up, talked to, and played with in these family circles.

Attachment versus Individuation

A major difference in the child-rearing practices between Middle Eastern families and Western families can be seen in the nature of parent–child attachment and separation/individuation. In the United States, a great emphasis usually is placed on early individuation and independence of the child from the parents. Among Middle Eastern families, the emphasis is often on attachment and parent–child bonding.

Kagan (1984) suggested that there is a general tendency to attribute to infants characteristics that are opposite of those valued by adults in the culture. Americans, he argued, valuing independence and individuality, tend to view the baby as dependent and undifferentiated from others. In contrast, many Eastern cultures, valuing a close interdependence between people, see the infant as potentially too autonomous and needing to be developed into a dependent role in order to encourage the mutual bonding necessary for adult life.

These differences in outlook and valuing can be a source of confusion and misunderstanding between the Middle Eastern parent and the Western interventionist. Independent achievement, privacy, and physical distance from others are generally valued by most adult Anglo-European Americans and seem to be the norms. This is reflected in the practice of having separate rooms for each child, emphasis on early toilet training, self-feeding, bathing, regular schedules for sleeping, and less physical contact. Middle Eastern mothers are less concerned about early toilet training of their children. They do not press for their children to eat, bathe, or put on their clothes independently at an early age. Thus, Middle Eastern children may differ from European-

Six-year-old Yusef, the second child of a young couple from the Middle East, has very little functional language and manifests some behaviors associated with autism; however, he has shown that he can learn certain things quite quickly. For example, he recognizes musical notes and can write his name. Yusef receives special education services and speech therapy.

Yusef's parents are both educated; however, they spend very little time, if any, promoting Yusef's intellectual growth at home. Yusef's father works all day; at home, he rarely spends time on any one planned, purposeful activity with his son. The family recently had a new baby who keeps the mother busy for a good part of the day. Yusef's mother, who believes in traditional roles for women, says that cooking, washing, and organizing the house leave little time for her to work with Yusef.

These parents have put their trust in the school to take full responsibility for Yusef's education and do not believe that it is part of their role to encourage the intellectual growth of a child with Yusef's difficulties at home. The parents also are busy with work and other family members and cannot see how they could add on responsibility for teaching Yusef. One of their friends has observed Yusef's eagerness to learn new tasks at home and has seen how much his behavior improves when he is engaged in "helping." This friend suggested that Yusef's mother ask the teacher for some suggestions on "homework" for Yusef. At her friend's urging, Yusef's mother agreed.

Yusef's teacher was excited by the opportunity to blend school and family goals, and she asked if she could talk with them about family expectations and routines during a home visit. The parents agreed, and the teacher gathered information about their expectations for Yusef and their other children in the home, their current routines, and the time constraints that each parent feels. She then worked with them to decide on several activities that they could work on with Yusef as they carried out their normal, daily routine. For example, after Yusef's mother set out placemats, Yusef could be taught to add place settings to get ready for dinner; as his father raked the yard, Yusef could be responsible for removing dead blossoms from the flower beds. They could also read to him and ask him to identify things around the house.

In this case, a friend and teacher were able to help Yusef's parents find ways to supplement their son's school experience with activities at home. Even though the parents did not want to assume the role of teachers or tutors, they were very comfortable having Yusef participate in the family's normal routines.

American children in the chronology of self-help skills. On the one hand, Western interventionists should not interpret this as a deficiency in the child but as a difference in parental attitude toward the child's independence. On the other hand, many Middle Eastern parents may misinterpret an emphasis on early separation and individuation as neglect and a lack of adequate love in parental duty.

Likewise, different attitudes are held regarding the need for privacy. In most Middle Eastern cultures, social interaction and connectedness take precedence over the need for privacy. This does not mean that people from the Middle East do not value their privacy, however. Whereas for many Americans privacy requires actual physical distance, many Arabs, for example, achieve it by becoming silent and temporarily tuning out in a crowd (Safadi & Valentine, 1985). Such silence or tuning out

may be interpreted as rude or as daydreaming by many Americans. For example, in an American family, a long period of silence or a pause during a family gathering such as dinner may create uneasiness and may be a sign of tension. In many Middle Eastern families, however, talking too much, talking too loudly, and talking while eating is discouraged among children.

In summary, Middle Eastern parents generally prefer to see their children grow as interdependent members of the family rather than as independent individuals. This perspective requires a different pattern of child care from that typically emphasized in the United States. In general, Middle Eastern children have strong and relatively secure emotional bonds with their parents, particularly with their mothers. They also are generally dependent on their parents for a longer period of time than are most American children. Middle Eastern sons and daughters, for example, do not leave their parents' home before they are married. It is very common for Middle Eastern sons and daughters to live in their parental homes into their twenties and thirties. Graduation and employment, which, in most Western societies, automatically result in an individual's separation from the family unit, are not reasons for such a change in the Middle East. Unmarried working individuals who live with their parents often give their earnings to their parents. A single man or woman who lives independently is often looked on as pitiful or suspicious; this is particularly true for single women whose modesty and reputation usually become questioned.

Death and Dying

The death of a loved one brings extreme sadness to a Middle Eastern family, regardless of religious background. Followers of different religions, however, have different ceremonies and manifest different behaviors during the mourning process. In most Muslim societies, mourning ceremonies are long and sorrowful, and especially for a very close or a young member of the family, they may be associated with overt manifestations of emotion. Crying, screaming, scratching one's face, pulling one's hair, and pounding on the chest are some behaviors frequently observed among traditional Muslim women during the early hours or days after the death of a child. The same behaviors are less frequently observed among Muslim men, however. Crying, however, is common among men during the burial and the service, which is usually held in a mosque or at the family's home.

The "owners of the grief" usually stay at home, and the rest of the family and friends can come and pay their condolences. It is common for the family and friends to rush to the grieving family's home in the early hours to help prepare food and other necessities. Food is often abundant in such times, and some visitors may stay for long hours.

The burial usually takes place in a designated place in a cemetery. In Islam, the body of the deceased is usually carried in a coffin called a *taboot* to a place in the mortuary where the body is washed thoroughly and stripped of any ornaments, including gold-plated teeth; this is to prepare the deceased to meet his or her creator. Similar to swaddling a newborn, the body is then tightly wrapped in a white cotton cloth called *Kafan* and, facing Mecca, it is placed directly into the grave, which is usually dug for the size of the deceased. Death, as Muslims believe, cleanses the deceased from mistakes and sins, and the white cloth represents this notion. In many Muslim countries, the body is first taken to a holy shrine before being placed in the grave. A gravestone is placed on the pile of dirt after 40 days, within which time the body is believed to have decomposed.

Wearing black, Muslims usually mourn the death of a loved one for at least 1 year by organizing big gatherings of relatives and friends on the 3rd day, the 40th day, and the 1-year anniversary of the death of the loved one. A Muslim priest, commonly referred to as a *mufti* among Sunnis and a *mulla* among Shi'as, is usually invited to read verses of the *Qur'an* related to death and dying. In most traditional Muslim families, women and men are in separate quarters during these ceremonies. Arab women in mourning typically sit in circles and collectively pound on their half-bare chests, scratch their faces, or move their heads in a circular motion often with their hair uncovered and loose. It also is common in many Arab countries to bring in "professional mourners"; it is thought that by maintaining a mournful atmosphere and making people cry, professional mourners help release some tension, particularly among those who do not cry easily.

Jews, Christians, Zoroastrians, Bahais, and other religious groups in the Middle East may manifest extreme emotions depending on the severity of the tragedy. The strong family bonds that exist in all religious groups in the Middle East warrant such emotions. Different religions, however, follow their respective rituals. In traditional Zoroastrian societies, for example, the dead body was placed on a stone platform in what used to be called a tower of silence, which exposed the body to the sun and the vultures. Today such practice is rare, and, under pressure from Islam, Zoroastrians bury their dead in concrete graves. Zoroastrians, however, continue to closely observe other rituals such as wearing white and holding memorials on the 10th and the 13th day after death and each month thereafter until the 1-year anniversary. After this, this ritual is repeated annually until the 30th anniversary.

Similar to Muslims, Middle Eastern Jews practice the interment of the dead, which must take place within 24 hours of the death. The body is thoroughly washed (*Taharah*) and dressed in a white linen shroud (*Takhrikhin*). The best-known memorial prayer is the *Kaddish,* which is said at the gravesite and on various occasions for 11 months. In general, a 7-day period of full mourning (*Shiva*) and 30 days of lesser mourning are observed. (For more information on religious rituals, the reader is referred to *Encyclopedia of World Cultures* [Levinson, 1991].)

For interventionists providing services to a grieving family from the Middle East, the most sincere gesture is to be present during important ceremonies in the early days of grief. Offering help and assistance in the organization of the ceremony in the early days usually is regarded as a sign of true friendship. Sending flowers also may be appreciated by more Westernized families; this, however, may not be the case with some traditional Muslim or Jewish families from the Middle East. All groups appreciate condolences offered over the telephone or in a card.

THE CHILD IN THE CONTEXT OF THE FAMILY

The emphasis on relationships and interdependence as opposed to separation and independence also is evident in the Middle Eastern family's pattern of social interaction. Middle Eastern parents, particularly mothers, rarely have social and recreational activities separate from their children. Family gatherings, picnics, cinemas, and, to a lesser extent, sports events are among the most common social events in the Middle East; children are usually included in all of them. Most Middle Eastern boys do not start to have activities of their own until after puberty; for unmarried girls, this may come even later. Many American parents, in contrast, have social, recreational, and leisure activities independent of their children.

Entertainment

Family get-togethers are the most important and common form of entertainment in the Middle East. Marriages, national and religious feasts, or even gatherings to remember the deceased loved ones are all occasions for family members and friends to get together and socialize. On many of these occasions, food is the central theme of the festivity or gathering, and, depending on the kind of ceremony, music and dance usually abound. Backgammon and chess are two popular games in many Middle Eastern countries and are most commonly played during family events by male members. Family gatherings, however, need not be justified by particular occasions. In most Middle Eastern countries, family members and friends tend to visit one another on a regular basis. In these gatherings, children are not usually given a particular place or realm separate from the adults. They are, in general, expected to find other children and entertain themselves in any way they can.

Middle Eastern children, similar to most immigrant families, fall under the magic spell of commercial television as soon as they arrive in the United States. In most Middle Eastern families in the United States, television becomes the main entertainment, at least in the first few years. Often, parents are as attracted to the television as their children and, before they know it, have lost control of the children's viewing habits. This is particularly true among less-educated families from the Middle East. The old ways of entertainment such as storytelling, hide and seek, or board games soon pale and, if children do engage in such activities, it is through great effort on the part of the parents.

Middle Eastern families in the United States observe their religious and national events very closely. The most significant feast among Muslims is *Eid-Ghorban,* which marks the termination of the Hajj or pilgrimage to Mecca, the Muslim house of God. *Eid-al-Feter* is the second most important Muslim feast, which terminates the fasting month of *Ramadan.* These events, however, fall on variable dates of the year because the Muslim calendar is a lunar calendar. The most significant feast for most Iranians in the United States is the Iranian New Year on March 21 or the Day of Equinox. *Norooz,* originally a Zoroastrian tradition celebrating spring, is observed by all Iranians, Afghans, and some Lebanese and Central Asian societies regardless of religious faith or ethnic origin. Middle Eastern families generally welcome guests at these events. An interventionist's knowledge of and participation in some of these events can help bridge the cultural difference and improve mutual respect and cooperation during the course of intervention.

The Importance of Guests

In the tradition of most Middle Eastern cultures, guests are to be honored and respected. A Middle Eastern family always has time for a guest or a visitor. A guest is usually given the best place, is offered the best food, and is treated with the utmost respect. Many Middle Eastern cultures have proverbs emphasizing the importance of guests. Muslims especially believe that guests are "endeared by God" and must be well treated. Middle Eastern hospitality, however, goes beyond differences in religion or social class. A poor Middle Eastern family may go as far as offering to the guests the only food available in order to maintain dignity in so important a matter. Children, similar to their parents, are expected to try to accommodate a guest. If the guest is staying overnight, they may have to give up their regular bed or room. They are expected to interact with the guest and not to retreat into their separate quarter or corner.

In general, a Middle Eastern child spends more time with his or her parents and other adults than the average American child; and on the average, an American child spends more time alone than the average Middle Eastern child. Less space, however, is not the only reason for more adult–child contact in the Middle Eastern family. Many Middle Eastern parents coming home from work prefer to spend more time with their children rather than put them to bed early. Young children, particularly before school age, can stay up as long as they can keep up with their parents. When they do go to bed early, an adult, usually the mother, grandmother, or an older sibling, accompanies them until they go to sleep. They are allowed to fall asleep on the parents' bed or in the midst of a gathering and are then transferred to their beds. Middle Eastern children rarely express the desire to take a teddy bear or a toy to bed, a need that is commonly observed among American children.

In summary, the sleeping and waking patterns of young children in Middle Eastern families generally follow that of their parents very closely. These patterns may allow greater contact and bonding between parents and children. Unfortunately, very often they persist even after the children start school. A Middle Eastern child not performing well in school on a particular day may well have been socializing the night before. Afternoon naps are very common for children and adults in the Middle East and, in fact, naps are expected of young children.

Children's Responsibilities and Work

Children are usually encouraged to take up responsibilities within the family at an early age. The degree and types of responsibilities expected from children, however, differ according to social class and the family's degree of adherence to tradition. Children as young as 4 or 5 years old from rural or poor urban sectors often have to learn various tasks necessary for survival. In many rural areas, little boys are expected to help with the farming tasks or help with family subsistence. They may work for other people outside of the house to earn extra money. Little girls as young as 5 or 6 years old may do a variety of household activities, such as taking care of younger siblings, cleaning the house, or even cooking. However, this is generally true of poor, overburdened families all over the world.

The Middle Eastern families who reside in the United States usually come from economically advantaged backgrounds. Children in such families are primarily expected to study and to succeed in school. This expectation, however, is very uneven for boys and girls, depending on the family's belief system. Highest achievement is usually expected for boys, whereas girls are expected to receive only a modest education. In general, girls are expected to learn household activities at approximately 5 or 6 years of age. Boys are usually exempt from doing household chores. Attitudes toward girls' education differ according to the family's educational standards and values. In some very traditional Muslim families, a girl's education may not extend beyond elementary school or may end just before puberty. Among other reasons for this differential treatment is a concern for a girl's modesty—that is, a fear that a girl attending school may be unguarded or exposed.

In contrast, many nontraditional Middle Eastern families who value education highly may have similar aspirations for both girls and boys. Having higher aspirations for girls does not usually change the division of labor in the family, however; girls continue to have more household responsibilities than do boys.

Role of the Father

The father is usually the head of the family. He is seen as the parent who controls the family finances, the agent of socialization with the world outside the family, the moral authority, and the final disciplinary agent in the family. All of these roles help put the father at a much higher level than the mother and the children and separate him from most of the day-to-day activities that bind the mother with the children.

Patriarchy is dominant in almost all religions and cultures in the Middle East. It is present in varying degrees depending on the level of education and traditionalism among the family. Some of the most extreme forms of patriarchy are prevalent among traditional Muslim families in the Persian Gulf region. In these families, women and children often are put into the same category and live under the authoritarian rule of the father. Women in these families have minimal economic power. Their roles are strictly limited to childbearing and child rearing, and they have very little contact with the outside world. They look to their husbands for major and even minor decisions. The fathers in these families are primarily disciplinary agents in their contact with their children. Although fathers often enjoy playing and spending time with their infants and toddlers, they rarely engage in caregiving activities and have very little awareness of the intellectual and psychological development of their children.

Most Middle Eastern families in urban and rural regions, however, fall outside of this extreme category. This is particularly true in families in which women have economic productivity. In many parts of the Middle East, women work with men and have substantial authority inside the family. However, in many instances, the power of these women is invisible, and the title of "all powerful" remains with the father.

The power of women is further limited if they have a lower level of education and less contact with the outside world. This equation, however, begins to change once the family is in the United States. In the absence of pressure from the traditional society in the United States, many Middle Eastern women thrive personally by seeking education and economic independence. So, whereas in some very traditional Muslim families men remain the authority figures, in others, their traditional status may be eroding.

Contrary to the general perception in the West, the level of education among women is high in most countries of the Middle East. All over the Middle Eastern countries, educated women can be found in professional, political, business, and scholarly spheres. In Iran, for example, the number of female college and university students exceeds those of males. Middle Eastern women's quest for education and autonomy, however, does not automatically translate into a changing view of the traditional family values.

Regardless of high achievements and financial autonomy, a Middle Eastern woman in the United States may choose to preserve the values transmitted by her faith or cultural tradition. Many women, however, inside their countries and out, are working hard to break down the barriers to their equal rights under the law imposed by religion and tradition. Issues such as the right to divorce, child custody, and inheritance are on the priority list of many women's organizations in the Middle East.

With the advances in communication and information technology, in recent years, these organizations have become more visible and powerful. Middle Eastern women are trying to find the balance between their basic human rights on the one hand, and their need to preserve some of the valuable traditions endorsed by their religions and cultures on the other hand. Organizations such as the Iranian Women's Studies Foundation (http://www.iwsf.org) and the Revolutionary Association of the Women of Afghanistan (http://rawa.org) are only a few places for information on advancing the rights of Middle Eastern women.

Many interventionists visiting a Middle Eastern family in the United States may find themselves talking with the father rather than the mother, even though the real authority over the children's lives may be the mother. One reason, of course, is that among recent immigrants from the Middle East, many mothers do not speak English. The other reason, however, is that many Middle Eastern men, particularly those from traditional Muslim families, see themselves as the sole agents of communication between the family and the "stranger." This allows the Middle Eastern father to control the type and the amount of information that leaves the family territory and to define the family ideology. Concern for family honor, dignity, and integrity is so great among some Middle Eastern men that they commonly forbid their wives and children to talk to strangers. Survey researchers, for example, have found it particularly difficult to collect information on Middle Eastern families through formal channels (Bozorgmehr & Sabagh, 1988). These researchers have emphasized the use of informal channels, such as contacting the religious and community leaders and requesting that they endorse a certain survey.

The father's level of education and his level of belief in the intervention may interfere with the effectiveness of communication if he is acting as a mediator between the interventionist and the mother. For instance, an early interventionist complained that during a visit the father kept summarizing her lengthy instructions into one or two brief sentences. Even though she did not speak the language, she believed that her message was not effectively translated to the mother. Although this is an isolated example, it also is a reminder that in some cases, using an English-speaking friend or a relative who is trusted by the family may be a reasonable alternative to direct communication between the interventionist and the mother.

Discipline

American parenting styles have been described in terms of three types: authoritative, permissive, or authoritarian (Baumrind, 1971; Satir, 1972). The most commendable parenting, or the authoritative form, is said to be characterized by high demands; control based on setting clear rules, routines, and standards; and high warmth. The permissive parents are usually low in both demand and control and are high in warmth. The authoritarian parents are high in demand, high in control, and low in warmth. Although Middle Eastern parenting may represent all of these forms, the general pattern among Middle Eastern families falls outside of the three categories. Middle Eastern parents are, in general, high in demand, high in control, and high in warmth.

The first signs of discipline appear with toddlers' exploration around the house. Before this time, a very permissive atmosphere prevails. No rules or rigid schedules requiring disciplinary action exist. Children are toilet trained when they demonstrate readiness. The mother usually places them on the toilet routinely, but no punishment for lapses in toilet training is administered before the age of 3. Similarly, children are not subject to much discipline regarding their eating, dressing, or sleeping.

During these early years, fathers have very little influence in shaping the behavior of the child. When the child cries, wets, or disrupts, the father usually calls on the mother to correct the situation. Toddlers may be scolded or spanked for touching breakable objects, putting things in their mouths, or moving toward a dangerous area in the house.

The father takes more direct responsibility, especially once a boy reaches the age of 4 or 5 years. Discipline and punishment vary depending on the father's belief system and level of education. Before the turn of the century, physical punishment was believed to be a viable way of disciplining boys and was commonly used in religious schools and even by regular teachers. Today, however, physical punishment is an exception rather than the rule, particularly among educated families. Parents who use it, however, usually are not subjected to legal or social scrutiny. The general attitude in the Middle East is that children "belong" to the parents and all parental behavior is motivated by love.

In families governed by strict tradition, rules are often to be obeyed without much explanation given by the parents. In less traditional families, however, children have much more freedom and rules are subject to revision by parents. Generally, Middle Eastern children learn what is expected of them by watching the interaction among family members. The following are some of the major disciplinary rules among Iranian families:

- Older family members should be respected.

- Children must not disobey the parents or talk back to them.

- Children should not interrupt when adults are talking.

- In the presence of a guest or during a visit, children should not make a lot of noise or touch the food without permission.

- Children should take very good care of their toys, clothes, and school materials.

- Children should not touch objects that do not belong to them.

- When siblings fight, the older sibling usually has to give in.

- Children should cooperate with the parents and other family members.

- Parents must know and approve of their children's friends and acquaintances.

- Girls in particular are not allowed to spend time outside of the house unsupervised.

In summary, Middle Eastern children are required to follow few rules prior to age 3. Middle Eastern children start learning the rules by watching parental reactions. In general, rules are not explained to the child through intimate parent–child talk. Such rules as respect and obedience are not to be questioned or explained. Parents typically expect the children to learn about rules by watching the pattern of interaction in the larger family. Children often are reminded of a good or bad behavior of a certain child in the family. Other members of the family also act as disciplinary agents.

The absence of an extended family poses serious discipline problems for Middle Eastern parents in the United States. Without the support of the extended family, parents have a hard time controlling their children or setting examples of desired behavior. Many may have a hard time sharing their power with a school or a teacher they barely know. Furthermore, communication may become difficult as a result of language barriers between parents and children, particularly when parents have little education. Children's acculturation through television and schooling is sometimes much faster than the parents can handle or even tolerate. In general, however, Middle Eastern parents have less concern about the acculturation of their sons than their daughters. The belief in a woman's piety and virtuosity is strong among adherents of all faiths in the Middle East (Armanios, 2002). One of the greatest fears of most Middle Eastern families in the United States is what they regard as peer pressure that girls experience in school to engage in early sexual activities. The author of this chapter knows a number of families with daughters who have decided to return to their home countries solely on the basis of this concern.

Intellectual Development and Schooling

The Middle Eastern infant typically comes in contact with a great deal of natural stimulation in the environment. Surrounded by adults, the infant is constantly touched, moved, and talked to within the first 2 years of life. Toddlerhood, however, brings a number of restrictions in the infant's world. Parents may limit their toddler's independent explorative behavior because they fear the child will become injured. Children are generally discouraged from touching objects that belong to adults. The family's economic status determines for the child the availability of toys. During the toddler years, children often receive verbal stimulation from adults other than their parents. The Middle East is rich with history, legends, literature, and poetry; storytelling is particularly common. In most parts of the Middle East, rhymed poems about everything are shared in the oral tradition, and children learn to recite them from an early age. Middle class and more educated parents are more likely to share picture books and read to children than are their less wealthy, less educated counterparts.

Most Middle Eastern parents assume that their children should do well in school. When children achieve, however, parents generally provide less overt praise or material rewards than are common in the United States; children are doing what is expected of them. When children do not do well, however, parents may present a variety of attitudes, including denying the problem, blaming the school, blaming the child, and/or feeling ashamed.

Attitudes Toward Disability

Guilt and shame are two common feelings when a child with a disability is born to a Middle Eastern family. Guilt is felt by the mother who is usually held responsible for the birth of a child with a disability. Fathers often feel shame because they may view their child's disability as a personal defeat and a scar on the family's pride. The results of guilt and shame are usually overprotection, continuous denial, isolation, or even total abandonment of the child. These attitudes, however, are often mediated by the family's familiarity with the field of special education.

Uneducated mothers may feel that they are being punished for some wrongdoing committed during or even before the pregnancy. A previous abortion, for example, may be linked to the birth of a child with a disability. Among less-educated women, lifting heavy objects, unsuccessful attempts at abortion, eating special types of food, or even thinking about certain taboos during pregnancy may be associated with birth defects. In reality, the causes of disability in the Middle East are not any different from those in other places, with one exception. Although on the decline, marriage between first cousins is permissible among the Middle Eastern Muslims and Jews, and, in some instances, it has contributed to genetic abnormalities in the offspring.

Social attitudes vary depending on the kind and degree of disability. Blindness, deafness, or paralysis may arouse pity for the individual and sympathy for the family; an overprotective, charitable, but nonetheless cooperative attitude may be directed toward these individuals.

Children with mild cognitive and/or learning disabilities that have no apparent physical signs can usually lead a near-typical life under the strong protection of the family. If the family does not stress education, many such disabilities may even go unnoticed. Girls may marry and form a family; boys may learn a trade and earn a living under the supervision of a family member. Boys with cognitive disabilities, however, are much more likely to be part of a typical life than girls. When a child has a severe cognitive disability, however, it often engenders pity for both the child and the family and may lead to alienation.

Strong negative stereotypes against severe mental disability often result in families isolating themselves from many social activities. Parents hesitate to take their child to public places for fear that the child and the family will become objects of pity. For example, when talking to a stranger, an Iranian father may leave out mention of his child with severe disabilities and talk instead only about his other children. Such isolation and limited contact with other adults make caregiving particularly difficult and stressful for the mother. The child with a disability often gets used to one or two people, usually the mother and female siblings. Members of the extended family may be less eager to take responsibility for fear they may not know how to respond to the child's special needs.

The social isolation also is motivated by the common assumption that children with severe disabilities do not understand their situation and do not care. Many Middle Eastern families have little faith that children with mental disabilities can become relatively self-sufficient. Thus, little attempt is made to educate such children at home.

The idea of special schools for children with disabilities, however, is not new in the Middle East. In Iran, for example, Shahnaz Shahnavaz, a pioneer Iranian female child psychologist, established the first center for children with mental disabilities during the late 1950s. Despite parental support and appreciation, the center had to battle against a multitude of obstacles often created by a lack of government support. Today, many schools and centers for children with special needs are in operation all over the Middle East; however, offering widespread services for children with disabilities continues to be a low priority on the agenda of many Middle Eastern governments.

Social acceptance and widespread support for children with disabilities in the United States relieve immigrant Middle Eastern parents of many of the tensions at home. Blame, guilt, shame, and denial, however, still may be observed in many of these families, depending on their level of education and traditional beliefs. Parents may be reluctant to talk about their child with a disability, particularly with other Middle Easterners. Some families may even prefer an American interventionist for fear they may "lose face" with a Middle Eastern interventionist. This, however, is open to speculation. Language continues to be a major barrier to adequate services to such families. This is particularly true for Middle Eastern children with speech difficulties who are caught between the language spoken at home and the language used by the therapists at their school.

In summary, Middle Eastern parents accept the reality of having a child with a disability less readily than most American parents. Denial, guilt, and shame persist for a long time and may interfere with an effective and positive intervention. Societal acceptance and support can help change this attitude among many immigrants, particularly those with less traditional concerns and a longer history in the United States.

LANGUAGE AND COMMUNICATION

The Middle East is rich in language diversity, and many Middle Easterners are bi- or multilingual. Arabic, Turkish, Farsi, Kurdish, Armenian, Hebrew, and Assyrian are commonly spoken, as are dialects of each of these languages. Because schools in some Middle Eastern countries include English instruction in their curriculum, many educated Middle Easterners come to the United States fluent in English.

Cultures of the Middle East are high-context cultures in which what is left unsaid is as important as what is said. Individuals rely heavily on shared experience, the situation, and nonverbal cues in communicative interactions. Although no generalization applies to all individuals, there are several things to keep in mind when interacting with families with Middle Eastern roots. A direct "no" is considered to be impolite for it could result in confrontation or hurt feelings. A weak "yes," "maybe," or "perhaps" may commonly replace a direct "no." However, a weak "yes" also may indicate agreement; therefore, individuals communicate their preferences very indirectly, relying on the listener to understand the intended meaning. This may be further complicated by the formality of the cultures, which demands that all of the behavioral codes be followed. For example, in interactions with professionals, respect requires that the family give the impression that they are not in conflict with the professionals' recommendations. Therefore, instead of saying "no" or "that won't work in our family," families may give the impression that they are in agreement but may not act on the suggested interventions.

Indirect communication also applies to saying "yes." When offered something, individuals from Middle Eastern cultures may verbally deny that they want it. For example, if a hostess offers tea, instead of saying "yes, please," a Middle Eastern guest may say "thank you" or "don't trouble yourself," expecting the hostess to understand that such a response is a polite assent. The confusion that direct communicators may experience as they try to sort out what is really being said may require the use of an interpreter who understands the culture until the interventionists are familiar enough with the families and the culture to understand their communication style and intent.

Social distance, or the distance between speakers in conversation, is less than the distance maintained by Anglo-European Americans or those speakers socialized

Avisa is a 6-year-old Iranian girl with a developmental age of 4 years. Avisa has no observable physical disability. Her mental disability, however, is immediately indicated through her speech and in certain aspects of her behavior. Avisa goes to a school for children with special needs, in which she learns academic skills. Her mother, Nahid, is a housewife who has devoted her life to her daughter. Keivan, Nahid's husband and the girl's father, has very little involvement with his family and is gone most of the time on business trips.

Even though Avisa is developing pre-academic skills, Nahid still complains about her daughter's slow progress. She believes that Avisa should be doing higher level reading and arithmetic, and if she is not, it is because of poor teaching. She continually sends Avisa for psychological testing and has changed her school a number of times. In addition, Nahid is in a constant state of anxiety over the future of her daughter, and her continued focus on Avisa has hurt her relationship with her older daughter, Sara.

Sara is a bright high school student who sees Avisa's situation very differently from her mother. She is extremely critical of her mother's overprotective attitude toward Avisa and believes that Avisa needs to be more independent. She blames her mother for many of Avisa's behavioral problems and, at times, she stops talking to her mother. Sara, however, confides with Neda, her aunt who lives in another state but who shares Sara's concern. They both believe that Nahid needs to receive some counseling, an idea that Nahid rejects based on her traditional beliefs.

Recently, through a concerted effort of Neda and Sara, Neda spoke with the psychologist who was to test Avisa and explained some of the tensions at home. The psychologist soon recognized Nahid's distress, and based on Neda's recommendation, tried to establish a rapport with Nahid. The psychologist gently described Avisa's strengths and weaknesses, communicated positively on Nahid's strong advocacy for her daughter, and talked a bit about how Sara might be experiencing things. She then asked if Nahid would be willing to come back soon to discuss all of these issues. Nahid reluctantly agreed by stating that she "would do whatever it takes to get what Avisa needs." Nahid has continued to meet with the psychologist approximately twice a month for the past year. Although there have been no miraculous changes, Nahid is less stressed, she and Sara are talking and doing things together, and Keivan has spent more time at home in the last 3 months. Avisa is doing well, and her mother has decided to let her stay at her current school until summer.

in the United States. Middle Easterners may stand much closer in face-to-face interactions, and this proximity is not viewed as threatening or aggressive.

Greetings and touch among Middle Easterners also differ from those of mainstream culture in the United States. It is common for men to kiss each other on both cheeks in greeting and for women to exchange hugs and kisses; however, such a public show of affection between men and women would be uncommon unless they were close family members. It also is common for male friends to hold hands and for female friends to hold hands. This does not indicate sexual orientation but rather is a way of showing friendship and support.

The guidelines for translators and interpreters presented in Chapter 3 are relevant to working with families from Middle Eastern cultures. In addition, it is important to recognize the importance of gender roles in these cultures. A traditional Middle Eastern woman would find it extremely difficult to discuss issues that are considered private to women, such as details of her pregnancy or child's birth, with a male translator. Likewise, traditional men, particularly young men, would find it difficult to speak with a female interpreter about personal information that is considered to be private to men. In arranging for interpreting and translation, these gender roles must be honored.

Language, both verbal and nonverbal, is one of the most important features of any culture. By learning and understanding the communication style and the preferences of families from the Middle East, interventionists can gain additional insights into the various cultures of the Middle Eastern families whom they serve.

SUMMARY

The Middle East is both a geographic and cultural designation that is rich in diversity. Differences in language, religion, and social and political systems have shaped groups of people who hold widely varying worldviews. There also is considerable diversity within each of the groups. Educated, urban individuals may be quite different in their beliefs and practices than those from more traditional, rural areas. Despite the differences within and across groups, however, certain bonds link people of Middle Eastern heritage. Of particular importance are the values and beliefs pertaining to family interactions and child-rearing practices that are shared among many Middle Eastern societies.

The extended family is the most important institution in the Middle East; the foremost loyalty among many Middle Easterners is the family, clan, or kin. The rules of family interaction are, in turn, shaped by religion, with Islam being the primary religious influence among many from the Middle East. Children are highly valued, and mothers have primary responsibility for nurturing and caring for them. Fathers usually are the head of the family and the primary agent of socialization with the outside world. Although fathers typically enjoy playing with and spending time with their young children, they rarely engage in the day-to-day responsibilities of caregiving. Sons are more valued than daughters. The birth of a child with a disability is cause for guilt and shame within the family of very traditional Middle Easterners.

The importance of family interactions and the high value placed on caring and providing for young children are strengths that families with Middle Eastern roots bring to intervention. As interventionists become familiar with general beliefs and practices common to families from the Middle East and the ways in which those traditions are expressed among the individual families with whom they work, effective partnerships can be developed.

RECOMMENDATIONS FOR INTERVENTIONISTS

The Middle Eastern population of the United States is increasing in number, representing a multitude of nationalities, languages, religions, and cultures. This chapter has been written to promote an understanding of some of the values and practices shared by a majority of people in the Middle East. The following recommendations provide some specific suggestions to assist interventionists in their interactions and relationships with their clients from the Middle East.

- *Try to learn the family's history of immigration.* Is the family newly arrived in the United States? If not, what generation are they? Are the parents American born; and, if so, how close are the family ties? Middle Eastern parents born in the United States are more likely to be Westernized. Do not assume, however, that newly arrived or first-generation Middle Easterners are a homogeneous group. They are different in their level of education, traditional background, religious beliefs, and attitudes toward adopting Western values. Certain traditional values may persist even among highly educated people from the Middle East.

- *Establish relationships with the family and observe the family's patterns of interaction to help understand the family's position and orientation.*

- *Gather information about the extent of the family's support system.* Are members of the extended family present? Is there a grandmother or an aunt on her way to the United States? Are there any fellow countrymen in the neighborhood who can or do help? What are some of the role divisions in the family? What is the relative status of the father and the mother in the family?

- *Try to establish a direct contact with the mother, but never discount the father or his role.* Whenever possible, use a nonbiased interpreter to communicate information to the mother so that the information that she receives related to the child and the intervention program are not filtered through the father.

- *Use informal, personalized forms of communication with Middle Eastern families rather than direct, assertive communication.* Establish rapport and confidence before moving ahead with the intervention, keeping in mind that it is far more effective to come into the family as a friend who wants to help rather than as an authority figure.

- *Use tactful inquiry to be sure that the family has clearly understood the message and to learn whether they have accepted it.* Politeness requires that the family members show agreement even though they may disagree; however, once the interventionist departs, the parents may continue their preferred practice. The inquiry should be gentle and carefully worded to avoid putting family members on the spot or pointing out disagreement within the family.

WHAT WOULD YOU DO?

Mona, a 2-year-old girl from a Middle Eastern family, showed signs of speech delay. For some time, both the parents and the child care provider attributed the speech delay to the child's confusion between the language spoken at home and that spoken at the center, each thinking that the child could speak the other language better. When the parents and child care provider learned of each other's concern, they arranged to have Mona tested by a speech-language therapist. The testing, which was conducted in English, resulted in a recommendation that Mona receive special services and a suggestion that speaking to her in English at home might help her. Both the diagnosis and the recommendations were unacceptable to Mona's family. They did not think that their daughter had mental retardation (the only reason that they were aware of that necessitated receiving special services), and speaking in their native language at home was a strong and important value to them.

What might the therapist do after hearing the parents' objections?

How can the therapist, in a culturally sensitive way, explain Mona's problem to the family, assure them that Mona does not have mental retardation, and affirm the importance of continuing to use their native language in the home?

REFERENCES

Armanios, F. (2002). The "virtuous woman": Images of gender in modern Coptic society. *Middle Eastern Studies, 38*(1), 110–130.

Aswad, B.C., & Bilge B. (1996). *Family and gender among American Muslims*. Philadelphia: Temple University Press.

Batmanglij, N. (1986). *Food for life: A book of ancient Persian and modern Iranian cooking and ceremonies*. Washington, DC: Mage.

Baumrind, D. (1971). Current patterns of parental authority. *Developmental Psychology Monograph, 1,* 1–103.

Blum, W. (1999). *A brief history of U.S. interventions: 1945 to the present. The National Security Archives*. Retrieved March 12, 2004, at http://www.Thirdworldtraveler.com/Blum/Us_Interventions_Wblumz.html

Bozorgmehr, M., & Sabagh, G. (1988). High status immigrants: A statistical profile of Iranians in the United States. *Iranian Studies, 21*(3,4), 5–37.

Bozorgmehr, M., & Sabagh, G. (1989). Survey research among Middle Eastern immigrant groups in the United States: Iranians in Los Angeles. *Middle East Studies Association Bulletin, 23*(1), 23–34.

Byrne, M. (2000). *The secret history of Iran coup, 1953*. The National Security Archives.

Cainkar, L. (2002, Fall). No longer invisible: Arab and Muslim exclusion after September 11. *Middle East Report,* 22–29.

Cainkar, L. (2003, March). Target Muslims, at Ashcroft's discretion. Middle East Report Online. Retrieved April 11, 2003, from http://merip.org/mero/mero 031403.html.

Economist of London (2003, January 11–17), Is torture ever justified? p. 9.

The Europa World Yearbook. (1996). London: Europe Publication Ltd.

Fata, S., & Rafii, R. (2003, September). *Strength in numbers: The relative concentration of Iranian Americans across the United States*. Retrieved May 9, 2004 from http://www.niacouncil.org/pressreleases/press116.asp

Feldman, K. (Fall, 2002). American justice, Ashcroft-style, *Middle East Report,* 30–31.

Fisher, S.N. (1969). *The Middle East*. New York: Alfred A. Knopf.

Hourani, A. (1991). *A history of the Arab peoples*. Cambridge, MA: Belknap Press.

Immigration and Naturalization Service. (1996). *Annual report: Statistical yearbook*. Washington, DC: U.S. Government Printing Office.

Immigration and Naturalization Service. (2000). *Annual report: Statistical yearbook*. Washington, DC: U.S. Government Printing Office.

Kagan, J. (1984). The nature of the child. New York: Basic Books.

Lane, E.W. (1963). *The manners and customs of the modern Egyptians*. London: J.M. Dent and Sons.

Lewis, B. (1995). *The Middle East: A brief history of the last 2000 years*. New York: Scribner.

Levinson, D. (Ed.). (1991). *Encyclopedia of world cultures*. Boston: G.K. Hall & Co.

Madani, A. (2000). Depiction of Arabs and Muslims in the United States news media. *Dissertation Abstracts International, 60*(B), (UMI No. 2000-95006-352).

Menocal, M.R. (2002). *The ornament of the world*. New York: Little, Brown.

Moore, K. (2002, Fall). A part of US or apart from US? Post September 11 attitudes toward Muslims and civil liberties. *Middle East Report,* 32–35.

Mostyn, T., & Hourani, A. (1988). *The Cambridge encyclopedia of the Middle East and North Africa*. New York: Cambridge University Press.

Nawa, F. (2002, November–December). Afghanistan: Herat is where the heart lives. *Saudi Aramco World,* pp. 26–29.

Prothro, E.T., & Diab, L.N. (1974). *Changing family patterns in the Arab East*. Beirut, Lebanon: American University of Beirut.

Sabagh, G., & Bozorgmehr, M. (1987). Are the characteristics of exile different from immigrants? The case of Iranians in Los Angeles. *Sociology and Social Research, 71*(2), 77–84.

Safadi, M., & Valentine, C.B. (1985). *Contrastive analysis of American and Arab nonverbal and paralinguistic communication* (Position paper). (ERIC Document Reproduction Service No. ED272 935)

Salah, D.H. (2002, Fall). Arabs, race and the post September 11 national security state. *Middle East Report,* pp. 16–21.

Satir, V. (1972). *Peoplemaking*. Palo Alto, CA: Science and Behavior Books.

Suleiman, M. (2001). Image making of Arab Americans: Implications for teachers in diverse settings. (ERIC Document Reproduction Service No. ED 452310)

Thernstrom, S., Orlov, A., & Handlin, O. (Eds.). (1980). *The Harvard encyclopedia of American ethnic groups*. Cambridge, MA: Belknap Press.

Torbat, A. (2002). The brain drain from Iran to the United States. *Middle East Journal, 56*(2), 275–294.

U.S. Bureau of the Census. (1994). 1990 census of populations, social characteristics of foreign-born. Washington, DC: U.S. Government Printing Office.

U.S. Bureau of the Census. (2003). *2000 census of popoulations, ancestry*. Washington, DC: U.S. Government Printing Office.

Young, R.F. (1987). Health status, health problems, and practice among refugees from the Middle East, eastern Europe and Southeast Asia. *International Migration Review, 21*(3), 760–782.

CONTRASTING BELIEFS, VALUES, AND PRACTICES

Middle Eastern	Mainstream culture
Informal support system	Formal support system
Children are brought up to live interdependently	Children are brought up to live independently
Identity is defined more by family achievement	Identity is defined more by individual achievement
Mothers are more willing to allow children to be picked up	Mothers are more reluctant to allow children to be picked up
More flexible time schedule for eating, sleeping, and toilet training	More regulated time schedule for eating, sleeping, and toilet training
Less freedom for independent learning and exploration	More freedom for independent learning and exploration
Respect for old age, spiritual maturity, and wisdom	Respect for youth, physical fitness, and intelligence
Children not permitted to make many independent decisions	Children permitted to make more independent decisions
Older parents live with adult children	Older parents have independent living arrangements

APPENDIX B

CULTURAL COURTESIES AND CUSTOMS

In a Middle Eastern house, it is not appropriate to

- Walk into the home with shoes, unless family members do the same
- Sit with your back to an adult who is present
- Sit with your feet up or legs crossed in front of elders
- Continue to sit when new guests, particularly elders, arrive
- Reject the food, unless there is a good health or religious reason

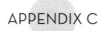

SIGNIFICANT CULTURAL EVENTS/HOLIDAYS/PRACTICES

ALL OF THE MUSLIM WORLD

Eid-al-Adha
(also known as *Eid-Ghorban*)

A feast of sacrifice; the "big feast" of all Muslim believers. It marks the end of the *Hajj* or the pilgrimage to Mecca.

Eid-al-Feter

Marks the end of the month of Ramadan in which Muslim believers observe fasting every day from sunrise to sunset

Eid-al-Moled-e-Nabi

Marks the birth of the Prophet. National holiday in all Muslim countries.

Arab Muslims use a lunar calendar. The dates of these holidays, therefore, vary each year on a solar or a Christian calendar.

IRAN, AFGHANISTAN, AND PARTS OF IRAQ, LEBANON, CENTRAL ASIA, AND AZERBAIJAN

Norooz (The New Day)

Begins on March 21 and lasts 13 days

A spring festival and originally a Zoroastrian tradition, it is the major feast for Iranians, Afghans, most of the Central Asian countries, Azerbaijan, as well as pockets of populations of Iraq, Lebanon, and the Persian Gulf states. It marks the beginning of the solar calendar in Afghanistan and Iran. Norooz is a national feast celebrated by all ethnic and religious groups in Iran.

MIDDLE EASTERN CHRISTIANS

Easter is the major celebration of all the Christians in the Middle East.

VOCABULARY

English	Arabic	Farsi	Turkish	Kurdish
Mother	Ŏomm	Mädar	Änne	Däy'k
Father	Abb	Pedar	Bäbä	Bäo'k
Brother	Akh	Barädar	Kärdes	Brrä
Sister	Ŏokht	Khähar	KizKärdes	Khoishak
Family	Äĕlá	Fäml	A ēlá	Mäll
Hello	Marhabä	Saläm	Merhabä	Chōni
Good-bye	Maa, salami	Khōdä, häfez	Güle Güle	Sar ch āo
Thank you	Sh ōkran	Sepasgozaram	Sagol	Sep āset
Please	Rejä, an	Khähesh	Lutfen	Shäyanineya Mikōnam
How are you?	Kif-Hälak	Chet ōrid?	Nasilsiniz?	Chōnich āki?
Has a disability	Äjz	Nätaväni	Äjz	Nätaväni

CHAPTER 12

FAMILIES WITH SOUTH ASIAN ROOTS

Namita Jacob

Work hard, achieve success.
—BHAGAVAD-GITA

The wise man is like a sieve. He keeps the grain
and discards the chaff.
—KABIR

Atithidevo bhava. (May your guest be a God to you.)
—UPANISHAD

To what we have not said, we are the master.
To what we have said, we are the servant.
—ARABIC PROVERB

Individuals with Asian roots represent one of the fastest growing populations in America, making up about 4.2% of the population in the beginning of the 21st century (U.S. Bureau of the Census, 2000). Asian Americans include people from many nations in the Asian continent who have come to America at various periods in response to different needs and desires. Naturally, this group includes people who differ significantly in economic, social, cultural, linguistic, and religious facets of life, all of which have implications for service provision. Asian Americans constitute 26% of the foreign born population in the United States and are rivaled in number only by those from Latin America. This adds substantially to the diversity of experiences within this group. Rather than treating Asian Americans as a single group, considering the countries and regions of origin is a first step toward tracing the unique experiences and beliefs that define these groups. Many researchers who are interested in families and parenting acknowledge the diversity represented by immigrants and subsequent generations from this vast region, and a small body of literature on each group of immigrants is slowly growing.

The term *South Asian American* has been used to describe people from various nations situated within or near the Indian subcontinent, including India, Pakistan, Bhutan, Nepal, Bangladesh, and Sri Lanka (Shinagawa & Jang, 1998; Thernstrom, 1980). Indians and Pakistanis form the greatest number of immigrants from this region and, therefore, are the focus of this chapter. In the special education literature, this group has received little attention and members typically are grouped within the larger Asian category. People from South Asia come from a region of great cultural, linguistic, and religious diversity. Among South Asian Americans, social and political conditions in their countries of origin and in the United States at the point of their arrival have resulted in the preservation of many of these features. Thus, any attempt to articulate beliefs and values of people with such diverse experiences and origins will necessarily be simplified and limited.

BACKGROUND

Geographical and Historical Origins

Although guarded in the north by the grand Himalayan ranges and surrounded on the remaining three sides by the Arabian Sea, Indian Ocean, and the Bay of Bengal, a great diversity of beliefs, religions, customs, and traditions is represented in the nations that comprise this region. Home to one of the oldest known civilizations in the world, this region has contributed to much of the world's knowledge of sciences such as mathematics, navigation, astronomy, medicine, and architecture. Aspiring scholars from all over the world lived and studied in the world's first university, which was established in 700 B.C. in Takshila, situated in present-day Pakistan, and the University of Nalanda, in present-day India, which was built in the 4th century B.C. Known for spices, precious stones, and skilled artisans, the region's contact through trade with the world beyond the oceans and mountains dates back to the earliest civilizations.

Although each nation that composes the South Asian region today is distinct in character, these nations share many aspects of their historical, political, religious, and linguistic origins. India and Pakistan, in particular, share history and experiences dating back to the Dravidians, who, prior to 2000 B.C., had established the first cities in the Indus Valley with evolved systems of government, irrigation, and pottery. The tradition of formal trade existed at this time with the civilizations in Mesopotamia. The history of the region is one of constant invasions, vigorous trade, and innovative scientific, religious, and philosophical thought. Around 1700 B.C., Aryan invasions from the northwest forced many Dravidians south, where their descendants still live today. Others remained in the north and intermarried with the Aryans. Over the next several hundred years, the Aryans evolved the Hindu philosophy and beliefs and another several hundred years saw the birth of Buddhism and Jainism, faiths that grew out of the prevailing belief system. About 300 B.C., the majority of the Indian subcontinent was united under the Mauryan Dynasty. In the period that followed, foreign invaders, internal rebellions, and trade resulted in the constantly changing kingdoms and the growth of different customs, religious practices, and languages. People in this region were active traders and businessmen and the substantial influence of architecture, language, and religion from this region can be seen in countries such as Thailand, Myanmar (Burma), and Cambodia, as well as in many African nations.

Around A.D. 1300, the region experienced the first attempts at settling by the Muslim invaders, who until then, invaded and plundered but left after each incursion for the northern kingdoms. The Turkish Sultanate was established in Delhi, and Muslim rule quickly covered the north and began pushing south past the Narmada River and the Deccan plateau. Under the Moghul rulers, many independent Hindu kingdoms were conquered and united into one extensive kingdom that covered the northern river valleys and extended far south into the modern day Indian states of Karnataka and Andhra Pradesh. Muslim architecture, language, religion, and art forms such as miniature paintings flourished during much of this period. Arabs were familiar in the kingdoms of the far south, having come as traders over sea routes as early as the 8th century A.D. Because their concern was not political power, they settled into the land and its customs peaceably, adapting their practices to include local ones and merging into the ever-accommodating culture of the south. Defeat of southern kingdoms by the massive Turkish armies led to anti-Turkish rather than anti-Islamic sentiments (Basham, 1959). The wars in the south resulted in the creation of the Muslim Bahmani and the Hindu Vijaynagar kingdoms. Unlike the northern rulers, the Bahmani kings constructed unique architecture, created and built by artisans brought in from Turkey and Persia, leaving Hindu places of worship and main cities untouched. The Vijaynagar kingdom, which lasted until the 17th century, covered much of present day Karnataka, Andhra Pradesh, and Tamil Nadu and parts of Kerala. The prosperity the kingdom enjoyed is legendary, and trade, governance, literature, and music flourished under the Hindu rulers who were able to preserve the Hindu faith in the south.

The rivalry of the Hindus and Muslims and the rigid rules and practices that defined their differences led to much persecution and distrust between the communities, especially in the northern regions of the subcontinent. In the 15th century in the Punjab, Nanak, a follower of Ramananda and Kabir—philosophers who opposed the rigid caste system of the Hindus and emphasized the essential humanity of followers of all religions—organized a group called the *Sikhs*, meaning *Disciples*. This group grew rapidly through the 16th century under the leadership of a succession of gurus or teachers. By the 17th century, the Mughul emperor, worried about his growing power over the region, engaged in several skirmishes and the martial nature of the Sikhs became more pronounced. Under Guru Gobind Singh, the tenth and last guru, this became a defining character of the Sikhs although the simple faith outlined by Guru Nanak was still the foundation of their beliefs.

The British, who had—along with the French, the Portuguese, and the Dutch—come as traders in the 1700s, soon took political control of the region and the British Raj was established, growing until it covered a vast area that included present-day India, Pakistan, and Bangladesh. During this period, the British contributed to the development of roads, railways, and the education system, and their influence can still be seen in these areas. A growing dissatisfaction with the British rule led the people of that region to a desire for independent statehood, and throughout the land, people united to fight for freedom. In 1947, when Britain finally granted autonomy to the region, two nations—India and Pakistan—were formed. In response to the religious conflicts between the Hindus and the Muslims, the northwestern portion of the region, with a strong Muslim majority, chose to become an independent nation called Pakistan. East Bengal, a section of the Indian state of Bengal with a largely Muslim population, also chose to become part of Pakistan at that time. Later, East Bengal fought for independence from Pakistan and, in 1971, became an independent nation called Bangladesh.

Early immigrants from these regions left for America for reasons ranging from better economic opportunity to escaping political persecution and instability. Today, the vast majority of immigrants from South Asia leave for reasons of economic advancement, and the United States has become the favorite destination for many seeking education and wealth. These immigrants tend to be well-educated, although some South Asian businesspeople in America import low-wage laborers from their native villages who tend not to be well educated. Such immigrants may not be educated or know English and will work in return for minimal pay and poor living standards. Young men who first come as students to America and then return to South Asia to get married may bring women who are not as well educated or exposed to the English language and Western ways of thinking. Grandparents, uncles and aunts, and other relatives brought over to help in the house or because of family obligations to care for these extended family members may likewise not be conversant in English or well educated.

RELIGIOUS ORIGINS

India

India is a secular democratic republic, the birthplace of and home to many of the world's major religions. The vast majority of the population in India is Hindu. Islam is the largest minority religion, and Muslims are found through the length and breadth of the nation today. Sikhs, Christians, Jains, Buddhists, Jews, and Zoroastrians are also represented in India. In the United States, Hindus and Sikhs represent a significant percentage of the Indian American population, whereas Muslims, Parsis (Zoroastrians), and Christians from India form a smaller percentage. Because religion is such an important part of life for many Indians, even among the smaller communities, immigrants take great pains to preserve and support their beliefs and traditions (see, e.g., Fenton, 1988).

Unlike the majority of the world's religions, Hinduism is not associated with the teachings of a particular founder. The religion has a deep ethnic character, shaping and being shaped by the lives and needs of the people of the region through the centuries. Religious scholars trace the roots of Hindu practices and philosophy to the earliest civilizations on the plains of the River Indus, 2,000 years before Christ (Basham, 1959). Over the centuries, it spread across the region, taking many forms as individuals and communities chose to stress or expand on its various aspects. Thus, today, many primitive aspects of the religion still exist together with a highly developed philosophical system, and the variety of practices and beliefs that are followed by Hindus makes its definition difficult. The chapter on Hinduism in the *Encyclopedia of Living Faiths* offers this definition,

> We can perhaps best briefly describe a Hindu as a man who chiefly bases his beliefs and way of life on the complex system of faith and practice which has grown up organically in the Indian sub-continent over a period of at least three millennia. (Basham, 1959, p. 225)

Because the faith accepts that there are many paths to *moksha* or freedom from the cycle of life and rebirth, the practices and beliefs of Hindus vary greatly. Hinduism describes God as one who presides over the world and governs it utilizing the numerous lesser gods, who are considered by theologians to be manifestations of His various aspects. Worship of one or the other deity, such as Vishnu or Shiva, as the supreme God, has led to sects within Hinduism such as the Vaishnavites or Shaivites. Monotheism is maintained not by rejecting other gods, but rather by assimilating them into their vision of the supreme God. For example, in the Bhagavad-Gita, one of the religious texts, Krishna, the reincarnation of Vishnu, declares, "If any worshipper do reverence with faith to any God whatever, I make his faith firm, and in that faith he reverences his God and gains his desires, for it is I who bestow them" (Radhakrishnan, 1977, pp. vii, 21–22). This allows the Hindu to take his worries or wishes to any deity and even accept gods of other religions with no sense of contradiction or betrayal to his essential faith, because all gods or sacred things are but manifestations of one. Thus, many Hindus make regular pilgrimages to the Christian shrine of Mary at Velangani in India because it is said to be a place of miracles. They make vows, keep vigils, and make offerings out of respect for her perceived power of intercession on behalf of the needy.

Belief in rebirth and the ultimate goal of *moksha*, or freedom from this cycle, is central in Hinduism and the related faiths of Buddhism and Jainism. The circumstances and the form that a person's life takes are seen as the result of the actions in a previous life. Whereas Western thinking sees time as linear and life begins with birth and ends with death, Hindu philosophy views time as cyclic. Life is thus conceptualized as intertwined and endless, with the actions of one life having the power to influence the form and nature of future lives. In addition, each being exists to support another and each one doing his or her duty ensures harmony. The individual is not whole except as part of a family, and the family is part of a larger caste, which in turn contributes to the functioning of society.

Sages and philosophers have written treatises and laws that provide the individual with a guide to right living. Great emphasis is placed on the duty and obligations of individuals (*dharma*). Relationship, age, and context dictate the priority of one duty or duty toward one person over the other. Unlike the Western value of equality for all, Eastern thought acknowledges that differences are inherent in each person and, thus, different expectations are attached to each individual.

The philosophy specifies the three aims of man—religious merit, prosperity, and pleasure—in which the demands of the first supersede that of the second, the first two override that of the third, but all three are legitimate and desirable for the ordinary man. The three aims are subordinate to the primary aim of life, which is escape from the cycle of rebirth (*moksha*). Thus, all activities undertaken by the individual or the group are fundamentally religious activities and no part of life is divorced from *dharma* (Basham, 1959).

Rituals and Practices   Because the performance of a person's duty carries such importance, in many communities it is the markers of the attainment of maturity that are celebrated rather than actual age. Thus, ceremonies mark the time when the child gets head control, when the first solid food is introduced, when the child is taught his or her first alphabet, and when a girl begins her menstrual cycle. The rites remind children as they grow that they are part of a larger society and have a part to play in it. Many second-generation Hindus in America reject the formal rituals of Hinduism, although they affirm the importance of the values that they associate with it (Agarwal, 1991; Gawlick, 1997).

Food   Many Hindus do not eat meat because they see this as a violation of the principle of *ahimsa,* or nonviolence. Very traditional Hindus may also avoid garlic, onions, and other root vegetables that can only be obtained by killing the plant. When health concerns lead doctors to prescribe such foods, traditional families may not comply, often feeling that it is better to undergo suffering in this life rather than to commit a sin that will result in a worse fate in the next life. These traditional individuals may then choose to look for alternate remedies offered by *Ayurvedic* and other traditional forms of medicine, as one alternative. Consulting with community elders and those with in-depth knowledge of the religion in which the family identifies is usually helpful in finding alternate and mutually acceptable health care remedies.

Other Hindus have a tradition of eating meat, although most will avoid beef because the cow is considered by some to be holy and is respected as an animal that serves man in numerous ways. Hindus often undertake fasts on certain days or parts of the year, or during certain festivals. Such fasts may entail total abstinence from food or just the avoidance of certain foods. Fasts, which are usually done by the mother, are usually undertaken for a purpose, such as to improve the well-being of the family in general, or the spouse in particular.

Prayer   Prayer is largely a private affair. Individuals go to the temple or conduct prayer, or *pooja,* in their homes. Unlike many other religions in which the temple is a place for formalized group worship, in Hindu temples, except during specific festivals or pilgrimages, *pooja* is an individual affair. Hindi people's concern that their children will have little access to the beliefs and traditions of their land has caused temples in America to become places of group worship where people come together regularly and use the opportunity to teach language, dance, and music. Families undertake to prepare food, organize youth meetings, and reach out to the older adults. People make pilgrimages to well-known temples in the United States to propitiate the Gods and to mark important events such as marriage, birth, or a first job, car, or house.

Pakistan

Pakistan is officially a Muslim nation, and the majority of Pakistanis are Sunni Muslims, although a small percentage of Shiite Muslims, Ahmadis, Hindus, Sikhs, Christians, and Buddhists are also represented there (Ghayur, 1980). Sunnis form the majority of Pakistanis in America and follow the *sunna* or "way of life" of the Prophet Muhammad and the first four caliphs who followed him.

In America, Pakistanis have a strong sense of community, typically settling close together and providing help and support to the new immigrants. In worship, they tend to maintain ethnic or religious differences, and the Sunnis, Shia, and Ahmadis have different mosques. The mosques provide a common space for people to meet and typically run religious schools for the children. Most Pakistani Muslims are devout followers of their faith and create the infrastructure required to support their beliefs. The mosques ensure that the children have a source of religious instruction including the teaching of Arabic, which is the language of the *Qur'an* (also spelled Quran or Koran), the holy book of the Muslims. In the major cities in America, Muslims prepare *halal* meat, in which the animal is killed and prepared in ways that are prescribed by the religion. Muslims maintain their private practices such as prayer five times per day, and with the growing awareness in America of the practices of this religion, many schools, universities, and businesses provide facilities for individual prayer during the day.

Although there is great variety in how Muslims may practice Islam, all practicing Muslims accept and follow five basic practices (Esposito, 2002). These include 1) the acknowledgement of one God, *Allah;* 2) worship of Allah five times per day; 3) *zakat,* or the responsibility of a Muslim to give a part of his wealth to the poor; 4) fasting during the month of Ramzan (the ninth month of the Islamic calendar during which the first revelation of the Qur'an was made to Muhammad, the prophet); and 5) the pilgrimage to Mecca in Saudi Arabia. The observance of these simple practices is meant to remind the individual of his or her duties to God and his or her fellow Muslims.

Religion is an intimate part of the lives of most Muslims. The laws of Islam guide individuals in how to live their lives, listing their duty toward their God, the Islamic community, and their families. Rules that govern the appropriate behavior of women and toward women, when interpreted strictly, can restrict women's interactions with people outside their immediate family. This can create a difficult situation when a child has a disability and the mother is required to interact with a variety of people, many of whom might be male. Men are given primary responsibility for the well-being of their family, and thus, most decisions in very traditional families have to be made by them, although the actual caregiving will be done by the women.

LANGUAGE/LINGUISTIC ORIGINS

Each nation in the South Asian region is home to several languages, many of which are common across the different countries. For example, Urdu, the Pakistani national language, and Punjabi, one of the most commonly spoken languages there, are both spoken in India. Tamil is spoken in Sri Lanka and India, and Bengali is spoken in India as well as Bangladesh. India officially recognizes 15 languages, whereas there are 5 major languages in Pakistan. Most languages have distinct scripts and the majority of languages in this region come from two language roots—the Indo-Aryan and the Dravidian. Urdu, Hindi, Bengali, Punjabi, and Telegu are some of the most commonly spoken languages in America. Numerous dialects exist, and there can be great regional differences in the language forms used. Still, language is one way in which people from this region identify with each other. Thus, there are several associations created to represent and maintain various South Asian languages in America, such as the Bengali Association, the Telegu Association, and the Malyalali Association, which keep the language alive through language classes, libraries, music, movies, and other activities.

Most foreign-born South Asians who come from wealthier economic backgrounds have had the opportunity to study in schools in their native country in which English is the medium of instruction. As a result, they are fluent in spoken and written English and have little trouble gaining access to or using information in English. In fact, English is often the language of choice when South Asians who have different mother tongues meet. Many South Asians, particularly older women who come from traditional homes or individuals who could not afford to attend English medium school, however, may not be able to read, write, speak, or understand English with much fluency.

CONTEMPORARY LIFE

Prior to 1900, few South Asians lived in America. Most immigrants during this period were scholars, traders, professionals, or religious men, and came mostly from the north of the subcontinent. Between 1900 and 1920, close to 7,000 emigrants, mostly young rural men from the Malwa and Doab regions of the Punjab, came to the west coast through Canada (Jensen, 1980). Men from these regions had a reputation of loyalty and bravery, and many served in the British army in various British territories. These men were educated and learned about the world as they traveled with the army. When the Canadian timber mills were looking for cheap labor, these men encouraged their families in the villages to send the younger sons, who tended to be illiterate, in search of occupations and sources of income. Thus, scores of young South Asian men left to work in the Canadian mills. From there, these immigrants pushed far south into America, past the persecution and harassment they faced in Washington State, to California, where they quickly took to farming, the work they knew so well (Hess, 1976). They pooled their money, lived and ate together in order to save, and whenever possible, put together their savings and bought land as collectives. Many Punjabis married Mexican women and became well established in the fertile valleys of California.

Most immigrants who came as political refugees were from the northern parts of the Indian subcontinent, including present-day India, Pakistan, and Bangladesh. They typically came to the United States to attend the University of Washington, in Seattle, and University of California, Berkeley. These young men forged strong relationships with the Punjabi farmers, to whom they turned for economic support and summer jobs. In return, the farmers looked to the students to fight for them against the social and legal discrimination they faced. The students organized political groups and published newspapers broadcasting their concerns and demands for independence from the British. Sikhs, Hindus, and Muslims from different parts of the country were united in this fight and a strong sense of community was apparent during this period (Jensen, 1980).

The Immigration and Nationality Act in 1965, which eliminated discrimination based on national origin, led to the second major influx of immigrants from this region. The U.S. Census in 1970 recorded 51,000 foreign-born and close to 25,000 native-born Americans of South Asian descent. The preference given to trained professionals resulted in an influx of educated men and their families. Coming mostly from the major cities of India and Pakistan, the men and many of the women were educated in English and used to urban life. This group was better prepared for life in

America than the early immigrants, for whom the urban life, strange language, social antagonism, and vast cultural differences presented tremendous challenges (Agarwal, 1991; Jenson, 1980).

Since 1965, many regions, including Sri Lanka, Bangladesh, Tibet, and the Punjab, have had periods of political upheaval, and many families who emigrated during that time came seeking asylum and escape from the uncertainty of life in their own lands. Adaptation to life in America; knowledge of English and academic or technical skills; association with others from the same country, community, or religious groups; and access to support networks at home are all areas in which this group may show great differences (Agarwal, 1991).

The primary impetus for recent emigration from South Asia has been for economic advancement. The majority of immigrants entered the United States with strong academic credentials and work skills that supported an easy entry into the economic mainstream. At the same time, the existence of a large, well-established South Asian community has enabled them to maintain their cultural identity (Bacon, 1996; Saran & Eames, 1980). Especially in the major cities of America, a South Asian person can easily obtain food, clothes, movies, and magazines from his or her country or community. Places of worship; social and voluntary organizations; and schools that teach dance, art, and languages of their culture are popular, especially among first-generation South Asians, who see them as ways of transmitting cultural values to their children (Fenton, 1988; Gawlick, 1997).

VALUES

As members of a culture, individuals are exposed to and adopt, to varying degrees, certain values and ideas that are shared by the group. These ideas, or cultural models, are typically not explicitly taught or formulated but instead, are implicit in the practices and traditions of that culture. A child grows up exposed to these ideas from multiple sources, including his or her family, peer group, and other adults. He or she is also exposed in multiple ways, including reinforcement for actions, the expected tasks of childhood, daily routines, and stories (Harkness, 1980; Harkness & Super, 1995; Rogoff & Morelli, 1989; Shore, 1996). Thus, the degree to which individuals adopt these models will vary depending on their personality, life experiences, and the variety of alternate models to which they may have access. The pertinence of the values discussed in this section to each individual and family must therefore be determined on an individual basis.

Family Structure and Functioning

For both Indians and Pakistanis, the family is the center of their social life. Families tend to be hierarchically organized and male-dominated in that the oldest male in the family has authority over all other members (Ghayur, 1980; Jensen, 1980). The women are responsible for maintaining the home and rearing the children, responsibilities that often remain primarily theirs, even when they are educated, hold jobs, and contribute economically to the household. The presence of a child with a disability does not automatically release a woman from her responsibilities in her other roles. Religion and tradition dictate the roles and responsibilities of the various family members and these vary from community to community. Fulfilling one's duty toward the family, rather than seeking personal fulfillment, is the primary goal of all action (Zaehner, 1959).

Traditionally, the man is responsible for his parents, who may often move from their home in order to be with their son. The grandparents may then become the primary caregivers for the children, allowing the husband and wife to go out and earn. Other siblings of the father may also move in, especially when they are unmarried or have recently arrived in the country (Ghayur, 1980). Often, the mother will add caring for her in-laws to her existing responsibilities as wife and mother.

Extended family members play an important role in child rearing. Although economic necessity may foster nuclear families living separately, when possible, family members try to live near each other, visit often, and take care of each other. Even when extended family members do not live nearby, they may still play an important role in major decisions (Bacon, 1996; Fenton, 1988).

Kinship in South Asian countries carries with it strong obligations and responsibilities. These obligations and responsibilities vary greatly in what they are, as well as to whom they are extended. In some communities, responsibility will extend beyond relatives to members of the same religion or temple, caste group, or village (Bacon, 1996; Gibb, 1959; Mandelbaum, 1970). Age, wealth, education, and gender determine an individual's specific duties and obligations to other members of his or her family and community. These obligations lead families to place different priorities than those of the teacher on intervention and other activities.

Specific duties and hierarchies of responsibility and authority are tied into relationships between people. In fact, many South Asian languages have specific words that distinguish between relationships, such as father's younger brother from older brother and maternal from paternal uncles, aunts, and cousins. Children are socialized young and are typically present at all social and religious occasions so that they may have many opportunities to learn these complex relationships and the correct way to behave toward each individual (Gawlick, 1997).

Education and Schooling

Education is seen as the key to success in America and is highly valued among South Asians (Gawlick, 1997). Most South Asians have high educational aspirations for their children and a deep respect for professional qualifications. The child's teacher and the school are highly respected. South Asian parents are typically conscientious about following instructions that are sent home and will oversee their children's homework, even when they are not educated themselves.

The primary responsibility of young children is to apply themselves diligently so that they may do well in school, get a professional education, and thus attain economic stability. Discipline, hard work, and a strong focus on academic skills are all encouraged. Parents go to great lengths to ensure that their children attend good schools, often living with minimal facilities so that they can afford a school that has a reputation for discipline and academic excellence.

Parent–Professional Partnerships

South Asians are deeply respectful of professionals, particularly teachers and doctors. Parents will often name their child after his or her doctor and will ask the teacher and doctor to be present at significant family events. Traditionally in both India and Pak-

Katy had been Naveen's therapist at a learning center for about 6 months. Naveen was a sweet-natured, 1½-year-old child. Katy communicated mostly with Shireen, Naveen's mother, because Naveen's father, Abdul, was usually busy at the software company where he worked. Both parents were college graduates from India, and both spoke excellent English. They had moved to America soon after Naveen was diagnosed with cerebral palsy at age 1, believing that he would receive the best services in the United States. Shireen was quick to learn and was very consistent in carrying out the therapy that was taught to her. She was unwilling to attend early intervention sessions at the center, however, and also resisted the idea of a home teacher. Unable to understand this reluctance from a mother who was so engaged in her child's well-being, Katy began chatting with Shireen about child-rearing practices in India with very young children. As Shireen described the ways in which children were cared for, she prefaced many of her descriptions with remarks such as, "No doubt you will find this funny," or "You may be shocked at how we pamper our children." Katy soon realized that Shireen worried that if she attended the early intervention class, she would be required to make her child do things such as sleep alone, which she felt he was too young to do. By not attending class, Shireen avoided having to disagree with her child's teacher. After convincing Shireen to attend, Katy invited a pediatrician to speak to the parent group about child-rearing practices around the world and their effect on development and learning. The parents and teachers were fascinated and turned repeatedly to Shireen to ask about what she did. In this nonconfrontational situation, Shireen was comfortable discussing what she did with Naveen and why. By the end of the meeting, it was easy for Shireen to promise to be part of the infant group the next morning.

istan, teachers had a major responsibility in child rearing, providing religious education and guiding the development of values as well as the mind. Although, with the advent of the formal school system, this relationship has become more impersonal, parents will still appeal to a teacher for help, guidance, or blessings when the teacher is seen as learned or is one who has been involved with the child for many years. Disagreeing with such a person is therefore very difficult, and asserting one's own wishes or desires is considered highly inappropriate. The individualized family service plan (IFSP) and the individualized education program (IEP) processes, which expect the parents to articulate their goals for their children, can therefore be a very difficult and unnerving process for these parents.

Parents are usually grateful for the concern, interest, and guidance offered by the early interventionist and in such a situation may find it hard to be assertive about their needs or desires. South Asians are rarely direct, especially in formal situations, and may clothe their requests in statements that are disparaging or indifferent. For example, a mother may say, "This silly child doesn't even know the difference between his uncle and his father's uncle!" By this statement the mother is implying that she is worried that her child has not yet learned to use these terms appropriately. She is signaling that it is something on which she would like the teacher to focus.

Although home-based services are professional visits, to the South Asian, anyone entering his or her home is a guest. Both Islam and Hinduism instruct their followers to treat guests as those sent by God. Guests are therefore honored, and their comfort while in the home is important. Parents may offer the teacher food or drink and will often engage in social conversation during home visits. The teacher is expected to take the lead in the interaction and will be deferred to out of respect for his or her status as a teacher as well as a guest. South Asians raised in America are better able to negotiate professional interactions, having had experiences throughout their lives interacting with the larger society.

BELIEFS

Understanding the cultural models of parenting that a parent is exposed to is important for family services professionals because these values inform parents' beliefs and attitudes toward child rearing; similarly, it is helpful to understand parents' perceptions of the boundaries of the parenting role. This idea is particularly relevant when considering parent beliefs about child rearing when the child has a disability because the concept of disability itself is one that is socially constructed. Understanding cultural beliefs and immigration history provides the interventionist with a context within which to understand family responses to having a child with a disability, anticipate family needs, and provide appropriate services. The cultural themes described in this chapter are meant to alert the interventionist to alternate perspectives that a family may hold, rather than providing a prescriptive list with which to understand families. In this section, three areas are discussed that are most relevant to interventionists who work closely with families: parenting practices and child rearing, health practices, and causation and disability.

Parenting Practices and Child Rearing

According to most South Asian traditions, having and raising children is one of the primary duties of a man and his wife. This is the main goal of marriage and, therefore, the relationship between husband and wife is not the primary one. The coming of the first child is often anticipated within the first year of marriage, and, as previously mentioned, the mother is expected to devote herself to caring for the child in addition to her duties toward her husband and household. Having children gives a mother status, and children are highly valued and loved. Children's behavior and accomplishments are taken to be a reflection of the mother's skills. Older siblings and relatives, however, may play a primary role in child rearing and often it may be an older sister, a grandmother, or the mother's younger sister who provides primary care for the younger child. Because child rearing is seen as the responsibility of the mother, interaction with medical and other support services will often fall to her. Among more traditional households, the mother may be reluctant to face strangers, or if she does not speak the language of the service providers, this may result in the father attending all official meetings while the mother provides the child care.

Sons are particularly valued among Hindus because they play an essential part in the death rites of the parents. Those who have no sons are pitied. Sons are valued in most communities because they are expected to take responsibility for caring for their parents in their old age. Thus, when a child is born with a disability, parents are often urged to have more children so that there are more opportunities to have boys to take on the responsibilities and duties toward the parents. In addition, having more children ensures that the child with the disability will always have a family member to care for him or her. Many present-generation South Asian Americans reject these ideas of filial duty, however, preferring to focus their energies on supporting their child. The resulting clash of opinions may make family and community support systems less available.

Relationships and interdependence are emphasized and evident in many child-rearing practices. Infants and young children are nurtured constantly and kept in close physical proximity with the mother or other adults. The mother often carries out a daily ritual with her infant of massage with oil and herbal preparations. Children are indulged greatly and are often carried and fed by a parent or a sibling many years past the age when they can do these things by themselves. They typically sleep with their parents and may do so through much of their childhood years. Adults are very tolerant of children during infancy and toddlerhood, placing no restrictions on behavior, and, contrary to the Western insistence on independence, do not insist on toilet training, independent eating, or stay-

ing alone without a parent or family member nearby. Few parents are comfortable with child care or babysitters, and parents socializing without the child is rare.

In contrast to a child's early years, by age 6 or so, a child is expected to understand and obey strict social rules, and apply him- or herself diligently to schooling (Kakar, 1978). Obedience and respect are valued child characteristics, and great emphasis is given to understanding relationships and speaking with due respect to elders. Parents exercise great control over their children, overseeing friendships and activities outside of the school, even into the teenage and young adult years. Decisions are made for children in all areas ranging from what clothes they wear to what profession they should undertake. Although the individual's desire is considered when elders make decisions for the children, it does not take precedence over what is best for the larger family unit.

Health Practices

Several well-developed medical systems date back to ancient times and are still in use in India and Pakistan today. The ancient settlers in the region had well-developed and detailed theories and practices of healing the body. Twenty-six hundred years ago, Sushruta, considered the father of modern-day surgery, and other health scientists of his time conducted surgeries like cesarean sections, nose reconstruction, cataract removal, the repairing of fractures, and the removal of kidney stones; and the use of anaesthesia was well known in the region. The system of *Ayurveda* dates back to the Vedic Age after the arrival of the Aryans, whereas *Unani Tibb* came to the region through the Arabs and is influenced by the work of Hippocrates (*Unani* means Greek). *Ayurveda* emphasizes the importance of physical and mental or spiritual balance and sees illness as a manifestation of imbalance. An *Ayurvedic* practioner takes a detailed history of a person's life, daily practices, and personality, from which he or

Walking into the house, Julie, a therapist, said "What a wonderful smell!" Beroz was cooking dinner and told her what dishes she was making. Julie, who loved learning about different dishes, asked her about each dish and what went into it. Beroz pressed her to try them, but Julie, conscious of the time, refused, and they spent the hour with the child. When she was ready to leave, Julie found Beroz had packed up a box of food for her, a practice she maintained in every visit after that. Julie was unwilling to hurt Beroz, who poured her heart into creating a variety of dishes, yet uncomfortable with receiving these constant gifts. When she explained her discomfort, Beroz said simply, "You are my child's teacher. It is the least I can do." Respecting this sentiment, Julie suggested that instead of cooking for her, Beroz could teach her how to make the dishes so that she could always make them herself. Beroz happily wrote out detailed recipes that Julie faithfully tried, occasionally bringing her latest experiment to Beroz to try.

she develops a prescription that could include suggestions on changing sleeping or eating patterns, specific foods and herbs, and oils and extracts of various plants to restore the balance within the system.

Unani Tibb considers the balance of the *akhlaat*, or four humors (i.e., fire, air, earth, and water), and the state of the body, which encompasses the concepts of health, disease, and "neutral" (in which the symptoms have not yet been manifested) in understanding and describing illness (Irfan, 2002). Herbal and mineral preparations are selected to restore the balance of the four humors and move the body to health. In addition, massages; manipulation; and the application of cold, heat, and suction cups to specific body points may also be done (Australian Unani Medicine Society, 2000). Thus, in both *Ayurveda* and *Unani Tibb*, the cure is targeted at the system rather than the symptom, the opposite of what is common in *allopathic* or Western medicine. Many South Asians prefer these traditional forms of treatment, especially for young children, and often undertake several forms of treatment simultaneously. Many families do not tell their doctor about alternative treatments because they fear that they will be ridiculed or that the doctor will feel slighted at their lack of confidence in his or her treatment. Families may also give their child traditional herbs and supplements without consciously registering it as a treatment and, thus, may not report it to the doctor. Maintaining a nonjudgmental attitude and gathering information in great detail about the foods and practices that families may be using to support their child's health and development is, therefore, an important component of understanding the child's health status.

Causation and Disability

Disability is often attributed to the anger of the gods or some sin of the parent or child in a past life. Among the educated, however, such beliefs have given way to more mainstream attitudes regarding the causes of disability, including ill health, consanguinity, or other medical reasons. Even so, in a family with a child with a disability, if members of the extended family hold on to old beliefs, parents may be reluctant to tell them about the nature or extent of the child's problem. Many parents do not return to their native land or visit with relatives in America so that they do not have to tell them about the disability. Thus, access to typical sources of practical and emotional support may be unavailable to many families.

Because, according to tradition, illness and disability are often attributed to the gods' anger, the evil eye, past sins, or numerous other reasons, people of South Asian descent often view prayer, vows, and pilgrimages as essential to the child's ultimate well-being. Both Hindus and Muslims wear amulets; bracelets; or black, red, or yellow threads on arms or around the neck to ward away evil, protect the child, or suck out the illness.

Death and Dying

Although the beliefs and rituals that surround death differ depending on the religion and community to which the family belongs, the general cultural emphasis on being part of a greater community or society is evident in all South Asian customs of mourning. When a member of a family dies, the entire community comes forward to express their sorrow. Neighbors, friends, and extended family members take over all arrangements that have to be made, allowing the immediate family to mourn. The stove is not lit in the house, and the community members bring food for as many days as the family requires.

The open expression of sorrow is permissible among men and women, adults and children in most traditional South Asian communities. Mourning for a family member is usually a public and openly emotional affair. Both men and women may cry, and some may beat their chests and talk aloud about their grief and memories. Family and friends who come to pay respects and show solidarity also demonstrate their sorrow in similar public displays of grief. Visiting the home during this period of mourning is a sign of your respect and affection for the individual and is greatly appreciated by the family.

Muslims and Christians bury their children; Hindus either bury or cremate a child. If cremation is chosen, the ashes are usually released into a flowing body of water. Cremation is usually done before sunset on the day of death. Rituals that follow death vary from community to community and often last a certain number of days when close family members observe deep mourning. This deep mourning is followed by a cleansing ritual or a blessing, depending on the community. At this time, the family invites people from the community for a meal and often gives charity in memory of the person who died. Many families do not participate in any celebrations or festivals for a year after the death of a family member. Every year, the day is usually commemorated by prayer or by giving charity.

ISSUES OF LANGUAGE

Just as in the mainstream culture, conversations serve as a vehicle for sharing information, but at all times, conversations are social events and embody the individual's respect for people, sense of duty, and correctness. South Asians often ask many questions about a person's work, life, and family that seem invasive to most Americans. However, these questions help them place the person with whom they are speaking in the complex social hierarchy and this gives them the context within which they will relate to the individual and understand his or her interactions. The meandering,

context-heavy, and complicated rituals of conversation among South Asians contrast with the forthright and direct conversational style of the mainstream culture. For example, when a South Asian person is offered something, politeness requires that person to refuse it. The person who offers must press again so that the individual may accept the favor gracefully. As a result, many South Asians remain standing in crowded waiting rooms, stay hungry, or wait patiently and endlessly for a service because their instinctive answer is taken literally.

Another source of confusion is with the use of the affirmative "yes." When asked if they will do something or if they understood something, South Asians may say "yes," which is typically taken to mean agreement. "Yes," however, can mean several things and is often used to indicate that the person is listening, understands your perspective, or appreciates your intention.

Although most South Asians speak English well, interpreters may be necessary to reach all of those who care for the child. In many families, the older parents, the child care provider, or the mother who cares for the child may not speak English or may lack fluency. In such cases, the quality of interaction will be enhanced if interpreters of the same gender are used.

SUMMARY

The countries that form the Indian subcontinent and those that abut it have over the years grown into distinctly different political entities; however, strong family ties and obligations, education, social harmony, and the maintenance of cultural practices are values commonly held by people in these diverse lands (Agarwal, 1991; Saran, 1985; Saran & Eames, 1980). The degree to which an individual or a particular family may hold these values is, of course, determined by their own experiences and upbringing. Furthermore, the degree to which these values will influence their child-rearing and parenting decisions will also vary depending on the individuals and the circumstances.

RECOMMENDATIONS FOR INTERVENTIONISTS

As with many communities in America today, South Asians represent a great diversity in background, faith, and tradition. Many South Asians raised in America have experience in interacting with the mainstream culture. Therefore, these guidelines will be most useful to the interventionist who works with those who grew up in their own land or within more traditional family systems and are less comfortable with mainstream methods of communication and functioning.

PARENT-PROFESSIONAL PARTNERSHIPS

Tolerance and accommodation are valued characteristics among South Asians, to whom being assertive and making demands of teachers, therapists, or doctors is particularly difficult because these individuals are viewed with respect. Family service professionals may have to take the initiative in finding out practices important to Asian families they serve because many families will not feel comfortable making demands or requests, and they will tolerate a high degree of inconvenience rather than do so. It is important to take time to understand the rituals and practices associated with the religions of South Asia. Setting aside a time and place for prayer; being aware that the mother may be fasting; and ensuring that food, medicines, and practices prescribed for or given to the child do not offend the family are some ways in which family service providers can easily accommodate their needs.

With some families and communities, drawing on the elders or respected members of the community may be a useful way of addressing problems that may arise during service provision. Many families resent the inclusion of "outsiders," although they may be from the same community or religion. Ask the family whom they would turn to if confused or worried about making decisions regarding their child. Especially because disability carries such a stigma with it in many communities, involvement of other community members could be a source of tension and great discomfort rather than a source of support.

Talking about emotional needs in a group situation is uncomfortable for many South Asian parents, and thus they may not enjoy being part of parent groups. They are typically uncomfortable with the sharing that is part of such groups, although they appreciate access to information.

Children are cherished in South Asian families, and parents will undertake activities and actions that would typically be considered taboo or strange by their communities. The sensitivity of the interventionists to their own biases, beliefs, and prejudices as well as to the possible desires, goals, and beliefs of the families will determine the quality of the interaction they have with families (Hanson, Lynch, & Wayman, 1990).

WHAT WOULD YOU DO?

Rajesh and Prema had lived and worked in America for several years, having come when they got married 5 years ago. When their child, Ashok, was born with several medical complications, they were glad to be in America, where they had access to a variety of medical services. When the doctor, Derek, recommended a complicated surgical procedure that had to be carried out as soon as possible, Rajesh and Prema asked for time to think about it. They researched the condition and the recommended procedure on the Internet and consulted with other physicians. Having decided that this was the only chance for their son, they agreed. When they realized that his head would have to be shaved for the operation, however, they were very upset and refused to give permission. They explained that they had vowed to take their son to a temple in India when he was 1 year old to offer his hair in thanks to God. Until that was done, his hair was not to be cut. At first, Derek was taken aback at what he saw as unreasoning superstition from an educated couple.

If you were Derek, how would you handle this situation in a culturally sensitive way?

How might your emotions change as you look at the situation in different ways?

How might this families' traditional ways be accommodated?

REFERENCES

Agarwal, P. (1991). *Passage from India: Post 1965 Indian Immigrants and their children.* Palos Verdes, CA: Yuvati Publications.

Australian Unani Medicine Society. (2000). http://www.traditionalmedicine.net.au/unani.htm

Bacon, J.L. (1996). *Life lines: Community, family and assimilation among Asian Indian immigrants.* New York: Oxford University Press.

Basham, A.L. (1959). Hinduism. In R.C. Zaehner (Ed.), *The concise encyclopedia of living faiths* (pp. 225–260). London: Hutchinson & Co.

Esposito, J. (2002). *What everyone needs to know about Islam.* New York: Oxford University Press.

Fenton, J. (1988). *Transplanting religious traditions: Asian Indians in America.* New York: Praeger.

Gawlick, M. (1997). Silicon Valley connections: Asian immigrants and sojourners. Adaptation strategies of second generation Asian Indians. *Journal of history and computing web ring.* Retrieved June 9, 2002, from http://mcel.pacificu.edu/aspac/papers/scholars/Gawlick/gawlick.html

Ghayur, A. (1980). Pakistanis. In S. Thernstrom (Ed.), *Harvard encyclopedia of American ethnic groups* (pp. 768–770). Cambridge, MA: Harvard University Press.

Gibb, H. (1959). Islam. In R.C. Zaehner (Ed.), *The concise encyclopedia of living faiths* (pp. 178–208). London: Hutchinson & Co.

Hanson, M., Lynch, E., & Wayman, K. (1990). Honoring the cultural diversity of families when gathering data. *Topics in Early Childhood Special Education, 10,* 112–131.

Harkness, S. (1980). The cultural context of child development. In C.M. Super & S. Harkness, (Eds.), *Anthropological perspectives on child development* (Vol. 8, pp. 7–13). San Francisco: Freeman.

Harkness, S., & Super, C. (1995). Culture and parenting. In M.H. Bornstein (Ed.), *Biology and ecology of parenting* (Vol. 2, pp. 211–234). Mahwah, NJ: Lawrence Erlbaum Associates.

Hess, G. (1976). The forgotten Asian Americans: The East Indian community in the United States. In N. Hundley (Ed.), *The Asian American* (pp. 157–178). Santa Barbara, CA: Clio Books.

Irfan, H. (2002). *Hikmat. (Unani medicine).* Retrieved from http://www.islamonline.net/English/Science/2002/06/article15 .shtml

Jensen, J. (1980) East Indians. In S. Thernstrom (Ed.), *Harvard encyclopedia of American ethnic groups* (pp. 296–301). Cambridge, MA: Harvard University Press.

Kakar, S. (1978). *The inner world.* Delhi, India: Oxford University Press.

Mandelbaum, D.G. (1970). *Society in India: Change and continuity* (Vol. 2). Berkeley: University of California Press.

Radhakrishnan, S. (Trans.) (1977). *The Bhagavadagita.* Bombay, India: Blackie and Sons Limited.

Rogoff, B., & Morelli, G. (1989). Perspectives on children's development from cultural psychology. *American Psychologist, 44,* 343–348.

Saran, P. (1985). *The Asian Indian experience in the United States.* Cambridge, MA: Schekman Publishing Company.

Saran, P., & Eames, E. (Eds.). (1980). *The new ethnics: Asian Indians in the United States.* New York: Praeger.

Shinagawa, L., & Jang, M. (1998). *Atlas of American diversity.* Walnut Creek, CA: Alta Mira Press.

Shore, B. (1996). *Culture in mind: Cognition, culture, and the problem of meaning.* New York: Oxford University Press.

Thernstrom, S. (Ed.). (1980). *Harvard Encyclopedia of American ethnic groups.* Cambridge, MA: Harvard University Press.

U.S. Bureau of the Census. (2000). *Profile of general demographic characteristics: 2000.* Washington, DC: U.S. Government Printing Office.

Zaehner, R.C. (Ed.). (1959). *The concise encyclopedia of living faiths.* London: Hutchinson & Co.

CONTRASTING BELIEFS, VALUES, AND PRACTICES

South Asian

Importance of group/family goals

Value age and learning

Solve problems by contemplation and internal adjustment

Support networks drawn from own family or community

Primacy of parent–child relationship

Value of interdependence

Belief that not all people are equal

Mainstream culture

Importance of individual goals

Value youth and performance

Solve problems by actively seeking to cause external change

At ease with accessing professional and non-family sources of support

Primacy of husband–wife relationship

Value of independence

Belief that all people are equal

CULTURAL COURTESIES AND CUSTOMS

Greetings

- Physical contact is not customary, especially when greeting a stranger or a person of the opposite gender.

- Shaking hands as a way of greeting is often uncomfortable to South Asians, to whom the traditional form of greeting is with the palms pressed together and held at about chest level.

- Some South Asians may be comfortable with shaking hands since they may have grown up in America or been exposed to Western customs in other ways.

- Do not assume that all family members will have the same degree of comfort with one method of greeting because they may come from very different experiential backgrounds.

- Traditionally, in the South Asian culture, it was seen as bad luck to talk of leaving without speaking of meeting again. Even today, when leaving a house, it is customary to talk of returning rather than focus on departing. In many of the South Asian languages, the phrase used when leaving after a visit typically translates into "I am coming again" rather than "I'm leaving." When speaking in English, however, it is quite usual to use the typical phrase "good-bye."

Nonverbal communication

- Sustained eye contact between people of the opposite gender, of different ages and of different social standing is seen as impolite, aggressive, or flirtatious.

- Nodding the head indicates that the person is listening to you, rather than agreeing with or answering you.

- Standing up when a person of greater age or status (such as a teacher or doctor) enters the room is a sign of respect. The person may remain standing until asked to sit down.

- Allowing the leg or foot to touch symbols of learning (such as books or bags), food (or utensils), or people is very disrespectful.

Conversation

- Direct questions and statements are viewed as aggressive. Important issues are almost always discussed in a circuitous manner.

- When asked a direct question, the person may feel obligated to respond with what he or she believes you want to hear so as to diffuse the situation.

Private Homes

- South Asians are proud of their hospitality and will go to great lengths to ensure your comfort.

- Typically, footwear is left outside the door.

- Although your visit is for a professional purpose, that is, you are in their house to provide intervention services or for a meeting about the child, the family is likely to treat it as a social event, offering you food and drink and making small talk.

- Commenting enthusiastically on the beauty of items in the house or talking about something you desire will often be interpreted as a request for that object, which will then be presented to you as a gift. Refusal of such gifts is often viewed as insulting or condescending.

- Giving gifts to teachers is a traditional part of celebrations in some communities. Such gifts are tokens of the givers' appreciation and acknowledgment of the important role you play in their child's life.

SIGNIFICANT CULTURAL EVENTS/HOLIDAYS/PRACTICES

Certain festivals typically follow the lunar calendar, and there are no fixed dates for their celebration.

HINDU FESTIVALS/EVENTS

Diwali

The festival of lights; celebrates the triumph of good over evil, with the lighting of lamps and the preparation of sweets and food. It is usually in October or November.

Holi

The spring festival is celebrated with colors, music and dance. It occurs in March or April.

MUSLIM FESTIVALS/EVENTS

Ramzan (Ramadan)

The month during which the first revelation of the Qur'an came to Muhammad. It is commemorated by fasting from dawn to dusk.

Eid ul fitr (Ed-al-Feter)

A great day of feasting that marks the end of the month. It occurs around November.

Eid al Moled e Nabi (Eid-al-Moled-e-Nabi)

Celebrates the birth of the Prophet Mohammed.

PAKISTANI CELEBRATIONS

Independence Day	August 14
Pakistan Day	March 23
Birthday of the founder of the nation	December 25

INDIAN CELEBRATIONS

Independence Day	August 15
Republic Day	January 26

APPENDIX D

VOCABULARY

Hindi, Punjabi, and Urdu share many words in common. Some useful web sites are given below to find specific words in each language. See also Chapter 12 for some Arabic words.

Urdu is spoken differently by different communities, so if you are using an interpreter, please ensure that the Urdu spoken is understood by the family.

English	Hindi	Punjabi	Urdu
Greeting	namaste	sat sri akal	assalam-o-alaikum
Yes	haan	haan	haan
No	nahein	nahein	nahein
Thank you	dhanyavaad	sukr	shukran
Father	baap	baap	baap
Mother	ma	ma	ma
Family	kutumba	kutmb	kunba

Web site for Hindi: http://www.wordanywhere.com

Web site for Punjabi: http://www.punjabonline.com/servlet/library.language?
  Action=Main

Web site for Urdu: http://www.urduword.com

CHILDREN OF MANY SONGS

Eleanor W. Lynch and Marci J. Hanson

The culture writes us first, and then we write our stories.
—CHUCK MEE (2002)

Intercultural couples find themselves choosing not to
choose between their own cultures of origin; instead, they
move among cultures, between struggles and harmony,
accepting what they can and negotiating what they
cannot, articulating what they can and trusting the
inarticulable to somehow make itself known.
—JESSIE CARROLL GREARSON AND LAUREN B. SMITH (1995)

Cultures are like organisms. They grow, change, adapt, and evolve. An individual's cultural beliefs and practices are challenged daily by competing beliefs and practices, although often on an unconscious level.

A British zoologist, Richard Dawkins (1989), coined the term *meme* to describe a unit of memorable cultural information. Memes have physical bases but they serve as cultural building blocks that are passed from generation to generation in a Darwinian process (Pollan, 2001). Sometimes the old gives way to the new, and at times the old prevails. Most often, however, the old is modified and changed so that it is something different—neither the old nor the new. According to Pollan, "culture at any given moment is the 'meme pool' in which we all swim—or rather, that swims through us" (2001, p. 148).

Nowhere is this evolution more evident than among families whose members come from more than one cultural, ethnic, and/or racial background. Sometimes referred to as bicultural, biracial, interracial, mixed race, or multiracial, families in this group include the many in which the parents come from different ethnic, cultural, or racial backgrounds, as well as those parents of foster or adoptive children who come from different ethnic, cultural, or racial backgrounds than the children's natural parents. For some couples, the differences in these backgrounds are perceived as great; for others, they are perceived as small. Yet, whatever the magnitude of the differences, even more service delivery practices may have to be negotiated than when husband and wife, partner and partner, and/or parent and child share similar backgrounds. Differences in religious beliefs may require similar negotiations, but they are addressed here only secondarily. This short section provides a brief overview of bi- or multicultural families—those families with children of many songs.

DEMOGRAPHICS

The growing segment of the U.S. population that is multicultural and/or multiracial highlights the inappropriateness of the often-seen instruction on forms: "Ethnicity, please check one." Although a new census category—"multiracial"—was proposed for the 2000 census, it was rejected in 1997 (Gross, 1996). However, the 2000 Census did expand the range of options for reporting race to enable respondents to identify themselves in more than one category. Census data confirmed that the number of children in mixed-race families had more than doubled between 1970 and 1980, growing from 460,000 to 996,070 (U.S. Bureau of the Census, 2001). By 1990, almost 2 million—4% of all children in households—lived in mixed-race homes (U.S. Bureau of the Census, 2001). In 2000, the number climbed to 4.5 million (Nakazawa, 2003). The growth of university courses, popular writing, and professional literature devoted to issues of mixed heritage attest to the growth of this population. A Google search of related items resulted in more than 13,000 entries that ranged from books about multiracial families to activist organizations in support of multiracial and interracial families, to information about interracial adoptions. Periodicals as well as Internet sites have been established to give voice to a multicultural society. Although the Supreme Court overturned the last of the laws in 16 states that prevented marriage or cohabitation between people of different races (commonly called miscegenation) in the 1960s, discussion about multicultural, multiethnic, and multiracial families has only recently become a topic in public discourse (Gross, 1996). The importance of the topic is underscored by the American Academy of Child and Adoles-

---

The term *children of many songs*, learned from Sam Chan, has been selected to describe children who are members of bi- or multiracial families. The term, we believe, emphasizes the strengths that unique combinations and blends of people contribute to our society.

cent Psychiatry's posting on their web site of a "Facts for Families" link about rearing mixed-race children (http://www.aacap.org/publications/factsfam/71.htm).

The number of individuals engaged in interracial relationships in the United States has continued to grow. At the beginning of the 21st century, at least 3 million interracial couples had married (Root, 2002), and many young people report dating outside their own ethnic or racial group. A 1997 Gallup Poll (as cited by Root, 2002) found the highest ever approval rating for interracial marriage among both African Americans and Anglo-European Americans. For all ethnic and racial groups, out-marriage, or marriage outside of one's ethnic or racial group, appears to be increasing. According to Holmes (1996), 12% of Asian men and 25% of Asian women have non-Asian spouses, and approximately 8% of married African American men and 2% of married African American women are married to individuals from other racial groups. Because these data include only married couples, they clearly under-represent the number of "children of many songs" as well as their families who are part of U.S. communities and service systems.

ISSUES

Understanding any family is complex; however, as this text points out, understanding families different from one's own is even more complicated. When the family is bi- or multicultural or multiracial, the complexity may increase. It is especially important for service providers, then, to recognize such a child's or family's uniqueness when providing intervention. When working with families that represent more than one ethnic, cultural, or racial group, the service provider must take the family's lead. How is the family approaching the issues of cultural identity, complementary or competing values, and differences in behaviors and beliefs? To what extent do they feel accepted by parents, siblings, and other extended family members? Is the neighborhood and community supportive or hostile? As service providers work with an increasing number of multicultural families, a number of issues surface. The paragraphs that follow highlight some of these.

Race is scientifically irrelevant, but it continues to exert a powerful influence over the experiences, opportunities, and lives of children, families, and professionals in the United States. Although scientific evidence clearly shows that there is no genetic material that accurately predicts racial traits per se and that race is indeterminable in human blood groups, racial labels continue to be assigned based on phenotype and the "one-drop rule" of the 1800s (Zack, 1995, p. xvii). The one-drop rule held that a single drop of blood inherited from a nonwhite parent determined the racial status of the child. This rule was a sociopolitical construct designed to enslave American-born African Americans (Zack, 1995). Since 1990, the one-drop rule has been applied in reverse to individuals with some traceable American Indian ancestry (Zack, 1995). Because of the entitlements accorded to American Indians, limiting the number who can claim such ancestry reduced the number of individuals who can claim rights and benefits. As a result, the federal government used the notion of "blood quantum" to determine tribal membership (Wilson, 1992). Thus, many American Indians who are listed on tribal rolls do not qualify as certified Indians according to federal standards and, therefore, do not qualify for any government-sponsored tribal benefits (Clements, 1995). These rules, made to support the sociopolitical context and power bases of the time, demonstrate the ways in which race, a biologically irrelevant issue, is a factor in daily life. As a result, families that include members of more than one racial group are often forced to struggle with others' perceptions of their child's identity. It is important that service providers be aware of and empathic about the struggle, and that they support interventions and approaches that are congruent with the family's wishes related to the healthy development of the child's identity.

Another issue the service provider may want to consider is the way in which families help children develop cultural identities and affiliations. For many families in which parents come from different cultural backgrounds, both cultures will be equally acknowledged, valued, and treated as part of daily life. Some families may blend different practices, whereas others will adopt and rely on one set of cultural

practices to the exclusion of the other. In still other families, cultural values, practices, beliefs, and behaviors will be situational or contextual. For example, in a family in which one parent is Anglo-European and the other is Chinese American, the family may use Western medicine, follow Buddhist beliefs, and combine their Chinese and Anglo-European American heritages as they cook meals or celebrate important life events. For the service provider, the important issue is to understand the family's relationship to the cultures that they represent and the ways in which this relationship is interpreted in daily life.

Service providers may find that multiracial families and their children are not accepted by other families in the program. Helping multiracial families feel comfortable and encouraging other families to accept differences may become goals for the program and the providers. Including representations of multiracial families in photos, pictures, and materials in the program can help increase their comfort. Ensuring that families are welcomed and included in all activities in which they choose to participate and introducing them to staff members or other families who are part of multiracial families can provide additional support. Programs for all families, curricular activities for children, and an inclusive attitude held by administrators and staff members may encourage families who are less accepting to be more supportive of differences.

In some instances, providers may sense or clearly recognize that there is tension within a multiracial family related to identity, values, beliefs, and behaviors. If these issues are directly shared with the provider, he or she can assist families to find resources to help resolve those differences. Counselors, pastors, priests, imams, rabbis, trusted elders, or families who have encountered similar challenges may be able to assist a family to work through their concerns and differences. When the issues are not presented to the provider, she or he may need to determine to what extent she or he should discuss them with the family. If the tensions significantly affect the child, the provider may need to address them sensitively and perhaps with the aid of a cultural mediator or cultural broker. With each family the need and approach will be different, and the provider's judgment and clinical skills will be critical in determining the appropriate steps.

Finally, service providers need to be aware of the prejudice and discrimination that multiethnic and multiracial children and families often encounter. The stares, looks of disapproval, and intrusive questions from strangers are well documented by children and adults in interracial families (Nakazawa, 2003). In spite of an increased focus on the importance of pluralism in the United States, old beliefs, biases, and behaviors remain. In any intervention, it is important to consider the family's immediate concerns and priorities and the sociopolitical context in which they live. Interventions must be matched to each family's comfort level within the larger society. For example, establishing eye contact between the child and an adult may be a goal that service providers view as important; however, if the family has experiences that suggest that direct eye contact is considered a sign of disrespect that leads to trouble in the community, it is not a goal to be pursued. At a more global level, one role of the service provider is to work effectively with the family but also to be an agent of change within the community and to work toward greater tolerance and acceptance for families who are not viewed as part of the mainstream.

The previous chapters in this section focus on the multiple dimensions and diversity within each of the groups addressed. Yet, for many families, the diversity is multiplied by the different cultures, ethnicities, races, and languages within the family. As the family's composition and complexity increase, so does the job of the service provider. The need to be culturally competent is magnified and so are the rewards. In explaining the title of their book, *Swaying*, Grearson and Smith shared their image of intercultural relationships:

> Swaying suggests both the problem, the instability of these intercultural relationships, and its provisional solution, flexibility. It suggests a bending between different realities and different worlds, a movement that is graceful but suggests uncertainty, insecurity, even trouble. A tree sways in a storm. We sway with the music. We allow ourselves to be swayed. [It] suggests the kind of multiple movements that the renegotiation of boundaries requires—both swaying and being swayed, the ability to be flexible while remaining rooted in our own cultural identities. (1995, p. xv)

Although viewed from a different perspective, their image is remarkably similar to the one we see as a prerequisite for effective intervention.

REFERENCES

American Academy of Child and Adolescent Psychiatry. (1999, October). *Multiracial children*. Retrieved July 9, 2003, from http://www.aacap.org/publications/factsfam/71.htm

Clements, S. (1995). Five arrows. In N. Zack (Ed.), *American mixed race* (pp. 3–11). Boston: Rowman & Littlefield.

Dawkins, R. (1989). *The selfish gene*. Oxford: Oxford University Press.

Grearson, J.C., & Smith, L.B. (Eds.). (1995). *Swaying: Essays on intercultural love*. Iowa City: University of Iowa Press.

Gross, J. (1996, January 9). UC Berkley at crux of new multiracial consciousness. *The Los Angeles Times*, pp. A1, A11–A12.

Holmes, S.A. (1996, August 3). Marriages between blacks and whites increasing rapidly. *San Diego Union-Tribune*, p. A26.

Mee, C. (2002, August). *Performing arts*. CA: LaJolla Playhouse.

Nakazawa, D.J. (2003, July 6). What young people of mixed race can tell us about the future of our children. *Parade Magazine*, p. 4.

Pollan, M. (2001). *The botany of desire: A plant's eye view of the world*. New York: Random House.

Root, M.P.P. (2002). The color of love: The Tiger Woods generation is far more accepting of racial intermarriage. Is this a gain for tolerance and openness or a prologue to a new backlash? The politics of family, *The American Prospect*. Retrieved July 9, 2003, from the LexisNexis™ Academic Database.

U.S. Bureau of the Census. (2001, March 14). *Questions and answers for census 2000 data on race*. Retrieved July 9, 2003, from http://www.census.gov/Press-Release/www/2001/raceqandas.html

Wilson, T.P. (1992). Blood quantum: Native American mixed bloods. In M.P.P. Root (Ed.), *Racially mixed people in America* (pp. 108–126). Beverly Hills: Sage Publications.

Zack, N. (Ed.). (1995). *American mixed race*. Boston: Rowman & Littlefield.

SUMMARY AND IMPLICATIONS

Part III of this text synthesizes the information presented in Parts I and II and provides recommendations for service providers working in service delivery systems. It walks the reader through the steps in the service delivery process from beginning contact with families to the implementation and evaluation of services. The recommendations for this process are made with the intent of enhancing the sensitivity and awareness of service providers to issues of variability across families with respect to child rearing, health care, and communication. Through this knowledge, sensitivity, and positive action, it is hoped that service providers will be able to engage in fruitful interactions and provide effective and culturally competent services to families from a wide range of cultural, ethnic, and linguistic groups.

CHAPTER 13

STEPS IN THE RIGHT DIRECTION

Implications for Service Providers

Eleanor W. Lynch and Marci J. Hanson

On a deeper level the process of coming to know another
culture allows us to gradually become ourselves again. Many
of us, not knowing which of our behaviors may be culturally
acceptable (or neutral) and which may not, err on the side of
caution and move through intercultural situations in a state
of semiparalysis. . . . We are, quite literally, not ourselves.
—CRAIG STORTI (1989)

Time is neutral and does not change things. With courage
and initiative, leaders change things.
—JESSE JACKSON (IN BELL, 1995)

The American landscape is a kaleidoscope of cultures, and the changing patterns of color, customs, and language have introduced new energy, new concepts, and new challenges. One of the greatest concerns associated with increasing diversity is how human services agencies and programs can respond sensitively and effectively to families whose language, experience, and needs differ from those of the dominant culture in the United States. Defining, creating, and maintaining caring, culturally competent services is one of the most challenging tasks that agencies and service providers face; and as the 21st century unfolds, those challenges will increase.

REVIEWING THE THEMES

This final chapter reviews basic themes of the book and recommends practices that individual service providers can adapt or adopt to make the intervention process more appropriate for families with whom they work from diverse cultures and socio-cultural experiences. It is true that much of what needs to occur in order to develop and implement high-quality services that are cross-culturally appropriate and effective must be accomplished at the systems level. To encourage the entrance of people of color and individuals who are bilingual into the human services professions, training and support must begin early. Young adults need to be mentored throughout their school years, supported to stay in school, and encouraged to enter university programs in the human services. At the same time, comprehensive educational, health, and social programs that prevent failure, illness, and the hopelessness of poverty need to be put into place. Organizational policies that support the recruitment and hiring of individuals from a full range of cultural and ethnic backgrounds, staff development that increases intercultural competence throughout the organization, and a commitment to changing practices that compromise or discriminate against those from differing backgrounds must be incorporated into each agency's way of thinking and doing business. A great deal remains to be done to help systems embrace diversity; however, this book is about diversity at the interpersonal level—the face-to-face level of the service provider and the family.

Cross-Cultural Competence Defined

Throughout this book, several phrases have been used interchangeably—*cross-cultural competence, intercultural effectiveness,* and *ethnic competence.* All refer to ways of thinking and behaving that enable members of one cultural, ethnic, or linguistic group to work effectively with members of another. Green defined *ethnic competence* as being "able to conduct one's professional work in a way that is congruent with the behavior and expectations that members of a distinctive culture recognize as appropriate among themselves" (1982, p. 52). This includes 1) an awareness of one's own cultural limitations; 2) openness, appreciation, and respect for cultural differences; 3) a view of intercultural interactions as learning opportunities, 4) the ability to use cultural resources in interventions; and 5) an acknowledgment of the integrity and value of all cultures (Green, 1982). Barrera and Kramer (1997) expanded the definition to include the sociocultural contexts in which children and families operate, reinforcing the perspective that economic, lifestyle, and regional differences between service providers and families may have an impact as powerful as cultural, ethnic, or racial differences.

Respect for difference, eagerness to learn, and a willingness to accept that there are many ways of viewing the world are the hallmarks of a culturally competent individual. In describing the characteristics of counselors who are effective cross culturally, Sodowsky, Kuo-Jackson, and Loya include flexibility in approach and "tolerance for cultural mysteries" (1997, p. 9).

Just as cultural competence can be characterized as many things, there are several things that cultural competence is *not*. It is not becoming a member of another culture by a wholesale adoption of another group's values; attitudes; beliefs; customs; or manners of speaking, dress, or behavior. In fact, such overidentification would "be manipulative and patronizing" (Green, 1982, p. 52). Abandoning one's own cultural identity and substituting another is not a form of respect but rather a statement that culture can be easily shed. Furthermore, cultural competence does not imply that individuals can be categorized into groups and that little variability within cultural groups exists. Rather, cultural identification incorporates many dimensions and is viewed as only one variable that guides an individual's lifeways, not a total prescription for a way of life (Rowe, Behrens, & Leach, 1995). Finally, being culturally competent does not mean knowing everything about every culture; complete cultural competence can never be fully attained; rather, it is a lifelong process of learning, growing, and changing.

Transactional and Situational Nature of Cultural Identity

In 1969, Barth suggested that ethnic identity is transactional and situational. Instead of being a category to which one automatically does or does not belong, ethnic or cultural identity is defined by the boundaries that group members use in their interactions with the larger society. Considerable research and theory on identity development has followed (for a review, see Rowe, Behrens, & Leach, 1995). However, characteristics, traits, ceremonies, and so forth are important only insofar as they are markers of inclusion or exclusion used by the group to define itself from others.

As service providers work with families, the influence of the family members' cultural identity may change based on a given situation. For instance, a family of an infant may be eager for early educational intervention for their child, and, as a result, they may actively participate in the child's education program. In this situation, the family chooses a practice that is consistent with the view generally held in the dominant culture of valuing early intervention. A family whose cultural background is different regarding the need for early education may decide to adopt new values that it has encountered. However, if a surgical procedure were to be suggested to correct a malformation of the child's hands, then the same family members may elect not to have the surgery. It may be their belief that the child's hands are spiritually significant. In this situation, the family's decision may be at odds with the values of many others in the mainstream society but highly consistent with the values held by the cultural group with which they identify. Another family may enroll their child in a preschool program, but the mother may not participate in "Kinder Gym" programs or parent support groups because of a cultural belief that only the father should interface with the community. Thus, the family may accept dominant-culture beliefs related to services for their child but may not choose to participate in the kind of parent involvement activities that are common in the dominant culture.

Given the diversity of U.S. society, families may be monocultural (identify with one primary group), bicultural (identify with two different groups and move comfortably between these groups), or even multicultural (identify with more than two groups and move from group to group). Even families whose values and beliefs are tied strongly to a particular cultural group may, on occasion, adopt the values or practices of another group. Bi- or multicultural, bi- or multiracial, or bi- or multiethnic families may adapt, adopt, or create a completely unique way of identifying. Thus, as the previous examples demonstrate, belief systems in one area of family life (e.g., early educational experiences) may be consistent with those held by one cultural group, and beliefs and practices in another area of family life (e.g., health care practices, the role of women) may reflect the values of another group. The degree of exposure to other cultural groups—and, in the case of immigrants, the length of time in this country and place of residence—may influence the degree of mixing cultural practices.

The type of situation also may influence the degree to which an individual responds according to cultural traditions or to the assumed expectations of others. The degree of formality, the size of a group, the potential for embarrassment, or other negative consequences all influence an individual's behavior. It is simply a matter of human nature that individuals respond differently in different situations. This phenomenon is easily observed in young children. Parents often remark how good their child was at school or when visiting someone else's house, yet they lament about the child's difficult behavior at home with the parents. The situational nature of behavior is equally applicable to adult behavior. Parents may agree to give an antibiotic, to feed the child a particular food, or to provide an opportunity for a child with a disability to play with peers without disabilities, yet their actual behavior may differ. When meeting with professionals from the society's service delivery systems, they may agree to recommendations made by these professionals; however, they may practice very different methods of care at home or within their own cultural community. Because cultural identity can be situational and occur (or not occur) in a variety of transactions that families have with service providers who come from cultures that differ from their own, it is important to learn about the family's cultural boundaries.

The recognition of the transactional and/or situational nature of cultural identity may be the most important point to consider in working with families from a variety of cultures. This point guides the service provider away from overgeneralizing about families or stereotyping families based on their ethnic, cultural, or racial background. The behavior of each individual is dynamic and modified by each interaction. Many factors other than cultural identity also influence an individual's behavior. It is this acceptance of the constant dynamic interplay of the individual's beliefs and background with the daily demands of the society that will guide service providers to greater understanding and effectiveness in their work with families. This focus, in turn, will better support families in their transactions with the human services system.

Sociocultural Factors and Cultural Identification

Although a person's cultural identity exerts a profound influence on his or her lifeways, it is not the only critical factor. Each individual and family member is defined by more than these characteristics, and the influence of cultural identity may vary from one time to another. As pointed out in Chapter 1, sociocultural factors also shape the ways in which individuals and families live, as well as the way in which they identify themselves and wish to be identified. These factors include the following:

- Socioeconomic status

- Educational level

- Time of arrival in the United States

- Premigration and migration experiences

- Proximity to other members of their cultural or ethnic community

- Proximity to other cultural groups

- Age

- Gender

- Language proficiency

- Sociopolitical climate, including the extent of societal bias, distrust, and racism

- Locus of control

These factors may strongly influence an individual's life practices, and they may support or interfere with healthy cultural, ethnic, and racial identity as well as the ability or willingness to participate in intervention services.

For example, some families who fled their country of origin because of war and came to the United States seeking a safe haven may choose to put the pain of the past behind them. They may work diligently to adapt to a new way of life and identify with the mainstream culture of the United States. Other families who had similar migration experiences may seek to keep their original cultural identity alive and strong in their families and in their children. They may place considerable emphasis on maintaining the beliefs, customs, and language of their country of origin and plan to return if that should ever become possible.

Socioeconomic status and education also may influence identification with one's native culture. These variables may interact with cultural considerations in influencing individuals' and families' interactions with the larger community and their access to the community's resources. Affluent families whose members are highly educated may have a broad worldview and may move comfortably among two or more cultures and languages. Families with very limited resources, however, may have more difficulty finding educational opportunities, health care, employment, housing, and services for their children and family. Being poor and non–English speaking, for example, is a considerable disadvantage throughout the Unites States. These families may be compromised even in gaining access to services that are designed to assist families in overcoming obstacles. For many of these families, issues of survival such as obtaining adequate food and shelter may dictate their lifeways far more than their cultural identification.

Each individual and each family is different, and culture-specific information cannot be assumed to apply in every situation. However, culture-specific information can raise issues to consider, pose questions that may need to be answered, and underscore the service providers' desire to respond sensitively and effectively to each family and each family member.

Personal Growth and Change

The importance of self-awareness is emphasized throughout this book. Until one understands the impact of his or her own culture, language, race, and ethnicity on attitudes, beliefs, values, and ways of thinking and behaving, it is not possible to fully appreciate the cultures of others (e.g., Baruth & Manning, 1991; Campinha-Bacote, 1994; Chan, 1990; Hanson & Lynch, 1995; Harry, 1992b; Lynch & Hanson, 1993; Patterson & Blum, 1993; Randall-David, 1989). Thus, examining one's own roots is the place to begin any journey toward increased cross-cultural competence.

This exploration may uncover many insights regarding attitudes and behaviors that can help to reframe practice. For example, anyone who has grown up hearing, "Where there's a will, there's a way"; "He pulled himself up by his own bootstraps"; "God helps those who help themselves"; and "Never say 'I can't,' say 'I'll try,'" has a dramatically different view of the world (and of intervention) than someone who has heard, "It's God's will" or "The nail that stands up gets hammered down."

Studying one's own culture is not easy because it is so much a part of one's identity. Many of the beliefs and behaviors that are taken for granted in the United States are really the long-term influence of culture. There is, for example, no inherent reason to drive on the right-hand side of the road, to use knives and forks rather than chopsticks, or to eat cereal rather than beans or fish for breakfast. Yet, when one is confronted with behaviors that are different, the most common first response is that the other person or culture is wrong. As Adams and Carwardine said,

> Assumptions are the things you don't know you're making . . . the shock is that it had never occurred to you that there was any other way of doing it. In fact, you had never even thought about it at all, and suddenly here it is—different. The ground slips. (1990, p. 141)

Moving past these little differences allows us to consider the larger differences that can lead to cross-cultural misunderstanding.

Increased self-awareness also helps service providers discover unknown prejudices that can have subtle but pervasive effects on intercultural interactions. The long-standing tensions between and among various cultural groups sometimes emerge when least expected. This became most evident when one of the authors' close friends, a normally cheerful, adventurous, and open-minded traveling companion, became increasingly grumpy and ill-tempered on a trip through England. After several oblique attempts to determine the cause of this change of attitude, the author gently asked, "What in the world is the matter with you?" The answer tumbled out, "I can't stand being in this country because of what they've done to the Irish!" An unknown feeling and deep-seated prejudice had popped out, surprising both people. The Irish roots and childhood memories of conversations about the English occupation and oppression of Northern Ireland expressed themselves years later in a negative feeling about a country, its people, and its culture.

No one is free of prejudices. In spite of our best attempts to alter negative attitudes, expunge stereotypes, and accept others without regard to any of their external characteristics, human nature interferes. Perhaps the best way to monitor prejudices is to attend to the subtext that is part of our thinking and processing. We may say one thing aloud, but what is the subtext that we hear when we listen to that little voice in our heads? For example, when a driver cuts us off, what is the subtext coming from that little voice? Is it "He certainly must be having a bad day," or is it "Wouldn't you know, a foreign driver." When we are delayed in line at the grocery store while someone's groceries are sorted by food-stamp eligible and food-stamp ineligible, are we saying, "It certainly is good that families who could not afford food are getting support," or is that little voice saying, "Looks like my taxes are paying for their groceries, too—why aren't they working as hard as I am?" The world will never be without prejudice; discrimination; and cultural, racial, and sociocultural misunderstanding until we are able to change the subtext as well as our overt behaviors.

Learning about one's own culture, weeding out prejudices, and understanding the profound impact of culture on all aspects of life prepares individuals for change. For all service providers who work with families whose backgrounds are different from their own, some changes in practice are probably necessary.

CREATING A CULTURALLY APPROPRIATE INTERVENTION PROCESS

The intervention process has multiple components. Although the process may be lengthy in some systems, such as education or social services, and compressed in others, such as health care, all systems follow a similar model in planning, implementing, and evaluating intervention services. Regardless of the service system, the process typically begins with a family–professional exchange of information and planning for assessment. Once the relationship with the family is initiated and the family's concerns and priorities are determined, assessment planning begins, followed by the actual data gathering and assessment. This is followed by implementation of the intervention or treatment plan and monitoring and evaluation of the procedures (Hanson & Lynch, 1995; Lynch, Jackson, Mendoza, & English, 1991). Cross-cultural competence is an important aspect of each step. The paragraphs that follow briefly discuss each of the components in terms of the service provider's role in making the interaction sensitive to those from a variety of cultural and sociocultural groups.

Establishing Family–Professional Collaboration and Assessment Planning

The importance of family–professional collaboration has become one of the underpinnings of effective services for children (e.g., Beckman, Newcomb, Frank, & Brown, 1996; Dunst, Trivette, & Deal, 1988; Erwin & Rainforth, 1996; Rosin et al., 1996; Walker & Singer, 1993). Although its value has been discussed for children of all ages and in a variety of service delivery systems, it has particular relevance to working with young children with disabilities and their families. Learning more about the ethnic and cultural groups represented in one's community and working with a cultural mediator or guide can help service providers begin to develop a collaborative relationship with families. Determining where family members are on the cultural continua also can provide clues about the extent of participation and involvement that families may choose and help the service provider separate cultural differences from lack of information or personal preferences. Knowing some words and phrases in the family's language and recognizing patterns of family interaction; religious practices; and views about health, healing, and causation can increase the service provider's ability to interact sensitively and effectively with the family, thus increasing the likelihood of forming a successful partnership.

A partnership with the family provides the basis for planning an assessment that addresses its concerns. Although it is still common for assessments to be driven by preestablished protocols based on systems' regulations, a number of changes in this process are emerging (e.g., Haney & Cavallaro, 1996; Linder, 1993; Lynch, Mendoza, & English, 1990; Schwartz & Olswang, 1996). These changes would tailor assessments to the child's needs and the family's concerns and priorities. Although this reconceptualization of how assessments should be planned is a far more sensitive and effective approach to working with *all* families, it is particularly relevant to families from diverse cultures. Basing assessments on family concerns and priorities helps to ensure that their cultural perspective is honored.

To make this component of the intervention process more culturally appropriate, a service provider can

- Learn about the families in the community served. Which cultural groups are represented? Where are they from? When did they arrive? How closely knit is the community? What language(s) is(are) spoken? What are the cultural practices associated with child rearing? Are there any commonly held cultural beliefs surrounding health and healing, disability, and causation? Who are the community leaders and/or spiritual leaders, and what are their roles in advising and counseling families?

- Work with cultural mediators or guides from the families' cultures to learn more about the extent of cultural identification within the community at large and the situational aspects of this identification and regional variations.

- Learn and use words and forms of greeting in the families' languages if families are English-language learners; ensure that trained interpreters are present for assessments and meetings with family members.

- Allow additional time to work with interpreters to determine families' concerns, priorities, and resources, and to determine the next steps in the process. Remember that rapport building may take considerable time but that it is critical to effective intervention.

- Recognize that some families may be surprised by the extent of parent–professional collaboration that is expected in intervention programs in the United States. Do not expect every family to be comfortable with such a high degree of involvement. However, never assume that they do not want involvement and are not involved from their own perspective. Likewise, do not assume that they will become involved or will feel comfortable doing so.

- Use as few written forms as possible with families who are English-language learners or non–English speaking. If forms are used, then be sure that they are available in the family's language. Rely on the interpreter, your observations, and your own instincts and knowledge to know when to proceed and when to wait for the family to signal their readiness to move to the next step.

- Recognize the power differentials that many families experience between agency representatives and themselves; be aware of the larger sociopolitical climate that is influencing families' comfort and decision making.

Data Gathering and Assessment

Cultural bias is often most evident in the assessment process. Instruments that have been designed for use with English-speaking children and families who are part of the dominant culture in the United States are not always appropriate for children and families with other life experiences and languages. Instruments must be selected with care because developmental norms and expectations may differ from group to group. This is especially true in situations in which children have not had the opportunity to practice behaviors that are reflected in the test or they have not been expected to perform at those levels. For example, in some cultures, children are expected to "behave" and control their impulses from early in the preschool years. In other cultures, few demands are made on children until they are 6 or 7 years of age.

In some cultures, language is the primary way in which family members communicate with young children and, as a result, children become language oriented at a very early age. In other cultures, touch is the primary mode of communication and far less emphasis is placed on verbal input and output. As a result, tests with mainstream U.S. norms may not adequately measure the child's performance or potential in these areas. Furthermore, the child's prior experiences may influence his or her responses in the assessment. For example, in the experience of one of the authors, a young child whose family had recently moved to California from Samoa was observed to exhibit clumsiness and delayed motor development during an assessment conducted by an early intervention team. When the child was observed later in his home, he was able to move more freely and functionally. The home was furnished like a traditional Samoan home with mats and low-lying furniture and had none of the furniture or large obstacles found in most American homes. The interventionists realized that the child had never been exposed to or practiced ambulating around the types of objects found in most homes or test situations. Without a greater knowledge of the family's cultural background and practices, the staff members would not have been able to appropriately assess this child's developmental status and areas of need.

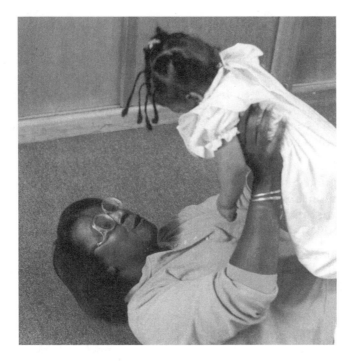

In other instances, the language of the assessment instrument is a barrier to its use. Tests that are not available in bilingual and/or bicultural editions cannot be assumed to be appropriate when directly translated. Perhaps the best strategy for gathering information is to interview the family through a trained interpreter. If formal assessments are used, then they should be conducted in the child's and/or the family's primary language, and missed items, especially related to vocabulary, in one language may need to be repeated in the second language. As Barrera and Corso (2003) pointed out, in bilingual homes children may know different words in different languages. For example, they may know the words for family members in their native language and words for colors in English.

Even the process of interviewing can be inappropriate for some families. This is true in terms of both the manner in which the interview is conducted and the content of the questions (e.g., questions related to marital relationships). One of the authors observed an illustrative example in her local community: Families were selected from each of the early intervention programs in the community to respond to a community services needs assessment, and information was gathered through structured interviews. For interviewees whose primary language was not English, community interpreters conducted the interview in conjunction with the professional who was performing the needs assessment. At one point, a mother indicated to the interpreter that she was very uncomfortable being singled out and embarrassed when asked questions about her child's disability and her thoughts about service needs. She indicated that it reflected badly on her to have a child with a disability and that it was inappropriate for parents to be questioned about services because "that was the job of the professionals to decide." In this case, the process of interviewing this mother was not culturally sensitive and had a negative influence on her "face saving" with respect to her child's disability, even though the professional conducting the needs assessment had the best of intentions in gathering input from families in the community. It is the service provider's job to determine, often with the help of cultural mediators, when and how data gathering and assessment can be conducted in a culturally competent manner, which can be challenging in many situations.

Hanson, Lynch, and Wayman (1990) proposed a paradigm of ethnic competence in data gathering and assessment that includes values clarification by the service provider, collection and analysis of ethnographic information regarding each family's cultural community, determination of the degree to which each family operates transculturally, and examination of each family's orientation to specific issues of child rearing. Using this model would help to ensure that the assessment process is both family focused and conducted in a manner desired by families, both practices of which are prerequisites to culturally competent services.

In the data-gathering and assessment phase of the intervention process, there are several ways to gather more accurate information and to make the experience more responsive to and appropriate for families from diverse cultures.

- When selecting commercially available assessment instruments, choose only those that are appropriate for the language and culture of the child and family.

- If the family members are English-language learners or non–English speaking, then work with a trained interpreter who can interpret language as well as cultural cues, and follow the guidelines suggested for working with interpreters presented in Chapter 3. Remember that what is *not* said can be as meaningful in some cases as what *is* said.

- Arrange the assessment at a time that allows the people important to the family to be present. For example, although the father may not have any direct caregiving responsibilities for the child, it may be important for him to be present during an assessment. In fact, it may be the father or another family member such as the grandmother who holds the decision-making powers in the family with respect to the child's education or treatment.

- Conduct the assessment where the family will be most comfortable. Although the home is typically the preferred place, if the family is not comfortable with outsiders visiting, then use the program site or some other place that is comfortable for the family.

- Gather only the data necessary to begin to work with the child and family. Limit the numbers of forms, questionnaires, and other types of paperwork.

- Include as few assessors as possible. Although the wisdom of all of the team members can be used to contribute to understanding the child and family's needs, a group of assessors is probably too demanding for everyone involved, especially if the interactions are being conducted through an interpreter. Additional observations or information can be obtained at another time as trust and comfort are established.

- Gather information in those areas in which the family has expressed concern. Tending to the family's issues first is a sign of respect for *all* families.

- Explain every step of the assessment and its purpose to the family. Explanations may need to occur several times and be made in several different ways.

Developing the Intervention Plan

Regardless of whether the intervention plan is a medical treatment or an educational program, the intervention will be only as effective as those who implement it; therefore, it is important that each person be involved in implementation "buy in" to the plan. When plans are based on highly valued behaviors and perceived concerns, it is much easier to obtain follow-through and support. As the family and other members

of the team formulate goals and objectives for the child or outcomes for the family, it is essential to have the family's point of view represented. Although this representation is usually assumed to be direct, verbal participation in the planning meeting, involvement may be different for families from other cultures or families from sociocultural groups other than the mainstream. A third party may serve as the family's representative, and the family may or may not elect to participate actively. As Harry (1992a) and Lynch and Stein (1982) pointed out, families from different cultures have very different ways of understanding and participating in interventions for their children. What may be considered active participation by one group is viewed as passive by another. For example, for some families, following the teacher's suggestions and making no demands is considered active participation; for others, involvement is conducting research on recommended practices in service delivery, asking questions, and constantly advocating for their child's needs in person and in writing.

Most families report that planning meetings (e.g., meetings to develop individualized education programs [IEPs] or individualized family service plans [IFSPs]) are intimidating. This may be even more true for families whose cultural and language background differ from that of the majority of others present at the meeting. The emphasis in education and early intervention on parent–professional collaboration, joint decision making, and family-focused plans makes this planning process even more complicated. Service providers throughout the United States have been working to increase their skills in family-centered practice, yet there will be many families from different cultures who do not expect, or prefer not, to take such an active role. Without ruling out these families' desire to participate, service providers may have to rethink their interpretation of family-centered practice. That is, if a family does not wish to participate in joint decision making, then this does not mean that the service provider has failed. To help make planning meetings more culturally responsive, the service provider may wish to incorporate some of the following practices:

- Brief the family about the meeting, its purpose, and who will be present well in advance of the meeting.

- Reduce the number of professionals present unless the family has requested that others be present.

- Encourage families to bring those people who are important to them—relatives, spiritual leaders, friends, and so forth—and be sure that a skilled interpreter is present if families are English-language learners or non–English speaking.

- Incorporate practices that are culturally comfortable for the family, such as serving tea, taking time to get acquainted before beginning the more formal aspects of the meeting, or conducting the meeting in a highly formal manner.

- Be sure that family input is encouraged without creating embarrassment. If it is felt that family members will not interact comfortably in such a public forum, then be sure that the service provider who knows the family best has spoken with them ahead of time and can represent their perspective at the meeting.

- Ensure that the goals, objectives, or outcomes that are being developed are matched to the family's concerns and priorities.

- Use appropriate resources that are designed for or are a part of the family's cultural community; for example, child care sponsored by the religious group to which they belong or referral to a health care provider who shares the same language and culture. Use cultural mediators or guides to help determine which matches are likely to be appropriate. Coming from the same country does not ensure that individuals share the same beliefs, values, behaviors, or language.

- Allow time for questions, but be prepared to discuss the kinds of questions that other families often ask. This allows questions to be answered without having to be asked by family members who may feel uncomfortable about public questioning.

Implementation

Putting the intervention or treatment into action is the most critical component of the intervention process. Assessments are conducted to determine what the intervention should be, and monitoring and evaluation are used to ensure that the intervention is working. Yet, implementation may be the area in which the greatest likelihood for cultural conflicts exists. If assessment and intervention planning are done well, then the chance of conflicts arising during implementation is significantly decreased, but they still may occur.

If family members had a different understanding of the goals, if they viewed their roles in implementation differently from the service providers, or if they were simply too polite to disagree at the time that the goals were being written, then conflicts may arise. The signs of conflict vary dramatically from one person to another as well as from one culture to the next, so it may be important for a cultural mediator or a guide to work with the service provider and the family to determine what each wants and what each believes is occurring. For example, the intervention plan for a young child may include a goal related to toilet training. At the time that the goal was written, everyone seemed to agree that it was a desired outcome; however, the family has chosen to keep the child in diapers at home and is making no attempt at scheduling potty breaks, something that is encouraged at the preschool program. After closer examination, the service provider may discover that such a goal was of no importance to family members. Although they had nothing against it and felt that it was acceptable because it was what the service provider wanted to do, they also saw no reason for it and simply continued their original practices regarding toileting.

In another instance, the child's weight gain and nutrition were of concern both to the parents and to the health care professionals. The nutritionist working in conjunction with the primary care physician recommended a new diet for the child. A visiting nurse later found that the family was not following the recommended regimen because some of the foods were considered to be "hot" foods or "cold" foods in that culture and, therefore, were not believed to be appropriate for the child's condition. Cultures may differ radically in terms of daily life practices such as food selection and preparation. In fact, a practice such as eating bananas may be encouraged in one culture and absolutely forbidden in another. Once again, if the service provider gathers cultural- and family-specific information, works with cultural guides, and attempts to work with rather than against other practitioners or care providers who are important to the family—whether they are healers, shamans, medicine men, *curanderos(as)*, or priests—the likelihood of designing and implementing appropriate interventions will be maximized.

Implementation can be made more effective by incorporating some of the following practices in the program:

- Put time and energy into ensuring that the goals and outcomes proposed are those that are of primary importance to the family.

- Adjust typical goals for children to match the family's priorities; for example, learning to eat with chopsticks rather than with a spoon and fork, behaving in cooperative rather than competitive ways, learning words in the language of the home, being taken to the bathroom rather than independently toileting, or sleeping and napping in the parents' bed rather than alone.

- Involve the family to the extent that they choose to be involved in all aspects of the program; try to determine how the family defines involvement.

- Continue to provide information to the family members about the program and their child's progress through cultural mediators, photos, and/or videotapes (even if families choose to take a less active role).

- Create a program that fits into the cultural communities that it serves. Use the multicultural aspects of the program to strengthen its implementation through creating a community center where people want to be and partnering with other community services such as child care and health clinics.

- Involve the various cultural communities' leaders in the program and invite their participation and advice through advisory boards, roundtables, and councils.

Monitoring and Evaluating

The final component of the intervention process is monitoring and evaluating the services provided to each child and family. It may mean determining whether the child has met the specified objectives and/or whether family members are satisfied with the degree to which they have reached the outcomes that they specified. Monitoring and evaluating can be made more effective by attempting to gather enough information to answer the following questions:

- Has the child met the full range of objectives that are a part of his or her individual plan?

- Is the child's rate of success consistent with his or her predicted rate of gain, or has the rate of gain been accelerated?

- Are adaptations being made to enable each child to participate in activities considered to be typical for the child's chronological age and culture?

- Have families been assisted and psychologically supported to meet any outcomes that they have specified for themselves? For example, if family members felt that they needed more information to explain their child's disability to other family members, then has that occurred? Or, if families felt that they needed additional child care, then have they been assisted in finding resources within the community?

In addition to evaluating the effectiveness of individual services, the effectiveness of the program or agency as a whole should be included in the evaluation.

- Is the work of the program/agency still consistent with the mission? Is the mission consistent with providing the highest quality service to *all* families, including those from diverse cultural, ethnic, linguistic, and sociocultural backgrounds?

- Is the program/agency effective as determined by client success, staff perceptions, families' satisfaction, and the perceptions of other agencies?

- Do families from diverse groups continue to enroll in the program or are their numbers declining despite no changes in the community's demographics? If the numbers are declining, then what are the reasons?

- Are resources allocated in the most effective way?

- Has staff development been effective in keeping service providers up to date with recommended practices?

- Do changes in staffing or overall program implementation need to occur?

- Is there a plan for increasing the number of staff members who represent the cultures and languages of the children served? Has the plan resulted in staffing changes?

The suggestions that follow provide specifics related to program monitoring and evaluation at the individual child and family level as well as the programmatic level:

- Ensure that individual child progress or change is systematically monitored and evaluated to determine if goals are met within prescribed timelines and conditions.

- Develop an evaluation plan using culturally competent, external evaluators to assist in the design and analysis. External evaluators have no vested interest in the program/agency and may provide a helpful and objective examination of the practices that are effective and those that need revision.

- Develop ways to examine the degree to which families are accomplishing the outcomes that they have specified. Consider practices such as goal attainment scaling; interviews; or other unobtrusive, family-oriented approaches to gather this information.

- Be sure that families' perceptions of the program/agency are assessed on an annual basis. Find a system for doing this that is most appropriate for the families being served. Consider using a combination of face-to-face interviews, short questionnaires in the families' languages, and parent-led focus groups.

- Seek input from other community members (e.g., human services agencies, university personnel, and members of cultural advocacy groups) regarding their perceptions of the program/agency and its effectiveness.

- Maintain logs of staff development activities, new initiatives, and innovative ideas on which the program/agency is working and revisit the program's/agency's progress at least annually.

The overall goal of all intervention programs is to provide high-quality services that have been demonstrated to be effective and to provide those services in ways that are culturally appropriate, caring, and cost-effective. Regardless of the service system or environment, when this goal is accomplished, children will make progress, families will be satisfied participants and consumers, and the community as a whole will profit from the efforts.

CONCLUSION

This book emphasizes the importance of intervention that is culturally responsive and suggests specific skills that service providers can learn and incorporate into their practice to increase their cross-cultural competence. It also provides cultural information to help service providers learn more about the range of attitudes, values, and beliefs that shape individuals' and families' views of the world. It is the authors' hope that this information will be used and shared by staff and parents in programs for young children and their families, especially in those programs that provide services to young children with disabilities and their families. Yet, this book is only the beginning—it is only a vehicle for helping readers consider the value of cultural diversity and its impact on the programs in which service providers work.

Skills and information also are only the beginning, a first step in the never-ending journey toward cross-cultural competence; this is an area in which the head is less important than the heart. After all of the books have been read and the skills learned and practiced, the cross-cultural effectiveness of each of us will vary. And it will vary more by what we bring to the learning than by what we have learned. Enthusiasm, openness, respect, awareness, the valuing of *all* people, and the willingness to take time are underlying characteristics that support everything that can be taught or learned. These are the characteristics that distinguish those individuals who can understand the journey from those who will actually take it.

You make the road by walking on it.
—NICARAGUAN PROVERB
(AS QUOTED IN MALECKA, 1993, P. 21)

REFERENCES

Adams, D., & Carwardine, M. (1990). *Last chance to see.* New York: Harmony Books.

Barrera, I., & Corso, R.M. (2003). *Skilled Dialogue: Strategies for responding to cultural diversity in early childhood.* Baltimore: Paul H. Brookes Publishing Co.

Barrera, I., & Kramer, L. (1997). From monologues to skilled dialogues: Teaching the process of crafting culturally competent early childhood environments. In P.J. Winton, J.A. McCollum, & C. Catlett (Eds.), *Reforming personnel preparation in early intervention: Issues, models, and practical strategies* (pp. 217–251). Baltimore: Paul H. Brookes Publishing Co.

Barth, F. (1969). *Ethnic groups and boundaries.* Boston: Little, Brown.

Baruth, L.G., & Manning, M.L. (1991). *Multicultural counseling and psychotherapy—A lifespan perspective.* Upper Saddle River, NJ: Prentice Hall.

Beckman, P.J., Newcomb, S., Frank, N., & Brown, L. (1996). Evolution of working relationships with families. In P.J. Beckman (Ed.), *Strategies for working with families of young children with disabilities* (pp. 17–30). Baltimore: Paul H. Brookes Publishing Co.

Bell, J.C. (1995). *Famous black quotations.* New York: Warner Press.

Campinha-Bacote, J. (1994). Cultural competence in psychiatric mental health nursing. *Mental Health Nursing, 29*(1), 1–8.

Chan, S. (1990). Early intervention with culturally diverse families of infants and toddlers with disabilities. *Infants and Young Children, 3*(2), 78–87.

Dunst, C.J., Trivette, C.M., & Deal, A.G. (1988). *Enabling and empowering families: Principles and guidelines for practice.* Cambridge, MA: Brookline Books.

Erwin, E.J., & Rainforth, B. (1996). Partnerships for collaboration: Building bridges in early care and education. In E.J. Erwin (Ed.), *Putting children first: Visions for a brighter future for young children and their families* (pp. 227–251). Baltimore: Paul H. Brookes Publishing Co.

George, C.D. (1989). *My heart soars.* Blaine, WA: Hancock House Publishers.

Green, J.W. (1982). *Cultural awareness in the human services.* Upper Saddle River, NJ: Prentice Hall.

Haney, M., & Cavallaro, C.C. (1996). Using ecological assessment in daily program planning for children with disabilities in typical preschool settings. *Topics in Early Childhood Special Education, 16,* 66–81.

Hanson, M.J., & Lynch, E.W. (1995). *Early intervention: Implementing child and family services for infants and toddlers who are at risk or disabled* (2nd ed.). Austin, TX: PRO-ED.

Hanson, M.J., Lynch, E.W., & Wayman, K.I. (1990). Honoring the cultural diversity of families when gathering data. *Topics in Early Childhood Special Education, 10*(1), 112–131.

Harry, B. (1992a). *Cultural diversity, families, and the special education system.* New York: Teachers College Press.

Harry, B. (1992b). Developing cultural self-awareness: The first step in values clarification for early interventionists. *Topics in Early Childhood Special Education, 12,* 333–350.

Linder, T.W. (1993). *Transdisciplinary play-based assessment: A functional approach to working with young children* (Rev. ed.). Baltimore: Paul H. Brookes Publishing Co.

Lynch, E.W., & Hanson, M.J. (1993). Changing demographics: Implications for training in early intervention. *Infants and Young Children, 6*(1), 50–55.

Lynch, E.W., Jackson, J.A., Mendoza, J. M., & English, K. (1991). The merging of best practices and state policy in the IFSP process in California. *Topics in Early Childhood Special Education, 11*(3), 32–53.

Lynch, E.W., Mendoza, J.M., & English, K. (1990). *Implementing individualized family service plans in California: Final report.* (Available from Early Intervention Programs, Department of Developmental Services, 1600 9th Street, Sacramento, CA 95814).

Lynch, E.W., & Stein, R.C. (1982). Perspectives on participation in special education. *Exceptional Education Quarterly, 3*(2), 56–63.

Malecka, J. (1993). The multicultural treasury. Portland, ME: J. Weston Walch.

Patterson, J.M., & Blum, R.W. (1993). A conference on culture and chronic illness in childhood: Conference summary. *Pediatrics, 91,* 1025–1030.

Randall-David, E. (1989). *Strategies for working with culturally diverse communities and clients.* Bethesda, MD: Association for the Care of Children's Health.

Rosin, P., Whitehead, A.D., Tuchman, L.I., Jesien, G.S., Begun, A.L., & Irwin, L. (1996). *Partnerships in family-centered care: A guide to collaborative early intervention.* Baltimore: Paul H. Brookes Publishing Co.

Rowe, W., Behrens, P.T., & Leach, M.M. (1995). Racial/ethnic identity and racial consciousness: Looking back and looking forward. In J.G. Ponterotto, J.M. Casas, L.A. Suzuki, & C.M. Alexander (Eds.), *Handbook of multicultural counseling* (pp. 218–235). Beverly Hills: Sage Publications.

Schwartz, I.S., & Olswang, L.B. (1996). Evaluating child behavior change in natural settings: Exploring alternative strategies for data collection. *Topics in Early Childhood Special Education, 16,* 82–101.

Sodowsky, G.R., Kuo-Jackson, P.Y., & Loya, G.J. (1997). Outcome of training in the philosophy of assessment. In D.B. Pope-

Davis & H.L.K. Coleman (Eds.), *Multicultural counseling competencies: Assessment, education and training, and supervision* (pp. 3–42). Beverly Hills: Sage Publications.

Storti, C. (1989). *The art of crossing cultures.* Yarmouth, ME: Intercultural Press.

Walker, B., & Singer, G.H.S. (1993). Improving collaborative communication between professionals and parents. In G.H.S. Singer & L.E. Powers (Eds.), *Families, disability, and empowerment: Active coping skills and strategies for family interventions* (pp. 285–316). Baltimore: Paul H. Brookes Publishing Co.

SUGGESTED READINGS
AND RESOURCES

Now, she calls out each [name] as best as she can, taking
care of every last pitch and accent, and I hear her speaking
a dozen lovely and native languages, calling all
the difficult names of who we are.
—CHANG-RAE LEE (1995)

One does not worship, display, or teach culture;
one acknowledges it as a whole way of life grounded
in the past, and one necessarily lives a culture.
—HOUSTON BAKER, JR. (1990)

Our understandings of culture, ethnicity, religion, and race are often based on limited experience, impressions, misinformation, and mythology that are passed from generation to generation. Sometimes we are fortunate enough to learn from bicultural people, those who walk in two worlds and are able to communicate their life experience across cultural boundaries. We can also learn from those with whom we share a common culture, race, or ethnicity as we explore and discover our commonalities and differences. Lucky indeed are those who have the opportunity to walk in other worlds and participate in other cultures or to be with those from different ethnic, cultural, racial, and language backgrounds. But even if these opportunities do not exist, we can still learn a great deal about worldviews and lifeways that may be similar to or different from our own through the growing number of books in the popular press, web sites accessible in libraries and at home, films that reach audiences beyond the art cinemas, and live theater. These media bring cross-cultural experiences and interactions closer to all of us and allow us to think, feel, and reflect on who we are within the rich texture of the universal tapestry. Almost daily, a new book of fiction or nonfiction, poetry or prose, enters the market and invites us to accompany the author on a cultural odyssey—an adventure of the spirit that brings us closer to understanding ourselves and others.

The world is getting smaller, but small spaces require heightened civility and increased competence. This brief list of books, plays, and films is intended to open doors, to provide a sampling of media that can expand the heart and challenge the mind to increase our understanding of what it means to live in someone else's culture. This list includes works of fiction and nonfiction in which culture, cultural differences, and adapting to other cultures serve as the focus or the backdrop. Many of the resources listed here describe the life experiences of people of color in America; others chronicle experiences of Anglo-Europeans adjusting to life in unfamiliar cultures. Some detail cultures from a historical perspective; a few highlight cultural values, beliefs, and attitudes through words, pictures, and performance. This list is neither exhaustive nor equally representative of every group discussed here. Rather, it is hoped that it will help readers find truths on a long journey . . . one that will take them down many roads and lead to much satisfaction.

BOOKS

ANGLO-EUROPEAN

A Connecticut Yankee in King Arthur's Court

Mark Twain (Samuel L. Clemens, 1889; now available through Bantam, New York, 1981)
A comic satirical novel that describes a quintessential New Englander who brings the inventions and ingenuity of the American 19th century to King Arthur's age of chivalry.

Thanks to Dawn Thompson for her assistance in assembling this list in the first edition and to Valerie Bourque for her assistance in the second edition. Suggestions in this edition have been supplemented by Leslie Eckard and the Paul H. Brookes Publishing Co. "family."

A Tree Grows in Brooklyn

Betty Smith (Harper & Row, New York, 1947)
The experiences of an Irish American family in Brooklyn, New York, and their struggles with ethnic identity, poverty, and politics. An important work on Anglo-European immigration and acculturation.

Angela's Ashes

Frank McCourt (Scribner, New York, 1999 [2nd ed.])
Compelling tales of experiences of an Irish family growing up in poverty and experiences of Irish-American immigrants. Other books include *'Tis: A Memoir* and *Brotherhood.*

At Home in Mitford

Jan Karon (Penguin Books, New York, 1994)
Set in the safety of a small U.S. town where people still know one another, this book describes the United States that people recall but that may never have existed. Although the town is filled with unique "characters," it is remarkably lacking in diversity. *These High Green Hills* is a sequel and many more follow.

Centennial

James A. Michener (Random House, New York, 1974)
The epic saga of the origins, founding, and shaping of the United States from prehistoric to contemporary times. Generations of families are followed throughout the course of the nation's history.

Chesapeake

James A. Michener (Random House, New York, 1978)
The complete history of the Chesapeake Bay region from the days of the original American Indians to contemporary times. This book gives a flavor to the arrival of settlers from the British Isles and the clashes and blending of their culture with those of the American Indian population.

Lake Wobegon Days

Garrison Keillor (Viking Penguin, New York, 1985)
An amusing chronicle of the history of small-town American life.

My Ántonia

Willa Cather (Houghton Mifflin, Boston, 1918)
A powerful chronicle of pioneer life in the Midwest and the experience of European immigrants who moved to the United States. Other books by Cather include *O Pioneers!, Death Comes for the Archbishop,* and *Song of the Lark.*

On the Road with Charles Kuralt

Charles Kuralt (Putnam, New York, 1985)
Wonderful descriptions of American life as told by the late Charles Kuralt, a reporter, during his travels around the country. Another book by Kuralt, *A Life on the Road,* continues to chronicle these experiences.

Taking It Home: Stories from the Neighborhood

Tony Ardizzone (Sunsinger Books, University of Illinois Press,
Urbana & Chicago, 1996)
A collection of short stories about growing up Italian American and Catholic in Chicago during the 1950s and 1960s. From laugh-out-loud childhood memories to the sadness of losing a father in the war, this book helps readers realize that Anglo-European American culture is not monolithic.

Texas

James A. Michener (Random House, New York, 1985)
The history of the state of Texas from the first Spanish explorers and settlers to its separation and independence from Spain to its becoming a state.

The Life of an Ordinary Woman

Anne Ellis (Houghton Mifflin, Boston, 1929)
Chronicles one woman's life in the mining camps of the Rocky Mountains.

The Poisonwood Bible

Barbara Kingsolver (HarperCollins, New York, 1998)
A compelling story of an American missionary family in Africa, cross-cultural interactions, and outcomes.

The Stone Diaries

Carol Shields (Penguin Books, New York, 1993)
The 1995 Pulitzer Prize winner for fiction, this book describes one woman's life in the United States and Canada from the early 1900s to her death in the 1980s.

Undaunted Courage: Meriwether Lewis, Thomas Jefferson, and the Opening of the American West

Stephen E. Ambrose (Touchstone, published by Simon & Schuster, New York, 1996)
Chronicle of the Lewis and Clark expedition, its perils, discoveries, and the social and political context of the time.

AMERICAN INDIAN

A Thief of Time

Tony Hillerman (Harper & Row, New York, 1988)
One among several of Tony Hillerman's well-crafted mysteries that are centered in the Southwest and provide some insight into the culture of the Navajo nation. Although not an American Indian, Hillerman presents readable and colorful accounts of aspects of contemporary Navajo life. See also *Skinwalkers, People of Darkness, Talking God,* and others by Hillerman.

Alaska

James A. Michener (Random House, New York, 1988)
A journey from prehistoric times to the present-day state of Alaska. This novel describes the crossing of the Bering Strait and settlement of what is now Alaska and gives a good account of the history and life experiences of Native Alaskan Indians and Eskimos.

Earth Song, Sky Spirit

Clifford E. Trafzer (Ed.) (Anchor Books, New York, 1992)
An anthology of 30 short stories from contemporary American Indian writers with an introduction to each piece and each author by the editor.

Love Medicine

Louise Erdrich (Holt, Rinehart & Winston, New York, 1984)
Multigenerational family portrait of two American Indian families that gives a moving account of their lives and experiences in contemporary times in the United States. Other books by Erdrich that describe American Indian life include *The Beet Queen, Tracks,* and *The Last Report on the Miracles at Little No Horse.*

Mother Earth Spirituality: Native American Paths to Healing Ourselves and Our World

Ed McGaa (Harper SanFrancisco, San Francisco, 1990)
Ed (Eagle Man) McGaa, an Ogalala Sioux, draws on centuries of American Indian wisdom to describe practices and ceremonies that reestablish a nurturing relationship with nature.

My Heart Soars

Chief Dan George (Hancock House Publishers, Surrey, British Columbia, 1989)
Poetic wisdom on life and on being Indian in America.

Native American Wisdom

Kent Nerburn & Louise Mengelkoch (Compilers) (New World Library, San Rafael, CA, 1991)
A compilation of observations made by American Indians drawn from speeches, first-person accounts, and government documents. Comments on government, the environment, lifeways, and prejudice.

Spider Woman's Granddaughters

Paula Gunn Allen (Ed.) (Fawcett Columbine, New York, 1989)
An anthology of stories by American Indian women from long ago to contemporary times. Each reflects the influence of cultural bonds and traditions and the influence of contact with Anglo-Europeans on the culture.

The Bean Trees

Barbara Kingsolver (Harper Perennial, New York, 1988)
The story of a young woman from rural Kentucky who travels west and in the process becomes the caregiver for a 3-year-old American Indian girl. Subsequent books *Animal Dreams* and *Pigs in Heaven* continue the story.

The Lone Ranger and Tonto Fistfight in Heaven

Sherman Alexie (The Atlantic Monthly Press, New York, 1993)
A chronicle of life on the Spokane Indian reservation with no punches pulled—humor and harsh reality combined. This is the basis of the film *Smoke Signals* listed in the film section of Suggested Readings and Resources.

AFRICAN AMERICAN

A Lesson Before Dying

Ernest J. Gaines (Vintage Books, New York, 1993)
A poignant picture of life in the segregated South of the 1940s, the racial injustices of the judicial system, and the lives of those caught up in it. Other books by Gaines include *The Autobiography of Miss Jane Pittman, A Gathering of Old Men,* and *In My Father's House.*

Can't Quit You, Baby

Ellen Douglas (Atheneum, New York, 1988)
Cornelia, a rich southern woman, and Tweet, her storytelling housekeeper, create a unique and supportive relationship through adversity.

Coming of Age in Mississippi: An Autobiography

Anne Moody (Dial, New York, 1968)
A powerful autobiographical account of a young girl that describes the experiences of growing up black in Mississippi.

Disappearing Acts

Terry McMillan (Washington Square Press, New York, 1989)
An unromanticized look at an African American couple's efforts to escape their individual pasts. Also by McMillan, *Waiting to Exhale*, available in print and as a film.

Every Good-Bye Ain't Gone

Itabari Njeri (Vintage Books, New York, 1990)
An autobiography of Njeri and her family that describes the diversity of the African American experience with humor, power, and finely drawn characterizations.

Having Our Say—The Delany Sisters' First 100 Years

Sarah Delany and A. Elizabeth Delany, with Amy Hill Hearth
(Kodansha International, New York, 1993)
With a combined age of 204, the late Delany sisters share their stories from childhood in North Carolina to the heyday of the Harlem Renaissance to life at the end of the 20th century. Their memories and commentary on contemporary life make for page-turning reading. Also produced on stage throughout the United States.

On the Pulse of Morning

Maya Angelou (Random House, New York, 1993)
A poem of inclusivity written and read by Maya Angelou on the inauguration of President Bill Clinton in 1993. Other must-read books from Maya Angelou include *I Know Why the Caged Bird Sings, Gather Together in My Name, All of God's Children Need Walking Shoes, I Shall Not be Moved, Maya Angelou Poems, The Heart of a Woman*, and *Wouldn't Take Nothing for My Journey Now*.

Once Upon a Time When We Were Colored

Clifton L. Taulbert (Council Oak Book, Tulsa, OK, 1989)
Recollections of life in a small Mississippi town before integration, with emphasis on the strength of kinship and friendship bonds.

Roots

Alex Haley (Dell Books, New York, 1974)
An epic story that spans seven generations. This major novel chronicles the African American experience from life in a small village in Africa through slavery and into contemporary life. *Roots* is also available on videotape and DVD.

Song of Solomon

Toni Morrison (Alfred A. Knopf, New York, 1977)

A novel about four generations in an African American family, the importance of family bonds, and one man's search for knowledge of his own heritage. *Beloved,* another of Morrison's books, tells the story of Sethe, a runaway slave who is haunted by her past and the ghost of her murdered daughter and provides an exploration of some of the less well-known horrors of slavery. Other books written by Morrison that also bring to life the African American experience include *Tar Baby, Sula,* and *The Bluest Eye.*

Talk that Talk: An Anthology of African-American Storytelling

Linda Goss & Marian E. Barnes (Eds.) (Simon & Schuster, New York, 1989)

Stories of history remembered, home and family, and the supernatural, along with fables, anecdotes, sermons, and rhymes. Includes works by Maya Angelou; Langston Hughes; Zora Neale Hurston; Martin Luther King, Jr.; and Winnie Mandela. A tour de force of African American storytelling.

The Autobiography of Malcolm X

As told to Alex Haley (Ballantine Books, New York, 1964)

The story of Malcolm X, leader of the Nation of Islam and civil rights activist in the 1960s. From childhood as the son of a minister through his affiliation with the Nation of Islam and his calls for separatism through a period of profound change following his trip to Mecca, this book provides an important piece of American history. The movie *Malcolm X,* directed by Spike Lee, is available on videotape and DVD.

The Bondwoman's Narrative

Hannah Crafts, edited by Henry Louis Gates, Jr. (Warner Books, Inc., New York, 2002)

Believed to be the first novel written by a fugitive slave, the manuscript for the book was purchased in an auction by scholar Henry Louis Gates, Jr. The introduction by Gates provides the background and historical context. The book continues with Crafts' story written in the styles of the times.

The Cheneysville Incident

David Bradley (Harper & Row, New York, 1981)

A young African American historian returns to his hometown to care for his father's old friend and begins an irresistible search into his family's past.

The Color Purple

Alice Walker (Harcourt Brace Jovanovich, New York, 1982)

A moving account of the struggles and joys in the life of an African American woman from childhood through adulthood as told through her letters. *The Temple of My Fa-*

miliar, another book by Walker, weaves together stories told by the central characters to portray the heritage and experiences of several families. Other books by Walker, *Meridian* and *The Third Life of Grange Copeland,* describe African American experiences in a similar vein. A film version of *The Color Purple* is also available.

The Measure of Our Success—A Letter to My Children and Yours

Marian Wright Edelman (Beacon Press, Boston, 1992)
In this readable and quotable book, Edelman, the founder and president of the Children's Defense Fund, reminds us of our responsibility to serve others in a nation that may have lost sight of that value.

The Sanctified Church

Zora Neale Hurston (Turtle Island Foundation, Berkeley, CA, 1981)
About folklore in the "Blacksouth" of the 1920s, 1930s, and 1940s, this book of essays represents one of the many genres that Hurston mastered in her lifetime. These volumes cover topics such as herbs and herbal medicine, the language of African Americans, and the church. Other books by Hurston include *Their Eyes Were Watching God, Mules and Men,* and *Jonah's Gourd Vine.*

Through the Ivory Gate

Rita Dove (Vintage, New York, 1992)
Winner of the Pulitzer Prize for Poetry and Poet Laureate of the United States from 1993 to 1995, Rita Dove tells the story of a young black actress who returns home to teach in her midwestern town.

Words to Make My Dream Children Live: A Book of African American Quotations

Deirdre Mullane (Ed.) (Anchor Books, New York, 1995)
A comprehensive collection of quotations from African Americans including humor, inspiration, scholarship, and faith.

LATINO

Bless Me, Ultima

Rudolfo Anaya (Warner Books, New York, 1981)
A haunting story of custom and culture about the relationship of a young boy and Ultima, a curandera who comes to live with his family and helps him shape his identity. Hailed as one of the foremost Chicano writers, Anaya has also written *Albuquerque.*

Breath, Eyes, Memory

Edwidge Danticat (Vintage Books, New York, 1994)
A literary plunge into Haitian life with characters that combine love and tyranny. Also by Danticat, *Krik? Krak!*

Cuba and the Night

Pico Iyer (Vintage Books, New York, 1995)
A novel by travel writer and essayist, Pico Iyer, set in contemporary Cuba.

Getting Home Alive

Aurora Levins and Rosario Morales (Firebrand Books, Ithaca, New York, 1986)
A collection of poetry, stories, and comments on geography, politics, and culture by a Puerto-Rican, American-Jewish mother and daughter.

Hunger of Memory—The Education of Richard Rodriguez

Richard Rodriguez (Bantam Books, New York, 1982)
An autobiography that chronicles the loss of Rodriguez's Mexican American culture as he climbs the ladder of academic success.

Like Water for Chocolate

Laura Esquivel (Translated by Carol Christensen & Thomas Christensen)
(Doubleday, New York, 1992)
A sensual novel of food, fantasy, and family life centered around Tita, the youngest daughter of a Mexican family at the beginning of the 20th century. Responsible for caring for her mother and forgoing marriage to honor this obligation, Tita's cooking expresses her passion. *Like Water for Chocolate* is also available on videotape and DVD. Also by Esquivel, *The Law of Love.*

Love in the Time of Cholera

Gabriel García Márquez (Translated by Edith Grossman)
(Penguin Books, New York, 1988)
A master storyteller, Márquez creates rich characters and steamy settings evocative of his native Colombia. This is the story of lost love and a kind of reunion. Also by Márquez, *One Hundred Years of Solitude* and *The General in His Labyrinth.*

Our House in the Last World

Oscar Hijuelos (Washington Square Press, New York, 1991)
The tale of the immigration of the Santinios, a rural Cuban couple, to New York City, as told by their American-born son.

Stones for Ibarra

Harriet Doerr (Penguin, New York, 1984)
A tender story of love and culture about an Anglo-European couple who go to Mexico to reopen an old family mine. Also by the late Harriet Doerr, *Consider This, Señora,* and *Tiger in the Grass.*

Tales of the Shaman's Apprentice

Mark Plotkin (Penguin Books, New York, 1993)
A nonfiction account of ethnobotanist Plotkin's search for medicines in the rain forest of the Amazon. An account of the people and places of Latin America that are often left untold.

The Latino Reader: An American Literary Tradition from 1542 to the Present

Harold Augenbraum & Margarite Fernandes Olmos (Eds.) (Houghton Mifflin, New York, 1997)
A new anthology of the body of Latino literature that stretches back to the 1500s and encompasses poetry and prose.

The Wise Women of Havana

José Raúl Bernardo (HarperCollins, New York, 2002)
A story of three Cuban women and their families set in the late 1930s, as told by composer, author, and architect, José Raúl Bernardo.

When I Was Puerto Rican

Esmeralda Santiago (Vintage Books, New York, 1993)
Santiago's autobiography that tells of her life in two worlds. From the lush, languid setting of her native island through the wrenching move to New York City where her talents are ultimately recognized, the story pulls the reader into her experiences.

Woman Hollering Creek

Sandra Cisneros (Random House, New York, 1991)
An excursion into a wonderful variety of lives in the Hispanic community. Cisneros is the author of several other novels including *The House on Mango Street* and *Caramelo.*

ASIAN

Growing Up Asian American—An Anthology

Maria Hong (Ed.) (William Morrow & Co., New York, 1993)
Life stories of Asian Americans of literary note provide individual perspectives on common themes such as language, stereotype, and identity.

In the Year of the Boar and Jackie Robinson

Bette Bao Lord (Harper Trophy Books, New York, 1984)
In 1947, a young girl moves from China to Brooklyn. She discovers Jackie Robinson and baseball.

Iron and Silk

Mark Salzman (Vintage Departures, New York, 1990)
Salzman recounts his experiences as a young English language teacher in the Hunan Medical College. Open to the cultural differences that he experiences, this well-told story is truly a celebration of diversity. *Iron and Silk* is also available on videotape. Another Salzman book, *The Laughing Sutra,* is a humorous adventure novel that uses the clash between Chinese and American culture as a backdrop.

Learning to Bow: Inside the Heart of Japan

Bruce Feiler (Ticknor & Fields, New York, 1991)
A witty and insightful book by a young American teacher working in Japan and the cultural clashes that occur as he and his students and colleagues learn more about each other.

Native Speaker

Chang-Rae Lee (Riverhead Books, New York, 1995)
A novel by Korean-American Lee set in New York City provides insight into life within and between two cultural worlds through an exploration of family life and city politics. Other books by Lee include *A Gesture Life* and *Aloft.*

Snow Falling on Cedars

David Guterson (Harcourt Brace & Company, New York, 1994)
A lyrically written book of suspense that depicts the prejudice against Japanese American fishermen and strawberry farmers in Puget Sound following World War II. Also available on videotape and DVD.

Strangers from a Different Shore: A History of Asian Americans

Ronald Takaki (Penguin Books, New York, 1989)
Stories from many Asian groups, including Japanese, Chinese, Korean, Pilipino, Indian, Vietnamese, Cambodian, and Laotian as told through oral history.

The Joy Luck Club

Amy Tan (G.P. Putnam's Sons, New York, 1989)
Four Chinese women come together in San Francisco and meet regularly over a game of mah jongg. Their marvelous stories chronicle relationships between generations and friends, and the interface between experiences from the old world (China)

and those of a new life in America. *The Joy Luck Club* is also available on videotape. More recent works by Tan include *The Kitchen God's Wife, The Hundred Secret Senses,* and *The Bonesetter's Daughter.*

The Spirit Catches You and You Fall Down

Anne Fadiman (Farrar, Straus & Giroux, New York, 1997)

A must read for any service provider about a Hmong child with epilepsy and her family, who transplanted to Merced, California, and the misunderstandings and cultural clashes between medical professionals and family members. A true account of the differences in meaning that professionals and new refugees take from each encounter.

The Woman Warrior

Maxine Hong Kingston (Alfred A. Knopf, New York, 1976)

An enthralling description of Chinese immigrant life in California and the conflicts and paradoxes of the Chinese American experience as told often through the mother's "talking story." Another book by Kingston, *China Men,* also portrays the Chinese American experience, particularly that of the early Chinese who came to America and labored in the development of this country.

Thousand Pieces of Gold

Ruthanne Lum McCunn (Beacon Press, Boston, 1981)

A biographical novel about Lalu Nathoy, a Chinese woman, who was sold by her father into slavery and taken to a mining town in Idaho in 1872. The novel describes her struggles, survival, and growth as a woman, as well as her experiences as a Chinese woman in the American West. *Thousand Pieces of Gold* is also available on videotape. Also by McCunn, *Wooden Fish Songs.*

Wild Swans: Three Daughters of China

Jung Chang (Anchor Books, New York, 1991)

A memoir of three generations of Chinese women from Imperial China through and beyond the Cultural Revolution. A beautifully crafted personal story with a sociopolitical backdrop.

PILIPINO

Dogeaters

Jessica Tarahata Hagedorn (Penguin, New York, Reissue 1991)

A raw, harsh, and sometimes humorous look at Manila's seamier side along with the politics of the times. Also performed as a stage play.

Video Night in Katmandu

Pico Iyer (Vintage Departures, New York, 1989)
A series of essays on the interplay between Eastern and Western culture. In the essay devoted to the Philippines, Iyer presents a grim picture of the influence of American ways on the lives of Pilipinos.

NATIVE HAWAIIAN AND SAMOAN (AND PACIFIC ISLANDER)

Amerika Samoa—An Anthropological Photo Essay

Frederic Koehler Sutter (University of Hawaii Press, Honolulu, 1985)
A beautiful photographic essay captioned with Samoan proverbs.

Changes in Latitude—An Uncommon Anthropology

Joan McIntyre Varawa (Harper & Row, New York, 1989)
An Anglo-European American marries a Fijian and chronicles her life with him and his extended family in the village. The cultural clashes that inevitably occur are discussed and inform the reader about the power of culture and cross-cultural learning.

Conversations with the Cannibals

Michael Krieger (The Ecco Press, Hopewell, NJ, 1994)
A travel story of Krieger's attempts to chronicle the fading way of life on the islands of the Pacific. Much of the book is based on interviews with islanders and time spent in remote areas of Melanesia and Polynesia.

Where We Once Belonged

Sia Figiel (Kaya Press, New York, 2000)
The first Samoan woman to be published in the United States, Figiel tells a coming-of-age story in stark contrast to that told by Anglo-European anthropologists.

Hawaii

James A. Michener (Random House, New York, 1959)
A saga of the history of the Hawaiian islands from settlement by the first Polynesians to statehood and contemporary life. The novel chronicles the range and experiences of the many cultural and ethnic groups that make up contemporary Hawaii.

The Happy Isles of Oceania—Paddling the Pacific

Paul Theroux (G.P. Putnam's Sons, New York, 1992)
Famous travel writer and novelist Theroux provides a fascinating, witty, and sometimes cynical picture of the South Pacific.

MIDDLE EASTERN

A History of the Arab Peoples

Albert Hourani (The Belknap Press of Harvard University Press, Cambridge, MA, 1991)
A comprehensive book that chronicles the history of Arab-speaking parts of the Islamic world from the 7th century into the 1980s. For each time period, there is an emphasis on society and culture.

Arabian Jazz

Diana Abu-Jaber (Harcourt Brace & Company, New York, 1993)
A novel about a Jordanian family transplanted in upstate New York with humorous characters who struggle with the demands of the old and the new customs and cultures.

Baghdad without a Map

Tony Horowitz (Dutton, New York, 1991)
A freelance journalist describes his search for stories throughout the Middle East. As each chapter unfolds, so, too, do the differences between the West and the Middle East, as well as the diversity among the Middle Eastern countries that in some ways are linked only by geographical designation.

Daughter of Persia

Sattareh Farman Farmaian, with Dona Munker (Crown Publishers, New York, 1992)
Farmaian, a social worker, recounts her life from a privileged childhood in the harem compound on the grounds of her formerly wealthy father's land to her experience as the first Persian woman to study at the University of Southern California. Her return to Iran is marked by extraordinary accomplishments in the male-dominated university system followed by the upheaval of the revolution.

Motoring with Mohammed

Eric Hansen (Houghton Mifflin, Boston, 1991)
In search of his travel journals buried after a shipwreck 10 years earlier, Hansen returns to Yemen to find them. The direct and demanding Anglo-European American approach is gradually smoothed by the Yemeni culture, customs, and people.

Reading Lolita in Tehran: A Memoir in Books

Azar Nafisi (Random House, New York, 2003)
In 1995, after resigning from her job as a professor at a university in Tehran due to repressive policies, the author invited some of her female students to attend weekly sessions of great Western literature (banned by the government) in her home. The book is part memoir, part literary criticism, and is a testament to the power of art to change lives.

The Hadj

Michael Wolfe (Atlantic Monthly Press, New York, 1993)
The story of his pilgrimage to Mecca, Wolfe, an Anglo-European American Muslim, explains the religious significance and rituals of the Hadj.

The Kite Runner

Khaled Hosseini (Riverhead Books, New York, 2003)
An Afghan American writer struggles with his past and returns to his homeland to find redemption in a time of turmoil.

SOUTH ASIAN

Arranged Marriage

Chitra Banerjee Divakaruni (Anchor Paperbacks, New York, 1996)
A collection of short stories of Indian-born women in America. Describes conflicts between old beliefs and new. Other books written by Divakaruni include *Mistress of Spices* and *Sister of My Heart.*

Hindoo Holiday: An Indian Journal

J.P. Ackerley (New York Review of Books, New York, 2000)
Originally published in 1932 and written as a travel tale by a wealthy British merchant during the time of the Raj. Valuable for helping readers understand colonialism with its misunderstandings and demands, and enjoyable for its series of unusual characters.

Midnight's Children

Salman Rushdie (Avon Books, New York, 1980)
A mystical story about all of those children born at the stroke of midnight on August 15, 1947, when India obtained independence. The birth of the children and the birth of a nation are intertwined in mystical and magical ways.

The Namesake

Jhumpa Lahiri (Houghton Mifflin Co., Boston, 2003)
A novel about two young Americans fitting into the world of their Indian and Bengali families and the world of the United States. Lahiri is also the author of *The Interpreter of Maladies.*

The Spirited Earth—Dance, Myth, and Ritual from South Asia to the South Pacific

Victoria Ginn (Rizzoli International Publications, Inc., New York, 1990)
A beautiful photographic anthology of the rituals of South Asia and the Pacific as enacted through myth and dance.

MULTICULTURAL, BIRACIAL, AND MULTIETHNIC

The Color of Water: A Black Man's Tribute to His White Mother

James McBride (Riverhead Books, New York, 1997)
A man born in the late 1950s recalls his life as the son of an African American pastor and his white Jewish mother. The story recounts the life lessons imparted by his mother, who raised 12 children, all of whom attended college and lived successful lives.

American Mixed Race: The Culture of Microdiversity

Naomi Zack (Ed.) (Rowman & Littlefield Publishers, Lanham, MD, 1995)
A remarkable collection of stories and essays by and about multiracial Americans.

Swaying: Essays on Intercultural Love

Jessie Carroll Grearson & Lauren B. Smith (Eds.) (University of Iowa Press, Iowa City, 1995)
A richly enlightening series of essays on love across cultural boundaries as written by "international families." The essays range from negotiations over the little issues to some of the profound similarities, differences, attitudes, and perspectives that must be examined.

The Night My Mother Met Bruce Lee: Observations on Not Fitting In

Paisley Rekdal (Vintage Books, New York, 2000)
A contemporary view of life as the daughter of a Chinese American mother and Norwegian father.

MISCELLANEOUS

Do's and Taboos Around the World (Second Edition)

Roger E. Axtell (Ed.) (John Wiley & Sons, New York, 1990)
Compiled by the Parker Pen Company for employees in their overseas offices, this book provides basic information about the customs and etiquette of greetings, gifts,

conversations, gestures, and punctuality in countries throughout the world as well as tips for visitors to the United States. Also by Axtell, *Gestures: The Do's and Taboos of Body Language Around the World.*

Multicultural Manners: New Rules of Etiquette for a Changing Society

Norine Dresser (John Wiley & Sons, New York, 1996)
An up-to-date guide for negotiating a multicultural world in personal and professional interactions. Short vignettes highlight cross-cultural conflicts and provide explanations of the differing perspectives.

The Graywolf Annual Five: Multicultural Literacy—Opening the American Mind

Rick Simonson & Scott Walker (Eds.) (Graywolf Press, St. Paul, MN, 1988)
An anthology of short stories from writers of color who seek to ensure that we expand cultural literacy to include multicultural literacy.

The Graywolf Annual Seven: Stories From the American Mosaic

Scott Walker (Ed.) (Graywolf Press, St. Paul, MN, 1990)
Fifteen fictional stories that focus on diverse cultures' interactions with mainstream U.S. culture. The various stories highlight misunderstanding, confusion, conflict, and the beginning of mutual respect and understanding. This Graywolf publication has tales from the New Europe, another way of viewing the dynamism of culture.

Urban MO•ZA•IK—Life in a Modern Multicultural Society

Carolyn Quan (Ed. and Creative Director) (Studio Q International, New York)
A print and on-line magazine (http://www.indypress.org/mstand/titles/urbanmozaik .html) that celebrates life in a multicultural world and addresses challenging issues of pluralism.

Working Together—How to Become More Effective in a Multicultural Organization

George Simons (Crisp Publications, Los Altos, CA, 1989)
A workbook of exercises to help organizations and the people in them to examine their own feelings about diversity and develop ways to improve their cross-cultural effectiveness.

PLAYS/THEATER

Adoration of the Old Woman

José Rivera
A cultural, political piece based on Puerto Rico and its relationship to the United States.

Blues in the Night

Sheldon Epps
A chronicle of the blues and singers of the blues that traces the African American experience.

Overtime

A.R. Guerney
With its *Merchant of Venice* plot line, *Overtime* confronts racial, ethnic, religious, and sexual orientation stereotypes. It is very funny, but you wonder if you should be laughing. It hits all groups equally.

Pentecost

David Edgar
The discovery of a church painting in an Eastern European country brings together experts from England and the United States, curators and cultural emissaries from the country, and a group of stateless people seeking asylum. The issues of culture, class, power, and statelessness are presented in hard-hitting action and dialogue that is often spoken in languages other than English.

Redwood Curtain

Lanford Wilson
Set in the redwoods of northern California, the play tells the story of an adopted daughter who is a gifted pianist. Born during the Vietnam War to an enlisted soldier and Vietnamese mother, her heritage is revealed in the redwoods. Also available on videotape.

The Gate of Heaven

Lane Nishikawa and Victor Talmadge
The compelling story of the unexpected reunion of a Japanese American soldier and a German Jew whom he had liberated from the Dachau concentration camp. Based on an actual event in World War II in which members of the 442nd Regiment of the U.S. Army, made up of Japanese Americans, were some of the first to reach Dachau.

The Piano Lesson

August Wilson
An African American family and the piano in their house.

Voire Dire

Joe Sutton
A multicultural jury debates a case amid their own racial, cultural, and gender struggles.

FILMS

In addition to the films based on many of the books listed in the first section of Suggested Readings and Resources, there are a number of other films that address cross-cultural issues or provide insight and understanding about worldviews that may be different from one's own. A short list without annotation is provided below. Many have been released commercially; some have not. Like the books and plays listed previously, many of the films are written and produced for adults, not children.

Avalon	*My Left Foot*
Balseros	*Osama*
Bend It Like Beckham	*Rabbit-Proof Fence*
Cinema Paradiso	*Real Women Have Curves*
Eat Drink Man Woman	*Secrets and Lies*
Farewell My Concubine	*Smoke Signals*
Frida	*The Killing Fields*
Gangs of New York	*The King of Masks*
Himalaya	*The Last Emperor*
Il Postino	*The Long Road Home*
In America	*The Milagro Bean Field War*
Indochine	*The Scent of Green Papaya*
Lone Star	*Tortilla Soup*
Monsoon Wedding	*Whale Rider*
My Big Fat Greek Wedding	*Windtalkers*

WEB SITES

Readers are encouraged to explore the sites on the web that address culture, linguistic diversity, and ethnic diversity. Because of the rapidly changing nature of the Internet, we have chosen not to make specific recommendations. However, the numbers and the diversity are growing.

REFERENCES

Baker, H.A., Jr. (1990). *Long black song—Essays in black American literature and culture.* Charlottesville: The University Press of Virginia.

Lee, C.R. (1995). *Native speaker.* New York: Riverhead Books.

AUTHOR INDEX

SUBJECT INDEX

Page numbers followed by *t* indicate tables.

Understanding
FAMILIES
Approaches to Diversity, Disability, and Risk
By Marci J. Hanson, Ph.D., & Eleanor W. Lynch, Ph.D.

Also Available

Learn how to develop effective partnerships with families of many different beliefs, backgrounds, and value systems. With this accessible text, early childhood professionals will get research on diverse families and family-centered services combined with ready-to-use suggestions for working with caregivers, especially those whose young children are at risk or have disabilities. Two trusted experts thoroughly prepare professionals to work respectfully with today's families, giving readers practical knowledge on: demographics and diversity, including factors such as socioeconomic status, culture, ethnicity, and language; how disability influences family life; factors that contribute to family resilience and strength; risk factors such as poverty, addiction, and violence; and how to form alliances with other professionals.

Enhanced by vignettes that paint vivid pictures of the challenges families face today, this comprehensive blend of research and practice is every professional's expert guide to meeting the needs of diverse families with young children.

US$32.00 • Stock Number: 6997 • 2004 • 264 pages • 7 x 10 • paperback • ISBN 1-55766-699-7

Please send me:

Quantity	Stock #	Title	Price
_____	6997	*Understanding Families*	US$32.00

Name:_____ **Daytime Phone:** _____

Street Address: _____

☐ Residential   ☐ Commercial

Complete street address required.

City/State/ZIP_____ **Country:** _____

E-mail Address: _____

☐ *Yes!* I want to receive special website discount offers. My e-mail address will not be shared with any other party.

If you know your customer number (please refer to your invoice for this product), provide it below, along with your professional title and field of practice.

Customer number (4 or 6 digits): __ __ __ __ __ __

Title: _____

Specialty: ☐ Birth–5   ☐ K–12   ☐ 4-year College/Graduate   ☐ Community College/Vocational
☐ Clinical/Medical   ☐ Community Services   ☐ Association

Credit Card #: _____ **Exp. Date:** _____

Signature (required with credit card use): _____

MAIL it to:
Brookes Publishing Co.,
P.O. Box 10624, Baltimore,
MD 21285-0624, U.S.A

ᵀAX: 410-337-8539

ᴸLL: 1-800-638-3775
⟍–5 P.M. ET) or
⟍7-9580 (outside
⟍ Canada)

⟍LINE at:
⟍publishing.com

Shipping & Handling

For subtotal of	Add*	For CAN
$0.01 – $49.99	$5.00	$7.00
$50.00 – $69.99	10%	$7.00
$70.00 – $399.99	10%	10%
$400.00 and over	8%	8%

*calculate percentage on product total

Shipping rates are for UPS Ground Delivery within continental U.S.A. For other shipping options and rates, call 1-800-638-3775 (in the U.S.A. and CAN) and 410-337-9580 (worldwide).

Subtotal $_____

5% sales tax, Maryland only $_____

7% business tax (GST), CAN only $_____

Shipping Rate (see chart) $_____

Total (in U.S.A. dollars) $_____

155 is your list code

Policies and prices subject to change without notice. Prices may be higher outside the U.S. You may return books within 30 days for a full credit of the product price. Refunds will be issued for prepaid orders. Items must be returned in resalable condition.